SUICIDOLOGY:
CONTEMPORARY DEVELOPMENTS

SEMINARS IN PSYCHIATRY

Series Editor
Milton Greenblatt, M.D.
Chief, Psychiatry Service
Veterans Administration Hospital
Sepulveda, California, and
Professor of Psychiatry
University of California, Los Angeles

Other Books in Series:

SUICIDOLOGY:
CONTEMPORARY DEVELOPMENTS

Edited by

Edwin S. Shneidman, Ph.D.

Professor of Thanatology,
Director, Laboratory for the Study
of Life-Threatening Behavior,
University of California, Los Angeles

Foreword by

Milton Greenblatt, M.D.

Chief, Psychiatry Service
Veterans Administration Hospital
Sepulveda, California, and
Professor of Psychiatry
University of California, Los Angeles

GRUNE & STRATTON 1976
A Subsidiary of Harcourt Brace Jovanovich, Publishers
New York   San Francisco   London

Library of Congress Cataloging in Publication Data

Main entry under title:

Suicidology.

  (Seminars in psychiatry)
  Includes bibliographical references and index.
  1. Suicide—Addresses, essays, lectures.
I. Shneidman, Edwin S.
RC569.S94   616.8′5844   76-7031
ISBN 0-8089-0930-4

Grune & Stratton, Inc.
111 Fifth Avenue
New York, New York 10003

Library of Congress Catalog Number 76-7031
International Standard Book Number 0-8089-0930-4
Printed in the United States of America

To
JACQUES CHORON, LOUIS DUBLIN and ERWIN STENGEL
scholars and gentlemen who personified all the best
contemporary developments in Suicidology

Acknowledgments

Appreciation is acknowledged to the following for permission to reproduce materials that appear in this volume:

American Journal of Psychiatry for "Symptomatology and Management of Acute Grief" by Erich Lindemann.

American Psychological Association for *Technical Recommendations for Psychological Tests and Diagnostic Techniques* by Lee Cronbach *et al.*

D. Appleton and Company for *Suicide: An Essay on Comparative Statistics* by Enrico Morselli.

Jason Aronson, Inc. for "Dead to the World" by Henry A. Murray from *Essays in Self-Destruction* edited by Edwin S. Shneidman.

Basic Books for *Black Rage* by William Grier and Price Cobb.

Boni and Liveright for *Beyond the Pleasure Principle* by Sigmund Freud.

George Braziller, Inc. for *How Could I not Be Among You?* by Ted Rosenthal.

Doubleday Anchor Books (Doubleday Publications) for *Values in a Universe of Chance (Philosophic Writings of Peirce)* by Charles Sanders Peirce edited by Philip P. Wiener.

Encyclopaedia Britannica, Inc. for "Suicide" by Henry Harvey Littlejohn from the 1910-1911 Edition of the *Encyclopaedia Britannica*.

The Free Press for *Suicide* by Emile Durkheim.

Harcourt, Brace and Jovanovich for *Man Against Himself* by Karl A. Menninger.

Jossey-Bass, Inc. for "Suicide Prevention" by Louis I. Dublin from *On the Nature of Suicide* edited by Edwin S. Shneidman.

Social Science Research Council for *The Use of Personal Documents in Psychological Science* by Gordon Allport.

Stanford University Press for *The Gifted Child Grows Up. Volume IV, Genetic Studies in Genius* by Lewis M. Terman and Melita H. Oden.

University of California Press for "The Specific Laws of Logic in Schizophrenia" by Ellard von Domarus from *Language and Thought in Schizophrenia* edited by J. S. Kasanin.

Vintage Books for *The Myth of Sisyphus* by Albert Camus.

A number of good people cheerfully helped me with the preparation of this volume, but two, Melinda Bertolet and Maureen Katz, were as indispensibly helpful as they are describably lovely. David Pallack graciously prepared the name index. And, as she has done a dozen times before, my peerless wife Jeanne supported my idiosyncratic ways of trying to produce a useful book.

Contents

Contents

Foreword

Ed Shneidman—brilliant, creative, irrepressible—the first Professor of Thanatology ever in history, has consented to do this book for us on *Suicidology: Contemporary Developments.* Drawing upon a lifetime of energetic scholarship and research, and his world-wide network of scientific colleagues who have distinguished themselves in the field, he has collated and updated all the essential work, in a most attractive and readable form.

Although the main course is *contemporary developments,* this is spiced with delightful and highly literary historical selections that precede and enrich every chapter. Thus, he creates a book of both scientific and artistic merit.

I have found it delightful reading, and I hope the reader will receive it with equal satisfaction.

MILTON GREENBLATT, M.D.
Editor-in-Chief
Seminars in Psychiatry

Preface

In the Introduction to Freud's Beyond the Pleasure Principle, writing about the function of introductory remarks, Gregory Zilboorg says: "An introduction is not supposed to explain in advance what is said in the book; still less is it meant to interpret it. Rather, it is intended to clarify some shadows and point to certain lights which will possibly set the book in proper perspective."

What strikes me most about this brief passage is the visual quality of its imagery: shadows, lights, perspective. To read is to use one's eyes; to learn and to know is to see; to look at life is to understand its bitter-sweet gustatory nature in visual terms, of lights and shadows, of peaks, depressions and plateaus. A dying poet said:

> Step lightly, we're walking home now.
> The clouds take every shape.
> We climb the boulders; there is no plateau.
> We cross the stream and walk up the slope.
> See, the hawk is diving.
> The plain stretches out ahead, then the hills, the valleys,
>   the meadows.
> Keep moving people. How could I not be among you?*

The very topic of suicide is addressed to the poet's poignant question. The suicidal person (and thus the clinical suicidologist) focuses on the valleys and troughs in the waves of the human voyage. The larger, professional question of "What is new?" needs (in order to be candid and complete) to touch upon the lugubrious and on the failures as well as the bright successes.

In this volume of contemporary developments and current perspectives I have attempted, by means of inviting almost a score of currently active suicidologists—granting immediately that a few eminent ones may not be represented in the final listing—to write original essays specifically for this volume (with one exception: my own three chapters) to display some of the important contemporary problems: areas of

---

*Reproduced from Ted Rosenthal's *How Could I Not Be Among You?* and reprinted with the kind permission of the copyright owners, George Braziller, Inc.

theoretical interest, foci of professional and ethical concern, and targets for empirical investigation to any reader interested to know and learn about current issues in suicide theory and suicide prevention work. This book is obviously not a manual; not a "how to do it" (i.e. prevention) book, nor is it a polemic or a tract.

I can recite the history of this volume rather quickly: Dr. Milton Greenblatt, formerly Commissioner for Mental Health of the Commonwealth of Massachusetts and now Chief of Psychiatry at Sepulveda Veterans Administration Hospital and Professor of Psychiatry at UCLA asked me—as part of his avocational efforts as an editor at Grune and Stratton—if I would develop a book on current perspectives in suicidology. This volume is the result of my efforts. The book belongs entirely to the contributors. All I did was to provide the hall; they brought the viands and the potables. To them I am enormously grateful, not only for their generous response in sharing but grateful because they have increased my own pride in being a suicidologist.

A few words about the "interstitial" materials may be in order: I had first thought, as editor, to introduce each contributed chapter by writing some appropriate comments, perhaps placing it in a larger context or suturing it more securely into the body of the book-as-a-whole. But then the idea occurred to me that it would give much more enjoyment and meaning (both to me and to the reader) instead to choose some "classic" piece from the entire literature of suicidology that in some direct or arcane way illuminated the contributor's chapter; some well-known or historically important (or perhaps even not so well known) passage that emphasized (in other words or at some previous time) some main point in that chapter, or was propaedeutic to the conceptual idea of that chapter, or was simply similar or sympathetic in timbre or tone to that chapter, or even was in opposition to the chapter—in other words, some relevant historic piece that, in some way, resonated to the chapter and served as a kind of palate-whetting morsel preceding the chapter itself.

E.S.S.

U.C.L.A.
March, 1976

Contributors

Richard B. Brandt, Ph.D.
Professor and Chairman
Department of Philosophy
University of Michigan
Ann Arbor, Michigan

Warren Breed, Ph.D,
Research Sociologist
Scientific Analysis Corporation
San Francisco, California

James C. Diggory, Ph.D.
Professor of Psychology
Chatham College
Pittsburgh, Pennsylvania

Richard Fox, M.B., M.R.C.P., F.R.C. Psych, D.P.M.
Consultant Psychiatrist
Severalls Hospital,
Colchester, Essex, England
Hon. Psychiatric Consultant
The Samaritans
United Kingdom Representative
International Association for Suicide Prevention

David C. Heilbron, Ph.D.
Supervising Statistician
Office of Information Systems
University of California
San Francisco, California

Herbert Hendin, M.D.
Director
Psychosocial Studies
The Center for Policy Research and
Visiting Professor of Psychiatry
New York Medical College
New York, New York

Robert Kastenbaum, Ph.D.
Professor of Psychology
University of Massachusetts
Boston, Massachusetts

Ari Kiev, M.D.
Clinical Associate Professor of Psychiatry
New York Hospital, Cornell Medical Center
Director
Social Psychiatry Research Institute, Inc.
New York, New York

Leonard L. Linden, Ph.D.
Associate Professor
Department of Sociology
University of Georgia
Athens, Georgia

Robert E. Litman, M.D.
Chief Psychiatrist
Suicide Prevention Center and
Professor of Psychiatry
University of California at Los Angeles

Richard K. McGee, Ph.D.
Director
Alachua County Drug Programs
Gainesville, Florida

Jerome A. Motto, M.D.
Professor of Psychiatry
University of California
School of Medicine
San Francisco, California

Charles Neuringer, Ph.D.
Professor of Psychology
University of Kansas
Lawrence, Kansas

Thomas L. Shaffer, J.D.
Professor of Law
University of Notre Dame
Notre Dame, Indiana

Edwin S. Shneidman, Ph.D.
Professor of Thanatology
Director of the Laboratory for
    the Study of Life Threatening Behavior
Department of Psychiatry
University of California at Los Angeles

Michael A. Simpson, M.B., B.S.,
  M.R.C.S., M.R.C. Psych., D.P.M.
Assistant Professor of Psychiatry
Academic Department of Psychiatry
The Royal Free Hospital
Senior Lecturer and
Honorary Consultant
Medical School
London University
London, England

William C. Swanson, Ph.D.
Associate Professor of Sociology
Tulane University
New Orleans, Louisiana

Peter Tripodes, Ph.D.
Consultant
Social Science Research Center
University of California at Los Angeles

Carl I. Wold, Ph.D.
Director of Clinical Research
Suicide Prevention Center
Los Angeles, California

J. William Worden, Ph.D.
Assistant Professor of Psychology
Harvard Medical School and
Research Director
Project Omega
Massachusetts General Hospital
Boston, Massachusetts

SUICIDOLOGY:
CONTEMPORARY DEVELOPMENTS

Edwin S. Shneidman

Introduction
Current Over-View of Suicide

The editor's article in the *Encyclopaedia Britannica*, 14th ed., on "Suicide," serves as the introduction to this volume. Preceding the article, however, is a complete reprinting of the comparable article from the *Encyclopaedia Britannica*, 11th ed., on "Suicide," written by Henry Harvey Littlejohn, M.A., F.R.C.S. (Edin.)., F.R.S. (Edin.)., late professor of Forensic Medicine and Dean of the Faculty in Medicine at the University of Edinburgh. Both articles are reproduced here with the kind permission of *Encyclopaedia Britannica*, 14th ed., © 1973 and 11th Ed., © 1910–1911.

SUICIDE (from Lat. *sui*, of oneself, and *cidium*, from *caedere*, to kill), the act of intentionally destroying one's own life. The phenomenon of suicide has at all times attracted a large amount of attention from moralists and social investigators. Its existence is looked upon, in Western civilization, as a sign of the presence of maladies in the body politic which, whether remediable or not, deserve careful examination. It is, of course, impossible to compare Western civilization in this respect with, say, Japan, where suicide in certain circumstances is part of a distinct moral creed. In Christian ethics and Christian law it is wrong, indeed illegal, as a *felo de se*, self-murder. It is within comparatively recent years that the study of suicide by means of the vital statistics of various European countries has demonstrated that while the act may be regarded as a purely voluntary one, yet that suicide as a whole conforms there to certain general laws, and is influenced by conditions other than mere individual circumstances or surroundings. Thus it can be shown that each country has a different suicide-rate, and that

1

while the rate for each country may fluctuate from year to year, yet it maintains practically the same relative proportions to the rates of other countries. The following table shows the suicide-rate for various European countries (Bertillon):—

TABLE I.

Country.	Period of Observation.	Annual Number of Suicides per Million Inhabitants.
Saxony	1878–1882	392
Denmark	1880–1882	251
Switzerland	1878–1882	239
Baden	,,	198
Württemberg	1877–1881	189
France	1878–1882	180
Prussia	,,	166
Belgium	,,	100
Sweden	,,	92
England and Wales	,,	75
Norway	,,	69
Scotland	1877–1881	49
Ireland	1878–1882	17

In addition to furnishing materials for an approximately accurate estimate of the number of suicides which will occur in any country in a year, statistics have demonstrated that the proportion of male to female suicides is practically the same from year to year, viz. 3 or 4 males to 1 female; that it is possible to predict the month of greatest prevalence, the modes of death adopted by men on the one hand and women on the other, and even the relative frequency of suicide amongst persons following different professions and employments; and that in most of the countries of Europe the suicide-rate is increasing. In England and Wales the annual death-rate per million from suicide has steadily advanced, as is shown by the following figures for quinquennial periods:—

1861–1865	. .	65 per million living.
1866–1870	. .	66 ,, ,,
1871–1875	. .	66 ,, ,,
1876–1880	. .	74 ,, ,,
1881–1885	. .	75 ,, ,,
1886–1890	. .	79 ,, ,,
1891–1895	. .	88 ,, ,,
1896–1900	. .	89 ,, ,,
1901–1905	. .	100 ,, ,,

The next table illustrates the continued increase in recent years, and at the

TABLE II.

Total Suicides—Male and Female—in England and Wales, 1886-1905,
together with the annual rate per million living (Registrar-General's Reports).

Year.	Male.	Female.	Total.	Suicide-rate per Million Living.
1886	1694	560	2254	82
1890	1635	570	2205	77
1895	2071	726	2797	92
1896	1979	677	2656	86
1897	2090	702	2792	90
1898	2166	711	2877	91
1899	2121	723	2844	89
1900	2166	730	2896	90
1901	2318	803	3121	96
1902	2460	807	3267	99
1903	2640	871	3511	105
1904	2523	822	3345	99
1905	2683	862	3545	104
Total.	28,546	9564	38,110	—

same time shows the total number and the number of male and female suicides each year from 1886 to 1905.

The reason of the high suicide-rate in some countries as compared with others, and the causes of its progressive increase, are not easily determined. Various explanations have been offered, such as the influence of climate, the comparative prevalence of insanity, and the proportionate consumption of alcoholic drinks, but none satisfactorily accounts for the facts. It may, however, be remarked that suicide is much more common amongst Protestant than amongst Roman Catholic communities, while Jews have a smaller suicide-rate than Roman Catholics. A point of considerable interest is the increase of suicide in relation to the advance of elementary education. Ogle states that suicide is more common among the educated than the illiterate classes. It is also more prevalent in urban than in rural districts. A curious feature in large towns is the sudden outbreak of self-destruction which sometimes occurs, and which has led to its being described as epidemic. In such cases force of example and imitation undoubtedly play a considerable part, as it is well recognized that both these forces exert an influence not only in causing suicide, but also in suggesting the method, time and place for the act. No age above five years is exempted from furnishing its quota of suicidal deaths, although self-destruction between five and ten years is very rare. Above this age the proportion of suicides increases at each period, the maximum being reached between fifty-five and sixty-five. Among females there is a greater relative prevalence at earlier age periods than among males. The modes of suicide are found to vary very slightly in different countries. Hanging is most common amongst males; then drowning, injuries from fire-arms, stabs and cuts, poison and precipitation from heights. Amongst females, drowning comes first, while poison and hanging are more frequent than other methods entailing effusion of blood and disfigurement of the person. The methods used in England and Wales by suicides during 1888–1897, and in Scotland during the years 1881–1897, are given in the following table:—

TABLE III.
Modes of Suicide in England and Wales, 1888–1897.

Order of Frequency.	Males.		Females.		Both Sexes.	
	Mode.	Number.	Mode.	Number.	Mode.	Number.
1	Hanging	5669	Drowning	2089	Hanging	7005
2	Stab-cut	3594	Poison	1652	Drowning	5532
3	Drowning	3443	Hanging	1336	Stab-cut	4365
4	Poison	2264	Stab-cut	771	Poison	3916
5	Fire-arms	2152	Fire-arms	52	Fire-arms	2204
6	Otherwise	1773	Otherwise	527	Otherwise	2300
	Total	18,895	Total	6427	Total	25,322

Modes of Suicide in Scotland, 1881–1897.

Order of Frequency.	Males.		Females.		Both Sexes.	
	Mode.	Number.	Mode.	Number.	Mode.	Number.
1	Hanging	741	Drowning	430	Drowning	1060
2	Drowning	630	Hanging	257	Hanging	998
3	Stab-cut	556	Poison	145	Stab-cut	700
4	Poison	257	Stab-cut	144	Poison	402
5	Fire-arms	245	Fire-arms	6	Fire-arms	251
6	Otherwise	207	Otherwise	100	Otherwise	307
	Total	2636	Total	1082	Total	3718

The season of the year influences suicide practically uniformly in all European countries, the number increasing from the commencement of the year to a maximum in May or June, and then declining again to a minimum in winter. Morselli attempts to account for this greater prevalence during what may well be called the most beautiful months of the year by attributing it to the influence of increased temperature upon the organism, while Durkheim suggests that the determining factor is more probably to be found in the length of the day and the effect of a longer period of daily activity. The suicide-rate is higher in certain male occupations and professions than in others (Ogle). Thus it is high amongst soldiers, doctors, innkeepers and chemists, and low for clergy, bargemen, railway drivers and stokers. The suicide-rate is twice as great for unoccupied males as for occupied males.

AUTHORITIES—Morselli, *Il Suicidio* (Milan, 1879); Legoyt, *Le Suicide ancien et modern* (Paris, 1881); Westcott, *Suicide: its History, Literature, &c.* (London, 1885); Ogle, "Suicides in England and Wales, in relation to Age, Sex, Season, and Occupation," *Journal of the Statistical Society* (1886), vol. xlix.; Strahan, *Suicide and Insanity* (London, 1893); Mayr, "Selbstmord statistik," in *Handwörterbuch der Staatswissenschaften* (Jena, 1895); Durkheim, *Le Suicide* (Paris, 1897).   (H. H. L.)

SUICIDE. No one really knows why human beings commit suicide. Indeed, the very person who takes his own life may be least aware at the moment of decision of the essence (much less the totality) of his reasons and emotions for doing so. At the outset, it can be said that a dozen individuals can kill themselves and "do" (or commit) 12 psychologically different deeds. Understanding suicide—like understanding any other complicated human act such as drug or alcohol misuse or antisocial behaviour—involves insights drawn from many fields that touch on man's entire psychological and social life.

DEFINITION OF SUICIDE

In this article the definition of suicide will be treated in two ways: first, a definition is put forward and, then, some of the difficulties and complexities involved in defining the term are discussed. Briefly defined, suicide is the human act of self-inflicted, self-intentioned cessation.

Suicide is not a disease (although there are those who think so); it is not, in the view of the most detached observers, an immorality (although, as noted below, it has often been so treated in Western and other cultures); and, finally, it is unlikely that any one theory will ever explain phenomena as varied and as complicated as human self-destructive behaviours. In general, it is probably accurate to say that suicide always involves an individual's tortured and tunneled logic in a state of inner-felt, intolerable emotion. In addition, this mixture of constricted thinking and unbearable anguish is infused with that individual's conscious and unconscious psychodynamics (of hate, dependency, hope, etc.), playing themselves out within a social and cultural context, which itself imposes various degrees of restraint on, or facilitation of, the suicidal act.

This definition implies that committing suicide involves a conceptualization of death; that it combines an individual's conscious wish to be dead and his action to carry out that wish; that it focuses on his intention (which may have to be inferred by others); that the goal of action relates to death (rather than self-injury or self-mutilation); and that it focuses on the concept of the cessation of the individual's conscious, introspective life. The word "suicide" would seem to be clear enough, although such phrases as "self-inflicted" (in the incident in which Saul asked another soldier to kill him) and "self-intentioned" (when Seneca was ordered by Nero to kill himself) add to the complications of finding a clear-cut definition of suicide.

Complexities and Difficulties with Definitions.—If the definition of suicide is complicated, there are even more confusions of meaning when the adjective "suicidal" is used. Some of the current confusions relating to the term "suicidal" are as follows:

(1) The word "suicidal" is used to cover a number of categories of behaviour. For example, it may convey the idea that an individual has committed suicide, attempted suicide, threatened suicide, exhibited depressive behaviour—with or without suicidal ideation—or manifested generally self-destructive or inimical patterns.

(2) There also is confusion with respect to the temporal aspects of suicidal acts. One sees "suicidal" used to convey the information that an individual was self-destructive, is currently self-destructive, or will be so. Most diagnoses in this field are post hoc definitions, labeling an individual as "suicidal" only after he has attempted or committed suicide.

(3) Serious confusion relating to suicidal phenomena may occur if the individual's intentions in relation to his own cessation are not considered. "Suicide" may be defined for medical, legal, and administrative purposes. In the United States and Great Britain (and most of the countries reporting to the World Health Organization), suicide is defined (by a medical examiner or coroner) as one of four possible modes of death. There are 140 possible causes of death but only four modes. An acronym for the four modes of death is N-A-S-H: natural, accident, suicide, and homicide. This traditional fourfold classification of all deaths leaves much to be desired. Its major deficiency is that it emphasizes relatively adventitious details in the death. Whether the individual is invaded by a lethal virus (natural), or a lethal bullet (homicide), or a lethal steering wheel (accident) may be a trivial difference to the deceased, who may be more interested in the date of his death. More importantly, the N-A-S-H classification of death erroneously treats the human being in Cartesian fashion, as a biological machine, rather than appropriately treating him as a motivated psychosocial organism. It also obscures the individual's intentions in relation to his own cessation and, further, completely neglects the contemporary concepts of psychodynamic psychology regarding intention, purpose, and the multiple determination of behaviour including unconscious motivation.

It may make more sense eventually to eschew the category of suicide entirely—along with the other N-A-S-H categories—and instead to classify all deaths in terms of the role of the individual in his own demise: (1) intentioned, (2) subintentioned—cases in which an individual has played partial, latent, covert, or unconscious roles in hastening his own demise—or (3) unintentioned. The problems of certification would then be no more difficult than they are at present, but such a classification would serve to put man back into his own dying and death and, in addition, would reflect the 20th-century view of man that emphasizes both the conscious and unconscious aspects of his intentionality.

The Word.—Suicide is a relatively recent word. According to *The Oxford English Dictionary*, the word was first used in 1651 by Walter Charleton when he said, interestingly enough, "To vindicate ones self from . . . inevitable Calamity, by Sui-cide is not . . . a Crime." The exact date of its first use is open to some question. Edward Phillips in the 1662 edition of his dictionary,

A New World in Words, claimed invention of the word: "One barbarous word I shall produce, which is suicide." Curiously enough he does not derive it from the death of oneself but says it "should be derived from 'a sow' . . . since it is a swinish part for a man to kill himself."

The British poetry critic Alfred Alvarez in 1971 claimed that he found the word was used even earlier, in Sir Thomas Browne's *Religio Medici*, written in 1635 and published in 1642, in the following passage: "Herein are they not extreme that can allow a man to be his own assassin and so highly extoll the end by suicide of Cato."

The word "suicide" does not appear in Robert Burton's *Anatomy of Melancholy* (1652 edition) nor in Samuel Johnson's *Dictionary* (1755). Before the introduction of the word, other terms, mostly circumlocutions and euphemisms relating to self-murder, were used—among them self-destruction, self-killing, self-slaughter, *sibi mortem consciecere* (to procure one's own death), *vim sibi inferre* (to cause violence to oneself), and *sui manu cadere* (to fall by one's own hand). Burton's phrases for suicide include "to make way with themselves" and "they offer violence to themselves." The traditional (and current) German term is *Selbstmord*—self-murder.

It may well be that in light of current concepts and facts about human self-destruction a new (and more accurate) term may eventually come into general usage. In the 1960s a relatively new word, suicidology, was introduced. *Suicidologie* was used in a text by a Dutch professor, W. A. Bonger, in 1929, but did not become widely known. Independently, the word was used by Edwin S. Shneidman in a book review (1964) and then in the *Bulletin of Suicidology* (1967) and at the first convention of the American Association of Suicidology, which met in 1968. Since then the word has come into general use. Suicidology is defined as the scientific study of suicidal phenomena.

MAIN THREADS OF SUICIDAL STUDY

The modern era of the study of suicide began around the turn of the 20th century, with two main threads of investigation, the sociological and the psychological, associated with the names of Émile Durkheim (1858-1917) and Sigmund Freud (1856-1939), respectively. Much earlier, during classical Greek times, suicide was viewed in various ways, but in classical Rome, in the centuries just before the Christian era, life was held rather cheaply and suicide was viewed either neutrally or even positively. The Roman Stoic Seneca said: "Living is not good, but living well. The wise man, therefore, lives as well as he should, not as long as he can. . . . He will always think of life in terms of quality not quantity. . . . Dying early or late is of no relevance, dying well or ill is . . . even if it is true that while there is life there is hope, life is not to be bought at any cost."

Historically it seems that the excessive martyrdom and penchant toward suicide of the early Christians frightened the church elders sufficiently for them to introduce a serious deterrent. That constraint was to relate suicide to crime and the sin associated with crime. A major change occurred in the 4th century with a categorical rejection of suicide by St. Augustine (354-430). Suicide was considered a crime, because it precluded the possibility of repentance and because it violated the Sixth Commandment relating to killing. Suicide was a greater sin than any sin one might wish to avoid. This view was elaborated by St. Thomas Aquinas (1225–74), who emphasized that suicide was a mortal sin in that it usurped God's power over man's life and death. Although neither the Old nor the New Testament directly forbids suicide, by 693 the Council of Toledo proclaimed than an individual who attempted suicide was to be excommunicated. The notion of suicide as sin took firm hold and for hundreds of years played an important part in Western man's view of self-destruction.

The Christian injunctions against suicide seemed paradoxically to rest on a respect for life (especially the life of the soul in the hereafter) and were a reaction to the light way in which life was held by the Romans. If those were the church's original motivations, however, they went awry and the results were excessive and counterproductive, and resulted in degrading, defaming, impoverishing, torturing, and persecuting individuals (who had attempted suicide, committed suicide, or were the survivors) whom they had originally tried to protect and succor.

The French philosopher Jean Jacques Rousseau (1712–78), by emphasizing the natural state of man, transferred sin from man to society, making man generally good (and innocent) and asserting that it is society that makes him bad. The disputation as to the locus of blame—whether in man or in society—is a major theme that dominates the history of suicidal thought. David Hume (1711–76) was one of the first major Western philosophers to discuss suicide in the absence of the concept of sin. His famous essay "On Suicide," published in 1777, a year after his death, was promptly suppressed. That well-reasoned essay is a statement of the Enlightenment position on suicide. The burden of the essay is to refute the view that suicide is a crime; it does so by arguing that suicide is not a transgression of our duties to God, to our fellow citizens, or to ourselves. He states that ". . . prudence and courage should engage us to rid ourselves at once of existence when it becomes a burden. . . . If it be no crime in me to divert the Nile or Danube from its course, were I able to effect such pruposes, where then is the crime in turning a few ounces of blood from their natural channel?"

Whereas Hume tried to decriminalize suicide, Rousseau turned the blame from man to society. In the 20th century, the two giants of suicidal theorizing played rather different roles: Durkheim focused on society's inimical effects on the individual, while Freud—eschewing the notions of either sin or crime—gave suicide back to man but put the locus of action in man's unconscious.

Durkheim's best-known work, *Le Suicide* (1897), established a model for sociological investigations of suicide. There have been many subsequent studies of this genre. The monographs and books by R. S. Cavan on suicide in Chicago (1926), of Calvin F. Schmid on suicide in Seattle (1928) and Minneapolis (1933), of Peter Sainsbury on suicide in London (1955), of Louis I. Dublin and Bessie Bunzel (1933), and of Andrew F. Henry and James F. Short, Jr., on suicide in the U.S. (1954) all fall within the sociological tradition

Durkheim's
Types
Suicide

of taking a plot of ground—a city or a country—and figuratively or literally reproducing its map several times to show its socially shady (and topographically shaded) areas and their differential relationships to suicide rates.

According to Durkheim suicide is the result of society's strength or weakness of control over the individual. He posited three basic types of suicide, each a result of man's relationship to his society. In one instance, the "altruistic" suicide is literally required by society. Here, the customs or rules of the group demand suicide under certain circumstances. Hara-kiri and suttee are examples of altruistic suicides. In such instances, however, the persons had little choice. Self-inflicted death was honourable; continuing to live was ignominious. Society dictated their action and, as individuals, they were not strong enough to defy custom.

Most suicides in the United States are "egoistic"—Durkheim's second category. Contrary to the circumstances of an altruistic suicide, egoistic suicide occurs when the individual has too few ties with his community. Demands, in this case to live, do not reach him. Thus, proportionately, more individuals, especially men, who are on their own kill themselves than do church or family members.

Finally, Durkheim called "anomic" those suicides that occur when the accustomed relationship between an individual and his society is suddenly shattered. The shocking, immediate loss of a job, a close friend, or a fortune is thought sufficient to precipitate anomic suicides; or, conversely, poor men surprised by sudden wealth also have been shocked into anomic suicide.

The students and followers of Durkheim include Maurice Halbwachs in France and Ronald W. Maris and Jack D. Douglas in the United States. Douglas, especially, has argued that Durkheim's constructs came not so much from the facts of life and death as from official statistics, which themselves may distort the very facts they are supposed to report.

As Durkheim detailed the sociology of suicide, so Freud fathered psychological explanations. To him, suicide was essentially within the mind. Since men ambivalently identify with the objects of their own love, when they are frustrated the aggressive side of the ambivalence will be directed against the internalized person. The main psychoanalytical position on suicide was that it represented unconscious hostility directed toward the introjected (ambivalently viewed) love object. For example, one killed oneself in order to murder the image of one's loved-hated father within one's breast. Psychodynamically, suicide was seen as murder in the 180th degree.

In an important exegesis of Freud's thoughts on suicide by Robert E. Litman (1967, 1970), he traces the development of Freud's thoughts on the subject, taking into account Freud's clinical experiences and his changing theoretical positions from 1881 to 1939. It is evident from Litman's analysis that there is more to the psychodynamics of suicide than hostility. These factors include the general features of human condition in Western civilization, specifically, suicide-prone mechanisms involving rage, guilt, anxiety, dependency, and a great number of specifically predisposing conditions. The feelings of helplessness, hopelessness, and abandonment are very important.

Psychodynamic explanations of suicide theory did not move too much from the time of Freud to that of Karl Menninger. In his important book *Man Against Himself* (1938), Menninger (in captivating ordinary language) delineates the psychodynamics of hostility and asserts that the hostile drive in suicide is made up of three skeins: (1) the wish to kill, (2) the wish to be killed, and (3) the wish to die. Gregory Zilboorg refined this psychoanalytic hypothesis and stated that every suicidal case contained strong, unconscious hostility combined with an unusual lack of capacity to love others. He extended the concern from solely intrapsychic dynamics to the external world and maintained that the role of a broken home in suicidal proneness demonstrated that suicide has both intrapsychic and external etiological elements.

In addition to the sociological and psychological approaches to the study of suicide, there is a third main contemporary thrust that might be called the philosophical or existential. Albert Camus, in his essay *The Myth of Sisyphus*, begins by saying: "There is but one serious philosophic problem and that is suicide." The principal task of man is to respond to life's apparent meaninglessness, despair, and its absurd quality. Ludwig Wittgenstein also states that the main ethical issue for man is suicide. To Camus, Wittgenstein, and other philosophers, however, their ruminations were never meant as prescriptions for action. Arthur Schopenhauer (1788-1860), the philosopher of pessimism, lived to a fairly ripe age and died of natural causes.

PSYCHOLOGICAL CHARACTERISTICS OF SUICIDE

Suicide has been related to many emotions: hostility, despair, shame, guilt, dependency, hopelessness, ennui. The traditional psychoanalytic position, first stated by Wilhelm Stekel at a meeting in Vienna in 1910, is that "no one kills himself who has not wanted to kill another or at least wished the death of another." This thought became translated into the psychoanalytic formulation that suicide represented hostility toward the introjected (ambivalently identified) love object. Currently, even psychodynamically oriented suicidologists believe that although hostility can be an important psychological component in some suicides, other emotional states—especially frustrated dependency and hopelessness and helplessness—often play the dominant role in the psychological drama of suicide. If there is one general psychological state commonly assumed to be associated with suicide it is a state of intolerable emotion (or unbearable or "unrepeatable despair")—what Herman Melville, in his masterpiece on self-destruction, *Moby Dick*, called "insufferable anguish."

Over and above the emotional states related to suicide, there are three important general psychological characteristics of suicide:

(1) The first is that the acute suicidal crisis (or period of high and dangerous lethality) is an interval of relatively short duration—to be counted, typically, in hours or days, not usually in months or years. An individual is at a peak of self-destructiveness for a brief time and is either helped, cools off, or is dead. Although one can live for years at a chronically elevated self-destructive

level, one cannot have a loaded gun to one's head for too long before either bullet or emotion is discharged.

(2) The second concept is ambivalence. Few persons now dispute that Freud's major insights relating to the role of unconscious motivation (and the workings of what is called the unconscious mind) have been one of the giant concepts of this century in revolutionizing our view of man. The notion of ambivalence is a critical concept in 20th-century, psychodynamically-oriented psychiatry and psychology. The dualities, complications, concomitant contradictory feelings, attitudes, and thrusts toward essentially the same person or introjected image are recognized hallmarks of psychological life. The dualities of the mind's flow constitute a cardinal feature of man's inner life. One can no longer ask in a simple Aristotelian way, "Make up your mind." To such a question a sophisticated respondent ought to say: "But that is precisely the point. I am at least of two, perhaps several, minds on this subject." A law has equal force whether it is passed in the Senate by a 100-0 or a 51-49 vote; so has a bullet. The paradigm of suicide is not the simplistic one of wanting to or not wanting to. The prototypical psychological picture of a person on the brink of suicide is one who wants to and does not want to. He makes plans for self-destruction and at the same time entertains fantasies of rescue and intervention. It is possible—indeed probably prototypical—for a suicidal individual to cut his throat and to cry for help at the same time.

(3) Most suicidal events are dyadic events, that is, two-person events. Actually this dyadic aspect of suicide has two phases: the first during the prevention of suicide when one must deal with the "significant other," and the second in the aftermath in the case of a committed suicide in which one must deal with the survivor-victim. Although it is obvious that the suicidal drama takes place within an individual's head, it is also true that most suicidal tensions are between two people keenly known to each other: spouse and spouse, parent and child, lover and lover. In addition, death itself is an extremely dyadic event.

The cold sociological truth is that some modes of death are more stigmatizing to the survivors than are other modes of death and that, generally speaking, suicide imposes the greatest stigma of all upon its survivors. The British physician John Hinton deals with this in his book *Dying* (1967). Hinton also comments that the notes left by the suicidal subject often cause further anguish.

Suicide notes provide an unusual window into the thoughts and feelings of a suicidal person. Various surveys in different places indicate that about 15% of individuals who commit suicide leave suicide notes—although the actual range is from 2 to 20%. By the 1970s fewer than 20 systematic studies of suicide notes had been completed. One of the first scientific studies of suicide notes was by W. Morgenthaler (1945) in a monograph that reported 47 suicide notes (in German) from Bern, Switz. The best-known reports in the United States are by Edwin S. Shneidman and Norman L. Farberow (1947, 1970) in their studies of genuine suicide notes and elicited matched notes written by nonsuicidal persons. Suicide notes have been subjected to a number of types of analyses: by emotional states, logical styles, "reasons" stated or implied, death wishes, language characteristics, relations to persons, and by computer count of key "tag words." In general these analyses indicate that (1) it is possible to distinguish between genuine and simulated suicide notes, and, more importantly, (2) genuine suicide notes are characterized by dichotomous logic, greater amount of hostility and self-blame, use of very specific names and instructions to the survivor, more decisiveness, less evidence of thinking about thinking, and more use of the various meanings of the word "love."

The Two Fundamental Aspects of Death and Suicide.—Twentieth-century philosophers, especially Percy Bridgman (1938), pointed out that there is an epistemological characteristic unique to death, specifically that there are two fundamental aspects of death: the private aspect, as an individual lives it himself (my death); and the public aspect, as one can experience, in reality, the death of another (your death). In death (and suicide) there is a key difference between the principal actor and the observer. One major implication of this key difference is that I can observe and experience your death (just as you can observe and experience my death), but I can never experience my own death for if I could, I should still be alive.

Some of this kind of thinking operates in suicide, especially when it is seen as a psychologically magical act. Just as Melville wrote that "All evil, to crazy Ahab, were visibly personified and made practically assailable in Moby Dick," so to the suicidal mind, using this same tortured logic, the whole world is "made practically assailable" and can be thought to be expunged by destroying oneself.

The fantasies of one's own suicide can represent the greatest possible combination of omnipotence and potential realization of effectiveness—greater even than one's fantasies of the assassination of another, group revenge, mass murder, or even genocide. Any "average" individual can say: "From my point of view, suicide destroys all"—and it can be done.

These inferred psychodynamics of suicide (relating to delusions of annihilation) are thought by psychoanalysts to have their origins in the earliest notions of an individual's infantile omnipotence. The literature of suicide in Western man, however, continually emphasizes that suicide can be an individual's final act, his final escape hatch, his final revenge—often misconstrued as a final "right." This unique epistemological dual characteristic of death (the difference between my death and your death) is fundamental to an understanding of suicide.

ATTEMPTED SUICIDE

Although it is obvious that one has to "attempt" suicide in order to commit it, it is equally clear that often the event of "attempting suicide" does not have death (cessation) as its objective. It is an acknowledged fact that often the goal of "attempted suicide" (such as cutting oneself or ingesting harmful substances) is to change one's life (or to change the "significant others" around one) rather than to end it. On the other hand, sometimes death is intended and only fortuitously avoided. After that, one's life—what has been called "a bonus life"—is forever somewhat different. Alfred Alvarez who himself made a serious suicide attempt, said that survivors have a changed life, with entirely different standards.

Erwin Stengel, a student of attempted suicide, in his arguments and statistical presentations, seems to suggest, in the main, that persons who attempt suicide and those who commit suicide represent essentially two different "populations"—with admittedly some overflow from the first to the second. It is useful to think of two sets of overlapping populations: (1) a group of those who attempt suicide, few of whom go on to commit it, and (2) a group of those who commit suicide, many of whom have previously attempted it. A great deal has to do with the lethality of the event. Lethality is roughly synonymous with the "deathfulness" of the act and is an important dimension in understanding any potentially suicidal person. Avery D. Weisman in 1972 distinguished three aspects of lethality: that of intention (ideation and involvement); that of implementation (risk and rescue); and that of intercession (resources, relief, and reorientation). The ratio between suicide attempts and commits is about 8 to 1—1 committed suicide for every 8 attempts.

Suicide attempts have many meanings and, whatever their level of lethality, ought to be taken seriously. A person who attempts suicide because he believes that there is no use living may not necessarily mean that he wants to die but that he has exhausted the potential for being someone who matters.

PARTIAL DEATH AND SUBSTITUTES FOR SUICIDE

Sometimes the very life-style of an individual seems to truncate and demean his life so that he is as good as dead. Often alcoholism, drug addiction, mismanagement of physical disease (such as diabetes or Buerger's disease), and masochistic behaviour can be seen in this light. A study of gifted individuals (with IQ's over 140) indicated that conspicuous failure in adult life—a kind of "partial death"—was sometimes the "price" for life as a substitute for overt suicide.

The chief theorist of the concept of partial death is Karl Menninger. Much of his conception is explicated in *Man Against Himself.* Menninger writes of (1) chronic suicide, including asceticism, martyrdom, neurotic invalidism, alcohol addiction, antisocial behaviour, and psychosis; (2) focal suicide—focused on a limited part of the body—including self-mutilations, malingering, multiple surgery, purposive accidents, impotence, and frigidity; and (3) organic suicide, focusing on the psychological factors in organic disease, especially the self-punishing, aggressive, and erotic components. In the 1970s, the focus was on concepts such as indirect self-destructive behaviour. There have been many studies of alcoholism and drug addiction and diabetes and on aspects of homicide (on both the murderer and the victim) as suicidal equivalents. In relation to the role of the homicidal victim in his own death, the work of Marvin Wolfgang (1958) has been particularly interesting.

A related concept is that of "subintentioned death." That concept asserts that there are many deaths that are neither clearly suicidal nor clearly accidental or natural but are deaths in which the decedent has played some covert or unconscious role in "permitting" his death to occur, sort of "accidently," or by "inviting" homicide, or, by unconsciously disregarding what could be life-extending medical regimen, and thus dying sooner than "necessary." Losing the "will to live" and so-called voodoo deaths—as well as many deaths in ordinary society—can be viewed as subintentional deaths. Obviously, this view of death changes the nature and statistics of suicide dramatically.

This concept of a reduced level of life as a substitute (or psychological "trade") for suicide itself presents fascinating philosophic, social, psychological, and moral questions that relate to whether or not there actually is an irreducible suicide rate among human beings. Is there a price for civilization? Indeed, a price for life? Litman, reflecting on Freud's work, agrees with Freud's general schematic view and that there is a suicidal trend in everyone. This self-destructiveness is controlled through constructive habits of living and loving, but when they break down, the individual may easily be forced into a suicidal crisis. To keep alive one must keep his thoughts, feelings, and aspirations in a vital balance.

SUICIDE AND RELIGION

In the Western world it has been traditionally said that the suicide rate is higher among Protestants than among Catholics or Jews and that the latter group shows significantly low suicidal figures. By the 1970s it was known, however, that the role of religion in relation to suicide is more complicated and that religious affiliation serves both to inhibit and, at other times, to facilitate suicide. At the outset it is important to distinguish between religious beliefs and religious (social) affiliation. Durkheim not unexpectedly emphasized the sociological aspects of religion. He stated: "If religion protects one from the desire for self-destruction, it is not because it preaches to him, with elements of religious origin, respect for one's person; it is because it forms a social group." A nationwide study in the United States indicated that the pro rata suicide rate among veterans—a fairly representative group of U.S. citizenry—for Catholics and Protestants was about equal to the numbers (and percentages) of Protestants and Catholics in the country generally. Much more important than nominal religious affiliation would be a number of subtleties of religious belief: the feeling of group belongingness, belief in an omnipotent God, belief in the efficacy of prayer, belief in a hereafter or existence after death, and other issues relating to death in general. Results of a national U.S. survey of 30,000 persons reported by Shneidman in 1970 indicated that a sizable percentage (57%) of individuals of all religious backgrounds (and with a variety of intensities of religious belief) did not believe in any life after death and that over one-third indicated that religion had played either a relatively minor role or no role at all in the development of their attitudes toward death (and toward suicide). Just as in the 20th century there has been an enormous "secularization" of death—the physician and hospital in many ways replacing the clergyman and the church in relation to the anxieties surrounding death—so too has there been a secularization of suicide. Few of the current debates about suicide are on primary religious grounds; when the ethics of suicide are debated, those usually are in terms of such concepts as "freedom" and "life," *i.e.*, how free an individual should be to take his own life and how far "benign intervention" should go in an attempt to save an individual's life before the intervention is intrusive and robs him of more than his life is worth.

When Durkheim spoke of religion as a source of social organization (holding individuals together with common beliefs and practices), he was not only speaking of social integration but he was also, from a psychological point of view, referring to personal identification. Walter T. Martin and Jack P. Gibbs (1964) proposed a theory relating status integration with suicide and Henry and Short (1954) discussed the positive relationship between suicide and status and the negative relation between suicide and the strength of a relational source. In general it appears that a person who is uneasy in his religion (or in his irreligion) or changes his religion several times (like a person who is uneasy in his marriage or has several marriages) is more likely to commit suicide, not so much on purely religious (or marital) grounds but because of his general perturbation and lack of good self-concept, which underlie his uneasy search for certainty and stability in his life.

SUICIDE AND THE LAW

Not surprisingly, the history of suicide and the law closely parallel and reflect—often with significant lags—the major cultural and philosophic attitudes toward suicide. Probably the most important recent legal change was the passage of the Suicide Act in England in 1961 that (1) finally abolished criminal penalties for committing suicide—considering that in the 19th century (as late as 1823), a London citizen who committed suicide was buried at a crossroads in Chelsea with a stake pounded through his heart; (2) no longer made survivors of suicide attempts liable to criminal prosecution; and (3) as a kind of quid pro quo for the liberalization of the first two measures, increased the penalties (up to 14 years' imprisonment) for aiding and abetting a suicidal act. Earlier, the Homicide Act of 1957 changed the charge against a survivor of a suicide pact from murder to manslaughter.

In the United States, most aspects of suicide are not against the law. As of the early 1970s a comparatively small number of states (9) listed suicide as a crime, although no penalties (such as mutilation of bodies or forfeiture of estates) were exacted. In such states suicide attempts are either felonies or misdemeanours and could result in jail sentences, although such laws are selectively or indifferently enforced. Two states (Nevada and New York) repealed such laws, stating in effect that although suicide is "a grave social wrong" there is no way to punish it. Eighteen states—Alaska, Arkansas, California, Florida, Kansas, Louisiana, Michigan, Massachusetts, Minnesota, Mississippi, Missouri, Montana, Nevada, New Mexico, New York, Oregon, Wisconsin, and Wyoming—have no laws against either suicide or suicide attempts but specify that to aid, advise, or encourage another person to

commit suicide is a felony. In the more than 20 other states, there are no
penal statutes referring to suicide.

In the early 1970s, especially in Great Britain, there was some movement
(among some eminent lawyers, theologians, philosophers, and physicians)
toward the legalization of voluntary euthanasia; proposals were to repeal
the aiding and abetting aspect of suicide laws so that a physician might,
on a patient's request, assist him to his own voluntary death.

SOME ODDITIES OF SUICIDE

The lore about suicide contains a large number of interesting and esoteric
items about various cultures. Suicide was thought, for example, to be absent
among so-called primitive cultures, but it is evident that this is not so. Studies
were made of suicide in Africa (Paul Bohannan, 1960), India (Verrier Elwin,
1943; Upendra Thakur, 1963), Hong Kong (Yap Powmeng, 1958), and Japan
(Ohara, 1961). Practically every popular article on suicide routinely contains
a statement about the kamikaze pilots who flew and died for Japan in World
War II. Also, in relation to Japan, one often reads of the practice of harakiri
or seppuku, which is the ritual act of disemboweling oneself and was limited
to the samurai warrior and noble classes. General Tōjō, who attempted hara-kiri
at the end of World War II, was saved by U.S. doctors, only to be hanged
later by a military tribunal. In 1970 the well-known Japanese author Mishima
Yukio (q.v.) committed seppuku (with ritual self-disemboweling and decapita-
tion) at the age of 45. In general, however, suicide in contemporary Japan
is more "Western" than otherwise—often done with barbiturates. In a
discussion of suicide in 19th-century India one finds references to suttee,
the custom in which Hindu widows threw themselves onto the funeral pyres
of their husbands.

Six suicides are recorded in the Old Testament: Abimelech, Samson, Saul,
Saul's armour bearer, Ahithophel, and Zimri. The most famous and among
the most frequently cited suicides perhaps, are Socrates' drinking hemlock
and Cato's throwing himself upon his sword. The apocryphal stories of
Bismarck's contemplating suicide, Napoleon's attempting suicide, Washington's despondency, and Lincoln's depression keep reappearing in articles
on suicide—including this one.

Myths of Suicide.-—Following is a summary of some of the more outstanding
misconceptions of suicide:

Fable: Persons who talk about suicide do not commit suicide. *Fact:* Of
any ten persons who will themselves commit it, eight have given definite
warnings of their suicidal intentions.

Fable: Suicide happens without warning. *Fact:* Studies reveal that the suicidal
person gives many clues and warnings regarding his suicidal intentions.

Fable: Suicidal persons are fully intent on dying. *Fact:* Most suicidal persons
are undecided about living or dying, and they "gamble with death," leaving
it to others to save them. Almost no one commits suicide without letting
others know how he is feeling.

Fable: Once a person is suicidal, he is suicidal forever. *Fact:* Individuals who wish to kill themselves are suicidal only for a limited period of time.

Fable: Improvement following a suicidal crisis means that the suicidal risk is over. *Fact:* Most suicides occur within about three months following the beginning of "improvement," when the individual has the energy to put his morbid thoughts and feelings into effect.

Fable: Suicide strikes much more often among the rich, or, conversely, it occurs almost exclusively among the poor. *Fact:* Suicide is neither the rich man's disease nor the poor man's curse. Suicide is represented proportionately among all levels of society.

Fable: Suicide is inherited or "runs in the family." *Fact:* It follows individual patterns.

Fable: All suicidal individuals are mentally ill, and suicide always is the act of a psychotic person. *Fact:* Studies of hundreds of genuine suicide notes indicate that although the suicidal person is extremely unhappy, he is not necessarily mentally ill.

Romantic Suicide and the Artist.—Since at least the 16th century, specifically in the Italian commedia dell'arte, there has been a character named Harlequin who typically wears a multi-coloured suit and a black mask—and has a connection with death. Indeed to be loved by Harlequin was to be married to death. This is the idea of death as a lover; it relates to the romanticization of death itself. As a refinement of this idea, suicide has historically been thought to be a romantic kind of death. One specific myth is that suicide is caused by unrequited love. Suicide pacts (portrayed romantically in *Mayerling* and in *Elvira Madigan*) are depicted as the essence of intense love. One result of this mystique is a belief that especially sensitive people, artists—poets, painters, and writers—are unusually prone to commit suicide and, indeed, add to their reputations as artists by committing suicide. Perhaps the best-known novel of this genre is Goethe's *The Sorrows of Young Werther,* published in 1774 when the author was 24 years old and credited, in the mythology of suicide, with having created a veritable epidemic of romantic suicides throughout Europe. By the 1970s the list of suicides of artists was sufficiently long and vivid to persuade an uncritical student of suicide that the sensitivity of the artist is somehow related to the special nature of a romantic suicidal death. The list includes Van Gogh, Virginia Woolf, Hart Crane, the Italian writer Cesare Pavese, Randall Jarrell, Modigliani, Jackson Pollock, Mark Rothko, Ernest Hemingway, John Berryman, Sylvia Plath, Mishima, and Kawabata Yasunari. Perhaps the best description and analysis of suicide and the creative literary artist is by the English poetry editor and critic Alfred Alvarez in his book *The Savage God: a Study of Suicide* (1971). Maksim Gorki attempted suicide when he was 19. One of the most romanticized suicides in Western literature is that of the English poet Thomas Chatterton (1752-70), who took poison at the age of 17. This particular death illustrates the notion (or myth) "that those with more life and passion go soon"—that the best die young. It reminds one of those who have died "too young"—Byron, Shelley, Keats, Mozart—and the particular poignancy of an untimely death of an especially beautiful or gifted person. We tend to be essentially undemocratic about death and suicide—because we tend to believe that some deaths level (or elevate) certain people more than others.

STATISTICS ON SUICIDE

The demographic use of statistics on suicide perhaps were given their greatest impetus by John Graunt and Johann Peter Süssmilch. Graunt was a London tradesman who, in 1662, published a small book of observations on the London bills of mortality. He separated various bits of information contained in these rolls of names of the dead into separate categories and organized the information systematically, finally constructing mortality tables—the first attempt to organize data in that manner. Of great significance was his success in demonstrating the regularities that can be found between medical and social phenomena when one deals with large numbers. He demonstrated how an analysis of the mortality statistics could be used to the advantage of physicians, businessmen, and government.

Much of what is known today as statistical information came into existence with the work of Süssmilch, a Prussian clergyman who in 1741 in his analyses of vital data from church registers created political arithmetic, or what is now called vital statistics. It is important to keep in mind that statistics, particularly statistics on suicide, are in part socially manufactured data—mostly by coroners and physicians. Suicidal deaths are notoriously underrepresented and obviously vary from country to country dependent not only on the number of suicides that in fact occur in each country but also on deeply ingrained cultural folkways relating to the social, cultural, and religious attitudes of that country.

There are several sources of suicide statistics. Louis Dublin's text, *Suicide* (1963), is a standard source; the World Health Organization (WHO) booklet, *The Prevention of Suicide* (1968), is another. *Suicide in the United States, 1950-1964* (1967) and *The Facts of Life and Death* (1970), both published by the U.S. Department of Health, Education, and Welfare, are standard sources in the United States. In general, the reported suicide rate for the United States is between 10 and 12 per 100,000, which places the United States about in the middle of the countries that report to the United Nations. Austria, West Germany, Hungary, Japan, Czechoslovakia, Denmark, Finland, Sweden, and Switzerland report rates of over 25 per 100,000 population, and Italy, the Netherlands, and Spain report rates under 10 per 100,000. The number of suicides in the United States per year is given at about 22,000 but many experts believe the actual number to be at least twice as high.

In any discussion of the statistics of suicide—keeping in mind their tenuous character—it is important to distinguish among rank, rate, and number. Currently, in the United States, suicide is ranked among the first five causes of death for white males from 10 to 55. For example, suicide is the second-ranked cause of death for white males age 15-19, but one must appreciate that the first leading cause of death, accidents, yields 627 chances in 100,000 of the individual's dying from that cause, while suicide yields (only) 88 chances in 100,000. Generally, in the early ages when suicide is high, it occupies that rank because the other killers like heart disease, malignant neoplasms (cancer), vascular lesions of the central nervous system (stroke), and cirrhosis of the liver are not then common.

In general, statistics on suicide in the 19th and 20th centuries indicate that more men than women commit suicide (about 3 to 1) and that more women than men attempt suicide (again about 3 to 1). In the early 1970s there was evidence that the ratio for committed suicide seemed to be changing, moving toward (but not yet achieving) an equal proportion between the sexes. Statistics relating to race and ethnic origin seem to be undergoing changes, probably reflecting general changes in attitude toward the concept of race and ethnicity. In the United States it was reported for years that Caucasian suicides far outnumbered Negro suicides, but the rate for Negroes seems to be changing, moving closer to that for Caucasians. Whether this reflects the effects of urban ghetto living, the effects of identifying with "the white man's problems," or simply better and more accurate recordkeeping are all issues for further study. Some studies (conducted in England and Australia) that followed individuals who emigrated either to the United States or to Australia seem to indicate that the suicide rates of specific groups such as Hungarians, Italians, Poles, and Irish appear, for a generation or so, to be closer to the rates of the homeland than to the rates of the adopted country. In these data, there are many methodological issues that are also yet to be resolved.

In relation to suicide statistics, a standard textbook on sociology published in 1972 reported thats sociologists still made continuous reference to the work of Durkheim. Rates derived from Durkheim's studies show that suicide rates for Protestants have been consistently higher than those for Jews or Catholics. In the early part of the 20th century the Jewish rate in the Netherlands was higher than the Protestant, and during the depression, in Toronto, Can., Catholic rates also were higher than Protestant. The inference is that the time, the place, and the social circumstances are all important factors.

In the matter of comparative national statistics, Alvarez points out that U.S. Pres. Dwight D. Eisenhower blamed the high Swedish suicide rate on what too much social welfare can do. But the present rate in Sweden, Alvarez notes, is about the same as it was in 1910, before comprehensive social welfare programs were begun and is actually ranked ninth on a table published by WHO. The countries of Central Europe show the highest rates: Hungary has the highest national rate; Austria and Czechoslovakia are third and fourth. The highest suicide rate in the world is that of West Berlin; its rate is more than twice that of West Germany as a whole. The city, it has been suggested, is a model of what Durkheim called anomie—alienated not only geographically but also in cultural, social, and political aspects. Countries like Ireland and Egypt, where suicide is considered by many a mortal sin, have rates among the lowest in the world, bearing out Stengel's conclusion that highly industrialized and prosperous countries tend to have comparatively high suicide rates. Alvarez concludes that official statistics reflect only a fraction of the true figures, which a number of authorities reckon to be anywhere from a quarter to a half again as large. Because of religious and bureaucratic prejudices, family sensitivity, differences in the proceedings of coroners' hearings and postmortem examinations, the shadowy distinctions between suicides and accidents—in short, the unwillingness to recognize the act for what it is—knowledge of the extent to which suicide pervades modern society is diminished and distorted.

A certain sizable percentage of deaths that are certified by coroners or medical examiners—estimated to be between 10 and 15%—are equivocal as to what the actual mode of death ought to be; this uncertainty usually lies between suicide or accident. A procedure, called the psychological autopsy, has been developed to deal with these equivocal deaths. Essentially, the psychological autopsy involves the use of social and behavioural scientists (psychologists, psychiatrists, social workers, and other trained personnel) who interview relatives and friends of the decedent with the goal of developing information about the decedent's intention vis-à-vis his own death in the days just before the death. Clues—verbal ("You won't be seeing me around"); behavioural (*e.g.*, giving away prized possessions or marked changes in patterns of eating, sexuality, interests); or situational (*e.g.*, the loss of a loved one)—are deemed to point more to suicide than to accident. In the absence of such clues, a recommendation for a non-suicidal or "undetermined" mode of death should be made to the certifying official.

SUICIDE VENTION (PREVENTION, INTERVENTION, POSTVENTION)

The Latin word *venire* means "to come" or "to do." In relation to any event (*e.g.*, suicide) one can act before, during, or after—corresponding to prevention, intervention, and postvention. These terms also correspond roughly to the public health concepts of primary, secondary, and tertiary prevention.

Prevention.—If, as this article has suggested, suicidal phenomena are existential-social-psychological-dyadic events, then obviously primary prevention is enormously complicated—almost tantamount to preventing human unhappiness. Some students of human nature believe that the urge toward self-destruction is ubiquitous and that a certain amount of it is an inevitable and constant price of civilization, if not of life itself. Primarily, prevention would relate to the principles of good mental hygiene in general.

Intervention.—Intervention relates to the treatment and care of suicidal crises or suicidal problems. On this score, suicide prevention centers could be more accurately labeled suicide intervention centers. A great deal has been learned about practical techniques for effective suicide intervention. There is a vast literature on therapy and treatment of suicidal persons in various settings—in the community, in suicide prevention and crisis intervention centers, in poison-control centers, in outpatient offices, and in both medical and mental hospitals. In general, most of the suggestions for care have in common the stressing of good rapport, working with the "significant others" in the suicidal person's life, using the available community resources for referral (for emotional support, legal aid, financial help, employment, individual and group psychotherapy, hospitalization), and focusing on the reduction of the person's "lethality" during the period of suicidal crisis. Much of the suicide prevention work borrows from the theory of crisis intervention developed by Erich Lindemann (1944) and Gerald Caplan (1964). In the United States, the theoretical and empirical work of the Los Angeles Suicide Prevention Center, established in 1955, and in Great Britain, the work of the Samaritans, established in 1953, has been widely emulated.

In 1960 there were fewer than a half-dozen suicide prevention centers in the United States; a decade later there were over 200. Typically they are telephone-answering centers; maintaining 24-hour service, they serve as short-term resources, are theoretically modeled in terms of the concept of crisis intervention, and use both professional and lay volunteer staff.

Suicide is best understood as a socio-psychological, existential human event that calls for compassionate response to an individual in an emotional and philosophic crisis. Obviously suicide is not solely a medical problem and many kinds of persons including volunteers—provided they are carefully selected, well-trained, and continuously supervised—can serve as lifesaving agents in the prevention of suicide. The lay volunteer has been described as probably the most important single discovery in the history of suicide prevention. Nonetheless, professionally trained persons—psychologists, psychiatrists, social workers—continue to play the primary roles in suicide prevention and especially in research.

Postvention, a term introduced by Shneidman in 1971, refers to those things done after the dire event has occurred that serve to mollify the aftereffects of the event in a person who has attempted suicide, or to deal with the adverse effects on the survivor-victims of a person who has committed suicide. It is offering psychological services to the bereaved survivors. It includes work with the surviving children, parents, and spouses. Much of postventive work has been focused on widows. Studies show that survivors are apt to have a higher morbidity and mortality rate in the year following the death of their loved one than comparable persons who are not survivors of such a death. It may well be that the major public mental-health challenge in suicide lies in offering postventive help to the survivor-victims. The development of postvention is part of the current new view of the special psychological needs relating to death.

BIBLIOGRAPHY.—Émile Durkheim, *Suicide* (1897; Eng. trans. by J. A. Spaulding and G. Simpson, 1951); Sigmund Freud, "Mourning and Melancholia" (1917), in *The Standard Edition of the Complete Psychological Works*, vol. 14 (1965); Karl A. Menninger, *Man Against Himself* (1938); Edwin S. Shneidman and Norman L. Farberow (eds.), *Clues to Suicide* (1957), *The Cry for Help* (1961); Glanville Williams, *The Sanctity of Life and the Criminal Law* (1957); Louis I. Dublin, *Suicide: a Sociological and Statistical Study* (1963); Erwin Stengel, *Suicide and Attempted Suicide* (1964); Paul Friedman (ed.), *On Suicide* (1967); Jack D. Douglas, *The Social Meanings of Suicide* (1967); Robert E. Litman, "Sigmund Freud and Suicide," Henry A. Murray, "Dead to the World," in E. S. Shneidman (ed.), *Essays in Self-Destruction*

(1967); U.S. Public Health Service, *Suicide in the United States, 1950–1964* (1967); Arnold Toynbee *et al.*, *Man's Concern with Death* (1969); World Health Organization, *Prevention of Suicide* (1968); Edwin S. Shneidman, "Suicide, Lethality and the Psychological Autopsy," in E. S. Shneidman and M. Ortega (eds.), *Aspects of Depression* (1969); N. L. Farberow, *Bibliography on Suicide and Suicide Prevention* (1969); E. S. Shneidman (ed.), *On the Nature of Suicide* (1969); E. S. Shneidman, N. L. Farberow, and R. E. Litman, *The Psychology of Suicide* (1970); A. Alvarez, *The Savage God: a Study of Suicide* (1971); Jacques Choron, *Suicide* (1972).(E. S. Sh.)

PART I

Demography of Suicide

James C. Diggory

1
United States Suicide Rates, 1933–1968: An Analysis of Some Trends

The introductory passages to this chapter are taken from John Graunt's *Observations on the London Bills of Mortality* (1662), chaps. II and III.

In my Discourses upon these *Bills*, I shall first speak of the Casualties, then give my Observations with reference to the *Places* and *Parishes* comprehended in the *Bills*; and next of the *Years* and *Seasons*.

1. There seems to be good reason, why the *Magistrate* should himself take notice of the numbers of *Burials* and *Christnings*, *viz.* to see whether the City increase or decrease in People; whether it increase proportionably with the rest of the Nation; whether it be grown big enough, or too big, &c. But why the same should be made known to the People, otherwise than to please them, as with a curiosity, I see not.

2. Nor could I ever yet learn (from the many I have asked, and those not of the least *Sagacity*) to what purpose the distinction between *Males* and *Females* is inserted, or at all taken notice of? or why that of *Marriages* was not equally given in? Nor is it obvious to every body, why the Accompt of *Casualties* (whereof we are now speaking) is made? The reason, which seems most obvious for this later, is, That the state of health in the City may at all times appear.

3. Now it may be Objected, That the same depends most upon the Accompts of *Epidemical Diseases*, and upon the chief of them all, the *Plague*; wherefore the mention of the rest seems only matter of curiosity.

4. But to this we Answer, That the knowledge even of the numbers which

dye of the *Plague*, is not sufficiently deduced from the meer Report of the *Searchers*, which only the Bills afford; but from other Ratiocinations, and comparings of the *Plague* with some other *Casualties*.

5. For we shall make it probable, that in the Years of *Plague*, a quarter part more dies of that *Disease* than are set down; the same we shall also prove by other *Casualties*. Wherefore, if it be necessary to impart to the world a good Accompt of some few *Casualties*, which since it cannot well be done without giving an Accompt of them all, then is our common practice of so doing very apt and rational.

6. Now, to make these Corrections upon the, perhaps, ignorant and careless *Searchers* Reports, I considered first of what Authority they were of themselves, that is, whether any credit at all were to be given to their Distinguishments: and feeling that many of the *Casualties* were but matter of sense, or whether a child were *Abortive* or *Stilborn;* whether men were *Aged*, that is to say, above sixty years old, or thereabouts when they died, without any curious determination; whether such *Aged* persons died purely of *Age*, as for that the *Innate heat* was quite extinct, or the *Radical moisture* quite dried up (for I have heard some Candid *Physicians* complain of the darkness which themselves were in hereupon) I say, that these Distinguishments being but matter of sense, I concluded the Searchers Report might be sufficient in the Case.

7. As for *Consumptions*, if the *Searchers* do but truly Report (as they may) whether the dead Corps were very lean and worn away, it matters not to many of our purposes, whether the Disease were exactly the same, as *Physicians* define it in their Books. Moreover, In case a man of seventy five years old died of a *Cough* (of which had he been free, he might have possibly lived to ninety) I esteem it little errour (as to many of our purposes) if this Person be in the Table of *Casualties*, reckoned among the *Aged*, and not placed under the Title of *Coughs*.

8. In the matters of *Infants* I would desire but to know clearly, what the *Searchers* mean by *Infants*, as whether Children that cannot speak, as the word *Infant* seems to signifie, or Children under two or three years old, although I should not be satisfied, whether the *Infant* died of *Wind*, or of *Teeth*, or the *Convulsion*, &c. or were choaked with *Phlegm*, or else of *Teeth*, *Convulsion*, and *Scowring*, apart, together, which, they say, do often cause one another; for, I say, it is somewhat to know how many die usually before they can speak, or how many live past any assigned number of years.

9. I say, it is enough, if we know from the *Searchers* but the most predominant Symptoms; as that one died of the *Headach*, who was sorely tormented with it, though the *Physicians* were of Opinion, that the Disease was in the *Stomach*. Again, if one died *suddenly*, the matter is not great, whether it be reported in the Bills, *Suddenly*, *Apoplexy*, or *Planet-strucken*, &c.

10. To conclude, In many of these Cases the *Searchers* are able to report the Opinion of the *Physician*, who was with the Patient, as they receive

the same from the Friends of the Defunct: and in very many Cases, such as *Drowning, Scalding, Bleeding, Vomiting, making away themselves, Lunaticks, Sores, Small-pox, &c.* their own senses are sufficient, and the generality of the World are able pretty well to distinguish the *Gout, Stone, Dropsie, Falling sickness, Palsie, Agues, Pleuresie, Rickets,* one from another.

11. But now as for those Casualties, which are aptest to be confounded and mistaken, I shall in the ensuing Discourse presume to touch upon them so far, as the Learning of these Bills hath enabled me.

12. Having premised these general Advertisements, our first Observation upon the *Casualties* shall be, That in Twenty Years there dying of all Diseases and Casualties 229250, that 71124 died of the *Thrush, Convulsion, Rickets, Teeth* and *Worms;* and as *Abortives, Chrysomes, Infants, Livergrown,* and *Overlaid;* that is to say, that about $\frac{1}{3}$ of the whole died of those Diseases, which we guess did all light upon Children under four or five years old.

13. There died also of the *Small Pox, Swine Pox,* and *Measles,* and of *Worms* without *Convulsions,* 12210, of which number we suppose likewise, that about $\frac{1}{2}$ might be Children under six years old. Now, if we consider that sixteen of the said 229250 died of that extraordinary and grand Casualty, the *Plague,* we shall find that about thirty six *per Centum* of all quick conceptions died before six years old.

14. The second Observation is, That of the said 229250 dying of all Diseases, there died of *acute* Diseases, (the *Plague* excepted) but about 50000, or $\frac{2}{9}$ parts. The which proportion doth give a measure of the State, and disposition of this *Climate* and *Air* as to health; these *acute* and *Epidemical* Diseases happenning suddenly and vehemently, upon the like corruptions and alterations in the *Air.*

15. The third Observation is, That of the said 229250, about seventy thousand died of *Chronical* Diseases, which shews (as I conceive) the State and Disposition of the Country (including as well its *Food* as *Air*) in reference to health, or rather to *longevity:* for as the proportion of *acute* and *Epidemical* Diseases shews the aptness of the *Air* to sudden and vehement Impressions; so the *Chronical* Diseases shew the ordinary temper of the place: so that upon the proportion of *Chronical* Diseases seems to hang the judgment of the fitness of the Country for *long life.* For, I conceive, that in Countries subject to great *Epidemical* sweeps, men may live very long, but, where the proportion of the *Chronical* distempers is great, it is not likely to be so; because men being long sick, and alwaies sickly, cannot live to any great Age, as we see in several sorts of *Metal-men,* who, although they are less subject to *acute* Diseases than others, yet seldom live to be old, that is, not to reach unto those years, which *David* says is the Age of Man.

16. The fourth Observation is, That of the said 229250, not 4000 died of outward Griefs, as of *Cancers, Fistula's, Sores, Ulcers, broken and bruised Limbs, Imposthumes, Itch, King's Evil, Leprosie, Scald-head, Swine Pox, Wens, &c. viz.* not one in sixty.

17. In the next place, whereas many persons live in great fear and apprehension of some of the more formidable and notorious Diseases following;

I shall only set down how many died of each: that the respective numbers, being compared with the total 229250, those persons may the better understand the hazard they are in.

Table of Notorious Diseases.

Apoplex	1306
Cut of the Stone	38
Falling Sickness	74
Dead in the Streets	243
Gout	134
Head-ach	51
Jaundice	998
Lethargy	67
Leprosie	6
Lunatick	158
Overlaid and Starved	529
Palsie	423
Rupture	201
Stone and Strangury	863
Sciatica	5
Suddenly	454

Table of Casualties.

Bleeding	69
Burnt and Scalded	125
Drowned	829
Excessive drinking	2
Frighted	22
Grief	279
Hanged themselves	222
Kill'd by several accidents	1021
Murdered	86
Poysoned	14
Smothered	26
Shot	7
Starved	51
Vomiting	136

18. In the foregoing Observations we ventured to make a Standard of the healthfulness of the *Air* from the proportion of *acute* and *Epidemical* Diseases, and of the wholsomness of the food, from that of the *Chronical.* Yet, for as much as neither of them alone do shew the *longevity* of the Inhabitants, we shall in the next place come to the more absolute Standard and Correction of both, which is the proportion of the Aged, *viz.* 15757 to the Total 229250. That ‖ is, of about 1 to 15, or 7 *per Cent.* Only the question is, What number of years the *Searchers* call *Aged*, which I conceive

must be the same that *David* calls so, *viz.* 70. For no man can be said to die properly of *Age*, who is much less. It follows from hence, That if in any other Country more than seven of the 100 live beyond 70, such Country is to be esteemed more healthful than this of our City.

19. Before we speak of particular *Casualties*, we shall observe, That among the several *Casualties* some bear a constant proportion unto the whole number of *Burials*; such are *Chronical* Diseases, and the Diseases whereunto the City is most subject; as for Example, *Consumptions, Dropsies, Jaundice, Gout, Stone, Palsie, Scurvy, Rising of the Lights* or *Mother, Rickets, Aged, Agues, Fevers, Bloody Flux* and *Scowring:* nay, some Accidents, as *Grief, Drowning, Men's making away themselves,* and being *Kill'd by several Accidents, &c.* do the like; whereas *Epidemical* and *Malignant* Diseases, as the *Plague, Purples, Spotted Fever, Small Pox* and *Measles* do not keep that equality: so as in some Years, or Months, there died ten times as many as in others . . .

My first Observation is, that few are *starved*. This appears, for that of the 229250, which have died, we find not above fifty one to have been *starved*, expecting helpless *Infants* at Nurse, which being caused rather by carelessness, ignorance, and infirmity of the Milch-women, is not properly an effect or sign of want of food in the Country, or of means to get it. . . .

The *Lunaticks* are also but few, *viz.* 158 in 229250, though I fear many more than are set down in our *Bills*, few being entred for such, but those who die at *Bedlam*; and there all seem to dye of their *Lunacy*, who died *Lunaticks*; for there is much difference in computing the number of *Lunaticks*, that die (though of *Fevers* and all other Diseases, unto which *Lunacy* is no *Supersedeas*) and those that dye by reason of their *Madness*.

So that, this *Casualty* being so uncertain, I shall not force my self to make any inference from the numbers and proportions we find in our Bills concerning it: only I dare ensure any man at this present, well in his Wits, for one in a thousand, that he shall not dye a *Lunatick* in *Bedlam* within these seven years, because I find not above one in about one thousand five hundred have done so.

The like use may be made of the Accompts of men that made away themselves, who are another sort of Mad men, that think to ease themselves of pain by leaping into *Hell*; or else are yet more Mad, so as to think there is no such place; or that men may go to rest by death, though they dye in *Self-murther*, the greatest Sin . . .

United States Suicide Rates, 1933–1968: An Analysis of Some Trends*

The data presented and discussed here are from the annual volumes of *Vital Statistics of the United States* representing the years 1900–1968.† Although the data are thus easily available, not all have been published in a form to make them readily accessible and useful to students of suicide. Although there have been some special studies of levels and trends in suicide rates of various subdivisions of the population,[1-5] neither the ordinary reader or the expert on suicide has found it feasible to consult the data on which these special studies were based. One function of the present article is to make these

*This chapter was written while the author was principal investigator of NIMH Grant No. MH-17367, awarded to Information and Volunteer Services (IVS) of Allegheny County. Special acknowledgments and thanks are hereby rendered to Miss Marian Marconyak, former Research Assistant on the project, who helped in the research, transcription, and preliminary analysis of some of the data; Mr. Thomas Brezny, former Computer Programmer on the project, who performed the trend analyses; Mrs. Mary Lou Charlton, Librarian of the Health and Welfare Association of Allegheny County, for research and frequent advice about sources; and Mrs. Catherine O. Saxe, former Office Manager for the project, who organized and assisted in many ways, including typing the manuscript. The matter presented in this chapter is not necessarily representative of the opinions of the National Institute of Mental Health.

†Some data on U.S. suicide rates are available through 1971 but not in the detail needed for the analyses presented here. Some data for the later years of the range discussed here were not published at the time they were needed for this compilation. They were made available as computer printouts from the National Center for Health Statistics through the good offices of Mrs. Gwendolyn M. Rucker, of their Office of Information.

data easily accessible so that with only a little additional effort a reader can quickly compare his local suicide statistics to those for the entire nation.

A second function of this chapter is to display the results of systematic analytical trend analyses as applied to successive annual suicide rates for the indicated subdivisions of the population. Although many people are interested in whether the annual suicide rates of particular subgroups are[2,4,5] rising or falling, the most responsible discussions of the relevant data have not employed genuine trend analysis techniques. The present chapter attempts to repair that deficiency for some subgroups of the United States population and indicates some of the possibilities for trend analyses in other subgroups.

DEFINITION OF UNITED STATES VITAL STATISTICS

Prior to 1900 there were no *annual* compilations of number and rate of deaths from various causes for the total United States population. Beginning with the census of 1850 and continuing through 1900, decennial US mortality statistics were published, based on reports of census enumerators. In 1880, a system parallel to that of the census enumerators was established—a Death Registration Area (DRA) which included some entire states and some cities in other states from which mortality returns were received *in addition* to the information from census enumerators. Beginning with the calendar year 1900, annual mortality statistics were compiled from the DRA. Admission to the DRA was determined by the willingness of state or local authorities to use certificates and certification criteria which met minimum standards suggested by the Federal Bureau of Vital Statistics. The importance of this certification procedure to the nation at large is ably discussed by Moriyama and Israel.[6]

The DRA of 1880 included Massachusetts, New Jersey, and the District of Columbia. By 1890 it added Connecticut, Delaware, New Hampshire, New York, Rhode Island, and Vermont. Beginning in 1900 every annual volume included information about the growth of the DRA. In 1933, with the addition of Texas, the DRA finally came to represent 100 percent of the population and land area of the United States[7] and the volume for that year contains a summary of the growth of the DRA. As already indicated, the District of Columbia was included in the DRA from the beginning, and the territories were added subsequently; the Virgin Islands in 1924 and Puerto Rico in 1932. Hawaii was added as a territory in 1917. Generally, the DRA represented a steadily increasing proportion of the population and land area of the United States year by year, but there were some regressions. For example, Delaware was dropped from the area in 1900 and readmitted in 1919; South Dakota was admitted in 1906, dropped in 1910, and readmitted in 1930; in 1910 North Carolina was represented by municipalities with a population of 1,000 or more (about 16 percent of its total population) and the remainder of the state was added in 1916. Although Texas did not completely enter the area until 1933, it had for several years prior been represented by eight of its larger cities. In 1900 the DRA included only 40.5 percent of the total US population, a proportion which rose to 58.3 percent in 1910, 82.3 percent in 1920, 96.2 percent in 1930, and 100 percent from 1933 onward.

Thus, prior to 1933 available mortality data do not represent the entire nation. Seiden[5] said that it was, nevertheless, "accepted practice . . . to regard the statistics from the expanding group of registration states as the best approximation to the national figures and to use them to make comparisons over a long period." The figures from the expanding DRA are the *only* data on US mortality but, in a variety of ways, they may be poor approximations for those causes of death which show systematic regional differences. Seiden, commenting on his data which give age-adjusted rates for the United States, 1900–1964, observed that total population suicide rates rose from 11.3 per 100,000 in 1900 to 17.9 per 100,000 in 1915 (a 58 percent increase in 15 years). Since the 1900 DRA included only slightly more than 40 percent of the US population and probably a considerably lower proportion of US suicides (for it did not include the Mountain and Pacific regions which have consistently had the highest suicide rates in the nation), some of the increase may have resulted from the addition of California and Colorado to the DRA in 1906. In 1910 the California suicide rate was 28.9 per 100,000.[1] In this chapter the basic data are presented in Appendix A as raw rates per 100,000 for the years 1933–1968 for the total population divided by 5-year age groups. Appendix A also contains the basic 4-way subdivision of the population into white and nonwhite males and females and separate totals for all males and all females (races combined), and all white and all nonwhite (sexes combined). The rates are also given for each of these population subgroups with all ages combined.

DESCRIPTIONS OF SECULAR TRENDS

Figure 1-1 presents a graphic display of the 36 successive annual suicide rates for the total population of the United States, all ages combined, with the corresponding rates for the total male, total female,

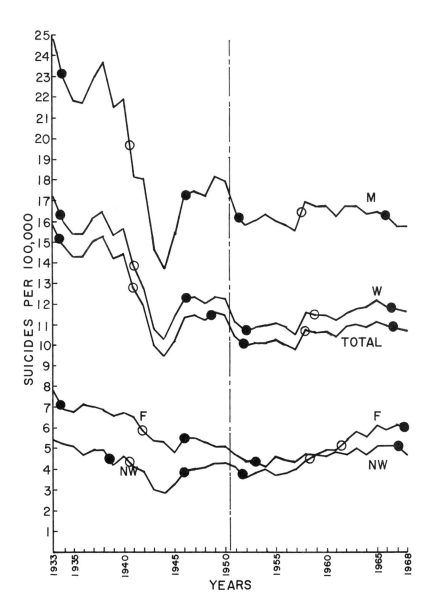

Fig. 1. Annual suicide rates for United States, 1933–1968 for total population, white population (W), nonwhite population (NW), male population (M), and female population (F). The open circles on each polygonal line are centered on the best-fitting straight lines for the entire 36-year period. The closed circles to the left of the vertical centerline are centered on the best-fitting straight lines for the first 18-year period, 1933–1950; those to the right of the centerline are on the best-fitting straight lines for the second 18-year period, 1951–1968.

33

total white, and total nonwhite components. The solid polygonal lines which connect the data points contain some pitfalls which interpreters of the data should avoid. The primary trap involves selecting particular years (e.g., decennial census years) and considering variations between them as representative of a trend. For example, in Figure 1-1 the graph for the total population shows the year 1950 with a higher rate than 1960 and yet those years belong to a generally *rising* trend, though the increase was by no means steady. A special case of this type of error is the attempt to manufacture trends from the magnitude and direction of change in any two successive years; e.g., all segments of the population represented in Figure 1-1 had suicide rates which rose between 1945 and 1946, but, in every instance, 1945 and 1946 belong to a period where suicide rates were generally declining.

Another practice which may lead to erroneous impressions about trends in suicide rates is the practice of presenting a long sequence of annual rates taken at selected intervals, say of 5 years or 10 years. Seiden[5] gives an example of the use of 5-year periods. Comparison of his Figure 2 with our Figure 1-1 shows that by selecting data points spaced 5 years apart he has produced a polygonal trend line which is smoother than it ought to be and specifically supresses both the fact that the rates for the total white and total male populations were maximal in 1938 and the deep trough in all of the trend curves between 1940 and 1945. Only the single-year presentation exemplified in Figure 1-1 indicates that the year 1944 was the nadir of suicide rates for the total US population, as well as for the white, nonwhite, and male populations. The total female population in the period considered had a lower suicide rate in 1945 than it did in 1944 but its lowest rate occurred in 1954.

For the entire 36-year period the average of the annual white suicide rate was 12.5 per 100,000 and 4.4 per 100,000 for nonwhite. The average for the total population was 11.6. That is, in every year the suicide rate for the total population is much closer to that of the white population than to that of the nonwhite population, and this is due to the fact that the white population is larger. This fact depends only on the size of the base population, not on the number or proportion of suicides generated by that population, a point illustrated by the fact that the data points for the total male population and the total female population (which are approximately equal in size) are annually approximately equidistant from, and on opposite sides of, the total population data points. Thus, although on the average male suicide rates have been 3.18 times those of females, the form of the national trend for the total population has been almost equally determined by the male and female population components. This is particularly evident in the second 18-year period under consideration in which there is no change (zero slope) in the male suicide rate, while the significant increase (positive slope) of the female suicide rate reflects itself in a significant positive slope for the total population. The finer details of the sex-by-race breakdown shown in the last four sections of Appendix B indicate that during the second 18-year period the white male population component shows no significant increase in suicide rates while white female, and nonwhite males and females all show significant increases. The largest increase occurs among white females and the smallest increase among nonwhite females.

THE ANALYSIS OF TRENDS*

As the caption for Figure 1-1 indicates, the open and closed circles on the polygonal lines of the figure indicate the position of the idealized trend line associated with each polygonal line. These ideal trends are straight lines, represented by the general equation $y = a + bx$, where y represents a point any distance above the horizontal axis of the graph, a is a function of the height of the line above the horizontal axis, and b is the number of units by which y changes for each unit change in x. Thus b is the slope of the straight line.

The choice of a straight line, or any other analytical function, to represent a trend is completely arbitrary. Any one of a number of types of curves could have been fitted to the data by the familiar statistical routine known as the method of *least squares*—a segment of a circle, an ellipse, a parabola or a hyperbola, or a trigonometric or exponential function. If it is interpreted cautiously, the best-fitting (least-squares) straight line gives the most direct and uncomplicated answer to the question most often asked: Are the successive rates year-by-year getting lower or higher? Since the fitting procedure is statistical it also has a built-in method for deciding whether the trend is significantly different from zero. Thus for the total population, for the total white population, and the total male population, there can be little doubt that the best-fitting straight lines indicated by the open circles on each of the curves just mentioned verifies what

*A good presentation of the topics dealt with in this section is given by Draper and Smith.[8]

common sense would say about the general trend of the polygonal
lines for the 36-year period, i.e., that the trend is downward.

The numerical slopes and means of all trend lines are shown
in Appendix B where the slopes are marked with an asterisk if they
are significantly different from zero. It can be determined from
Appendix B that generally the trend of US suicide rates from 1933
to 1968 was significantly downward for the total population and for
all components of the population except for the total nonwhite
component which showed no change.

Although, as already indicated, the choice of a straight line is
arbitrary, the original data shown by the polygonal lines of Figure
1-1 can be compared with the best-fitting straight line and a decision
can be made as to whether the differences between the two can
be considered as merely random fluctuations of the true data around
the idealized trend line or whether the pattern of deviations of data
from trend is so systematic as to suggest that some sort of curved
lines would better fit the data. In other words we want to know
whether the deviations of the original data points from the straight
line are so systematic (non-random) that we can decide that the two
are significantly different. The handiest method for making this decision
under the present circumstances is the Runs Test[9] the application
of which will be illustrated here with a single example.* For the
total population data shown in Figure 1-1 the best-fitting straight line
runs through the two open circles located approximately at years
1940 and 1958. With that trend line actually extended it can be seen
that the real data point for 1933 is above the trend line, that is,
it has a positive residual. If the residuals simply alternated between
positive and negative in successive years, then intuition would prompt
the decision that a straight line is the best description of the data
and the residuals, independent of their magnitude, were merely chance
fluctuations around the linear trend. No matter what the nature of
the raw data, the method of least squares indicates that the numbers
of positive and negative residuals around a trend line are approximately
equal. There are a few instances in the present data where the
occurrence of a few very large deviations produces distributions of
residuals where the numbers of positives and negatives are not exactly
equal. It is also possible, though it is a rare occurrence, that some
of the residuals equal zero. The tables of the Runs Test give the
probabilities of observing various numbers of *runs* in ordered sequences

---

*The minimum instructions and tables needed to apply the Runs Test are included
in most collections of tables for nonparametric statistics.

of events where each event can be of one class, e.g., positive or another class, e.g., negative. In the instance under consideration here, a *run* is a set of contiguous residuals all of which have the same sign. The smaller the number of runs the smaller the probability that the observed data are well represented by the best-fitting straight line. In that case, the decision that the data would be better represented by some other curve is justified, but there is no way to specify which of the many possible types of curves that might be. If simple alternation positive-negative-positive-negative, etc. prevailed, then, in the present data, there would be as many runs as there are residuals because each data point would be preceded and followed by a sign opposite to its own (or by no sign at all). Each would constitute a run of one unit, and thus the total number of runs would be 36 which is the largest possible number available for the data being described. But for the total population data it is obvious that there are only three runs; all the residuals from 1933 to 1941 are positive, all those from 1942 to 1957 are negative, and all those from 1958 through 1968 are positive. For 19 positive and 17 negative residuals the probability of observing as few as 3 runs is less than 1 in 100,000, so the data are significantly nonlinear.

Inspection of the five sets of real data points represented by the polygonal lines in Figure 1-1 suggests that the course of US suicide rates decreases sharply between 1933 and 1944 and thereafter rises slightly. Appendix B shows that, with the exception of the data for the nonwhite population, all of the real trends shown in Figure 1-1 depart significantly from linearity in the sense just described.

Given the nature of the departure of the real data trends from linearity as described in the previous paragraph it is possible to see each total 36-year trend line as consisting of two branches, the first one rapidly declining and the second one either declining less rapidly or actually rising. Each of these branches was separately fitted with its own straight line. Since the data provide no clear guides about where to divide the 36-year trends they were arbitrarily separated into the first 18 years (1933-1950) and the second 18 years (1951-1968). Given the data in Appendix A anyone who wants to make a different analysis can do so. It is likely that if the first period were defined as running from 1933 to 1944 and the second period from 1945 through 1968, all the trend lines for the first period would have large negative slopes and in the second period the trend line for the total male population would have a small negative slope, the trend line for the total nonwhite population would have the largest positive slope, and the other slopes—total population, total white population, and total female population—would be approximately zero. Given the break-down made here between first and second 18-year periods, all of the trend lines for the first 18 years are significantly negative and significantly non-linear except that for the total nonwhite population where the slight negative slope ($-.09$) does not differ significantly from zero or from linearity. For the second 18-year period all the linear trends have significant positive slopes except that for the total male population which does not differ significantly from zero. With the exception of the curve for the total population (9 positive residuals, 9 negative residuals, 6 runs, $\alpha = .0445$) none of the second-half trends differs significantly from a straight line.

In view of the considerations so far adduced in the trend analyses, the following conclusions seem justified. As long as there have been any true total US mortality data, the general trend of suicide rates for the whole population and for its white, male, and female components has been downward. The decrease occurred primarily in the first half of the 36-year period and the second half is characterized by a general rise in the suicide rates of all population components except for males. The total nonwhite population component shows no net trend either for increase or decrease in suicide rates for the whole 36-year period; the trend of nonwhite suicide rates is not significantly different from zero in the first half of the period and it shows a significant increase in the second half. In the first part of the 36-year period the decline in suicide rates was greater for males than for females and it was also greater for the white population than for the nonwhite population. In the second half of the period the total female population component had the largest rate of increase, the male component had the smallest rate of increase, and the nonwhite population suicide rate rose somewhat faster (.09 per year) than that of the white population (.07 per year).

FORECASTING

Since we are dealing here with the special variety of trend analysis known as *time series* analysis it is important to bear in mind the truth of the witticism that, in spite of all the impressive things that statisticians know how to do, "when it comes to time series, there is no Santa Claus."[10] Those who follow the daily, weekly, monthly, or annual fluctuations in stock market prices, whether motivated by hope of gain or mere intellectual curiosity, are baffled in their efforts to discover a rational analytical function or formula which would enable them to predict future fluctuations in average market prices. At present the student of changes in suicide rates is in no better position. There was no way in 1933 to predict the course described previously for the successive annual suicide rates of the US population or its components through 1968. Our present knowledge is all hindsight; there is no method for predicting. Regardless of these limitations in our knowledge of the future course of time series, students of suicide who think they have discerned trends in their data often refer to them as though they were relatively durable, perhaps permanent, phenomena. Following are some forecasts made on the assumption, weak almost to the point of total impotence, that the most recent trends will continue forever. Each trend for the second 18-year period is represented by its own particular values of a and b inserted into the equation given previously. If two linear trends have different slopes it can be determined by inspection whether they will diverge forever or converge at some time in the future. If they are convergent we can calculate how many years it will take for the suicide rates of the two population components to be identical. This is done by taking the difference between the equations for the two population groups, setting the difference equal to zero, and solving for x, the number of years. A few illustrations will enable every reader to make these highly suspect "forecasts" for himself. The equation used is $x = -[(a - c)/(b - d)]$, where a and b are, respectively, the level and slope of one straight line and c and d are, respectively, the level and slope of the other. During the final 18-year period the total male suicide rates had a positive slope of .0058 (not significantly different from zero) and the overall female rates increased significantly with a slope of .1117. In 1968 the overall male suicide rate was 15.7 and 5.9 for women. To apply the formula subtract the female suicide rate from the male suicide rate for an obtained difference of 9.8. Then subtract the female slope from the male slope for a difference of $-.1059$. Divide the difference between the suicide rates by the difference between their slopes (taking the signs into account) to get the positive quotient of 92.5 years, the length of time (after 1968) it would take for male and female suicide rates to coincide. By the same argument it will take 408.3 years for the white and nonwhite suicide rates to converge, 106.2 years for the white and nonwhite male suicide rates to converge, and 84.5 years for white male and female suicide rates to converge. There would be no convergence between white and nonwhite females or between nonwhite males and females.

AGE-SPECIFIC SUICIDE RATES

Appendixes A and B present the data in uniform 5-year age categories, beginning with the 10-14 year-old group. Suicide rates at ages under 10 are negligible. The decision to combine all persons at least 75 years old was arbitrary and done for convenience. It does not adversely affect the resultant picture of age-specific trends other than suppressing the fact that interannual fluctuations in the suicide rates of persons over 85 years of age are larger and more irregular than those at younger ages, largely because of the relatively small number of people over 85.

It has been commonly accepted that when no distinctions of sex or race are made annual suicide rates are likely to be higher in older age groups. This is confirmed, with few exceptions, in the sections of Appendix A which show total population suicide rates and male suicide rates. In neither the total population or any of its components is the age-specific increase purely monotonic since there are instances where, in the same year, an older age group has a lower suicide rate than some younger age group. More important, in US component populations, the relation of suicide rates to age depends upon both race and sex.

Among white males the highest suicide rates were in the group at least 75 years old, with two exceptions—in 1933 and 1934 the maximum white male suicide rates occurred in the 70-74 year age category. The white female suicide rates were considerably more varied in the locus of the maximum rates, which ranged from the 45-49 year age group to the 60-64 age group. In 24 of the 36 years being considered (1933-1968) the US white female suicide rate was maximal in the 50-54 year age group and in one of those years, 1953, the 50-54 and the 55-59 year age groups shared the maximum suicide rate, 9.4 per 100,000. Despite the relative uncertainty as to which age group consistently contained the maximum white female suicide rate a fair description is that suicide increased in likelihood with increasing age up to about 45 years of age; from there until about 65 years of age it showed only a slight tendency to change with age (the direction of the change is uncertain); and from 65 years of age onward there was a definite tendency for white female suicide rates to become increasingly lower at higher ages.*

The age-specific locus of maximum suicide rates for US nonwhite

---

*Bolander[11] describes quite similar age-specific relations in the statistics on female suicides in the four Scandinavian nations, 1966-1968 averages. In comparison with her data on Scandinavian males, US male suicide rates, especially for white males, have the stronger tendency to increase after 50 years of age.

males was more variable from year to year than that of white females. In 9 of the 36 years the highest nonwhite male suicide rate was in the age group at least 75 years old. (In one of those 9 years an equally high rate occurred in the 55-59 year age group.) In 17 of the 36 years the maximum suicide rates of nonwhite males occurred in the 60-64 year age group. In 1964 and 1967 the nonwhite male maximum suicide rates were in the 25-29 year age group and in 1966 the maximum was in the 30-34 year age group. Taking the modal age group for maximal nonwhite male suicide rates as 60-64 years there is no consistent trend of lowering the age for the maximum suicide rate throughout the 36-year period; the three lowest ages for the maximum suicide rate were in the second half of the 36-year period but in the same period there were more deviations of maximal suicide rate above the modal age group than below it. Although there are many exceptions, an adequate summary of age differences in nonwhite male suicide rates is that they increased irregularly from the earliest ages until approximately 60 years of age after which there was either a marked slowing of the increase with age or a tendency for suicide rates to decline with advancing age after 60. The choice between the latter options depends on which year is being examined.

The age bracket which contained the largest number of maximum suicide rates for nonwhite females during the 36-year period is 30-34 years, 30 years below the modal age of maximal nonwhite male suicide rates. While the choice of a function relating suicide rates to age among nonwhite males must be approached with circumspection it appears hopeless in the case of nonwhite females where the locus of the maximum suicide rate ranged from 20-24 to at least 75 years of age, and only the 65-69 year age group and the two age groups under 20 never contained the maximum suicide rate in that 36-year span. Generally speaking, among nonwhite females there was an irregular increase in suicide rates up to somewhere between 25 and 40 years of age and at higher ages there was an irregular decrease, but even so general a statement can be justified only by averaging age-specific suicide rates over the entire 36-year period. There is no generally consistent pattern for the nonwhite female suicide rates as a function of age nor any systematic change in pattern throughout the 36-year period.

SECULAR TRENDS IN AGE-SPECIFIC SUICIDE RATES

Seiden[5] points out that, in recent years, suicide rates have risen in many countries, including the United States, at younger ages, and increases have been greater for females and nonwhites. ''The dramatic

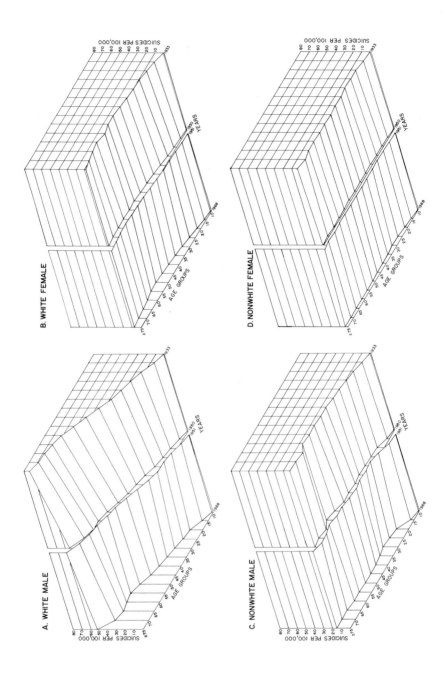

42

increase has occurred among nonwhite teenagers who show only slightly lower suicide rates than their white peers.'' For this discussion recent years means the second half of the 36-year period under consideration (1933-1968). Analysis of the slopes of the linear trend lines for the age-specific groups by sex and race (Appendix B) shows that the largest rates of increase do not occur among teenagers if "teenagers" are interpreted as persons under 20 years of age. Indeed in the 10-14 year age bracket there is a significant increase (slope = .03) only for white males; the slope for nonwhite males is negative, not significantly different from zero and the slopes for females of both races are positive but not significantly different from zero. In the 15-19 year age bracket all slopes for the four sex-by-race groups are positive and significantly different from zero and their order of magnitude is: white male (.24), nonwhite male (.18), nonwhite female (.08), and white female (.04). As Appendix B indicates all of these trends may be regarded as linear. For the total population, without regard to race or sex, there have been significant increases in the suicide rates of persons under 20 years of age between 1951 and 1968.

With respect to the above suggestion that the relatively close approximation between white and nonwhite teenage suicide rates is a relatively recent event, the means shown in Appendix B indicate that the ratios of white to nonwhite average teenage suicide rates are nearly identical in 1951-1968 and 1933-1950.

The entire picture of the age specific *trends* in the 36-year period requires the simultaneous appreciation of three variables—the two "independent" variables, age and year and the "dependent" variable, suicide rate. This can be most easily visualized by the aid of three dimensional graphs such as those presented in Figure 1-2. The surfaces shown in Figure 1-2 were constructed by drawing the straight line trends for each age category through the first and final years of each of the two 18-year periods. The graphs were drawn without perspective—they are isometric. The surfaces for the first 18 years and the second 18 years are distinguished by the gap between them; the width of the gap shows the standard one-year interval.

For the white male population the surface for the earlier period

←――――――――――――――――――――――――――――――――――――――

Fig. 2.   Age-specific trends in US suicide rates by sex and race, 1933-1950 and 1951-1968. The "ribs" of each surface are the best-fitting least-squares straight lines with slopes as shown in Appendix B. The beginning and ending points for each line are the predicted suicide rates for the indicated years. The actual rates are given in Appendix A.

slants downward toward the observer's point of view, showing that, in the years 1933-1950, the suicide rates in all age groups had negative slopes, and the surface rises along the age axis showing the general tendency for suicide rates to increase with age. The surface for the second 18-year period presents a twisted aspect because beginning with the youngest ages and continuing up through the 40-44 year bracket the age-specific suicide rates are increasing significantly year-by-year from 1951-1968. From 45 years of age through 59 years of age there are three 5-year age groups in which the rate of change did not differ significantly from zero. In all age categories above 60 the age-specific suicide rates declined significantly in successive years. In other words the suicide rates of white males under 45 years of age all declined significantly from 1933-1950 and since then, until 1968, they have all increased significantly, though at slower rates than those of their previous declines. Between 45 and 60 years of age suicide rates declined precipitously from 1933-1950 and from 1950-1968 remained nearly constant. The suicide rates of all age categories above 60, which declined steeply between 1933-1950 have continued to decline until 1968, with the later rates of decrease being less than the earlier ones. All features of this description would apply to the graph for the total population as can be seen in Appendix B.

During the first 18-year period there was a much less pronounced decline in the age-specific suicide rates of nonwhite males than among white males. In neither period were age-specific decreases in nonwhite male suicide rates as durable or as steep as those of white males and during the second period more of the age-specific nonwhite male suicide rates showed positive trends than did those of white males.

The surfaces for the white and nonwhite females are much less elevated than those for the two male groups, corresponding to the generally lower suicide rates among women than among men. For both groups of females, differences in slope of the age-specific trends in the two 18-year periods are very small and are barely discernable in the graphs.

SIGNIFICANCE OF AGE-SPECIFIC SECULAR TRENDS

In a previous section an exercise in forecasting was carried out to determine whether and how soon the most recent secular trends in annual suicide rates would produce equality of rates between the sexes and between white and nonwhite race groups. Superficially it appears inviting to try some similar forecasting to determine whether and when suicide rates of younger and older groups might coincide.

That exercise will not be attempted here. Sex and race are biological facts which probably are more intimately related to differences in behavior, temperament, and rates and types of physical and psychological development. Age is a transient condition, a series of arbitrarily separated temporal stages, loosely correlated with behavior, through which all standard members of a species pass.* What happens in the course of psychobiological development at any particular age is more materially caused by factors associated with sex and race of that individual than the other way around. It is possible that some aspects of the observed differences in age-specific suicide rates already commented on are dependent upon differences between the sexes and races, and there may be even a sex-by-race interaction, various differences between male and female age-specific trends depending on the race being considered.

Some students of suicide have informally expressed the view that the recent increases in suicide rates among persons below age 45 are signs that we are entering an era of rising suicide rates in all segments of the population. This is not an inevitable conclusion in view of the recent US experience in which the suicide rates of those under 45 and those over 60 are compensatory so that the overall national suicide rate in the last 18 years has risen significantly, but so slowly that it would take 86.7 years from 1968 for it to regain its 1933 level. Possibly there is a mechanism which produces lower suicide rates in older age groups when the rates are high or increasing in younger groups. For instance, if a relatively large proportion of people under 40 commit suicide, then those who survive to later ages may contain a lower proportion of suicide-prone individuals. This hypothesis cannot be tested adequately with the present total US data (Appendix A) nor its derived parameters (Appendix B). A more adequate test of that hypothesis would be to follow several age cohorts from the year of their birth, tracing their mortality experience year-by-year until 80 percent or 90 percent of them had died. Moriyama and Gustavus[12] in their pioneering study of cohort mortality from all causes point out that (1) cohort survivorship is generally higher than what would be expected from conventional "period" survivorship tables; (2) the percentage of excess cohort survivorship increased steadily through the birth cohorts of 1901, 1910, 1920, and 1930 for the latest age data available for all cohorts (40 years); and (3) in the three latter cohorts the preponderance of cohort survivorship lies with females rather than males, and with

---

*A standard individual is a typical survivor who dies at an age not younger than the mean age at death for his group.

nonwhite rather than white persons. These findings, together with
the age-by-race-by-sex suicide rates analyzed in this chapter, suggest
that a high priority be given to cohort mortality and survivorship
studies with emphasis on details of various causes of death including
suicide. It is entirely likely that such a study would reveal relations
between the likelihood of suicide and other causes of death.

Though their data are inadequate by modern standards (which
themselves are far from perfect) most commentators on 19th century
suicide statistics indicate that there was a great increase in suicide
rates during that century.[13-15]* According to Achté and Lönnqvist[13]
Finnish suicide statistics show a compensatory relation between
younger and older age groups which is opposite to that found in
the United States; since the 1920s, suicide rates of younger Finnish
age groups have either declined or remained unchanged whereas rates
in older age groups have risen clearly and steadily. To understand
the significance of changes in suicide rates in specific age groups
we should find out how changes in general mortality and mortality
from specific causes are related to suicide rates. For example, if
it can be firmly established that suicide rates were generally rising
in European countries throughout the 19th century it will probably
follow that there is a significant positive correlation between suicide
rates and increasing life expectancy, but there are no firm grounds
for interpreting such a correlation in this way. The relation between
age-specific suicide rates and total death rates from all causes in
various age groups would no doubt be complex. Moriyama[17] presents
data (Figs. 6A and 6B, p. 8-9) which indicate that from 1930-1960
total death rates per 100,000 declined in all age groups, both sexes,
and in white and nonwhite population components; the rate of decline
was steeper in the younger age groups and decreased with advancing
age. Thus, since the suicide rates of individuals under 45 years of
age have been generally rising throughout the same period, the
correlation between suicide rates and total mortality should be negative
for the population under 45, and it should be increasingly positive
for groups older than 45. The author has noted a large *negative*
correlation ($>$.70) between US annual infant mortality rates and suicide
rates of people under 20 for the 36-year period covered in this report.
The correlation just cited and others suggested are among the highest
correlations between suicide rates and any other phenomena so far
reported. Presumably, they have some significance for our under-

*According to Retterstöl[16] no systematic increase occurred in Norwegian suicide
rates since 1885, so any increase in Norway during the 19th century must have occurred
before this date.

standing of suicide. However, rather than pointing to the end of our bewilderments about the causation of suicide and changes in its rates, these correlations and all others indicated in this report point to the very great magnitude of the labor that still lies between us and our understanding of suicidal phenomena.

REFERENCES

1. Allen NH: Suicide in California, 1960–1970. California State Department of Public Health, 1973
2. Kalish RA: Suicide: An ethnic comparison in Hawaii. Bull Suicidol: 37–43, 1968
3. MacMahon B, Johnson S, Pugh TF: Relation of suicide rates to social conditions: Evidence from US vital statistics. Public Health Reports 78: 285–293, 1963
4. Massey JT: Suicide in the United States. Washington, D.C., US Public Health Service, 1967
5. Seiden RH: Suicide among youth. Bull Suicidol, 1969
6. Moriyama IM, Israel RA: Problems in compilation of statistics on suicides in the United States. Proceedings 4th International Congress Suicide Prevention. Los Angeles, International Association for Suicide Prevention, 1968, p 16
7. United States Bureau of the Census: Mortality Statistics, 1933. Washington, D.C., US Government Printing Office, 1935
8. Draper N, Smith H: Applied Regression Analysis. New York, Wiley, 1966
9. Swed FS, Eisenhart C: Tables for testing randomness of grouping in a sequence of alternatives. Ann Math Stat 14: 66–87, 1943
10. Wallis WA, Roberts HJ: Statistics: A New Approach. New York, Free Press, 1956
11. Bolander AM: Nordic suicide statistics, in Waldenström J, Larsson T, Ljungsted N (eds): Suicide and Attempted Suicide. Stockholm, Nordiska Bokhandelns Förlag, 1972, p 57
12. Moriyama IM, Gustavus SO: Cohort mortality and survivorship: United States death registration states, 1900–1968. Washington, D.C., US Public Health Service, 1972
13. Achté KA, Lönnqvist I: Cultural aspects of suicide in Finland. Psychiatr Fenn: 291–294, 1972
14. Durkheim E: Suicide. Glencoe, Illinois, Free Press, 1951
15. Morselli H: Suicide: An Essay on Comparative Moral Statistics. New York, Appleton-Century-Crofts, 1882
16. Retterstöl N: Suicide in Norway, in Waldenström J, Larsson T, Ljungsted N (eds): Suicide and Attempted Suicide. Stockholm, Nordiska Bokhandelns Förlag, 1972, p 89
17. Moriyama IM: The change in mortality trend in the United States. Washington, D.C., US Public Health Service, 1964

Appendix A
US Total Population Suicide Rates per 100,000 by Five-Year Age Groups, 1933–1968

Year	10-14	15-19	20-24	25-29	30-34	35-39	40-44	45-49	50-54	55-59	60-64	65-69	70-74	≥75	All ages
1933	0.3	4.2	10.6	12.8	15.0	18.8	24.6	31.5	35.3	41.3	44.9	44.9	47.4	42.7	15.9
1934	0.4	4.5	10.6	13.5	15.5	17.9	22.6	27.4	32.0	35.6	38.9	39.6	42.0	38.4	14.9
1935	0.4	4.2	10.3	13.1	15.5	17.6	21.1	27.1	30.3	34.2	35.7	35.7	35.4	36.5	14.3
1936	0.5	4.3	9.6	13.0	16.0	18.1	21.9	25.7	29.8	33.8	34.3	35.6	33.0	35.8	14.3
1937	0.6	4.0	10.2	13.0	15.9	18.5	23.6	28.8	31.4	34.3	36.6	35.5	32.6	36.4	15.0
1938	0.3	4.1	9.5	13.0	16.0	18.6	24.1	28.5	33.0	36.6	38.3	35.8	32.1	34.4	15.2
1939	0.5	3.7	8.3	11.4	14.6	17.3	20.9	25.6	31.1	33.3	35.7	33.8	34.1	34.0	14.2
1940	0.4	3.5	8.9	12.2	15.0	18.1	20.7	26.1	29.5	34.0	34.9	33.1	33.4	33.3	14.4
1941	0.4	3.5	8.2	11.3	13.7	16.2	18.2	21.5	25.2	29.0	30.7	29.9	32.0	32.9	12.8
1942	0.5	3.1	7.1	9.8	13.2	14.7	17.6	20.0	22.7	28.3	28.5	26.7	29.2	31.8	11.9
1943	0.5	3.0	5.8	7.5	10.1	12.2	13.8	15.8	19.5	22.7	25.1	24.8	26.7	30.2	10.0
1944	0.4	2.7	5.3	7.2	9.4	11.9	14.3	15.8	18.9	21.5	22.0	22.0	24.3	28.8	9.5
1945	0.4	2.6	5.6	7.3	10.9	13.3	15.7	17.7	21.6	23.0	24.7	24.5	27.8	29.2	10.1
1946	0.5	2.9	7.3	8.8	11.1	14.0	16.6	18.9	23.5	24.7	27.9	24.1	28.8	28.9	11.3
1947	0.5	2.9	6.3	8.1	10.9	13.7	16.6	20.0	22.5	26.2	27.9	27.6	28.0	33.0	11.4
1948	0.4	2.8	6.6	7.8	10.3	12.8	16.4	19.6	22.7	25.7	27.2	25.3	29.5	30.0	11.2
1949	0.5	2.5	6.5	7.8	9.9	13.6	17.1	19.0	23.0	27.0	29.4	28.9	27.7	30.4	11.5
1950	0.3	2.7	6.2	8.1	10.2	13.1	15.9	19.5	23.0	25.9	28.8	29.0	29.9	30.8	11.4

Appendix A (continued)

Year	10-14	15-19	20-24	25-29	30-34	35-39	40-44	45-49	50-54	55-59	60-64	65-69	70-74	≥75	All ages
1951	0.4	2.6	6.1	8.0	9.1	11.5	15.2	17.8	19.8	21.8	24.8	26.7	27.8	28.9	10.4
1952	0.3	2.8	5.6	7.9	9.0	11.3	13.5	16.7	20.0	20.9	24.3	25.0	26.5	29.1	10.0
1953	0.5	2.8	6.0	8.4	8.6	11.0	14.3	17.4	20.3	21.0	24.0	24.7	26.5	28.7	10.1
1954	0.3	2.4	6.0	8.5	9.0	10.8	14.4	17.9	20.8	22.2	25.8	24.5	26.0	26.3	10.1
1955	0.3	2.6	5.6	7.9	8.9	10.3	14.5	17.6	21.9	24.4	25.2	25.2	24.7	28.6	10.2
1956	0.4	2.3	5.9	7.6	9.4	10.6	13.8	17.2	20.1	23.4	25.1	25.4	25.1	28.1	10.0
1957	0.5	2.5	5.8	7.6	9.7	10.9	14.6	16.4	20.3	22.2	22.6	23.1	24.4	27.5	9.8
1958	0.5	3.0	7.0	9.2	10.3	12.0	15.6	18.9	22.8	23.5	24.7	24.4	26.0	28.5	10.7
1959	0.5	3.4	6.8	9.1	10.5	12.3	15.0	18.1	21.7	23.9	24.8	24.5	25.2	28.8	10.6
1960	0.5	3.6	7.1	9.0	10.9	13.2	15.2	19.1	22.6	23.6	23.8	21.4	25.0	28.9	10.6
1961	0.4	3.4	7.1	9.2	11.3	13.2	15.6	18.6	22.2	23.8	22.3	21.7	22.3	27.2	10.4
1962	0.6	3.7	8.2	9.9	12.6	13.8	16.3	19.4	22.8	24.0	23.3	21.9	22.6	28.4	10.9
1963	0.6	4.0	8.5	11.0	12.6	15.5	16.6	19.1	23.3	24.6	22.4	21.5	23.4	26.2	11.0
1964	0.5	4.0	8.5	10.7	13.1	14.6	16.5	19.5	21.7	23.5	21.7	22.1	22.1	25.0	10.8
1965	0.5	4.0	8.9	11.3	13.3	15.8	17.5	18.7	22.8	24.7	22.8	22.3	21.6	25.0	11.1
1966	0.6	4.3	9.2	11.4	13.3	14.6	16.9	19.0	21.1	23.0	22.8	21.6	21.5	24.7	10.9
1967	0.6	4.7	9.7	11.8	12.9	15.7	17.5	18.2	21.0	22.6	22.1	19.4	20.3	21.8	10.8
1968	0.6	5.1	9.6	11.4	12.8	15.2	17.1	18.6	20.7	22.1	21.4	19.6	19.6	21.4	10.7

Appendix A (continued)
US Male Suicide Rates per 100,000 by Five-Year Age Groups, 1933–1968

Year	10-14	15-19	20-24	25-29	30-34	35-39	40-44	45-49	50-54	55-59	60-64	65-69	70-74	≥75	All ages
1933	0.4	4.5	13.5	17.5	21.5	27.8	36.8	49.5	56.6	66.5	74.7	76.5	84.5	80.7	24.9
1934	0.5	4.8	14.2	18.5	22.2	25.9	33.7	41.2	49.5	57.9	62.6	67.3	75.0	71.2	22.9
1935	0.6	4.6	14.0	18.6	20.9	24.8	31.4	41.5	47.1	54.1	56.8	59.8	59.8	68.8	21.8
1936	0.7	5.2	12.8	17.4	22.2	27.0	32.3	38.9	45.1	53.6	55.1	59.5	55.6	66.4	21.7
1937	0.9	4.8	13.7	18.1	22.9	26.9	35.3	43.2	47.9	53.1	59.5	58.9	56.5	67.7	22.8
1938	0.5	5.0	13.4	18.6	23.5	27.3	36.1	43.1	51.3	57.9	63.0	59.5	55.7	63.9	23.6
1939	0.8	4.8	12.1	17.1	20.9	24.8	31.1	37.6	47.2	52.4	57.8	55.8	57.4	64.3	21.5
1940	0.7	4.2	13.0	17.3	21.1	26.3	30.1	38.6	45.0	54.4	56.9	53.7	56.1	61.7	21.9
1941	0.5	4.0	11.4	16.1	19.1	23.5	26.4	30.8	37.5	45.0	49.4	50.0	54.8	62.0	18.1
1942	0.7	3.8	10.3	13.6	18.9	21.3	26.1	26.6	33.4	44.4	45.5	45.1	49.7	56.8	18.0
1943	0.7	3.9	7.8	10.3	13.9	17.6	18.7	21.9	27.6	34.1	37.3	40.0	43.5	56.2	14.7
1944	0.6	3.1	6.5	9.8	12.2	16.2	19.8	22.3	27.0	31.7	33.2	35.5	40.8	52.3	13.7
1945	0.7	3.5	7.3	9.6	14.1	18.6	22.4	24.6	31.2	34.6	39.2	39.7	46.8	53.9	15.3
1946	0.9	3.5	10.4	13.1	14.0	19.5	24.5	27.9	34.4	38.2	44.4	49.2	49.2	61.2	17.2
1947	0.8	3.9	9.2	11.6	15.3	20.1	24.4	29.0	33.6	42.3	45.5	45.2	47.8	63.5	17.4
1948	0.7	3.5	9.8	11.7	14.4	18.6	23.6	30.0	34.7	40.8	45.4	43.0	52.4	56.0	17.2
1949	0.7	3.6	9.6	11.9	14.4	20.3	26.1	29.0	36.0	42.7	48.3	49.1	49.2	58.8	18.1
1950	0.5	3.5	9.4	11.8	15.5	19.6	24.0	30.0	35.7	42.3	47.5	49.4	52.6	58.8	17.9

Appendix A (continued)

Year	10–14	15–19	20–24	25–29	30–34	35–39	40–44	45–49	50–54	55–59	60–64	65–69	70–74	≥75	All ages
1951	0.7	3.5	9.6	11.9	13.2	16.9	22.4	27.2	30.1	35.0	40.6	45.1	50.1	54.4	16.3
1952	0.5	4.4	9.0	11.9	12.9	16.9	20.3	25.1	31.2	33.2	40.5	42.4	47.2	57.5	15.8
1953	0.7	3.9	9.7	12.6	12.8	16.7	22.4	27.0	31.9	33.3	39.9	42.8	47.5	56.5	16.0
1954	0.4	3.6	10.3	13.1	13.8	16.6	21.4	28.8	33.6	35.9	43.1	42.2	45.8	52.0	16.3
1955	0.4	4.0	8.8	12.1	12.6	16.6	21.4	28.8	33.7	39.2	41.7	42.2	43.8	54.4	16.0
1956	0.6	3.3	9.6	11.3	14.0	15.6	21.0	25.8	31.2	37.4	40.9	42.7	44.7	56.6	15.7
1957	0.7	4.0	9.3	11.0	14.3	16.1	22.3	25.5	37.2	35.0	37.0	38.7	45.2	56.0	15.5
1958	0.8	4.3	11.1	13.3	14.9	18.3	24.1	29.3	35.2	27.9	41.6	41.3	46.1	57.5	16.9
1959	0.9	5.1	11.0	13.1	15.6	18.4	22.7	28.2	34.2	38.4	40.7	41.0	44.7	58.1	16.7
1960	0.9	5.6	11.5	13.7	15.6	19.1	23.1	28.5	35.2	37.7	38.6	36.4	43.9	56.1	16.7
1961	0.7	5.3	11.2	13.5	16.2	19.4	23.2	28.1	34.1	38.4	36.2	36.4	39.5	54.2	16.2
1962	1.0	5.5	12.5	13.9	17.8	19.9	23.3	28.0	34.1	38.3	37.5	37.7	40.3	57.4	16.7
1963	0.9	6.0	12.8	13.8	17.5	21.2	23.6	27.2	34.6	38.5	35.8	35.6	41.6	53.0	16.7
1964	0.9	6.3	12.9	15.4	18.5	19.2	23.3	28.2	34.8	36.7	35.4	35.9	38.4	51.9	16.3
1965	0.9	6.1	13.8	16.3	18.3	21.1	24.0	25.5	33.1	37.8	36.8	36.5	38.5	50.1	16.4
1966	0.9	6.5	14.2	16.3	18.4	20.1	23.0	26.3	30.9	35.5	37.0	36.0	37.9	51.5	16.2
1967	0.9	7.0	14.9	17.1	17.4	21.3	24.4	25.3	29.9	33.5	35.0	30.6	35.9	44.4	15.7
1968	0.9	7.6	14.8	16.3	18.1	20.9	23.1	25.5	29.1	33.8	34.3	33.7	35.6	53.5	15.7

Appendix A (continued)
US Female Suicide Rates per 100,000 by Five-Year Age Groups, 1933–1968

Year	10–14	15–19	20–24	25–29	30–34	35–39	40–44	45–49	50–54	55–59	60–64	65–69	70–74	≥75	All ages
1933	0.2	3.8	7.7	8.2	8.6	9.6	11.8	12.1	12.0	14.1	13.4	12.4	9.8	8.3	6.8
1934	0.2	4.1	7.1	8.5	8.9	9.9	11.1	12.7	13.1	11.5	13.9	11.4	8.9	8.9	6.9
1935	0.3	3.9	6.7	7.9	10.1	10.1	10.4	11.8	12.1	12.5	13.5	11.2	11.0	7.5	6.8
1936	0.4	3.3	6.5	8.7	9.9	9.2	11.2	11.6	13.2	12.6	12.6	11.3	10.3	8.5	7.1
1937	0.3	3.1	6.8	8.1	9.0	10.1	11.6	13.5	13.7	14.1	12.8	12.0	8.8	8.6	7.0
1938	0.1	3.3	5.7	7.7	8.7	10.0	11.8	13.1	13.3	13.9	12.7	12.1	8.9	8.2	6.9
1939	0.2	2.5	4.8	6.0	8.4	9.8	10.5	13.0	13.8	12.9	13.0	12.0	11.2	7.1	6.6
1940	0.1	2.8	4.9	7.3	9.0	10.0	11.2	13.1	13.0	12.4	12.2	12.7	11.2	8.3	6.7
1941	0.3	2.9	5.0	6.7	8.5	9.0	9.9	11.8	12.2	12.2	11.5	10.1	10.0	7.5	6.5
1942	0.2	2.4	4.1	6.1	7.5	8.2	9.1	13.3	11.4	11.5	11.1	8.8	9.5	10.3	5.8
1943	0.3	2.2	3.9	4.8	6.5	6.9	8.8	9.6	10.6	10.9	12.7	10.2	10.8	7.9	5.4
1944	0.2	2.3	4.0	4.7	6.7	7.8	8.7	9.3	10.5	10.9	10.8	9.2	8.8	8.8	5.3
1945	0.2	1.7	4.1	5.1	7.8	8.3	9.2	10.7	11.7	11.2	10.0	10.1	10.1	8.4	4.8
1946	0.2	2.3	4.2	4.7	7.1	8.7	8.8	9.9	12.4	11.2	11.4	5.1	9.9	7.9	5.5
1947	0.1	1.9	3.5	4.7	6.7	7.6	9.0	11.1	11.5	10.1	10.5	11.1	9.9	8.0	5.5
1948	0.1	2.2	3.7	4.2	6.3	7.3	9.4	9.3	10.8	10.7	9.1	8.7	8.8	8.6	5.3
1949	0.3	1.4	3.6	3.9	5.7	7.2	8.2	9.2	10.1	11.5	10.6	10.0	8.3	7.2	5.1
1950	0.1	1.8	3.3	4.7	5.2	7.0	8.1	9.3	10.5	9.7	10.3	10.2	9.6	8.0	5.1

Appendix A (continued)

Year	10-14	15-19	20-24	25-29	30-34	35-39	40-44	45-49	50-54	55-59	60-64	65-69	70-74	≥75	All ages
1951	0.2	1.7	2.9	4.3	5.3	6.3	8.1	8.6	9.6	8.6	9.0	9.3	7.6	7.8	4.7
1952	0.2	1.3	2.6	4.2	5.2	5.9	6.9	8.5	8.9	8.8	8.5	8.7	7.9	6.6	4.4
1953	0.2	1.8	2.8	4.4	4.6	5.5	6.5	8.0	8.7	8.8	8.7	7.8	7.8	6.9	4.3
1954	0.1	1.3	2.3	4.1	4.4	5.2	7.6	7.2	8.3	8.8	9.3	8.1	8.5	6.2	4.1
1955	0.2	1.3	2.6	3.8	5.4	5.4	6.9	8.9	10.3	10.1	9.5	9.6	7.9	7.9	4.6
1956	0.1	1.3	2.5	4.0	4.9	5.7	6.9	8.8	9.3	9.8	10.1	9.5	8.0	6.2	4.4
1957	0.2	1.0	2.6	4.3	5.2	6.0	7.1	7.5	8.6	9.8	9.3	9.0	6.3	5.8	4.3
1958	0.2	1.7	3.1	5.2	6.0	6.1	7.3	8.9	10.7	9.6	9.2	9.3	8.7	6.6	4.7
1959	0.1	1.6	2.8	5.2	5.7	6.4	7.6	8.2	9.6	10.0	10.1	9.9	8.5	6.9	4.7
1960	0.2	1.6	2.9	4.6	6.4	7.6	7.7	10.0	10.4	10.2	10.2	8.1	8.9	8.6	4.9
1961	0.2	1.5	3.2	5.0	6.6	7.4	8.3	9.4	10.6	9.8	9.7	9.0	7.9	7.4	4.9
1962	0.1	2.0	4.0	6.1	7.6	8.1	9.6	11.1	12.0	10.5	10.4	8.4	8.0	7.5	5.4
1963	0.2	1.9	4.4	6.4	8.0	9.9	10.0	11.3	12.5	11.4	10.2	9.6	8.5	7.6	5.8
1964	0.1	1.7	4.2	6.1	7.8	10.2	10.1	11.3	12.8	11.1	9.3	10.5	9.0	6.2	5.6
1965	0.2	1.9	4.3	6.5	8.4	10.8	11.4	12.3	13.1	12.4	10.2	10.4	8.3	7.6	6.1
1966	0.2	2.1	4.4	6.8	8.4	9.4	11.2	12.2	11.8	11.4	10.0	9.6	8.9	6.7	5.9
1967	0.3	2.4	4.8	6.8	8.6	10.4	10.9	11.5	12.7	12.3	10.6	10.1	8.5	6.5	6.1
1968	0.2	2.2	4.7	6.7	7.7	9.9	11.4	12.1	12.8	11.5	10.0	7.9	7.6	6.1	5.9

Appendix A (continued)
US White Suicide Rates per 100,000 by Five-Year Age Groups, 1933–1968

Years	10-14	15-19	20-24	25-29	30-34	35-39	40-44	45-49	50-54	55-59	60-64	65-69	70-74	≥75	All ages
1933	0.4	4.3	11.0	13.5	15.8	19.9	25.9	33.5	37.6	43.8	47.5	47.6	49.6	45.2	17.1
1934	0.4	4.7	10.9	14.2	16.2	19.2	24.1	29.2	34.2	37.4	41.1	42.0	44.5	40.2	16.0
1935	0.5	4.5	10.7	13.7	16.3	18.5	22.5	29.0	32.3	36.0	37.4	38.0	37.4	38.5	15.4
1936	0.8	4.7	10.1	13.8	16.9	19.3	23.4	27.7	31.7	35.7	35.8	37.9	34.6	37.8	15.4
1937	0.6	4.2	10.8	13.7	16.8	19.8	25.1	30.9	33.3	36.2	38.4	37.8	34.2	38.5	16.1
1938	0.3	4.3	9.9	13.8	16.9	19.9	25.8	30.6	34.9	38.8	40.0	38.3	38.3	36.0	16.4
1939	0.5	3.9	8.7	12.0	16.6	18.5	22.3	27.2	33.1	37.3	37.6	36.3	36.0	35.7	15.3
1940	0.4	3.7	9.2	12.8	15.7	19.6	22.1	27.7	31.3	36.0	36.8	35.4	35.2	35.2	15.6
1941	0.4	3.6	8.5	12.0	14.5	17.5	19.4	22.8	26.7	30.7	32.3	32.0	33.9	34.6	13.8
1942	0.5	3.2	7.3	10.2	13.9	15.9	18.7	21.6	24.2	29.8	29.8	28.6	31.0	33.7	12.8
1943	0.5	3.2	6.0	7.9	10.7	13.1	14.8	17.0	20.8	24.0	26.2	26.8	38.9	26.3	10.8
1944	0.4	2.8	5.4	7.7	9.9	12.9	15.3	15.7	20.2	22.6	23.1	23.7	25.7	30.4	10.3
1945	0.5	2.8	5.7	7.8	11.3	14.4	16.8	19.0	23.0	24.5	25.9	26.3	29.3	30.6	11.3
1946	0.6	3.1	7.5	9.2	11.6	14.9	17.8	20.2	25.1	26.1	29.2	25.9	30.3	30.4	12.2
1947	0.5	3.0	6.4	8.4	11.4	14.6	17.7	21.3	24.1	27.6	29.3	29.5	29.6	34.8	12.3
1948	0.4	3.0	6.8	8.1	10.6	13.5	17.5	20.7	24.2	27.3	28.7	27.0	31.1	31.6	12.0
1949	0.5	2.6	6.8	8.1	10.3	14.3	18.2	20.3	24.5	28.5	30.6	30.8	29.1	31.9	12.3
1950	0.3	2.8	6.4	8.4	10.5	13.8	17.0	20.7	24.5	27.3	30.1	31.2	31.2	32.6	12.2

Appendix A (continued)

Year	10-14	15-19	20-24	25-29	30-34	35-39	40-44	45-49	50-54	55-59	60-64	65-69	70-74	≥75	All ages
1951	0.5	2.7	6.1	8.1	9.5	12.0	16.2	19.1	21.0	22.9	26.1	28.5	29.5	29.8	11.1
1952	0.3	3.1	5.7	8.1	9.3	11.9	14.5	18.0	21.4	22.1	25.5	26.8	28.0	30.3	10.7
1953	0.5	3.0	6.2	8.6	8.9	11.6	15.3	18.6	21.5	22.2	25.3	26.2	28.0	29.6	10.8
1954	0.3	2.5	6.1	8.5	9.3	11.3	15.4	19.0	22.2	23.7	27.1	26.0	27.3	27.5	10.9
1955	0.3	2.7	5.5	8.1	9.2	10.9	15.4	18.7	23.5	26.1	26.5	26.9	26.1	29.7	11.0
1956	0.4	2.3	6.1	7.7	9.7	10.9	14.7	18.3	21.5	25.0	26.4	27.0	26.6	29.5	10.8
1957	0.5	2.6	5.9	7.7	9.9	11.5	15.5	17.4	21.8	23.6	23.8	24.6	25.2	28.7	10.5
1958	0.5	3.2	7.1	9.4	10.6	12.5	16.6	20.1	24.4	24.9	26.1	25.8	27.5	29.9	11.5
1959	0.6	3.5	6.8	9.1	10.9	12.9	15.9	19.1	23.1	25.4	26.1	25.8	26.7	29.9	11.4
1960	0.6	3.8	7.4	9.3	11.2	13.8	16.1	20.4	24.2	25.1	25.0	22.5	26.5	30.2	11.4
1961	0.5	3.5	7.0	9.1	11.5	13.9	16.5	19.8	23.5	25.4	23.4	22.9	23.8	28.4	11.2
1962	0.7	3.9	8.2	10.3	13.2	14.7	17.5	20.8	24.8	25.8	24.6	23.3	24.0	28.9	11.5
1963	0.6	4.2	8.6	10.3	13.0	16.4	17.8	20.7	25.1	26.5	24.1	22.7	24.4	26.6	11.7
1964	0.5	4.2	8.6	10.7	13.6	15.4	17.5	20.9	23.1	25.1	23.0	23.2	23.4	26.3	11.8
1965	0.6	4.1	9.0	11.5	13.8	16.7	18.5	19.8	24.4	26.4	24.2	23.3	22.9	26.1	12.1
1966	0.6	4.4	9.2	11.4	13.5	15.5	18.2	20.1	22.5	24.4	24.2	22.7	22.6	26.0	11.8
1967	0.7	4.9	9.7	11.9	13.1	16.6	18.5	19.4	22.5	24.0	23.6	20.4	21.4	23.0	11.7
1968	0.6	5.3	9.7	11.6	13.2	16.2	18.2	19.8	22.1	23.6	22.8	20.7	20.4	22.6	11.6

Appendix A (continued)
US Nonwhite Suicide Rates per 100,000 by Five-Year Age Groups, 1933–1968

Year	10-14	15-19	20-24	25-29	30-34	35-39	40-44	45-49	50-54	55-59	60-64	65-69	70-74	≥75	All ages
1933	0.1	2.1	7.2	7.1	8.0	8.6	11.4	11.5	10.3	9.1	8.8	7.3	12.9	6.6	5.4
1934	0.2	3.1	7.7	7.8	9.3	7.5	7.9	9.0	8.6	12.1	8.3	8.6	3.1	12.8	5.2
1935	0.4	2.0	6.9	8.7	8.2	8.8	8.0	8.2	8.5	9.4	12.4	5.9	5.8	6.2	5.1
1936	0.6	3.2	5.4	6.7	7.4	8.0	7.7	5.3	9.0	9.5	12.5	5.6	8.4	6.7	4.7
1937	0.5	2.2	5.7	7.4	7.8	7.4	9.3	7.1	10.7	9.2	10.9	7.2	7.3	5.9	4.9
1938	0.4	2.3	6.2	6.5	8.6	7.6	8.0	6.9	11.0	8.8	14.3	6.5	5.1	10.3	4.9
1939	0.1	1.6	5.0	6.7	6.3	6.8	7.3	8.4	8.7	5.9	9.2	5.5	6.8	8.2	4.2
1940	0.4	2.4	6.1	6.6	8.0	6.2	7.3	9.6	8.7	8.2	7.4	7.5	7.1	4.9	4.6
1941	0.2	2.0	5.7	5.9	6.7	5.3	7.0	7.7	8.3	11.2	10.6	7.8	12.0	7.0	4.1
1942	0.4	2.1	5.7	6.5	6.4	5.2	7.4	5.1	5.1	8.6	9.4	5.1	3.9	3.9	3.9
1943	0.4	1.9	4.4	4.2	4.7	4.5	4.2	4.1	4.3	5.7	8.5	2.3	5.3	5.3	3.0
1944	0.2	1.5	3.9	4.0	4.3	4.8	5.0	4.9	5.0	7.1	6.9	3.7	5.2	5.1	2.9
1945	0.0	1.1	5.4	3.1	7.2	4.7	5.9	5.1	5.8	4.8	7.3	5.2	7.0	7.8	3.3
1946	0.2	1.7	5.5	5.5	6.8	6.3	5.1	6.6	6.7	7.9	9.2	4.8	7.3	5.6	3.9
1947	0.4	2.5	5.1	5.5	6.5	6.4	6.9	5.3	5.7	8.7	8.5	7.5	6.1	7.6	4.0
1948	0.1	1.7	5.1	6.0	6.2	7.2	7.1	8.7	7.5	6.4	6.7	6.5	8.7	5.6	4.1
1949	0.2	1.6	4.6	5.8	6.4	7.3	6.3	7.4	6.8	8.9	12.1	7.5	8.5	8.3	4.3
1950	0.2	1.9	4.9	5.6	7.1	7.2	5.9	8.7	6.9	9.0	10.8	5.7	11.3	5.6	4.3

Appendix A (continued)

Year	10-14	15-19	20-24	25-29	30-34	35-39	40-44	45-49	50-54	55-59	60-64	65-69	70-74	≥75	All ages
1951	0.3	1.7	5.8	7.0	5.7	7.1	6.0	5.8	8.0	8.3	6.6	6.5	5.3	7.3	4.1
1952	0.5	1.3	4.3	6.8	6.1	6.1	4.9	5.0	6.6	7.8	9.1	5.0	6.3	6.6	3.6
1953	0.4	1.7	4.5	6.2	5.4	6.1	5.4	6.3	8.2	7.2	6.8	7.6	6.0	10.1	3.8
1954	0.1	1.7	5.2	8.3	6.5	6.3	5.9	6.3	7.9	6.1	9.5	7.3	9.0	6.3	4.0
1955	0.1	2.4	5.8	5.6	6.3	5.0	6.0	6.2	7.0	7.1	8.3	6.0	7.2	7.1	3.7
1956	0.1	2.2	4.7	6.6	6.2	7.3	5.9	5.8	7.0	6.9	8.8	6.6	5.6	6.2	3.8
1957	0.1	1.9	5.1	6.6	8.1	6.3	6.2	6.7	6.0	7.8	7.9	6.4	13.8	8.9	4.0
1958	0.3	1.1	6.3	7.4	8.2	8.0	6.6	8.1	7.5	9.7	8.0	8.4	7.5	7.4	4.4
1959	0.3	2.5	6.5	9.4	7.9	6.7	6.5	8.3	8.2	9.5	9.4	10.2	6.3	11.1	4.7
1960	0.1	2.4	4.5	7.5	8.2	8.7	7.9	7.8	8.0	10.2	9.8	8.5	7.2	8.3	4.6
1961	0.3	2.4	7.6	9.6	9.2	8.1	6.9	7.2	9.3	8.2	10.0	8.9	4.9	9.1	4.8
1962	0.2	2.8	8.3	7.6	9.2	8.4	7.7	7.9	7.5	7.3	11.6	8.0	10.1	8.2	4.7
1963	0.5	2.9	7.7	9.0	11.1	10.1	7.9	6.8	9.2	8.0	6.6	10.5	11.8	9.6	5.0
1964	0.2	3.8	7.7	10.6	9.4	8.2	8.1	7.0	7.9	7.5	8.7	8.8	6.9	6.6	4.7
1965	0.3	3.6	8.4	10.0	9.7	9.4	9.1	8.6	8.5	7.4	9.3	10.6	5.9	9.4	5.1
1966	0.3	3.7	8.6	11.5	11.9	7.7	6.1	9.4	7.5	9.5	8.0	8.7	8.3	9.8	5.1
1967	0.3	3.7	9.4	11.4	11.4	9.1	9.0	7.6	7.1	9.2	6.8	7.9	6.8	7.1	5.1
1968	0.3	3.5	8.5	16.0	16.1	12.0	13.2	12.1	12.6	13.3	11.4	12.8	18.1	7.2	4.7

Appendix A (continued)
US White Male Suicide Rates per 100,000 by Five-Year Age Groups, 1933-1968

Year	10-14	15-19	20-24	25-29	30-34	35-39	40-44	45-49	50-54	55-59	60-64	65-69	70-74	≥75	All ages
1933	0.5	4.7	14.0	18.3	22.5	29.2	39.0	52.6	60.6	70.9	79.3	81.4	88.3	85.4	26.8
1934	0.6	5.0	14.8	19.4	23.1	27.6	36.1	43.9	53.0	60.9	66.6	71.6	79.5	74.6	24.6
1935	0.7	4.8	14.7	19.2	22.2	26.0	33.6	38.6	50.1	57.3	59.6	63.9	63.1	73.2	23.3
1936	0.8	5.4	13.4	18.5	23.4	28.5	34.4	42.0	48.1	56.7	57.6	63.7	58.5	70.5	23.3
1937	1.0	5.0	14.5	19.1	24.1	28.4	37.5	46.4	50.8	56.2	62.6	62.9	59.6	71.5	24.5
1938	0.6	5.2	14.0	19.8	24.8	29.0	38.6	46.2	54.2	61.3	66.2	64.0	58.9	66.8	25.4
1939	1.1	4.9	12.5	17.8	22.1	26.3	33.2	40.1	50.1	55.8	61.2	60.1	60.7	67.7	23.4
1940	0.8	4.3	13.6	18.0	22.0	28.3	32.0	40.7	47.8	57.6	60.2	57.5	59.3	65.2	23.5
1941	0.6	4.3	11.7	16.7	20.0	25.2	27.8	32.6	39.6	47.6	52.1	53.7	58.1	65.5	20.7
1942	0.8	4.0	10.5	14.2	19.9	22.8	27.7	30.9	35.8	46.7	47.6	48.4	52.9	60.1	19.4
1943	0.8	4.0	7.9	10.6	14.5	18.9	20.2	23.4	29.9	36.1	39.0	43.3	45.9	59.6	15.7
1944	0.7	3.3	6.7	10.3	12.8	17.2	21.2	23.7	28.8	33.3	34.7	38.3	43.3	55.4	14.7
1945	0.8	3.7	7.3	10.1	14.5	19.8	23.8	26.2	32.3	36.8	41.2	42.3	49.4	56.7	16.5
1946	1.0	3.7	10.7	13.5	15.8	20.5	26.1	29.8	36.8	40.2	46.5	42.5	52.0	57.0	18.3
1947	0.9	4.1	9.4	12.0	15.9	21.1	25.8	31.1	35.9	44.6	47.7	48.0	50.5	66.7	18.8
1948	0.8	3.7	9.9	12.0	14.9	19.2	25.0	31.5	36.9	43.2	47.9	45.8	55.2	59.2	18.4
1949	0.8	3.7	10.0	12.2	14.8	21.2	27.8	30.8	38.4	45.0	50.7	52.4	51.7	62.0	19.2
1950	0.6	3.7	9.5	12.0	15.9	20.4	25.5	31.8	38.3	44.4	49.7	52.9	55.3	62.5	19.2

Appendix A (continued)

Year	10-14	15-19	20-24	25-29	30-34	35-39	40-44	45-49	50-54	55-59	60-64	65-69	70-74	≥75	All ages
1951	0.7	3.8	9.7	11.9	13.7	17.5	23.8	29.0	31.8	37.0	42.8	48.2	53.4	57.4	17.3
1952	0.5	4.7	9.2	11.9	13.3	17.7	21.7	26.8	33.2	35.0	42.4	45.2	50.0	60.0	16.9
1953	0.8	4.2	9.9	12.9	13.1	17.5	23.8	28.7	33.8	35.2	42.0	45.4	50.5	58.5	17.2
1954	0.5	3.8	10.3	13.0	14.1	17.2	22.7	30.5	35.9	38.4	45.2	44.7	48.3	54.5	17.5
1955	0.4	4.0	8.7	12.5	12.8	16.3	23.5	28.0	36.1	41.7	44.0	45.0	46.3	57.7	17.2
1956	0.7	3.5	9.6	11.3	14.4	16.2	22.1	27.5	33.3	40.1	43.0	45.6	47.5	59.8	16.9
1957	0.8	4.1	9.4	10.9	14.3	16.7	23.6	26.8	34.4	37.4	38.9	41.1	46.7	59.0	16.5
1958	0.8	4.7	11.2	13.6	15.0	18.8	25.6	30.9	37.6	40.2	43.9	43.6	48.7	60.9	18.0
1959	1.0	5.4	11.0	12.8	15.9	19.3	24.0	29.8	36.2	40.7	43.1	43.2	47.4	60.7	17.7
1960	1.0	5.9	11.9	13.8	15.9	19.6	24.3	30.2	37.6	39.9	40.6	38.5	46.7	59.2	17.6
1961	0.7	5.5	11.0	13.0	16.2	20.1	24.7	29.8	36.0	41.1	38.0	38.2	42.1	57.5	17.1
1962	1.1	5.8	12.6	14.5	18.4	20.8	24.9	30.2	37.0	41.4	39.4	40.1	42.8	59.2	17.8
1963	1.0	6.3	12.9	16.2	17.7	22.2	25.0	29.4	37.0	41.5	38.7	37.8	43.4	54.7	17.8
1964	1.0	6.6	12.8	15.2	18.9	20.0	24.5	30.0	33.8	39.3	37.5	37.8	40.6	55.5	17.2
1965	1.0	6.3	13.9	16.5	18.9	21.8	25.0	26.7	35.2	40.3	38.9	37.8	41.2	53.4	17.4
1966	1.1	6.7	14.2	16.1	18.4	21.0	24.4	27.5	32.8	37.6	39.3	37.8	40.0	54.8	17.2
1967	1.0	7.5	14.9	16.9	17.5	22.2	25.4	26.8	31.8	35.7	37.4	32.2	37.9	48.1	16.8
1968	1.0	8.3	15.0	16.3	18.3	22.0	24.2	27.0	30.8	35.8	36.5	35.6	37.0	48.0	16.9

Appendix A (continued)
US White Female Suicide Rates per 100,000 by Five-Year Age Groups, 1933–1968

Year	10–14	15–19	20–24	25–29	30–34	35–39	40–44	45–49	50–54	55–59	60–64	65–69	70–74	≥75	All ages
1933	0.2	3.9	8.1	8.7	9.1	10.4	12.5	13.0	12.7	13.1	14.2	13.1	10.4	8.8	7.3
1934	0.3	4.3	7.2	9.0	9.3	10.6	11.8	13.6	14.0	10.4	14.5	11.9	9.4	9.1	7.3
1935	0.3	4.2	6.8	8.3	10.5	10.9	11.1	13.0	13.1	11.0	14.3	11.8	11.7	7.4	7.2
1936	0.4	3.4	6.8	9.2	10.5	10.0	12.1	12.5	14.1	10.6	13.3	12.1	10.8	8.5	7.3
1937	0.3	3.3	7.0	8.4	9.6	11.0	12.4	14.5	14.5	11.7	13.4	12.9	9.2	9.1	7.5
1938	0.1	3.5	5.8	8.0	8.9	10.8	12.7	14.1	14.3	11.2	12.9	12.7	9.3	8.6	7.4
1939	0.2	3.0	5.0	6.3	9.0	10.8	11.3	13.8	14.8	10.2	13.5	12.7	11.9	7.3	7.1
1940	0.1	3.0	4.9	7.8	9.5	10.9	12.1	14.1	13.8	9.5	13.0	13.6	11.8	8.7	7.3
1941	0.3	3.0	5.3	7.3	9.1	9.8	10.9	12.7	13.0	9.7	12.2	10.7	10.7	7.8	6.8
1942	0.2	2.4	4.1	6.3	8.0	9.0	9.6	11.8	12.1	9.5	11.8	9.4	10.1	10.9	6.3
1943	0.3	2.3	4.1	5.3	7.0	7.5	9.4	10.4	11.4	9.3	13.4	10.9	11.5	8.2	5.9
1944	0.2	2.4	4.2	5.2	7.1	8.6	9.4	10.1	11.3	9.6	11.4	9.8	9.3	9.2	5.8
1945	0.2	1.9	4.1	5.5	8.2	9.1	9.9	11.7	12.7	10.3	10.6	11.0	10.8	8.9	6.2
1946	0.2	2.4	4.4	5.1	7.5	9.4	9.4	10.6	13.3	10.4	12.0	10.1	10.5	8.4	6.1
1947	0.1	1.9	3.6	5.0	7.0	8.2	9.8	11.5	12.4	9.7	11.1	12.0	10.6	8.5	5.9
1948	0.1	2.2	3.9	4.3	6.7	8.0	10.1	10.1	11.6	10.8	9.7	9.5	9.3	9.1	5.6
1949	0.2	1.5	3.7	4.2	6.0	7.7	8.9	10.0	10.9	11.8	10.9	10.8	8.9	7.6	5.5
1950	0.1	1.9	3.5	5.1	5.4	7.6	8.9	9.8	11.2	10.4	10.9	11.0	9.9	8.4	5.5

Appendix A (continued)

Year	10-14	15-19	20-24	25-29	30-34	35-39	40-44	45-49	50-54	55-59	60-64	65-69	70-74	≥75	All ages
1951	0.2	1.7	2.9	4.6	5.5	6.8	8.7	9.3	10.3	9.0	9.5	10.0	7.9	7.9	5.0
1952	0.1	1.4	2.7	4.4	5.5	6.3	7.4	9.2	9.6	9.4	9.0	9.5	8.4	6.9	4.7
1953	0.1	1.8	2.9	4.6	5.0	6.0	7.1	8.6	9.4	9.4	9.2	8.4	8.1	7.2	4.6
1954	0.1	1.2	2.4	4.2	4.7	5.6	8.2	7.8	8.8	9.3	9.7	8.7	8.7	6.4	4.5
1955	0.2	1.4	2.6	3.9	5.8	5.8	7.6	9.6	11.1	10.9	9.9	10.2	8.3	8.2	4.9
1956	0.1	1.2	2.8	4.2	5.3	5.9	7.5	9.4	9.9	10.4	10.7	10.1	8.4	6.6	4.8
1957	0.2	1.0	2.7	4.5	5.6	6.5	7.7	8.2	9.4	10.3	9.8	9.7	6.5	6.0	4.6
1958	0.2	1.8	3.1	5.3	6.3	6.5	7.8	9.5	11.5	10.3	9.8	9.9	9.2	6.8	5.1
1959	0.1	1.6	2.8	5.4	5.9	6.8	8.2	8.7	10.4	10.7	10.5	10.4	9.0	7.2	5.0
1960	0.2	1.6	3.1	4.8	6.7	8.2	8.1	10.8	11.1	10.8	10.9	8.5	9.3	8.9	5.3
1961	0.2	1.6	3.2	5.3	7.0	7.9	8.7	10.2	11.4	10.5	10.2	9.6	8.4	7.4	5.3
1962	0.2	2.0	4.1	6.3	8.1	8.8	10.3	11.8	13.1	11.1	11.1	9.0	8.5	7.5	5.9
1963	0.2	1.9	4.6	6.6	8.4	10.9	10.9	12.3	13.6	12.3	10.9	10.0	8.9	7.1	6.3
1964	0.1	1.7	4.5	6.2	8.3	10.9	10.9	12.2	12.9	11.7	9.9	10.9	9.7	6.4	6.1
1965	0.1	1.8	4.3	6.6	8.7	11.7	12.3	13.2	14.0	13.4	10.9	11.2	8.6	7.8	6.6
1966	0.2	2.1	4.5	6.8	8.8	10.2	12.3	13.1	12.8	12.1	10.7	10.1	9.3	6.9	6.3
1967	0.3	2.2	4.8	7.0	8.9	11.2	11.9	12.3	13.8	13.2	11.3	10.7	8.9	6.7	6.5
1968	0.2	2.2	4.8	7.0	8.1	10.6	12.3	13.1	13.9	12.3	10.7	8.3	8.0	6.3	6.3

Appendix A (continued)
US Nonwhite Male Suicide Rates per 100,000 by Five-Year Age Groups, 1933-1968

Year	10-14	15-19	20-24	25-29	30-34	35-39	40-44	45-49	50-54	55-59	60-64	65-69	70-74	≥75	All ages
1933	0.2	2.7	9.5	10.7	12.2	14.6	18.6	19.7	16.1	13.2	14.8	11.9	24.9	12.3	8.3
1934	0.3	3.7	9.2	10.8	13.5	10.9	11.9	14.6	13.1	21.0	11.2	12.9	5.9	21.0	7.6
1935	0.4	2.5	8.0	11.9	9.6	13.7	12.2	15.4	14.4	15.7	20.8	9.7	11.3	8.8	7.4
1936	0.7	3.9	7.5	8.6	10.3	13.2	13.3	8.2	13.7	15.0	21.8	9.2	13.4	5.7	7.0
1937	0.7	2.8	6.4	6.7	10.8	12.9	14.7	11.2	15.7	15.2	17.1	12.3	12.9	11.1	7.4
1938	0.6	3.0	8.3	8.7	11.3	12.4	13.1	10.5	18.3	14.9	20.5	9.0	8.6	20.4	7.4
1939	0.0	1.7	6.4	10.6	9.6	11.9	11.7	11.8	14.6	9.6	15.3	7.9	11.9	13.3	6.5
1940	0.9	3.0	7.6	10.7	12.3	9.6	11.8	16.1	13.3	13.6	13.3	11.9	12.5	7.8	7.2
1941	0.1	1.8	9.0	10.1	10.6	8.4	13.0	12.6	12.7	11.9	19.4	10.4	10.0	11.1	6.6
1942	0.4	2.1	8.2	8.6	9.9	8.7	10.7	9.2	6.7	14.6	17.2	8.9	7.5	8.2	5.9
1943	0.7	2.8	7.0	7.5	7.7	6.8	5.4	6.7	7.1	8.8	14.6	3.5	10.4	7.8	4.7
1944	0.3	1.7	5.5	6.5	6.8	6.8	7.3	8.0	7.9	12.3	12.0	5.1	8.1	7.5	4.6
1945	0.0	1.9	7.0	4.9	10.6	8.2	8.7	8.4	10.1	8.0	12.8	10.5	12.8	14.3	5.3
1946	0.4	1.6	8.6	9.5	10.2	10.4	7.3	9.7	10.2	12.9	15.6	8.6	12.5	11.7	6.1
1947	0.7	2.8	7.6	8.7	9.9	10.4	12.0	8.6	10.0	14.5	15.8	14.2	12.1	16.0	6.6
1948	0.0	1.7	8.7	9.1	9.8	13.2	11.2	15.4	12.6	11.2	12.5	12.4	15.4	11.8	6.9
1949	0.1	2.4	7.0	10.0	10.1	12.2	10.6	12.4	11.5	14.7	21.5	13.6	16.0	15.7	7.2
1950	0.3	2.3	8.5	9.6	11.0	12.2	10.5	13.3	10.0	16.9	19.1	10.9	18.2	9.2	7.1

Appendix A (continued)

Year	10-14	15-19	20-24	25-29	30-34	35-39	40-44	45-49	50-54	55-59	60-64	65-69	70-74	≥75	All ages
1951	0.7	1.8	9.0	12.4	8.8	12.3	9.1	10.0	13.0	12.4	11.6	11.2	8.3	13.7	6.6
1952	0.7	1.9	7.4	11.8	9.5	9.8	7.8	8.3	11.6	13.0	16.2	10.5	12.0	12.4	6.1
1953	0.3	1.6	7.5	10.2	9.9	10.5	10.1	11.0	14.3	12.2	11.8	14.5	8.5	20.8	6.4
1954	0.1	1.7	10.1	13.9	11.7	11.4	9.7	10.9	11.9	9.6	15.7	13.8	13.4	12.1	6.8
1955	0.2	4.0	9.5	8.6	10.6	8.4	10.9	9.7	11.4	12.6	12.8	9.9	12.2	13.8	6.1
1956	0.1	2.5	9.6	11.0	10.6	10.6	10.5	8.4	11.3	10.7	14.4	10.6	9.0	11.9	6.1
1957	0.1	3.3	8.5	11.5	14.4	10.5	10.6	12.8	10.8	10.9	13.2	12.2	25.5	15.4	6.8
1958	0.4	1.4	10.4	11.4	13.8	13.6	10.8	13.7	11.7	15.9	14.3	15.0	13.0	12.4	7.1
1959	0.4	3.4	10.6	15.7	13.1	11.0	11.0	13.3	14.6	15.7	13.5	17.3	11.3	21.6	7.5
1960	0.2	3.4	7.8	12.6	13.2	14.7	12.2	13.2	12.3	16.8	17.0	13.8	10.8	12.8	7.2
1961	0.2	3.6	12.8	17.1	15.6	13.1	9.8	12.6	15.1	13.6	16.8	16.0	9.2	17.3	7.6
1962	0.3	3.7	12.7	10.9	14.7	14.0	11.5	12.0	12.9	10.9	19.4	15.2	18.9	14.4	7.2
1963	0.6	3.7	12.5	14.2	17.6	16.6	13.1	11.7	15.8	13.8	11.3	16.6	20.1	19.0	7.9
1964	0.3	4.0	13.5	16.7	15.6	12.4	13.1	11.1	12.5	10.7	14.2	13.4	13.5	11.8	7.2
1965	0.5	5.2	13.1	14.9	13.5	15.3	14.8	14.2	12.8	12.9	15.7	21.1	8.2	15.7	7.7
1966	0.2	4.8	14.1	17.3	18.8	12.6	10.2	15.1	12.9	14.6	14.1	14.6	13.5	18.8	7.8
1967	0.4	3.8	14.4	18.3	17.0	14.0	15.5	11.6	11.5	15.8	10.4	12.7	11.8	12.0	7.6
1968	0.3	4.7	13.1	16.0	16.1	12.0	13.2	12.1	12.6	13.3	11.4	12.8	18.1	11.6	7.3

Appendix A (continued)

US Nonwhite Female Suicide Rates per 100,000 by Five-Year Age Groups, 1933–1968

Year	10-14	15-19	20-24	25-29	30-34	35-39	40-44	45-49	50-54	55-59	60-64	65-69	70-74	≥75	All ages
1933	0.1	3.1	5.1	3.8	4.1	3.0	4.2	3.7	3.2	3.8	1.6	2.1	0.0	1.4	2.5
1934	0.1	2.5	6.3	5.1	5.3	4.4	3.9	3.3	3.2	1.2	4.8	3.8	0.0	5.4	2.9
1935	0.3	1.6	5.8	5.9	7.0	4.1	3.8	0.9	1.6	1.8	2.3	1.8	0.0	3.9	2.7
1936	0.6	2.6	3.4	5.0	4.7	3.1	2.2	2.4	3.5	2.9	1.5	1.7	1.5	7.7	2.4
1937	0.3	1.7	5.1	5.6	3.5	2.3	3.9	2.9	4.9	2.2	3.7	1.6	1.4	1.2	2.5
1938	0.3	1.6	4.3	4.6	6.1	3.2	2.9	3.2	2.6	1.6	7.2	3.7	1.3	1.2	2.5
1939	0.3	1.6	3.9	3.2	3.2	2.1	2.9	4.8	2.2	1.6	2.1	2.8	1.3	3.6	2.0
1940	0.0	1.8	4.8	3.0	4.1	3.2	2.8	2.8	3.6	2.0	0.7	2.7	1.3	2.3	2.2
1941	0.3	2.1	3.0	2.2	3.1	2.4	1.1	2.7	3.2	3.5	1.3	2.6	0.0	3.3	1.7
1942	0.3	2.2	3.6	4.6	3.2	2.0	4.0	1.1	3.4	1.9	0.6	1.2	0.0	0.0	2.0
1943	0.1	1.0	2.2	1.4	2.0	2.3	3.1	1.6	1.3	2.3	1.9	1.2	0.0	3.0	1.3
1944	0.1	1.3	2.6	1.4	3.0	1.4	2.8	1.8	1.9	1.4	1.2	2.3	2.1	2.9	1.4
1945	0.0	0.3	4.1	1.5	4.2	1.5	3.2	1.7	1.3	1.2	1.2	0.0	1.0	1.8	1.4
1946	0.0	1.9	2.8	1.9	3.8	2.7	2.9	3.6	3.0	2.6	2.3	1.0	2.0	1.8	1.8
1947	0.1	2.2	3.0	2.7	3.5	2.8	2.0	2.1	1.2	2.5	0.6	1.0	0.0	0.0	1.6
1948	0.1	1.6	2.0	3.2	3.0	1.8	3.2	2.1	2.3	1.2	0.5	1.0	1.8	0.0	1.5
1949	0.3	0.9	2.4	2.0	3.0	2.9	2.2	2.2	2.0	2.8	2.1	1.9	0.9	1.6	1.5
1950	0.1	1.5	1.9	2.0	3.7	2.7	1.5	4.2	3.9	0.8	2.0	0.9	4.3	2.3	1.7

Appendix A (continued)

Year	10-14	15-19	20-24	25-29	30-34	35-39	40-44	45-49	50-54	55-59	60-64	65-69	70-74	≥75	All ages
1951	0.0	1.7	3.2	2.2	3.0	2.4	3.0	1.7	2.9	4.0	1.4	2.2	2.4	1.5	1.7
1952	0.3	0.8	1.8	2.5	3.0	2.7	2.2	1.7	1.5	2.4	1.8	0.0	0.8	1.4	1.3
1953	0.5	1.8	2.2	2.8	1.5	2.1	1.1	1.7	2.0	2.0	1.7	1.3	3.6	0.7	1.3
1954	0.0	1.8	1.3	3.5	2.0	1.6	2.4	1.9	3.9	2.5	3.3	1.3	4.8	0.6	1.5
1955	0.0	1.0	2.7	3.1	2.6	1.9	1.5	2.9	2.6	1.5	4.0	2.5	2.6	1.2	1.5
1956	0.1	1.8	0.6	2.8	2.4	4.2	1.7	3.3	2.8	3.2	3.4	2.8	2.5	1.2	1.6
1957	0.0	0.7	2.1	2.4	2.7	2.4	2.2	1.2	1.4	4.7	3.0	1.2	3.1	3.3	1.4
1958	0.1	0.8	2.8	4.0	3.2	2.8	2.7	2.8	3.4	3.5	2.1	2.3	2.4	3.2	1.8
1959	0.2	1.7	2.9	4.0	3.5	2.9	2.5	3.7	2.0	3.3	5.5	3.8	1.7	2.1	1.9
1960	0.0	1.5	1.6	3.1	3.8	3.4	4.0	2.7	3.9	3.7	3.0	3.7	3.9	4.5	2.0
1961	0.3	1.3	2.9	3.2	3.8	3.6	4.3	2.3	3.1	2.9	3.5	2.6	1.0	2.3	1.9
1962	0.1	1.9	4.3	4.6	4.6	3.4	4.4	4.2	2.3	3.7	4.1	1.5	2.5	3.1	2.2
1963	0.1	2.0	3.2	4.5	5.5	4.5	3.4	2.5	3.0	2.5	2.1	5.2	4.8	2.1	2.2
1964	0.1	1.8	2.3	5.2	4.1	4.5	3.7	3.2	3.6	4.5	3.4	4.7	1.4	2.4	2.2
1965	0.2	2.4	4.0	5.6	6.4	4.4	4.0	3.7	4.6	2.3	3.3	1.2	4.0	4.5	2.5
1966	0.3	2.4	3.6	6.4	6.0·	3.6	2.6	4.4	2.6	4.7	2.2	3.4	4.1	2.9	2.4
1967	0.3	3.5	4.7	5.2	6.6	5.0	3.5	3.9	3.1	3.2	3.5	3.6	2.8	2.7	2.1
1968	0.3	2.2	4.4	4.5	4.8	4.7	4.2	3.8	3.4	3.1	2.4	3.5	2.4	3.9	2.4

65

Appendix B
Slopes (S) and Means (M) of Trend Lines for U.S.
Suicide Rates by Age, Sex, and Race, 1933–1968.
(Parameters of best-fitting straight lines are shown for
the whole 36-year period, the first 18 years, and the
second 18 years; * = slope differs significantly from
zero, c = trend departs significantly from a straight line.)

		10–14	15–19	20–24	25–29	30–34	35–39	40–44
1933–1968	S	.004*	.003c	−.03c	−.06c	−.10*c	−.12*c	−.18*c
	M	0.5	3.4	7.6	9.9	12.0	14.2	17.3
1933–1950	S	.001	−.12*	−.31*	−.42*c	−.42*c	−.41*c	−.54*c
	M	0.4	3.4	7.9	10.3	13.0	15.6	19.0
1951–1968	S	.02*	.14*	.26*c	.25*c	.32*c	.33*	.21*
	M	0.5	3.4	7.3	9.4	11.0	12.9	15.6
Male								
1933–1968	S	.01*	.06*c	.02c	−.07c	−.13*c	−.20*c	−.30*c
	M	0.7	4.6	11.3	14.1	16.9	20.6	25.3
1933–1950	S	.01	−.10*c	−.36*	−.53*	−.61*c	−.60*	−.83*c
	M	0.7	4.1	11.0	14.6	18.2	22.6	27.9
1951–1968	S	.03*	.23*	.36*	.31*c	.38*	.32*	.15*
	M	0.8	5.1	11.5	13.7	15.7	18.6	22.7
Female								
1933–1968	S	−.002	−.05*c	−.08*c	−.05*c	−.06*c	−.03c	−.04c
	M	0.2	2.2	4.1	5.7	7.1	8.1	9.3
1933–1950	S	−.01	−.14*	−.29*	−.29*	−.24*	−.19*	−.21*
	M	0.2	2.7	4.8	6.2	7.8	8.7	9.9
1951–1968	S	.002	.05*	.15*	.19*	.25*	.34*	.29*
	M	0.2	1.7	3.4	5.3	6.5	7.6	8.6
White								
1933–1968	S	.004	.001c	−.04c	−.08*c	−.12*c	−.14*c	−.20*c
	M	0.5	3.6	7.8	10.2	12.5	15.1	18.4
1933–1950	S	−.004	−.13*c	−.33*	−.45*	−.46*	−.44*c	−.57*c
	M	0.5	3.6	8.2	10.9	13.7	16.6	20.2
1951–1968	S	.02*	.15*	.26*c	.25*	.32*c	.36*	.22*
	M	0.5	3.6	7.4	9.5	11.3	13.6	16.6
Nonwhite								
1933–1968	S	−.002	.03*c	.06*c	.14*c	.11*c	.07*c	.01c
	M	0.3	2.3	6.1	7.4	7.8	7.2	7.1
1933–1940	S	−.01	−.05*	−.13*	−.17*	−.14*	−.11c	−.22*
	M	0.3	2.1	5.6	6.1	7.0	6.7	7.1
1951–1968	S	.002	.14*	.28*	.39*	.46*	.25*	.28*
	M	0.3	2.5	6.6	8.7	8.7	7.8	7.2

45-49	50-54	55-59	60-64	65-69	70-74	≥75	All ages
−.28*c	−.29*c	−.38*c	−.48*c	−.49*c	−.48*c	−.38*c	−.13*c
20.4	23.9	26.5	27.7	27.0	27.9	30.0	11.6
−.76*c	−.79*c	−.88*c	−.90*c	−.95*c	−.80*c	−.60*c	−.32*c
22.7	26.4	29.8	31.8	30.9	31.9	33.2	12.7
.07	.10	.10	−.20*	−.35*	−.41*	−.36*	.06*c
18.1	21.4	23.1	23.6	23.1	23.9	26.8	10.5
−.43*c	−.46*c	−.64*c	−.77*c	−.83*	−.78*c	−.52*c	−.19*c
30.4	36.5	41.4	44.9	45.4	48.7	58.3	17.8
−1.21*c	−1.31*c	−1.44*c	−1.46*c	−1.53*c	−1.41*c	−1.00*c	−.48*c
33.7	40.0	47.0	51.2	52.1	54.9	62.5	19.4
−.06c	−.04c	.07c	−.42*	−.67*	−.76*	−.36*c	.01
27.1	33.0	35.9	38.5	38.7	42.6	54.2	16.2
−.06*c	−.04c	−.07*c	−.11*c	−.08*	−.07*	−.06*	−.04*c
10.6	11.4	11.1	10.7	9.7	9.0	7.6	5.6
−.22*	−.16*c	−.19*	−.23*	−.20*	−.04	−.02	−.14*c
11.4	12.0	11.9	11.8	10.5	9.8	8.2	6.1
.28*	.28*	.21*	.08*	.07	.04	−.01	.12*
9.8	10.7	10.3	9.7	9.0	8.2	7.0	5.0
−.29*c	−.31*c	−.40*c	−.50*c	−.54*c	−.55*c	−.41*c	−.14*c
21.8	25.5	28.1	29.1	28.7	29.8	31.3	12.5
−.82*c	−.84*	−.95*c	−.96*c	−1.00*c	−.85*	−.65*c	−.34*c
24.2	28.1	31.6	33.3	33.1	34.4	34.7	13.7
.12*	.11	.12c	−.19*	−.40*	−.44*c	−.36*	.07*
19.4	22.9	24.6	24.9	24.4	25.2	27.9	11.3
.02	−.001c	.003c	−.043	.113*	.07	.05	.007c
7.3	7.8	8.4	9.2	7.2	7.7	7.5	4.4
−.12c	−.25*	−.15	−.11	−.08	.06	−.12	−.09
7.2	7.6	8.4	9.6	6.1	7.3	6.9	4.3
.24*	.12	.16	.08	.27*	.24	.06	.09*
7.4	8.0	8.4	8.7	8.3	8.2	8.2	4.4

Appendix B (continued)

		10–14	15–19	20–24	25–29	30–34	35–39	40–44
White male								
1933–1968	S	.01*c	.06*c	.003c	−.09c	−.17*c	−.23*c	−.33*c
	M	0.8	4.9	11.5	14.5	17.5	21.6	26.9
1933–1950	S	.01	−.10*c	−.40*	−.58*	−.65*c	−.65*c	−.89*c
	M	0.8	4.3	11.4	15.2	19.1	23.9	29.7
1951–1968	S	.03*	.24*	.36*	.32*	.38*	.35*	.13*
	M	0.8	5.4	11.6	13.9	15.9	19.3	24.1
White female								
1933–1968	S	−.002	−.06*c	−.08*c	−.06*c	−.06*c	−.03c	−.04c
	M	0.2	2.2	4.3	6.0	7.5	8.8	10.0
1933–1950	S	−.01*	−.15*	−.25*	−.30*	−.25*	−.20*	−.22*c
	M	0.2	2.8	5.1	6.6	8.2	9.5	10.7
1951–1968	S	0.004	.04*	.15*c	.19*c	.26*c	.37*	.32*c
	M	0.2	1.7	3.5	5.4	6.8	8.1	9.3
Nonwhite male								
1933–1968	S	−.003	0.05*	.18*c	.22*c	.18*c	.07c	−.01c
	M	0.4	2.9	9.4	11.3	12.0	11.6	11.3
1933–1950	S	−.01	−.07*	−.04	−.10c	−.12	−.15c	−.34*
	M	0.4	2.5	7.8	9.1	10.3	10.9	11.3
1951–1968	S	−.004	.18*	.39*	.38*	.49*	.23*	.29*
	M	0.3	3.3	10.9	13.6	13.6	12.4	11.3
Nonwhite female								
1933–1968	S	−.002	.001c	−.05*c	.02c	.01c	.04	.01
	M	0.2	1.7	3.2	3.6	3.9	3.0	2.9
1933–1950	S	−.01c	−.07	−.21*	−.21*c	−.13*	−.08	−.09*
	M	0.2	1.8	3.7	3.3	3.9	2.7	2.9
1951–1968	S	.01	.08*	.14*	.19*	.25*	.16*	.13*
	M	0.2	1.7	2.8	3.9	3.7	3.3	3.0

45–49	50–54	55–59	60–64	65–69	70–74	≥75	All ages
−.45*c	−.51*c	−.64*c	−.80*c	−.90*c	−.82*c	−.57*c	−.22*c
32.2	38.7	44.2	47.3	48.1	51.5	61.1	19.1
−1.23*c	−1.39*c	1.55*c	−1.57*c	−1.73*c	−1.48*c	−1.12*c	−.53*c
35.7	42.6	49.7	53.9	55.2	57.9	65.5	20.9
−.05c	−.05	.05c	−.41*	−.75*	−.82*	−.48*	.001
28.6	34.7	38.8	40.6	41.0	45.0	56.6	17.3
−.06c	−.04c	.04*c	−.11*c	−.09*c	−.07*c	−.06*	−.05*c
11.3	12.2	10.7	11.3	10.6	9.5	7.9	6.0
−.25*	−.16*c	−.06	−.24*	−.15*	−.04	.000	−.13*c
12.1	12.8	10.5	12.4	11.4	10.3	8.6	6.6
.30*	.30*	.23*	.10*	.04	.05	−.02	.13*c
10.5	11.5	11.0	10.3	9.7	8.6	7.1	5.4
−.002c	−.02c	−.03	−.10	.19*	.07	.12*	.02c
11.8	12.4	13.3	15.3	12.1	12.8	13.4	6.9
−.22c	−.37*c	−.17	−.03c	.02	.08	−.05	−.08
11.8	12.1	13.6	16.4	10.2	12.5	11.9	6.7
.21*	.05	.13	−.04	.24	.22	.01	.09*
11.8	12.7	13.1	14.3	14.0	13.2	14.9	7.1
.03	.01	.05*	.03	.04c	.09*	−.003	−.01c
2.7	2.8	2.6	2.0	2.2	1.9	2.4	1.9
−.02	−.06	−.04	−.13	−.11	.10	−.18	−.08*
2.6	2.7	2.1	2.1	1.9	1.1	2.4	2.0
.14*	.07	.05	.04	.15*	.03	.15*	.07*c
2.9	2.9	3.2	3.0	2.6	2.8	2.4	1.9

Leonard L. Linden
and Warren Breed

2
The Demographic Epidemiology
of Suicide

The introductory words for this chapter are taken from the 1903
English version of *Il Suicido* by Enrico Morselli, first published in
1879. These sections, from the Introduction to Morselli's *Suicide:
An Essay on Comparative Moral Statistics* are reproduced with the
kind permission of Prentice-Hall, Inc.

SUICIDE is one of the voluntary human acts on which statistical works
have dwelt with special predilection, and is one of the chief subjects of
social physics. The psychological meaning of this moral fact has always
been enveloped in great metaphysical obscurity, because suicide appears less
susceptible of positive appreciation than all other expressions of the human
will.

The social significance of voluntary death began to be evident when a
comparison was made between *homicide* and *suicide*, and therefore the true
literature of suicide did not arise before the time of the philosophic movement
which distinguished the second half of last century.

Nevertheless, mention was made of it amongst the ancients; Greek and
Latin civilization had often seen their best representative men lost to them
by means of suicide. But it is certain that the subject of self-destruction
did not enter into its positive phase until after statistical researches. . . .

This new aspect of suicide could not become clear where metaphysical
systems prevailed; it was necessary to collect all the facts, to unite them
together, to consider their analogy and differences, to do, in short, precisely
the reverse of what philosophy had done up to that time. That is not to
start from a preconceived system, but to base arguments on facts supplied
by observation and, when possible, by experiment.

In the natural sciences the experimental method was already introduced, and in the exact sciences the calculation of probabilities; thus the conviction came to be formed that to obtain knowledge of the true natural characters of phenomena, thought must remodel itself in its own way and recommence patient but productive analysis; that is to say, it must return to the natural process by which practical knowledge has been built up from generation to generation. For the phenomena of social life this aim can only be attained by statistics. The great reforms in habits and ideas which marked the second half of the eighteenth century prepared the ground, and the initiation of the people to a more direct participation in political events especially helped it.

And since nations are constituted, by developing, and transforming themselves through millions of individuals, it was natural that the science of order and numbers should be applied in a uniform way to the progression of living and operating numbers. From this was brought to light that perpetual element of force and development, the principle of organic and functional transformation, or the *dynamics of population.*

The old philosophy of individualism had given to suicide the character of liberty and spontaneity, but now it became necessary to study it no longer as the expression of individual and independent faculties, but certainly as a social phenomenon allied with all the other racial forces.

The real statistics of suicide began only in our century, and even late in it. It is true that from the end of the eighteenth century data were being collected in Switzerland and Paris (Mercier, 1783), but they were isolated figures, and perhaps on account of little exactitude not serviceable for analysis; later they were of value, however, in establishing the important statistical law of the progressive growth of suicide in civilized countries. To Switzerland belongs the credit of having been the first to gather its facts from the entire population; while France has the honour of having undertaken the regular and uniform publication of them in the registers of the Minister of Grace and Justice (1817-27). At the same time official statistics were begun in some other European States—Mecklenburg (1811), Prussia (1816), Norway (1816), and Austria (1819); which examples, on account of the impulse given to statistical works by the courage of the first sociologists, were followed by Hanover, the Canton of Geneva, Belgium, Saxony, Denmark, Bavaria, England, and so on by all the European States, from the most powerful to the smallest. The Southern States were the last to follow.

On the first statistical data of suicide Quetelet and Guerry were able to found the bases of that part of moral statistics, finding therein, indeed, the laws making known new grounds of comparison between State and State, between race and race, whence a marvellous reformation of ideas relative to voluntary death arose, recognized immediately as a most important element of social dynamics. This reform was aided by the simultaneous foundation and identification with the objective sciences of a new science which took for study the normal and morbid functions of the human mind. We find similarity of origin neither small nor indifferent between sociology and psychological physical pathology, both the progeny of our times, both arisen out of the ruins of the metaphysics of the schools, and united in the intention to get rid of the everlasting question of the relations between man and the rest of nature. It would be worth while, as far as it deserves, to investigate the historical and scientific relations between madness and suicide, and to show how often philosophical, religious, and judicial opinions relative to the morality and criminality of suicide clash with its obvious connection with the morbid perturbation of the mind; but ours is not a work intended to collect and explain the reason for suicide from the psychiatric side, which elsewhere has been fully treated by Esquirol, Falret, Lisle, Brierre de Boismont, Cazanvieilh, Petit, Des Étangs, Stark, Schürmayer, and a hundred other alienists, medical jurists, and moralists. It is true that statisticians and alienists have heretofore derived advantage from each other's works in studying the psychological and racial laws of self-destruction, arriving at synthetical results previously unforeseen and unexpected. The knowledge of suicide, or rather of suicidal tendency, was only then received among the positive results of social psychology, and ceased to depend *exclusively* on the systems of philosophers and jurists.

At the same time, however, the objections with regard to the insufficiency of the method of observation apply more to the statistics of suicide than to those of other things. The difficulties of gathering exact data of various times and various places are great. Not only is it sometimes impossible to assign the true cause of death, not only is the medico-forensic question of the distinction between suicide or homicide or accidental death (especially in the case of drowning) difficult of solution, but with respect to violent death statistics encounter obstacles in the prejudices, habits, indifference, or bad faith of the public. It is more than ever apt to excite hostility and deceit; a feeling of shame and the remembrance of the infamy attached for a long course of years to this act, impel families, relations, and friends to hide or to falsify the true cause, the manner, and particulars of death.
. . .

In the meantime it is certain that as long as facts are collected in their, so to speak, objective aspect, and, with regard to suicide, the sex, age, social condition, the race and religion of the individual, the time, place, and mode of death are registered, statistics can answer triumphantly to all these objections. Tangible and numerical facts are in question, and up to this point the subject matter lends itself to the measurement and elaboration of demography.

But there is one defect in the statistics of suicide which can be easily pointed out, and on which it is well to say something; we refer to the limits and classification of *individual motives*. It is true that dealing here with the inward phenomena of conscience, statistics cannot presume to learn the true mental state or psychical movement which has preceded the act of suicide; it is necessary to limit ourselves to an approximation, which often errs by deceit, sometimes changes and sometimes forces the meaning of the facts.

In that part of our work relating to causes it will however be seen that statistics do not assume undue powers and merits; the deductions on the psychological side are much more modest than its adversaries find it convenient to confess. If statistics speak of motives and seek their cause in sex, age, and race, it is because in the cases considered the determining causes of the act are evident, whether treating of physical causes or whether there remains unsuspected proofs of them by the act of the suicide himself. Brierre de Boismont in 4,595 cases of suicide has found that 1,328 of them (1,052 men and 276 women) left their last thoughts written, to which must be added those who expressed them by word of mouth, and the life and habits of most of whom were so well known as to leave no doubt to those who wished to deduce a reason from them to explain the moving cause of their last act; for instance, those suicides who had always led dissolute lives, who had strong passions or domestic dissensions, or who had suffered financial catastrophes. The motives then which may lead a man to take away his life are nearly the same which lead him to crime; his passions, his overpowering needs, and his inclination are too well known to us. There is also an abundant number of predisposing causes which give no support to the usual scepticism, and are dependent upon a morbid organization, either congenital or acquired— heredity, mental alienation, pellagra, delirium, drunkenness, hypochondria, physical disease. But also among the causes which touch rather upon the psychological aspects of cerebral activity (*moral causes*), not a few have been made plain by an exaggerated display, and are all the impulsive passions—love, jealousy, ambition, shame, religious or political fanaticism, the fear of punishment, &c. Nevertheless the motive of every suicide is not alone that which is apparent; there are other more secret causes whose existence and influence elude even the suicide himself, because they act upon him almost unconsciously (such as education, moral contact, imitation, physical and moral atmosphere), and which statistics have had no means hitherto of investigating. Experimental psychology also meets nearly the same difficulties when the objective method is applied to the study of the passions, of the instincts, of human or animal habits; but neither psychology nor moral statistics claim to discover the nature of psychical activity, knowing well that such a metaphysical enquiry is beyond their aim and the powers of reason. Both arrive at positive knowledge by considering the protean prism of the human conscience through all its phases, but they stop short at phenomena, that is, at sensible phases; and it is unquestionable that even when the numerical element should happen to fail, or should appear inadequate for psychological deductions, we should draw the same results from the moral analysis of men and nations as those that the rough numbers of statistics would have furnished. . . .

The uniformity, the regularity, and the constancy of the results constitute in fact the best answer to many objections. All the means agree perfectly, and this is how the study of the great series of facts gives to statistics that character of an exact science and of social psychology which we attributed to it at starting.

By its means the individual variations disappear, and our view takes in the whole of society in the expression of its wants and tendencies, that is, in the functions of its complicated organism.

The most fatal and at the same time the apparently most arbitrary human actions, suicide and crime, show themselves to us in their similarity subject to numerous influences, which the examination of every single case would not suffice to reveal to us, and which collectively are universal, perpetual, and intense, and such as the most positive mode of psychological study would fail to discover in the individual. The charges and objections made against statistics of suicide take their rise from the individual thought which ethics and philosophy have ever had; they conceal the fear that with such synthetical enquiries the limits of human freedom, before so unbounded, would become restricted to acknowledging that the apparent spontaneity of moral acts depends only on the individual and egotistical character of the determining motives.

These fears are not without cause for those who consider the results of sociology; with the laws that regulate social organism, the individualism of human activities disappears, as in a most complicated piece of mechanism the movement of one single wheel constitutes a small part of the whole work.

From the examination of the many and various causes which influence these things, statistics trace the indications of the prophylactics and therapeutics of suicide against which laws and philosophy show themselves powerless. The terrible increase of suicide at the present time is the first result brought to light by statistics, and would be sufficient to establish their value as a branch of social science. . . . With respect to suicide, the analysis may be based on facts under three different aspects; either they may be considered collectively as the dynamic element of population, or we may study their variations under the influence of cosmic, ethnic, social, intellectual, historical, and individual factors, or investigate the different modes of action in relation to the factors above indicated. Wagner, who has written the most complete statistical work on suicide that has hitherto appeared, develops it according to an ideal scheme taken from Engel, in which are indicated three classes of influences, external or natural, biological, and social.

But many of these statistics neither give nor can yet give positive information, so that many columns of his table remain blank, or are filled up by the imagination of the writer. We wish to be more prudent, and in our analysis we limit ourselves to those influences on which alone sufficient knowledge is furnished by statistics. After having shown the increase of suicide during this century, we shall employ ourselves especially with:

1. *Cosmic or natural influences.*

2. *Ethnic or social (demographic) influences.*
3. *Social influences.*
4. *Individual biological influences.*
5. *Individual psychological influences (determining motives).*

Studying finally the mode and place of suicide, we shall see how even in the choice of these man is subject to the numerous influences just named.

The Demographic Epidemiology of Suicide

The use of demographic data in studies and discussions of suicide is a revered tradition. However, the manner in which these statistics have been utilized has resulted in comparatively little progress in the advancement of knowledge of the epidemiology of suicide. While the accumulation of literature devoted to the subject is almost over-whelming at this time,[1] the serious student of suicide quickly finds that most of the materials are repetitious descriptions of oft-published relationships. For example, without detracting from the contributions of the respective authors, it can be noted that the reader of Morselli's work[2] which was first published in 1879, is well-equipped to anticipate most of the major findings presented more than eighty years later by Dublin[3] and the National Center for Health Statistics.[4]

The relative lack of progress in epidemiological investigations of suicide can be attributed to three basic sources: (1) the fragmentation of knowledge due to differences in the theoretical approaches and underlying assumptions of the various professional disciplines involved in the study of suicide; (2) the lack of understanding of the limitations and potentials inherent in demographic statistics; and, (3) the non-use and misuse of an epidemiological approach that has, in fact, contributed substantially to a greater understanding of the processes involved in other causes of death such as heart diseases and cancer.

It is an impossible task to attempt to remedy these serious problems in a short chapter. Instead, we will confine our efforts to four general topics—a brief discussion of the role of the epidemiological approach in the development of increased knowledge of the process of suicide, a commentary on the limitations of demographic statistics and the precautions to be taken in their use and interpretation, a critical examination and presentation of recent statistics on suicide in the United States, and finally some suggestions for directions to be taken in a meaningful epidemiological investigation of suicide.

AN INTERDISCIPLINARY EPIDEMIOLOGICAL APPROACH

Most previous studies of suicide tended to develop knowledge of this cause of death in a manner very analogous to the early investigations of the cause of infectious diseases. There is the assumption, usually implicit, that the cause of suicide is an etiological agent that needs only to be labeled in order to be understood. Thus, conditions labeled as depression, frustration, anomie, etc., are suggested as the causative agents by the proponents of various disciplines. This procedure is quite reminiscent of the explanation that the damp night air is the cause of malaria and yellow fever.

Modern epidemiology is no longer bound by the concept of uni-causality. Instead, it acknowledges the possibility of etiological agents which may be necessary but not in themselves sufficient to initiate a disease process. Thus, a full understanding of the disease process may involve the knowledge of individual differences, group (social activities), and environmental conditions.

An adaptation of this concept[5] to the study of suicide might be expressed in the formula

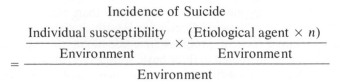

$$\text{Incidence of Suicide}$$
$$= \frac{\dfrac{\text{Individual susceptibility}}{\text{Environment}} \times \dfrac{(\text{Etiological agent} \times n)}{\text{Environment}}}{\text{Environment}}$$

This formula does *not* imply an exact mathematical relationship since most of the factors involved have not yet been identified, much less quantified. However, the statement of possible relationships in this form forces us to recognize that there are many dimensions involved in the analysis of the phenomena of suicide.[6]

Individual susceptibility is fixed by the interaction between the biological organism and the environment. In terms of suicide, biological susceptibility is modified by the presence or absence of psychological and social factors that influence the development of personality.

There may be just one type of etiological agent or many types. The concentration of the agent(s) can be increased, decreased, or even eliminated by environmental conditions. For example, if it is assumed that frustration is an etiological agent, a particular type of social environment might serve to enhance the development of conditions of frustration. Conversely, another type of social environment might reduce them.

The presence of both susceptible individuals *and* the etiological agent(s) is necessary, but not sufficient, for suicide to take place. The environment, including the psychosocial environment, determines the degree of exposure of individuals to the causative agents.

Thus, variations in the rates of suicide may result from high levels of susceptibility (or psychological resistance) in a population, the presence of high or low concentrations of etiological agents, and the degree of exposure of individuals to the causative agents.

The presence of comparatively large differences in the rates of two populations serves to alert investigators to possible conditions and situations that warrant intensive and/or extensive scrutiny in the quest for increased knowledge of the factors involved in the suicidal process. The existence of these differentials might also indicate potential laboratory areas for critical tests of hypotheses.

Most importantly, the use of this statement of relationships forces us to abandon simplistic explanations of suicide and to be more comprehensive in our statements and analyses of factors that are possibly involved in suicide. In addition, it compels us to recognize that any hypotheses of causation, no matter how appealing in terms of theoretical consistency and logic, must ultimately be tested by the facts, i.e., the observed rates of suicide.

STATISTICS ON SUICIDE: THE USE AND ABUSE

It is difficult to imagine any set of observations that has been subjected to more abuse and misuse than suicide statistics. While there never seems to be any reluctance to use these data when they offer support for the advocacy of a particular theory, type of research, or ameliorative service activity, we quickly deny the reliability and validity of these observations when they cast some doubt upon our own favored ideas.

Much of the abuse of suicide statistics results from what might be described as innocent ignorance. The excellent clinician, who develops a hypothesis of the cause of suicide based upon years of practice and does not find support for it in the data, is more likely to attack the reliability of the statistics than to take the time to develop the skills to use them properly. Similarly, a behavioral scientist might find that his personal opinions about the desirability of certain psychosocial conditions might overwhelm his scientific judgment so that he cannot accept observations that contradict these opinions. Suicide statistics are a readily available scapegoat in these cases.

An appreciation of the problems and potentials inherent in the use of suicide statistics is gained when it is understood that they are the byproduct of the legal requirement that all deaths be registered. The registration process involves the legal certification by a physician or other appointed person (such as a coroner or medical examiner) that death did occur to the described individual. The certifier is also asked to offer his judgment as to the cause of death based on the best available evidence. Absolute certainty is neither expected or anticipated. Many causes of death can be established with certainty only when there is a long diagnostic history available and a complete post-mortem examination.[7] This situation exists only for a relatively small percentage of deaths.

The information deemed to be important on the certificate is then coded and the information is placed into a storage-and-retrieval system such as punch cards or magnetic tape. The cause-of-death information, which is entered on the certificate in terms of medical nomenclature, is coded into statistical categories which are based upon those in the International Classification of Diseases, Injuries, and Causes of Death (I.C.D. categories). The logic underlying the establishment of the specific categories is that each will provide statistics of maximum utility to the largest number of users of the data.

While these procedures provide international uniformity in the statistical coding and tabulation processes, variations in the medicul-cultural norms of the certifiers, as well as legal requirements, may influence propensities favoring one type of diagnosis over another. Thus, comparisons of the actual rates of suicide among countries may be misleading. It is usually much more fruitful to study the patterns of variation of rates within a single nation since there is greater uniformity in legal requirements and medical-cultural norms within nations than between them.

It must be emphasized that the focus of analysis must be upon the observed patterns rather than upon minor differentials in rates or absolute numbers. The minor differences may be due to slight variations in certification practices and/or allowable clerical errors in the coding of mass data.[8] The errors of certification and coding can only be important if it is demonstrated that they are not uniformly distributed among the social and demographic categories being considered.

There are periodic revisions of the I.C.D. categories and coding rules that influence the continuity of mortality statistics over time. For example, with the introduction of the Seventh Revision of the I.C.D. in 1958, all deaths due to self-inflicted injury were classified as suicides if no statement that it was accidental was noted. Deaths where the certifier expressed uncertainty, accidental or intentional, were automatically coded as suicides. This resulted in an overall increase of approximately 3 percent in the number of deaths classified as suicide.[9] In addition, deaths to persons younger than eight years of age were not classified as suicide even if the certifier entered this as a cause of death.

With the introduction of the Eighth Revision of the I.C.D., in 1968, deaths due to self-inflicted injuries were no longer classifed as suicide unless the certifier specified intentionality. This change in procedure resulted in a decrease of approximately 6 percent in the number of deaths attributed to suicide.[10]

We have been discussing the factors that might change the numbers of suicides. However, since the suicide rate is calculated using the formula

$$\text{Suicide rate} = \frac{\text{Number of suicides}}{\text{population}} \times 100,000$$

possible errors in the denominator are of equal importance in determining accurate rates. While the population is usually underenumerated in a census, the proportion of those who are not counted is usually small. However, underenumeration is not randomly distributed, but rather tends to be concentrated in certain demographic categories. For example, nonwhites tend to be underenumerated to a greater extent than do whites, and young people are less likely to be counted than are older people.[11] Any interpretation of differences in suicide rates should take these factors into account.

The magnitude of the numbers, in both the numerator and denominator of the formula used in calculating the rates, must be considered in any comparative analyses between categories or over time. Where the numerator is small, as it is for the younger ages, relatively greater changes in the rates can occur due to random fluctuations of a comparatively rare event. When the denominator is small, as it is for the oldest ages, minor errors of underenumeration or age misstatement can produce large differences in the suicide rates.

DEMOGRAPHIC CHARACTERISTICS OF SUICIDE IN THE UNITED STATES

The most recent available suicide statistics in the United States are for the years 1969, 1970, and 1971. A detailed examination of differentials in suicide rates is possible when these data are used in conjunction with population bases from the 1970 Census of Population. Even if more recent suicide statistics were available at this time, they could only be used with estimates of the population until the 1980 census data are available. The calculated rates would then be less reliable than rates using census-based populations.

There were totals of 22,364, 23,480, and 24,093 deaths in 1969, 1970 and 1971, respectively which were coded to the categories of suicide and self-inflicted injuries (I.C.D. statistical categories E950–E959). The increase in the number of deaths in each successive year generally parallels the increases in the size of the population most susceptible to suicide.

Any examination of the suicide rates of the total population is inherently deceptive since approximately two-thirds of the suicides in any year are white males. Therefore, the rates for the total population will tend to reflect the characteristics and trends of the rates of white males, the differentials in patterns of suicide by sex and color will be obscured (see Table 2-1).

The suicide rates presented in this chapter are calculated whenever possible by using the average annual number of suicides for the three-year period centering on a census year, e.g., 1969–1971. This procedure tends to minimize fluctuations in the rates due to chance, but it does obscure short-term trends in suicide rates. The trade-off between obtaining greater reliability of the rates and ignoring sudden changes is worthwhile in early stages of epidemiological investigations when the factors producing changes are still unknown or immeasurable.

Sex Differentials in Suicide

The most important and consistent differential to be found in suicide rates is between the sexes. The rate for males usually ranges from approximately two to seven times greater than that for females.

The only exceptions noted to this general rule have been for areas of the world where the accuracy and completeness of mortality registration is open to serious question[12] or for specific age categories where the rates are based upon small numbers subject to relatively large fluctuations.

In 1969-1971, the ratio between the rates for the white male and female populations was 2.4; for nonwhites the ratio was 2.8. The white ratio ranged from 2.5 for the 15-24 age category to a ratio of 10.5 for those over 85 years of age. The ratio between the sexes for nonwhites ranged from 1.5 in the 5-14 age group to 4.6 in the 64-74 age category. The greater range of the ratio of the suicide rates by sex among nonwhites is due to the high suicide rates for older white males.

The existence of male suicide rates that are consistently higher than those for females means that in addition to the possibility of the operation of a biological factor in tendencies toward self-destruction, two factors are worthy of serious consideration. First, it may be that the psychological development and socialization process of females differs from that of males, and this difference may result in a personality type that is less susceptible to suicidal forces.

The second additional item is that females are possibly less frequently exposed to the forces or conditions that might promote suicide. This possibility contains the implicit assumption that when and where females and males have equal exposure to these forces, the female rate will start to approximate that of males.

Since there are a multitude of suggestions in the literature, both popular and scientific, that in the United States females in increasing numbers are entering occupations and playing roles previously reserved for males, there is the expectation that the female suicide rate might be increasing in relation to that of males. There is little indication that this increase has occurred over the last 30 years in the 15-44 year age groups where the social changes may have the greatest impact (see Table 2-2). However, no definite conclusions can be drawn until it is possible to control for important characteristics such as marital status, etc.

Age Differentials in Suicide

The second most important, and relatively consistent, patterns to be found in an examination of suicide rates are those associated with age. The suicide rates of white males tend to increase directly with age with the highest rates being found among the elderly. In

Table 2-1

Suicide Rates by Age, Sex, and Color, in the United States, 1939–1941, 1949–1951, 1959–1961, and 1969–1971
(Rates per 100,000)

Color and Sex	5–14	15–24	25–34	35–44	45–54	55–64	65–74	75–84	85+ Years	All ages
White males										
1939–1941[a]	0.4	8.4	19.3	28.6	41.6	55.4	57.9	67.3	60.0	22.6
1949–1951	0.3	6.7	13.2	22.3	32.8	44.1	51.9	58.5	69.8	18.5
1959–1961	0.4	8.2	14.6	21.9	33.1	40.7	42.2	55.6	62.4	17.5
1969–1971	0.5	13.8	19.3	23.0	29.0	34.9	37.9	47.2	47.1	17.8
White females										
1939–1941[a]	0.1	4.0	8.1	10.9	13.7	13.1	12.0	8.3	6.3	7.1
1949–1951	0.1	2.6	5.1	8.0	10.2	10.5	10.0	8.2	7.4	5.3
1959–1961	0.1	2.3	5.8	8.0	10.4	10.6	9.2	8.2	4.9	5.2
1969–1971	0.2	4.2	8.7	12.9	13.8	12.2	9.8	7.4	4.4	7.1

Nonwhite males

Period										
1939–1941[a]	0.2	4.7	10.6	11.0	13.5	12.1	11.4	11.8	6.8	6.8
1949–1951	0.2*	5.0	10.3	11.2	11.7	15.9	12.7	12.9	12.5*	6.9
1959–1961	0.1*	6.5	14.4	12.1	13.6	15.8	13.6	17.6	12.8*	7.5
1969–1971	0.3	11.0	18.1	14.2	12.1	10.8	12.4	12.4	13.8	8.4

Nonwhite females

Period										
1939–1941[a]	0.1	2.8	3.1	2.4	3.3	1.8	2.2	3.1	3.3	1.9
1949–1951	0.1*	1.9	2.6	2.5	2.8	2.3	2.0	2.3*	0	1.6
1959–1961	0.1*	1.9	3.6	3.5	2.9	3.6	2.9	3.0*	4.1*	1.9
1969–1971	0.2*	4.5	6.1	4.9	4.1	2.5	2.7	3.5	4.2*	3.0

* Based on less than 20 deaths. Not indicated for 1939–1941 period.
[a] Average annual rate for the 3-year period. Rates shown for other periods are based on the average annual number.

Sources:
1969–1971 Compiled and computed from unpublished data from the National Center for Health Statistics.
1959–1961 Compiled from National Center for Health Statistics, "Suicide in the United States: 1950–1964," Vital and Health Statistics, 20, 5. Washington, D.C., U.S. Government Printing Office, 1967.
1949–1951 Compiled from National Office of Vital Statistics, "Suicide," Vital Statistics—Special Reports, 49, 61. Washington, D.C., U.S. Government Printing Office, 1959.
1939–1941 Compiled and computed from National Office of Vital Statistics, "Death Rates by Age, Race, and Sex: United States, 1900–1953: Suicide," Vital Statistics—Special Reports, XLIII, 30. U.S. Government Printing Office, 1956.

Table 2-2
Ratio of Male to Female Suicide Rates in the United
States, 1939-1941, 1949-1951, 1959-1961, and 1969-1971,
by Color and Age (15-24 years and 25-34 years)

Color and Age	1939-1941	1949-1951	1959-1961	1969-1971
White				
15-24	2.1	2.6	3.6	3.3
25-34	2.4	2.6	2.5	2.2
Nonwhite				
15-24	1.7	2.6	3.4	2.4
25-34	3.4	4.0	4.0	3.0

Source: Computed from Table 2-1.

contrast, the rates for white females increase until ages 45-64, and
then they usually decrease slightly.

The chronological aging process is important because it is associated with changes in individual psychodynamic patterns due to
exposure to an increasing variety of personal experiences. In addition,
age determines the probabilities that individuals will be exposed to
factors associated with the life cycle. For example, marriage is rare
before the age of 15, but it is the predominant marital status during
the ages of 30-40; widowhood is a comparative rarity prior to age
40, but it becomes common after that age; and being a grandparent
may be an exceedingly common characteristic after age 50, but it
is as equally rare before age 30.

The age patterns of nonwhites reach their highest points in the
25-34 year age groups and then either decline or remain reasonably
level. Great caution must be exercised in the interpretation of differences in suicide rates by age for nonwhites since the rates are
based upon a relatively small number of occurrences which is subject
to extreme fluctuation. For example, in the age category 35-44 for
nonwhite males, 190 deaths were classified as suicide in 1969, 158
in 1970, and 185 in 1971. These fluctuations can result in correspondingly large changes in the rates.

Recent attention has been focused on the relatively great increases
in the suicide rates of younger persons. There has been an increase
of over 100 percent in the suicide rate of white males aged 15-24
between 1949-1951 and 1969-1971 and an approximately 50 percent
increase for white males aged 25-34 in the same time period.

While these increases are interesting and possibly important, they must be viewed in a larger perspective. First, it should be observed that the suicide rates of young people were at a low point during the early 1950s. If an earlier time period is used as the base, the increase by 1969-1971 is not nearly as large. Second, the suicide rates of young people are exceedingly low. Therefore, an increase of only five suicides per 100,000 can result in a relatively great increase in the rate. However, the age patterns of suicide rates would be virtually unchanged.

The consistent and substantial decrease in the suicide rates of persons older than age 35 is equally, if not more important than the slight increase at the younger ages. This trend over the last 30 years is most apparent for white males and is worthy of more intensive investigation.

Color Differentials in Suicide

Accurate biological descriptions of race are not used in either death reporting or census enumerations. Rather, the racial designations tend to be those in common usage and represent a mixture of self-declared race and nationality, i.e., white, black, Chinese, Japanese, etc.[13] While this procedure is reasonably satisfactory for the analysis of differentials between blacks and whites, it can result in errors of interpretation in analyses of suicide among other racial categories. For example, while most officials in California may be able to specify accurately whether a suicide victim is of Chinese or Japanese descent from the name if there is no reliable informant, it is unlikely that this distinction would be made in North Dakota. Consequently, the likely designation of Oriental might be classified to "other races" in the absence of additional information. Similarly, persons of mixed parentage might report themselves as white while alive, but in case of death the family informant may offer another designation.

Since the precision needed for an investigation of racial differences is beyond the scope of this chapter, we are forced to focus upon the differentials in suicide for the white and nonwhite categories. Blacks comprise almost 90 percent of the nonwhites in the United States and the two categories may be equated in analyzing national data. An investigator of suicide rates in some states, such as California, Hawaii, and New Mexico would not have the same freedom. In addition, the very small numbers of suicides, with great random fluctuations, make it almost impossible to calculate accurate and meaningful suicide rates for categories such as American Indians, e.g., in 1967 there were 227 deaths classified to suicide among all nonwhites other than blacks in all of the United States.

Students of suicide have usually tended to accept the dictum that the suicide rate of blacks is substantially below that of whites. This repeated finding is based upon national data and ignores the variations to be found in various parts of the country. The observation that the nonwhite rate in the Northeastern region of the nation was relatively high and approximated that of whites in the early years of this century was ignored.[14]

Present claims that the suicide rate of young blacks is higher than that of whites, even in some states of the Northeast, must be critically examined.[15] Since young people are underenumerated in the census to a greater degree than older persons and young nonwhites are underenumerated to a greater extent than whites, their rates are artificially inflated. Table 2-3 shows that when a correction for underenumeration is made, the suicide rates of young white and nonwhite males are approximately equal among the metropolitan population of New York State.

Based on the New York data and the national statistics (Table 2-1), it can be concluded that the suicide rates of young blacks now approximate those of young whites, but the suicide rates of blacks above age 45 are below those of whites of the same age. A tentative conclusion is that young blacks are now exposed to the same suicidal forces as young whites, but older blacks do not now have the same exposure to these forces as do older whites.

Rural-Urban Differentials in Suicide

The existence of urban suicide rates that are higher than corresponding rural areas has become so traditional in the literature that this phenomenon has been used to explain other differentials in suicide, e.g., the low suicide rates of blacks in the South.[16] The rare exceptions to the expected findings are looked upon as mere curiosities.[17]

There was some indication in the 1950 suicide statistics that the rural suicide rates were higher than the urban in some of the states of the United States. Since this might have been due to age and sex differences in the respective populations, proof for this finding was unavailable.

Awareness of two problems inherent in the computation and gathering of the statistics deterred a direct test until this time. The first problem was that rural deaths were sometimes mistakenly attributed to nearby cities even though the coding is supposed to be by usual place of residence. The second problem, equally serious,

Table 2-3
Reported and Estimated Suicide Rates by Color for the Male Metropolitan Population of
New York State, 1960
(Rates per 100,000)

Age category	Whites			Nonwhites		
	Number of suicides	Reported suicide rate	Estimated suicide rate	Number of suicides	Reported suicide rate	Estimated suicide rate
5–14	1	0.1	0.1	1	0.7	0.7
15–24	42	5.8	5.6	5	5.9	5.1
25–34	85	10.5	10.3	17	16.1	13.5
35–44	108	12.4	12.1	14	13.6	11.4
45–54	189	23.0	23.0	8	10.8	9.4
55–64	193	28.6	28.5	9	18.2	15.8
65–74	170	39.8	43.0	7	31.2	33.7
75–84	62	42.8	46.3	—	0	0
≥85	16	71.9	77.7	—	0	0

Sources: Compiled and computed from National Center for Health Statistics unpublished data and U.S. Bureau of the Census, U.S. Census of Population, 1960. Washington, D.C., U.S. Government Printing Office. Correction estimates from National Academy of Sciences, America's Uncounted People. Washington, D.C., National Academy of Sciences, 1972, p. 28.

was that the urban population as defined by the Bureau of the Census included more people than did the definition of urban used by the vital statistics agencies. Thus, the deaths in the numerator of the urban suicide rate were from a population that was smaller than the population used in the denominator. In contrast to the first problem which inflated the urban rate, the second problem tended to reduce the suicide rate for urban populations. The magnitude of these two distortions of the suicide rate was unknown.

One possible resolution of these two problems is to consider the populations of metropolitan areas as most urban. The rural populations of nonmetropolitan counties can be considered most rural since the largest city in the county has a population of less than 50,000. This procedure minimized, but did not eliminate, the problem of the misallocation of rural deaths to nearby urban areas. In addition, the procedure made it possible to calculate the populations used in the denominator of the rate so that they would be consistent with the definition used by the vital statistics agencies.

Table 2-4 demonstrates that males in rural areas have equal or slightly higher suicide rates than do those in metropolitan (most urban) areas. Although the difference is small, rural females still tend to have lower suicide rates than their most urban counterparts. The rates for the nonmetropolitan, urban populations are not meaningful since they still reflect some misallocation of rural deaths to nearby urban areas. When rates in the nonmetropolitan urban residence category are high, it only means that the true rural rate is probably higher than that shown.

Although it is not shown in the table, the higher rural suicide rate for males in 1960 was due primarily to white suicides since the nonwhite rural rates were slightly lower, or just equal to the corresponding metropolitan rates. It is not possible to repeat this test for 1970 since the National Center for Health Statistics has now included urban places of less than 10,000 population with the rural areas.

In any event, based on this demonstration it is no longer correct to assume that there is an inherent relationship between urban living and high suicide rates. Nor can the assumption be made that ruralism necessarily implies the existence of low suicide rates.

Some Other Differentials in Suicide

Epidemiological studies of suicide in the United States received a severe blow with the decision to restrict the coding of individual and social characteristics to age, sex, race, and residence for the

Table 2-4

Suicide Rates by Place of Residence, by Age and Sex in
the United States, 1960
(Rates per 100,000)

Age categories	Metropolitan	Nonmetropolitan urban	Nonmetropolitan rural
Males			
All ages	15.7	17.8	17.6
5–14	0.4	0.7	0.4
15–24	8.6	8.3	7.2
25–34	14.2	15.4	16.0
35–44	19.7	26.0	22.2
45–54	30.0	35.4	31.8
55–64	36.2	38.4	49.2
65–74	37.8	39.8	43.5
≥75	51.3	52.9	56.9
Females			
All ages	5.5	4.4	3.6
5–14	0.1	0	0.2
15–24	2.3	1.8	2.1
25–34	5.9	5.3	4.3
35–44	8.7	6.2	5.2
45–54	11.2	8.6	8.0
55–64	10.9	10.8	7.9
65–74	9.6	6.4	6.5
≥75	9.7	7.1	5.8

Source: Suicides compiled and computed from unpublished data from the National Center for Health Statistics. Population based, compiled, and computed from U.S. Bureau of the Census, U.S. Census of Population, 1960. Washington, D.C., U.S. Government Printing Office.

1969–1971 time period. The other characteristics listed on the death certificates were not coded due to limitations of budget and personnel. This means that analyses of the relationships between these other characteristics and suicide must wait at least until the 1980 census period. It is an impossible task to add codes to the certificates once they are processed.

It will not serve a useful purpose to reiterate the findings of investigations based on the statistics for earlier time periods since they are readily available.[18] However, previous discussions of the

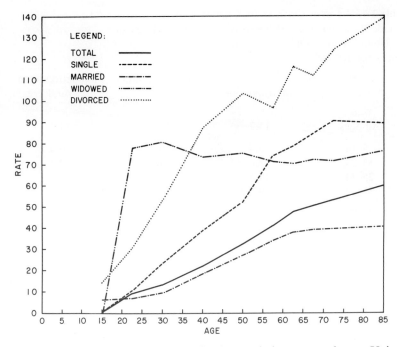

Fig. 2-1. Suicide rates of white males by marital status and age, United States, 1949–1951

association between suicide and marital status and migration should be supplemented.

While it has long been noted that married people have the lowest suicide rates, the differences among the unmarried are also worthy of attention. Those persons who have never married have a lower suicide rate than those whose marriage has been disrupted, however the rate for older white males who have never married approximates, and even exceeds, the rates for those who are widowed.

The suicide rates for both white males and females are relatively high when compared to the age categories for those who are married (see Figs. 2-1 and 2-2). However, the rates for the widowed remain level, or even decrease with increasing age. This suggests the possibility that there is a period of maximum risk just after the death of a spouse, and this risk declines with increasing time after the death of the partner. The magnitude of suicide among nonwhites is so small that there is great fluctuation in these rates by marital status. No

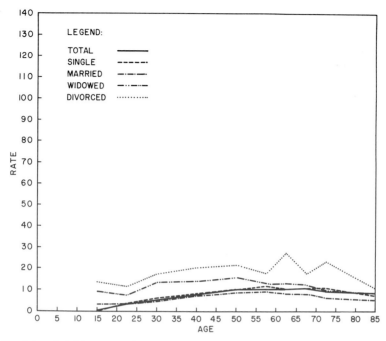

Fig. 2-2. Suicide rates of white females by marital status and age, United States, 1949–1951

valid conclusions can be drawn until techniques are devised to overcome the erratic patterns.

The possibility of a strong association between suicide and migration has often been noted.[19] However, there has never been a direct test of the relationship. Since international migration probably represents the most drastic changes associated with moving, there is the expectation that the suicide rates of the foreign-born would be substantially higher than those of the native-born. This assumption is correct for females, although not to the expected degree. Native-born, middle-aged males have rates of suicide approximately equal to the comparable foreign-born males. The suicide rates of the foreign-born are only higher than the native-born rates in the youngest and oldest age categories (see Fig. 2-3).

This finding casts some doubt upon the thesis that suicide is directly associated with migration. It is more likely that there is an indirect relationship, i.e., there is a relationship between suicide and other factors that are often associated with migration.

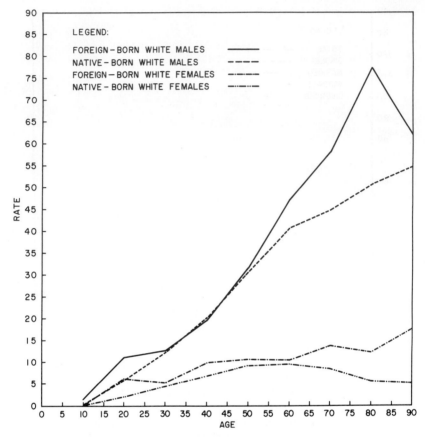

Fig. 2-3. Suicide rates by age for males and females of the native and foreign-born white population, United States, 1950

DIRECTIONS FOR THE FUTURE

Suicidology should abandon the use of demographic statistics solely for descriptive purposes and instead focus upon the use of these data in an epidemiological approach that is capable of testing the many suggestive (but obviously incomplete) hypotheses of the etiologies of suicide and their concomitants. To do otherwise means that we will continue to have a plethora of inconclusive studies with contradictory findings.

This is not to suggest that suicidologists abandon the training, experience, and approaches of their respective disciplines, and that all suicidologists should become epidemiologists. Rather, they should endeavor to use epidemiological findings to serve as critical rather than supportive tests of their hypotheses. In addition, the findings of demographic epidemiology can be used to stimulate the development of new hypotheses and approaches leading to a better understanding of this facet of human behavior.

For example, a suggestion found repeatedly in the literature is that ". . . when those psychological defense mechanisms, effective in earlier life, fail because of the impact of the biopsychosocial changes that come with increasing age, the older person is more likely to feel that time is running out and that his achievements in a general sense never have reached the level of his earlier aspirations. At this point he somehow turns his anger against himself."[20]

If one is talking about white males, then there is certainly substantial support for this position. However, a critical test would be to examine this hypothesis in the light of the epidemiological statistics for white females and/or nonwhites. If this is done, then the numerous contradictory implications of the statement start to become obvious, and these lead to questions worthy of serious investigation. Is it possible that females have a higher level of psychological defense mechanisms than do males and that these mechanisms are not reduced by the concomitants of the aging process? Do females have a lower level of aspiration than males and, conversely, are females more likely to achieve their aspirations than are males? Is there no sharing by the female of the aspirational levels of her spouse? The answer to these and other pertinent research questions generated by a critical examination of the original thesis would result in a substantial increase of our knowledge of the suicidal process and it would result in a modification of the hypothesis.

Another hypothesis frequently encountered is that suicide is associated with the loss of a loved one. Certainly the higher suicide rates of those who are widowed and divorced would support this suggestion. However, given our cultural patterns of age at marriage and the sex differential in mortality, it is the female that is more likely to lose a loved one and at an earlier age than the male. In addition, females are less likely to find a replacement spouse than males. Given the original thesis and this additional information, a critical comparison of male and female suicide rates reveals either that the assumption that females have greater resistance to suicide must be tentatively accepted or the hypothesis must be severely modified. An epidemiological approach would also demand an answer to a fundamental assumption inherent in the original hypothesis, Do those who have suffered the loss of a loved one have higher rates of suicide than those who have not had such a loss?

Although the two preceding examples have focused upon hypotheses offered by scholars of individual behavior patterns, sociologists and other scholars of social behavior have been just as guilty of avoiding a critical test using a demographic epidemiological approach. For example, the narrowing of rural-urban differentials in suicide has been attributed to the increasing poverty of rural areas.[21] If poverty per se is an etiological factor, then one would expect to find the highest suicide rates among blacks and in the South since these two population categories have relatively high levels of poverty. The data do not support this hypothesis.

It is beyond the scope of this chapter to attempt to examine the vast number of hypotheses that can be subjected to a critical test using the available demographic statistics in an analytical epidemiological approach. At most, we only can offer some guidelines and indicate some of the advantages of using this approach. In turn, we must deny that we are suggesting that the behavioral scientist is bound by the present restrictive limitations of available demographic analyses. Rather, we feel that it is time for the demographic epidemiologist to abandon the constant repetition of previously demonstrated relationships. The epidemiologist must start to examine the data that he has used for hidden assumptions inherent in the statistical gathering and processing techniques. Equally, and perhaps more important for the future, the demographic epidemiologist must start to devise and apply techniques that will make some of the more recent hypotheses of suicide amenable to critical tests. An example of this might be found in the area of recent suggestions that suicide is the result of a culmination of many events occurring earlier in a persons' life. That is, suicide is regarded as the final event of a processional chain rather than as an event occurring at a single temporal point. The demographic epidemiologist can adapt techniques using a cohort approach to test this type of hypothesis. For simple illustrative purposes it might be asked how economic adversity encountered at an early stage of life influences the probabilities of suicide in the later years of life.

Similarly, the assumption that some individuals have a high self-destructive potential might be examined by observing the rates of a cohort of men who served in a war. Since the hypothesis that war offers an avenue of legitimate self-destruction has been offered, one would expect that the post-war survivors would have lower suicide rates than those who did not engage in combative activities. Cohort analysis techniques can be developed to test these and other types of hypotheses.

In conclusion, we would like to offer three comments: (1) demographic epidemiology can play a very important role in the development and testing of a wide variety of hypotheses of the etiology and concomitants of suicide. While the proper categorization, calculation, and analyses of statistics are time-consuming and expensive, it is still less expensive than most other epidemiological techniques since the basic data are gathered as a byproduct of the legal requirement of death registration; (2) improvements in the quality and quantity of the statistics will only be achieved through the careful, continued analyses and constructive criticisms of the available data. No agency will make an effort to improve a product in the absence of a demand for it; (3) demographic epidemiology is not a panacea or a substitute for other types of epidemiological investigations, but rather it is complementary and supplementary to them.

REFERENCES

1. Farberow NL: Bibliography on Suicide and Suicide Prevention. Washington, D.C., US Government Printing Office, 1972
2. Morselli H: Suicide: An Essay on Comparative Moral Statistics (ed 2). London, Kegan Paul, Trench, 1883
3. Dublin LI: Suicide: A Sociological and Statistical Study. New York, Ronald Press, 1963
4. National Center for Health Statistics: Suicide in the United States, 1950-1964. Vital and Health Statistics 20, 5. Washington, D.C., US Government Printing Office, 1967
5. Wilson WG, Kilbourne ED: Preventive Medicine and Public Health (ed 3). New York, Macmillan, 1963, p 76
6. Breed W: Suicide and Loss in Social Interaction, in Shneidman ES (ed): Essays in Self-Destruction. New York, Science House, 1967, p 188
7. Moriyama IM, Baum WS, Haenszel WM, et al: Inquiry into Diagnostic Evidence Supporting Medical Certifications of Death. Am J Public Health 48:1376-1387, 1958
8. National Center for Health Statistics, Vital Statistics: Demographic Classification and Encoder Instructions for Death Records, 1969-1971. Instruction Manual, Data Preparation, Part 4. Rockville, Maryland, National Center for Health Statistics, 1971, p 6
9. National Center for Health Statistics, Comparability of Mortality Statistics for the Sixth and Seventh Revisions: United States, 1958. Vital Statistics Special Reports 51, 4, 1965
10. National Center for Health Statistics, Provisional Estimates of Selected Comparability Ratios Based on Dual Coding of 1966 Death Certificates by the Seventh and Eighth Revisions of the International Classification of Diseases. Monthly Vital Statistics Report 17, 8, 1968

11. Advisory Committee on Problems of Census Enumeration, America's Uncounted People. Washington, D.C., National Academy of Sciences, 1972, p 28
12. Shah JH: Causes and Prevention of Suicide. Indian Conference of Social Work, Hyderabad, 1959. Cited in Clinard MB: Sociology of Deviant Behavior (ed 4). New York, Holt, 1974, p 634
13. National Center for Health Statistics, Vital Statistics: Demographic Classification and Encoder Instructions for Death Records, 1969-1971. Instruction Manual, Data Preparation, Part 4. Rockville, Maryland, National Center for Health Statistics, 1971, p 28
14. National Office of Vital Statistics, Death Rates by Age, Race, and Sex: United States, 1900-1953: Suicide. Vital Statistics Special Reports, 43, 3, 1956
15. Hendin H: Black Suicide. Arch Gen Psychiatry 21:407-422, 1969
16. Clinard MB: Sociology of Deviant Behavior (ed 4). New York, Holt, 1974, p 635
17. Schroeder WW, Beegle JA: Suicide: An Instance of High Rural Rates. Rural Sociology 18:45-52, 1953
18. Kramer M, Pollack ES, Redick RW, Locke: Mental Disorders/Suicide: A.P.H.A. Vital and Health Statistics Monographs. Cambridge, Massachusetts, Harvard Univ Press, 1972, p 173
19. Sainsbury P: Suicide in London. London, Chapman and Hall, 1955, p 76
20. Weiss JMA: Suicide in the Aged, in Resnik HLP (ed): Suicidal Behaviors: Diagnosis and Management. Boston, Little, Brown 1968, p 264
21. Dublin LI: Suicide: A Sociological and Statistical Study. New York, Ronald Press 1963, p 51

William C. Swanson
and Warren Breed

3

Black Suicide in New Orleans

The introductory comments to this chapter are a section from Chapter
X of *Black Rage* by psychiatrists William H. Grier and Price M.
Cobbs. It is reproduced with the permission of Basic Books.

. . . The tone of the preceding chapters has been mournful, painful, desolate,
as we have described the psychological consequences of white oppression
of blacks. The centuries of senseless cruelty and the permeation of the black
man's character with the conviction of his own hatefulness and inferiority
tell a sorry tale.

This dismal tone has been deliberate. It has been an attempt to evoke
a certain quality of depression and hopelessness in the reader and to stir
these feelings. These are the most common feelings tasted by black people
in America.

The horror carries the endorsement of centuries and the entrie lifespan
of a nation. It is a way of life which reaches back to the beginnings of
recorded time. And all the bestiality, wherever it occurs and however long
it has been happening, is narrowed, focused, and refined to shine into a
black child's eyes when first he views his world. All that has ever happened
to black men and women he sees in the victims closest to him, his parents.

A life is an eternity and throughout all that eternity a black child has
breathed the foul air of cruelty. He has grown up to find that his spirit
was crushed before he knew there was need of it. His ambitions, even in
their forming, showed him to have set his hand against his own. This is
the desolation of black life in America.

Depression and grief are hatred turned on the self. It is instructive to
pursue the relevance of this truth to the condition of black Americans.

99

Black people have shown a genius for surviving under the most deadly circumstances. They have survived because of their close attention to reality. A black dreamer would have a short life in Mississippi. They are of necessity bound to reality, chained to the facts of the times; historically the penalty for misjudging a situation involving white men has been death. The preoccupation with religion has been a willing adoption of fantasy to prod an otherwise reluctant mind to face another day.

We will even play tricks on ourselves if it helps us stay alive.

The psycholgical devices used to survive are reminiscent of the years of slavery, and it is no coincidence. The same devices are used because black men face the same danger now as then.

The grief and depression caused by the condition of black men in America is an unpopular reality to the sufferers. They would rather see themselves in a more heroic posture and chide a disconsolate brother. They would like to point to their achievements (which in fact have been staggering); they would rather point to virtue (which has been shown in magnificent form by some blacks); they would point to bravery, fidelity, prudence, brilliance, creativity, all of which dark men have shown in abundance. But the overriding experience of the black American has been grief and sorrow and no man can change that fact.

His grief has been realistic and appropriate. What people have so earned a period of mourning?

We want to emphasize yet again the depth of the grief for slain sons and ravished daughters, how deep and lingering it is.

If the depth of this sorrow is felt, we can then consider what can be made of this emotion.

As grief lifts and the sufferer moves toward health, the hatred he had turned on himself is redirected toward his tormentors, and the fury of his attack on the one who caused him pain is in direct proportion to the depth of his grief. When the mourner lashes out in anger, it is a relief to those who love him, for they know he has now returned to health.

Observe that the amount of rage the oppressed turns on his tormentor is a direct function of the depth of his grief, and consider the intensity of black men's grief.

Slip for a moment into the soul of a black girl whose womanhood is blighted, not because she is ugly, but because she is black and by definition all blacks are ugly.

Become for a moment a black citizen of Birmingham, Alabama, and try to understand his grief and dismay when innocent children are slain while they worship, for no other reason than that they are black.

Imagine how an impoverished mother feels as she watches the light of creativity snuffed out in her children by schools which dull the mind and environs which rot the soul.

For a moment make yourself the black father whose son went innocently to war and there was slain—for whom, for what?

For a moment be any black person, anywhere, and you will feel the waves of hopelessness that engulfed black men and women when Martin Luther King was murdered. All black people understood the tide of anarchy that followed his death.

It is the transformation of *this* quantum of grief into aggression of which we now speak. As a sapling bent low stores energy for a violent backswing, blacks bent double by oppression have stored energy which will be released in the form of rage—black rage, apocalyptic and final.

White Americans have developed a high skill in the art of misunderstanding black people. It must have seemed to slaveholders that slavery would last through all eternity, for surely their misunderstanding of black bondsmen suggested it. If the slaves were eventually to be released from bondage, what could be the purpose of creating the fiction of their subhumanity?

It must have seemed to white men during the period 1865 to 1945 that black men would always be a passive, compliant lot. If not, why would they have stoked the flames of hatred with such deliberately barbarous treatment?

White Americans today deal with "racial incidents" from summer to summer as if such minor turbulence will always remain minor and one need only keep the blacks busy till fall to have made it through another troubled season.

Today it is the young men who are fighting the battles, and, for now, their elders, though they have given their approval, have not joined in. The time seems near, however, for the full range of the black masses to put down the broom and buckle on the sword. And it grows nearer day by day. Now we see skirmishes, sputtering erratically, evidence if you will that the young men are in a warlike mood. But evidence as well that the elders are watching closely and may soon join the battle.

Even these minor flurries have alarmed the country and have resulted in a spate of generally senseless programs designed to give *temporary summer jobs!* More interesting in its long-range prospects has been the apparent eagerness to draft black men for military service. If in fact this is a deliberate design to place black men in uniform in order to get them off the street, it may be the most curious "instant cure" for a serious disease this nation has yet attempted. Young black men are learning the most modern techniques for killing—techniques which may be used against *any* enemy.

But it is all speculation. The issue finally rests with the black masses. When the servile men and women stand up, we had all better duck.

We should ask what is likely to galvanize the masses into aggression against the whites.

Will it be some grotesque atrocity against black people which at last causes one-tenth of the nation to rise up in indignation and crush the monstrosity?

Will it be the example of black people outside the United States who have gained dignity through their own liberation movement?

Will it be by the heroic action of a small group of blacks which by its wisdom and courage commands action in a way that cannot be denied?

Or will it be by blacks, finally and in an unpredictable way, simply getting fed up with the bumbling stupid racism of this country? Fired not so much by any one incident as by the gradual accretion of stupidity into fixtures of national policy.

All are possible, or any one, or something yet unthought. It seems certain only that on the course the nation now is headed it will happen.

One might consider the possibility that, if the national direction remains unchanged, such a conflagration simply might *not* come about. Might not black people remain where they are, as they did for a hundred years during slavery?

Such seems truly inconceivable. Not because blacks are so naturally warlike or rebellious, but because they are filled with such grief, such sorrow, such bitterness, and such hatred. It seems now delicately poised, not yet risen to the flash point, but rising rapidly nonetheless. No matter what repressive measures are invoked against the blacks, they will never swallow their rage and go back to blind hopelessness.

If existing oppressions and humiliating disenfranchisements are to be lifted, they will have to be lifted most speedily, or catastrophe will follow.

For there are no more psychological tricks blacks can play upon themselves to make it possible to exist in dreadful circumstances. No more lies can they tell themselves. No more dreams to fix on. No more opiates to dull the pain. No more patience. No more thought. No more reason. Only a welling tide risen out of all those terrible years of grief, now a tidal wave of fury and rage, and all black, black as night.

Black Suicide in New Orleans

Three questions seem paramount in the study of suicide among blacks: Why do blacks commit suicide? Why is the rate so low? What has changed since the civil rights movement of the past 15-20 years? We have data and a conceptual perspective on the first two questions; these will permit speculation on the third.

If the black suicide rate were high there would be no difficulty explaining it. In western culture suicide is highest among the divorced and separated, Protestants, the unemployed, persons in poor physical health, and persons who live in the central cities.[1,2,3] Many blacks fall into these categories sometime in life. Blacks have high rates of infant mortality, their life expectancy is below that of whites, and they are more prone to sickness and injury. Unemployment rates of blacks exceed those of whites, more blacks are separated or divorced, and a higher percentage of blacks are Protestants than are whites. Blacks *should* have higher suicide rates. In fact, however, they do not. The demography of suicide at the national level indicates that the rate of self-inflicted death among blacks is less than half that of whites (4.6 versus 11.3 per 100,000 annually); in New Orleans the white/black ratio is 3:1 (see Table 3-1). While white suicide rates increase with age, the black rate reaches a plateau between the ages 25-29 with a slight, nearly steady decline after that. Black males, however, have a much higher suicide rate than black females (6.4 versus 1.6 at the national level).

Table 3–1
Suicide Rates in New Orleans by Age, Race, and Sex*
1966–1970 (rates per 100,000)

	White		Black	
Age	Male	Female	Male	Female
14 and under	30.0	9.5	11.3	2.5
15–24	16.8	4.7	11.8	1.1
25–34	24.9	13.8	13.9	4.7
35–44	27.9	14.7	8.8	2.6
45–54	26.6	13.9	9.2	1.5
55–64	50.0	11.0	12.1	2.7
65 and over	43.5	3.6	11.2	3.5

*Overall white rate is 18.9, overall black rate is 6.4.
Source: Louisiana State Department of Health, Division of Public Health Statistics.

Our first question was Why do blacks commit suicide? We have data from 1954–1963 on 42 black males who committed suicide in New Orleans. Only 2 of the total 44 black male suicides during this period could not be traced. All 42 were between the ages of 18 and 60 and had lived in the city for at least 6 months. Interviews were conducted with persons who knew these men (relatives, friends, neighbors, coworkers). Details of the survey procedure are given in Breed.[4] Although these men died before the flowering of the civil rights movement during the 1960s, the data are still relevant. Social life for most people does not undergo rapid change; the lives of millions of blacks are not yet very different from what they were in the 1950s. Further, the correlates of black suicide are probably quite relevant for other forms of self-destructive behavior—drug abuse and alcoholism. Very little is known about alcohol abuse among blacks[6] and the materials reported here should provide hypotheses for study on these related topics. For example, we would hypothesize that considerable alcohol abuse is a response to what we here call fatalistic oppression felt by blacks.

COMPARING SUICIDES OF BLACK AND WHITE MALES

Since more is known about white male suicides, they will constitute a point of reference to describe black male suicides. Table 3–2 contains percentages on some important items. Taking first the area of the family, no great differences between whites and blacks appear; both

Table 3-2

Some Characteristics of Black Male, White Male, and
White Female Suicides in New Orleans 1954–1963 (data
in percentages)

Characteristics	Black males	White males	White females
Age			
20–39	57%	26%	53%
40–49	17	34	25
50–60	26	40	22
Occupation			
White collar	12	36	51*
Craftsmen and foremen	10	14	11
Semiskilled	38	17	17
Service and labor	40	32	22
Education (less than high school			
graduate)	88	60	50
Marital status			
Single	24	17	7
Married	43	51	56
Widowed	0	2	7
Divorced or separated	14	27	20
Common-law	19	3	9
Size of household			
'One person	19	18	20
Two people	20	27	43
No children in household	60	53	62
Born in New Orleans	54	50	37
Seldom attend church	34	62	48
Visiting and informal social contacts			
(top two ranks—most frequent on			
four point scale)	69	45	44
Mental instability (hospitalized, saw			
psychiatrist, used tranquilizers)	32	37	69
Alcohol problems	42	31	23
Worried about debts	40	19	14
Threatened suicide (reported)	21	38	49
Attempted suicide (reported)	17	17	47
Not working full time	43	47	—
Income trend (last 2 years)			
Up	22	8	21
Down	34	51	21
Same	44	41	57
Number	42	103	107

*These figures refer usually to husband's occupation

groups evidenced a great deal of family instability. As to interpersonal affairs, the blacks showed less of the isolation typical of the whites who had committed suicide (both male and female); they attended church more often and did more socializing. In the area of personal problems, the black males showed somewhat more alcohol problems than the whites, both groups were about equal with respect to mental illness, and neither group contained many men with drug problems (recall that the period 1954-1963 predates the recent drug boom). One significant difference concerned bodily injuries due to accidents, usually at work. Ten blacks had suffered accidents, usually to the head area. Seven of these were among the younger half of the sample and six had occurred in the last year of life. The greater frequency of jobs involving manual labor among blacks probably accounts for this pattern and seems a definite factor in black male suicide. This possibility becomes important when one recognizes that the younger black suicides tended to have a more violent lifestyle than their elders—a pattern generally associated with the lower classes. The older black suicides had a profile very similar to that of the whites.

The white males had enormous difficulties in one particular area of their lives—their work roles. In an earlier paper[4] it was demonstrated that three-fourths of white suicides had experienced at least one kind of downward mobility—holding an occupational position lower than their father, having dropped from a position they had held earlier, or having a lower income at time of death than at some previous period. Only half were fully employed at time of death. In case after case, the white males gave evidence of work-role failure.

Many of the black male suicides suffered similar losses but work problems were less frequent among blacks than among whites. However, when persons who had known the deceased were asked if the victim had worried about debts, it was found that 40 percent of the blacks versus 19 percent of the whites had been so preoccupied. From this information we suggest that while prestige and respectability were of concern to the white suicides, it was actual economic distress that disturbed the blacks. Much closer to the subsistence-survival level than the whites, as can be seen in the occupation section in Table 3-2, the blacks worried in terms of immediate dollars, rather than "what others might think" about skidding or unemployment. Although 4 percent more of the blacks than whites were working full-time when they died, their economic level during life was substantially lower than that of the whites as indicated by the kinds of jobs that blacks had. Also, the black men, by a 2 to 1 margin, were more likely to worry about debts. This distinction between the two groups as to the consequences of work and money problems also appears when the cases are examined individually.

A significant difference was found in the life histories of the black and white male suicides in one other area—relationship with police and authority. Since this is the major area of contrast, it will be discussed in more detail.

THE BLACK MALE AND OVERREGULATION

Blacks in the United States, particularly in the Deep South, have been subjected to discrimination and all of its attendant difficulties and humiliations for centuries. Yet their suicide rate is low. They have managed to survive by accommodating to, if not accepting, white-dominated institutions. Dollard[7] stated that, ". . . every Negro in the South knows that he is under a kind of sentence of death." Nevertheless, the black man is not as likely to kill himself as the white man whose suicide rate continues to climb steeply reaching its peak near age 85. After age 30, the black male suicide rate rises very little and, it appears that once the young black accepts the black role he is relatively immune to overt self-destructive behavior.

What appears to be important here is the position of the black man in the community at large, in a situation of ultimate threat on his life and liberty. The black suicide case materials illustrate one particular area of contrast between blacks and whites—an overwhelming majority of the blacks who killed themselves were involved with the police and/or the courts. While only 10 percent of the white cases had such difficulties, 72 percent of the black male suicides (30 of 42 cases) had problems with the authorities. In 21 cases there had been some direct confrontation between the victim and the police. For example, 4 men hanged themselves in jail, 1 killed himself in a hospital after being taken there by police, and 4 others killed themselves while being chased by police. On a more indirect and less dramatic level, 6 of the men had been arrested 1 or more times (most had been arrested shortly before their deaths), 2 others had received several traffic tickets for speeding, and 1 had had his driver's license revoked.

Interviewers did not ask more questions about the police when dealing with black suicides than with white suicides, but the interviews abound with comments about the black victims' fear of the police. Several were quoted as having said they would kill themselves before going to jail. In some cases the respondents charged that the police had beaten and even killed the dead man. Some respondents made it clear that they, too, feared the police.

Breed[5] describes the prototypical altercation between the police and the black citizen:

> Sociologically, it is not difficult to imagine that a destructive form of social relationship has been institutionalized. Picture an altercation between Negroes, perhaps in a bar, at night. Policemen arrive. The Negroes fear the police. The police, on their part, are apprehensive of Negroes; the lower-class Negro is traditionally viewed as a 'weapon carrier' by police. The police will be more on guard, more ready to respond forcefully to an ambiguous stimulus, than with middle class whites. A vicious cycle of interaction goes into motion. Both parties commence with apprehension and perhaps hostility, and the threshold for violence is lowered. Over the years, myths of whatever justification develop in both camps.

The point here is not to assign blame. The problem is systemic; it grows out of a long history of misperception and misapprehension. The salient aspect of this problem is that blacks regard the policeman as the operant enforcer, and perhaps even more importantly, as the symbol of white authority over institutions in the black community. The word *authority* is used here because in several cases the immediate source of stress involved authorities other than the police. For example, one man was prevented from reopening his café after remodeling when the black church next door gained a court injunction; another man had 25 percent of his monthly wages garnished to make payments on his son's car. One young man was angered and committed suicide after a white priest accused him of stealing, another killed himself after being caught claiming illegitimate children as tax exemptions. Another man, charged with raping a young black girl, killed himself the day before his trial was to begin. The men in these latter cases tended to hold higher occupational status than those whose problems grew out of direct confrontation with the police.

One important fact is that, typically, these black men had little knowledge of community resources which might have helped them with their problems. No doubt they had even less confidence that they, as blacks, could gain access to these agencies. Many of these black men faced dilemmas which would not have been so severe for the white person. It is possible, for example, that some could have solved, or at least ameliorated, their problems by seeking free and available legal aid. The man with the tax problem could have consulted the Internal Revenue Service; others qualified for assistance from social welfare, clinics, credit bureaus, job advisers, etc. Nevertheless, as the interviews illustrate, these blacks made only sparing use of these resources. It is entirely possible that black attitudes toward white-controlled authorities extend to relief agencies as well. In a recent survey[8] designed to determine why people would or would not use the services of suicide prevention centers, one young black militant said he would not use such a center because, "They [white people] couldn't understand my problems. They can't know how I feel, being white and affluent." In addition to the lack of knowledge, then, blacks lacked trust in the community agencies. The latter were perceived as something alien to their experience, and were not meant "for people like me."

The black and white suicides, as we have seen, show basic similarity in individual and intragroup characteristics. However, they are very different in the relationship to controlling institutional processes.

> The white man need not identify with the Negro community or be subject to its rules. The Negro is subject to the imperatives of two communities, and when his difficulties extend outside the Negro sphere, he is faced with authorities who are white—to him an alien force. He bears a 'double burden' of social regulation. A white man can feel trapped, too, but the data demonstrate the much lesser frequency of the 'authority' stress factor in white male suicide.[5]

The black man is subject to more regulation by the social structure (a double burden) than is the white man. More than 70 years ago Durkheim recognized that excessive regulation of an individual by the social system increased the individual's suicidal risk. He called this type of suicide *fatalistic*. Durkheim[10] explicitly discussed fatalistic suicide, the least known of his four types, only in a footnote*

> . . . there is a type of suicide the opposite of anomic suicide. It is the suicide deriving from excessive regulation, that of persons with futures pitilessly blocked and passions violently choked by oppressive discipline. It is the suicide of very young husbands, of the married woman who is childless . . . But it has so little contemporary importance and examples are so hard to find aside from the cases just mentioned that it seems useless to dwell

*Barclay Johnson[9] points to other somewhat less explicit discussions of fatalism by Durkheim in *Suicide*.[10]

upon it. However it might be said to have historical interest. Do not the suicides of slaves . . . belong to this type, or all suicides attributable to excessive physical or moral despotism? To bring out the ineluctible and inflexible nature of a rule against which there is no appeal, and in contrast with the expression 'anomy' which has just been used, we might call it fatalistic suicide.

It seems fair to call these authority suicides fatalistic. These black men, of course, were no slaves, but their relationships to white authority figures were restrictive enough to resemble the slavery situation. During the period that these data were gathered, 1954-1963, New Orleans was bifurcated by race. One hundred years of *de jure* emancipation had not eliminated the excessive regulation of blacks by white-controlled institutions. The rules regulating blacks were, at this time, relatively inflexible and could be conceived of, in Durkheim's terms, as moral despotism. There is no effective rebuttal to the proposition that *de facto* discrimination was the general rule in the South during the decade of this study. The majority of these men (30 of 42) were in situations characterized by the absence of freedom from unjust and arbitrary authorities. Lacking the power to control the conditions of their existence, they committed fatalistic suicide.

Durkheim aptly described and well understood the theoretical importance of fatalistic suicide but he failed to recognize its empirical importance in modern society. He believed that the end of slavery, free urban institutions, and the extensive division of labor had made fatalistic suicide obsolete.

Most cases of suicide everywhere involve a mixture of Durkheim's four types and indeed this is the case with the black suicides in New Orleans. In some of these cases the victim had limited affective or solid relationships with others—possibly an indication of egoistic factors. Anomie, as will be discussed later, is not a primary characteristic of blacks. They are largely alienated from white society but certainly not unregulated by it. Altruism in the usual sense is not a prominent feature of these black suicides, although, the black man is stereotyped by whites as one member of a large racial group indistinct from his companions. [10]

In summing up the evidence which indicates that fatalistic suicide is the most common of Durkheim's four types among southern black males, Breed[5] states

We commenced with the low Negro rate and the lower age at death. We found rough similarities between characteristics of white and Negro male suicides as to relative class position, family, and assorted 'difficulties,' although Negro suicides showed less 'work-role failure' and downward mobility than whites. We added one new fact: the high frequency of 'authority problem' suicides, mainly *vis-à-vis* the police, among the southern Negro suicides. All of these facts are doubtless a consequence of one paramount circumstance: the Negro's position in society—inferior, segregated, powerless, less protected from arbitrary authorities. Thus suicide among young, low-class single Negro males is frequently fatalistic suicide.

THE LOW SUICIDE RATE AMONG BLACK PEOPLE

For decades sociologists have wondered about the reasons for the low black suicide rate—the second question raised at the beginning of this chapter. Is it that the black suicide rate is really low or that it is low by comparison to that of whites? The answer must be relative. Robins[11] has provided a perspective by pointing out that while the black rate is generally considered to be low it is an epidemiological fact that, as Figure 3-1 shows, the discrepancy is due almost entirely to the high suicide rate of older white males. Blacks of both sexes and white women have difficulties with their work, families, and physical and mental health. Blacks have more profound (from a white point of view) difficulties in these areas but they remain less self-destructive than their white counterparts. This is the paradox we will analyze.

Whereas black males often commit fatalistic suicide, white people most often commit suicide for reasons rooted in anomie and egoism—loneliness, loss, depression, and a lack of regulation at some point in their lives. As blacks move into the mainstream of American life, their coping problems will increasingly take these forms.

Durkheim[10] has pointed out that once we get beyond the maintenance of physical life, our human capacity for wanting and feeling is an "insatiable and bottomless abyss." If this capacity to want is not externally regulated our insatiable desires become a source of constant torment. "Inextinguishable thirst is constantly renewed torture," says Durkheim, of the social condition he called anomie. But what provides this vital factor of regulation? The answer for Durkheim is truly sociological: society. *Vis-à-vis* suicide, some groups within society are better regulated than others and are therefore less anomic. Clearly then, all aspirations must be limited, be they for water, sex, wealth, prestige—whatever. If a society is not well

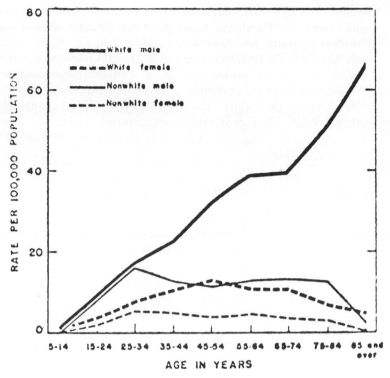

Fig. 3-1.   Suicide rates by color, sex and age, 1964.[29]

integrated, if its norms and values are not clear and widely shared, its regulating function is weakened and suicide rates climb.

The Durkheimian proposition is deceptively simple: the suicide rate varies inversely with the degree of social integration. The challenge, of course, is to determine the degree of social integration. Working backward, from the knowledge that blacks have a low suicide rate, we might speculate that they are more highly integrated, i.e., share norms and values more fully than whites. However, the evidence is complex and contradictory.

HOW MUCH SOLIDARITY IN THE BLACK COMMUNITY?

A number of researchers[12,13,14,15,16,17] have commented upon the solidarity, or lack of it, among blacks. The problem has been approached from many angles and at many levels and the conclusions vary. But a plurality of writers has described the competition, suspiciousness, rage, cross-class (as opposed to caste) conflict, and self-hate that seem to characterize the black community.

Myrdal's[15] deeply probing analysis of America's black communities of the early 1940s has contributed to the view that poor integration can be found within the black caste.

> It is revealing of the nature of the system of superior and subordinate castes that this Negro cohesion is defensive instead of offensive, and that, compared with white solidarity, it is imperfect. The individual Negro, as a member of the lower caste, feels his weakness and will be tempted, on occasion, to split Negro solidarity by seeking individual refuge, personal security, and advantages with the whites.[15]

It would seem, given this type of observation, that blacks are hardly a solid group.

However, Myrdal also says:

> Negroes, as a consequence of the bonds of caste in which they are enclosed, feel a larger degree of interest solidarity in relation to society. It is true that the Negro community is stratified into social classes and that, in general, Negroes are much at variance in political issues, interests, and ideals. But the lower classes are, because of the caste situation, a great majority, and the upper classes have strong interests in the economic welfare of the lower classes who constitute the basis of their economic sustenance. As regards Negro issues, therefore, the internal differences have little significance . . .[15]

Seeing solidarity or fragmentation among black people depends on one's focus of attention. Solidarity at one level and fragmentation at another can and does exist at the same time in the same community. Grier and Cobbs state

> The bickering, the sniping, the backbiting so often said to characterize black people in their relationship with one another seems so very much to be the rivalry of siblings. Underlying it all is a feeling that 'your're no better than I.' It is an unfortunate corollary of such a feeling of 'sibship,' but it is probably a small price to pay for the comfort and the web of support provided by brotherhood.[16]

Further supporting the notion that blacks have strong group ties, Kardiner and Ovesey[14] say the blacks who are above the level of

lower class have a sense of guilt to other blacks and consider their
success a betrayal of their less fortunate brothers. The successful
black man ". . . has frequently what might be called a 'success phobia'
. . . ."[14] If this success phobia is a reality, it limits aspirations or
is the concomitant of an active limiting force among blacks. This
could mean, in the Durkheimian sense and with regard to a utilitarian
type of success orientation, that black people are more regulated
(and therefore less anomic) than whites.

ATTITUDES TOWARDS SUCCESS

There is some evidence [14,13,16] that there is an anti-success orientation rooted in group ties that is dominant in the black community.
Many blacks do not merely accept their lack of material success
as a part of racial discrimination, but consciously or unconsciously
avoid educational and occupational success which would set them
apart from or above their peers. The successful black man not only
runs the risk of feeling guilty because of his success but also risks
losing the support of his peers—his brotherhood. As Grier and Cobbs[16]
state, "One may feel that to outstrip one's brothers is a wicked thing.
To announce oneself as an exception is to bring calumny down on
one's head."

Rohrer and Edmonson, in their study of the culture and personality
of New Orleans blacks show the anti-success orientation clearly at
work in a lower-class black gang:

> Acceptance by the gang provides almost the only source of
> security for its members, but such acceptance is conditional upon
> continual proof that it is merited, and this proof can only be
> furnished through physical aggressiveness, a restless demon-
> stration of sexual prowess, and a symbolic execution of these
> illegal deeds that a 'sissy' would not perform. These activities
> victimize women, but it would seem that they are not specifically
> directed toward women. Rather the enemy of the gang is the
> world of people (especially men) too unmanly for survival in
> what has often been described as a social jungle.[13]

The gang, they add, "Scorns religion and occupational and
educational achievement as effeminate."

Between gang members and the peripheral hangers-on who sub-
scribe to the gang ethic, more than half of New Orleans black males
could be affected by this anti-success attitude. The fact that such
an orientation exists and that it touches such a large proportion of

the black community has deep and thorough ramifications. Unfamiliarity with this caste-based outlook is probably why Durkheim felt fatalistic suicide had "little contemporary importance."

In socialpsychological terms, the black man does not invest his identity into a job as do whites. The black man plays the role, but protects his private self by segmenting it from the job. Nobody expects him to succeed, so he survives by separating self and role. If he is fired, the self remains protected by ostensible noninvolvement. Self-esteem and feelings of accomplishment must come from other quarters—such as outmaneuvering the white man in his own environment.

A CONCEPTUAL BASIS FOR UNDERSTANDING THE LOW BLACK SUICIDE RATE

The basic question remains, Why is the suicide rate among blacks so relatively low? We offer here a tentative answer, based on two kinds of research: our study of suicides and our analysis of in-depth interviews with blacks about the problems they face and their response to these problems.

Our studies of suicide among whites have led us to the following conclusion. Briefly stated, suicide is the result of a combination of factors occurring over time and along several dimensions[18] including a psychological trait, the relation of a person to his roles as defined by his culture, his performance in these roles, his response to this performance, and his consequent state of interpersonal relations between himself and significant persons.

The five components of a suicide syndrome can be singled out as[18]

1. *Rigidity*—a psychological trait often found among those who commit suicide indicating that the person is relatively inflexible, unable to shift roles and goals from one line of activity to another or from a high aspiration to a more feasible one. The rigid person is unable to break out of established patterns and feels that other persons have stamped him into a mold; he cannot discern a solution—a change to something different and more satisfying. This inflexibility reinforces the second component of the syndrome—commitment to a given goal.

2. *Commitment*—individuals who have committed suicide frequently seem to have had high aspirations—a strong desire to succeed at some endeavor or role. All humans play many roles, but certain

roles predominate for a given person. For males in Western society, the occupational role is paramount. For women, especially before the 1970s, it is the family-based roles of wife and mother. But each individual must work out in a social context how deep his commitment to each role will be. Most men, but not all, e.g., lower-class blacks make a deep commitment to occupational success, as with Durkheim's overweening ambition. Goffman[19] has observed that when a person is heavily committed to a role he "becomes locked into a position and coerced into living up to the promises and sacrifices built into it. To embrace a role is to be embraced by it."

3. *Failure*—an individual experiences failure when the quality of his role performance falls short of his goals or his commitments. When this occurs and the person feels that he has failed and feels that it is his own fault, the risk of suicide rises. This is true only when the person has been heavily committed to the goal and when he is so rigid that he cannot shift into new pursuits. Among Western males this role failure is usually specific to the occupational sphere, a culturally-imposed expectation, but failure in family roles may also raise the suicidal risk. Among women the failure almost always occurs in one of the roles most closely related to the family—mother and wife. The term *failure* combines role performance below the high standards the individual has set for himself with culpability felt by the individual when he has not reached these high standards of performance.

4. *Shame*—when failure occurs in a role to which a person has been highly committed and it is a publicly recognizable event, he may feel shame. Shame can be more shattering to the self than guilt. Guilt involves a specific transgression of a norm, and can be expiated by paying a penalty. Shame involves the whole self and occurs when a goal presented by the ego ideal is not being reached.[20] Shame is a real shortcoming—exposing the self without ego defense mechanisms to the self and others. In Erikson's terms[21] one is suddenly "caught with one's pants down." It is the sudden exposure of weakness in the eyes of significant others that hurts most deeply. The person feels disgrace and a loss of honor, integrity, and self-esteem. He perceives not just error or dereliction but a generalized sense of worthlessness. He sees himself as exposed to the pitying reflections of others.

5. *Isolation*—failure and the response to it, shame, do not occur in a vacuum. The individual feels that he has failed in a role that he wanted to succeed in and he responds with the feeling

of shame. The response pervades his awareness because he knows, whether justified or not, that other persons share his assessment of failure. In George Herbert Mead's terms, he "takes the attitude of the other" toward himself. In his state of despair he is all too prone to conclude that the others, too, are evaluating him negatively. Not only does he feel impotent, he emphasizes the strength of others.[22] When this happens a process of withdrawal often follows and the person becomes more and more isolated from other people. On the other hand, the non-shamed person is free to play many roles and to relate to many significant others. This flexibility shields him when crisis hits. Change is only change, not disaster for the person who does not feel shame. However, failure and negative role taking, in the rigid and committed person, add enormously to the suicidal potential.

These five components of suicide do not, of course, constitute a formula for suicide. However, they do describe the basic pattern of suicide that we have observed. Other components such as unfortunate parent-child relations in the individual's early life, psychopathology, and feelings of hopelessness and despair after the shame certainly also enter the picture.

What is of immediate importance about this syndrome is that we do *not* find it characteristic of the blacks we have studied. This is most true among lower-class blacks. Some middle-class blacks may be found to show and experience all five traits, as do many whites, but we expect the distribution to be small relative to whites.

Of the five components the key omission with respect to blacks is probably commitment. Our interviews revealed the strikingly low aspirations of blacks. Their commitment is to survival rather than to success in a major role. We state this is an extreme form to emphasize the direction the data take. For the sociological and historical reasons already discussed, blacks could not, dared not, allow themselves the luxury of being committed to roles and goals which would put them into dangerous conflict with the white hegemony. If the person has no commitment to specific goals fear of failure becomes obsolete. Such being the case, one will not experience shame and will not imagine that other persons define him as a failure. Clearly, no social isolation will be indicated.

We have held that white male suicide often follows failure related to work role. On the other hand, black men who kill themselves are overwhelmingly in lower echelon jobs to begin with and have little opportunity for downward mobility and the sense of culpability and shame which accompanies occupational failure. Blacks clearly have not had the same opportunities for occupational success afforded whites. The black man could legitimately blame the system for his inability to achieve lofty occupational goals but he seldom seems to have the aspiration to achieve these goals. Rather, he appears to be limited in his aspirations not only by the crushing reality of the black-white caste system but by an equally pervasive and profound nonutilitarian world view which lessens his risk of becoming anomic and consequently lessens his risk of suicide. The latter orientation is doubtless a historic reaction to the caste imposition. The black suicide rate is elevated in cities in the northern part of the United States where caste lines are not so severely drawn and where blacks are more likely to assume white values. Important to realize is that not only are black Americans prevented, except in rare cases, from achieving a great occupational success, but that the social structure militates against high aspirations and thus mollifies the pangs of status failure. The intense desire for the achievement of occupational prestige is an aspiration confined, for all practical purposes, to whites and the relatively small number of middle- and upper-class blacks. The proposition here is that to commit suicide one must be blocked in his aspirations; he must want to achieve very badly but cannot, or, having once made it, slips in prestige. For males in white America achievement almost always indicates occupational success.

Rohrer and Edmonson[13] have documented the anti-success orientation of at least half of the lower-class black males in New Orleans. Similarly, a 1970–1971 survey of 50 black males who lived in New Orleans shows that their aspirations related primarily to maintaining their subsistence level of survival. Most of the men surveyed had not scored notable success on the job. However, they did not have the same feeling of failure that the average white man would have had in the same situation. They did not define themselves as work failures. Almost all said that their biggest current problem was getting enough money to make ends meet. They were fighting to get the income to pay the most pressing bills and to live without any frills like doctors or expensive drugs. They were often looking for a better job, but this meant a job with more pay *not* more prestige.

Having low aspirations has clear-cut survival value for the black man. In the South, it was generally unwise for a black man to put himself in a position which would bring him into direct competition with a white man. "Today black boys are admonished not to be a 'bad nigger.' No description need be offered; every black child knows what is meant. They are angry and hostile."[16] Grier and Cobbs say that the black child is socialized to have limited aspirations and that his characteristics are so connected to employment that they call it the "postal-clerk syndrome." The opposite type, the rageful black man, ". . . no doubt accounts for more worry in both races than any other single factor."[16]

HISTORICAL SOURCES OF LOW ASPIRATIONS

Although it is not possible to develop a thorough historical analysis here, it is possible to show briefly that a number of factors have conspired to orient the black American to a non-utilitarian point of view and to the docile "postal-clerk syndrome."

During the process of taking, transporting, and selling slaves there was a calculated and successful effort to obliterate black African culture and language and to resocialize the slaves toward obedient compliance.[23] Most blacks held positions of little or no power, rights, or control over their own destiny; some were "free men of color" and some were slaves; from 10 percent to as much as 20 percent held positions as foremen, managers, artisans, etc.[24] African cultural norms and values were not applicable or were not allowed to apply. In essence, a cultural vacuum was created by dividing slaves up by language and tribal groups.

This vacuum was filled of necessity by a new black culture—of survival. The black men and women who reached North America had already demonstrated their tenacity and ability to cling to life. Some would-be slaves did kill themselves (fatalistic suicide) rather than become slaves. But those who survived forged a new culture the very genius of which was to maximize survival under appalling conditions.[16] To survive, the newly arrived slaves had no choice but to accept important elements of the host white culture. They had little choice of any kind in interacting with whites. The African cultures and languages were useless to them in the cotton fields of Mississippi or in the streets of New Orleans. Blacks had to do the menial jobs and play the compliant role of "Uncle Tom." They learned to act dumb, to smile when they were not happy, to work patiently, and to express thanks to their white masters for what little they had—in short to be perceived by the whites as "good niggers."

These customary, necessary ways of behaving, when coupled with religious beliefs, geared the black man and his culture for survival. They reinforced his non-utilitarian world view which was, and still is conducive not only to survival in relation to the white power structure but to reduction of anomie and egoism—and therefore the risk of suicide.

THE ROLE OF RELIGION IN THE NEW BLACK CULTURE

Religion, primarily fundamentalist Protestant, as practiced by southern black people, did not dispose them to a Protestant ethic. Southern black folk religion performed a different function; it helped make the black man's position as slave more tolerable. The black man's religion in America could not encourage acquisitiveness and a utilitarian approach to life. To have done so would have placed him in competition with whites, a competition he could not win. Religion, then, made life safer and more tolerable. To envision green pastures in the next world was not only comfortable, it was also safe. However, the white American, from the eighteenth and nineteenth centuries to today, has become evermore committed to the idea of utility and worldly success. This is important *vis-à-vis* suicide because as Gouldner[25] points out, anomie is a normal pathology of utilitarianism. This work-role failure, as we have hypothesized, did not play an important part in black male suicides. The black American is not yet committed to utilitarianism as is the white. We are asserting that the utilitarian ethic did not develop among black people because the system encouraged them to adopt the old-fashioned, more traditional morality of Christianity.

The conditions under which slaves were given instruction in religion were controlled in large measure by slavemasters who, particularly in the early part of the nineteenth century, feared insurrection and rebellion. Slave owners allowed the clergy to convert slaves to Christianity under the condition that the gospel be presented, ". . . in its original purity and simplicity."[23]

HOW NEW ORLEANS BLACKS VIEW SUICIDE AND RELIGION TODAY

Religion is still an important factor in helping blacks cope with their problems, particularly those involving finances, health, and relationships with other people.[26] In the white community it is precisely these problem areas which are often associated with suicide. In the black population the pain and frustration caused by these difficulties are such widely shared experiences that they often form the nexus for mutually supportive social interaction.

In our survey designed to determine attitudes toward and experiences with suicidal behavior, 100 black and 100 white adults living in New Orleans were randomly selected and interviewed. The blacks were clearly less suicidal than the whites. Only 8 black respondents stated that they had any history of suicidal behavior or ideation, whereas 23 white respondents said that they had experienced suicidal thoughts or engaged in suicidal behavior. Only two blacks (one male and one female) had made a suicide attempt. Fourteen percent of the black respondents and 6 percent of the white respondents could not conceive of ever being suicidal. Blacks are also much less likely to see suicide, under any circumstances, as a justifiable act. Seventy-six percent of the blacks versus 59 percent of the whites said that suicide was *never* justified and blacks were quicker and more likely to cite religious proscriptions against suicide.

The answers our respondents gave to questions about religious beliefs and practices support our thesis that the more orthodox, old-fashioned Christian intention-morality is more pervasive in the black community than it is in the white. For example, using chi-square as our measure of difference, blacks are significantly more likely than whites to see religion as truth rather than myth (p. < .001); to participate in church activities (p. < .01); to pray often (p. < .02); and to believe that everything and every person has a divine purpose (p. < .01). These data, taken in the context of the entire interview, indicate that blacks are more concerned than whites with the supernatural sanctions related to the motives behind their actions than about the consequences of their actions in the social marketplace. In other words, they do not, except in the relatively small middle-class, have the same utilitarian orientation of their white brothers and, as a consequence, are less likely to be anomic and isolated from interpersonal relations.

METHODS OF SUICIDE

Blacks and whites employ different methods of killing themselves, as shown in Table 2-3. The largest difference by sex and race occur in the most frequently used method, gunshot. Seventy-one percent of all white male suicides shot themselves. Gunshot accounted for a smaller percentage, 54 percent, but still a majority of all black male suicides. Officials in the New Orleans coroner's office report that the use of guns by females as a means of suicide has increased in recent years. Forty-eight percent of the white females and 40 percent of the black females killed themselves with guns. There may be an overall trend, at least in New Orleans, of increased use of firearms

Table 3-2
Methods of Suicide in New Orleans by Race and Sex
1966-1970 (data in percentages)

	White		Black	
Method	Male	Female	Male	Female
Gunshot	71.0	48	59	40
Stabbing	4.0	0	1	0
Poison (solid/liquid)	7.0	35	8	60
Asphyxiation	2.0	0	0	0
Drowning	2.0	2	0	0
Hanging	7.0	8	10	0
Jumping	6.0	2	15	0
Fire	0.0	0	5	0
Suffocation	0.5	1	0	0
Other and unspecified	2.0	4	2	0
Total	165	80	39	10

*Source: Coroner's office, city of New Orleans

as a method of suicide. The national statistics for 1964 show that 55.8 percent and 25.2 percent of all white male and female suicides, respectively, were due to gunshot wounds. According to the 1967 national statistics of the Public Health Service, the percentage of black males and females killing themselves with guns in 1964 was 54.0 percent and 30.3 percent, respectively. Comparison of these nationwide data with the data in Table 2-3 shows that, with the exception of the black females, firearms predominate as a method of suicide in New Orleans.

Another interesting comparison is the large percentage of black females, 60 percent, in New Orleans who poisoned themselves with drugs or other types of toxic chemicals. The use of poisons, especially analgesic and soporific substances, commonly accounts for a large, often the largest percentage of female suicides. However, national statistics indicate that white females are more apt to use such a method than black females and that the black females are more likely to use guns. In New Orleans the pattern, for the five years we studied, is reversed. The black females who poisoned themselves most often did so with a toxic substance used in the home, such as rat poison, roach poison, lye, paint thinner, etc. On the other hand, the white females most often swallowed large doses of prescription drugs. Presumably, the difference is financial.

There were two cases of self-immolation by fire in New Orleans during the period 1966–1970. Both victims were black males. There were two other cases of self-immolation investigated by the New Orleans coroner's office of Louisiana but they were not New Orleans residents. One was a black male, the other a white female.

Alcohol played a major part in the lives and deaths of the New Orleans black male suicides. This was particularly true of the 20 men who had greatest involvement with the police. Recall that these men were predominantly young, lower-class, and not strongly oriented to regular work routines. Their greater orientation was to the neighborhood and their gang. Typically they lived a kind of underground life, giving only secondary thought to the deferred gratifications of the future. Life had conferred very little upon them from the outset and their response was to wrest from it whatever "meaning" and "kicks" they could.

Alcohol played a predominant role in their demise. Although only 2 of the 20 were considered to be alcoholics 9 others were seen as having alcohol problems—a very high proportion for any group. Post-mortem examinations showed 6 of them had more than .10 percent alcohol in the blood, another 3 had from .01 percent to .09 percent, 3 were not tested, and the remainder had no trace of alcohol.

Several of the 20 had adopted a pattern of weekend drinking, a program that would start shortly after the four o'clock payday on Friday and continue until some time before work Monday morning. Moreover, during the frequent periods of unemployment drinking would include weekdays as well.

SUICIDE AMONG BLACK FEMALES

Black female suicide, especially in the South, is a rare event. In the 10-year period of our study only 12 such events occurred, as compared to 107 suicides among white females during the same period. Study of the 12 cases produced no patterns. There was some indication that they were not too different from suicide among white women—less turbulence connected with men as the women became older—but even that remains vague. The 12 women suffered from a variety of problems and had lived very unrewarding lives. Such a low rate deserves an attempt at explanation. What would have been Durkheim's evaluation? He probably would have proceeded to his four types of suicide and hypothesized that the black females would have scored rather low on each. This will be our first and main approach. Considering first anomic suicide, in which society is unable to regulate the individual and his ambitions, it is safe to say that black females in the South were not encouraged to develop lofty aspirations and were well regulated. According to Durkheim the opposite of anomic suicide was fatalistic suicide, in which society controlled the individual with oppressive discipline. We have found this in the lives of many black male suicides, but we do *not* find it among the females the reason being that the black male must more frequently cross the race boundary in his job and circumstances find him confronting white authorities such as police, landlords, and white employers. Typically the black female remains in the black community, most often finding work within the confines of a white home—not a place noted for outright racial battles. Nor does she face the dangers of white outrage in regards to sexual expression; it is the black male that has been seen by the whites as the dangerous character in this area, not the black female.

The third type of suicide, egoistic, is most frequent in Western society and occurs when the individual is insufficiently integrated into family, community, and cultural patterns. Typically, the black female has played a traditional role, often close to her mother and sisters, rearing children, and having strong ties to the local church. Finally, altruistic suicide has not been blamed for high rates in any society of the modern world.

The same conclusion can be reached by the use of Breed's[18] basic suicide syndrome. Three of the five components of this syndrome, commitment, failure, and shame, are found to be largely absent in the lives of the southern black female. If an individual does not have lofty aspirations she cannot fail and therefore has a low likelihood of feeling shame over failure to attain them. We feel that these theoretically-based approaches greatly aid our understanding of the low black female suicide rate. Close study of personality characteristics and early life experiences would add to our knowledge of course, but on this specific topic it appears that the concept of socio-cultural role, the kind of life the black female in the South is expected to lead and in fact often does, is extremely useful.

SPECIAL CIRCUMSTANCES

We have shown that in New Orleans few substantial differences distinguish black male from white male suicides in the areas of individual difficulties such as mental disturbance, physical health, alcoholism, drug addiction, and gambling. Generally speaking, in terms of individual problems related to suicidal risk, similarities between the black and white suicides prevailed over differences. The black suicide has clearly suffered more in one area: bodily injuries due to accidents, usually associated with work. As stated previously, of the 42 black male suicides studies, 10 had suffered a serious accident, usually to the head. Because black men are concentrated in lower-class occupations they are clearly more exposed to bodily injury at work than are whites. These injuries appear to be an important factor in the black suicide rate. The risk of physical injury among black working men may also be related to the fact that they commonly work for small companies where safety rules are not as strictly enforced as they are at large companies. The fact that the black man is exposed to greater probability of bodily harm at work is directly related to the social and economic caste system which forces them into more dangerous, lower paying, and less attractive jobs.

Three counterbalancing forces, making life for New Orleans blacks somewhat less enervating, can be mentioned.

1. Sociability—black residential areas are closely packed in the city due to poverty and the fact that good land is scarce in the city primarily because New Orleans is below river level and flooding used to be a major problem.[27] As a consequence families live close together and in good weather there is much socializing and chatting across front porches and verandas. In addition, most neighborhoods have one or more gathering places for the men such as a bar, restaurant, barber shop, vacant lot, etc. On Sundays church is an all-day center for social as well as spiritual activity.
2. Sex-segregation and competition—much of this sociability is sex-segregated. As described in Rohrer and Edmonson[13] the women predominate in church-related activities while the men gather in bars and athletic centers. A considerable amount of the activity also contains an emotional overtone, taking the form of a battle of the sexes. The time and energy devoted by members of each sex group to excoriating the other, as seen by Rohrer and Edmonson, is remarkable. This rivalry could, we feel, have resulted in increased morale among both sexes, much as adherents of any teams and groups in competition build cohesion by praising their own side while damning the other.
3. Ethnic identity—blacks in New Orleans are not of one ethnic background. Of course most stem from African heritage, but notable proportions of two other ethnic groups, Indian and Creole, serve to shield about one-quarter of the "blacks" from feeling affront at racial slights. This pluralistic identification is also described by Rohrer and Edmonson.[13]

SPECULATION ABOUT THE FUTURE

The third and last question raised at the beginning of this chapter is What has changed since the civil rights movement of the past 15-20 years? At the outset, several qualifications must be made. First, the data are not firm. Black suicide and suicide attempt rates have increased in recent years but the extent of the rise is not well established. Recent studies further show these rates to be incorrectly high because of the under-enumeration of blacks, especially young blacks, by the US census. Suicide rates of young black males have been high for several decades, as seen in New York rates.[17] Second, when making any generalizations about blacks in the United States one must recognize the vast diversity among this group of well over 20 million persons. There is great differentiation among blacks not only as to age, sex, and class, but also as to many social, psychological, and behavioral variables. The single advantage in the present issue is that our focus can be on young blacks—those who are now, or will be soon, starting on the path toward adulthood. This group should be investigated for the ways it employs to cope with the new racial situation. It may be that these younger blacks will bear some resemblance to the second generation problem of many millions of European immigrants earlier in the century, those who abandoned traditional behaviors and struggled to assume new ones.

The civil rights movement has not yet ended. Discrimination and prejudice are still with us although attitudes of prejudice have decreased markedly as seen in surveys going back to the 1930s. The amount and virulence of discrimination varies by sector (housing, jobs, education, services), industry, and geographical location. The effect on individual blacks varies according to the specific situation. Blacks cannot feel secure in their relationships with whites and white institutions. Thus there will remain occasions for failure, shame, isolation, and resentment owing to racial slights and injustice.

What changes seem likely? Speculations about the near future can be viewed along three paths. The first is quite plain—suicide in any group will always be affected by interpersonal difficulties. Individuals will conflict with, misunderstand, and alienate each other in any society and this can lead to thoughts of self-destruction. It can involve parents and children, young people dating, spouses, and any other relationship. There is no indication that such sources of friction are lower among blacks than among other ethnic groups.

The other two sources of future suicidal behavior among blacks can be seen along the two principal Durkheiman dimensions, egoism and anomie. Egoism may become important because as more blacks proceed toward the national mean, they will have to sacrifice some roots in the community. Ties with mother, siblings, and old friends will break as upwardly mobile young people follow the path of millions of other Americans in the search for career achievement. This exchange of one lifestyle for another and the mobility and new roles it implies, may be especially difficult for young black females, as data on suicide attempts in one northern county suggest.[28] Attempt rates there during the years 1964-1967 were much higher for young black females than for young white females and were six times higher than rates for young black males.

One final change emerging from the black revolution intersects with the key reason for the traditionally low suicide rate among blacks. This is the low level of commitment to career aspirations. Freed from the bonds of automatic discrimination in education, work, and profession, the young black can today aim higher and is encouraged by the many notable cases of nationally-recognized achievement among blacks in recent years. The postal clerk syndrome, and the anti-success orientation can scarcely retain its present hold. It seems inevitable that more young blacks, male and female, will have higher aspirations, possibly, in individual cases, to unrealistic heights. To the extent that our syndrome involving commitment-failure-shame-isolation holds in such cases, suicide among blacks will probably increase.

REFERENCES

1. Schmid C: Suicides in Seattle, 1914-1925: On Ecological and Behavioristic Study. Univ Washington, 1938
2. Cavan R: Suicide. Chicago, Univ Chicago Press, 1928
3. Maris R: Social Forces in Urban Suicide. Homewood, Illinois, Dorsey, 1969
4. Breed W: Occupational mobility and suicide among white males. Am Sociol Rev 28: 179-188, 1963
5. Breed W: The Negro and fatalistic suicide. Pacific Sociol Rev 13: 156-162, 1970
6. Harper F: Alcohol and blacks: state of the periodical literature. School of Education, Howard Univ, 1975
7. Dollard J: Caste and Class in a Southern Town. New York, Harper, 1937
8. Swanson W, Breed W: Barriers to the use of suicide prevention centers. International Association for Suicide Prevention Sixth Proc. Mexico, 1972, pp 330-336

9. Johnson B: Durkheim's one cause of suicide. Am Sociol Rev 30: 875–886, 1965
10. Durkheim E: Suicide. Glencoe, Illinois, Free Press, 1951
11. Robins F: Suicide and violence: Explaining the low Negro suicide rate. Paper presented at American Sociological Association Roundtable, San Francisco, 1967
12. Davis A, Dollard J: Children of Bondage. New York, Harper, 1940
13. Rohrer J, Edmonson M: The Eighth Generation Grows Up. New York, Harper, 1960
14. Kardiner O, Ovesey L: The Mark of Oppression. New York, World, 1951
15. Myrdal G: American Dilemma. New York, Harper, 1944
16. Grier W, Cobbs P: Black Rage. New York, Basic Books, 1968
17. Hendin H: Black Suicide. New York, Basic Books, 1969
18. Breed W: Five components of a basic suicide syndrome. Life-Threatening Behavior 2: 3–18, 1972
19. Goffman E: Encounters. Indianapolis, Bobbs-Merrill, 1966
20. Lynd H: On Shame and the Search for Identity. New York, Science Editions, 1958
21. Erikson E: Childhood and Society. New York, Norton, 1950
22. Neuringer C: Attitudes toward self in suicidal individuals. Life-Threatening Behavior 4: 96–106, 1974
23. Elkins S: Slavery. Chicago, Univ Chicago Press, 1959
24. Fogel, Engerman S: Time on the Cross. Boston, Little, Brown, 1974
25. Gouldner A: The Coming Crisis of Western Sociology. New York, Basic Books, 1970
26. Swanson W, Harter C: How do elderly blacks cope in New Orleans? Aging and Human Development 2: 210–216, 1971
27. Gilmore H: The old New Orleans and the new. Am Sociol Rev 9: 385–394, 1944
28. Pederson A, Awad G, Kindler A: Epidemiological differences between white and nonwhite suicide attempters. Am J Psychiatry 130: 1071–1076, 1973
29. United States Public Service Publication: Suicide in the United States, No 1000, Series 20, No 5

PART II

Methodological Developments in Suicidology

J. William Worden

4
Lethality Factors and the Suicide Attempt

The introductory piece to this chapter is The Suicide Attempt from Dr. Erwin Stengel's *Suicide and Attempted Suicide*. It is reproduced here with the kind permission of Penguin Books © 1964.

The conventional notion of a genuine suicidal act is something like this: 'A person, having decided to end his life, or acting on a sudden impulse to do so, kills himself, having chosen the most effective method available and having made sure that nobody interferes. When he is dead he is said to have succeeded and the act is often called a successful suicidal attempt. If he survives he is said to have failed and the act is called an unsuccessful suicidal attempt. Death is the only purpose of this act and therefore the only criterion of success. Failure may be due to any of the following causes: the sense of purpose may not have been strong enough; or the act may have been undertaken half-heartedly because it was not quite genuine; the subject was ignorant of the limitations of the method; or he was lacking in judgment and determination through mental illness.' Judging by those standards only a minority of fatal and very few non-fatal suicidal acts would pass muster, as both serious and genuine. The rest have to be dismissed as poor efforts some of which succeeded by chance rather than design. Obviously, this approach cannot do justice to a very common and varied behaviour pattern.

If a visiting scholar from one of the inhabited planets came to earth to study the human species, he would sooner or later notice that some humans sometimes commit acts of self-injury. He would observe that occasionally this self-damaging behaviour causes the person's death, but it would hardly occur to him that this relatively rare outcome is the main purpose of that

131

behaviour. Having been taught that careful observation of as many subjects as possible is essential before one draws conclusions about the purpose of a certain type of behaviour, and having also learned that the subjects' explanations can be highly misleading, he would watch as many such acts as possible, together with their antecedents and consequences, without preconceived ideas, over a fairly long period. His report on his observations would read like this: 'There are some humans who damage themselves more or less badly and in about one in eight cases the damage is so severe that they die. Whatever the outcome, most of them give a hint or a clear warning to one or several of their fellow humans well before the act, telling them that they are thinking of killing themselves. Those fellow humans may or may not take notice of this warning. But once a person is found to have committed an act of self-damage there is invariably a great commotion among the other humans. They clearly show that they wish the act had never been committed. They do everything to keep him alive and to undo the damage that he did to himself. They go even further than this. While they usually do not show much concern about and sympathy with the suffering of fellow humans, an act of self-injury by one of themselves seems to make them take a profound and most active interest in him, at least for a time. They behave as if they had to help him and to put him on his feet. As a result, his situation is transiently or permanently transformed for the better. These helpful reactions are particularly marked in the members of his family group, but the larger community to which the human belongs also takes part.

'If one looked at the acts of self-damage alone one would be led to believe that self-destruction is their only purpose. But if one considers certain antecedents and the consequences of these acts, this simple explanation cannot be sustained. Why should these humans so often warn others of their intention to damage themselves, especially as they must know that this kind of behaviour is dreaded in their family group and the community? They must also know that, once they have injured themselves, everybody will be upset and will want to help them, and if they should die, many other humans will feel they ought to have helped them. It looks as if their peculiar behaviour cannot be derived from one single tendency but is probably due to a combination of at least two tendencies, one of which might be the urge to self-damage and possibly self-destruction, the other the urge to make other humans show concern and love and act accordingly. There are other peculiar features in the self-damaging behaviour of humans, but these seem the most important.'

The purpose of this fictitious report from unprejudiced space is to bring home the need for a new and very careful look at suicidal behaviour. The most striking difference between the conventional view of suicidal acts and that of the unprejudiced observer lies in his emphasis on the reactions of the environment. The possibility of such reactions and their occasional exploitation has long been known, but this is believed to occur only in suicidal attempts regarded as non-genuine. All genuine suicidal acts are understood to aim at death alone. It is this notion which the uncommitted observer refuses to accept. On what facts does he base his challenge?

The death of a person by suicide gives rise to a great number of questions all of which are concerned with facts and events preceding the act. This is why all suicide research has been retrospective, like any other post-mortem investigation. As such, it has considerable limitations because the chief source of information is no longer available. Only in a minority of cases can records such as hospital case notes be obtained which are of help in the reconstruction of the antecedents. Usually one has to rely on whatever information the victim left behind and on hearsay. Attempted suicides have often been used for research into the causes and motives of suicide, the assumption being that they are minor suicides. Therefore, investigations of suicidal attempts were purely retrospective and concerned with the same problems as those of suicide. This line of inquiry is perfectly legitimate and necessary, but until recently research workers ignored the obvious difference between suicides and attempted suicides, i.e. that the former are all dead while the latter are alive. At least, they have survived the suicidal act.

Studies into the fate of people who attempt suicide have been carried out only during the last two decades. They are the follow-up investigations undertaken by Dahlgren at Malmö, by Pierre B. Schneider at Lausanne and by Stengel and his associates at London. These studies have thrown light on how many members of large groups of people who had attempted suicide finally killed themselves.

The London team also investigated the social significance and effects of suicidal attempts. They started from the hypothesis that those who attempted and those who committed suicide constituted two different groups or 'populations.' They set themselves the task of investigating the following questions: 'What is the relationship between the two populations: those who commit suicide and those who attempt suicide? How many kill themselves later, and what makes them liable to do so? How does the suicidal attempt affect the patient's mental state? If suicide was motivated by a crisis in human relations, were those modified by the suicidal attempt, and if so, how? What is the effect of the suicidal attempt on the patient's group and what are their reactions to it? Sociologists have stated that suicide is due to social disintegration and isolation. Do these factors hold good for the suicidal attempt, and, if so, are they influenced by it? Some of these questions are of immediate practical interest for the clinician. The study of others might help us to understand the function of the suicidal attempt in our society.' (Stengel)

Research carried out since these questions were first posed in 1952 makes it possible to answer some of them tentatively today. The hypothesis that those who attempted and those who committed suicide constituted two different groups or 'populations' was confirmed when unselected samples of both were compared statistically. The formulation concerning the two populations has nevertheless given rise to serious misunderstandings. It has in fact been borrowed from epidemiology, which is the study of disease phenomena in groups or 'populations' which may overlap. It was, for instance, perfectly legitimate at the time when tuberculosis was a killing disease to divide patients into two populations, i.e. those who died from the disease and those who recovered, which did not mean that only the former were genuine cases; this division led to a better understanding of the various factors on which the outcome of the disease depended, and it also focused attention on the problems of the survivors. Or, to give an example relevant to the suicide problem, it has been stated quite correctly, that patients suffering from depressive illness and persons committing suicidal acts present two different populations (Sainsbury). This simply states, in the language of epidemiology, the well-known truth that not everybody who commits a suicidal act is suffering from depressive illness, nor vice versa. However, many members of the former group, or population, belong also to the latter. For the investigation of certain problems it may be essential to study those two groups separately, as was done by Walton who showed that they differed with regard to the history of a broken home.

Unfamiliarity with this use of the term 'population', and the preference for the simple over complex proposition, have led to the misconception that those two 'populations' were meant to consist of altogether different and mutually exclusive types of individuals. Some students of suicide readily, though erroneously, accepted this notion, while others, quite rightly, contested it, although it had never been put forward by the present author. That those who committed and those who attempted suicide differed statistically by age and sex had first been noted in a small sample by S. Peller, one of the pioneers of epidemiology, in 1932.

The *definition* of what constitutes a suicidal attempt is far from simple. If a person is taken to hospital in a drowsy or comatose state, having left a suicide note behind, and if he admits that he wanted to take his life, there is no problem about the nature of his action. However, if another person, having been admitted in a similar condition denies suicidal intentions and contends that he took an overdose by mistake, or because he wanted to have a good sleep, is he to be regarded as a suicidal attempt? Or if a teenager, after a row with her boy-friend, swallows a boxful of her mother's sleeping pills in his presence, with the obvious intention of impressing him, is she to be classed as a suicidal attempt? Or was this only a demonstrative suicidal gesture or threat? In practice the layman's answer to this question will depend on the effect of the pills and on the reactions of the environment. If the girl falls into a coma, has to be rushed into hospital and survives, the incident will be called a suicidal attempt. If she dies it will be a case of suicide. But if the boy-friend has the presence of mind to make her drink a tumbler of concentrated salt water immediately after she has swallowed the tablets and thus to make her vomit them before they have been absorbed, the whole episode may be over in a few minutes and be dismissed as just another lovers' tiff. However, it will be remembered if she should repeat the act at some later date, perhaps with a less harmless outcome. This example illustrates that the degree of damage and even the outcome of a suicidal act may depend on outside intervention, irrespective of the seriousness of the suicidal intent.

Many people deny suicidal intention after an act of self-damage, because they feel ashamed and guilty. They may not want to tell the truth, or their intention may have been confused at the time. It is generally believed that most if not all people who commit suicidal acts are clearly determined to die. The study of attempted suicides does not bear this out. Many suicidal attempts and quite a few suicides are carried out in the mood 'I don't care whether I live or die,' rather than with a clear and unambiguous determination to end life. A person who denies, after what seems an obvious suicidal attempt, that he *really* wanted to kill himself, may be telling the truth. Most people, in committing a suicidal act, are just as muddled as they are whenever they do anything of importance under emotional stress. Carefully planned suicidal acts are as rare as carefully planned acts of homicide. Many are carried out on sudden impulse, although suicidal thoughts were usually present before. At any rate, the person concerned cannot be the sole guide to the interpretation of his conduct. Doctors and others who have to make up their minds about acts of self-damage have to adopt a definition like this: '*A suicidal act is any deliberate act of self-damage which the person committing the act could not be sure to survive.*' Clinicians as well as lay persons ought to regard all cases of potentially dangerous self-poisoning or self-inflicted injury as suicidal acts whatever the victim's explanation, unless there is clear evidence to the contrary. 'Potentially dangerous' means in this context: believed by the 'attempter' possibly to endanger life. For instance, if a person who is ignorant of the effects of drugs takes double or three times the prescribed dose, this might have to be regarded as a suicidal attempt because in taking that overdose the person took a risk which may have proved fatal. However, if a doctor or a nurse took the same dose, the act may not be regarded as a suicidal attempt but only as a gesture. The same applies to injuries with cutting instruments, and to other means of self-damage. To draw an example from literature, the blind Gloucester's jump in *King Lear* from what he thought to be the cliffs of Dover was subjectively a serious suicidal attempt, but in reality quite harmless.

Was it a serious suidical attempt? This is a question immediately asked in every case by everybody who gets to know about the attempt. The question may have various meanings. It may refer to the chances of survival while the outcome is still in the balance. As the term suicidal attempt is in this book used only for nonfatal suicidal acts, this version of the question need not be discussed here.

There is a good deal of confusion about the criteria of the seriousness of a suicidal attempt, even among experts. Should the degree of self-inflicted damage, i.e. the depth of the coma, the amount of blood lost, in short, the degree of the danger to life, be the sole yardstick? If so, a carefully planned act of self-destruction which was prevented from taking effect by timely intervention may have to be classed as harmless.

Some writers call an attempt serious if it caused severe physical dysfunction of if the suicidal intention was serious. But, there is another aspect which has to be taken into account, i.e. the possibility of intervention from the environment. A lethal dose of a narcotic taken with genuine intent in a situation in which immediate counter-measures can be instituted may not seriously endanger life. On the other hand, a relatively small overdose taken half-heartedly by a person in poor health in a situation where help is not available may be fatal. If danger to life is to be the criterion of the seriousness of a suicidal act, the following aspects, which can be recorded with the help of rating scales, have to be taken into account. (1) The risk taken, i.e. the degree of danger to life the person could subjectively have believed he would incur. This factor is closely related to the conscious suicidal intent if there was any. (2) The hazard actually incurred. This can be assessed only by experts. Often there is a marked discrepancy between (1) and (2). If the latter was nil or slight, the suicidal act is often dismissed as non-genuine or negligible, while (1) may in fact have been considerable. Doctors often make the mistake of taking it for granted that their patients' and their own knowledge of the effects of drugs do not differ. (3) The damage suffered, e.g. degree and duration of disturbance of consciousness and of other effects of the poison, degree of the injury, etc., and (4) the social constellation at the time of the act, i.e. the chances of intervention and rescue as they could have been perceived by the person committing the act. The majority of the fatal or almost fatal suicidal acts have a high rating in at least two of those three criteria. To give an example: a suicidal attempt by a person who takes a heavy overdose of sleeping tablets with strong suicidal intention in his home and is found unconscious by a member of his family will not rank as highly on the dangerousness or 'lethality' scale as a similar act undertaken in a hotel room or on a lonely moor. From this point of view, only a minority of suicidal acts, fatal and non-fatal, qualify for top scores. Ettlinger and Flordh, two Swedish investigators, found that of 500 attempted suicides only four per cent could be regarded as well planned, but only seven percent were more or less harmless.

The classification of the vast number of non-fatal potentially suicidal acts has exercised the minds of many workers ever since attempted suicide has received special attention. The acts subsumed under this term not only differ greatly in dangerousness but also in the degree and clarity of conscious suicidal intention. Should they all be classed as attempted suicides even if the hazard incurred and the physical damage inflicted were negligible? Some writers distinguish between (a) 'suicidal gestures' in which the communicative and the manipulative purpose of the act is prominent and self-destructive intention apparently absent, (b) ambivalent attempts in which the person was aware of his indecision and apparently could not make up his mind whether he wanted to die or to live, and (c) the determined deliberate suicidal attempt which was intended and could be expected to be fatal by both the attempter and by others. There is also the problem of drawing a line between a suicidal gesture and the pretence of such a behaviour pattern undertaken with due safeguards and without any risk. Shneidman classifies non-fatal suicidal acts according to the person's statements about his intentions to bring about his death as follows: intentioned, subintentioned, unintentioned and contra-intentioned, the last category referring to those only pretending and having made sure of survival. It can be argued that the latter, the contra-intentioned group, should be excluded from this grouping, as the person takes no risk. They are nevertheless of interest to the student of suicidal behaviour because they give rise to the question why some people choose this particular type of malingering and attention-seeking. It could also be questioned whether the 'unintentioned' group, i.e. the gestures, should be included if the assessors are satisfied that self-destructive intentions were absent.

This approach which uses professed or apparent intention rather than overt behaviour as criterion is full of pitfalls which have already been referred to in this chapter. It also has far-reaching consequences for statistics and prevention. This is illustrated by the following case, reported in the *Guardian* in the autumn of 1968. As the names mentioned in the newspaper report are not relevant for this presentation they are not reproduced here.

> A man found dead in his cell at W. Prison, three weeks ago made a suicide gesture rather than a deliberate attempt on his life, and accidentally killed himself, the deputy Coroner, Mr. G. A. E., said yesterday. A verdict of misadventure was recorded on G. G. R., serving a two-year sentence for theft.
>
> Dr. B., pathologist, said R. had died from vagal inhibition, pressure on the vagal nerve in the neck causing the heart to stop. He had been on the floor, near a broken table, with prison uniform straps round his neck.
>
> Dr. W. S., senior medical officer at the prison, said R. was given to histrionic displays to draw attention to himself. In July he inflicted a wound on his wrist and said it was a suicide attempt. The doctor thought this a 'gesture to gain admission to hospital' not a 'genuine suicide attempt.'

It was a misjudgement to classify the first act of self-injury as a purely manipulative gesture, i.e. as 'unintentioned or contraintentioned' in spite of the man's assertion to the contrary. The warning was ignored. The doctor obviously saw only the appeal component of the motivations and dismissed the self-destructive tendency as non-existent. It can be assumed that this view was conveyed to the prison staff who were not alerted to the risk of suicide. At any rate, the man was left with the means of hanging himself. At the inquest the doctor stuck to his guns and the case was duly registered as an accident, the onus being put squarely on the victim and on Providence. Everybody else who might otherwise have been involved and who could have prevented this death, if only they had heeded the warning, i.e. the medical officer and the prison administration, was cleared. Public opinion was reassured. One case was lost to the suicide statistics. Society's collusion in evading a sense of guilt for ignoring the appeal for help was all too obvious.

Considering the importance of precedent in legal matters, one can safely assume that more such "accidents" will occur in prisons in this country unless the people who are responsible for the care of the prison population, and also HM. Coroners, are better informed about the complexity of motivations of suicidal acts. This kind of occurrence shows the need for an operational definition of suicidal attempt, and indeed of any suicidal act. Such a definition was proposed earlier in this chapter. It really implies that any act of self-damage inflicted deliberately which looks like a suicidal attempt ought to be regarded and treated as such. Only if there is evidence that the person took no risk subjectively should the act be regarded as falling outside the categories of suicidal acts. This kind of definition leaves plenty of scope for the study of the great variety of behaviour patterns subsumed under the terms of suicidal act, suicidal attempt and suicide. The present author advises workers in this field to accept a basic proposition which he has found helpful. *Most people who commit suicidal acts do not either want to die or to live; they want to do both at the same time, usually the one more, or much more, than the other.* It is quite unpsychological to expect people in states of stress, and especially vulnerable and emotionally unstable individuals who form the large majority of those prone to acts of self-damage, to know exactly what they want and to live up to St James' exhortation: 'Let your yea be yea and your nay, nay.'

Lethality Factors and the Suicide Attempt

In a broader study of terminal illness and suicide we wanted to look at the relationship between various presuicidal factors and the quantitative assessment of severity in an actual suicide attempt. A number of studies have been conducted comparing individuals who have attempted suicide with individuals who have completed suicide but few studies have focused on the lethality level of those who attempt suicide.

In an earlier study, Farberow and Shneidman[1] compared threatened, attempted, and completed suicides in which the attempters were treated as a single group with no separation as to the lethality of their attempts.* Although the groups did not differ with respect to demography or early family environment, it was found they differed significantly on psychiatric diagnosis, method of attempt, and previous medical history.

In a study of 109 suicide attempters, Schmidt, O'Neal, and Robins,[3] discriminated high-level attempts from low by calling a serious attempt "one in which the patient has done to himself enough damage to

This work was supported by a research grant from the National Institute of Mental Health (MH 15903)—Avery D. Weisman, Principal Investigator. The research staff included Frederick G. Guggenheim, M.D., Harry S. Olin, M.D., Joe P. Lemon, M.S.W., Mary Vallier, R.N., Lee C. Johnston, Ph.D. and Robert Sterling-Smith, Ph.D.

*Elsewhere, Shneidman[2] has written of the importance of distinguishing among various degrees of lethality in suicide attempts.

put him in a serious medical or surgical condition . . . or in which the psychiatrist was convinced the patient had fully intended to commit suicide." The serious attempters were found to be older and differed from the less serious group in psychiatric diagnosis, mental status, current life problems, reasons for the attempt, how serious they saw the attempt, alcohol use at attempt, and in informing another about the attempt.

Dorpat and Boswell[4] evaluated 121 suicide attempts and rated them on an ordinal scale of seriousness of attempt from 1 to 5, based on the degree of risk taken by the subject. A rating of 1 indicated a suicide gesture, 3 an ambivalent attempt, and 5 a serious one. They found high-intent suicide to be associated with males, older persons, and frequently, with a diagnosis of psychosis. Low-intent attempters tended to manipulate others by their act. The ambivalent middle group also used the attempt to test the affection and care of others.

In our study of suicide we wanted to develop a scale which would measure the relative severity of suicide attempts with respect to the probability of inflicting irreversible damage and death. We did this by creating the Risk-Rescue Rating.[5]

The Risk-Rescue Rating is a measure of what the person did and the context in which he did it. It is based on external criteria and is not subject to the phenomenology of the attempter. Intent may well be implied by the severity of the act in terms of danger to life and limb but it is not necessary to measure intent when examining the lethality of implementation.

Any suicide attempt entails a calculated risk. Because it takes place in a psychosocial context, survival may depend upon resources for rescue as well as upon the specific form of the attempt. Jumping off a relatively high bridge into the water has about the same level of risk whether it is done at 3 o'clock in the afternoon or 3 o'clock in the morning. However, the possibilities for rescue are reduced in the early morning hours where darkness may obscure the act and fewer people are around to effect a rescue.

The Risk-Rescue Rating scores 5 factors of risk and 5 factors of rescue. Factors of risk (on a 3-point scale for each) include the agent used, the degree of impaired consciousness, level of physical damage, reversibility, and the level of treatment required. Rescue factors, also on a 3-point scale, include the location of the act, the person initiating the rescue, the probability of discovery by any rescuer, accessibility of the person to being rescued, and the delay until discovery. (Specific definitions of these concepts and scoring instructions can be found in the original paper.) Risk-Rescue scores range from 17–83.

All suicide attempts are serious if they mean that a person has no other options than to harm himself. However, some suicidal attempts portend a higher probability of damage and death than do others. We wanted to investigate characteristics which differentiate high-level attempters from low-level attempters when lethality is treated as a continuous measure. We made the assumption that all suicide acts fall on a continuum of lethality and that this continuum can be quantified as a function of risk to rescue. There is also a broad range of suicidal attempts of intermediate lethality which, when placed on a continuum, may help to further differentiate characteristics of the low, the moderate, and the high attempter.

Lester[6] states that lethality can be seen on a continuum rather than suicide attempters and suicide completers being two distinct but overlapping groups. He argues that many completers were previous attempters and many attempters would be found to be completers if follow-ups were carried out for a sufficient period of time. He also points out that variables, such as sex, which tend to discriminate attempters from completers, increase monotonically as the seriousness of the attempt increases. He concludes that "suicidal behaviors fall on a continuum and that it is possible to order the different forms of suicidal behavior on a dimension of lethality of seriousness." This is exactly what the risk-rescue rating purports to do. Our main task is to show the relationship of certain significant presuicidal factors to the severity of an attempt as measured by the Risk-Rescue Rating.

Subjects

Forty patients who had made suicide attempts and were admitted to the Massachusetts General Hospital were investigated by our project team of 3 psychiatrists, 3 psychologists, a social worker, and a nurse clinician. Although each patient could be interviewed and tested, 4 died during hospitalization because of irreversible damage sustained in the suicide attempt.* These 40 patients were selected from the total population of attempters passing through the hospital on the basis of the lethality level of their attempt as determined by the risk-rescue rating. We wanted to have more or less equal numbers of patients in each of three lethality categories—high lethality: R^3 = 57-83, (N = 15); moderate lethality: R^3 = 40-56, (N = 14); low lethality: R^3 = 17-39, (N = 11).** Because the broader aim of the study was a comparison of lethality and terminality rather than strictly

*Psychological Autopsy reports on some of these cases can be found in Weisman.[7]
**R^3 = Risk Rescue Rating.

a comparison study of suicide attempters and suicide completers, only patients alive after an attempt were included in this study. The demography of these patients can be seen in Table 4-1 and does not differ significantly from the demography of the total population of suicidal patients admitted to the Massachusetts General Hospital during that period with respect to age, sex, race, religion, or marital status. However, there was an important difference with regard to the distribution of risk-rescue scores. Although we chose to include as close to equal numbers in each of the three lethal categories, a previous study of suicide at the Massachusetts General Hospital revealed that the number of low-level lethal attempts is twice as great as high-level attempts.

Procedures

Patients and families were given a series of interviews by a psychiatrist and social worker. The nurse clinician reported on hospital behavior based on observations and interviews with the staff members directly concerned with patient care. Patients were tested by the psychologist with the Thematic Apperception Test (TAT), a sentence completion test, and the Profile of Mood States (POMS). Patients were seen immediately after the attempt and observed for an average of 6 months. Data from interviews, observations, and testing were shared at a Psychological Autopsy Conference and then coded and recorded in the Terminality-Lethality Index, a research instrument for compilation of data on suicidal and terminal patients. Sections of the Index used in this study were background and personality data (section A), suicidal data (section S), and demographic data (section D). Because of the large amount of information representing events before, during, and after the attempt, we decided to submit the data to a series of factor analyses in order to identify the redundancy among variables. Psychosocial information from sections A and S of the Index were submitted to separate principal component factor analyses with Varimax rotation solution. As a result we found 13 factors related to A (background) variables and 14 factors related to S (suicide) variables.* These factors and their loadings can be seen in Tables 4-2 and 4-3. Only those factors whose Eigenvalues

*The data in the A factor analysis came from 86 patients—40 suicidal, 40 terminal cancer patients with no history of attempted suicide, and 6 patients with terminal cancer and history of recent suicide attempts. This was done to meet the broader objective of this study which was to compare lethality and terminality in suicide and cancer patients.

Table 4-1
Demography of Suicide Patients ($N = 40$)

		Male		Female		Total	
		N	%	N	%	N	%
Sex		15	38	25	62	40	100
Age	10–19	3	20	3	12	6	15
	20–29	4	27	6	24	10	25
	30–39	3	20	4	16	7	18
	40–49	3	20	3	12	6	15
	50–59	1	6	5	20	6	15
	60–69	1	6	2	8	3	7
	70–79	0	0	1	4	1	3
	≥80	0	0	1	4	1	3
Race	Caucasian	15	100	24	96	39	97
	Negro	0	0	1	4	1	3
Religion	Catholic	9	60	13	52	22	55
	Protestant	4	27	6	24	10	25
	Jewish	1	6	3	12	4	10
	Other	1	6	3	12	4	10
Marital status	Single	10	67	7	28	17	43
	Married	5	33	10	40	15	37
	Widowed	0	0	4	16	4	10
	Separated or divorced	0	0	4	16	4	10
Socioeconomic class	I	2	13	4	16	6	15
	II	2	13	3	12	5	12
	III	7	47	5	20	12	30
	IV	0	0	10	40	10	25
	V	4	27	3	12	7	18
Risk-Rescue rating	Low (17–39)	7	47	8	32	15	37
	Moderate (40–56)	5	33	9	36	14	35
	High (57–83)	3	20	8	32	11	28
Mortality	Living	14	94	22	88	36	90
	Dead	1	6	3	12	4	10

Table 4-2
Rotated Factor Loadings—Background and Personality
Variables (A)

Factor A-1—Poor Social Relationships

44. Patient has shown lifelong inability to maintain warm mutually interdependent relationships	.78
36. Estimated number of friends in the vicinity	−.72
48. Clear history of mental illness	.65
38. Patient admits to trouble getting along with people	.63
47. Received psychiatric treatment prior to admission	.57
45. Has mutually destructive interdependence with another person	.50
11. Family members close, mutually supportive	−.41
46. History of rage toward himself and others	.41

Factor A-2—Few Family Ties

08. Age patient permanently left home	−.69
12. Number of family moves during childhood	.54
21. Age when first parent lost by death	−.46

Factor A-3—Family Deaths

29. Suicide of a relative	.73
20. Recent family deaths	.65

Factor A-4—Cancer Deaths

25. Cancer death of relative	.57
22. Cancer death of mother	−.45
09. Actual or felt childhood rejection by parents	−.41
49. History of physical handicaps	.40

Factor A-5—Aggressive Narcissism

40. High need to control situations and others	.70
43. Excessive interest in appearance, comfort, importance, abilities	.70
41. Passively accepted pre-illness / suicide situation	−.62
46. History of rage towards himself and others	.57

Factor A-6—Birth Order

05. Birth order rank	−.71
03. Number of siblings	−.67
19. Number of sibling deaths	−.51
02. Patient was foreign born	−.49
10. Destructive parent / child relationships	.47
01. Parents were foreign born	−.46

Factor A-7—Parental Separation

07. Childhood separation from one or both parents	.78
06. Age of childhood separation from parent(s) (1–18)	.71

Table 4-2 (continued)
Rotated Factor Loadings—Background and Personality
Variables (A)

Factor A-7—Parental Separation	
42. Disparity between aspirations and accomplishments	.56
50. Seriously ill in childhood	.43
Factor A-8—Unstable Family	
17. Reformed alcoholic	.71
04. Step siblings	.57
15. Multi-problem family	.52
24. Cancer death of a friend	.52
10. Destructive parent/child relationships	.43
13. School difficulties (academic and behavioral)	.41
Factor A-9—Life-Threatening Behavior	
39. Engaged in physically dangerous activities	.69
28. Suicide of a friend	.60
18. Drug abuse	.47
21. Age when first parent lost by death	−.42
Factor A-10—Social Deviance	
32. Number of arrests	.78
16. Heavy current alcohol use	.71
30. Number of moves in the past 5 years	.56
45. Mutually destructive relationship with another person	.44
34. Dropped all traditional religious affiliation	.41
Factor A-11—NonParticipation	
35. Participant in many social group activities	−.62
37. Decreased contact with friends over past year	−.59
13. School difficulties (academic and behavioral)	.54
31. Planning to move at time of illness/suicide	.40
Factor A-12—Maternal Suicide	
26. Suicide of mother	.67
34. Dropped traditional religious affiliation	.41
50. Seriously ill in childhood	.40
Factor A-13—Religious Change	
33. Changed from family religion	.70
23. Cancer death in family	.45

Table 4-3
Rotated Factor Loadings—Suicide Variables (S)

Factor S-1—Intent to Die	
28. Stated intent to kill self	.88
29. Expected serious injury or death (Comstock scale)	.87
46. Beck Intent Scale—self report	.74
43. Delusional hopelessness	.59
33. Depression—affective aspects	.55
27. Clear idea as to why attempt was made	.51
26. Admits to and remembers attempt	.48
36. Length of depression prior to suicide	.40
Factor S-2—Help Negation	
65. Family ambivalent towards patient, post attempt	.75
42. Patient negates help, from significant other	.69
66. Family accepts patient, post attempt	−.68
41. Patient denies dependency needs	.64
20. Weekend suicide	−.46
Factor S-3—Disabled and Depressed	
51. Many physical symptoms, pre-attempt	.82
45. Attempt to please by conformatory social behavior	−.60
36. Lengthy depression prior to suicide	.57
35. Depression—social aspects	.47
34. Depression—somatic aspects	.45
54. Number hospital admissions prior to suicide	.41
52. High level physical disability, post attempt	.40
Factor S-4—Severe Damage	
22. Dead or disabled following attempt	.73
53. Permanent damage from attempt	.72
06. Elaborate advance planning for attempt	.69
07. Plan to thwart rescue	.63
52. High level physical disability, post attempt	.60
13. Left a note to be discovered after death	.50
40. Long-standing marital discord	.44
57. Placed on the danger list	.43
Factor S-5—Speaks of Suicide	
11. Direct communication of distress to another	.82
12. Significant other attempts to understand and to help	.76
10. Specific and direct threat of suicide	.63
44. Communicates intent only to significant other	.55
31. Probability of another attempt, clinic evaluation	.41
03. Lengthy period of suicidal ideation	.40
36. Length of depression prior to suicide	.40

Table 4-3 (continued)
Rotated Factor Loadings—Suicide Variables (S)

Factor S-6—Multiple Attempters

01. Was a multiple attempter	.82
02. Number of previous attempts	.78
30. Ideation remains high following attempt	.53
43. Delusional hopelessness	−.45
19. Homicidal ideation	.43
54. Number hospital admissions prior to suicide	.43

Factor S-7—Daytime Dejection

21. Nighttime suicide	−.66
34. Depression—somatic aspects	.58
25. Suicide in public place	.55
17. Saw social worker past month	.54
50. Persistent expression of shame for attempt	.47

Factor S-8—Recourse to Treatment

55. Number of hospital days—medical	.81
58. Number of hospital days—psychiatric	.78
24. Delivered self to medical intervention	.54
23. Delayed rescue	−.54
26. Admits to and remembers attempt	.50
05. Highly specific	.47
27. Clear idea as to why attempt was made	.45
25. Suicide in public place	.44

Factor S-9—Regressive Symptoms

08. Presence of hallucinations/delusions	.81
48. Paranoid features	.56
38. Anxiety level prior to attempt—high	.52
56. Placed on suicidal precautions	.40

Factor S-10—Reconciliation with Relief

49. Suicide attempt improved relationship with significant other	.84
32. Staff judgment of high lethality on discharge	−.52
40. Long standing marital discord	−.45

Factor S-11—Family Indifference

59. Patient indifferent to family, post attempt	.80
63. Family indifferent to patient, post attempt	.66
14. Saw physician past month	.46
50. Persistent expression of shame for attempt	−.41

Factor S-12—Family Repudiation

62. Patient accepting of family, post attempt	−.88

Table 4-3 (continued)
Rotated Factor Loadings—Suicide Variables (S)

Factor S-12—Family Repudiation	
37. High level of anger prior to attempt	.46
18. Had or believed he had terminal illness	.44
39. Lifelong inability to maintain warm relationships	.40

Factor S-13—Psychiatric History	
47. History of psychosis	.81
16. Saw psychotherapist past month	.48
19. Homicidal ideation	.46
14. Prior professional resources—physician	−.41
44. Communicates intent only to significant other	.40

Factor S-14—Tactical Failure	
56. Placed on suicidal precautions	−.67
64. Family rejects patient following suicide	.54
20. Weekend suicide	−.48

exceeded a criterion level of 1.00 and for which there seemed to be significant breaks in their latent roots were included in the rotation.† Factor scores were computed by the direct (non-estimation) equations outlined by Harmon.[8]

Findings

The 13 factors which related to background and personality information were defined as follows

A-1—poor social relationships. These patients have few friends and show a lifelong difficulty in getting along with people. They often engage in mutually destructive but strongly dependent relations with their few intimates. Many outbursts of rage are reported. Mental illness is sometimes present.

A-2—few family ties. Family changed residences frequently when patient was a child. With few family ties, the patients left home at earlier ages.

A-3—family deaths. Patient experienced a recent death in the family which may have been a suicide.

---

†These meet the generally acceptable criterion that the number of factors should not exceed one-third the number of subjects.

A-4—cancer death. Loss of a family member (not the mother) by cancer death.

A-5—aggressive narcissism. The patient shows an active need to actively control his situation and other people. He may overemphasize and overinvest in his own importance and abilities.

A-6—birth order. Families are usually very small and the patient is either an only or oldest child of an American-born family.

A-7—parental separation. These patients were separated from their parents at an early age either by leaving voluntarily or through family disruption.

A-8—unstable family. The patient comes from a multi-problem family which may include divorce, alcoholism, truancy, and destructive parent-child relationships.

A-9—life-threatening behavior. These patients were involved in conspicuously dangerous physical activities which might result in serious illness or injuries. Drug abuse is common and a friend may have met death through suicide.

A-10—social deviance. Difficulties with the law, heavy alcohol use, transiency of residence, and mutually destructive relationship with another person.

A-11—nonparticipation. These patients do not like to participate in group activities and have experienced conflict and isolation with peers over the years. Relationships are not so much marked by conflict as they are by nonexistence.

A-12—maternal suicide. Suicide of the mother loads high.

A-13—religious change. These patients report abandoning their family religion or making a change from their family religion into another faith.

The factor analysis on the suicide data yielded the following 13 factors*

S-1—intent to die. These patients were depressed, saw their situation as hopeless, and expected to die or to be seriously injured as the result of their action.

---

*These factors are not necessarily stable and may not apply to another sample of suicidal patients. Factor analysis was used to get a better descriptive picture of how variables on these particular patients intercorrelated, to reduce the number of variables, and to eliminate some of the redundancy between variables.

S-2—help negation. These patients negated help from significant others prior to and after the suicide. Families of these patients were either ambivalent toward or rejective of the patient after the attempt.

S-3—disabled and depressed. These patients showed both somatic and social aspects of depression prior to the attempt, the depressions sometimes being lengthy. Physical illness, physical symptoms, and prior hospitalizations frequently accompanied the depression.

S-4—severe damage. This measures the degree of physical damage as a result of the attempt. Patients with a high degree of physical damage often made elaborate advance plans for the suicide including plans to thwart rescue. If a note was left it was left to be discovered only after death.

S-5—speaks of suicide. These patients make specific and direct threats of suicide to significant key others in their lives with a positive helpful response from such a person.

S-6—multiple attempters. Although not feeling their cause was hopeless, these patients were multiple attempters often having made a series of attempts.

S-7—daytime dejection. This factor discriminates patients whose suicide occurred in the daylight hours and often in a public place. Somatic aspects of depression may have also been present.

S-8—recourse to treatment. Patients scoring high on this factor spent considerable time in the hospital for both medical and psychiatric treatment following the attempt. The suicide was made for some highly specific reason and in some cases there was self-rescue.

S-9—regressive symptoms. This discriminates the attempt where anxiety, hallucination, and/or delusions preceded the attempt. In such cases the patient was frequently placed on special suicide precautions while in the hospital.

S-10—reconciliation with relief. Here the attempt resulted in some improvement in relationship with a significant other and the patient was judged to be unlikely to make another attempt when evaluated by the hospital staff.

S-11—family indifference. Indifference marks the interrelation between the patient and his family after the attempt with little shame expressed on the part of the patient. The patient may have been seen by a physician within a month of the attempt.

Table 4-4
Regression of Selected Variables on Risk-Rescue Rating

Variable (by order of entry)	β-weight	t
S-13—psychotic history	.37	2.26
A-9—life-threatening behavior	−.34	2.06
S-1—intent to die	.14	.85
Married	.19	1.30
A-13—religious change	−.19	1.31
A-6—birth order	.19	1.20
A-1—poor social relationships	.13	.77
S-12—family repudiation	−.09	.60

$R = .69$
$R^2 = .48$
$F = 3.54$, $df\ 8/31$, $p < .01$

S-12—family repudiation. A high level of anger is directed towards the family prior to the attempt.

S-13—psychiatric history. These subjects report episodes of psychoses but with different degrees of therapeutic contacts. Homicidal thoughts and impulses were frequently noted.

S-14—tactical failure. Suicide fails to rally support of the failing and the patient is rejected because of the attempt.

To determine the relative contribution of each factor score towards the Risk-Rescue Rating, a series of multiple regression analyses were done. The A factor scores were regressed against R^3 and those with significance were extracted. The same was done with significant S factor scores. The final regression equation which includes the significant A and S factor scores and one demographic variable can be seen in Table 4-4.* Multiple regression analysis was done not only to eliminate further redundancy in the data but also to see which variables might be acting as suppressor variables with respect to the rest.[9] Zero-order correlations between the demographic variables and factor scores with Risk-Rescue can be seen in Table 4-5.

The final regression equation consists of 4 A factors, 3 S factors, and one demographic variable. Factors showing influence on higher lethal attempts were A-1—poor social relationships, A-6—birth order,

*This procedure admittedly skews the data toward maximum predictability and is based on assumptions similar to those found in stepwise regression analysis. We know R and F are not true tests of significance. Factor S-4—severe damage—was eliminated because of its redundancy with the Risk-Rescue Rating.

Table 4-5

Correlation of Demographic Variables and Factor Scores
with Risk-Rescue Rating ($N = 40$)

Sex ($M = 1$, $F = 0$)	−.07
Age	−.06
Socioeconomic status	−.13
Religion	
Prostestant	.23
Catholic	−.15
Jewish	.00
Marital status	
Single	−.17
Married	.32
Widowed	−.06
Separated or divorced	−.19
A *Factor scores* (personal history)	
A-1—poor social relationships	.31*
A-2—few family ties	−.27
A-3—family deaths	−.17
A-4—cancer deaths	−.26
A-5—aggressive narcissism	−.07
A-6—birth order	.25
A-7—parental separation	.00
A-8—unstable family	−.03
A-9—life-threatening behavior	−.27
A-10—social deviance	.26
A-11—nonparticipation	.13
A-12—maternal suicide	.05
A-13—religious change	−.20
S *Factor scores* (suicidal history)	
S-1—intent to die	.30*
S-2—help negation	−.08
S-3—disabled and depressed	−.08
S-4—severe damage	.53†
S-5—speaks of suicide	−.19
S-6—multiple attempters	−.15
S-7—daytime dejection	−.15
S-8—recourse to treatment	.15
S-9—regressive symptoms	.03
S-10—reconciliation with relief	−.11
S-11—family indifference	.05
S-12—family repudiation	−.20
S-13—psychiatric history	.40†
S-14—tactical failure	−.18

*$p < .05$
†$p < .01$

Table 4-6
Factors Associated with Lethality

High Lethality	Low Lethality
High intent to die	Low intent to die
Life-threatening behavior	Less life-threatening behavior
Married	Marital status other than married
Psychiatric history	No psychiatric history
Lower birth order	Higher birth order
History of poor social relationships	No history of poor social relationships
Little repudiation of family	Repudiation of family
No change of family religion	Change from family religion

S-1—intent to die, S-13—psychiatric history, and married. Those showing influence in lower lethal attempts were A-9—life-threatening behavior, A-13—religious change, S-12—family repudiation.

If we construct a composite picture contrasting persons who made high-level lethal attempts with persons who made low-level lethal attempts, we find that high-level attempts are associated with persons who had expected serious injury or death from the attempt. These persons had few friends and showed a lifelong difficulty in getting along with others. Any relationships they had could be defined as mutually destructive. A mental illness history, sometimes with accompanying psychosis, was frequently present. Homicidal thoughts, impulses, and frequent outbursts of rage were often found. Often they were the only or oldest child coming from a small family.

Persons who had made low-level lethal attempts had not expected serious injury or death from the attempt. They came from larger families with whom they were angry prior to the attempt and from whom they refused offers of help. Some had expressed rebellion by leaving the family religion. They had less history of psychiatric care but much more involvement in life-threatening behavior.

DISCUSSION

In this discussion the focus will be on those variables that met the criterion of either significant zero-order correlation or a significant t in the final regression equation.*

*Kerlinger, Fred N. and Pedhazur, Elazar J.: Multiple Regression in Behavioral Research, Holt, Rinehart and Winston, Inc., New York, 1973.

Psychiatric Illness

It is not surprising that psychiatric illness should be associated with high-level lethal suicide attempts. An earlier survey study done by Sainsbury[10] indicated that psychiatric illness was often a significant aspect of self-destruction. Both Dorpat and Ripley[11] and Robins et al.[12] studied a series of completed suicides making special note of psychiatric symptoms. After interviewing significant survivors and examining hospital records, Dorpat and Ripley concluded that 90 percent of the suicides they were studying were psychiatrically ill at the time of the suicidal act. Robins' findings were similar. There is a wide range of findings in the literature as to psychopathology among suicidal persons. The results are not consistent due to the various approaches used by the researchers and the various definitions of pathology.

In a study cited earlier, Dorpat and Boswell[4] differentiated gestural, ambivalent, serious, and completed suicides. They found that psychoses were significantly more prevalent in the serious-attempt group than in the gestural and ambivalent groups. Sifneos et al.[13] supported this idea when they posited that neurotics were not as efficient as psychotics when attempting suicide. For example, they found that neurotics ingested smaller doses of barbiturates than psychotics, who tended to ingest large amounts.

Another study, made in the emergency room of a general hospital by Rubenstein et al.,[14] reported that the suicide attempts of psychotics were more severe than those of the general suicidal population who made their way into the same hospital emergency room. One problem in exploring this phenomenon is that suicidal behavior was a factor under consideration in arriving at a psychiatric diagnosis. However, in this study patients who scored high on factor S-13 had a diagnosis of psychosis sometime *prior* to the suicide attempt though they may have been receiving some kind of psychiatric treatment at the time of the attempt. This raises the interesting issue as to whether or not our patients were receiving psychiatric treatment because of a previous suicide attempt. Most of them were not. However, in a study of multiple suicide attempters we did find that psychiatric treatment at the time of the first attempt plays a significant role with regard to later attempts.[15] If one had no prior history of psychiatric treatment and was not given treatment after the first attempt, the second attempt would be one of increased lethality as measured by the Risk-Rescue Rating. On the other hand, those given treatment following their first attempts were more likely to make a second attempt of a lower lethality. This seems to suggest that if the first attempt is not taken as seriously as the patient wishes (no treatment is offered), the patient may make a more serious attempt in his second effort. Although psychotherapy may not prevent a second attempt it may make a difference in lowering the lethality of subsequent attempts.

Life-Threatening Behavior (LTB)

In this study, life-threatening behavior (LTB) was associated with lower levels of lethality. Many researchers have considered physically dangerous behavior to be suicidal equivalents. Farberow[16] suggests that certain physical activity be considered as indirect self-destructive behavior because of its consistent presence in the life of the person and because the person is not aware of or denies any intention to harm himself. "The result may be seen in physical effects, such as illness, loss of limb or sensory ability, surgeries, addictions, shortening of life, and pain; or in psychological effects, such as depression, psychosis, inability to tolerate success, gambling, smoking, antisocial behavior, etc." Menninger[17] uses the term *chronic suicide* to refer to persons who manifest long-term self-destructive behaviors such as alcoholism and accident proneness.

Although we defined life-threatening behavior in its more gross form and disregarded subtle self-inimical behavior, we found a clear association of LTB with low-level lethal attempts in the group of patients we studied. Were life-threatening behavior clearly a suicidal equivalent, it would have been more evenly distributed throughout the lethal spectrum. Therefore we might infer that life-threatening behavior is not primarily a suicidal behavior but a group of dangerous acts that might culminate in fatality. However, since it is a phenomenon less associated with intermediate and high lethality, one might also argue that frequent participation in dangerous behavior may prevent high lethality.

In support of the first possibility, that LTB is largely a non-suicidal entity, we found several patients who not only made multiple suicide attempts but also faced considerable self-imposed danger in their lives. These patients were able to number and identify the suicide attempts and to distinguish them from other risky behavior in which some other motive or painful emotion was involved. The non-suicidal behavior was termed suicidal by clinicians although the patients did not agree. They did concur that they were guilty of other kinds of reckless, risky behavior that could have been fatal but distinguished this from attempted suicide.

In support of the second possibility, that LTB diminished the lethal level, many highly lethal attempters are strongly inhibited, socially isolated, restricted individuals who do not reach out for recognition or help, but repudiate the world as well as their few contacts within it. They live and die within themselves, not by performing dangerous acts.

Life-threatening behavior covers such a wide range of acts that general conclusions about its suicidal component are scarcely justified. Likewise, in certain cases a low-level attempt may merely be a dramatic but not necessarily dangerous episode in the life history of an erratic individual. What is needed is a more precise definition of life-threatening behavior that can be quantified without falling into a semantic trap in which almost every hazardous endeavor becomes labeled as suicidal equivalent. We might then find LTB present not just in individuals who are prone to notorious acting out but also in the person who engages in this type of activity when his lethal level reaches a high degree of intensity.

Intent to Die

To classify suicidal behavior on the basis of intent to die, the intensity of the wish to terminate one's life, is difficult. Some make an attempt of a highly lethal nature but calculate that they will be rescued before they die. Others make an attempt of relatively low risk but the attempt is successful due to miscalculation of rescue. It is not uncommon to have attempters come into the emergency ward and tell the attending physician not to do anything to save them because they want very much to die. These same patients, when seen a day or so later, may totally deny any intent to die suggesting only that they began to take some medication and forgot just how many pills they had taken. One attempter was recently admitted to the hospital with a serious lesion in his chest from a knife wound. When I asked him about the wound he said that he was in the kitchen with his wife, went to embrace her, and the knife got in between them and he was stabbed!

The Risk-Rescue Rating was developed in such a way so that an intent rating would not be needed to rate the lethality of implementation. We were interested in intent to die, but wanted to keep intent as a separate measure so that it could be compared with the Risk-Rescue Rating. We initially assumed that the higher the R^3 rating the more we might infer intent to die. To assess intent to die we used various ratings including Beck's Intent Scale.[18] All of these ratings load high on factor S-1 (intent to die). Our findings suggest a strong relationship, though obviously not a perfect one, between the lethal level of the attempt and the report of the patient as to his intent following the act. It should also be noted that patients scoring highest on factor S-1 were also seen as the most clinically depressed and expressed a great deal of delusional hopelessness, an unrealistic belief that there was no way for them to escape their plight.

Beck et al. suggest that "the degree of intent reflected in an individual's overt behavior is a compromise between the wish to live and the wish to die. A balance between suicidal wishes and life preservative wishes may lead to an ambivalent suicide attempt." We believe that the Risk-Rescue Rating is a good measure of such ambivalence especially when an attempt falls into the range of intermediate lethality—40 to 56.

Marriage

Most of the suicide research suggests that the incidence of completed suicides among married persons is low. This seems to be true for both males and females and for almost all age groups.[19] However, in our group of patients marriage was significantly associated with high lethality. Just looking at this demographic fact can be misleading; it is important to study the kinds of marriage these patients had.

We found that most high lethal attempts were associated with the marriages in which there was emotional divorce and a chronic inability to communicate with the partner, where partners were living together merely from habit. Attempts of a low and intermediate level were associated with marriages in which there was considerable emotional investment yet also considerable conflict. Marital discord was generally more acute than chronic; communication patterns prior to the suicide seemed to break down between family members.

Poor Social Relationships

The importance of negative social interaction as a lethal contingency is substantiated in two recent, well-conducted studies. Breed[20] lists isolation as one of the five major components in a Basic Suicide Syndrome along with commitment, rigidity, failure, and shame. Breed considers isolation to be not only self-imposed social isolation but also the anger that accompanies frustrated dependency needs which cannot be adequately communicated.

Maris and Lazerwitz,[21] in a careful and statistically sophisticated comparison of completed suicides, suicide attempters, and natural deaths, found that negative interaction accounted for much of the variance in their prediction of completed suicides. Their concept of negative interaction is similar to what Breed calls isolation combined with his notion of interpersonal failure.

In our study, poor social relationships illustrate a lifelong inability on the part of the person to maintain warm, mutually interdependent relationships. These persons have few friends and admit to having trouble getting along with people. Those relationships which they do have are usually marked by destructive interdependence with another person. They report that their families are not close and mutually supportive. Patients with high scores on this factor also had attempts of a high lethal nature. This lifelong inability to maintain warm interdependent relationships not only influences lethality in suicidal patients but also effects the life span of the terminally ill (terminality). In our study of terminal illness and suicide we had A factor ratings on patients who were dying with cancer as well as suicidal patients. This same factor (A-1) was a significant predictor of short survival. That is, patients who died much sooner than expected when medical and treatment variance were carefully controlled showed significantly higher scores on this same poor social relationship factor than did people who lived much longer than medically expected.[22] It reminds one of Paul Federn's comment, "All that is living must be loving so as not to die." Or as Freud wrote, "In the last analysis we must love in order to not fall ill and must fall ill when, in the consequence of frustration, we cannot love."

Birth Order

Birth order is one variable which was not significant but since it neared significance for this small a sample of patients it is worth commenting on. This variable has been of continuing interest in suicide research. Again research evidence is not clearcut. In a study of school children who killed themselves, Jan-Tausch[23] found a greater proportion of firstborn than second born. However, in a study of alcoholics, Ritson[24] found that there were more latterborn persons among alcoholics who killed themselves than among alcoholics who did not. Two studies which found no difference in birth order in two different samples of completed suicides were that of Kallman et al.[25] and Paffenbarger and Asnes.[26]

In a recent study Cantor[27] investigated a random selection of young adults 18-25 years of age in an eastern university. Out of 200 she found 58 who had a history of suicide attempt. The remaining 142 were divided into two groups—those who thought of suicide frequently (high thinkers) and those who did not (low thinkers). Most of those in the attempt and high thinkers groups were firstborns. It is interesting to note that all firstborns who had absent fathers were either attempters or high thinkers.

Though it is not conclusive, there is some evidence that firstborn children may be more likely to be suicidal than latter born siblings. Lester and Lester[28] suggest that firstborn children tend to be overdependent on others, especially in times of stress. Suicide is a way of crying for help from significant others. They also suggest that latter borns can more easily direct their aggression outward because they are less hampered by social restraint while firstborns tend to turn aggression inward on themselves because of oversensitivity to social sanctions.

In addition to having a low birth order, patients scoring high on factor A-6 (birth order) also came from smaller families where there were fewer siblings. This raises the interesting notion of sibling socialization as a possible influence upon lethality. Sibling socialization, as an important developmental variable, was described by Harlow and Harlow in their famous monkey studies.[29] They found that monkeys deprived of their real mothers could survive and develop without emotional abberations if they had adequate sibling socialization. This was true even if the mother substitute was a wire mother rather than the softer, more cuddly, terry cloth mother-substitute. Sibling socialization has also been explored as an important variable in the development of certain psychoses. The lack of sibling socialization seems to be an important correlate in certain types of schizophrenia.

Birth order and its relationship to lethality and suicide is still questionable. Rather than just looking at birth order as an individual variable family size, types of interactions, including aspects of sibling socialization, need to be explored before we can say anything definitive about this phenomenon and suicidal behavior.

Age and Sex

Age and sex are two demographic variables which are traditionally associated with highly lethal attempts, but do not show up as significant in this study. In our original paper on the Risk-Rescue Rating, cited earlier, age and sex were significantly correlated with lethality of implementation. Those with higher R^3 tended to be older and male. The fact that these two important variables do not show up as significant in this study is probably due to our selection procedure. Patients were selected according to the lethal level of their attempt as measured by the R^3. When these patients were selected for study there were a number of women and younger males admitted to the hospital with high-level attempts. Including these persons in the study significantly affected the findings with respect to age and sex. Although the total group of 40 patients does not differ significantly by age and sex with the total group of suicides seen at the hospital during that time, the age and sex distribution included in each of the three lethal categories is *not* representative of the total group.

CONCLUSIONS

There are significant characteristics which differentiate the high-lethal from the low-lethal attempter. The most important of these characteristics are a history of psychosis, poor social relationships, intent to die, and life-threatening behavior.

These findings replicate for the most part what other studies have found when looking at high- and low-level suicide attempts. The unique contribution of this study is its treatment of lethality of implementation as a continuous variable. One of the more interesting findings in this study is the relationship of life-threatening behavior to low-level attempts. Further investigation needs to be done to determine whether or not life-threatening behavior is simply a suicidal equivalent or if it is qualitatively different. Also, the possibility that engaging in life-threatening behavior may discharge lethality so that a person does not engage in suicidal behavior of a more serious consequence needs to be studied. There is evidence from psychoanalytic theory that this may be the case.

Our hypothesis that the Risk-Rescue Rating is a good measure of the intent to die seems to have been validated in this study. This is an important finding since a Risk-Rescue Rating can be made apart from the self-report of the attempter.

The methodology used here can be commended to other suicide researchers. All too frequently suicide data are compared in oversimplistic two-by-two variable comparisons and the subtle interrelationship of variables is missed; relationships which can be found through partial correlation, factor analysis, and multiple regression analysis.

If lethality as expressed in self-destructive behavior is viewed on a continuum, then we can identify those elements which increase as one moves up that continuum, in order to make better clinical interventions which will help reduce lethality and perturbation as well as to help us better understand the factors associated with self-destruction.

REFERENCES

1. Farberow NL, Shneidman ES: Attempted, threatened, and completed suicide. J Abnorm Psychol 50:230, 1955
2. Shneidman ES: Suicide, lethality, and the psychological autopsy, in Shneidman ES, Ortega M (eds): Aspects of Depression Boston, Little, Brown, 1969
3. Schmidt EH, O'Neal P, Robins E: Evaluation of suicide attempts as guide to therapy. JAMA 155:6 549-557, 1954
4. Dorpat TL, Boswell JW: An evaluation of suicidal intent in suicide attempts. Compr Psychiatry 4:117-125, 1963
5. Weisman AD, Worden JW: Risk-rescue rating in suicide assessment. Arch Gen Psychiatry 26:553-560, 1972
6. Lester D: Suicidal Behavior: A Summary of Research Findings. Buffalo, Suicide Prevention and Crisis Service, 1970
7. Weisman AD: The Realization of Death: A Guide for the Psychological Autopsy. New York, Jason Aronson, 1974
8. Harmon HH: Modern Factor Analysis. Chicago, Univ Chicago Press, 1967
9. Cooley WW, Lohnes PR: Multivariate Data Analysis. New York, Wiley, 1971
10. Sainsbury P: Suicide in London. London Chapman and Hall, 1955
11. Dorpat TL, Ripley HS: A study of suicide in the seattle area. Compr Psychiatry 1:349-359, 1960
12. Robins E, Gassner S, Kayes J, Wilkinson RH, Murphy G: The communication of suicidal intent: A study of 134 consecutive cases of successful (completed) suicides. Am J Psychiatry 115:724-733, 1959
13. Sifneos PE, Gore C, Sifneos AC: A preliminary psychiatric study of attempted suicide as seen in a general hospital. Am J Psychiatry 112:883-888, 1956
14. Rubenstein R, Moses R, Lidz T: On attempted suicide. Arch Neurol 70:103-112, 1958
15. Worden JW, Sterling-Smith RS: Lethality patterns in multiple suicide attempts. Life-Threatening Behavior 3:2 95-104, 1973
16. Farberow NL: Research in Suicide. Center for Studies of Suicide Prevention, National Institute for Mental Health, 1970. Mimeographed 83 pages.
17. Menninger K: Man against Himself. New York, Harcourt, 1938.
18. Beck AT, Schuyler D, Herman I: Development of suicidal intent scales, in Beck AT, Resnik HL, Lettieri DJ (eds): The Prediction of Suicide Bowie, Maryland, Charles Press 1974
19. Durkheim E: Suicide. Glencoe, Illinois Free Press, 1951
20. Breed W: Five components of a basic suicide syndrome. Life-Threatening Behavior 2:3-18, 1972
21. Maris R, Lazerwitz B: Toward a General Theory of Self-Destructive Behavior (unpublished manuscript), 1973

22. Weisman AD, Worden JW: Psychosocial analysis of cancer deaths. Omega 6:61-75, 1975
23. Jan-Tausch J: Suicide of Children 1960-1963. Trenton, N.J., Department of Education, 1963
24. Ritson EB: Suicide among alcoholics: Brit J Med Psychol 41:235-242, 1968
25. Kallman FJ, De Porte J, De Porte E, Feingold L: Suicide in twins and only children. Am J Hum Genet 1:113-126, 1949
26. Paffenbarger RS, Asnes DP: Chronic disease in former college students. Am J Public Health 56:1026-1036, 1966
27. Cantor PC: Personality and Status Characteristics of the Female Youthful Suicide Attempter PH.D. dissertation, Columbia University, 1972
28. Lester G, Lester D: Suicide: The Gamble with Death. Englewood Cliffs, N.J. Prentice-Hall 1971
29. Harlow HF, Harlow MK: Social deprivation in monkeys. Sci Am 207:136-146, 1962

Jerome A. Motto
and David C. Heilbron

5

Development and Validation of Scales for Estimation of Suicide Risk

To introduce this chapter excerpts from the American Psychological Association's *Technical Recommendations for Psychological Tests and Diagnostic Techniques* by Lee Cronbach et al. were selected. They are reproduced here with the kind permission of The American Psychological Association © 1954.

DEVELOPMENT AND SCOPE OF THE RECOMMENDATIONS

Psychological and educational tests are used in arriving at decisions which may have great influence on the ultimate welfare of the persons tested, and of the community. Test users, therefore, wish to apply high standards of professional judgment in selecting and interpreting tests, and test producers wish to produce tests which can be of the greatest possible service. The test producer, in particular, has the task of providing sufficient information about each test so that users will know what reliance can safely be placed on it.

Professional workers agree that test manuals and associated aids to test usage should be made complete, comprehensible, and unambiguous, and for this reason there have always been informal "test standards." Publishers and authors of tests have adopted standards for themselves, and standards have been stated in textbooks and other publications. Through application of these standards, tests have attained a high degree of quality and usefulness.

Until this time, however, there has been no statement representing a consensus as to what information is most helpful to the test consumer. In

163

the absence of such a guide, it is inevitable that some tests appear with less adequate supporting information than others of the same type, and that facts about a test which some users regard as indispensable have not been reported because they seemed relatively unimportant to the test producer. This report is the outcome of an attempt to survey the possible types of information that test producers might make available, to weigh the importance of these, and to make recommendations regarding test preparation and publication.

Improvement of testing has long been a concern of professional workers. In 1906, an APA committee with Angell as chairman, was appointed to act as a general control committee on the subject of measurements. The purpose of their work was to standardize testing techniques, whereas the present effort is concerned with standards of reporting information about tests.

In a developing field, it is necessary to make sure that standardizing efforts do not stifle growth. The words of the earlier committee are appropriate today:

> The efforts of a standardizing committee are likely to be regarded with disfavor and apprehension in many quarters, on the ground that the time is not yet ripe for stereotyping either the test material or the procedure. It may be felt that what is called for, in the present immature condition of individual psychology, is rather the free invention and the appearance of as many variants as possible. Let very many tests be tried, each new investigator introducing his own modification; and then, the worthless will gradually be eliminated and the fittest will survive.

Issuing specifications for tests could indeed discourage the development of new types of tests. So many different sorts of tests are needed in present psychological practice that limiting the kind or the specifications would not be sound procedure. Appropriate standardization of tests and manuals, however, need not interfere with innovation. The recommendations presented here are intended to assist test producers to bring out a wide variety of tests that will be suitable for all the different purposes for which tests should be used and to make those tests as valuable as possible. . . .

VALIDITY

Validity information indicates to the test user the degree to which the test is capable of achieving certain aims. Tests are used for several types of judgment, and for each type of judgment, a somewhat different type of validation is involved. We may distinguish four aims of testing:

1. The test user wishes to determine how an individual would perform at present in a given universe of situations of which the test situation constitutes a sample.

2. The test user wishes to predict an individual's future performance (on the test or on some external variable).

3. The test user wishes to estimate an individual's present status on some variable external to the test.

4. The test user wishes to infer the degree to which the individual possesses some trait or quality (construct) presumed to be reflected in the test performance.

Thus, a vocabulary test might be used simply as a measure of present vocabulary, as a predictor of college success, as a means of discriminating schizophrenics from organics, or as a means of making inferences about "intellectual capacity."

Four Types of Validity

To determine how suitable a test is for each of these uses, it is necessary to gather the appropriate sort of validity information. These four aspects of validity may be named content validity, predictive validity, concurrent validity, and construct validity.

Content validity is evaluated by showing how well the content of the test samples the class of situations or subject matter about which conclusions are to be drawn. Content validity is especially important in the case of achievement and proficiency measures.

In most classes of situations measured by tests, quantitative evidence of content validity is not feasible. However, the test producer should indicate the basis for claiming adequacy of sampling or representativeness of the test content in relation to the universe of items adopted for reference.

Predictive validity is evaluated by showing how well predictions made from the test are confirmed by evidence gathered at some subsequent time. The most common means of checking predictive validity is correlating test scores with a subsequent criterion measure. Predictive uses of tests include long-range prediction of intelligence measures, prediction of vocational success, and prediction of reaction to therapy.

Concurrent validity is evaluated by showing how well test scores correspond to measures of concurrent criterion performance or status. Studies which determine whether a test discriminates between presently identifiable groups are concerned with concurrent validity. Concurrent validity and predictive validity are quite similar save for the time at which the criterion is obtained. Among the problems for which concurrent validation is used are the validation of psychiatric screening instruments against estimates of adjustment made in a psychiatric interview, differentiation of vocational groups, and classification of patients. It should be noted that a test having concurrent validity may not have predictive validity.

Construct validity is evaluated by investigating what psychological qualities a test measures, i.e., by demonstrating that certain explanatory constructs account to some degree for performance on the test. To examine construct validity requires both logical and empirical attack. Essentially, in studies of construct validity we are validating the theory underlying the test. The validation procedure involves two steps. First, the investigator inquires: From this theory, what predictions would we make regarding the variation of scores from person to person or occasion to occasion? Second, he gathers data to confirm these predictions.

There are various specific procedures for gathering data on construct validity. If it is supposed that form perception on the Rorschach test indicates probable ability to resist stress, this supposition may be validated by placing individuals in an experimental stress situation and observing whether behavior corresponds to prediction. Another much simpler procedure for investigating what a test measures is to correlate it with other measures; we would expect a valid test of numerical reasoning, for example, to be substantially correlated with other numerical tests, but not to be correlated with a clerical perception test. Factor analysis is another way of organizing data about construct validity.

We can distinguish among the four types of validity by noting that each involves a different emphasis on the criterion. In predictive or concurrent validity, the criterion behavior is of concern to the tester, and he may have no concern whatsoever with the type of behavior exhibited in the test. (An employer does not care if a worker can manipulate blocks, but the score on the block test may predict something he cares about.) Content validity is studied when the tester is concerned with the type of behavior involved in the test performance. Indeed, if the test is a work sample, the behavior represented in the test may be an end in itself. Construct validity is ordinarily studied when the tester has no definitive criterion measure of the quality with which he is concerned, and must use indirect measures to validate the theory. Here the trait or quality underlying the test is of central importance, rather than either the test behavior or the scores on the criteria.

It is ordinarily necessary to evaluate construct validity by integrating evidence from many different sources. The problem of construct validation becomes especially acute in the clinical field since for many of the constructs dealt with it is not a question of finding an imperfect criterion but of finding any criterion at all. The psychologist interested in construct validity for clinical devices is concerned with making an estimate of a hypothetical internal process, factor, system, structure, or state and cannot expect to find a clear unitary behavioral criterion. Concern for validity is in no way a challenge to the dictum that prediction of behavior is the final test of any theoretical construction. But it is necessary to understand that *behavior-relevance* in a construct is not logically the same as *behavior-equivalence*. It is one thing to insist that in order to be admissible, a complex psychological construct must have some relevance to behavioral indicators; it is quite another thing to require that any admissible psychological construct must be *equivalent to* any direct operational behavior measure. Any position that cuts the test inference off from all possible nontest sources of confirmation appears to be an unreasonable one. If the test is to be interpreted in terms of internal constructs, there must be some facts, quantitative or not, that would argue for the existence of the particular internal system postulated. An attempt to identify any one criterion measure or any composite as *the* criterion aimed at is, however, usually unwarranted.

This viewpoint, while fraught with grave dangers and sometimes misused, is nevertheless methodologically sound. The clinician interested in construct validity has in mind an admittedly incomplete construct, the evidence for which is to be found roughly in such-and-such behavioral domains. The vagueness of the construct is an inevitable consequence of the incompleteness of current psychological theory, and cannot be rectified faster than theory grows and is confirmed. At a given stage of theoretical development, the only kind of prediction that can be made may be that certain correlations should be positive, or that patients who fail to conform to a group trend should be expected with considerable frequency to exhibit such-and-such an additional feature, or the like. It is clear that these deductions do involve behavioral prediction. They require the test-constructs to be behaviorally relevant. But they still do not necessarily *identify* any of the test-inferred constructs or variables with any criterion measure. A clinician may say, "I expect to find cases of psychosomatic ulcer showing large discrepancies between latent Succorance [need] as inferred from TAT stories and manifest Succorance [need] as revealed by the score on a questionnaire." Such a declaration leads to an empirical test.

The correlation or measure of discrimination obtained in studying construct validity is not to be taken as the "validity coefficient," in the same sense that prediction of washouts during flight training is *the* validity coefficient for the battery employed. Studies of many such predictions, possibly involving quite independent components of theory, will in the mass confirm or disconfirm the claims made.

One tends to ask regarding construct validity just what *is* being validated—the test or the underlying hypothesis? The answer is, *both*, simultaneously. If one predicts an empirical relation by supposing a certain personality organization, the verification of this prediction tends to confirm both the component suppositions that gave rise to it. True, there might be plausible alternative hypotheses, but this is always the case in science. The more alternatives there are, the more cumulated evidence is needed to justify confidence in the particular test-hypothesis pair. A further characteristic of this type of validity inference is that the construct itself undergoes modification as evidence accumulates. We do not merely alter our confidence in the correctness of the construct, or in the estimates of its magnitudes, but we actually reformulate or clarify our characterization of its nature on the basis of new data.

It must be kept in mind that these four aspects of validity are not all discrete and that a complete presentation about a test may involve information about all types of validity. A first step in the preparation of a predictive instrument may be to consider what constructs or predictive dimensions are likely to give the best prediction. Examining content validity may also be an early step in producing a test whose predictive validity is ultimately of major concern. Even after satisfactory predictive validity has been established, information relative to construct validity may make the test more useful. To analyze construct validity, our total background of knowledge regarding validity would be brought to bear.

Development and Validation of Scales for Estimation of Suicidal Risk*

INTRODUCTION

Every day in numerous different settings suicidal persons are evaluated, judgments are made as to degree of suicide risk, and decisions are arrived at regarding what action, if any, should be taken. The sequence proceeds primarily at a clinical-intuitive level, reflecting the evaluator's perceptiveness, knowledge, and experience with persons in suicidal states.

Past efforts to develop formal scales to assist the clinician in this task have not been lacking [1-9] but their acceptance has been limited. The reluctance of the clinical community to adopt any of these instruments for general use is due to a number of reasons, not the least of which is the difficulty of demonstrating their validity. This in turn is understandable on the basis of inherent characteristics of the problem, such as (1) the vast number of unknown, undefined, and uncontrollable variables which contribute to outcome; (2) the relative infrequency of completed suicide, even in a known high-risk population; [10] (3) the limitations of using completed suicide as a validating criterion without regard for the effect of special interventive efforts necessarily directed toward high-risk subjects; [11] (4) the dif-

*This project was supported by Grant Nos. MH-16524 and MH-25080 from the Mental Health Services Development Branch of the National Institute of Mental Health. The assistance of Alan T. Bostrom, Ph.D., Linda W. Kwok, M.A., and Robert J. Jannerone, B.A. is also acknowledged with gratitude.

169

ferences in scales applicable to age, sex, racial, cultural, and various situation specific subgroups in the population;[8,12,13] and (5) the need for large samples, prospective design, control groups, and lengthy followup periods to explore a wide range of potential variables as well as to obtain a sufficiently large number of suicidal outcomes to statistically analyze their characteristics.[12] Attempts to deal with these obstacles to the development and validation of useful assessment instruments have led to a number of studies which reflect awareness of the problems but have been unable to avoid the handicap of an excessive proportion of high risk ratings,[3,5] or have depended on retrospective data with the attendant questions raised by obtaining information from records rather than subjects.[6]

In an effort to systematically avoid the recognized limitations of studies devised to generate and validate suicide risk scales, a project was undertaken in 1969 having as one of its goals the construction of such scales using a prospective design, relatively large samples, a wide range of variables, and enough follow-up time to provide sufficient completed suicides from the sample to permit meaningful statistical analysis for both identification of discriminating variables and for subsequent validation. The present discussion is a report of this project and the results of the initial validation procedures. The opportunity is taken to discuss some broader questions raised by validation efforts, including both statistical considerations and clinical limitations of a validation process with regard to estimation of suicide risk. It is important to emphasize that we cannot determine whether a given individual will or will not commit suicide. Rather, each person represents a given degree of risk that such an event will occur, according to his identified characteristics. Thus validation requires enough people at a given level of estimated risk to allow observation of their rate of suicide. We take the position that if this rate is in accord with the estimated risk the estimating instrument has done its job regardless of individual outcomes.

METHOD

The Sample

Subjects were defined as those persons seen on the inpatient services of 9 mental health facilities in San Francisco and whose admission was due primarily to a depressive state or a suicidal state (suicide was attempted, threatened, or contemplated). These are known to be high-risk populations for subsequent suicide with a rate of at least 1,000 per 100,000 annually. Each subject was thoroughly evaluated in a 1-hour to 3-hour interview, during which information was obtained regarding 162 demographic, social, and psychological characteristics (see Appendix A). These characteristics were comprised of those previously identified by workers in the field as indicative of high risk, supplemented by a number of refinements of those indicators and some intuitive hunches of the investigators. Two distinct time periods were considered, the first reflecting the person's status on admission and the second reflecting the circumstances at the time of discharge. The data were coded and punched on cards for analysis.

A systematic search of the California State Death Registry identified those subjects who died in that state and California residents who died in other states after entry into the study. Information from death certificates, family members, coroners' records, and clinical sources then permitted determination as to which of these were suicidal deaths.

The Index Set

The index set was comprised of (a) all subjects known to have committed suicide as of August 1, 1972 (40 men, 42 women) and (b) all subjects not known to have committed suicide by that date and who had been discharged from the in-patient setting, i.e., had been at risk to suicide, for a period of at least one year (487 men, 671 women). Non-suicidal deaths which occurred less than one year after discharge were excluded.

Development of Estimators of Suicide Risk

For this preliminary study we defined risk of suicide as the probability of suicide with time after evaluation not specified. On the assumption that risk factors would be strongly influenced by the sex of the person, data from male and female subjects were considered separately. Depression and resources subscales were generated from the variables included in the sections Present Depressive State and Resources (Appendix A) respectively, separately for each sex. Each subscale was generated as a linear logistic function estimator of the risk of suicide. The variables were also considered individually. Our goal was to generate two versions of a suicide risk estimator for each sex: the linear logistic function (LLF)—expected to be most accurate, and the linear discriminant function (LDF)—expected to be less costly to produce. These methods are considered further in the discussion of statistical methods below, and described and

compared in detail in Appendix B. It was felt that about 25 variables
was the maximum number a scale could include for clinical use, though
we wished to consider about 150 individual variables. It also seemed
desirable to consider appropriately defined products of pairs of
variables on the chance that such combinations might be better
discriminators of risk than the individual variables.[2,12]

The final strategy for selection of variables was determined largely
by considerations of cost and other properties of the computer programs
we planned to use for generating the estimators: BMDO7M[14] for
the LDF and DQUANT* for the LLF. Variables were selected
separately for each sex, in a three phase procedure. In Phase 1,
variables were defined and selected which, individually, were good
discriminators between suicides and non-suicides by statistical tests.
The criteria used depended on the measurement scale of the variables
considered.† Also, some variables were selected by clinical judgement,
including the depression and resources subscales and four dichotomous
variables based on age (<20 other; 20–39 other; 40–59 other; ≥ 60
other). These were not significant discriminators by the statistical
criteria. In addition a modest number of variables which had been
significant discriminators in combination with other variables in an
earlier study of project data was included.[16]

For Phase 2, all variables selected in Phase 1 were recoded,
if necessary, to have nonnegative values, with larger values indicating

*DQUANT was produced at the Office of Information Systems, University of
California, San Francisco. It is a substantially modified version of the QUANTR
program (Program Number MS/F7/1, author D. Clayton, Department of Medical
Statistics and Epidemiology, London School of Hygiene and Tropical Medicine), a
successor to the linear logistic regression program described by Armitage et al.[15]

†(i) Dichotomous variables—Fisher's exact test (see below) on the two way
classification of subjects by the given variable and outcome (suicide, non-suicide).
Variable selected if the one-tailed significance value $P \leq 0.05$; (ii) categorical variables
(with unordered categories) and ordinal variables—Fisher's exact test on each of the
dichotomous variables defined by a given category versus all other categories. For
ordinal variables, selected high-risk categories, i.e. having a higher than average
percentage of suicides were tested in combination with adjacent high-risk categories.
The dichotomy defined by this combination versus all other categories was selected
if it was clinically reasonable and $P \leq 0.05$; (iii) ordinal and interval scale variables—Wil-
coxon two-sample test comparing suicide and non-suicide groups; variable selected
if two-tailed $P \leq 0.1$. For Fisher's exact test, hypergeometric distribution P values
were generated by a computer program for specified values of N (total number of
cases) and n (number of suicides). A two way table of upper tail P-values was produced,
indexed by k (number in category) and x (number of suicides in category). For the
small number of variables with $k > 200$ or $x > 20$, the chi-square test was used
instead.

higher risk. Dichotomous variables were scored 1 on the high-risk category and 0 otherwise; the depression and resources subscales were each made integer with range 0–100. For each variable selected in Phase 1 for a given sex, stepwise linear discriminant analysis was used to determine the best four variables* in a set consisting of the given variable, its square, and its product with each of the other selected variables. A Phase 2 selection was then made from these best variables for consideration in Phase 3. As the specifications of these criteria indicate, considerable attention was paid to the differing properties of purely dichotomous and non-dichotomous variables.†

In Phase 3, final selections of variables were made using each of the two estimation methods, linear-logistic and linear-discriminant analysis. First the variables selected in Phase 2 for each sex were graded as either *must have* or *indifferent* in terms of clinical judgment of their importance as indicators of suicide risk. In refining the LLF and LDF estimators, variables were deleted one at a time. The deletion process, which utilized only statistical criteria,§ was carried out first

---

*These were the first four variables to enter the discriminant function in the stepwise selection using the largest F-to-enter criterion. For economy, the maximum number of steps was set at 4.

†On the collection of best variables from the separate discriminant analyses, the selection criteria were approximately: (i) all dichotomous variables with F-to-enter ≥ 15 and Fisher exact test significance $P \leq 0.001$ were selected. (Initially all variables with F-to-enter ≥ 15 were selected. For dichotomous variables, this was found to correspond roughly to $P \leq 0.001$ for the Fisher exact test); (ii) all non-dichotomous variables with F-to-enter ≥ 9 were selected. ($F = 9$ on 1 and infinite degrees of freedom corresponds roughly to one-tailed $P = 0.001$); (iii) variables with standard deviation of 0 in either group were excluded from the discriminant analyses. Dichotomous variables with 0 s.d. in the non-suicide group were selected if the Fisher exact $P \leq 0.001$; (iv) non-dichotomous variables arising as the product of a dichotomous variable (D) and a non-dichotomous variable (N) were selected only if the mean of N on subjects with variable D having value 1 was greater in the suicide group than in the non-suicide group; (v) in the set of variables selected by criteria i—iv the dichotomous and non-dichotomous variables were separately reanalyzed by discriminant analysis. The final selection included all variables in order of entry until F-to-enter dropped substantially below 1.

§LDF: after each BMDO7M run we deleted the variable with smalletst F-to-remove <0.25. For the final LDF estimator the prior probability of being from the suicide population was estimated by the proportion of suicides in the index set. LLF: after each DQUANT run we identified the variable with smallest absolute t value <0.5 (t = ratio of estimated coefficient to its estimated asymptotic standard error). The next run was started at final coefficient values of the first run with the identified variable not included. The identified variable was deleted if the decrease in due to regression chi-squares from the first run to the second was <0.25. Otherwise the procedure was repeated with the variable having next smallest absolute t in the first run.

considering only the *indifferent* variables as candidates for deletion and then the *must have* variables. This intentionally biased the selection procedure in favor of variables judged to be clinically important without sacrificing the principle that only those variables which demonstrated some statistical importance should be retained.

Assessment of goodness of Fit

Agreement of estimated and true probabilities of suicide was indirectly assessed by the method of Truett et al.[17] For each estimator of suicide risk, index set subjects were grouped into deciles of estimated risk (lowest 10 percent, next lowest 10 percent, etc.). In each of the 10 decile groups we determined the number of suicides and the sum of estimated risks—an estimate of the number of suicides expected under the fitted model. Observed and estimated numbers of suicides were also computed on other partitions of the sample as defined by categorical variables.

Validation

The purpose of validation was to obtain indications of the performance to be expected if these estimators of suicide risk were used on new presenting subjects from the same population. Primarily, performance was assessed in terms of classification of sample subjects with respect to suicide risk. Subjects were classified as high-risk if their estimated risk exceeded a criterion value of 0.5; those with values less than 0.5 were classified as not-high-risk. Other criterion values were also utilized.

As the index and validation sets were expected to differ in some respects, efforts were made to obtain valid estimates of performance through reuse of the index set. The Lachenbruch[18] procedure* was utilized to obtain estimates of the population probabilities of classification as high-risk for suicides and non-suicides for both the linear and quadratic discriminant functions (computed on the final sets of variables selected by the LDF). In this procedure for each subject in a sample, an estimation function computed on the data with that subject omitted was used to classify that one subject. The corresponding estimated probabilities of suicide from these modified discriminant functions were saved for further analysis.

It was not possible to utilize this general approach with the LLF

---

*Program obtained through the courtesy of Professor Peter Lachenbruch, University of North Carolina at Chapel Hill. For the linear discriminant function, this procedure is now available in another program, BMDP7M.[19]

because of cost. Instead, an analogous procedure was implemented in which the sample for each sex was randomly divided into 5 equal parts, each of which was omitted in turn and then classified by a linear logistic function computed on the other parts. Each of the 5 parts had the same numbers of suicides and non-suicides.

The Validation Set

Other validation efforts utilized an independent validation set of subjects. This was comprised of (a) all subjects known to have committed suicide as of August 1, 1974 and who were not included in the index set (28 men, 22 women) and (b) all subjects not reported to have committed suicide and who were at risk for at least one year and were not included in the index set (460 men, 587 women). Non-suicidal deaths which occurred less than one year after discharge were excluded. On this validation set we obtained classification results for the final LDF and LLF estimators generated on the index set. Some distributional comparisons with the index set were also made.

RESULTS

The variables included in the LDF and LLF estimators for males and females are shown in Tables 5-1 and 5-2. All of the variables selected are products except the variable—number of children in sibship—used in the estimator for females. The component variables of these products are either dichotomous, with the categories indicated in parentheses coded as 1 and all other categories coded as 0, or interval scale, with no parenthetical information.

The assessment of goodness of fit is presented in Tables 5-3 and 5-4, which show the observed and estimated numbers of suicides for each decile of estimated risk. For both males and females the fit of the LLF appeared to be good. The exact agreement between total suicides observed and total estimated by the linear logistic model is a constraint of the estimation method. Relative to the LLF, the LDF was markedly less satisfactory in fit tending to overestimate risk in the highest decile while underestimating in the first 9 deciles and in total suicides. Note that for the LLF, the decile of highest estimated risk included three-fourths of the observed suicides in the male sample and two-thirds in the female sample. The LDF was less satisfactory in this also.

Goodness of fit was also assessed by stratifying the index sets on several variables and comparing the observed and estimated

Table 5-1
Variables Entering into Estimation Functions for Males

1. Depression scale x race (Caucasian)
2. Depression scale x ability to relate to others*
3. Depression scale x resource scale†
4. Depression scale x present state of health as seen by subject (fair or poor)
5. Homosexuality (yes, but inactive or ideation only) x present state of health as seen by subject (fair or poor)
6. Homosexuality (yes, but inactive or ideation only) x resource scale
7. Homosexuality (yes, but inactive or ideation only) x age
8. Homosexuality (yes, but inactive or ideation only) x euphoria (moderate or severe)
9. Euphoria (moderate or severe) x verbal expression of anger (none)
10. Availability of method contemplated relative to present admission (method at hand) x job skills (high)
11. Availability of method contemplated relative to present admission (method at hand) x ability to relate to others
12. Availability of method contemplated relative to present admission (method at hand) x drug addiction or abuse (sporadic abuse)
13. Availability of method contemplated relative to present admission x age (40–59)
14. Degree of psychosis (moderate) x attitude toward interviewer (mixed or negative)
15. Degree of psychosis (moderate) x feelings of being a burden to others (yes)
16. Whom discharged to (other than self, friend, or family) x ideas of persecution or reference
17. Whom discharged to (other than self, friend, or family) x attitude toward suicide prevention center (would not call)
18. Guilt–shame–remorse (none) x ideas of persecution or reference
19. Discharge plan followed one month after discharge (no, but for reason other than patient leaving on own or staff initiative or patient readmitted) x suicidal impulses (severe)
20. Discharge plan followed one month after discharge (no, but for reason other than patient leaving on own or staff initiative or patient readmitted) x readiness to accept help (low or refuses or resents idea)*
21. Special isolating factor (moderate or severe) x from broken home (yes, death of father)
22. Special isolating factor (moderate or severe) x seriousness of present suicide attempt or intent (unequivocal)
23. Alcohol abuse (sporadic abuse) x effect of present attempt on consciousness (acute brain syndrome non-ambulatory or comatose)

*Enters into linear discriminant function only.
†Enters into linear logistic function only.

176

Table 5-2
Variables Entering into Estimation Functions for
Females

1. Suicidal ideation at time of discharge (mild, moderate, or severe) x interviewer's overall reaction to subject
2. Suicidal ideation at time of discharge (mild, moderate, or severe) x suicidal thoughts
3. Suicidal ideation at time of discharge (mild, moderate, or severe) x guilt-shame-remorse
4. Suicidal ideation at time of discharge (mild, moderate, or severe) x race (Caucasian)
5. Prior suicidal ideas x despondency (none)
6. Suicidal ideation at time of discharge (mild, moderate, or severe) x employment status, present—during present illness (unemployed chronic)*
7. Physical health for past year (severe impairment or severe impairment, getting worse) x employment status, past—prior to present illness (not in labor market or employed irregularly)
8. Physical health for past year (severe impairment or severe impairment, getting worse) x birth rank order (first)
9. Physical health for past year (severe impairment or severe impairment, getting worse) x zone of residence (non-residential or no local address)
10. Physical health for past year (severe impairment or severe impairment, getting worse) x race (Negro)
11. Physical health for past year (severe impairment or severe impairment, getting worse) x marital status (divorced)
12. Physical health for past year (severe impairment or severe impairment, getting worse) x duration of US residence
13. Age x depression scale
14. Age x number of children in sibship
15. Age x drug addiction or abuse (sporadic abuse)
16. Age x results of prior efforts to obtain help (variable, generally unsatisfactory, or uniformly poor)
17. Age (40-59) x employment status, present—during present illness (unemployed chronic)
18. Age (40-59) x special isolating factor (moderate or severe)
19. Duration of San Francisco residence x employment status, present— during present illness (unemployed chronic)*
20. Duration of San Francisco residence x employment status, past (not in labor market or employed irregularly)
21. Number of children in sibship
22. Despondency (none) x formal education, years*
23. Despondency (none) x prior suicide attempts
24. Prior suicide attempts x attitude toward discharge plan (no specific plan)

Table 5-2 (continued)
Variables Entering into Estimation Functions for
Females

25. Seriousness of present attempt or intent (ambivalence weighted toward suicide or unequivocal) x ideas of persecution or reference (moderate or severe)
26. Degree of psychosis (in past only, before present illness) x therapist or other known professional person available on discharge

*Enters into linear discriminant function only.

Table 5-3
Observed and Estimated Numbers of Suicides for Each
Decile of Estimated Risk of Suicide (males, index set)

Decile	n	Linear-logistic Function		Linear-discriminant Function	
		Observed	Estimated	Observed	Estimated
1	52	0	0.098	0	.002
2	53	0	0.164	0	.003
3	53	0	0.287	0	.005
4	53	0	0.450	0	.007
5	53	1	0.627	2	.009
6	53	2	0.886	0	.012
7	53	1	1.24	2	.019
8	53	3	2.08	2	.040
9	52	3	5.39	5	.297
10	52	30	28.8	29	32.3
	527	40	40	40	32.7

Table 5-4
Observed and Estimated Numbers of Suicides for Each
Decile of Estimated Risk of Suicide (females, index set)

Decile	n	Linear-logistic Function		Linear-discriminant Function	
		Observed	Estimated	Observed	Estimated
1	71	1	0.145	1	0.006
2	71	0	0.360	0	0.013
3	71	2	0.553	0	0.018
4	72	0	0.725	3	0.024
5	72	2	0.903	1	0.033
6	72	0	1.16	0	0.046
7	71	1	1.59	1	0.068
8	71	2	2.41	4	0.17
9	71	6	5.52	8	0.91
10	71	28	28.6	24	35.0
	713	42	42	42	36.3

Table 5-5
Classification of Suicides and Non-Suicides According to
Estimated Risk Exceeding 0.5 (index set)

Estimator		Males (40 Suicides, 487 Non-suicides)		Females (42 Suicides, 672 Non-suicides)	
		Classification		*Classification*	
		Not-high-risk	High-risk	Not-high-risk	High-risk
LDF	Non-suicides	98%	2%	98%	2%
	Suicides	48	52	52	48
LDF1	Non-suicides	97	3	97	3
	Suicides	55	45	62	38
LLF	Non-suicides	99	1	100	0
	Suicides	48	52	60	40

numbers of suicides within each stratum. These comparisons were made using age (<20, 20–39, 40–59, ≥59), suicidal state category (attempter, contemplator, non-contemplator), chronicity (acute, chronic, not applicable), and age by chronicity as stratifying variables. The agreement between observed and predicted numbers of suicides again appeared to be good for the LLF and, except for a consistent underestimation of the number of suicides, equally good for the LDF.

In our efforts to validate reusing the index set, the application of Lachenbruch's [18] procedure to the quadratic discrimination function* and the analog of the Lachenbruch procedure for the LLF were both unsuccessful. In each instance the small number of suicides in each index set was a source of difficulty. For the LLF, some of the 5 functions computed for each index set were extremely deviant as the omission of one-fifth of the suicides was sometimes sufficient to drastically alter the resulting function.

Classification results based on estimated risks from the linear logistic, linear discriminant, and modified linear discriminant functions are given in Table 5-5. Here, index set subjects were classified as high-risk if their estimated risk of suicide exceeded 0.5. These results show that approximately one-half of the suicides had estimated risks of suicide greater than 0.5. By lowering the criterion used to classify

---

*The quadratic discrimination function required the covariance structure of the independent variables to be estimated separately for suicides and non-suicides and the relatively small numbers of suicides and the dichotomous nature of many of the independent variables resulted in singular covariance matrices.

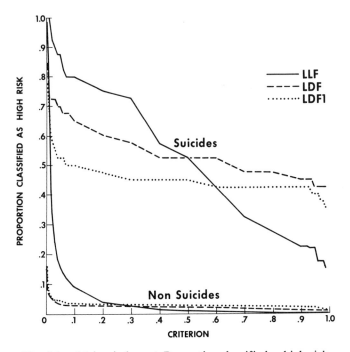

Fig. 5-1.   Males, index set. Proportion classified as high-risk
versus criterion used for high-risk classification. Proportions
are shown separately for suicides and non-suicides for the
linear-discriminant (LDF), linear-logistic (LLF) and modified linear-discriminant (LDF1) functions.

a subject as high-risk, more of the suicides could be classified as
high-risk at the expense of also including a greater number of the
non-suicides. The extent of this trade-off for different choices of
the criterion value is seen in Figures 5-1 and 5-2. These figures show
the proportion of subjects classified as high-risk (ordinate) as a function
of the criterion used (abscissa). Separate plots are shown for the
suicides and non-suicides for each of the predictors studied. The
best discrimination between the suicides and non-suicides resulted
from using the LLF and a criterion in the range from 0.05 to 0.3.
For the males, this resulted in classifying approximately 70 percent–80
percent of the suicides and 16 percent of the non-suicides as high-risk.
We assume these assessments to be overly optimistic.[20,21] More
conservatively, the modified linear discriminant functions (denoted
by LDF1) with a criterion of 0.1 classified 50 percent of the suicides

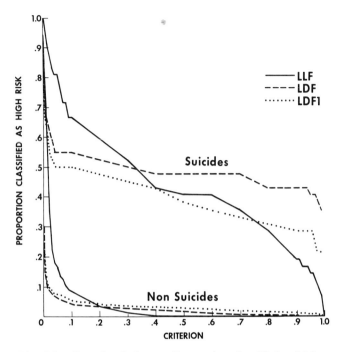

Fig. 5-2. Females, index set. Proportion classified as high-risk versus criterion used for high-risk classification. Proportions are shown separately for suicides and non-suicides for the linear-discriminant (LDF), linear-logistic (LLF) and modified linear-discriminant (LDF1) functions.

and 4 percent of the non-suicides as high-risk. The corresponding figures from the modified linear discriminant functions for the females were almost identical.

Means and standard deviations of LLF, LDF, and LDF1 estimates of suicide risk for suicides and non-suicides separately are shown in Table 5-6. Also shown is a statistic,* denoted $P_{S>NS}$, which estimates the probability that the estimated risk for a suicide will be larger than the estimated risk for a non-suicide in the population sampled. For example, for 93 percent of the 19,480 (40 × 487) male suicide/non-suicide pairings the estimated risk of suicide for the suicide subject

*This is the Mann-Whitney form of the rank sum statistic divided by the product of the sample sizes.[22]

Table 5-6
Comparisons of Estimated Risks for Suicides and Non-suicides (index set)

	Linear Logistic Function		Linear Discriminant Function		Modified Linear Discriminant Functions	
	Suicides	*Non-suicides*	*Suicides*	*Non-suicides*	*Suicides*	*Non-suicides*
Males						
Sample size	40	487	40	487	40	487
Mean risk	.51	.04	.54	.02	.45	.03
Standard deviation	.35	.10	.46	.13	.48	.16
$P_{S>NS}$	.93		.93		.93	
	Suicides	*Non-suicides*	*Suicides*	*Non-suicides*	*Suicides*	*Non-suicides*
Females						
Sample size	42	671	42	671	42	671
Mean risk	.44	.03	.48	.02	.39	.04
Standard deviation	.38	.07	.48	.11	.44	.15
$P_{S>NS}$	.88		.87		.82	

exceeded the estimated risk for the non-suicide for both the LLF and LDF.

Systematic differences between the populations from which the index and validation sets of subjects are sampled can be expected to reduce the performance of estimators on the validation set. For this reason comparisons were made between the index and validation sets on several variables, separately for each sex. The comparisons were made separately for suicides and non-suicides since discrepancies which would appear insignificant when comparing the total samples might be quite significant if a high proportion of the discrepant subjects were suicides. Chi-square tests of homogeneity of the index and validation set populations with respect to age, suicidal state category, chronicity, clinic where the subject was seen, and years at risk to suicide were carried out. Table 5-7 summarizes the findings from these tests. The two-way tables which generated the chi-square statistics with significance probabilities less than 0.05 are shown in Table 5-8(A–D).

The performance of the LDF and LLF estimators in estimating risk for validation set subjects was assessed using the procedures previously discussed. The validation set classification results are shown in Table 5-9. These can be compared with the index set results in Table 5-5.

Figures 5-3 and 5-4 show the results of using a classification criterion other than 0.5. For females, the best discrimination between suicides and non-suicides was obtained from the LLF and a criterion of 0.1, with approximately 32 percent of the suicides and 16 percent of the non-suicides being classified as high-risk. For the males a criterion of 0.04 yielded maximum discrimination with the LLF then classifying 60 percent of the suicides and 42 percent of the non-suicides as high-risk.

Table 5-10 compares the estimated risks for suicides and non-suicides in the validation sets. In all cases the mean estimated risks for suicides exceeded those for non-suicides, as expected. The differences, however, were not large. The measure $P_{S>NS}$ also indicated that the distribution of estimated risks for suicides was only slightly above the distribution for non-suicides.

DISCUSSION

For a suicide risk assessment scale which is to be scored by hand, the limit of complexity may be addition of scores of perhaps two digits for a one-page list of variables, each of which has no

Table 5-7
Results of CHI-Square Comparisons of Index and Validation Sets

	Suicides			Non-suicides		
	Chi-square	df*	Significance probability	Chi-square	df*	Significance probability
Males						
Age group	1.30	3	.73	1.75	3	.63
Suicidal state category	8.55	2	.014	11.66	2	.003
Chronicity	1.44	2	.49	16.05	2	<.001
Clinic	12.48	4	.014	138.72	6	<.001
Years at risk	6.52	3	.09	133.27	3	<.001
Females						
Age group	.15	2	.93	5.10	3	.16
Suicidal state category	.50	2	.78	27.38	2	<.001
Chronicity	.64	2	.73	2.25	2	.32
Clinic	10.17	4	.037	135.53	6	<.001
Years at risk	4.24	3	.24	144.03	3	<.001

*df = degrees of freedom

Table 5-8(A)
Data Set x Suicidal State Category

	Suicidal State Category		
	Attempter	*Contemplater*	*Non-contemplater*
Male Suicides			
Index set	18	18	4
Validation set	22	6	0
Male non-suicides			
Index set	266	173	48
Validation set	221	210	29
Female non-suicides			
Index set	369	193	109
Validation set	299	237	51

Table 5-8(B)
Data Set x Chronicity

	Chronicity		
	Acute	*Chronic*	*Not Applicable*
Male non-suicides			
Index set	214	248	25
Validation set	260	187	13

Table 5-8(C)
Data Set x Clinic

	Clinic Number*				
	One	*Two*	*Three and four*	*Five*	*Six and other*
Male suicides					
Index set	12	7	8	5	8
Validation set	2	7	3	1	15
Female suicides					
Index set	10	16	6	6	4
Validation set	2	4	2	7	7
Male non-suicides					
Index set	181	103	32	75	62	34
Validation set	66	97	69	23	102	103
Female non-suicides					
Index set	183	197	53	70	127	41
Validation set	56	187	73	13	153	105

*Clinic numbers—One-five are Community Mental Health Centers; six is San Francisco General Hospital.

Table 5-8(D)
Data Set x Years at Risk

	Years at Risk			
	1–2	2–3	3–4	4–5
Male non-suicides				
Index set	246	151	52	38
Validation set	186	274	0	0
Female non-suicides				
Index set	359	219	59	34
Validation set	236	351	0	0

Table 5-9
Classification of Suicides and Non-suicides According to
Estimated Risk Exceeding 0.5 (validation set)

		Males (28 Suicides, 460 non-suicides)		Females (22 Suicides, 587 non-suicides)	
		Classification		*Classification*	
		Not-high-risk	High-risk	Not-high-risk	High-risk
Estimator					
LDF	Non-suicides	86%	14%	94%	6%
	Suicides	82	18	91	9
LLF	Non-suicides	91	9	96	4
	Suicides	82	18	91	9

Table 5-10
Comparisons of Estimated Risks for Suicides and
Non-suicides (validation set)

	Linear-Logistic Function		Linear-Discriminant Function	
	Suicides	*Non-suicides*	*Suicides*	*Non-suicides*
Males				
Sample size	28	460	28	460
Mean risk	.17	.12	.18	.14
Standard deviation	.28	.21	.39	.34
$P_{S>NS}$	.56		.54	
Females				
Sample size	22	587	22	587
Mean risk	.19	.08	.10	.07
Standard deviation	.21	.15	.25	.21
$P_{S>NS}$	.58		.64	

186

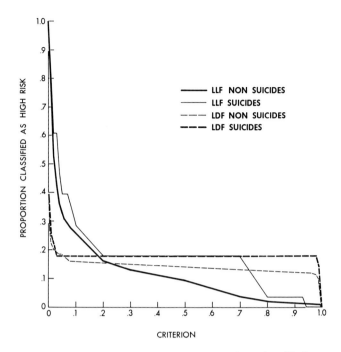

Fig. 5-3. Males, validation set. Proportion classified as high-risk versus criterion used for high-risk classification. Proportions are shown separately for suicides and non-suicides for the linear-discriminant (LDF) and linear-logistic (LLF) functions.

more than 3 or 4 possible scores.[7] This kind of reduction must be made for any scale intended for emergency use. Of the variables incorporated in the final estimators from this study (Tables 5-1 and 5-2), only the depression and resources subscales, each of which includes some 20 items, seem to be excluded from such applications. However, the discriminatory power of these subscales, in combination with other variables, suggests that they may be of use in other settings.

Variables which are products of dichotomous and interval scale variables are difficult to interpret and probably would not be included in any applied scale. In part, products involving a dichotomous variable were considered in this study as a simple way of obtaining suggestions from the Phase 2 variable selection process as to useful partitions of the sample for future studies.

This study afforded a somewhat limited test of the relative efficacy

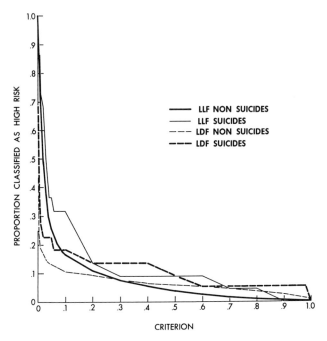

Fig. 5-4.   Females, validation set. Proportion classified as high-risk versus criterion used for high-risk classification. Proportions are shown separately for suicides and non-suicides for the linear-discriminant (LDF) and linear-logistic (LLF) functions.

of linear-logistic and linear-discriminant analysis as methods of scale generation, insofar as the latter was used for much of the variable selection process. Nevertheless, in spite of including fewer variables in the final version, the LLF achieved strikingly better results than the LDF in goodness of fit on groupings by estimated risk and slightly better indications with respect to expected performance on new subjects. We conclude that, for estimation of suicide risk, the linear-logistic function is worth the added expense of its application.

With respect to validation, we are faced with quite contrary indications of performance of the final estimators on the index and validation sets. Indications of performance which were obtained by applying the LLF and LDF estimators to the index set on which they were fitted were expected to be unrealistically favorable and were presented only to make that point. The Lachenbruch procedure which provided the LDF1 or modified LDF estimates of risk was designed to remove this favorable bias with respect to the expected performance of the LDF. However, we strongly suspect (on hindsight) that, because the index set was used for selection of variables as well as for fitting of the estimation model, the estimates of performance based on the Lachenbruch procedure are also favorably biased. Therefore, it appears that the performance on the validation set is the most reliable evidence at hand.

We of course cannot know the true risks of suicide which our full range of variables potentially define and hence can only surmise that it should be possible to achieve estimates of risk which have widely separated distributions for those who committed suicide and those who did not. Nevertheless, the weak separation which the final LLF and LDF estimators achieved on the validation set is difficult to accept as representing the true potential of these data. Although there is evidence of systematic differences between index and validation sets, the magnitude of any effects of this is impossible to assess. Such differences are primarily the result of evolution of institutions and social patterns. For increasing precision in our future efforts, we look principally to two areas—the variable selection process and the determination of the separate subpopulations of high-risk subjects for which risk scales are to be developed.

Some work on the definition of such subpopulations has been carried out by other investigators. Lettieri[7] derived special scales for age and sex specific groups from a sample of callers to the Los Angeles Suicide Prevention Center. Thus older (>39) men, older women, younger men, and younger women each have a specific set of variables for determination of high, moderate, or low risk. This clinically useful approach is further enhanced by a long and a short form for each scale, providing for those circumstances when only limited information can be obtained. However, no validation data have as yet been published. Wold[13] also pursued the definition of specific clinical subgroups using Suicide Prevention Center callers for a data base. In a somewhat impressionistic form, he has defined 6 basic clinical models for situation-specific recognition and has developed the concept of stratifying subjects as to age, sex, and chronicity of the suicidal state. Farberow and McKinnon[6] have reported validation of a scale for Veterans Administration in-patients with a prior history of hospitalization and Braucht and Wilson[5] have reported encouraging results with a scale designed for a Community Mental Health Center population. Though still in an early stage of study, these efforts to define specific subtypes of suicidal persons appear to point the way toward the most promising application of the statistical approach.

The idea of applying specific scales to discrete clinical subgroups is not a recent concept. Brown and Sheran[12] point out that many students of suicide over the past 75 years have recognized the need for this but that little suicide research has been based on this premise. The recent review of mathematical models for prediction of suicide risk by Litman[8] similarly concludes that suicide is too complex a phenomenon to be dealt with by any general or unitary scale or testing device and that "presumably the best prediction results from using scales consisting of different combinations of signs or cues that are found to be appropriate for each specific setting." These are the instruments that remain to be generated.

A practical problem of course, as Brown and Sheran point out, is that by defining limited subgroups to improve discrimination, the number of subsequent suicides available for validation is reduced, hence the size of the initial sample or the length of followup must be increased. Thus Lettieri,[7] simply by dividing his sample into 4 age-sex specific groups, was obliged to derive his estimation variable using data from 11 suicides in each group of women and from 13 and 17 suicides for his male groups. Adding 1 or 2 more screening variables would probably have strained his total of 52 suicides beyond its potential to yield statistically useful information.

It also seems clear that efforts to overcome this problem must accept the burden of a very large initial sample. Perseverance in followup will then provide an increasing number of subsequent suicides in a reasonable period of years for further validation or for reworking the data but a modest initial sample cannot provide this regardless of how long one studies it. Whether our total overall sample of 3,006 will eventually serve this purpose is yet to be seen.

An important issue, mentioned above, is the arbitrariness of the cut-off point for a high-risk classification. Some flexibility in this would be desirable, since with a small total caseload a larger proportion of high-risk persons can be managed. This would permit facilities or individual therapists to adapt the scale to their particular resources.

It appears that use of a wide range of variables for a relatively undifferentiated high-risk group may, contrary to expectations, reduce the success of validation efforts. The number of variables, including a number of low-frequency characteristics, permits so accurate a characterization of the suicides in the index set that the estimator may tend to assign low estimated risks to the validation set suicides, due to their chance variations from that precise characterization. The subjects comprising our sample come from a number of different settings, which may have exaggerated this problem.

An influence on validation is also exerted by the nature of the not-high-risk population. By using a sample made up entirely of known suicidal subjects, as was done here, differentiating between high-risk and not-high-risk is necessarily much less precise than discriminating between known high-risk and known non-suicidal persons, as in the Farberow and McKinnon[6] and the Miskimins and Wilson[4] studies. We feel that the most pressing clinical task is the delineating of degrees of a spectrum of risk rather than separating suicidal from non-suicidal.

A further consideration is that over the prolonged periods of time required for followup, changes occur in such variables as availability of specialized treatment programs, necessitating subsequent incorporation of variables that were not in evidence at the outset. We have found, for example, that high-risk persons discharged to an out-patient group therapy program geared specifically to their needs have a much lower rate of subsequent suicide than when discharged to traditional treatment programs.[23] Yet this special resource was not forseeable nor its influence considered in our preliminary period of scale construction.

The same issue arises in regard to the limited generality of discriminating variables.[12] For example, our findings can only be considered as applicable to persons admitted to an in-patient psychiatric setting by reason of a depressive or suicidal state. This is further complicated by the fact that the criteria for admission vary in different facilities and over a period of years they vary as a function of trends and policies in the mental health field.

Litman[8] calls for a two-stage process in which a general screening scale applied to a group in the general population would aim to identify the upper-2 percent in lethality and a second clinical scale would then be used for a guide to treatment and prognosis. We suggest that the upper-2 percent is now visible as Litman has already described, such as suicide prevention center callers, suicide attempters, or severely depressed persons. The instruments needed in a two-stage process are those which will characterize the person as to the situation-specific model that is represented, e.g., a person aged 40–60 with a stable background who is experiencing severe disruption and progressive constriction of a previously effective coping pattern and provide a scale that will estimate the degree of suicide risk over the near, intermediate, and long term for this particular member of a known high-risk population. This should allow narrowing the group to be provided treatment to a manageable number, even though it may only include 40 percent–50 percent of those who would be expected statistically to subsequently commit suicide.

SUMMARY AND FUTURE PROSPECTS

Current developments in the generation and validation of scales to assess suicide risk reflect efforts designed explicitly to overcome the recognized limitations of prior efforts in this field. Specifically they involve starting with large, prospective, clearly-defined samples and a broad spectrum of variables; lengthy follow-up periods permitting the study of outcome regarding suicide with due consideration for independent samples and pertinent intervening variables (e.g., treatment provided); experimentation with statistical approaches and instruments not previously used for this purpose; continued reconceptualizing of the prediction process, especially the limitations inherent in predicting risk rather than outcome; and progressive refinement of populations from which scales are derived and applied (e.g., age-sex specific, degree of chronicity, clinical models). It is clear from the data presented that the advantages of relatively large sample size, prospective design, a wide range of variables, and rigorous statistical treatment do not by themselves overcome the obstacles to generating and validating an efficient scale for estimating suicide risk.

The future development of more accurate measuring devices for suicide risk appears to lie in the gradual and progressive refinement of subpopulations from which the instruments are generated and to which they are applied. Some investigators have already moved in this direction but as yet the sample sizes have not permitted going beyond specified age-sex subgroups and clinically derived situation-specific models. These are still incompletely defined and are now in the process of systematic development.

The goal envisioned for the general clinician is a two-stage process providing first for identification of the situation-specific subgroup. A set of primary items would define the overall characteristics of this group. The second stage would require application of a set of secondary items that would both provide an estimate of the degree of risk within that specific model and indicate guidelines for clinical management. In this period of rapidly advancing technology it is not too early to envision use of a central computer that quickly provides information of this kind to terminals located in clinical settings.

As the limits to our potential for assessing suicide risk are approached, investigative efforts can be more fully focused on the challenge of developing improved therapeutic programs. Whether more accurate measurement of risk will reduce the occurrence of unnecessary and preventable suicides is still to be demonstrated. Yet that is the primary purpose of these investigative efforts and the goal that must eventually be served.

REFERENCES

1. Dean RA, Miskimins W, DeCook R, Wilson LT, Maley RF: Prediction of suicide in a psychiatric hospital. J Clin Psychiatry 23:296-301, 1967
2. Pöldinger W: Die Abschätzung der Suizidalität. Bern, Hans Huber, 1968, p 94
3. Tuckman J, Youngman W: A scale for assessing suicide risk of attempted suicides. J Clin Psychol 24:17-19, 1968
4. Miskimins R, Wilson L: The revised suicide potential scale. J Consult Clin Psychol 33:258, 1969
5. Braucht G, Wilson N: Predictive utility of the revised suicide potential scale. J Consult Clin Psychol 34:426, 1970
6. Farberow N, McKinnon D: Prediction of Suicide in Neuropsychiatric Hospital Patients, in Neuringer C (ed): The Psychological Assessment of Suicide Risk. Springfield, Illinois, Charles C Thomas, 1974
7. Lettieri D: Suicidal Death Prediction Scales, in Beck A, Resnik H, Lettieri D (eds): The Prediction of Suicide. Bowie, Maryland, Charles Press, 1974
8. Litman R: Models for Predicting Suicide Risk, in Neuringer C: The Psychological Assessment of Suicide Risk. Springfield, Illinois, Charles C Thomas, 1974
9. Zung W: Index of Potential Suicide, in Beck A, Resnik H, Lettieri D (eds): The Prediction of Suicide. Bowie, Maryland, Charles Press, 1974
10. Rosen A: Detection of suicidal patients. J Consult Clin Psychol 18:397-403, 1954
11. Neuringer C (ed): Psychological Assessment of Suicidal Risk. Springfield, Illinois, Charles C Thomas, 1974, p 12
12. Brown T, Sheran T: Suicide prediction: A review. Life-Threatening Behavior 2:67-98, 1972
13. Wold C: Subgroupings of suicidal people. Omega 2:19-29, 1971
14. Dixon W (ed): BMD Biomedical Computer Programs. Berkeley, Univ California Press, 1973
15. Armitage P, McPherson C, Copas J: Statistical studies of prognosis in advanced breast cancer. J Chronic Dis 22:343-360, 1969
16. Motto J: Refinement of Variables in Assessing Suicide Risk, in Beck A, Resnik H, Lettieri D (eds): The Prediction of Suicide. Bowie, Maryland, Charles Press, 1974
17. Truett J, Cornfield J, Kannel W: A multivariate analysis of the risk

of coronary heart disease in Framingham. J Chronic Dis 20:511-524, 1967

18. Lachenbruch P: An almost unbiased method of obtaining confidence intervals for the probability of misclassification in discriminant analysis. Biometrics 23:639-645, 1967

19. Dixon W (ed): BMDP biomedical computer programs. Berkeley, University of California Press, 1975

20. Weiner J, Dunn O: Elimination of variables in linear discriminant problems. Biometrics 22:268-275, 1966

21. Lachenbruch P, Mickey M: Estimation of error rates in discriminant analysis. Technometrics 10:1-10, 1968

22. Hollander M, Wolfe D: Nonparametric Statistical Methods. New York, Wiley, 1973

23. Billings J: The efficacy of group treatment with depressed and suicidal individuals in comparison with other treatment settings as regards the prevention of suicide. (PhD dissertation in clinical psychology, The California School of Professional Psychology, San Francisco), 1974

24. Cox D: Analysis of Binary Data. New York, Wiley, 1970

25. Halperin M, Blackwelder WC, Verter JI: Estimation of the multivariate logistic risk function: A comparison of the discriminant function and maximum likelihood approaches. J Chronic Dis 24:125-158, 1971

26. Mantel N: Synthetic retrospective studies and related topics. Biometrics 29:479-486, 1973

APPENDIX A

Data Coded for Each Subject

DEMOGRAPHIC DATA

Age
Sex
Race
Present marital status
Duration of present marital status
Number of living children
Age of youngest child
Number of times married
Number of times divorced
Birth rank order
Number of children in sibship
Age separation and gender of next older sibling
Age separation and gender of next younger sibling
Zone of residence (sociological category)
Type of residence
Number of moves in past 5 years
Duration of San Francisco residence
San Francisco residence lifelong?
Duration of California residence
California residence lifelong?
Duration US residence
US residence lifelong?

Country of acculturation
Present religious affiliation
Past religious affiliation
Formal education (years)
Occupation of subject
Occupation of subject's spouse
Last change in occupation
Present employment status
Past employment status
Owns own home?

SUICIDE ATTEMPT DATA
Method
Communication of intent
Help sought before attempt
Help sought after attempt
Suicide note left?
Seriousness (injury)
Seriousness (intent)
Effect of attempt on con-
sciousness
Attitude toward attempt

SUICIDAL THOUGHTS
Method contemplated
Availability of method contem-
plated
Preparation of contemplated at-
tempt
Action taken toward contemplat-
ed attempt
Termination behavior

**ROLE OF SUICIDE PREVEN-
TION CENTER**
Suicide prevention center called?
Number of calls to center
Duration of contact with center
Who called center?
Number of times seen by center
personnel
Perceived help from center
Attitude toward center

Referred to hospital by center?
Transportation to hospital arranged by center?

**CONSIDERATION OF FUTURE
SUICIDE ATTEMPT**
Method contemplated
Availability of method contem-
plated
Preparation of contemplated at-
tempt
Action taken toward contemplat-
ed attempt
Termination behavior

PRESENT LIFE SITUATION
Living arrangement
Acuteness of precipitating cir-
cumstances
Loss of significant person(s)
Threatened loss of significant
person(s)
Other significant loss
Other threatened loss
Subject to criminal prosecution?
Illigitimate children or preg-
nancy?
Alcohol abuse?
Drug addiction or abuse?
Homosexuality (overt)?
Special isolating factor
Present state of health
Other stress
Present occupation (lethality)

PAST LIFE SITUATION
From broken home?
Age when home broken
Emotional disorder in family:
relationship
Emotional disorder in family:
type of disorder
Suicide in family (number)

Suicide in family (relationship)
Prior psychiatric hospitaliza-
tion(s) (number)
Prior suicidal ideas
Prior suicide attempts (number)
Physical health for past year
Care required for physical illness
Prior efforts to obtain help
Results of prior efforts to obtain
help
Stability of job pattern
Stability of present marital rela-
tionship
Military record
Police record
Record of juvenile offences

PRESENT DEPRESSIVE STATE
Sleep
Appetite
Weight loss
Despondency
Euphoria
Crying
Loss of prior interests
Feelings of hopelessness
Guilt-shame-remorse
Apathy
Suicidal thoughts
Suicidal impulses
Acuteness of suicidal ideas
Feelings of confusion
Ideas of persecution
Fears of "losing mind," cancer,
or rare disease
Feelings of being a burden to
others
Intensity of feelings of anger
Verbal expression of anger
Motor expression of anger
Attitude toward hospitalization
Attitude toward interview

Diagnosis
Degree of psychosis
Readiness to accept help

RESOURCES
Other-person resource available
Financial resources
Ability to relate to others
Ability to relate to interviewer
Ability to communicate with
others
Ability to communicate with in-
terviewer
Overall stability of prior pattern
Capacity to control behavior
Motivation for help
Church as resource
Job available?
Living setting available?
Professional person available?
Eligible for public assistance?
Employability
Job skills
Intelligence
Capacity for self-scrutiny
Capacity for self-understanding
Interviewer's reaction to subject

**CIRCUMSTANCES OF DIS-
CHARGE**
Duration of hospital stay
Where discharged to
Whom discharged to
Attitude toward discharge plan
Discharge plan followed?
Suicidal ideation at discharge
Kind of hospital
Voluntary status?

SUPPLEMENTAL DATA
Change of life situation precipi-
tated by attempt
Stability of change

Twin?
Degree of present religious activity
Isolation or imprisonment
Lost parent figure replaced?
Age at which replaced
Suicidal behavior in family (number)
Suicidal behavior in family (rela-

tionship)
Anniversary phenomenon
Irritability
Somatic preoccupation
Death fantasies and dreams
Anxiety level
Biological crisis
Exhaustion of emotional resources

APPENDIX B

Theoretical Aspects of Estimation Methods

We have made use of two general statistical models for estimating risk of suicide, the linear-logistic function, and the linear-discriminant function. This section defines these models explicitly and discusses their suitability for estimating suicide risk.

Ideally, risk of suicide is defined as the probability that an individual (with given characteristics at the time of evaluation) will commit suicide within some fixed period of time after presenting himself for evaluation. This probability is the proportion of individuals who would commit suicide within that fixed period, among all those in the population being sampled who would present with the given characteristics. Let $X = (X_1, X_2,...,X_m)$ be the set of variables observed* at evaluation and let $x = (x_1,...,x_m)$ denote the particular values observed. Then any presumed relationship between the probability of suicide within the defined period and the characteristics of the presenting patient may be denoted by

$$P_x = f(\theta, x).$$

Here, P_x is the probability in question (labeled by the independent variable values x); f is some function; and θ is a sequence of population parameters, i.e., some numerical quantities which are assumed to have the same value for all individuals in the population of interest. By an estimator of the risk of suicide P_x we mean some particular

*In general, these variables may be products or other functions of directly observed variables. For the models considered here, the variables in principle should be dichotomous or interval scale.

choice of function f and values for its associated parameters θ. In practice, such estimators are obtained by assuming some convenient form for f then estimating θ for the population of interest from data on a sample of presenting individuals from that population. The data required are the values of the independent variables X and the suicide outcome variable Y, with value $y = 1$ if the individual committed suicide within the defined period after presenting, and $y = 0$ otherwise.

The simplest model relating P_x to x is the direct linear one,

$$P_x = \mu + \sum_{i=1}^{m} \beta_i x_i \tag{1}$$

where $\mu, \beta_1, ... \beta_m$ comprise the population parameters θ. This model may be fitted to the data by multiple linear regression* analysis of Y versus X. However, this approach has serious shortcomings for the estimation of probabilities, as discussed by Cox.[24] The validity of (1) is questionable as the right-hand side can have values outside the range 0–1 in which probabilities are defined. Most suicide risk probabilities are presumably on the order of 0.1 or less, so negative probabilities are a clear danger. Other objections concern the distribution† of Y and the reliability of standard statistical tests in linear regression analysis.

A linear function of the variables such as the right-hand side of (1) is relatively easy to compute, a virtue worth preserving when we consider applying estimation scales in emergency settings. Alternative models P_x can be defined by equating a linear function of the variables with some transformation of P_x which can take on any possible value. Cox[24] discusses several such transformations and concludes that the logistic is the most generally acceptable. We define the logistic transform or logit of P_x by

$$\lambda_x = \log \{P_x/(1 - P_x)\}$$

where log denotes natural logarithm. (If P_x is the probability of suicide, the quantity in brackets is the odds, hence the logit can also be called *log odds*.) The resulting linear-logistic model for P_x

---

*Equation (1) is a linear regression model for the expected value of Y, as the expected value of Y (given $X = x$) is P_x.

†The Statistical assumption of homogeneity of variance of Y is grossly violated for suicide data. Assuming conservatively that P_x is in the range of 0.001–0.1, there is approximately a 90-fold range in variance of Y.

$$\lambda_x = \mu + \sum_{i=1}^{m} \beta_i x_i \tag{2}$$

can be fitted to the data by maximum likelihood estimation. Estimated values for λ_x can be converted back to estimated values for P_x by use of the relationship

$$P_x = 1/\{1 + e^{-\lambda_x}\}$$

or the estimated λ_x can itself be thought of as an indicator of risk. Also, maximum likelihood estimation has an advantage over linear regression analysis in that only minimum assumptions* on Y are invoked; no distributional assumptions on X are made by either method.

Unfortunately, maximum likelihood estimation requires an iterative search for the best parameter values and therefore is usually far more costly than linear regression analysis, an important consideration when substantial numbers of variables and many data cases are to be studied. This led Truett et al.[17] to use of the linear-discriminant function for discriminating between two populations (in our context, the suicide and non-suicide subpopulations) to approximate the linear-logistic function.[2] The linear discriminant function is also a linear function of the independent variables, relatively quite inexpensive to compute (roughly as costly as linear regression analysis), and can be interpreted as a valid estimate of λ_x under certain conditions.† The conditions on X are quite restrictive and in particular are grossly violated if any of the variables are of the convenient "yes-no" (dichotomous) type. When these conditions are not met, the reliability of standard statistical tests in discriminant analysis is also questionable. Critical discussions of linear-discriminant versus linear-logistic functions as estimators have been given by Halperin et al.[25] and Mantel[26] among others. For suicide risk estimators employing dichotomous variables describing low-frequency characteristics, linear-logistic analysis should be considerably more accurate.

---

*The Y variables are assumed to be independent between subjects and, for each x, to have a common distribution.

†Under the standard assumptions for linear-discriminant analysis (X multivariate normal in each population with common covariance structure), the linear-discriminant function estimates the log posterior odds of being from the suicide population. If the prior probabilities are chosen to correspond the relative proportions of suicides and non-suicides in the population, then this log odds conceptually corresponds to λ_x.

PART III

Logical and Cognitive
Aspects of Suicide

Peter Tripodes

6
Reasoning Patterns in Suicide Notes

The introductory essay to this chapter is from E. von Domarus' paper The Specific Laws of Logic in Schizophrenia, *Language and Thought in Schizophrenia* (1944), J. S. Kasanin (ed). Appreciation is expressed to the University of California Press for permission to reproduce it.

When Dr. Kasanin invited me to speak before you he asked me to elaborate on the specific laws of logic in schizophrenia.

Because this topic involves an investigation of the question of whether or not psychiatric phenomena may be understood as deviations from the norm, or must be regarded as independent thereof, it seems to be of essential interest.

We shall proceed by investigating first the specific laws of logic in schizophrenia, and we shall then see what general aspects they may have for psychiatry. . . .

An elephant in a zoölogical garden, wishing to obtain a piece of sugar from a visitor, may be observed to go through the motions he would make had the piece of sugar already been obtained. He moves his trunk up and against the spectator, he plays with the snout as if grasping a piece of sugar, and he may move his trunk toward his mouth as if throwing a piece of sugar into it. All these motions are naturally understood as expressing the wish to obtain food from his visitors. . . .

A highly deteriorated schizophrenic patient who once spoke but had not done so for many years, ran her fingers through her hair when she saw an attendant, and the attendant correctly inferred from such an as-if motion that the patient thus expressed a wish to be combed. This schizophrenic patient, as did the mental defective, asked for food by going through the motions she would make if she had already obtained food. She pointed to it, put her fingers into her mouth, and licked them.

The significance of these and similar observations lies in the probable correctness of the assumption that the physical or mental defective phase of as-if expressions is ever so often repeated during the process of schizophrenic deterioration of thought and language, indicating that the thought and language of schizophrenics may be in the nature of an atavism.

With this idea in mind let us now turn to illustrations of so-called specifically schizophrenic disturbances of logic. . . .

Let us consider an illustration of this type of schizophrenic thinking. A schizophrenic patient of the Insane Asylum of the University in Bonn believed that Jesus, cigar boxes, and sex were identical. How did he arrive at that strange belief? Investigation revealed that the missing link for the connection between Jesus, cigar box, and sex was supplied by the idea of being encircled. In the opinion of this patient the head of Jesus, as of a saint, is encircled by a halo, the package of cigars by the tax band, and the woman by the sex glance of the man.

Apparently, our patient had the feeling that a saint, cigar package, and sexual life were identical; that is, the feelings which he experienced when he spoke of a saint, cigar package, or sex life were the same. Though an adult, mature person has never such a feeling of identity, it is to be noted that even for a normal person these so strangely unified objects have one particular in common. Were this not so, the schizophrenic could never be understood.

On the other hand, the difference between normal and schizophrenic thinking seems to be that, whereas for a normal person the particular of being encircled is only one of many accidentals, for the schizophrenic patient it is the quality expressing essence.

We are now prepared to discuss the illustrations of schizophrenic reasoning in respect to formal properties.

In its most precise form our logical thinking follows the so-called Mode of Barbara. If, in the figure, area A designates 'All men are mortal' and area B 'Socrates is a man,' then we conclude correctly that 'Socrates is mortal.'

From the figure it follows at once that the last statement yields no new knowledge. To the concept 'man' belongs by implication also the man Socrates, and hence, simply by definition, as it were, Socrates is mortal.

Experience shows that the conclusion is justified only if the major premise implicitly contains the minor premise. If thinking does not take this into consideration, we arrive at what seems to be contrary to, or other than, normal thinking, or to be paralogical.

An arbitrarily selected illustration, with the aid of the following figure, will elucidate the nature of paralogical thinking.

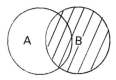

If A means 'Certain Indians are swift' and B means 'Stags are swift,' the area of intersection of A and B symbolizes the common element of swiftness.

It follows for the paralogical thinker that 'Certain Indians are stags,' and he will act as his conclusion directs him to do. A glance at the figure reveals a further, most important point. Because everything which lies outside the common intersection of A and B is irrelevant for the identification of A and B, the law of contradiction is excluded from paralogical thinking and its paragrammatical language.

Thus the above-mentioned patient asserted that a saint and a cigar box were identical because they were identified as surrounded. Neither the nature of the 'surroundings' nor that of the 'surrounded' made any difference in the conclusion drawn. The same mode of syllogistic reasoning also identified a saint and a cigar box with the male sex.

The difference between logical and paralogical thinking may be stated: whereas the logician accepts only the Mode of Barbara, or one of its modifications, as basis for valid conclusions, the paralogician concludes identity from the similar nature of adjectives. This idea might have been expressed by Vigotsky as follows: whereas the logician accepts identity only upon the basis of identical subjects, the paralogician accepts identity based upon identical predicates. In the logical example the identical concept was the subject man, and Socrates was mortal because he was a man. In the paralogical example concerning the identity of certain Indians and stags, the identification was made from what may be said about them, that is, from a common single predicate. Furthermore, when a schizophrenic patient identified a saint with a cigar box and the male sex, he did so because of what he could predicate upon each one of these different subjects; and, because this predicate was the same for the three subjects, they were held to be identical. Upon examination the same kind of reasoning may be found reappearing in all other examples of paralogical reasoning.

We are now in a position to evaluate Vigotsky's discoveries. We have seen that he distinguished five phases of thought and speech. The phase antecedent to the final phases of esophasy and endophasy was the so-called egocentric speech. In egocentric speech inner and outer speech are not yet separated. The inner speech proceeds by thinking in predicates rather than in subject-predicate sentences; but I just stated that the paralogical thinker finds identity of subjects whenever and wherever he finds identity of predicables. The paralogician expresses himself in egocentric speech habits, for his thinking is predicative and he has regressed to the egocentric speech of the child. We know that the child's speech has some elements of the speech of primitive peoples. Therefore we are once more driven to the conclusion that the specific paralogical thought and speech processes of the schizophrenic are in essence those of primitive peoples. When the patient deteriorates still further, he acquires modes of expressing himself which are still more primordial. An illustration of such a regression to an animal-like behavior is the as-if language and concomitant thought production. At the beginning of this discussion such production was exposed as atavistic.

The discussion set as its task to investigate first the specific laws of logic in schizophrenia, and then to see what general aspects the laws of logic may have for psychiatry.

The specific laws of language in schizophrenia show that they are the same as those of primitive people, or even those of higher animals. Of course, just as a decerebrized man does not become a fish, because the evolution and development of a cerebral cortex subsequently changed to a greater or lesser degree the function and structure of the entire central nervous system, so the regressive schizophrenic process does not make the patient a primitive. The patient exhibits only to a pathological degree some of the peculiarities of a primitive. It is this that makes it possible to understand in principle the laws of logic in schizophrenia as products of psychology, although of primitive rather than of adult psychology. It is the latter which makes it difficult, if not impossible, for an inexperienced adult to grasp the meaning of schizophrenic language; on the other hand, a scrutinizing study makes it possible, at least in favorable circumstances, to understand schizophrenic thought processes as deviations from a norm rather than to conclude that they are independent thereof. The general aspect of the laws of logic in schizophrenia seems to indicate that thought and language in schizophrenia are chapters in psychiatry.

Reasoning Patterns in Suicide Notes

INTRODUCTION

In this paper we describe some reasoning patterns occurring in suicide notes and indicate various psychological implications which can be drawn from them.

The materials examined consist of 33 pairs of matched genuine and simulated suicide notes. We utilize a method of analysis conceived by Edwin S. Shneidman[1-5] and developed jointly with the author which relates reasoning patterns and psychological mentational traits in a systematic way. The method of analysis specifies an inventory of reasoning patterns with respect to which the notes are scored. The incidence of reasoning patterns in the genuine notes is compared to that in the simulated notes and then, in accord with a technique the method specifies, certain psychological traits are associated with the genuine notewriter.

The method is concerned with relating the way that an individual thinks to certain of his psychological traits or to relate an individual's thinking behavior to his various dispositions to effect other behaviors. Of course, any unrestricted notion of thinking is far too broad to be workable; instead, the method uses, as a measure of an individual's thinking, certain explicit patterns he exhibits while verbally relating concepts. At first examination it is reasonable to suppose that, given a precise characterization of reasoning patterns, that some sort of inference concerning an individual's psychological makeup might be drawn from the fact that his statements manifest certain of these reasoning patterns. When a person is engaged in an argument, for example, he makes a decision at each instant to pattern the reasoning of his discourse. These decisions are not random or accidental but are assumed to be determined by psychological states which are in some sense characteristic of that person. It is further assumed that certain clues to these psychological states are in various ways manifested in the reasoning patterns which are the products of these decisions.

The method of analysis makes explicit the reasoning patterns it employs and provides a specific and uniform rationale for inferring psychological traits from reasoning patterns. In general, the method replaces *ad hoc* relationships between qualitative characterizations of thinking and psychological traits by a uniform and explicit relationship between specific reasoning patterns and psychological traits. Furthermore, the definitions of the various reasoning patterns used by the method appear to afford enough precision to yield a fairly good intra- and inter-rating reliability in the scoring of these patterns. Further efforts in sharpening these definitions should enhance this reliability. One of the most favorable features of the method, with respect to applications, is that it can be applied to almost any sort of verbal materials, such as letters, test protocols, suicide notes, interview materials, speeches, etc.

As used in this study, the method reflects its present state of development and so it might be better viewed as a specific formulation in a process of successive refinement rather than as the final statement of its underlying conception. Subsequent work will undoubtedly indicate modifications both in the inventory of reasoning patterns and in the mode of association of psychological dimensions to these patterns. Indeed, work has been undertaken regarding the problem of making various definitions of existing patterns more precise as well as extending the present inventory of patterns.[6,7]

The method is flexible and as more is discovered about its effectiveness through applications [10] and predictions it will undoubtedly be improved in various ways. The important thing is that the method points out a direction and structures a program for the analysis of verbal materials which has far-reaching possibilities. The degree of explicitness, completeness, and range of applicability it embodies distinguishes it markedly from other techniques purporting to relate thinking and personality.

The focus of this study is suicide and the results obtained indicate aspects of suicide phenomena previously untapped and illustrate the potentials of the method in psychological investigations.

In this study, a suicide note is treated as an argument. Its premises are the reasons for the suicidal act; its conclusion, often suppressed, is "therefore, I commit suicide."

METHOD OF ANALYSIS

Reasoning Patterns

The patterns the method employs have been chosen in such a way so that they are to the greatest extent possible, dependent on and reflective of only the *structure* of discourse and relatively independent of the content of the discourse and the language skills of the subject. The patterns are designed to reflect only how concepts are manipulated and how the sentences incorporating them are logically related. Assessments of reasoning patterns are based on the paradigm of *argument construction,* whereby an individual's verbal productions (relative to some stimulus or situational context) are regarded as embodying his attempts to establish one or more conclusions or positions. The method assumes that the individual producing the text is, in general, concerned with establishing certain conclusions or positions as true, plausible, agreeable, acceptable, etc. and that he effects these ends by constructing arguments for them. His dominant reasoning patterns are the devices he idiosyncratically uses in constructing these arguments. The paradigm of argument construction stems ultimately from the notion of a correct deductive argument which is comprised of a set of sentences called *premises* and a sentence called the *conclusion* which are so related that the conclusion follows from the premises according to certain inference rules. Arguments framed in English and arising in natural ways are scarcely ever deductively correct, strictly speaking, but can become so if the sentences are reformulated in certain ways and if certain additional premises are supplied. The necessity for reformulation arises from the fact that the inference rules we use come ultimately from the field of formal logic and are geared to the more limited structure of that discipline. These rules are too restrictive to apply to a language as English whose formation rules are exceedingly permissive; thus we allow ourselves to reformulate English sentences to analogues of a more uniform and limited structure. (The reader should not think that the necessity for reformulation would be obviated by supplying English with less limited inference rules, for the kinds of inference rules allowed in formal logic are the best available; that is, these are the only inference rules we know of which are truth-preserving, i.e., which yield true conclusions from true premises.) What we call an "argument" in English differs also in another way from the deductive case just described. In general, an argument in English is comprised of more than one premise set and a conclusion. The premises do not necessarily precede conclusions in the argument, the premise-conclusion relationship being primarily indicated by mode of phrasing rather than order. Generally the speaker or writer credits his audience with possession of background information necessary to follow his arguments; the nature of the premises he omits is a function of how much he so credits his audience which in turn is measured by some of the reasoning patterns the method employs. In deductive arguments as used by logicians in formal languages one rarely encounters redundant premises. However, in ordinary English arguments the use of redundant premises is common. We thus reconstruct an English argument in various ways to obtain correct deductions without redundant premises. In general, the reasoning patterns the method employs are devised to enable us to record: 1) the various kinds of modifications required to reconstruct the original English argument into one which is deductively correct and not redundant and 2) certain stylistic features of the argument relating to the order, relationships, and mode of presentation of the concepts involved in the argument. The patterns subsumed under the first might be thought of as logical characteristics of the argument while the patterns under the second might be thought of as stylistic characteristics of the argument. The method classifies the former under aspects of reasoning and the latter under cognitive maneuvers. Partial lists of these patterns with their definitions appear in Appendices A and B. However, in order that the reader might better see the motivation behind this classification we will remark on some of the considerations which underlie it.

Aspects of reasoning.   Here we are concerned with characteristics of a sentence which bear on its deductive role. For example, we are interested in whether a given sentence overlaps another sentence in content and, if so, whether it is consistent or inconsistent with it, follows from it, or implies it. We also ask whether an implication would hold if additional premises required to make it deductively correct were true, plausible, contestable, or false. In order to effect these comparisons we need to reconstruct the sentence, involving considerations of whether the sentence is absolute or modal, or descriptive or normative and whether it is literal or figurative. We also ask if its denoting terms are abstract or concrete and determine their mode of combination in addition to whether the reconstructed sentence is clear or ambiguous, true or false, empirical or definitional, absolute or probabilistic, direct or oblique, etc. The list of aspects of reasoning is designed to reflect these and similar considerations.

Cognitive maneuvers. Here we are concerned with relationships of concepts employed in the argument with respect to their mode of presentation, order, juxtaposition, introduction, termination, relatedness, and the like. In general, here we are interested in the modulation of content as reflected in, for example, the degree of repetition, digression, continuity, emphasis, specificity, etc. The list of cognitive maneuvers is intended to provide a broad spectrum of such stylistic features.

In consulting the list of aspects of reasoning, the reader will note that some of the entries are among those traditionally referred to as logical fallacies. Indeed, the list was originally composed around such entries and, as the reader will note, is considerably augmented. However, though the aspects of reasoning encompass some of the traditional logical fallacies, the method is not concerned in the evaluation of arguments as being good or bad, but rather with the kinds of modifications required for the reconstruction and rectification of arguments. As was noted earlier almost all arguments arising ordinarily in English are deductively incorrect; thus, to affirm only that an argument is incorrect is of little interest. Rather, we are interested in the *ways* that it is incorrect, that is, in the kinds of modifications ultimately required to rectify it. In general, different individuals require different sorts of modifications in their arguments to rectify them and tend to exhibit different stylistic features—different individuals have different reasoning patterns. An individual's reasoning patterns tend to be characteristic. The measurement of an individual's reasoning patterns appears to be fairly objective, repeatable, and applicable to almost any kind of verbal production. As the definitions of the various reasoning patterns are made more precise, their objectivity and assessment in verbal text will be further facilitated. Indeed, efforts are currently being directed towards greater precision, not only to expedite their handling by analysts, but also to make the assessment of certain of these patterns automatic so that ultimately we can employ the use of computers.[8] A manual has been developed for assessing reasoning patterns.[5] The listing in that manual (see lists in Appendices A and B) includes 28 aspects of reasoning and 42 cognitive maneuvers—70 reasoning patterns in all.

THE CATEGORIES OF ANALYSIS

The method is applied in three steps, idio-logic, contra-logic, and psycho-logic, each dealing with a separate category of analysis of the text.

Idio-logic

The idio-logic of a text sample is the overall picture of the way that the reasoning patterns with the highest and lowest relative frequencies (relative to some standard or control text) group together to form the dominant reasoning characteristics of that sample. These groupings take into account not only how the aspects of reasoning cluster with respect to each other but also how they relate to the cognitive maneuvers. The idio-logic thus describes how the profile of reasoning patterns in the sample text differs from the profile of reasoning patterns in the standard or control text. It describes what is distinctive in the reasoning patterns of the sample text or in the reasoning of the individual who produced the text. We then affirm that that individual's distinctive reasoning patterns or idio-logic is characterized by the properties accorded to the text he produced. For example, if his text evidences a high relative frequency in the aspect of reasoning Contradiction V-B, we say that he is prone to contradictions or prone to be contradictory. The idio-logic associated with a given text sample is not simply a list of the distinctive reasoning patterns of the sample but rather an integrated description of what they mean. In general, sample text will evidence three or four reasoning patterns with a high score and three or four with a low score, though there are cases which deviate considerably from this sort of balance. The idio-logic of the sample then takes into account how these various frequent and infrequent patterns relate to each other. There are many possible combinations of high and low scores, hence many possible idio-logics. The one ultimately assigned to a given individual is assumed to be characteristic of him. Indeed, previous studies strongly suggest that one's idio-logic is fairly constant, relative to samples of the same type of produced text.

Contra-logic

The contra-logic of a text sample is obtained from its idio-logic as an account of what sorts of beliefs might be consistent with that idio-logic. Each aspect of reasoning is accorded an associated philo-sophical belief or position which would be consistent with the tendency to commit or avoid that aspect of reasoning or which would account for that tendency in terms of more general beliefs. The contra-logic associated with a given aspect of reasoning is, roughly speaking, obtained by recasting the defining properties of that aspect of reasoning into a statement about the world, the relation between language and reality, etc. For example, consider the aspect of reasoning V-B, Contradiction. The contra-logic for this would be the belief or position that something can be the case and yet not be the case. Thus an individual's proneness for this pattern is accounted for by hypothesizing that that individual holds the general position that something can be the case and yet not be the case. A contra-logic is then associated with the entire sample, obtained as an integrated description of the various individual contra-logics associated with those aspects of reasoning which have a high or low relative frequency in the sample.

The construction of a contra-logic can thus be viewed as an attempt to recover, from the fact of an individual's propensity to commit or avoid some given aspect of reasoning, an explanation for this propensity in terms of his picture of the world. An individual would not necessarily consciously affirm his own contra-logic, but his contra-logic is, in a sense, the simplest picture of reality consistent with his distinctive aspects of reasoning. Just as an individual's behavior can be taken as an index or clue of his basic feelings and attitudes (not necessarily conscious), it can also be taken as an index or clue of his basic philosophic orientation. We might say then that the method regards an individual's contra-logic as an answer to the question, What kinds of things must this individual generally believe in order to be prone to particular, dominant aspects of reasoning?

The particular contra-logic associated with a given aspect of reasoning is a hypothesis subject to correction and amendment. On the other hand, the specific contra-logics associated with particular aspects of reasoning have at least *prima facie* reasonableness which would warrant their assumption pending further refinements.

Psycho-logic

The method is of course especially interested in the psychological traits* which would be associated with a given pattern of reasoning. The traits associated with a sample of text are called the psycho-logic of the sample and collectively are ascribed to the individual or group that produced the sample. The method arrives at them through the

---

*The psychological traits used in this study are based on what Shneidman calls mentational traits, i.e., psychological traits which might reasonably be related to thinking and, as such, represent a selected segment of the whole personality spectrum.

mediation of the notion of contra-logic. Roughly speaking, the psycho-logic associated with a sample is an answer to the question, What kind of person would have a particular contra-logic? Or What kind of person would believe the things constituted by the contra-logic associated with the sample? This technique of invoking the mediation of a construct follows a psychological tradition whereby one articulates a psychological picture of an individual in terms of the meanings underlying his behavior rather than the behavior itself. Returning to our example of contradiction where the contra-logic was that something can be the case and yet not be the case, the associated psycho-logic is partly that the individual is neutral and indecisive. This kind of person would appear* to hold this contralogical position. Every aspect of reasoning has an associated psycho-logic and an individual's psycho-logic is obtained from a sample of text he produces as a combination of the individual psycho-logics associated (via the contra-logic) with those aspects of reasoning which have a distinctively high or low relative frequency in the sample.

Again, just as the method is not wedded to a specific contra-logic as being the only one which might be associated with a given aspect of reasoning, it does not propose that a specific psycho-logic is the only one which might be associated with a given contra-logic. The method is flexible, self-corrective, and amenable to feedback from the outcome of predictions based on it.

MATERIALS AND RESULTS

We analyzed 33 pairs of suicide notes, each pair consisting of one genuine and one simulated note. These notes were collected and paired by Shneidman and Farberow (see the Appendix of their book[9]) and served as the basis for the analytical study entitled "The Logic of Suicide." They obtained the genuine notes from the office files of the Los Angeles County Medical Examiner-Coroner and the simulated notes from nonsuicidal individuals contacted in labor unions, fraternal groups, and the general community. All 66 genuine and simulated notes were written by individuals who were male, Caucasian, Protestant, native-born, and between the ages of 25 and 59. In addition, each of the 33 simulated notewriters was matched, man for man,

---

*Of course this question is ultimately an empirical one. At this point our assessments are largely an estimate of what we would expect to be true. These estimates would be refined through further research.

with a genuine notewriter who was not only the same age (within five years), but also of the same occupational level.

The 33 simulated notes are used as a control group against which we base our assessments of the distinctive reasoning patterns in the genuine notes. That is, we will consider a particular relative frequency associated with a given reasoning pattern found in the genuine notes as distinctive if it varies sufficiently from the relative frequency of that reasoning pattern as found in the simulated notes. For each reasoning pattern we will consider an increase (positive) or decrease (negative) of at least 30 percent in its relative frequency as constituting a distinctive variation, provided that the group with the higher relative frequency commits at least seven instances of the reasoning pattern in question. The data on which these analyses are based appear in Appendix B.

In the following description of results, we indicate the reasoning pattern in question and a designation of positive or negative (whether its relative frequency is distinctively higher or lower than that in the simulated notes). For example (AR I-A, positive) refers to *Aspect of Reasoning* I-A which (see Appendixes A and B), is Irrelevant Premise and the designation positive indicates that the relative frequency of its occurrence in the genuine notes was at least 30 percent higher than in the simulated notes. The expression "I-A" is simply its listing in Appendix A. Similarly (CM 256, negative) refers to *Cognitive Maneuver* 256, as listed in Appendix B.

Idio-logic of the Genuine Notewriter

The genuine notes evidence a high degree of irrelevancies, that is, the genuine notewriter tends to be subject to the use of irrelevant premises (AR I-A, positive). He brings in material which, while purporting to account for his decision to take his life, is in fact unrelated to that decision from a logical point of view. Thus, the genuine notewriter tends to give reasons which have no actual bearing on his decision to commit suicide. On the other hand, he tends to be explicit about various aspects of his decision rather than assuming that they are already known or acceptable to whomever will receive the note (AR I-J, negative). Thus, it appears that the genuine notewriter is unwilling to take for granted any disposition in his audience. He does not assume that the receiver of the note already shares his various beliefs and convictions that would account for his decision to commit suicide. He takes nothing for granted and writes the note in a very explicit way, as if it were intended for someone who would in no way understand his intentions. Furthermore, the genuine note-writer tends to avoid the use of indirect contexts; he rarely imbeds his affirmations in contexts which would in any way suggest that these affirmations are relative to his own beliefs, surmisals, conjectures, positions, or the like (AR II-D, negative). His affirmations tend to be absolute and unqualified and he treats his affirmations as objective rather than subjective. This tendency, in conjunction with the above-mentioned avoidance of "question-begging devices" (AR I-J, negative), suggests the picture of a person who is interested in describing a wholly objective situation to someone who knows nothing about it—he is describing something which, in his own mind, is a thorough and objective assessment which nevertheless could easily be misunderstood.

The genuine notewriter also tends somewhat toward amphiboly; his sentence structure tends to mask the content of his assertions (AR II-B, positive). Amphibolous constructions arise from the use of idiosyncratic phrasings which tend to juxtapose concepts in unnatural ways, the effect of which is to blunt the import of the communication. (The method treats amphiboly, like the other reasoning patterns, as an important index of the writer's reasoning processes; amphibolous constructions are not considered as accidental or resultant of limitations in the language skills of the writer but rather as an important feature of how the writer integrates his concepts.)

The genuine notewriter tends also to treat dichotomies in a special way; he tends not to oppose concepts (AR II-C1, negative; AR II-C2, negative). It is as if the genuine notewriter does not consider alternatives—suicide, once decided upon, marks the end of his considerations not to commit it.

Consonant with some of the themes mentioned above is the fact that the genuine notewriter also tends to avoid *ad populum* arguments (AR I-F, negative). He avoids appeals to popular acceptations, beliefs, attitudes, and the like. He elects not to elicit acceptance for his projected suicide by resorting to appeal to the general convictions of society. He attempts to ground his arguments for his projected act in other ways. The suggestion then, is that the suicidal person, at the point of suicide, regards himself as quite separate from the constellation of beliefs shared by those who will go on living.

The genuine notewriter is also very prone to mix his modes of discourse; he infuses the contexts in which his purely descriptive utterances take place with moral judgments and emotive declarations whereby he implies that the various moral positions he holds and the attitudes he maintains have some factual status (AR II-E, positive).

Mixing of modes occurs when the writer does not distinguish between what he claims to be the case and what he claims ought to be the case (in a preferential or moral sense). Instead, he confers the same logical status on both and views them as having the same objective import. It is as if the writer wants to elevate his moral beliefs and attitudes to the status of objective empirically-sanctioned positions. He is also very prone to cite circumstances he regards as tragic or pathetic as grounds for his projected suicide (AR I-E, positive), again reflecting his tendency to objectify values and attitudes. Another interesting feature is the genuine notewriter's proneness for using derogation; in justifying his suicide, he tends to incorporate irrelevant allegations to the effect that individuals or circumstances surrounding his projected suicide have some intrinsic fault or evil (AR I-K, positive). These allegations generally have the force of an objective assessment of negativism and are phrased, not in the framework of an expression or attitude, but rather as an affirmation of some objectively condemnable situation. His tendency toward derogation reiterates the genuine notewriter's general propensity for phrasing his personal attitudes in the form of objective assessment. We find that the genuine notewriter also tends to effect normative conclusions from descriptive premises (AR V-E, positive). In other words, he concludes that something is imperative or morally necessary from premises which state facts about the world. We might describe this penchant as a tendency to derive what *ought to be* from what *is*. This again might be taken as evidence of the genuine notewriter's tendency to objectify moral judgments.

The preceding description of the genuine notewriter's idio-logic concerned his aspects of reasoning; we will now discuss those of his reasoning patterns which concern stylistic properties or cognitive maneuvers. We find that the genuine notewriter tends to lack continuity; he tends to jump from one idea to an entirely unrelated idea (CM 210, positive). He tends to omit justifications for his assertions (CM 256, negative). Furthermore, the genuine notewriter tends not to conclude—he will argue a position and never affirm it explicitly (CM 265, negative). Thus we might say that the genuine notewriter will say things without justification and will engage in discourse which does not justify any position he explicitly states. The genuine notewriter is nonetheless very emphatic; he is prone to intensify his concepts (CM 100, positive) and to avoid attenuating them (CM 150, negative). It is as if he prefers his declarations to be couched in the strongest possible form. In conjunction with some of his previously mentioned cognitive maneuvers his style might be described as emphatic but undirected. This is not to say that he discourses with abandon, for we find that he also has a strong tendency to summarize what he has said, up to a certain point. That is, while he does not draw conclusions, he takes pains to integrate his premises (CM 252, positive). He is also prone to change the emphasis of his discourse at many junctures, suggesting some flexibility (CM 156, positive). He is also prone to use numerous examples illustrating the situations he is describing (CM 251, positive). Summarizing some of the stylistic patterns of the genuine notewriter, we find that he is intense, integrative, changeable in emphasis, somewhat erratic in the continuity of his content, and prone to allege and not substantiate. In general he avoids justification, employs numerous examples, and avoids discussing alternatives.

Contra-logic of the Genuine Notewriter

The genuine notewriter appears to hold the position that whatever one associates with a given state of affairs can be taken as a reason for it (AR I-A, positive). In other words, he believes that any two events, however associated, are such that one can be taken as an explanation for the other. He appears to presume that any sort of remarks he might make on a subject would be germane to whatever point he was driving at. He sees events as intrinsically related by the very fact of their cooccurrence; contiguous events, relative to space, time, or thought are seen by him as intrinsically connected. Furthermore, he believes that events and their significance are exactly what they appear to be, that if something appears to be important or related to something else, then it is so in fact (AR I-J, negative). He believes that things are very much what they appear to be. He seeks no mysterious linkages between events, feeling that nature is not at all subtle, and that access to knowledge is an uncomplicated affair.

The genuine notewriter also holds that objective assessments are to be made without any reference to the asserter's point of view as observer; truths about the world are direct and absolute and any statement which is relativized in any way to a belief system is to that extent not a statement about the world but a statement about that belief system (AR II-D, negative). The genuine notewriter might thus be accorded the view that only absolute reference systems are permissible. He would thus demand points of reference which are fixed; a thing is exactly what it is in itself and not what it might appear to be to some given observer or to some given idiosyncratic reference system. Neither of two conflicting points of view would be acceptable for the genuine notewriter; he is prone to accept only that which purported to be the real state of things, totally independent of observational contingencies.

Another of the genuine notewriter's reasoning patterns reiterates a position discussed earlier—he tends to see everything as obvious and unmysterious (AR II-B, positive). The emphasis in the currently considered contralogical position is however linguistic or communicational; namely, that people intend to say exactly what they in fact, do say. Communication tends to be accurate and subtleties or nuances of meaning are simply nonexistent. Thus the genuine notewriter would appear to believe that language is a straightforward and uncontaminating vehicle for communication and one which can be trusted to convey the precise intent of its user.

The genuine notewriter further believes that there is no need to distinguish between things which are distinct; there is no need to contrast what a thing is with what it is not and there is no need to belabor the nature of a concept once described (AR II-C1, negative). The genuine notewriter thus regards the making of distinctions as unnecessary, a belief which relates closely to some of the contralogical themes mentioned earlier. This theme is further amplified in the following: The genuine notewriter believes that no state of affairs is incompatible with or opposed to any other state of affairs; fact is not in contrast with an individual's belief that it is not fact (AR II-C2, negative). Thus we see that the genuine notewriter's disavowal of distinctions is further corroborated.

The preceding elements of the genuine notewriter's belief system comprise his extreme sort of epistemological system: namely, that truths about the world are thoroughly accessible, unsubtle, and obvious; that events in nature are unopposed discrete happenings which are all equally related or unrelated in the same way; and that there is no particular structure or patterning to the objective world, all events being discrete entities which may manifest certain accidental features like contiguity in space or time. In a sense, this position views nature as having a very simple structure for the very reason that nature has no particular structure at all. The constructions invented by science to expedite certain ends like prediction and control are seen by the genuine notewriter as practical devices which are relative to these ends and have no absolute sanction. He would take the very facts that science is a self-corrective process and that scientific theories have no absolute criterion for veridicality as simply further evidence of the fact that the more sophisticated ways of talking about the world are relative to given points of view, given ends, and as such, do not issue from an absolute base or coordinate system, hence they are unacceptable to him.

The above components of the belief system of the genuine notewriter suggest a reticence to accept the more orthodox ways of structuring and understanding the world that society has developed. This theme is picked up again in another of the genuine notewriter's positions, that factual assessments are independent of societal beliefs and attitudes; the mere fact that all or most men believe something is not reason for accepting it (AR I-F, negative).

We turn now to another component in the genuine notewriter's belief system. While he believes that truth is independent of societal sanction, he does not hold that human attitudes are wholly irrelevant. Indeed, it would appear that his own attitudes are of supreme importance, for an additional element of his belief system is that personal feelings and moral judgments issuing from one's self are relevant to assessments of factual truth (AR II-E, positive). Specifically, the genuine notewriter accords the same logical status to factual statements, expressions of personal attitudes, and the levying of moral judgments. Comparing the import of this belief with the others discussed, it might appear that the genuine notewriter's disavowal of idiosyncratic reference systems and his ready acceptance of his own, which seems to be currently implied, might be conciliated by ascribing to him the position that his own belief system is absolute. One might surmise that the genuine notewriter appropriates the entire world unto himself; he ultimately identifies that which is with that which he perceives. The genuine notewriter also presumes that personal feelings are relevant in the making of objective assessments (AR I-E, positive). We thus see that the preceding theme is reiterated in another of his reasoning patterns. Of interest is yet another element in his belief system; that the negative characteristics in any thing or event are relevant in assessing it; the aspects of a thing which one may wish to condemn or the occurrence of an event which one may lament are intrinsic characteristics of that thing or event and must be taken into account in its objective assessment (AR I-K, positive). A final component in the genuine notewriter's belief system is that which "is" implies that which "ought to be." Assertions of fact in some way determine, influence, imply, or suggest moral judgments concerning what ought to have happened or ought to happen (AR V-E, positive). This element further amplifies the present theme that for the genuine notewriter, factual assessments and expressions of attitudes and moral judgments merge together in such a way as to give all of his subjectively generated judgments an objective force or import. Indeed, it is as if the universe is united with and perhaps even emanates from or is dictated by the subjective states of the genuine notewriter. Moreover, it might be suggested further that the earlier mentioned position affirming that knowledge about the world was direct, immediate, and obvious, also arises from this suggested identification of his inner and outer world.

Psycho-logic of the Genuine Notewriter

The genuine notewriter tends to be diffuse, scattered and disorganized, and has difficulty in integrating his thoughts and actions to any given end (AR I-A, positive). He sees everything as bearing equally on any situation he wants to control or bring about. He cannot separate what is relevant from what is irrelevant and he is prone to considerations which just disperse his energies and leave the task undone.

The genuine notewriter trusts his own impressions and convictions (AR I-J, negative). He has a sense of righteousness about his beliefs. He is not mindful of subtlety or complexity and tends to take things at face value (AR I-J, negative; AR II-B, positive). He also tends to be rigid and dogmatic, expects others to understand him, and is impatient with them when they do not (AR II-B, positive). He views his statements as straightforward and feels that any lack of communication is the fault of his audience. Furthermore, he is opinionated and moralistic (AR V-E, positive), and feels that his moral judgments about the way things ought to be are in fact statements about the world rather than opinions based on his belief system. In this regard (AR V-E, positive), he is also prone to be fatalistic, feeling that what ought to be is somehow dictated by that which is.

He also tends to avoid making comparisons and distinctions (AR II-C1, negative); he feels that what he says is clear enough and does not need clarification by contrast with anything else with which his audience may confuse it. We also find that the genuine notewriter does not see his positions or beliefs as conflicting with anything else; he feels that his own convictions are in accord with each other and with his attitudes and moral beliefs (AR II-C2, negative). Thus he sees little internal conflict in the constellation of his own cognitive and subjective processes.

The genuine notewriter also tends to see his judgments about the world as being independent of his perceptive and cognitive processes (AR II-D, negative). He apparently disavows that his beliefs have anything to do with any idiosyncratic characteristics he possesses. He is not prone to surmisal or conjecture and feels simply that what he says is true. He would have difficulty in appreciating how his way of looking at things influences what he believes and says.

He also tends to be isolated and nongregarious (AR I-F, negative). He does not mix easily with others and feels that everything that is important to him is somehow provided by himself. He is prone not to need approval from others and will not, as a rule, seek it; he is somewhat withdrawn and self-sufficient. He tends to project his standards (AR II-E, positive). He projects his subjective attitudes and his moral beliefs but is oblivious to the fact that he does this. He is like a religious zealot whose religion is himself. He would feel that he is telling it the "way it is," and that what he says has nothing to do with his own needs or beliefs. Indeed, the genuine notewriter is very focused on the self and tends towards self-pity but endeavors to objectify his statements to that effect (AR I-E, positive). He bemoans his fate but puts it into an objective caste, as if his laments had an objective status rather than simply constituting an expression of feeling.

He also tends to be somewhat hostile and aggressive and to identify with his own beliefs and positions (AR I-K, positive). Again, the genuine notewriter masks the subjective import of his condemnations by somehow seeing them as objective truths. In conjunction with some of the previous remarks, we might say that the genuine notewriter is unable to distinguish between his feelings and the outside world.

The overall picture of the genuine notewriter is that of a person who is disorganized, unable to implement his impressions and convictions, tends to over-simplify and thinks that everything is obvious, tends to be focused and rigid, fatalistic and dogmatic, projects his standards on the world, and is unable to see any difference in his feelings and the outside world. It is as if the genuine notewriter encapsulates the world within himself, becoming the universe, or, projects his inner feelings outward onto the world and then "reads it back" as fact. The persistent thread in the personality of the genuine notewriter is his inability to distinguish subjective from objective while displaying a confidence, indeed an arrogance, in his estimation of the objective content of his assertions and his unrealistic expectations from others.

REFERENCES

1. Shneidman ES: Psycho-logic: A personality approach to patterns of thinking, in Kagan J, Lesser G (eds): Contemporary Issues in Thematic Apperceptive Methods. Springfield, Illinois, Charles C Thomas, 1961, pp 153-189

2. Shneidman ES: The logic of El: A psychological approach to the analysis of test data. J Proj Techniq 25: 390-403, 1961
3. Shneidman ES: The logic of politics, in Arons L, May MA (eds): *Television and Human Behavior.* New York, Appleton-Century-Crofts, 1963, pp 178-179
4. Shneidman ES: Logical content analysis: An explication of styles of "Concludifying," in Gerbner G, Holsti OR, Krippendorff K, Paisley WJ, and Stone PJ (eds): The Analysis of Communication Content. New York, Wiley, 1969
5. Shneidman ES: The Logics of Communication: A Manual for Analysis. China Lake, California, US Naval Ordnance Test Station, 1966
6. Tripodes PG: Natural Language Sentences. China Lake, California, US Naval Ordnance Test Station, 1969
7. Tripodes PG: Translation and Processing Algorithms. San Diego, California, US Naval Undersea Research Center, 1969
8. Shneidman ES, Tripodes PG: Feasibility Study on Computerizing Logical Patterns. China Lake, California, US Naval Ordnance Test Station, 1967
9. Shneidman ES, Farberow NL (eds): Clues to Suicide. New York, McGraw-Hill, 1957
10. Tripodes PG: Suicidal reasoning, content and clinical evaluation. Unpublished report, Los Angeles Suicide Prevention Center, 1970

APPENDIX A

Definitions of Aspects of Reasoning

I-A *Irrelevant Premise:* Premise is irrelevant to the conclusion it is purportedly instrumental in establishing

I-B *Irrelevant Conclusion:* Conclusion is irrelevant to the major body of premises which purportedly establish it

I-C *Argumentum Ad Baculum:* Appeal to force or fear in one or more premises where the conclusion in question does not involve these concepts

I-D *Argumentum Ad Hominem:* Appeal to real or alleged attributes of the person or agency from which a given assertion issued in attempting to establish the truth or falsity of that assertion

I-E *Argumentum Ad Misericordiam:* Appeal to pity for oneself or for an individual involved in the conclusion where such a sentiment is extraneous to the concepts incorporated in the conclusion

I-F *Argumentum Ad Populum:* Appeal to already present attitudes of one's audience where such attitudes are extraneous to the concepts incorporated in the conclusion

I-G *Argumentum Ad Verecundium:* Appeal to authority whose assertions corroborate or establish the conclusion where no premises are asserted to the effect that the authority is dependable or sound

I-H *False or Undeveloped Cause:* Falsely judging or implying a causal relationship to hold between two events

I-J *Complex Question:* A premise or conclusion of an argument containing a qualifying clause or phrase, the appropriateness or adequacy of which has not been established

I-K *Derogation:* A premise or conclusion containing an implicit derogation of an individual or group, where the concepts expressing derogation are neither relevant nor substantiated

II-A *Equivocation:* The use of a word or phrase which can be taken in either of two different senses

II-B *Amphiboly:* An unusual or clumsy grammatical structure obscuring the content of the assertion incorporating it

II-C1 *Complete Opposition:* The phrasing indicates an opposition or disjointedness of elements which are in fact opposed and disjointed

II-C2 *Incomplete Opposition:* The phrasing indicates an opposition or disjointedness of elements which are in fact not opposed or disjointed

II-D *Indirect Context:* Indirect rather than direct phrasing is used in contexts where the latter is appropriated

II-E *Mixed Modes:* An instance in which the context contains two or more of the following modes within the same context: descriptive, normative, or emotive-personal

III-A *Contestable Suppressed Premise:* A suppressed premise, necessary for rectifying initial validity of argument, is contestable

III-B *False Suppressed Premise:* A suppressed premise necessary for rectifying initial invalidity of argument is false, either logically or empirically

III-C *Plausible Suppressed Premise:* A suppressed premise necessary for rectifying initial invalidity of argument is plausible but not obvious

III-D *Suppressed Conclusion:* The conclusion, while determined by the context of discussion, is never explicitly asserted so that the point allegedly established by the argument is not brought clearly into focus

IV-A *Isolated Predicate:* A predicate occurs in a premise which occurs neither in the remaining premises nor in the conclusion, the function of such recurrence being to bind or relate the isolated predicate to other predicates

IV-B *Isolated Term:* A predicate occurs in the conclusion which does not occur in the premise

V-A1 *Truth-Type Identification:* A confusion between unquestionable assertions on the one hand—logically true assertions and definitions—with empirical assertions on the other hand

V-A2 *Logical Type Identification:* Confusion between general and specific or between abstract and concrete

V-B *Contradiction:* Making conflicting or contradictory assertions

V-C *Identification of a Conditional Assertion with its Antecedent:* Treating an assertion of the "If *A*, then *B*" as equivalent to *A*

V-D *Illicit Distribution of Negation:* Treating an assertion of the form "It is false that if *A*, then *B*" as equivalent to "If *A*, then it is false that *B*"

V-E *Illicit Derivation of Normative from Descriptive:* To derive a normative statement from a descriptive, i.e., a statement of the form, "It is necessary that *X*," "One should do *X*," "*X* ought to be," from ordinary descriptive statements, i.e., statements containing no words expressing imperativeness

APPENDIX B

Genuine Suicide Note Scores (33 Subjects)

Aspects of Reasoning

		Genuine Notes		Simulated Notes	
		Relative frequency	Number of instances	Relative frequency	Number of instances
I-A	Irrelevant Premise	12	32	6	10
I-B	Irrelevant Conclusion	5	14	4	6
I-C	Argumentum Ad Baculum	0	1	0	0
I-D	Argumentum Ad Hominem	7	19	5	7
I-E	Argumentum Ad Misericordiam	14	41	8	12
I-F	Argumentum Ad Populum	7	18	16	25
I-G	Argumentum Ad Verecundium	0	0	0	0
I-H	False or Undeveloped Cause	1	3	1	1
I-J	Complex Question	10	29	17	26
I-K	Derogation	5	14	3	5
II-A	Equivocation	1	3	1	1
II-B	Amphiboly	3	8	1	2
II-C1	Complete Opposition	4	10	6	9
II-C2	Incomplete Opposition	5	13	8	12
II-D	Indirect Context	7	19	16	25
II-E	Mixed Modes	8	21	4	6
III-A	Contestable Suppressed Premise	0	0	0	0
III-B	False Suppressed Premise	0	0	0	0
III-C	Plausible Suppressed Premise	0	0	0	0

	Genuine Notes		Simulated Notes	
	Relative frequency	Number of instances	Relative frequency	Number of instances
III-D Suppressed Conclusion	1	3	0	0
V-A1 Truth-Type Identification	1	2	1	2
V-A2 Logical-Type Identification	1	2	2	3
V-B Contradiction	1	2	0	0
V-E Descriptive-Normative Derivation	5	13	3	5
Totals	98	267	102	157

Cognitive Maneuvers

		Genuine Notes		Simulated Notes	
		Relative frequency	Number of instances	Relative frequency	Number of instances
100	Increase intensity	9	17	4	4
101	Allege but not substantiate	3	5	1	1
102	Deny or reject	0	0	0	0
104	Increase generality	2	4	3	3
150	Decrease intensity	5	10	18	18
151	Accept conditionally	3	6	5	5
152	Obstruct	0	0	0	0
153	Increase specificity	5	10	5	5
154	Change emphasis	12	22	9	9
155	Transfer Responsibility	4	8	0	0
201	Introduce new notion	1	1	0	0
202	Make a distinction	9	16	9	9
203	Branch-out	1	1	2	2

APPENDIX B (continued)

Cognitive Maneuvers

		Genuine Notes		Simulated Notes	
		Relative frequency	Number of instances	Relative frequency	Number of instances
204	Stop short and begin again	0	0	0	0
205	Interrupt	0	0	0	0
207	Shift from topic to audience	0	0	2	2
208	Shift from audience to topic	0	0	2	2
209	Digress	1	2	0	0
210	Initiate a discontinuity	88	15	1	1
211	Abruptly terminate	1	2	1	1
213	Take the initiative	0	0	0	0
250	Enlarge or elaborate	5	10	6	6
251	Analogize or illustrate	4	7	1	1
252	Synthesize or summarize	8	14	2	2
254	Paraphrase	0	0	0	0
256	Justify	9	17	15	15
257	Agree	0	0	0	0
258	Repeat	3	5	2	2
262	Partially agree	0	0	0	0
263	Partially disagree	0	0	0	0
264	Focus on the preceding	3	5	0	0
265	Deduce or purport to deduce	5	10	10	10
	Totals	101	187	98	98

Charles Neuringer

7
Current Developments in the Study of Suicidal Thinking

The introductory remarks to this chapter are from two papers by America's famous logician and philosopher, Charles Sanders Peirce— The Fixation of Belief (1877) and Issues of Pragmaticism (1905). They are reproduced with the permission of Doubleday.

Few persons care to study logic, because everybody conceives himself to be proficient enough in the art of reasoning already. But I observe that this satisfaction is limited to one's own ratiocination, and does not extend to that of other men.

We come to the full possession of our power of drawing inferences the last of all our faculties, for it is not so much a natural gift as a long and difficult art. The history of its practice would make a grand subject for a book. The mediaeval schoolman, following the Romans, made logic the earliest of a boy's studies after grammar, as being very easy. So it was as they understood it. Its fundamental principle, according to them, was that all knowledge rests on either authority or reason; but that whatever is deduced by reason depends ultimately on a premise derived from authority. Accordingly, as soon as a boy was perfect in the syllogistic procedure, his intellectual kit of tools was held to be complete.

To Roger Bacon, that remarkable mind who in the middle of the thirteenth century was almost a scientific man, the schoolmen's conception of reasoning appeared only an obstacle to truth. He saw that experience alone teaches anything—a proposition which to us seems easy to understand, because a distinct conception of experience has been handed down to us from former generations; which to him also seemed perfectly clear, because its difficulties had not yet unfolded themselves. Of all kinds of experience, the best, he

229

thought, was interior illumination, which teaches many things about nature which the external senses could never discover, such as the transubstantiation of bread.

Four centuries later, the more celebrated Bacon, in the first book of his *Novum Organum*, gave his clear account of experience as something which must be opened to verification and re-examination. But, superior as Lord Bacon's conception is to earlier notions, a modern reader who is not in awe of his grandiloquence is chiefly struck by the inadequacy of his view of scientific procedure. That we have only to make some crude experiments, to draw up briefs of the results in certain blank forms, to go through these by rule, checking off everything disproved and setting down the alternatives, and that thus in a few years physical science would be finished up—what an idea! "He wrote on science like a Lord Chancellor," indeed, as Harvey, a genuine man of science, said.

The early scientists, Copernicus, Tycho Brahe, Kepler, Galileo, Harvey, and Gilbert, had methods more like those of their modern brethren. Kepler undertook to draw a curve through the places of Mars; and his greatest service to science was in impressing of men's minds that this was the thing to be done if they wished to improve astronomy; that they were not to content themselves with inquiring whether one system of epicycles was better than another but that they were to sit down by the figures and find out what the curve, in truth, was. He accomplished this by his incomparable energy and courage, blundering along in the most inconceivable way (to us), from one irrational hypothesis to another, until, after trying twenty-two of these, he fell, by the mere exhaustion of his invention, upon the orbit which a mind well furnished with the weapons of modern logic would have tried almost at the outset.

In the same way, every work of science great enough to be remembered for a few generations affords some exemplification of the defective state of the art of reasoning of the time when it was written; and each chief step in science has been a lesson in logic. It was so when Lavoisier and his contemporaries took up the study of Chemistry. The old chemist's maxim had been *Lege, lege, lege, labora, ora, et relege*. Lavoisier's method was not to read and pray, not to dream that some long and complicated chemical process would have a certain effect, to put it into practice with dull patience, after its inevitable failure to dream that with some modification it would have another result, and to end by publishing the last dream as a fact: his way was to carry his mind into his laboratory, and to make of his alembics and cucurbits instruments of thought, giving a new conception of reasoning as something which was to be done with one's eyes open, by manipulating real things instead of words and fancies.

The Darwinian controversy is, in large part, a question of logic. Mr. Darwin proposed to apply the statistical method to biology. The same thing has been done in a widely different branch of science, the theory of gases. Though unable to say what the movement of any particular molecule of gas would be on a certain hypothesis regarding the constitution of this class of bodies, Clausius and Maxwell were yet able, by the application of the doctrine of probabilities, to predict that in the long run such and such a proportion of the molecules would, under given circumstances, acquire such and such velocities; that there would take place, every second, such and such a number of collisions, etc.; and from these propositions they were able to deduce certain properties of gases, especially in regard to their heat-relations. In like manner, Darwin, while unable to say what the operation of variation and natural selection in every individual case will be, demonstrates that in the long run they will adapt animals to their circumstances. Whether or not existing animal forms are due to such action, or what position the theory ought to take, forms the subject of a discussion in which questions of fact and questions of logic are curiously interlaced.

The object of reasoning is to find out, from the consideration of what we already know, something else which we do not know. Consequently, reasoning is good if it be such as to give a true conclusion from true premises, and not otherwise. Thus, the question of validity is purely one of fact and not of thinking. A being the premises and B being the conclusion, the question is, whether these facts are really so related that if A is B is. If so, the inference is valid; if not, not. It is not in the least the question whether, when the premises are accepted by the mind, we feel an impulse to accept the conclusion also. It is true that we do generally reason correctly by nature. But that is an accident; the true conclusion would remain true if we had no impulse to accept it; and the false one would remain false, though we could not resist the tendency to believe in it.

We are, doubtless, in the main logical animals, but we are not perfectly so. Most of us, for example, are naturally more sanguine and hopeful than logic would justify. We seem to be so constituted that in the absence of any facts to go upon we are happy and self-satisfied; so that the effect of experience is continually to counteract our hopes and aspirations. Yet a lifetime of the application of this corrective does not usually eradicate our sanguine disposition. Where hope is unchecked by any experience, it is likely that our optimism is extravagant. Logicality in regard to practical matters is the most useful quality an animal can possess, and might, therefore, result from the action of natural selection; but outside of these it is probably of more advantage to the animal to have his mind filled with pleasing and encouraging visions, independently of their truth; and thus, upon unpractical subjects, natural selection might occasion a fallacious tendency of thought.

That which determines us, from given premises, to draw one inference rather than another is some habit of mind, whether it be constitutional or acquired. The habit is good or otherwise, according as it produces true conclusions from true premises or not; and an inference is regarded as valid or not, without reference to the truth or falsity of its conclusion specially, but according as the habit which determines it is such as to produce true conclusions in general or not. The particular habit of mind which governs this or that inference may be formulated in a proposition whose truth depends on the validity of the inferences which the habit determines; and such a formula is called a *guiding principle* of inference. Suppose, for example, that we observe that a rotating disk of copper quickly comes to rest when placed between the poles of a magnet, and we infer that this will happen with every disk of copper. The guiding principle is that what is true of one piece of copper is true of another. Such a guiding principle with regard to copper would be much safer than with regard to many other substances— brass, for example.

A book might be written to signalize all the most important of these guiding principles of reasoning. It would probably be, we must confess, of no service to a person whose thought is directed wholly to practical subjects, and whose activity moves along thoroughly beaten paths. The problems which present themselves to such a mind are matters of routine which he has learned once for all to handle in learning his business. But let a man venture into an unfamiliar field, or where his results are not continually checked by experience, and all history shows that the most masculine intellect will ofttimes lose his orientation and waste his efforts in directions which bring him no nearer to his goal, or even carry him entirely astray. He is like a ship on the open sea, with no one on board who understands the rules of navigation. And in such a case some general study of the guiding principles of reasoning would be sure to be found useful. . . .

Pragmaticism was originally enounced in the form of a maxim, as follows: Consider what effects that might *conceivably* have practical bearings you *conceive* the objects of your *conception* to have. Then, your *conception* of those effects is the whole of your *conception* of the object.

I will restate this in other words, since ofttimes one can thus eliminate some unsuspected source of perplexity to the reader. This time it shall be in the indicative mood, as follows: The entire intellectual purport of any symbol consists in the total of all general modes of rational conduct which, conditionally upon all the possible different circumstances and desires, would ensue upon the acceptance of the symbol.

Two doctrines that were defended by the writer about nine years before the formulation of pragmaticism may be treated as consequences of the latter belief. One of these may be called Critical Common-sensism. It is a variety of the Philosophy of Common Sense, but is marked by six distinctive characters, which had better be enumerated at once . . .

Character III. The Scotch philosophers recognized that the original beliefs, and the same thing is at least equally true of the acritical inferences, were of the general nature of instincts. But little as we know about instincts, even now, we are much better acquainted with them than were the men of the eighteenth century. We know, for example, that they can be somewhat modified in a very short time. The great facts have always been known; such as that instinct seldom errs, while reason goes wrong nearly half the time, if not more frequently. But one thing the Scotch failed to recognize is that the original beliefs only remain indubitable in their application to affairs that resemble those of a primitive mode of life. It is, for example, quite open to reasonable doubt whether the motions of electrons are confined to three dimensions, although it is good methodeutic to presume that they are until some evidence to the contrary is forthcoming. On the other hand, as soon as we find that a belief shows symptoms of being instinctive, although it may seem to be dubitable, we must suspect that experiment would show that it is not really so; for in our artificial life, especially in that of a student, no mistake is more likely than that of taking a paper-doubt for the genuine metal. Take, for example, the belief in the criminality of incest. Biology will doubtless testify that the practice is inadvisable; but surely nothing that it has to say could warrant the intensity of our sentiment about it. When, however, we consider the thrill of horror which the idea excites in us, we find reason in that to consider it to be an instinct; and from that we may infer that if some rationalistic brother and sister were to marry, they would find that the conviction of horrible guilt could not be shaken off.

In contrast to this may be placed the belief that suicide is to be classed as murder. There are two pretty sure signs that this is not an instinctive belief. One is that it is substantially confined to the Christian world. The other is that when it comes to the point of actual self-debate, this belief seems to be completely expunged and ex-sponged from the mind. In reply to these powerful arguments, the main points urged are the authority of the fathers of the church and the undoubtedly intense instinctive clinging to life. The latter phenomenon is, however, entirely irrelevant. For though it is a wrench to part with life, which has its charms at the very worst, just as it is to part with a tooth, yet there is no *moral* element in it whatever. As to the Christian tradition, it may be explained by the circumstances of the early Church. For Christianity, the most terribly earnest and most intolerant of religions (see *The Book of Revelations of St. John the Divine*)—and it remained so until diluted with civilization—recognized no morality as worthy of an instant's consideration except Christian morality. Now the early Church has need of martyrs, i.e., witnesses, and if any man had done with life, it was abominable infidelity to leave it otherwise than as a witness to its power. This belief, then, should be set down as dubitable; and it will no sooner have been pronounced dubitable, than Reason will stamp it as false.
. . .

Current Developments in the Study of Suicidal Thinking

The hypothesis that the cognitive organization of self-destructive people is a critical variable leading to suicide has a great attraction for those interested in the nature and causes of suicide. This contention was most fully stated by Shneidman[1-4] and was elaborated upon and developed by others.[5-9] The ready acceptance of this hypothesis can be attributed to some disappointment with motivational constructs, which have not fulfilled their promise to explain the nature and dynamics of suicide.

It would appear that motivational dynamics and environmental stresses are impersonal in their measured effects on people. Their very universality (i.e., their disregard for age, race, sex, nationality, education, etc.) ensures that they are a common event in all men's lives. What is particular is the manner in which people perceive, interpret, and react to both their external stresses and affective pressures. It is an old adage that one man's stress is another man's triviality. A politely phrased rejection may lead to mild rueful disappointment in one person but be a major blow to another. It would be difficult to argue that the stress situation producing these varied response was objectively different. What is different is the manner in which the stress is interpreted. Each man has a cognitive coding system which serves to shape, mold, and interpret the inputs arising from the environment. It is that coding system, or cognitive-interpretative system, which supplies the dimensions to stress.

How life's experiences are perceived, coded, organized, and understood is the basic clue to the explanation of why a person acts

To end his existence. One important question in suicidology is what cognitive structures and what interactions between these cognitive structures lead a person to so interpret the world and his own feelings that he is impelled to seek surcease.

The whole field of suicidology seems to be moving toward an emphasis on prevention rather than one of understanding.[10,11] This movement reflects the direction found in most mental health endeavors and seems to be the product of the disappointments, equivocalities, and cul-de-sacs that have resulted from the failures associated with personality- and motivation-dominated research in suicide. These disappointments may be traced to the disregard of cognitive variables as they affect and determine the course of the individual's employment of his sensory inputs and affective systems.

At this point it is of interest to mention general intelligence in suicidal individuals. Level of general intelligence is directly related to the variety, richness, and differentiation of mental processes and activities. A consistently high or low intelligence level in one group might be enough of an explanatory variable to account for a variety of behaviors differentiating them from some other groups. The myth that suicide is the property of a precious intelligent and creative elite is found in a great number of literary and philosophical writing.[12] On the other hand, one often hears the characterization of suicide as being of immense stupidity. Evidence gained from suicidal persons via standard measures of intelligence indicate that there is no real difference in the distribution of general intelligence between suicidal persons and other people.[13-18] Therefore one must look to particular cognitive organizations rather than to the level of intelligence for the solution that will unravel the obscurities surrounding the problem of the meaning of suicide.

Progress has been made in the study of suicidal thinking. Cognitive variables that are directly related to suicidal behavior have been identified. The results of research in suicidal thinking can be organized into three general catetories—structures of suicidal thinking, rigidity and constriction, and time perception. The categorization is arbitrary and limiting, since all these areas are inextricably intertwined. But they are presented as separate areas only for expository purposes.

THE STRUCTURE OF SUICIDAL THOUGHT

The structure and organization of suicidal thinking has received the attention of various researchers because of a hypothesized link between self-destructive activity and various cognitive processes. One of the prime sources of data is the suicide note, which is in many cases the only source of information for individuals who have committed suicide. The suicide note also has the advantage of often being the last written communication by the suicide and as such probably reflects his psychological and cognitive state at that time.

Shneidman pioneered the study of suicidal thinking when he studied the logical substructures of the syntax found in real and simulated notes.[2,19] He felt that the suicidal decision is reached by reasoning based on essentially fallacious logic. After describing the various kinds of logical fallacies, he concluded that the suicidal person commits a certain type of logical error, which he called *catalogical.* This error was so named because it tends to destroy the logician. Catalogical reasoning is characterized by semantic errors, where the error is dependent upon the meaning of the terms occurring in the premise or conclusions of a syllogism and are not deductive fallacies. An example of self-destructive catalogic is: "If anybody kills himself then he will get attention; I will kill myself: therefore I will get attention."[19]

Shneidman says that the fallacy is concealed in the concepts contained in the word "I." Specifically, the confusion is between the self as it is experienced by the individual himself and the self as he feels himself thought of, or experienced by, others. Shneidman attempted to demonstrate the presence and extent of catalogical fallacies in suicidal thinking by a thematic analysis of suicidal notes. He and Farberow[4] subjected a matched set of real and simulated suicide notes to a mood analysis of the message statements using a technique developed by O. H. Mowrer.[20] The technique, known as the DRQ (Discomfort-Relief Quotient), characterizes message statements in terms of reflecting either discomfort, relief, or neutrality. Shneidman felt that the results of the analysis substantiated the presence of catalogic errors of thinking in suicidal individuals.

Shneidman's attempt to study the logic of suicidal thought was original and stimulating, especially in terms of dichotomous thinking. Questions have arisen about whether human thought follows syllogistic patterns,[6] and there has been some disagreement about whether the DRQ data substantiate the catalogic hypothesis,[13] p. 206. However, Shneidman's work has given great impetus to the investigation of the organization of suicidal thinking.

Spiegel and Neuringer[21] reported that suicidal individuals tend to use a series of cognitive strategies to avoid thinking about the dread associated with dying. One of the prime strategies they describe is *semantic disorganization.* They found this to occur to a greater extent in real notes as opposed to simulated notes. Osgood and Walker[22] also analyzed the language structure of real and simulated notes but did not report any appreciable differences in disorganization of the thought processes between the two. However, their method of measuring disorganization differed from that used by Spiegel and Neuringer. Osgood and Walker did find more ambivalent constructions (e.g., "but," "maybe," "except," etc.) in the real notes inferring the increased ambivalent vacillation in the thinking of suicidal individuals.

Osgood and Walker also reported that the real suicide notes reflected both a lower usage of verbs associated with the use of judgment and planning and a greater utilization of verbs dealing with simple action than did the simulated notes. This tendency was also found in the investigations of Gottschalk and Gleser[23] in their study of the verbal content of suicidal notes. These last findings are particularly significant for understanding the nature of the suicidal thought process. Evidently, one of the critical hallmarks of suicidal thinking is the inability of self-destructive persons to reflect upon or think through the implications or ramifications of their thoughts. They do not, or are reduced in their ability to use internal cogitation. This implies that the ability to utilize cognitive-reflective resources is severely limited and they seem to rely on action modalities. The suicidal individual doesn't seem to be able to think before he acts. It may be that the limitation is one of the conditions impelling them towards impulsive actions, one of which may be self-destructive. The findings of the impoverishment of the suicidal individual's capacity to utilize his judgmental and reflective cognitive capabilities is supported by the studies of dichotomous thinking and constriction and rigidity described below. Data from these studies indicate that the suicidal person is far too rigid, constricted, and polarized in his thinking to be able to make fine discriminations, modulate his thoughts, or to use his intelligence in an imaginative manner.

An interesting correlate of this impoverishment of internal judgmental processes is reported by Williams and Nickels[24] and Levenson.[25] They both report that suicidal individuals, more than other people, tend to be more controlled by outer stimuli than by inner promptings. Both investigations used Rotter's[26] Internal—External Scale. These data were reported for suicidal college students and for hospitalized serious suicide attempt patients.

The lack of cognitive differentiation is best reflected by the extensive presence of extreme polarized thinking found in suicide attempt individuals. The bulk of research in the study of polarized or dichotomous thinking has been carried out with suicide attempters using the semantic differential. However, it is of interest to note the continuity of cognitive structures found for completed suicides through suicide note analysis and attempted suicides via the study of the semantic differential. In their study of real and simulated suicide notes, Osgood and Walker[22] reported a difference between the two which is of great interest. They found that polarity syntax ("always," "never," "forever," etc.) occurred more often in the real notes than in the fake notes. Shneidman, in his discussion of the implications of catalogical thinking, argued that extreme dichotomous thinking should be present in suicidal individuals to a degree not found in normal or even psychiatrically ill non-suicidal persons.[19]

Dichotomous thinking, the tendency to polarize thought in an extreme manner, has been studied extensively by Neuringer[6,8,9] and has been found to be an important ingredient in the cognitive structure of suicidal individuals. It has also been found to exist in severely depressed persons.[5] Influenced by Shneidman's original work, Neuringer elaborated upon the concept of dichotomous thinking and argued that suicidal individuals organize their characterizations in polar dichotomies in a much more rigid and extreme manner than do non-suicidal persons regardless of neuropsychiatric status. All people think dichotomously but most individuals have the capacity to moderate or even ignore the dichotomies. He felt that suicidal individuals lack this flexibility and cling to extreme polarized views. Such rigid clinging to extreme polarized characterizations precludes the possibilities for moderation, compromise, and shifting of perspectives. This leads to diminished problem-solving adaptation as well as making the use of cognitive faculties extremely difficult. Dichotomous thinking can be lethal because if an individual is dissatisfied with something in his life he finds it difficult or impossible to modulate his extreme polarized expectancies—he cannot conceptualize compromise. If an individual lives in a world of only "all," "none," "always," "never," etc., without any intermediacy he finds himself backed into corners from which escape is difficult. Since the real world is not congruent with the psychological world of extreme dichotomous expectancies, it is essential that people compromise in order to survive. The rigid adherence to extremes, which cannot be realistically realized, makes life miserable for the suicidal individual.

Is there evidence for the existence of extreme dichotomous thinking in suicidal individuals? In a series of studies Neuringer[6,8,9] has produced evidence confirming its presence in self-destructive persons. He has used the semantic differential[27] to measure dichotomous thinking. The semantic differential is a measurement of meaning technique composed of a series of seven-step bipolar scales. A person is asked to rate a particular concept in terms of where he feels it belongs on each scale. For example ice cream can be rated from very good at one end to very bad at the other end. Any number of such scales may be used. Rating style is very important here. While the subject is free to use the whole range of interval steps, some tend to modulate their ratings whereas others tend to use the extreme steps or make absolute judgments. Excessive use of the extreme interval steps is considered an indication of dichotomous thinking. There are generally three types of factor dimensions reflected in the scales. The first of these is an evaluative factor—is the concept good or bad? The second factor is activity—Is the concept active or passive? The last factor is potency—Is the concept under consideration strong or weak?

The presence and extent of dichotomous thinking was evaluated in two ways, the extent of exclusive use of the extreme rating steps and the amount of divergency or gap on identical bipolar scales between semantically opposite concepts, e.g., Love and hate or God and devil.

Neuringer[6,8] administered the semantic differential to an unselected group of suicide attempters, psychosomatic patients, and normal patients and reported that both the suicidal and psychosomatic patients showed more extreme dichotomization on those scales dealing with the evaluative factor than did the normal patients. He also found that the suicide attempters were overwhelmingly more dichotomous in their thinking on the activity and potency factor scales than the other two groups of subjects. He concluded that extreme polarization of values is a common characteristic of individuals undergoing psychological stress but that extreme dichotomization of the activity and potency associated with events in the world was an exclusive hallmark of suicidal thinking. He felt that suicidal and other disturbed groups both polarize their value systems but that the suicidal individuals are more polarized in terms of their percepts of the power and malignancy of events, associated with their values. They experience things more keenly and poignantly and feel that the forces around them are either very influential and powerful or very impotent and weak. So it is not in the extreme organization of values that the suicidal individual runs into trouble but rather in his feelings about the extreme strength, virulence, and immutability of his already extreme value system.

In another study Neuringer[9] refined the methodology used in his previous investigations. He utilized only serious suicide attempters and compared them to psychosomatic and normal patients on the concepts which he felt were critical to the suicidal individual, e.g., life and death. Here he reported more extreme dichotomous thinking by suicidal subjects as compared to the other groups, on all the factors. In addition, he also reported that the concepts of life and death were more clearly polarized or perceived as clear alternatives by the suicidal patients.

Another study of extreme dichotomous thinking[28] revealed a disturbing aspect of this particular cognitive characteristic in suicidal individuals. Neuringer and Lettieri took daily measures of dichotomous thinking from high-risk, medium-risk, low-risk, and zero-risk suicidal individuals over a three-week period following a suicidal crisis. They reported that the high-risk suicidal group was distinctively different from the other subjects in that they were far more extreme in their dichotomizations than the other subjects and perceived a greater divergency between life and death than did the other less suicidal individuals. They also reported the somewhat alarming finding that extreme dichotomous thinking did not diminish over time. Neuringer and Lettieri interpreted this to mean that the extreme polarization of thinking found in suicidal individuals is not a temporary dislocation of the cognitive structures produced by stress but a dispositional cognitive characteristic of the suicidal individual. This latter finding suggests that the cognitive thought structures associated with suicidal action are always present, ready to continuously distort the world in such a way that suicide is an ever-present action possibility. Unless one can find evidence that indicates that dichotomous thinking is not related to high suicidal risk, or that it is amenable to change, one may have to accept the possibility that there are people who are suicidal because their cognitive organization makes them that way. They are not just reacting to situational stress alone but to an internal coding system that categorizes everything as a traumatic situation that is automatically insoluble and therefore forever unending.

RIGIDITY AND CONSTRICTION OF THINKING

It seems to have become part of the general folklore of suicide that suicidal individuals have a disposition to think in a somewhat rigid and inflexible manner.[2,19,29-32] It is generally felt that the suicidal individual, because of his rigid mode of thinking, finds it difficult to develop new or alternative solutions to debilitating emotional difficulties. As one can observe from the research presented below, there seems to be little doubt that rigidity of thinking and the correlative cognitive characteristic of constriction seem to be a major component of suicidal thinking.

Rigidity and constriction of thinking have debilitating consequences for all human beings but the consequences can be lethal for individuals disposed to suicide. A review of the data reveals that rigidity and constriction occur at significantly higher levels in suicidal individuals as compared to even those with major psychopathological diagnoses. The rigid person finds it difficult to change and to entertain new behavior options. His rigidity traps him in a closed system from which there is no escape. The constriction even further limits the possibilities within the rigidified range. One can imagine the suicidal person experiencing a continously narrowing world with fewer and fewer possibilities for relief and change. If possibilities for change are suggested to him, he finds it nearly impossible to accept them. One can imagine the rigid suicidal individual desperately clinging to what he has, even if it is anxiety-provoking and debilitating, rather than try something new. His rigidity and constriction may even make it impossible for him to perceive and contemplate anything other than his wretched state. Death can then be seen as an escape from an impossible situation.

Neuringer[7] administered the Rokeach Map Reading Problems Test and the California F Scale to groups of suicidal, psychosomatic, and normal hospitalized patients. The patients were equated for age, socioeconomic status, education, and intellectual level. The California F Scale[12] is thought to be a measure of social attitudinal rigidity, while the Rokeach[33] Map Reading Problems Test is designed to evaluate the ability to shift from one previously successful but not inappropriate problem-solving strategy to another plan of attack. The results demonstrated the suicidal individual to be significantly more socially rigid and inflexible and incapacitated in ability to shift problem-solving strategies than the other patients. This study was repeated by Levenson and Neuringer[34] using suicidal adolescents and the original finding was confirmed.

Levenson[25] went further and investigated the effect of rigidity on the constriction of range of concepts. He argued that rigid thinking restricted the scope of conceptualization, that is rigidity has a generalized narrowing effect on the whole conceptual schema. In order to test his hypothesis, Levenson borrowed techniques used to assess divergent thinking. Divergent thinking is a style of cognition characterized by freedom from restriction. Successful use of divergent thinking for problem solving calls for opening the range of conceptualization or finding as many correct solutions to a problem as is possible. On the other hand convergent thinking depends upon the capacity to eliminate unessentials and to focus on the only possible correct solution, such as the answer to a particular algebra problem.

The Unusual Uses Test and Word Association Test developed by
Getzels and Jackson[35] were used. The Unusual Uses Test consists
of five common objects such as bricks, pencils, paperclips, toothpicks,
and newpapers. The subject is instructed to write down as many
different uses for each object as he can devise. The instructions
for the Word Association Test call for as many associates as the
subject can produce. The two techniques were administered to serious
suicide attempters, psychiatric, and normal hospitalized patients
matched for age and IQ. The findings indicate that diminution of
creative flexibility and narrowing of the conceptual range is a predominating characteristic of suicidal individuals.

Two other studies conducted by Levenson[25] indicated that the
rigidifying effects of suicidal thinking may extend to and influence
the perceptual processes. Levenson administered the Perceptual Span
Test[36] to the patients mentioned in the previous study. The test is
composed of a square upon which various letters are scattered. The
subject sits in a head-movement control appartus very similar to that
used in evaluating the extent of peripheral vision and is asked to
enumerate the letters that he can perceive without moving his eyes.
Levenson felt that the general narrowing-rigidifying tendency extended
to the perceptual range and that suicidal individuals would not be
able to perceive the stimuli at the periphery of the visual field. His
expectations were confirmed. In a second study (field dependency)
Levenson evaluated the capacity of the suicidal individual to make
correct estimations of the upright in the absence of visual clues arguing
that rigidity restricted the individual from being able to use nonvisual
or internal cues. To test this hypothesis, the Rod and Frame Test[37]
was used. The subject is seated in a dark room with a tiltable luminous
rod placed before him at various angles. The subject can manipulate
the rod by instruments until it is in a position which he feels is
upright. Visual cues are not available and so other cues must be
used. Correct estimation of the upright position is not difficult for
most people. Individuals suffering from brain damage find this task
to be difficult, mostly because of their increased intellectual limitation.
If rigidity narrows the accessability of non-visual cues, then suicidal
individuals should have greater difficulty in finding the true upright
position than other subjects. This is exactly what Levenson found.
Levenson and Neuringer[38] found this to be also true for individuals
that had committed suicide. Since the Rod and Frame Test could
not be administered to those subjects who had committed suicide,
the Picture Completion, Block Design, and Object Assembly Subtests
from the Wechsler Adult Intelligence Scale[39] were used to assess

field dependency. These subtests have been found to be significantly related to field dependency as measured by the Rod and Frame Test and the Embedded Figures Test.[40,41] The lower the combined score of the three subtests, the greater the field dependency. The Wechsler Adult Intelligence Scale records of 84 male suicides and 84 nonsuicidal patients were examined and the subtest scores extracted and calculated. The combined score of the committers was found to be significantly lower than that of the comparison group.

One of the most dire consequences of rigidity and constriction is its capacity to limit problem-solving behavior. There has been only one direct study of the suicidal individual's problem-solving capacity. Levenson and Neuringer[34] found that suicidal adolescents had more difficulty solving arithmetic problems than a group of psychiatrically disturbed non-suicidal adolescents. In addition, these suicidal subjects also had greater difficulty with the Rokeach Map Reading Problems Test than their non-suicidal cohorts.

TIME PERCEPTION

One of the more fascinating constituents of suicidal thinking is that of time perception. That the organization and perception of time is peculiarly distorted by suicidal individuals has been one of the implicit assumptions made by writers concerned with the psychodynamics of suicide. However, very little research has been done to evaluate this assumption. Reviews of the suicidal bibliographical literature[13,42-45] revealed only eight explicit references to time perception in suicidal individuals.

Binswanger[29] inferred, from a single case study, that the suicidal individual is frozen in time, having a congealed past and an abortive future. Binswanger felt that the suicide lacked the capacity to reinterpret the past, look at it in a new way, or reevaluate it in the light of new experiences. Neither could the suicidal individual foresee a future for himself. And so the individual is immobilized in the present or frozen in time. Evidence for Binswanger's speculations have come from a variety of sources. Brockopp and Lester[46,47] and Greaves,[48] utilizing suicidal and non-suicidal patients empirically confirmed Binswanger's speculations by reporting that the suicidal patients were more present oriented as opposed to being past and future oriented than the other patients. Yufit et al.[49] and Melges and Weisz,[50] using the Time Questionnaire, both produced evidence that suicidal patients showed less projection into or fantasy about the future than did a variety of other types of patients. Interestingly enough only the

Brockopp and Lester[47] study used actual behavioral time estimation measures made by subjects. The other researchers reached their conclusions indirectly from a variety of verbal and written thematic and attitudinal measures. However, a high degree of consistency is found among the research results in this area. Evidently, fixation on the present and crippling of the capacity to deal with the future are hallmarks of the suicidal individual's temporal orientation. Such debilities would certainly interfere with both reevaluating the past and contemplating future possibilities.

Neuringer and his colleagues have attempted to tease out the mediating processes underlying the suicidal individual's distorted time perception processes. In a series of studies[11,51,52] they have taken extensive behavioral and attitudinal time perception and phenomenological time flow measures from suicidal, geriatric, terminal, and normal individuals. Their concern has been mostly with the speed or tempo of the movement of time for suicidal individuals.

Neuringer conjectured that time moves or is perceived as moving very fast by the suicidal individual and that this leads the self-destructive person to feel that his present condition is seemingly changeless and that the future is very far away. Such a condition leaves him caught in what he feels to be eternal agony since time seems to be passing so quickly but nothing changes in that elongated time period. If time appears to be moving rapidly and very little occurs during periods of accelerated time, then one feels that he is always in the present. It is very much like the constant present experienced by the bored person. If the suicidal person is enduring an always present presence, then his ability to contemplate and plan for the future is severely curtailed. If the suicidal individual cannot envision the future, he therefore cannot envision possible future solutions to his problems, or even worse, cannot imagine that there could be a change in his status in the future. He literally has no future. He is without hope since he feels trapped in a noxious present which he perceives will not change in any substantial way.

Neuringer and his associates theoretically derived the empirical literature findings of the suicidal's fixation in the present and inability to deal with the future from the perceived acceleration of the passage of time. They feel that the phenomenal acceleration of the speed of time to be the central mediating process underlying the observed time-perception distortions found in suicidal individuals. They also derived a pattern of behavioral consequences from their mediating process hypothesis, which will be described later.

Neuringer evaluated his hypothesis in two ways. He took behavioral time-elapse estimation measures from a series of death involved patients (suicidal, geriatrically ill, and terminal) and from a group of normal hospitalized patients. From these subjects he also gathered data about their attitudes and feelings concerning the speed of time passage. For the behavioral measures, patients were asked to verbally estimate the elapsed time of four standard intervals. two of the intervals were short (30 seconds and 60 seconds) and two were long (180 seconds and 300 seconds). The beginning and end of a trial were signaled by the experimenter. The patient was then asked to estimate the elapsed time. The patient's attitude about the passage of time was evaluated by a Time Opinion Survey method developed by Kuhlen and Monge.[53] The survey is composed of a series of images and questions dealing with projected future accomplishments, feelings of amount of available leisure time, and self-descriptions of the richness or poverty of one's life among others. The Time Opinion Survey yields a series of factor scores. The most important of these deals with the person's feelings about the speed of time passage. It was argued by the developers of the survey that the other factor score evaluated some of the conditions linked to the perception of the speed of passage of time. They argued that the rate of time flow would influence the ability to conceptualize and organize for the future, affect one's sense of urgency, determine a person's ability to inhibit his immediate needs, and determine one's state of acceptance of his lot.

It was from these last measures that the pattern of behavioral consequences associated with the acceleration of time passage was derived. These patterns fit the theoretical expectations and thus the hypothesized mediating process explained a series of behaviors reported in the suicide literature. Neuringer felt that such behaviors as inability to delay gratification, boredom, irritation, and restlessness observed in suicidal patients by Applebaum and Holzman;[54] Farberow, Shneidman, and Leonard;[55,56] Farberow, Shneidman, and Neuringer;[51] Neuringer[58] and others were direct consequences of the accelerated speed of time passage.

Does the phenomenon of fast perception of the passage of time actually occur in suicidal individuals? The data from the studies of Neuringer and his associates[11,51,52] seem to indicate that it does exist. It has evidently a much more powerful effect over short periods of time than for longer intervals. The acceleration of time passage is a reliable phenomenon among suicidal subjects for the short intervals[51,52] but the data are equivocal for the longer intervals.[11] In the latter study, the suicidal patients made longer estimates for the long intervals than did the geriatrically ill, terminal, and normal patients but the differences barely missed reaching statistical significance. The differences did reach statistical significance for all the intervals in an earlier study,[51] however. In the studies dealing with the speed of time passage attitude factor score of the Time Opinion Survey, it was found that the suicidal patients made the lowest scores of all the comparison groups, indicating that their attitudes about the passage of time reflected the greatest acceleration orientation. The reliability of these observations was demonstrated by the consistent heirarchial ordering of this measure among the four groups of patients in all the studies. In addition, the results dealing with the subsidiary factor scores on the Time Opinion Survey scores of the suicidal patients in the Neuringer studies indicated that suicidal patients expressed more impulsiveness and described themselves as feeling more wretched and miserable than did the other individuals.

The Neuringer data confirm the speculations and findings of previous investigators of time perception in suicidal individuals. From these studies several conclusions about suicidal time perception can be made: it has been reliably demonstrated that the suicidal person's time perception deviates in some manner from the norm; the suicidal person's time perception distortion is different from the distortions found in other pathological groups, e.g., psychiatric, geriatric, or terminal patients in that it is more extreme in its deviations from the norm; suicidal patients demonstrate a greater fixation or attachment to the immediate present than do other people; and suicidal individuals lack the ability to project, imagine, fantasize, or think about the future. Neuringer feels that all these findings can be traced to acceleration of the perception of the passage of time. He and his associates also feel they have demonstrated that other observations in the literature about suicidal patients such as increased impulsiveness and feelings of boredom, misery, and wretchedness are also related to this phenomena.

SELF-DESTRUCTIVE COGNITIONS

One of the general conclusions that can be drawn from a review of the research literature on suicidal thinking is that there is a difference in the cognitive structures and activities of suicidal individuals as compared to those of individuals who are considered normal and persons who are diagnosed as being psychiatrically disturbed but not self-destructive.

Several specific conclusions may also be drawn from the literature.

The conclusions that follow ought to be considered as working hypotheses that should stimulate further research and verification.

1. Suicidal individuals have difficulty in utilizing and relying on internal imaginative resources to a greater degree than non-suicidal persons.
2. Suicidal individuals polarize their value systems to a greater degree than normal people but not to a greater extent than other psychiatrically disturbed persons. However, suicidal individuals polarize their perceptions of the activity and strength of already polarized values to a greater degree than all other comparison groups.
3. Suicidal individuals are more rigid and constricted in their thinking than non-suicidal persons.
4. Suicidal individuals are much more present oriented as opposed to being past and future oriented than non-suicidal individuals. They show a startling lack of ability to projroject or imagine themselves into the future.

One might use a trilevel model for conceptualizing the role of cognitive disabilities in human beings. The first level is one of unstressed normal cognitive activities. The second is one of stress-associated cognitive disabilities. These may range from normal memory blocking in moments of mild stress to the kinds of intellectual losses associated with chronic psychopathology. One may describe this stage as the general psychopathology cognition breakdown level. The third level may be characterized as the specific suicide cognitive breakdown stage. Evidently, there is a third level which seems to be reached mostly by suicidal individuals where the extent of debilitation is greater than at any of the previous levels. Far too much of the research data reviewed here indicate that the suicidal subjects can be successfully differentiated from the psychiatrically disturbed and normal comparison subjects. If one assumes that an excrutiating high trauma level must be present in order for a person to contemplate killing himself, then one also has to assume that this stress level is higher for persons who are suicidal than for those who are not self-destructive. One can also then assume that the increased amounts of stress acting upon the suicidal individual affect the cognitive structures to a greater degree than the lesser perturbations affecting the non-suicidal person. Suicide is dangerous in many ways, but one of its insidious consequences is decreased cognitive capacity, which is desperately needed by the self-destructive person to help him deal with his painful existence.

One very suggestive point has arisen from the data. It may be that suicide attempters and suicide committers have common suicidal thinking styles. The traditional findings and methodological opinions[59,60] hold that there is a motivational and personality difference between committers and attempters; they are two distinctly different groups. This seems to be the state of affairs in terms of personality measures. However, the data for cognitive variables imply the reverse. The field dependency data gathered from suicide attempters[25] and suicide committers[38] are very similar. The findings of polarity and impoverishment of thinking garnered from suicide notes is echoed in the dichotomous thinking studies done on suicide attempters. There may be a core cognitive organization that is related to suicide. The level of suicidal activity, attempting versus committing, may be a consequence of the level of external crisis, or the greater the stresses on a certain cognitive organization, the greater the gravity of the level of consequent suicidal behavior.

One will have to grapple with the possibility that the suicidal cognitive pattern is one that is an essential organization in the self-destructive individual. Various writers have talked about the existence of a suicidal personality.[32,61,62] While such a concept is somewhat unpalatable, the finding of similarities in cognitive structures between committers and attempters as well as the data found by Neuringer and Lettieri indicating the essential stablity of cognitive characteristics in suicidal individuals over time raises the specter of a person doomed to make a certain kind of behavioral response to the environment because of an implacable cognitive coding system. That certain cognitive states accompany suicidal ideation and behavior has repeatedly been demonstrated. What is not known is whether these cognitive states appear only as a reaction to stress or are an enduring disposition in certain people. Are both the cognitive disabilities that accompany suicidal activity and the suicidal activity itself exacerbated responses to crisis; are they two different but interrelated consequences of another mediating process? Or is a stable and omnipresent suicidal cognitive style the cause of the appearance of suicidal behavior? Do cognitive collapses and suicidal behavior rise and ebb together in a never-ending parallelism, always being determined by some other mediational force, or does the very presence of one of them, cognitive organization cause the other, suicide, to be an inevitable effect? This is one of the prime questions for suicide researchers interested in cognition.

Other areas of cognitive patterning also need to be studied. Not enough has been done in the problem-solving area. The ability to solve problems would seem to be crucial for people under stress.

Is there a straightforward diminution of this capacity in suicidal individuals, or are particular but probably inefficient problem-solving techniques adopted by suicidal individuals when in crisis? Memory processes also need to be studied. Memory is a powerful cognitive process which has a wide variety of adaptive facets. Is there a selective diminution in recognition and recall among suicidal individuals? Diminished memory is known to limit problem-solving behavior. Is there an inability to inhibit and select memories in an adaptive fashion or just the opposite—a pervasive censoring of memories? Both of these would be maladaptive. Some of the characteristics of suicidal thinking bear a resemblance of those found among brain-damaged persons.[63,64] Might there be subtle inherited or traumatic neurological anomolies in suicidal individuals? The evaluation of the incidence and extent of neurological and psychoneurological deficit in suicidal individuals may prove to be of great interest. Very little is known about the cognitive organization of children who attempt or commit suicide. This is a particularly fruitful area for further research. Their limited cognitive range may prove to be an ideal simplified condition for investigation of stress and cognitive style interactions. Ease of learning and conditionability is another variable that merits study. There may be learning or conditioning blocks that occur in suicidal individuals that diminish their capacity to successfully deal with their environment. Linguistic analyses of the suicidal individuals' speech and thought may also prove to be illuminating. Are there particular linguistic patterns or breakdowns in the generations of grammar which appear in suicidal persons and which limit cognitive complexity? All of these questions are in need of answers if we are better to understand the thought processes which lead a person to say to himself that he wants to embrace the one event that most men fear and dread above all things—death.

REFERENCES

1. Shneidman ES: The logical, psychological, and ecological environments of suicide. Calif Health 17:193–196, 1960
2. Shneidman ES: Psycho-logic: A personality approach to patterns of thinking, in Kagan J, Lesser G (eds): Contemporary Issues in Thematic Apperception Methods. Springfield, Illinois, Charles C Thomas, 1961
3. Shneidman ES: Logical content analysis: An explication of styles of concludifying, in Gerber G et al (eds): The Analysis of Communication Content. New York, Wiley, 1969
4. Shneidman ES, Farberow NL: Comparison between genuine and simu-

lated suicide notes by means of Mowrer's DRQ. J Gen Psychol 56:251–256, 1957

5. Beck AT: Thinking and depression: Idiosyncratic content and cognitive distortion. Arch Gen Psychiatry 9:324–333, 1963
6. Neuringer C: Dichotomous evaluations in suicidal individuals. Consult Clin Psychol 25:445–449, 1961
7. Neuringer C: Rigid thinking in suicidal individuals. J Consult Clin Psychol 28:54–58, 1964
8. Neuringer C: The cognitive organization of meaning in suicidal individuals. J Gen Psychol 76:91–100, 1967
9. Neuringer C: Divergences between attitudes towards life and death among suicidal, psychosomatic, and normal hospitalized patients. J Consult Clin Psychol 32:59–63, 1968
10. Shneidman ES: New directions for suicide prevention centers, in McGee RK (ed): Planning Emergency Services for Comprehensive Mental Health Centers. Gainesville, Florida, Univ Florida Press, 1967
11. Neuringer C, Harris RM: The perception of the passage of time among death involved hospital patients. Paper delivered at the Annual Meeting of the American Association of Suicidology, Jacksonville, Florida, 1974
12. Adorno TW: Frenkel-Brunswick E, Levenson DJ, Sanford RN: The Authoritarian Personality. New York, Harper, 1950
13. Lester D: Why People Kill Themselves. Springfield, Illinois, Charles C Thomas, 1972
14. McDowall, AW: Subsequent suicide in depressed in-patients. Br J Psychiatry 114:749–754, 1968
15. Murthy VN: Personality and the nature of suicide attempts. Br J Psychiatry 115:791–795, 1969
16. Ravensborg MR, Foss A: Suicide and the natural death in a state hospital population. J Consult Clin Psychol 33:466–471, 1969
17. Rosenberg PH, Latimer R: Suicide attempts by children. Ment Hyg 50:354–359, 1966
18. Vinoda KS: Personality characteristics of attempted suicides. Br J Psychiatry 112:1143–1150, 1966
19. Shneidman ES, Farberow NL: The logic of suicide, in Shneidman ES, Farberow NL (eds): Clues to Suicide. New York, McGraw-Hill, 1957
20. Mowrer, OH: Psychotherapy: Theory and Research. New York, Ronald Press, 1953
21. Spiegel D, Neuringer C: Role of dread in suicidal behavior. J Abnorm Psychol 66:507–511, 1963
22. Osgood C, Walker EG: Motivation and language behavior. J Abnorm Psychol 59:58–67, 1959
23. Gottschalk LA, Gleser GC: An analysis of the verbal content of suicide notes. Br J Psychol 33:195–204, 1960
24. Williams CB, Nickels JB: Internal-external control dimensions as related to accident and suicide proneness. J Consult Clin Psychol 33:485–494, 1969

25. Levenson M: Cognitive correlates of suicidal risk, in Neuringer C (ed): Psychological Assessment of Suicidal Risk. Springfield, Illinois, Charles C Thomas, 1974

26. Rotter JB: Generalized expectancies for internal versus external control of reinforcement. Psychol Monog 80:1-28, 1966

27. Osgood CE, Suci GJ, Tannenbaum PH: The Measurement of Meaning. Urbana, Illinois, Univ Illinois Press, 1957

28. Neuringer C, Lettieri DJ: Cognition, attitude, and affect in suicidal individuals. Life-Threatening Behavior 1:106-124, 1971

29. Binswanger L: The case of Ellen West, in May R, Angel E, Ellenberger HF (eds): Existence. New York, Basic Books, 1958

30. Cavan R: Suicide. Chicago, Univ Chicago Press, 1928

31. Dublin L, Bunzel B: To Be or Not to Be: A Study of Suicide. New York, Random House, 1933

32. Menninger K: Man against Himself. New York, Harcourt, 1938

33. Rokeach M: Generalized mental rigidity as a factor in ethnocentrism. J Abnorm Psychol 43:259-278, 1948

34. Levenson M, Neuringer C: Problem solving behavior in suicidal adolescents. J Consult Clin Psychol 37:433-436, 1971

35. Getzels JW, Jackson PW: Creativity and Intelligence. New York, Wiley, 1962

36. Eysenck HJ, Granger GW, Brengelman JC: Perceptual Processes and Mental Illness. New York, Basic Books, 1957

37. Witkin HA: Perception of the upright when the direction of the force acting upon the body is changed. J Exp Psychol 40:93-106, 1950

38. Levenson M, Neuringer C: Suicide and field dependency. Omega 5:181-186, 1974

39. Wechsler D: Wechsler Adult Intelligence Scale Manual. New York: Psychology Corporation, 1955

40. Goldstein G, Neuringer C, Klappersack B: Sources of field dependence. J Gen Psychol 117:253-268, 1970

41. Witkin HA, Dyk RB, Faterson HR, Goodenough DR, Karp SA: Psychological Differentiation. New York, Wiley, 1962

42. Beall L: The dynamics of suicide: A review of the literature 1897-1965. Bull Suicido 2:2-16, 1969

43. Farberow NL: Bibliography on Suicide 1897-1957, in Farberow NL, Shneidman ES (eds): The Cry For Help. New York, McGraw-Hill, 1961

44. Farberow NL: Bibliography on Suicide and Suicide Prevention. Washington, D.C., National Clearinghouse for Mental Health Information, 1969

45. Neuringer C: Suicide: A selected bibliography. Books and Libraries 7:1-8, 1970

46. Brockopp GW, Lester D: Time perception in suicidal and nonsuicidal individuals. Crisis Intervention 2:98-100, 1970

47. Brockopp, GW, Lester D: Time competence and suicidal history. Psychol Rep 28:80, 1971

48. Greaves G: Temporal orientation in suicidal patients. Percep Mot Skills
     33:1020, 1971
49. Yufit RI, Benzies B, Fonte ME, Fawcett JA: Suicide potential and
     time perspective. Arch Gen Psychiatry 23:158-163, 1970
50. Melges FT, Weisz AE: The personal future and suicidal ideation. J
     Nerv Ment Dis 153:244-250, 1971
51. Neuringer C, Levenson M: Time perception in suicidal individuals. Omega
     3:181-186, 1972
52. Neuringer C, Levenson M, Kaplan JM: Phenomenological time flow
     in suicidal, geriatric, and normal individuals. Omega 2:247-251, 1971
53. Kuhlen RG, Monge RH: Correlates of estimated rate of time passage
     in adult years. J Gerontol 23:427-433, 1968
54. Applebaum SA, Holzman PS: The color-shading response and suicide.
     J Projective Techniques 26:155-161, 1962
55. Farberow NL, Shneidman ES, Leonard CV: Suicide among schiophrenic
     mental hospital patients. Veterans Administration, Medical Bulletin No.
     8, 1962
56. Farberow NL, Shneidman ES, Leonard CV: Suicide among general
     medical and surgical hospital patients with malignant neoplasms. Veterans
     Administration, Medical Bulletin No. 9, 1963
57. Farberow NL, Shneidman ES, Neuringer C: Case history and hospitali-
     zation factors in suicides of neuropsychiatric hospital patients. J Nerv
     Ment Dis 142:32-44, 1966
58. Neuringer C: Reactions to interpersonal crises in suicidal individuals.
     J Gen Psychol 28:54-58, 1964
59. Farberow, NL: Personality patterns of suicidal mental hospital patients.
     Genet Psychol Monog 42:3-79, 1950
60. Neuringer C: Methodological problems in suicide research. J Consult
     Clin Psychol 26:273-278, 1962
61. Bender L, Shilder P: Suicidal preoccupation and attempts in children.
     Am J Orthopsychiatry 7:225-234, 1937
62. Wahl CW: Suicide as a magical act, in Shneidman ES, Farberow NL
     (eds): Clues to Suicide. New York, McGraw-Hill, 1957
63. Goldstein K: The Organism. New York, American Book, 1939
64. Goldstein K: Human nature in the Light of Psychopathology. Cambridge,
     Massachusetts, Harvard Univ Press, 1951

Edwin S. Shneidman

8
Suicide Notes Reconsidered

The introductory passage to this chapter is Gordon Allport's Chapter 5, Why Do People Write Personal Documents?, *The Use of Personal Documents in Psychological Science* (1942). Acknowledgment is given to the Social Science Research Council for permission to reproduce it. Gratitude is also expressed to the William Alanson White Psychiatric Foundation for their kind approval to permit the reprinting of "Suicide Notes Reconsidered," which originally appeared in *Psychiatry*, 36: 379–394, 1973.

The following outline summarizes the forms in which personal documents are found. The many varieties of *third-person* case studies, life histories, interview-reporting, psycho-portraits, biographies, institutional records, etc., are not included, for it is only with first-person documents that we are here concerned. [They include:]

(I) Autobiographies (Comprehensive, Topical, and Edited); (II) Questionnaires; (III) Verbatim Recording (Interviews, Dreams, and Confessions); (IV) Diaries (Intimate Journals, Memoirs, and Log-Inventories); (V) Letters; and (VI) Expressive and Projective Documents (Literature, Compositions, Art Forms, Projective Productions, Automatic Writing, Various others). . . .

A gross dichotomy of motives could be made in terms of the original incentive to writing. Did the author spontaneously create his product or did he do so at the instigation of some outsider (perhaps a psychologist)? Since valuable documents have been secured under both types of instigation there is no special merit in making this distinction. More illuminating is a classification in respect to the *intention* of the author. Krueger and Reckless state that all personal documents are either *confessional* in character or *detached*, but this rough distinction fails to reveal subtler shades of motivation. Burgess suggests a slightly more elaborate set of motives in his fourfold classification of autobiographers: *chroniclers, self-defenders, confessants,* and *self-analysts.* The motives in diary writing are explored by Ponsonby; Burr has listed additional reasons for the writing of autobiographies. Combining these classifications, we may distinguish approximately a dozen motives that underlie the production of personal documents. In any concrete production, of course, it is likely that not one but several motives are operating.

1. *Special Pleading.* A writer may outdo himself to prove that he is more sinned against than sinning. He may blame others for failure to understand him, expatiate on their faults, and, not rarely, ascribe to them faults that are outstanding in himself. In their cruder forms such self-justification and projection are easy to detect, but not so in their subtler forms. . . .

2. *Exhibitionism.* Closely related is the document in which egotism runs riot. The author seeks always to display himself in as vivid a light as possible. Sins as well as virtues may be exposed with such relish and satisfaction that we are likely to dismiss the author as hopelessly narcissistic. . . .

3. *Desire for Order.* Just as there are people who continually tidy their rooms and order their possessions, so there are diary keepers who cannot sleep at night until certain experiences of the day are entered in writing. This motivation may become compulsive in character; it seemed to be so with Pepys. On the other hand, there are methodical individuals who like to record their experiences just as they like to budget their expenditures. Much of the product is dull and uneventful, but much of it, because of its very lack of dramatic accentuation, is true to life.

4. *Literary Delight.* The narrowly aesthetic motive can be traced in innumerable literary biographies wherein personal experience is revealed in a delicate and pleasing way. Symmetry, perfection of expression, artistic form, are obviously intended by the author. . . .

5. *Securing Personal Perspective.* Many sincere autobiographies are attempts to take stock at a crossroads in life, frequently in advanced years. H. G. Wells gives this as the prime motivation for writing his *Experiment in Autobiography.* . . . Documents written with this workmanlike incentive are likely to be dispassionate, sincere, and mature. It is a motive that might be appealed to by psychologists for obtaining a larger supply of documents from adults and elderly people, as well as from college students, especially seniors, who are facing a turning point in their lives.

6. *Relief from Tension.* Krueger maintains that catharsis is the underlying motive in the production of confessional documents. Through writing one secures relief from mental tension which often results from a distrubance of adjustments in human association bringing with it a loss of the sense of individuality and of personal worth. When no other relief is in sight the sufferer expresses himself in a rush of feeling. Some of the most vivid confessional documents in existence race along madly until the early death of their authors, sometimes by suicide. The journals of Bashkirtseff, Ptaschkina, and Barbellion are examples. . . .

7. *Monetary Gain.* To turn to an abrupt contrast in motives, we find documents secured in response to a prize competition or obtained for payment of money. Mercenary motives do not seem to diminish quality, although it seems probable that in all cases where payment has secured excellent documents the authors have been attracted to the task of other reasons as well.

8. *Assignment.* The investigator may have other holds on the writer. In college courses students can be required to write autobiographies. . . . Nearly all students like the assignment and are grateful for the incentive to produce a personal document.

9. *Assisting in Therapy.* It is obvious that the patient who produces an autobiography for a psychiatrist does so in order to assist in his own cure. He takes the physician into his confidence and has every reason to tell the truth. Documents of this type, however, are likely to be limited to the disordered condition for which relief is sought.

It is not only a psychiatrist who obtains autobiographical documents motivated by a desire for help. Counselors, teachers, social workers, clergymen, and friends find them offered for the same purpose. The catharsis of writing, the breaking of inhibitions, and the advice obtained, all contribute to the therapy. Over and over do we hear the personal document extoled for its hygienic merit.

10. *Redemption and Social Re-incorporation.* Confession is the pre-condition of absolution. Religious confession before the priest has as its aim a restoration of status as a child of God and a member of the Christian community. Secular confessions serve a similar purpose. The peccavis of the criminal, the spy, the social parasite, the ingrate, contain implicit pleas for forgiveness and social re-acceptance.

11. *Scientific Interest.* Cultivated individuals, notably college students, will frequently offer their diaries or their candid autobiographies to psychologists interested in problems of personality. Each is convinced that his life experience is unique, that he has suffered what others have not suffered, that scientists may find his story novel and significant. Sometimes the student of psychology feels that the science of human nature as he knows it has nowhere taken account of his own forms of experience, and he therefore yields up his document for the purpose of enlarging the outlook and sharpening the perspicacity of the science he finds so inadequate.

12. *Public Service and Example.* There are documents manifestly written to achieve a reform, to offer a model or a warning, to help others through their difficulties. Clifford Beers was interested in improving the lot of the insane; Booker T. Washington, that of the Negro; Jane Addams, that of the slum dweller. Though bent on reform and centered outward, these documents may disclose poignant reflections of human thought and feeling.

13. *Desire for Immortality.* Marie Bonaparte points out the significance of personal documents in man's "battle against oblivion." If "to be forgotten is to die a second and more complete death," we must expect to find diaries and autobiographies written for the purpose of assuring personal identity

after death. This motive clearly underlies Barbellion's *Journal of a Disappointed Man*, and is likewise explicit in Marie Bashkirtseff's journal. It seems, however, to be a motive which, if not rare, at least is seldom expressed.

The question of what *unconscious* motives may operate in the production of personal documents is puzzling. Speaking of confessional documents Darlington asserts that they are symptomatic of oral-eroticism. But he does not prove his assertion. Compulsive neuroticism, narcissism, latent aggression, may all operate in the production of documents. A detailed analysis of any given life would be necessary to establish their presence. It is true that the motives listed above express primarily *conscious intentions* and for this reason they are not to be taken as exhaustive. On the other hand, it is perilous to invoke unconscious motives where clearly manifest intentions provide adequate explanation for the document's existence. To do so prejudices the interpretation of a document. Often too, it will be found that the unconscious factors are merely deeper layers of the conscious motives listed above. For example, our category of *special pleading* seems to cover all of the projective and defense mechanisms of which psychoanalysts are fond of speaking.

There is one class of documents to which the discussion in this chapter does not apply—the unintentional or incidental document. . . . Literary compositions, paintings, moving pictures, sound-recordings, are, in a sense, personal documents. In these instances, however, the product is not intentionally self-revealing and does not deal directly with one's own life. The motivations operating are the motivations characteristic of creativity in general.

Suicide Notes Reconsidered

"I have read scores of letters from suicides, but none of them ever told the
truth."
—Isaac Bashevis Singer*

I'm sorry, but somewhere I lost the road, and in my struggle to find
it again, I just got further and further away.

There should be little sadness, and no searching for who is at fault;
for the act and the result are not sad, and no one is at fault.

My only sorrow is for my parents who will not easily be able to accept
that this is so much better for me. Please folks, it's all right, really it is.

1:30 P.M.—The ultimate adventure begins!

Mary, Betty, George, Harry, Bill, and Sue. Car to Helen or Ray (needs
a tune up). Money to Max and Sylvia. Furniture to George (plus $137.00
I owe him).

I wanted to be too many things, and greatness besides—it was a hopeless
task. I never managed to learn to really love another person—only to make
the sounds of it. I never could believe what my society taught me to believe,
yet I could never manage to quite find the truth.

2:15 P.M.—I am about to will myself to stop my heart beat and respiration.
This is a very mystical experience. I have no fear. That surprises me. I
thought I would be terrified. Soon I will know what death is like—how
many people out there can say that?

The above suicide note (reproduced with a few minor emendations)
was found a few years ago in the pocket of a 30-year-old psychiatrist
who committed suicide with sleeping pills, deep in a forest of a

*Isaac Bashevis Singer, The bishop's robe, The New Yorker, June 2, 1973, p.
39.

257

midwestern state. Later in this article we will compare this note with another, also written by a 30-year-old psychiatrist in the period preceding his death—but a death of a radically different kind.

Almost without a flagging of interest, for nearly 25 years I have been keenly concerned with trying to unlock the mysteries of suicidal phenomena using suicide notes as the possible keys. It is almost a basic tenet of suicidology that suicide notes are written in the context of the suicidal act, usually within a few minutes of the death-producing deed. Suicide notes would seem to offer a special window, unparalleled among sociopsychological phenomena, into the thoughts and emotions that encompass the deed. And yet, a dozen and a half research studies by a score of qualified investigators over the past 15 years have not produced those new insights and information which that amount of focus and effort would have lead us legitimately to expect. How can we account for these essentially disappointing results? That question is the topic of this paper.

Suicide notes are not like letters or diaries, which are written at leisure, often away from the scene of action. Suicide notes would seem to be comparable to battle communiques, filled with the emotion of the current scene and describing some special aspects of the contemporary dramatic event. And yet, as one reads hundreds of suicide notes, it becomes clear that many of them tell pretty much the same story. What is most disappointing is that most suicide notes, written at perhaps the most dramatic moment of a person's life, are surprisingly commonplace, banal, even sometimes poignantly pedestrian and dull. It is obviously difficult to write an original suicide note; it is almost impossible to write a note which is really informative or explanatory.

Without a doubt, suicide notes are valuable and fascinating documents. They furnish extremely important data for the study of suicide. But they are not the royal road to an easy understanding of suicidal phenomena. The perusal of a suicide note is usually a disappointing process. The large-scale study of notes has not yielded findings that have thrown completely new light on suicidal behavior in general.

Suicide notes are rather special documents. They obviously fall under the category of personal documents as discussed in the pioneer monograph of Gordon Allport.[1] It is interesting to reflect that in Allport's comprehensive listing of personal documents—autobiographies, confessions, diaries, memoirs, logs, letters,* etc.—it apparently did not occur to him to think of sucide notes. However, Allport's

---

*Allport GW: Letters from Jenny. New York, Harcourt, 1965.

monograph is to be recommended to any serious student of personal documents, suicide notes included. He lists over a dozen reasons why personal documents are written, which include the following: special pleading, exhibitionism, desire for order, literary delight, securing personal perspective, relief of tension, assisting in therapy, redemption and social reincorporation, scientific interest, public service and example, and desire for immortality. One can see that the writing of suicide notes encompass these reasons as well as others such as confession, attribution of blame, removal of guilt, pleading for understanding, coercive demand for action, etc.

The importance of the use of personal documents in psychological science is not to be underestimated. Indeed it may well be that we will learn more about suicidal phenomena from a close study of personal documents written over an extended period of time—diaries, journals, and autobiographies—than from any other sources. Nor should we neglect biographies of individuals who have committed suicide, for example the several biographies of Thomas Chatterton, the English genius who committed suicide at age 18.[2]

The study of suicide notes is a relatively recent occurrence although there is a nineteenth century study by Brierre de Boismont[3] which contains analysis of 1,328 suicide notes expounding essentially moralistic viewpoints. Almost a centry later Curt Michael[4] published a collection of 166 suicide notes written by known personalities from antiquity to modern times emphasizing the ubiquitous human elements and focusing on the changes in attitudes toward life and death of the prevailing culture. About the same time W. Morgenthaler[5] published a monograph on suicide notes in which he reproduced verbatim 47 notes from Berne, Switzerland, from 1928-1935.

Shneidman and Farberow[6] can be said to have begun the scientific study of suicide notes by employing Mill's methods of difference and residues,[7] specifically by eliciting suicide notes from non-suicidal individuals and then analyzing substantial numbers of both genuine and simulated notes in blind studies (where the identity of the note, genuine or simulated, was not known to the raters doing the analyses). A set of 33 paired and matched genuine and simulated suicide notes all written by Protestant, Caucasian male adults in Los Angeles County in the period 1945-1955 has been used in several different studies: studying the logics of suicide,[6] changes in suicidal dynamics over age,[6] the socioeconomic and psychological variables of suicide,[8] suicidal life-space,[9] a phenomenological study of suicide notes,[10] a re-study of suicide and age,[11] and the effects of knowledge of manner of death in judging suicide notes.[12]

There are recent studies of suicide notes from Denmark,[13] Wales,[14]

Pennsylvania[15] (focusing on the emotional content of suicide notes), and Illinois[16] (analyzing the effects of motivational level on language). In addition to the studies which have compared genuine notes with simulated notes, one of the studies sagaciously compared suicide notes with ordinary letters to friends and relatives.[16]

Suicide notes have been analyzed with a number of emphases: in terms of emotional states,[5,6,9,10,13] logical styles,[6, 17-22] stated or implied reasons for suicide,[14] levels of death wishes,[6] language characteristics,[11,15,16,23] relations to persons,[8] and computer count of key "tag words.[24]

One study[17] compared materials before suicide and at the time of suicide. (The former were Thematic Apperception Test protocols of individuals who subsequently committed suicide; the latter were genuine suicide notes, though of not the same individuals.) The most important finding of this study is that the styles of reasoning and the patterns of logic are different at the time of suicide than they are some weeks or months before; specifically, at the time of suicide an individual is more constricted, irrelevant, scattered and disorganized in his logical style. He simply is not at his cerebral best at the moment of truth.

As a whole, these studies indicate that it is possible to distinguish between genuine and simulated suicide notes and, more importantly, that genuine suicide notes are generally characterized by dichotomous logic, a greater amount of hostility and self-blame, more use of very specific names and instructions to the survivors, less evidence of thinking about how one is thinking, and more use of the various meanings of the word love.

Overall summary reports of suicide note studies have been listed by Bjerg,[9] reported in a concise summary by Frederick,[25] and presented and discussed by Lester.[26] But in general the results of all these studies have been fragmentary and not as illuminating as one would have wished. In almost every case, the results have reflected more the method of analysis than the suicidal state of man and, although some of the findings are extremely interesting from several theoretical points of view, they have not provided an open door into the understanding of human self-destruction. The results of these carefully done studies, taken as a whole, have been deeply disappointing.

If this assessment of the relative barrenness of most suicide notes is correct, what might account for this characteristic? In order to generate a hypothesis it is necessary to digress slightly and speak of a closely related topic—death, taking note of two recent books on death.[27,28] The main burden of Kubler-Ross's[27] book is her assertion that there are five stages of dying—denial, anger, bargaining, depression, and acceptance. While I was drawn to the human and compassionate aspects of her book, I could not completely agree with her five stages of dying. In my own experience with dying persons, admittedly less intensive than hers, I have never seen these five stages in any one person, much less seriatim. What I have seen is a variety of emotional postures, mood states, and existential positions in a variety of different orders, always interspersed, though not necessarily between each stage, by *denial*, i.e., denial of the fact that the individual is dying. The key concept is denial. Intermittent denial is the ubiquitous psychological feature of the dying process. During the dying process, there are periods of constricted focus, tunneled vision, blinded view, and simple denial of the life-threatening illness and of the threat of death.

As its very title indicates, Weisman's recent book[28] focuses on the pivotal and ubiquitous role of denial in the dying process. Dr. Weisman discusses the purposes of denial in the following words.

> . . . denial is expressed in words, actions, and fantasies, but these are what people *do* in order to counter, categorize, and orient themselves in the presence of danger. . . . Although a potential danger is about to evoke denial, a common threatened danger is a *jeopardized relationship with a significant key person.* Hence, the purpose of denial is not simply to avoid a danger, but to prevent loss of a significant relationship . . . even when there seems to be no one in particular who threatens or could be threatened by a patient's illness, termination, or death, the patient himself may deny because he wants to maintain the *status quo* of already existing relationships. . . .

Nor is denial seen as a unitary, unchanging process, at one or another point in the dying process. Weisman further says, "The balance between denial and accepting changes like a kaleidoscope during fatal illness; all fragments constantly re-arrange themselves into new patterns."

When a person commits suicide his faculties of attention are constricted. There is a narrowing of focus of his perceptual field and he suffers from what might be called tunnel vision. Ringel has written about the "narrowing of the field of consciousness." Alvarez[29] has called this "the closed world of suicide" which he describes as, "Once a man decides to take his own life he enters a shut-off, impregnable but wholly convincing world . . . where every detail fits and each incident reinforces his decision. . . . Each of these deaths has its own inner logic and unrepeatable despair. [Suicide is] a terrible but utterly natural reaction to the strained, narrow, unnatural necessities we sometimes create for ourselves."

This narrowing of the field of consciousness, the closed world of suicide, the constriction of focus of attention, or the tunnel vision that one finds during the actual moments of a suicidal deed are dramatically illustrated in the following excerpt of a 25-year-old woman who, in a transient period of acute confusion and panic, jumped several stories from a hospital balcony and miraculously survived. Two days previously she had ingested 50 100 mg Seconal tablets, and after being discovered by her landlady, was brought to the hospital and treated in the emergency room and then placed in a hospital room. About the attempt she remarked, "I was pretty isolated at that time. Precisely at the moment of my 25th birthday I sort of went into a kind of panic state and things got worse and worse." She stated that she was angry that she had complicated everything by winding up in a hospital. I asked her what happened then to which she replied

Well, after that I was out of danger more or less and at that point they pretty much let me wander around the hospital as I pleased. And there was some question about my husband letting me return home, to the apartment, because he thought I was going to make another attempt and he couldn't bear to live with that. And it was just all up in the air, it was sort of like, well you go and find a place to stay and there was no place for me to stay. And then it turned out that I was going to be staying in some sort of welfare kind of arrangement which was going to be fixed or arranged by the social worker. All of a sudden there I was out in the middle of nowhere without any money, and my husband wasn't going to let me come back to the house and I was desperate. And then I went into a terrible state. So at this point I was supposed to be making these arrangements myself. I could barely even speak, you know, the social worker was calling various agencies and then turning the telephone over to me so I could tell my story and I could even barely remember my name let alone my date of birth or anything like that and I thought my God in heaven, I can hardly even—and I was not functioning at all and these people are going to throw me into the street. And I didn't want to go to a psychiatric ward because I was really frightened that I would wind up—I would possibly have a psychotic episode or something like that. I was so desperate I felt my God, I can't face this thing. Going out, and being thrown out on the street. And everything was like a terrible sort of whirlpool of confusion. And I thought to myself there's only one thing I can do, I just have to lose consciousness. That's the only way to get away from it. The only way to lose consciousness, I thought, was to jump off something good and high. I just figured I had to get outside, but the windows were all locked. So I managed to get outside. I just slipped outside. No one saw me. And I got down to the ground by walking across that catwalk thing, sure that someone would see me, you know, out of all those windows. The whole building is made of glass. And I just walked around until I found this open staircase, and, as soon as I saw it I just made a beeline right up it. And then, I got to the 5th floor and everything just got very dark all of a sudden, and all I could see was this balcony. Everything around it just sort of blacked out. It was just like a circle. That was all I could see, was just the balcony. And I went over it. I climbed over it and then I just let go. I was so desperate. Just desperation. And the horribleness and the quietness of it. The quiet. Everything became so quiet. There was no sound. And everything sort of went into slow motion as I climbed over the balcony. I let go and it was like I was floating. I blacked out. I don't remember any part of the fall. Just, just going. I don't remember anything after going over that balcony. I don't remember crying or screaming. I think I was panting from the exertion and the strain of running up all those stairs. And then, when I woke up I was having a dream, which seemed very weird. At that point I was in intensive care and I was looking at the patterns on the ceiling, you know the sort of metal inserts that are like this, and there's a light in the middle of each one. . . .

Writing of the suicide of several young poets, Boris Pasternak[30] states:

A man who decides to commit suicide puts a full stop to his being, he turns his back on the past, he declares himself bankrupt and his memories to be unreal. They can no longer help or save him, he has put himself beyond their reach. The continuity of his inner life is broken, and his personality is at an end. And perhaps what finally makes him kill himself is not the firmness of his resolve but the unbearable quality of this anguish which belongs to no one, of this suffering in the absence of the sufferer, of this waiting which is empty because life has stopped and can no longer feel it.

If this sense of personal emptiness is at all true of the suicidal person, is it any wonder that suicide notes, written at the very moment when an individual has lost touch with his own past are concerned with the moment's emotions and minutiae and are relatively arid and psychologically barren?

One of the main functions of the personality is to protect itself from other aspects of itself. An individual cannot stare into the horrors of his own life; he needs to view them only tachistoscopically. At best, the topic of death is rather threatening and needs to be intermittently denied in order to maintain one's own mental balance and health. Denial is a necessary gyroscope in one's own psychic life.

Now to take the step from death to suicide (and to state my hypothesis about the reason for the relative barrenness of most suicide notes). In order for a person to kill himself he has to be in a special state of mind, a state of relatively fixed purposes (not gainsaying his ambivalence) and relative closemindedness. It is a psychological state which, while it permits suicide to occur, indeed, facilitates it, it obviously militates against insight or good communication. In other words, that special state of mind necessary to perform a suicidal act is one which is essentially incompatible with an insightful recitation of what was going on in one's mind that lead to the act itself.

Suicide notes are often like a parody of the postcards sent home from the Grand Canyon, the catacombs, or the pyramids—essentially unimaginative, *pro forma*, and not al all reflective of the grandeur of the scene being described or the grandeur of the human emotions that one might expect to be engendered by the situation. Melville, in his flawed masterpiece *Pierre*, (1852), described, in the language of genius, this special brand of emptiness

. . . we learn that it is not for man to follow the trail of truth too far, since by so doing he entirely loses the directing compass of his mind; for arrived at the Pole, to whose barrenness only it points, there, the needle indifferently respects all points to the horizon alike.

By vast pains we mine into the pyramid; by horrible gropings we come to the central room; with joy we espy the sarcophagus; but we lift the lid—and no body is there!—appallingly vacant as vast is the soul of a man!

Admittedly it is difficult to select a prototypical suicide note, but my analysis of suicide note materials leads me to believe that such a note might sound like a paraphrase of the pointedly empty conclusion of Ionesco's *The Chairs*.

Ladies and Gentlemen: I am unhappy to be here today. I guess that I am gathered here to bespeak myself. What shall I say? I had it so clearly in mind just a short while ago. Now all I can say is that actions will have to speak louder than words. I sign this note as one who will soon no longer be himself. George.

In fact, actual suicide notes typically contain such phrases as   I love you   I am sorry   I am in pain   I have lost the way   Please don't blame yourself   You drove me to this   Please be good to our child   Fix the spark plugs on the car   Don't come into this room. For one who seeks deep insights into the reasons for human self-destruction, the deep reasons why individuals intentionally end their own lives, these typical excerpts from genuine suicide notes are not very illuminating.

It is hypothesized that suicide notes cannot be the insightful documents which suicidologists would hope that they would be, mainly because they are written during a special psychological state, a state of focused purpose, narrow perception, and psychodynamic denial. It is a state which, by its nature, precludes the individual's having access to the full ambivalent details of his own self-destructive drama and thus diminishes the possibility of his sharing with others, in a suicide note, what is truly going on in his mind.

In order to commit suicide one cannot write a meaningful suicide note; conversely if one could write a meaningful note he would not have to commit suicide. Or, to be figurative, in almost every instance one has to be intoxicated or drugged in order to commit suicide and it is almost impossible to write a psychologically meaningful document when one is in this special disordered state.*

Obviously by no means are all suicide notes dross or barren. There are many conspicuous exceptions in which the suicide note is filled with psychodynamic information, genuinely explaining the human reasons for the act and giving rather clear hints as to the unconscious reasons behind it. Occasionally a suicide note can serve an important historical task as in the case of Percy W. Bridgman, the Nobel laureate in physics and famous American philosopher. He committed suicide when he was 80 years old on August 20, 1961. The suicide note, published in the *Bulletin of the Atomic Scientist* (1962), is an indictment of the medical profession for their being too loathe to practice voluntary euthanasia on request. His note states, "It isn't decent for Society to make a man do this thing himself. Probably this is the last day I will be able to do it myself. p.w.b."

Bridgman had cancer and was in great pain. Earlier he had said that the "disease has run its normal course, and has now turned into a well-developed cancer for which nothing can be done. . . . in the meantime there is considerable pain, and the doctors here do not offer much prospect that it can be made better." That he had cancer had been corroborated by two or three eminent physicians. He had asked them to give him a substance with which to end his life. They refused. The day before he shot himself he mailed to the Harvard University Press the index for the seven volume collection

---

*A few words about causes of suicide may be useful. If one thinks of a hierachy or multiplicity of causes involving several layers—precipitating causes, secondary causes, sustaining or resonating causes, and primary causes—then it is clear that most suicide notes (and practically all newspaper accounts of suicide), when they touch upon causes at all, seem to deal solely with precipitating causes, e.g., ill health, being jilted, etc., conditions which apply to many people, most of whom do not commit suicide. This fact, in some large part, accounts for the relative shallowness of most discussions of and many publications on this topic and for the somewhat superficial quality that one finds in most suicide notes.

of his complete scientific writings. In his earlier works he had discussed death. Writing about death a few years before in *The Way Things Are* (1959) he said, "If there is one thing which my own death is not, it's a form of my own experience—when I am dead I no longer have experiences. The man who says 'I shall never die' cannot be refuted."

About one-sixth of those who commit suicide write suicide notes.[6] What are the psychological differences between those who do write suicide notes and those who do not? We know from a previous study in Los Angeles by Shneidman and Farberow that the distribution for sex, age, marital status, and socioeconomic statistics of the two groups have been found to be essentially the same. Furthermore Tuckman, Kleiner and Lavell,[15] in a study of 165 notes collected in the Philadelphia area, found that a "comparison of those who left notes with those who did not showed no significant difference between the two groups with respect to age, race, sex, employment, marital status, physical condition, mental condition, history of mental illness, place of suicide, reported causes of unusual circumstances preceding the suicide, medical care and supervision, and history of previous attempts or threats."

It is reasonable to assume that the contents of suicide notes vary according to who is expected to read the note. They communicate a variety of messages such as apology, self-justification, revenge, anger, or even the wish to arouse curiosity or to create a mystery. What do some of the available data tend to show about the addressee of suicide notes? A survey was made of 906 suicide notes collected in the Los Angeles area in the 1940s and 1950s (this is the same set of notes from which the 33 genuine notes referred to previously were selected). The notes were examined in terms of the following categories of addressee, with the following overall findings: no addressee—20 percent; to whom it may concern—7 percent; police 5 percent; spouse 20 percent; parent 6 percent; progeny 8 percent; sibling 3 percent; friend 7 percent; a specific person (relationship not indicated) 15 percent; and other (such as landlord) 8 percent. Some additional results were: more men than women (20 percent versus 16 percent) had no addressee on their suicide notes or addressed their notes to their spouse (22 percent versus 15 percent); fewer men than women addressed their notes to their parents, children, or siblings. Not unexpectedly, the addressee differed among the various age groups— parents and friends sharply decreased after age 30; progeny increased after age 40; no addressee increased after age 60; and, conversely, spouse decreased after age 60.

What type of person writes suicide notes? Suicide note writers are people who typically had a penchant for elaborating the obvious, explaining the apparent, belaboring the given, and repeating the unnecessary. There is probably a pervasive subtle redundancy in their life style. To a "Quarantine—Measles" sign such a person might add the words, "Illness inside—please stay out." To a "House For Sale" sign, he might add "Owner moving, forced to sell." These addenda can be called information duplication, for, what can a suicide note pinned on the chest possibly add to the totality of information immediately conveyed by the hanging body itself? Seen in this light, a suicide note is one of the world's most unnecessary documents.

Professor Erwin Stengel[31] states, "Whether the writers of suicide notes differ in their attitudes from those who leave no notes behind, it is impossible to say. Possibly they differ from the majority only in being good correspondents." The latter hypothesis, which Dr. Stengel seems to have mentioned almost facetiously, has not so far been rigorously tested. It would seem to merit serious attention from students of suicide notes.

One can imagine at least two sets of motives for writing a suicide note—social motives, involving primarily the desire to have one's behavior understood by others, and personal motives, relating to the desire for self-expression for its own sake, self-loyalty, and to a number of secondary gains. In general, we cannot hope fully to understand suicide notes if we neglect the fact that the suicide note writer knew that he was writing a suicide note. So we need to keep in mind that some individuals will, each in his own idiosyncratic fashion, seek to exploit the latent possibilities inherent in making himself the focus of attention. It is not always clear in reading a suicide note which were the primary motives at work in the production of the note.

A "good" suicide note would have to be written in a more open frame of mind or at least a fortnight before the act. But then of course it might not strictly be a suicide note but rather a journal or a diary. There are a few extensive diaries in the public domain of individuals who subsequently committed suicide. Two of them are reproduced in a book by Ruth Cavan.[32] One is by a 26-year old woman whose diary of over 50,000 words was kept over a 7-year period. She subsequently committed suicide by shooting herself. The other is a diary kept by a young man, age 23, for a period of just over 18 months. His last entry was on the day of his death before he drowned himself.

Ponsonby[33] published the remarkable diary of the nineteenth-century painter B. R. Haydon which covered a period of 26 years, 1820–1846, including an entry about an hour before he killed himself by cutting his throat and shooting himself in the head. There is a 5 volume edition of Haydon's diary published by Harvard University Press.

These diaries are "the real thing."* They permit one to see life in its longitudinal workings. They are serial glimpses over extended time into what William James[34] called "the recesses of feeling, the darker, blinder strata of character which are the only places in the world in which we catch real fact in the making, and directly perceive how events happen and how work is actually done."

Perhaps the most extensive personal document relating to suicide is the famous *Confessions* of Jean-Jacques Rousseau.[35] The encyclopaedias of this century invariably list Rousseau's death as a natural death, although Choron[36] says that Rousseau "was rumored to have eventually committed suicide. . . . what seems certain is that Rousseau talked suicide at length with David Hume whose ungrateful guest he was in 1776–1777." However, if one goes back to the nineteenth century one finds that Rousseau's death is reported as a suicide. In a recent article, Fuller[37] quotes extensively from a textbook on suicide written by a French physician, Jean Pierre Falret, in 1822.[38] The relevant section is as follows

> . . . in some people the idea of suicide tortures them for months or even years. This affliction seems to have sapped the existence of the Geneva philosopher for a long time. Possessed of a happy temperament but gifted by a too high sensitivity Rousseau becomes affected by the miserable state he finds himself in and the most somber melancholia fills his heart. Apprehensive, fainthearted, timid, suspicious, he avoids the company of men because he believes they are all perverse, all his enemies. He seeks solitude and soon wishes for death. Let's look at some of his immortal writings to justify our assertion: 'Here I am all alone on earth, without relatives, friends or society. Thus the most loving of men has been banished by a unanimous agreement. I have been in this painful situation for more than twenty years; it still seems like a dream to me. I have head pains and continuous indigestion. The least thing scares me, upsets me and saddens me. Since my body is only an embarrassment, an obstacle to my rest I shall seek a way to divest

---

*C.S. Lewis presents a markedly contrary view on the usefulness of diaries, "If theism had done nothing else for me, I should still be thankful that it cured me of the time-wasting and foolish practice of keeping a diary. (Even for autobiographical purposes a diary is nothing as useful as I had hoped. You put down each day what you think important; but of course you cannot each day see what will prove important in the long run)."[39] Not much to gain from theism!

myself of it the sooner the better.' This great writer accomplished his fatal project. The morning of the day Rousseau died, Madame De Stael reported, 'he got up in his usual state of health, but he said he was going to see the sun for the last time.' He had taken some coffee he himself had prepared before going out. He came in a few hours later and began suffering horribly. He forbade anyone to call for help or to notify anyone. A few days before this sad day Rousseau had noticed the vile inclinations of his wife toward a man of very low social condition. This had crushed him and he had spent eight hours on the edge of the lake in deep meditation."

If indeed Rousseau did commit suicide then his extended *Confessions* may well constitute the most remarkable and the most complete "suicide note" that we know of. We shall need to study these documents, the confessions and the diaries, in greater detail to understand the psychological development of the suicidal drama.*

I move now from Rousseau to other philosophers, Bacon, Kant, Hume, and especially Hegel, for a brief epistemological aside. Hegel believed that the product of the interaction of thesis and antithesis, driven by the power of the negative, was a new synthesis. A contemporary psychodynamically-oriented psychologist would rather envisage the union of thesis and antithesis in terms of their continual coexistence, reflecting the psychological dualities in man, e.g., in many, simultaneous love and hate; in some few, at a special time, simultaneously wishing to live and wishing to die, etc. For this state or condition I would propose the word *ambithesis*. I believe it to be the most typical state of mind, and paradoxically, the least often represented in suicide notes, for the reasons which I have outlined in this paper. I would propose five possible epistemological kinds of suicide notes.

1. *Thetical.* Those notes which assert a thesis or are declarative or testimonial. One example would be Percy Bridgman's note declaring that doctors should be permitted to practice euthanasia upon request.

   Sample Note:† Dearest darling i want you to know that you are the only one in my life i love you so much i could not do without you please forgive me i drove myself sick honey please beleave me i love you again an the baby honey don't be mean with

---

*My deep and abiding debt to Dr. Henry A. Murray[40-42] for appropriately emphasizing the special usefulness of studying detailed data on a relatively few individuals over an extended period of time should be obvious.

†This actual suicide note and the following three notes are from the appendix of *Clues to Suicide.*[6]

me please I have lived fifty years since i met you, I love you—I love you. Dearest darling i love you i love you. Please don't discraminat me darling i know that i will die dont be mean with me please i love you more than you will ever know darling please an honey Tom i know don't tell Tom why his dady said good by honey. Can't stand it any more. Darling i love you. Darling i love you.

2. *Antithetical.* Those notes which rebut or deny a stated or implied thesis.

    Sample note: Good by Kid. You couldn't help it. Tell that brother of yours, When he gets where I'm going. I hope I'm a foreman down there. I might be able to do something for him.

3. *Synthetical.* Those notes which, in a new insight, combine, or attempt to combine, the basic tenets of a thesis and its antithesis.

    Sample note: To my wife Mary: As you know, like we've talked over before our situation, I'll always love you with all my heart and soul. It could have been so simple if you had have given me the help that you alone knew I needed.

    This is not an easy thing I'm about to do, but when a person makes a few mistakes and later tried to say in his own small way with a small vocabulary that he is sorry for what has happened and promises to remember what has happened and will try to make the old Bill come home again, and do his best to start all over again, and make things at home much better for all concerned, you still refuse to have me when you as well as I know that I can't do it by myself, then there's only one thing to do.

    I'm sorry honey, but please believe me this is the only way out for me as long as you feel as you do—This will put you in good shape. Please always take care of Betty and tell her that her Daddy wasn't too bad a guy after all. With all the love that's in me. Bill

    Yes, Mommie, now you have your car and a lot more too, even more than you had hoped for. At least you are better off financially than you were 6 years ago. The only pitiful thing about the whole situation is the baby and the nice car that I bought with blood money. I only hope I do a good job of it. Then your troubles will be over with. I know this is what you have been hoping for for a long time. I'm not crazy, I just love you too much!!!

    I love you—Daddy—Goodbye forever.

4. *Athetical.* A suicide note which lacks a point of view and simply contains instructions or directions.

Sample note: Dear Mary. I am writeing you, as our Divorce is not final, and will not be till next month, so the way things stand now you are still my wife, which makes you entitled to the things which belong to me, and I want you to have them. Don't let anyone take them from you as they are yours. Please see a lawyer and get them as soon as you can. I am listing some of the things, they are: A Blue Davenport and chair, a Magic Chef Stove, a large mattress, an Electrolux cleaner, a 9 x 12 Rug redish flower design and pad. All the things listed above are all most new. Then there is my 30-30 rifle, books, typewriter, tools and a hand contract for a house in Chicago, a Savings account in Boston, Mass. Your husband, William H. Smith

5. *Ambithetical.* Those notes which present the simultaneous coexistence of a point of view and its opposite—contrary, contradictory, antinomy. Ambithetical suicide notes come closer to the psychological realities of how the person really feels. This type of suicide note, from which we learn most about suicide, is relatively rare. The expression of the ubiquitous ambivalence of the human spirit needs time for contemplation. That is why it is seen only on occasion in some extended journals, some few diaries, some rare series of letters, and among some special ambithetical authors such as Stendhal (*The Red and The Black*), Tolstoy (*War and Peace*), Hesse (*Narcissus and Goldmund,* "Klein and Wagner"), and especially Melville ("The Paradise of Bachelors and the Tartarus of Maids," Lucy and Isabel in *Pierre*, and the stark white dualities of good and evil which permeate *Moby Dick*). The key is in the conjunction.

It may well be that for knowledge or science the Hegelian model of attempting to unify opposites (spirit and nature, universal and particular, ideal and real, thesis and antithesis) into a transcending synthesis has its own special merits, but to describe the stream of an individual's inner psychological life, it may make more sense to think in terms of thesis-antithesis-ambithesis—not serially as Hegel believed, but flowing and concomittantly as Freud implied. Synthesis is itself an ideal; ambivalence is the human condition.

For reasons which the reader should now be able to understand, I have advertently chosen not to illustrate ambithesis with a suicide note, but shall instead quote a pivotal passage from Melville's *White Jacket* (1850).

As I gushed into the sea, a thunder-boom sounded in my ear; my soul seemed flying from my mouth. The feeling of death flooded over me with the billows. The blow from the sea must have turned me, so that I sank almost feet foremost through a soft, seething, foamy lull. Some current seemed hurrying me away; in a trance I yielded, and sank deeper down with a glide. Purple and pathless was the deep calm now around me, flecked by summer lightnings in an azure afar. The horrible nausea was gone; the bloody, blind film turned a pale green; I wondered whether I was yet dead, or still dying. But of a sudden some fashionless form brushed my side—some inert, soiled fish of the sea; the thrill of being alive again tingled in my nerves, and the strong shunning of death shocked me through.

For one instant an agonising revulsion came over me as I found myself utterly sinking. Next moment the force of my fall was expended; and there I hung, vibrating in the mid-deep. What wild sounds then rang in my ear! One was a soft moaning, as of low waves on the beach; the other wild and heartlessly jubilant, as of the sea in the height of a tempest. Oh soul! thou then heardest life and death; as he who stands upon the Corinthian shore hears both the Ionian and the Aegean waves. The life-and-death poise soon passed; and then I found myself slowly ascending, and caught a dim glimmering of light.

Quicker and quicker I mounted; till at last I bounded up like a buoy, and my whole head was bathed in the blessed air.

Up to this point, I have spoken about individuals who have committed suicide. But if one is being pushed toward death, under the threat of a terminal disease or of execution, then apparently the psychological situation is quite different. One is then forced from the outside to marshall one's psychic energies and, being so affected, can speak with passion and relevance. Witness the letters from the German concentration camps (1950) and the letters, on the eve of their announced execution dates by John Brown, Feodor Dostoevsky (who was not executed), and Bartolomeo Vanzetti—all published in Schuster's book of letters[43]—and the poem,[44] written in 1586 in the London Tower by Chidiock Tichborne, a young nobleman who plotted against Queen Elizabeth I and who was caught, imprisoned, and beheaded. Of all these interesting pieces I reproduce only the second of the three verses from Tichborne's elegy written in the tower before his execution.

My tale was heard, and yet it was not told;
My fruit is fall'n, and yet my leaves are green;

My youth is spent, and yet I am not old;
I saw the world, and yet I was not seen;
My thread is cut, and yet it is not spun;
And now I live, and now my life is done.

Here is a relevant quotation from the Danish psychiatrist Frederik
F. Wagner.[13]

It is interesting to note a striking difference between such letters
and farewell letters of an entirely different category; letters from
people who were convinced of facing an immediate, inevitable,
unwanted death. In *Last letters from Stalingrad*[45] the German
soldiers openly express their feelings of despair and bitterness
against their leadership, but even more often they dwell upon
their "happy childhood," the "happy years" before the war or
prior to the Hitler period, and first of all: their love for their
relatives. In short: They stick to life. As an example of documents
of particular high human quality can be mentioned the letters
from members of the Danish resistance movement[46] during the
German occupation, written the night before their execution. These
letters reveal a positive, dignified, often religious attitude towards
life and a warm attachment to the family.

This special insight-giving quality is especially noteworthy in
documents written by people who knew that they were dying of a
fatal disease and who addressed themselves to their feelings about
dying and death. What is to be noted about these documents is the
amount of psychological information which they yield, in contrast
to suicide notes. This may be because they were written over a period
of time in which the individual had an opportunity to experience
and to communicate various emotional states, including periods of
denial. Whereas a level of denial characterizes the entire brief period
of writing a suicide note, it would seem safe to assume that when
a dying person is in a period of denial he simply does not turn to
the manuscript. Thus the dying person's manuscript is composed during
the more lucid periods. Recent articles of this genre include an article
by a dying housewife,[47] the recitation of a personal experience by
a psychiatric social worker dying of cancer,[48] reflections of a dying
professor,[49] and an account by 30-year-old psychiatrist who discovered
that he had acute myelogenous leukemia.[50] It is this last essay which
is alluded to in the opening paragraph of this article as a contrast
to a suicide note written by another individual of the same age and
occupation. The reader is encouraged to compare for himself that
suicide note with Dr. Trombley's extended personal reflections and
sharings. A few brief quotations must suffice.

. . . My reasons for writing this paper are to objectify and clarify my own feelings regarding my illness, to help crystallize my perspective on matters of living and dying, and to inform others in a subjective way about the psychological processes which take place in a person who has a life-threatening disease. . . . I have not yet found any enlightenment as to why people in our profession do not write about this. . . . In November 1966, I discovered that I had acute myelogenous leukemia. . . . My initial reactions are difficult to describe and still more difficult to recall accurately. However, I do remember feeling that somehow the doctor's remarks could not be directed to me but must be about some other person. Of course, I shook off that feeling very soon during this conversation and the full realization of the import of this diagnosis struck me, I was steeped in a pervasive sense of deep and bitter disappointment. I thought that I had been maliciously cheated out of the realization of all the hopes and aims that I had accrued during my professional career. . . . The next subjective feeling I can clearly identify is that I was increasingly apprehensive following the diagnosis about my inevitable decreasing body efficiency and thus very likely my decreasing efficiency and interest in my work. . . . This engendered some little guilt over my anticipating not being able to do the job I had been doing. . . . Nonetheless, I did have pangs of remorse when I finally had to stop seeing long-term patients because my physical symptoms interfered too much with appointments. Surprisingly, I did not feel consciously angry or frightened by the knowledge that I had a life-threatening illness. . . . I was gravely disappointed and terribly annoyed that this thing inside my body would interfere with my life, but at no time did I really feel, as one might put it, "angered at the gods" for having such sport with me. Nor did I find that I used denial as a defense to any extent early in the course of the illness, as I did later on when it appeared that some of the chemotherapeutic measures were having considerably good effect and I began to feel that I could go on interminably from drug to drug and not die of my disease. . . . One almost amusing idea came to light through one of my supervisors, namely that some of my colleagues might very well be wishing that I would drop dead and get it over with rather than continue to torment them as I was. For others there was a heightened awareness of a close relationship that had never been verbalized in the past. This occurred with two or three of my fellow residents and certainly we were all the better for it. Not only was there some clarification of feelings and a chance openly to discuss them between us, but also this produced a closer relationship. . . . People wrongly assume that a sick person should be "protected" from strong, and particularly negative feelings. The truth is that there is probably no more crucial time in a person's life when he needs to know what's going on with those who are important to him. . . . In the several months since the inception of my illness I became increasingly aware of a new sensitivity that had gradually but progressively developed in my interpersonal relationships, both with patients and with all my acquaintances. . . . One thing I noticed most pointedly was that I was very much more tolerant of the vagaries and inconsistencies of other peoples' attitudes and behavior than I had ever been before. . . . This heightened awareness of affect in others also extended to myself and I found that my own feelings were much more accessible to my conscious recognition than they had been in the past. I also found that all of my senses seemed more acute, though I believe that really I simply paid more attention to what was going on around me and, in a way, I found myself hungering for every sensory experience that I could absorb. In many ways the world seemed to offer more beauty and there was a heightened awareness of sounds and sights, which in the past I may have only casually observed or simply not have paid much attention to at all. . . . It would appear that the peace I made with myself during my illness and the maturing ability that I was developing to cope with life crises like this one, arose from several dynamic factors. One was the increasing capacity to sublimate the rage and aggression engendered by the impotency I felt regarding this invasion from within. . . . It was very seldom that I was conscious of any feelings of despair or depression. . . . Certainly there are rewarding aspects of facing life-threatening illness. I have learned much about the alterations in my own internal psychological processes, and the subtle metamorphorsis in interpersonal relationships which have occurred and are still occurring. I wish that other people in my position would write also subjectively about this. Perhaps this paper may encourage it.

It seems as though we tend to confuse the drama of the suicidal situation with our own expectations that there be some dramatic psychodynamic insights in the communications written during the moments of that drama. But the fact remains that memorable (authenticated) words uttered during battle or on one's deathbed are relatively rare. It seems to be true also of suicide notes. Understandably, however, we continue to hope that any individual, even an ordinary individual, standing on the brink of what man has always conceptualized as life's greatest adventure and mystery ought to have some special message for the rest of us. Western civilization has for centuries romanticized death;[51] we tend to read with special reverence and awe any words, however banal, that are part of a death-oriented document and thus we tend to think of suicide notes as almost sacred and expansive pieces of writing. And we are then understandably disappointed when we discover that, after all, suicide notes are always secular and usually constricted.

REFERENCES

1. Allport GW: The Use of Personal Documents in Psychological Science. New York, Social Science Research Council, 1942
2. Shneidman ES: Perturbation and lethality as precursors of suicide in a gifted group. Life-Threatening Behavior 1:23–45, 1971
3. de Boismont Brierre: Du Suicide et De La Folie Suicide. Paris, Bailliere, 1856
4. Michael C: Abschied: Briefe und Aufzeichnungen von Epikur bis Unsere Tage. Zurich, Verlag Oprecht, 1944
5. Morgenthaler W: Letzte Aufzeichnungen von Selbstmorden. Beheift fur Scheizerischen Zeitschrift fur Psychologie und Ihre Anwendungen 1. Berne, Hans Huber, 1945
6. Shneidman ES, Farberow NL (eds): Clues to Suicide. New York, McGraw-Hill, 1957
7. Mill JS: System of Logic. London, Routledge & Kegan Paul, 1892
8. Shneidman ES, Farberow NL: A sociopsychological investigation of suicide, in David H, Brengelmann JC (eds): Perspectives in Personality Research. New York, Springer, 1960
9. Bjerg K: The suicidal life-space: Attempts at a reconstruction from suicide notes, in Shneidman ES (ed): Essays in Self-Destruction. New York, Science House, 1967
10. Jacobs J: Phenomenological study of suicide notes. Social Problems 15:60–72, 1967
11. Darbonne AR: Suicide and age: A suicide note analysis. J Consult Clin Psychol 33:46–50, 1969
12. Hood RW: The effects of foreknowledge of manner of death in the assessment from genuine and simulated suicide notes of intent to die. J Gen Psychol 82:215–221, 1970
13. Wagner FF: Suicide notes. Dan Med J 7:62–64, 1960
14. Capstick A: Recognition of emotional disturbance and the prevention of suicide. Br Med J 1:1179, 1960

15. Tuckman J, Kleiner RJ, Lavell M: Emotional content of suicide notes. Am J Psychiatry 116:59-63, 1959
16. Osgood CE, Walker EG: Motivation and language behavior: A content analysis of suicide notes. J Abnorm Psychol 59:58-67, 1959
17. Tripodes P: Reasoning Patterns in Suicide. Los Angeles, Suicide Prevention Center, 1968 (unpublished)
18. Neuringer C: Dichotomous evaluations in suicidal individuals. J Consult Clin Psychol 25:445-449, 1961
19. Neuringer C: Rigid thinking in suicidal individuals. J Consult Clin Psychol 28:54-58, 1964
20. Neuringer C: The cognitive organization of meaning in suicidal individuals. J Gen Psychol 76:91-100, 1967
21. Neuringer C, Lettieri DJ: Cognition, attitude, and affect in suicidal individuals. Life-Threatening Behavior 1:106-124, 1971
22. Shneidman ES: Logical content analysis: An explication of styles of "concludifying," in Gerbner G et al (eds): The Analysis of Communication Content. New York, Wiley, 1969
23. Gottschalk LA, Gleser GC: An analysis of the verbal content of suicide notes. Br J Med Psychol 33:195-204, 1960
24. Ogilvie DM, Stone PJ, Shneidman ES: Some characteristics of genuine versus simulated suicide notes, in Stone PJ, Dunphy DC, Smith MS, and Ogilire DM (eds): The General Inquirer: A Computer Approach to Content Analysis. Cambridge, Massachusetts: MIT Press, 1966
25. Frederick CJ: Suicide notes: A survey and evaluation. Bull Suicidol 2:17-26, 1969
26. Lester D: Why People Kill Themselves. Springfield, Illinois, Charles C Thomas, 1972
27. Kubler-Ross E: On Death and Dying. New York, Macmillan, 1969
28. Weisman AL: On Dying and Denying. New York, Behavioral Publications, 1972
29. Alvarez A: The Savage God: A Study of Suicide. New York, Random House, 1972
30. Pasternak B: I Remember: Sketch for an Autobiography. New York, Pantheon, 1959
31. Stengel E: Suicide and Attempted Suicide. Baltimore, Penguin, 1964
32. Cavan RS: Suicide. New York, Russell & Russell, 1928
33. Ponsonby A: English Diaries. Longon, Methuen, 1923
34. James W: Principles of Psychology. New York, Holt, 1890
35. Rousseau Jean-Jacques: Confessions. Baltimore, Penguin, 1954
36. Choron J: Suicide. New York, Scribner's, 1972
37. Fuller M: Suicide past and present: A note on Jean Pierre Falret. Life-Threatening Behavior 3:58-65, 1973
38. Falret Jean Pierre: De l'Hypochondrie et du Suicide. Paris, Caroullebois, Libraire de la Societe de Medecine, 1822
39. Lewis CS: Surprised by Joy. London, Fontana, 1955

40. Murray HA: Research planning: A few proposals, in Sargent SS, Smith MW (eds): Culture and Personality. New York, Basic Books, 1949
41. Murray HA: Preparations for the scaffold of a comprehensive system, in Koch S (ed): Psychology: A Study of a Science, vol. 3. New York, McGraw-Hill, 1959
42. Murray HA: (Autobiography), in Boring EG, Lindzey G (eds): A History of Psychology in Autobiography, vol. 5. New York, Appleton-Century-Crofts, 1967
43. Schuster M (ed): The World's Great Letters. New York, Simon and Schuster, 1960
44. Tichborne C: Elegy written in the tower before his execution, 1586, in Ault N (ed): Elizabethan Lyrics. New York, Capricorn, 1960
45. Schneider F, Gullans C (eds): Last Letters from Stalingrad. New York, Morrow, 1962
46. Gollwitzer H, Kuhn K, Schneider R (eds): Dying We Live: The Final Messages and Records of the Resistance. New York, Pantheon, 1956
47. Helton L: Soon there will be no more me. Los Angeles Times, West Magazine 8-13, Jan 16, 1972
48. Harker BL: Cancer and communication problems: A personal experience. Psychiatry Med 3:163-171, 1972
49. Anonymous: Notes of a Dying Professor. Pennsylvania Gazette, March, 1972, pp 18-24
50. Trombley LE: A psychiatrist's response to a life-threatening illness. Life-Threatening Behavior 2:26-34, 1972
51. Shneidman ES: On the deromanticization of death. Am J Psychother 25:4-17, 1971

Part IV

Clinical Correlates of Suicide

Michael A. Simpson

9
Self-Mutilation and Suicide

The introductory paragraphs to this chapter are from the section on
Focal Suicide in Karl Menninger's *Man against Himself* (1938) and
are reproduced with the kind permission of Harcourt Brace Jovanovich.

In contrast to those forms of partial suicide in which the self-destructive
activity although attenuated in time is still generalized in its focus are those
in which it is concentrated upon the body, and usually upon a limited part
of the body. I have designated this localized self-destruction *focal suicide*.

Certain clinical phenomena familiar to all physicians belong—I believe—in
this category. I have in mind particularly self-mutilation, malingering, compulsive polysurgery, certain unconsciously purposive accidents resulting in local
injury, and sexual impotence. I believe it will be possible to demonstrate
that they are determined in general by the same motives and mechanisms
outlined for suicide proper, except in the degree of participation of the death
instinct. . . .

For the present we shall consider only those self-destructions which are
mechanically or manually produced in ways which are consciously recognized
and directed by the patient.

By *self-mutilations* I refer to (1) those deliberate destructive attacks upon
various parts of the body with which we are most familiar in the extreme,
bizarre forms occasionally manifested by patients in mental hospitals. In
the same category, also, we cannot omit (2) the various forms of self-inflicted
bodily injury to which neurotics are addicted. Biting the finger nails, for
example, is a degree short of biting the fingers, and some individuals have
a compulsion to bite themselves more or less severely in various other parts

of the body. Others scratch and dig at their flesh incessantly, pluck out their hair or rub their eyes or skin to the point of inflammation. Finally (3), we will consider the self-mutilations which are authorized, encouraged, or dictated by social custom and by religious ceremony. . . .

I must warn the reader that what follows in this chapter is not very pleasant subject matter. Our experience with pain makes the thought of self-mutilation even more repugnant than the thought of suicide, in spite of the great reality differences in favor of the former. We physicians, familiar from our daily experiences with these unlovely sights, often forget that for most persons the barriers imposed by these taboos are quite high, to be set aside only by the more intelligent, objective, and mature. . . .

It is absolutely essential to the development of our theory, however, that we demonstrate that the suicidal impulse may be concentrated upon a part as a substitute for the whole. Self-mutilation is one of the ways in which this is done and we must examine it.

A high school principal of thirty developed a severe depression with the delusion that all life was full of sorrow for which he was chiefly responsible. He was confined in a hospital and showed some improvement, whereupon his mother came one day and removed him against advice, insisting that she understood her own son better than did the physicians and knew that he was well. She took the patient home where a few nights later he quietly arose while the rest of the household slept, and murdered his own two-year-old child by beating it in the head with a hammer, saying that he wanted to spare the baby the suffering that he himself had endured. This led to his commitment to the state hospital. While in the hospital he repeatedly made attempts to injure himself and one day succeeded in thrusting his arm into some machinery in such a way as to bring about the amputation of his right hand. After this he made a rapid and complete recovery.

Although this case was not studied psychoanalytically it is possible to make certain general reconstructions on the basis of clinical experience regarding the unconscious mechanisms back of such behavior. This is always more nearly possible in psychotic persons than in neurotics for the reason that in the psychoses the unconscious tendencies are acted out or spoken out with less disguise, i.e., with less distortion.

It is strongly presumptive here that this patient was driven to make a spectacular atonement for an equally spectacular crime. By injuring himself in this terrible way, he paid the penalty for having murdered his child, that is, he cut off the offending arm, faithful to the Biblical command, "If thy right hand offend thee, cut it off." But the child whom he murdered was apparently his chief love object, and, in spite of the poet's comment that "each man kills the thing he loves," we know that he does so only if that love has become too strongly tinctured with (unconscious) hate. Destruction is not the fruit of love but of hate.

Then what is the explanation for hate so great as to drive this father to murder? Sometime after his recovery I talked with him. He seemed singularly unconcerned and unabashed about his forearm stump. But when I asked him about the death of his child, he showed more emotion; with tears gathering in his eyes he said, "You know, I shall always feel that my mother was partly responsible for that, some way. She and I never got along together."

This, I think, was undoubtedly the correct clue. The patient's mother was a very aggressive, and unsympathetic woman who had been apprised of the patient's condition and yet disregarded experienced advice. It is easy to understand how a person with such a mother would feel hatred toward her. But we know from everyday experience that when such hatred cannot be carried out toward the person who has given rise to it, it is often transferred to someone else. We know, too, from psychiatric and psychoanalytic experience that in melancholia, the disease from which this patient was suffering, the victims stew in the caldron of their own hate, turned back upon themselves from some unrecognized external object.

Whether this external object was more immediately the mother or the baby daughter is really of secondary importance here. What we clearly see is that this fellow hated someone so much that he committed murder, for which he then offered propitiation by mutilating himself. In his unconscious thinking and feeling, this man's mother, daughter, and self were all partially identified. If he killed his child to punish his own mother, he also cut off his own arm to punish himself.

The psychological mechanisms of this instance of self-mutilation, therefore, are like those of suicide to this extent, that hate directed against an external object was turned back upon the self and reinforced with self-punishment. It differs from suicide in that this punitive self-attack, instead of being concentrated upon the total personality, as is the case in suicide, was divided into two parts, one part upon the baby and one part upon the arm, each of which was played off against the other. Lacking, also, is any convincing evidence for a wish to die, which we found reason for believing to be dominant in the case of suicide.

"But," the reader may object, "this is a very interesting speculation logical enough but quite unsusceptible of proof. How can one be sure that these interpretations are correct? Other explanations might be constructed that would seem equally convincing, at least in a particular case which one might select."

Such a demurral is entirely justified. I cannot support the application of these explanations to this case except by analogy and inference because it was not accessible to study . . .

Let us now try to get together the evidence contained in these studies that points to the motivation for self-mutilation and attempt to answer some of the questions raised in the beginning.

We see that self-mutilation is to be found under widely varying circumstances and conditions, including psychosis, neurosis, religious ceremony, social convention, and occasionally as a behavior symptom in certain organic diseases. From representative examples of all of these we are able to detect certain motives in a fairly consistent pattern.

It would appear that self-mutilation represents the surrender or repudiation of the active ("masculine") role, accomplished through the physical removal or injury of a part of the body. Even if there were not already abundant psychoanalytic evidence to the effect that the prototype of all self-mutilation is self-castration, there would be strong reasons for inferring this from our material, in which we frequently find self-castration to be undisguised; and in the cases in which another organ or part of the body is the object of the attack, the associations, fantasies, and comparable analogies make it clear that the substituted organ is an unconscious representative of the genital. This may be, as we have seen, either the male or female genital but has the significance of activity generally associated with the male. This sacrifice of the genital or its substitute appears to satisfy certain erotic and aggressive cravings and at the same time to gratify the need for self-punishment by a self-inflicted penalty.

The aggressive element in self-mutilation can be of both the active and passive variety. The act of self-mutilation may be directed toward an introjected object, as in the example of the man who, hating someone else, cut off his own arm, a process epitomized in the familiar expression of "cutting off one's nose to spite one's face." The passive form of aggression is even more conspicuous because it is directed toward real and present rather than fantasied or distantly removed objects; the provocative behavior of nail-biting children or of malingerers who so exasperate their friends and physicians, clearly illustrates this.

The erotic gratification achieved by the surrender of the active in favor of the passive role is partly dependent upon the innate bisexuality of everyone and the unconscious envy on the part of men of the female role. There is also a tendency, however, on the part of the erotic instinct to make the best of a bad bargain and to exploit the consequences of this rash expression of the aggressive, destructive tendency by erotization. In this sense the erotic gratification of self-mutilation is both primary and secondary.

Finally, there is the self-punishment implicit in self-mutilation, which has the curious Janus-like property of looking both forward and backward. The self-mutilation atones or propitiates by sacrifice for the aggressive acts and wishes of the past, and it also provides an anticipatory protection as if to forestall future punishment and permit further indulgences by the advance payment of a penalty. Incident to the latter, self-mutilation by the sacrifice of the aggressive organ safeguards the individual against the possibility (and therefore the consequences) of further active aggressions.

Our material does not enable us to dilate upon the nature of the aggressive fantasies from which the sense of guilt arises beyond saying that they are connected with castrating or mutilating fantasy originally directed toward the parents and siblings. We know from the work of many analysts that these are usually connected with the *Oedipus* complex and arise from the wish to kill or castrate the father and take the mother, or to kill or mutilate the mother for "faithlessly" preferring the father or a sibling.

It would appear from this summary that self-mutilation is the net result of a conflict between (1) the aggressive destructive impulses aided by the super-ego, and (2) the will to live (and love), whereby a partial or local self-destruction serves the purpose of gratifying irresistible urges and at the same time averting the pre-logical but anticipated consequences thereof. The reality value of the self-mutilation varies greatly; the symbolic value is presumably much the same in all instances. To the extent that the psychological needs can be met by a symbolic self-mutilation with minimum reality consequences, as in such socialized forms as nail-trimming or hair-cutting for example, the device is a useful one; but in those individuals whose reality sense is diminished or whose conscience demands are inexorable the device is literally self-destructive.

In any circumstance, however, while apparently a form of attenuated suicide, self-mutilation is actually a compromise formation to avert total annihilation, that is to say, suicide. In this sense it represents a victory, even though sometimes a costly one, of the life instinct over the death instinct.

Self-Mutilation and Suicide

Self-mutilative behavior occurs in a wide variety of settings and for many different reasons—frightening an enemy or impressing an opponent, making oneself more attractive, initiation and acceptance into a group, religious sacrifice, and others. It may take the form of piercing and misshaping earlobes, nostrils, or lips; deforming head, neck, or foot; scarifying or tatooing the skin; circumcision, subincision or introcision of the genitalia[1,2]; or reshaping teeth or fingernails. Some varieties are culturally accepted as unremarkable—we bite our nails, cut hair and nails, and pierce earlobes without attracting much attention or interest.

However the common situation in which an emotionally disturbed person cuts himself usually attracts an inordinate amount of attention—upsetting, frightening, and annoying other people to a degree usually out of proportion with the gravity or lethality of the act itself. Such acts tend, with few exceptions, to be classified as suicide attempts and are rarely distinguished meaningfully from other varieties of suicidal behavior. Such individuals are usually badly managed by those members of the medical profession with whom they came into contact, in whom they tend to arouse a sense of hoplessness and hostility. They are at times treated as if of high lethality (although this is not true of most self-mutilators), and at other times regarded as indulging in highly manipulative, almost frivolous acting-out, both unhelpful responses, which tend to neglect the patient's real needs; which tend to expose the small and relatively distinct group of high lethality cutters to greater hazard; and which often generates further self-mutilation in the typical cutter.

In this chapter, we will consider in some detail what is known about self-mutilation especially its commonest form, wrist-cutting. We will identify the common features of wrist-cutting as a syndrome of low lethality and distinguish the smaller sub-groups of mutilators of significantly higher lethality.

INCIDENCE

Self-mutilation is seen in general and liaison psychiatric practice, in general medical and surgical as well as psychiatric wards, and in emergency rooms. However, there have been no really adequate studies of incidence. Phillips and Muzaffer[3] reported an incidence of 4.3 percent in a group of psychiatric patients, women outnumbering men 3 to 1, while Ressman and Butterworth[4] reported that 2.1 percent of the population of a school for the feeble-minded mutilated their skin. Barter et al.[5] studied suicide attempts in hospitalized adolescents and found self-inflicted injury accounted for 37.8 percent of attempts, cutting being equally used, proportionately, by boys and girls. Ballinger[6] found that 14.9 percent of patients in a mental subnormality hospital (13 percent males and 17 percent females) and 3.4 percent of general psychiatric patients (3 percent males and 4 percent females) had injured themselves over the course of one month.

Many cases fail to be reported or noted at all, as the wounds are usually minor and can be easily cared for by the patient or treated in emergency rooms as simple lacerations—with no consideration of the source of injury. Available figures certainly underestimate the true incidence. Whitehead, Ferrence, and Johnson,[7,8,9] in a thorough survey, collated many sources of information within a community in London, Ontario and estimated an incidence of self-injury (including suicide, overdose and self-mutilation) of 730 per 100,000 population annually—a figure much higher than earlier estimates which varied between 40 and 220 per 100,000 annually. Johnson,[10] studying the same population, found a high incidence of previous self-injury (60 percent) for these patients, although their physicians were aware of only 20 percent of such incidents (and unsure of a further 28 percent); only 46 percent of the patients themselves initially reported such previous episodes. Whitehead, Ferrence, and Johnson[8] discuss reasons for underreporting by physicians of unhospitalized self-injuries.

Apart from the typical wrist-cutter, described below, there are two other groups among which self-mutilation is relatively common.

High incidences have been reported in studies of subnormal[4,11] and schizophrenic children[12,13] and among prisoners.[14-18] In prisons, self-cutting and hanging are the favored means of suicide[19] partially due to the relative unavailability of other methods, but also, as Danto[20] has described, to manipulate one's way into better conditions by using the grammar of suicide, or as Cooper[21] stressed, as an expression of self-defense, to end severe corporal ill-treatment, or in a celebration of humiliation when there is nothing else to attack but oneself.

SEX DISTRIBUTION

Most clinical studies have been based on hospitalized populations, and in these groups females have markedly outnumbered males.[22-26] Green[12] found more girls than boys in his group of self-mutilating schizophrenic children. Fabian[27] classified self-injuries in a psychiatric hospital into categories: I—minor or superficial attempts, II—more serious attempts, and III—potentially or actually lethal attempts. Lacerations constituted 63 percent of category I attempts, 53 percent of category II, and 23 percent of category III. Women were responsible for 60 percent of all cases of self-injury—72 percent and 77 percent of categories I and II respectively, and only 30 percent of category III. However, it appears that a cut only needing suturing or butterfly bandages was placed in category III along with actually lethal cuts.

Clendenin[28] studied a large population of suicide attempters reported to the police and found that 11.5 percent of all attempts were by self-cutting. He found that the wrist-cutters, compared with other suicide attempters, were significantly younger, more often single, and more often male than non-cutters (40 percent versus 28 percent). Overall, women cutters still outnumbered males, 1.5 to 1. Ferrence and Whitehead[29] support these findings in their study. Of patients seen in medical facilities, a greater proportion of males cut themselves, although the number of males doing so was slightly less than the number of females.

There is thus a range of reported sex ratios among various studies, ranging from an overwhelming predominance of female cutters in clinical studies to more equal ratios in more epidemiological studies and less-selected groups. There may be a higher proportion of males among cutters than among other suicide attempters.

SUICIDAL LETHALITY

While the self-mutilator may show high perturbation, the act of self-cutting is usually of low lethality[20,22,24-26,30-36] and an alternate and generally preferred means of impulse discharge. The same individuals, of course, may also make suicide attempts in their own right and with varying risk, although wrist-cutters appear no more likely than non-cutters to make repeated attempts.[28] Ferrence and White-head[29] found that slightly more females than males said they had wanted to die as a result of their self-injury, though there was no sex difference in the proportion who still wanted to die at the time of interview. Many wrist-cutters when interviewed specifically deny frank suicidal intent, and more important, cite other specific motivations, as will be discussed below.

SYMPTOMATOLOGY

Rosenthal et al.[22] found that 23 out of 24 cutters studied listed their main symptom as depression; 16 complained of chronic feelings of emptiness, very rarely reported by the control group. In Simpson's study of 24 cutters,[36] as their first or second most serious symptom, 9 complained of depression, 21 of emptiness, and 18 of tension. The symptoms of Pao's patients[25] included eating problems, mild swings of depression and elation, brief moments of petit-mal-like lapse of consciousness, absconding from hospital, promiscuity, suicidal ruminations, ingestion of sharp objects or intoxicants, breaking window panes or furniture, burning themselves with lighted cigarettes, attempted arson, etc. Grunebaum and Klerman[31] have also emphasized the rapidly fluctuating mood swings which tend not to be prolonged into classical depression and tension, neither of which respond well to phenothiazine or other tranquillizers or anti-depressant medication except for short periods. In Simpson's series[36] 11 out of 24 cutters showed similar major mood instability.

DIAGNOSIS

Many diagnoses are allotted to these puzzling patients, most of them unhelpful. The process is somewhat like the fable of the blind men trying to describe an elephant. Some staff members concentrate on the "acting-out" behavior and incorrigibility and use the label psychopath; the psycho-analytically oriented staff note the uses of projection and denial, primitive aggressive and sexual fantasies, withdrawal and depersonalization, and may diagnose schizophrenia, as do some of the more impatient physicians who tend to regard any behavior that they don't immediately comprehend as psychotic. Others, especially sensitive to the theatrical aspects of the act of cutting and to the patient's seductive appeal, opt for hysteria.[31]

Schizophrenia and borderline personality state have been favored diagnoses in various published series.[22-24] Asch[34] considered the condition a primitive form of depression called Anhedonia;[89] while Siomopoulos[32] classified it as an impulse neurosis like kleptomania and pyromania. Clanon[37] proposed the term psychoschizopathic. Pao[25] has stressed that the cutters characteristically go "in and out of psychosis in a split second," and that when psychotic they may demonstrate "perceptual distortion, hallucinations, tenuously formulated delusional systems, and other primary process experiences," although several other authors have stressed the relative infrequency of hallucinations or delusions.

Pao,[25] and Goldwyn, Cahill, and Grunebaum[35], have emphasized the differences between high and low lethality groups. The low lethality group, Pao's "delicate cutter", will be described at further length in the next paragraph. The high-risk group consists of two distinct types of patients: Pao's group of course cutters[25]—the psychotically depressed, usually older and more frequently male, patients who cut to kill themselves, seldom needing more than one cut close to vital points such as the radial artery or jugular vein; and the overtly schizophrenic, who cut for various delusory reasons, and account for most of the more bizarre self-mutilations. For example, they include ocular self-mutilators,[38-41] some of whom literally obey and quote the St. Matthew injunction: "If thy right eye causeth thee to stumble, pluck it out, and cast it from thee." They, too, may be of high lethality, and run a high risk of serious permanent disfigurement.

THE TYPICAL CUTTER

A very clear composite picture of the typical wrist-cutter emerges from the classical studies of the syndrome. She is likely to be a young (typically 16-24 years old[25]), attractive, and intelligent woman. Often she had worked in a paramedical or related field[31,35] (5 out of 13 in McEvedy's series[43] and 10 out of 24 in Simpson's series[36] were nurses, medical secretaries, or had strong medical interests and connections). Waldenberg[44] found that significantly more cutters had a history of trauma at school and difficulties with the police. The self-mutilator is quickly labeled by patients and staff[45] and embraces the label "slasher" or "cutter" as an identification. Friedman et al.[46] described a characteristic "low self-esteem, excessive self-criticism and intense guilt," and ascribed the often strong self-denigration to "the presence of a severe, relentless, primitive superego." Many talk of hating their own bodies and feeling forced into their fantasies and the acts of mutilation by their bodies. Novotny[26] has seen them as having narcissistic infantile personalities with masochistic trends, and pointed out that they tend to act so as to involve others in their pathology, such as by absconding from hospital (9 out of 24 in one series absconded repeatedly[36]).

DYSOREXIA

The common incidence of major dysorectic symptoms in the self-mutilators has been more recently recognized. In the Rosenthal et al. series of 24,[22] 15 described either compulsive over-eating, severe anorexia, or periods of both and 7 had frequent nausea. In Simpson's series,[36] 75 percent reported dysorectic symptoms and others who have noted the association include Novotny,[26] Siomopoulos,[32] Asch,[34] McEvedy,[43] and Waldenberg.[44] In some cases, acts of cutting are temporally associated with binge-eating or its associated vomiting. Malcove[47] proposed a relationship between bodily mutilation and learning to eat. The cases of binge-eating described by Nogami[48] in the Japanese literature, show several similarities to the typical self-mutilator—28 percent cut themselves. He has suggested a similar origin in self-directed aggression for self-mutilation and hyperorexia. Shinosaka[49] has pointed out the incidence of mutilation in frank anorexia nervosa, and, as we shall see, there may be similar underlying disturbances of the experience of body image.

DRUG AND ALCOHOL ABUSE

In the series studied by Rosenthal et al.[22] Novotny,[26] Simpson,[36] and Waldenberg,[44] nearly 50 percent of the cutters used drugs and alcohol in excess, and others have also described the association.[24,25,31] Asch[34] has pointed out that hallucinogens, by their tendency further to dissolve distinctions between self and object (already a somewhat tenuous distinction in such persons), are often more anxiety-provoking for the cutter, while amphetamines are popular with them as they can amplify sensation and stimulate bodily awareness. Alcohol is still the drug most commonly abused by cutters.

SEXUAL IDENTITY AND BEHAVIOR

Confusion of sexual identification seems common. Rosenthal et al.[22] demonstrated a greater identification with the father than the mother in 65 percent of the female cutters versus 25 percent of the control group. On the Draw-A-Person Test, half the cutters drew a male first while only 20 percent of the control group did so. Pao[25] stressed the female cutters' repugnance toward their female sexuality. He described male cutters as "pretty boys" and Asch[34] also noted their effeminacy. On psychological tests both males and females showed uncertainty of sexual identity. In Simpson's group,[36] 66 percent showed significant disturbance of sexual identification and 25 percent were at one time actively homosexual or actively disturbed by homosexual impulses. Gardner and Gardner[58] also found more frequent psychosexual disorder in cutters.

Sexual behavior seems often to have an all-or-none quality. Several authors have been impressed by the degree of promiscuity[24,25,34,36,44] of some of the cutters, others seeming to have had no sexual experience.[24,36] Very few, at any rate, seem to have enjoyed their sexual encounters, whatever type they were. Grunebaum and Klerman[31] have suggested that "premature sexual experience, often incestuous, is typical" and Siomopoulos[32] asserts that the cutter is typically given, before puberty, to "excessive masturbatory experimentation," though these observations have not been confirmed by other investigators.

MENSTRUATION

Rosenthal et al.[22] report that 65 percent of female cutters had a negative reaction to menarche, feeling unhappy, disgusted, or frightened (unlike the majority of the control group), that almost half had always had irregular menstrual periods and frequent amenorrhea, and that the more frequent cutters had the more abnormal menstrual rhythms. Pao[25] found that menarche was usually established more than a year before the first cutting experiments, which seldom occurred before 12 or 14 years of age.

In the Rosenthal et al. series, more than 60 percent of the cuts occurred at the time of the patient's menses: 30 percent in the two days preceding menstruation, and 30 percent in the last two days of the period or the first post-menstrual day. Crabtree[45] also noted an increase in cutting at the time of menstruation, and Bettelheim[50] described a girl who cut herself only during her period. On the other hand, neither McEvedy[43] or Waldenberg[44] has been able to demonstrate any relationship between cutting and the phase of the menstrual cycle.

FAMILY BACKGROUND: DEPRIVATION IN CHILDHOOD

Waldenberg[44] found that significantly more cutters, as compared with the control group, came from broken homes and had cold, distant mothers, and that both groups had a striking history of maternal deprivation and felt unable to talk to their parents. (Rosenthal et al.[22] found half of both his cutters and his controls came from homes broken by divorce or death.) Lester[30,51] commented that while suicides typically have a history of childhood experiences of complete parental deprivation through divorce or death, self-mutilators more commonly experience partial loss through emotional distancing and inconsistent maternal warmth. Graff and Mallin[24] describe the typical cutters as having a "cold, domineering mother and a withdrawn, passive father." Lester described the fathers as timid, weak, aloof, and minor characters in the family; the mother as dominant, hostile, critical, and involved in a pathological relationship with the child. Grunebaum and Klerman[31] state that in many cases the father has been seductive and unable to set limits, intermittently indulgent, often inadequate at his occupation, and frequently alcoholic. They saw the mother as usually cold, punitive, and unconsciously provocative, setting high standards for the patient but acting out herself, and further claim that the most striking features of parental behavior are the open display of sexuality and aggression.

Friedman et al.[46] found the striking feature of these girls' relationship to their mothers was expressed in an unremitting need not to "give in" to the mother, and considered this to be a defense against regressive, passive, homosexual wishes in relation to the mother, who is experienced as a very powerful, frighteningly active person who threatens to overwhelm them. Pao[25] agreed with the mother's central role in the family constellation, and with the father's position on the periphery. Bach-y-Rita,[52] in a study of violent prisoners who cut themselves, found a common history of marked early environmental deprivation and violent tumultuous families and cruel parents. Half had lost a parent before the age of 1.

Deprivation of adequate parenting during childhood seems generally agreed to be a common experience in cutters. Rosenthal et al.[22] noted that 60 percent had had surgery, hospitalization for serious illness, or lacerations requiring multiple sutures before the age of 5, often before 18 months of age. None of the control group had similar experiences. Green[12] showed that self-mutilation in schizophrenic children was significantly associated with experience of physical abuse in the first 2 years of life; Mason and Sponholz[53] in an experimental study with monkeys showed a correlation between isolation in childhood and self-mutilating behavior. Grunebaum and Klerman[31] mention that their patients' conceptions were often illegitimate or the cause of their parents' marriages, and that histories of foster home placements are frequent. The patient feels unwanted and rejected by both parents. Friedman et al.[46] found as an invariable feature in all their patients, a constant underlying fear of abandonment. Pao[25] found screen memories of early traumatic experiences of being abandoned and a lack of maternal handling during infancy, as did Kafka.[54] Novotny[26] too, asserts that all his patients experienced "unusual traumatic experiences" during the first year of life, "reflecting a disturbance in the mother-child relationship frequently manifested by minimal physical and/or psychological contact between the child and parents," including very limited handling, and Siomopoulos,[32] in one of his cases, made the same observation. Early childhood desertion and deprivation were also noted by Asch,[34] Waldenberg,[44] and Vereecken.[55] McEvedy[43] found, in the absence of gross maternal deprivation, a high incidence of absence of the father. Dorn[56] has commented that the dreams of some mutilators are similar to those of children who have been abused in childhood.

VERBALIZATION

Graff and Mallin[24] considered that early maternal deprivation lead to a subsequent inability of the patient to give and receive verbal communication, and that many of their patients showed abnormalities of behavior during the preverbal stages of childhood and a later difficulty in verbally communicating their wants or in accurately understanding what was said to them. They felt that this made it difficult for the patient to respond to the usual verbal psychotherapy and that it required the therapist to make a special attempt to help the patient to use words rather than more primitive gestures to communicate. Grunebaum and Klerman[31] have described how the cutter "often does not or cannot verbalize the extent of her tension to her doctor . . . the ability to communicate discomfort is a critical variable in determining whether a slash will occur." In Simpson's series,[36] 66 percent of the patients showed significant difficulties in verbalization, and an improved facility in verbal expression was associated with clinical improvement and cessation of cutting.

Shodell and Reiter[13] postulated that the ability of schizophrenic children to verbalize would help them to use language as a substitute for action when releasing tension and frustration and thus to become frustrated less easily. In fact, they found that the verbal children were significantly less likely to mutilate themselves than the non-verbal children.

THE TYPICAL ACT OF SELF-MUTILATION

Pattern of Cuts

The "delicate cutter" (Pao's phrase) tends to make multiple superficial carefully-considered incisions, often so delicate as to heal without scarring, though a spidery network of dozens of fine scars may be seen. Bach-y-Rita[52] found an average of 93 scars per patient in his series, ranging from 3 to 150. It is rare for such a person to cut just once. In the Rosenthal et al. series,[22] half had cut themselves on more than 5 occasions, and 3 patients alone totaled more than 200 cutting episodes. Wrist-cutting is typical, though cutting right up the forearm to the antecubital fossa is quite common, and they may cut the legs, abdomen, neck or face. Other varieties of self-mutilation may occur in the same patients, especially burning themselves with cigarettes, dermatitis artefacta, and tattooing.[57] The cuts vary in depth, from very superficial scratching to full thickness lacerations, though blood is usually drawn even by the scratches. A proportion of patients may break windows and cut themselves with the glass; more usually, the instruments used are razor-blades or glass from broken glasses, mirrors, or light-bulbs. In a hospital setting, there is a tendency to favor objects obtained by breaking or bending hospital rules.

Motives and Precipitants

Offer and Barglow[59] have proposed several motives such as gaining attention, the need to be loved and cared for, attempts to control aggression, tension reduction, and gaining prestige among the social group in the ward. Elements of such motivations may well play a part in the dynamics of self-mutilation, but they are inadequate explanations—Why choose to gain attention or express the need for love by cutting one's wrist? Battle and Pollitt[60] divided self-inflicted injuries into three categories: (1) suicidal attempts of a determined and violent kind, (2) self-mutilation deliberately carried out for conscious gain (e.g., Clark and Campbell[61] report that about 2 percent of gunshot wounds among soldiers were probably self-inflicted), and (3) self-mutilation without conscious motive. We will discuss this last group now.

By far the major precipitant is an experience or threat of loss or abandonment—a mother hospitalized, being jilted by a boyfriend or girlfriend, separation, rejection, the loss of a meaningful person, or an impasse in interpersonal relations.[26,31,35,46] Asch[34] described how separation from important objects can produce severe panic and depression in these patients who "desperately need to maintain contact and closeness with their objects at any price." Rosenthal et al.[22] found that cutting was related to staff departures and absences. In their study, more than half of the episodes were on Friday or Saturday, with another peak on Wednesday afternoons when the resident staff left the wards to attend an outside clinic. Cutting occurred in two clear time periods: half between 10 A.M. and 2 P.M., and the other half between 4 P.M. and 8 P.M. Some occurred during active planning for discharge, and some were directly related to a quarrel or disappointment with the doctor, or when he went on holiday. Nelson and Grunebaum[23] also noticed that cuts were preceded by anger towards the staff, sometimes in the context of ungratified erotic transference reactions to their therapists. Watson[62] used a Repertory Grid Technique to study the motives of one mutilator and found cutting to be consistently associated with the constructs "feeling depressed, feeling angry, thinking people were unfriendly, *wanting to talk to someone and being unable to,* and having the same thoughts for a long time."

Two other themes have been noted with some consistency. One is the frustration of experiencing powerful emotions which cannot be expressed in words.[23] The other is the turning of active into passive—the passive experience of being left (which is feared) is transferred into the active experience of leaving (by absconding); the passive experience of being hurt by a malevolent world is transferred into the active process of hurting oneself. This latter construct is sometimes expressed directly: "The world has hurt me so much, so I thought I'd hurt myself."

Epidemic

Cutting behavior can be learned and propagated in a hospital, clinic, or institution, and often sustained by the responses of the hospital personnel, which Offer and Barglow[59] have described as "fragmented and diffuse, with widespread confusion, guilt, heated arguments, and breakdowns in communication"; the staff alarm exaggerating the patients' fears. Many patients learn about wrist-slashing while in the hospital, and as Grunebaum and Klerman[31] have emphasized, feelings of competition between patients may arise, the patient with the most stitches being the "chief cutter," a title for which there may be some competition, as patients cut to prove themselves the most unhappy. Matthews[83] has described such an epidemic of self-injury in an adolescent unit, and Simpson[36] has described an epidemic in a general hospital psychiatric ward that eventually involved 12 patients and 2 nurses who cut themselves.

While patients may claim afterwards that they do not wish others to know of their act, they often manage to flaunt the wound or their bandage like a newly-engaged girl wearing her diamond ring for the first time.

The Activity of Cutting

The circumstances of the act of cutting are almost stereotyped and many authors' descriptions show striking agreement.[24,25,31,32,44,46,54,64,65] The various precipitating factors contribute to feelings of anger, self-hatred, or depression, but tension is predominant, and rises steadily, especially when in isolation or when one cannot act on his or her feelings. During the phase of mounting tension, one becomes aware of the wish to cut himself and may struggle in conflict over whether or not to do so. Some describe "a feeling that something was going to happen," or that "I have to do something."[52] (Some patients describe a mild sense of relief experienced early in a day of tension when they decide to cut themselves later, or remember where they have hidden their razor-blade.) At this point the patient will usually seek solitude if not alone already. As the rising tension becomes unbearable, a transition into a depersonalization state occurs. "You feel a lot, but then you don't feel anything."[22] Words very commonly used to describe the state are "numb," "empty," "floating—as if I had no insides"—the person becomes totally self-engrossed and oblivious of the surroundings or other people. The flat, withdrawn, dead dissociated state is no more bearable. Suddenly, the patient cuts, often expressing lack of direct awareness of the cutting act. However, some control is clearly exercised, as the extent and depth of the wound is generally limited and its site carefully chosen. Some describe stopping cutting when they have had "enough blood" or just "enough."

Far from an act of suicide, such self-mutilators commit what amounts to anti-suicide, employing the wrist-cutting as a means of gaining reintegration, repersonalization, and an emphatic return to reality and life from the state of dead unreality. They seem to have some awareness of just what is needed to end the depersonalization— usually the sight and feel of blood, sometimes the sight of the wound gaping, "seeing what was inside." Rosenthal et al. have characterized the meanings of the act as "I bleed; therefore I am alive" or "I do have insides; I can see them."[22] Grunebaum and Klerman[31] have called wrist-slashing a "self-prescribed treatment that does not involve verbalizing feelings in psychotherapy."

Gero and Rubinfine's patient[64] described the experience as a pleasure in the sensation "of opening up, of creating a gap, and the sweet feeling of blood flowing out" and Kafka's patient[54] described "the exquisite border experience of sharply 'becoming alive'" with the flow of blood, "like a voluptuous bath, a sensation of pleasant warmth which, as it spread over the hills and valleys of [her] body, moulded its contour and sculpted its form." If any pain is felt, which, as we shall see, is uncommon, this also serves the function of return to reality. "To feel is reassuring that one is alive, even if that feeling is pain."[65]

A sexual metaphor is apparent and some patients explicitly liken cutting to sexual intercourse or masturbation[44,46,65] in the rising tension followed by the orgasmic quality of the relief and pleasure as the blood flows, followed by relaxation and calm to the point that they may even fall asleep.

Pain

The typical absence of pain during the actual cutting is a very common and intriguing feature, noted by many clinicians.[22,24,25,34,35,52] Gross lacerations may be inflicted without the patient appearing to experience any suffering; cutting tendons,[31] lacerating vagina and cervix,[67-70] or even performing a bilateral orchidectomy[71] or hysterectomy of a prolapsed uterus[72] without anesthetic or notable pain. One may be able to suture the wounds without needing further anesthetic. McKerracher, Loughnane, and Watson[11] reported that only 28 percent of their series admitted to feeling any pain when cutting, while only 2 out of 21 of Novotny's cases[26] and 2 out of 24 of Simpson's patients[36] felt pain. Pain may return anywhere from a few hours to a couple of days later.[11,67] Asch[34] has suggested that the boys in his series of cutters did experience pain on cutting, in comparison to the girls who outnumbered the boys 5 to 1. This observation has still to be confirmed by others; the four male cutters in Simpson's series[36] did not describe pain.

Blood

Blood has a special significance for the self-mutilator, functioning in part as a transitional object,[73] a "potential security blanket capable of giving warmth and comforting envelopment . . . carried within oneself"[54] and apparently a necessary component of the process whereby the cutting serves to recathect the depersonalized body-image and reestablish a functioning sense of the boundaries between inside and outside, self and not-self. Some patient descriptions of the part blood necessarily plays in this process have already been quoted. In Rosenthal et al.[22] many patients made spontaneous comments conveying positive reactions to the sight of the blood, a happy fascination with it and its warmth, as did those described by Pao,[25] Offer and Barglow,[59] Conn[74] ("I had to see blood. I wanted to see blood come out."), and Waldenberg[44] ("incredibly exciting, incredibly beautiful . . . it makes me feel very happy."). Goldwyn, Cahill, and Grunebaum's patients[35] felt that the flowing blood "drained something bad from them" and Simpson's[67] case of genital self-mutilation felt "something evil and tense within her, leaking away." There appears to be no interest in stale or clotted blood, in menstrual blood, or in other people's blood.

In Burnham and Giovacchini's case,[65] blood was experienced as "warm, comforting, and maternal" likened to the feeling of freshly voided urine when she wet the bed as a child. Some of Asch's patients[34] described the sensation of their surroundings becoming drained of color, and white during the phase immediately preceding the cut. One explained, "There was too much white, white nurses, white doctors, white sheets, white walls. It was such a relief to cut and see the red blood appear" adding a dimension of self-induced color-shock to the reintegrative process. The sought-after sensation may be described with great sensuality as in Richardson,[75] "The real thing that excites me most is to see my blood, the pleasure of it coming, crawling and dribbling over your flesh—you know that its really you coming out. Deep rich red, the color, the velvety warmness. Sometimes I give myself a nosebleed just to feel my nose being warmed, invaded by liquid rubies or a vintage claret—it moves slow like the birth of a child or like wearing an Afghan coat on a cold day. . . ."

Outcome

There have been no fully adequate follow-up studies. Novotny[26] comments that "the more frequently self-cutting occurred, the worse was the overall outlook for the particular patient." Grunebaum and Klerman[31] record that one outcome is the patient's transfer to a custodial institution "where the doors are not all open, limit-setting may be easier" and there is less intense staff involvement with the patients. Watson's case,[62] becoming more and more disturbed, was transferred to a long-stay mental hospital where the self-mutilation abruptly ceased. Others[31] are simply discharged abruptly, and "despite the hazard of suicide" some appeared to recover quite well. Only Nelson and Grunebaum[23] have managed to follow up 19 such patients for 5 to 6 years after their initial hospital contacts: 10 were regarded as well or improved, based on criteria of social adjustment and decrease of psychiatric symptoms. 4 showed no significant change in adjustment or symptoms and continued wrist-slashing, not responding to attempts at limit-setting, and requiring frequent hospital admissions; 3 who had been regarded as intermittently psychotic, 1 with psychotic depression, and two with strong self-destructive impulses and delusions of guilt, committed suicide.

THEORIES, MECHANISMS, AND EXPLANATIONS

The first significant attempt to conceptualize self-mutilating behavior was presented by Menninger.[76] He regarded self-mutilation as an example of self-destructive behavior that allows the person to live, a suicidal act in which the suicidal impulse is concentrated on part of the self as a substitute for the whole, which he termed *focal suicide*. With regard to the suicidal impulse, Menniger proposed that it had 3 components: the desire to hurt others, the desire to be punished, and the desire to escape from an unbearable situation. He considered that self-mutilation satisfied the first 2 motives: that the patient, angry at someone, was able to hurt the significant other; and, feeling the need to be punished for some actual or imagined offense or sin, caused pain to the self. Although this was a tidy theoretical formulation, it is not totally adequate to explain the phenomenology of self-mutilation. Pain, as we have seen, is often strikingly absent, and self-punishment does not appear as a prominent motive. Anger at a significant other is common but the anxiety the act may cause to others is seldom considered by the cutter. On the other hand, Menninger's third component is clearly seen—the desire to escape from an unbearable situation, first from growing tension, and then from the resultant depersonalization. Self-mutilation seems to represent an intense intrapersonal act in the context of a tense interpersonal situation.

Rosenthal et al.[22] felt that the common element was that an overwhelming situation, viewed by the psyche as catastrophic, is counteracted by a physical act performed by and against the self, as a means of regaining control; they linked it to Anna Freud's (and their) observation that adults in helpless and overwhelmingly passive situations often identify with the aggressor and act out against themselves, the victim.

In women, Deutsch[77] saw the act as one way of "solving the menstrual conflict," the choice being either to eliminate bleeding, as in amenorrhea (we have already seen that menstrual conflicts are common in these patients and amenorrhea is not uncommon) or what she called vicarious menstruation—invoking displacement and referral of the bleeding to a part of the body removed from the genitals, rendering the bleeding visible and explicable, with other psychological factors determining the choice of the substitute bleeding organ. Asch,[34] emphasizing how rare self-cutting was before menarche, also proposed a mechanism of displaced genital bleeding, commenting that "the relief in seeing the gaping, open wound may be part of the recreation, through an identification with the aggressor, of some conception of menstruation as a helplessly and passively experienced genital mutilation."

Siomopoulos[32] regarded repeated self-cutting as a distorted form of autoerotic activity, the cutter "opening up symbolically on her skin multiple little genitals . . . which become available for all sorts of autoerotic manipulations." Vereecken[55] also emphasized the poor Id control, the failure to regulate autoeroticism and autoaggression, and considered the mutilation a masturbation equivalent. He states that "Oedipal relationships have assumed very concrete forms in such cases." Friedman et al.[46] proposed that the typical unconscious fantasy was of "destroying the genitals seen as the source of the urges; through displacement, whichever part of the body is attacked then represents the genitals" whereas in a suicide attempt, he feels it is the whole body which is attacked as the source of the unwelcome urges. He points out that whereas a period of calm often precedes a suicide attempt, the self-mutilator describes a state of calm after the act. Friedman regards this as relief that, despite the injury, the genitals are safe.

McKerracher, Street, and Segal[66] studied a group of subnormal female prisoners diagnosed as psychopaths, a small sample biased further by the difficulty of finding patients who could complete the tests. They hypothesized that the mutilators were cutting themselves in response to boredom (hence the increase in cutting on weekends) and frustration. However, the mutilators did not rate themselves as more bored, tense, or anxious than did the non-mutilators, so the difference might lie in their response to boredom and tension. They did report themselves to be more phobic, obsessional, and preoccupied with bodily complaints than non-mutilators; there was no difference in I.Q.

Panton[18] compared MMPI scores in male self-mutilating and

non-self-mutilating prisoners. The mutilators appear to be more hostile, have more inner turmoil, and more maladjusted. He claimed that they were suffering more from personality disorders than from psychoses, although they scored significantly higher on the schizophrenia scale and on the MMPI scale of psychotic tendency. They didn't have elevated depression scores on the MMPI, so he felt they were not suicidal, although Lester[30] reviewing recent studies, has claimed that the depression score is not related to suicidal intent. Panton considered that the non-mutilators tended to show a hysterical reaction to stress rather than a self-destructive reaction, but his distinction is not altogether clear. These findings may be compared with Taylor's study[57] comparing tattooed and clear-skinned Borstal girls. The heavily tattooed girls were reported as more aggressive, uncooperative, unstable, and insecure; a statistically significant number had been involved in escaping and violence, were active homosexuals, and on the 16 P.F. test, were lower on Superego strength, more forthright, radical, with higher tension, and had a strong tendency towards paranoid ideation and low self-integration.

More recently, Gardner and Gardner[58] have reported a controlled study of 22 female habitual self-cutters. In comparison with non-cutting controls, the only significant difference was that the cutters more frequently showed psychosexual disorders. Using the Middlesex Hospital Questionnaire and the obsessive-compulsive section of the Tavistock Inventory, the cutters proved to be markedly obsessional. Siomopoulos[32] suggested that the irresistibility of the urge to cut was different from compulsive behavior in that the obsessive-compulsive person experiences his impulses as ego-alien, while the cutter feels his unavoidable behavior to be ego-syntonic, even if unwelcome.

Graff and Mallin[24] considered that in a single act, cutting served simultaneously to elicit therapeutic maneuvers from others, to attack and punish the rejecting mother, and to provide the self-stimulation needed for relief. Following Stekel they suggest that the patient had protected herself against maternal rejection by introjecting the mother, allowing her both to hold onto the lost object and to deal with it by destroying that part of it within herself. They also suggest that their patients had a great need to be held and cuddled, and regarded the cutting as a pre-verbal communication of rage to the mother and also as an alternative way of gaining stimulation when they were unable to get this through being held. Friedman et al.[46] stressed two meanings of the act, "destroying the body, regarded by the adolescent as the instrument through which actual expression can be given to the wish to kill the mother," and "turning the feeling of helplessness in the face of the aggressive and sexual urges into one of omnipotence" which is similar to the other aspects we have stressed of the technique of turning passive into active. Rado[78] referred to self-cutting as representing a symbolic castration in order to avoid real castration— "the choice of the lesser evil." Bettelheim[50] has emphasized the similarities between such mutilation and the cutting of the skin in primitive initiation rites.

Novotny[26] felt that as self-cutting is a hostile, aggressive action, it has to be seen (as far as it is a direct libidinal gratification) as a masochistic phenomenon. He also stressed the passive-to-active transformation, considering that the patient's rage was projected onto the environment and then the assault which is feared from the environment is carried out by the patient herself. He proposed that being in control by these means not only reduced tension, but that it required less energy than would be needed to cope with the state of rising tension using projective defenses alone. He identified the characteristic uses of the oral zone for symptom formation, the low frustration and anxiety tolerance, impaired impulse control, and related difficulties, suggesting that these implied a predominance of conflicts characteristic of the earliest phases of psychosexual development. He also raised the odd question, "Does the 'self-penetration' which is one aspect of the self-cutting also represent symbolically the wished for and feared penetration by the father?"

Kafka[54] emphasized the problems of limits—"the limits of her body, the limits of her power, and the limits of her capacity to feel." His patient treated parts of the surface of her body as if it were not quite living skin and he considered that she was preoccupied with what was for her the unfinished business of establishing her body scheme. Hoffer,[79] observing a tendency to self-mutilation in the first year of life, postulated a "pain barrier," a mechanism which normally protected the infant from its own destructive impulses until the boundaries between the self and the non-self had been established. He believed that impairment of this mechanism was responsible for self-mutilation in infancy and possibly in later life. Stengel[80] pointed out the puzzling discrepancy between the reactions to self-inflicted and extraneous noxious stimuli shown by low-grade subnormal and proposed that "self-inflicted pain is experienced differently from pain the source of which is outside the body."

Wahl[85] has illustrated the occasional belief that retaliation towards others can be effected by self-damage, as though everyone were a part of our own substance, in the case of a young schizophrenic boy who often slashed himself with a knife, smiling as he watched his blood flow. Asked why he did this, his reply was "All the world bleeds when I'm cut, but I have more blood than they do and I'll live when they are all bled out." Then he added, "But my parents and sister bleed most of all when I cut myself."

Offer and Barglow[59] stressed the extent of the secondary gain involved and some conscious effort to gain gratification from the environment, particularly increased prestige among the peer group, competition with other group members, expression of anger toward the family or hospital personnel, or desire for more attention from the staff. While such factors may play a part in the generation of the cutting act, primary internal gains far outweigh secondary gratifications in most instances, and the attention attracted is more often hostile and rejecting than satisfying. Declich[81] regarded self-mutilation as the expression of an altered sentiment of corporality which leads to "a rejection of the part of the body which the individual no longer recognizes as part of himself and which he really wishes to remove." Crabtree[45] considered repetitive self-mutilation as a particular form of sadomasochism in which "the core instinctual issue is expressed, initially in a self-enclosed way, such that the patient takes his own body as an object." By increase of skin cathexis and consequently increased cathexis of bodily ego boundaries, self-cutting can help the patient differentiate with greater clarity what is inside from what is outside, self from not-self. Dabrowski[82] tells of a little boy who mutilated himself by dropping boiling water on his hand and explained, "Only this can bring me back the feeling of myself."

Many theories deal with the central role of depersonalization in the phenomenology of self-mutilation, and there have been three main discussions of depersonalization, what Plath describes as "the thin papery feeling."[84] Asch[34] has described a process whereby, if the aggressive drives cannot be warded off successfully and become more intense and eventually overwhelming, depersonalization is brought into play as a typical and specific defense mechanism. He sees it as arising as the ego regresses from even that fragile, tentative distinction between self and object which these girls maintain even at the best of times, leading to further dissolution of these filmy boundaries as they depersonalize. Their acts are attempts to feel themselves again. Lacking the Cartesian confidence of "I think, therefore I am," they work on the principle of "I feel, therefore I am." Such reassurances of existence seem seldom, however, to last very much longer than they continue to feel the immediate sensation they have provoked, as they seem to lack the ability to firmly retain its memory.

Waltzer,[103] defining depersonalization as a state of splitting or fragmentation of the ego, involving an alteration in the state of consciousness, suggests that it can be viewed as an unconscious expression of self-destructive urges, an unconscious but incomplete withdrawal from both the external and intra-psychic worlds. During this state, "there is characteristically a temporary alteration of the capacity to feel, to react, and above all to control impulse." He considers the state to represent for the ego an unstable compromise between ambivalent feelings and thoughts of wanting to live and wanting to die. In this dissociated state, the person "acts as both participant and observer" and "responds as though his behavior were being carried out by another person." Although designed to ward off painful affect and anxiety, depersonalization can of itself precipitate "severe and overwhelming panic secondary to the sensations of unreality and fragmentation."

Pao[25] specified that the split in the ego was such that motor control was retained in the absence of full consciousness. He considered that under the stress of conflict, the patient gave up ego-directed interaction with the external environment and entered a regressed ego state, surrendering autonomous ego function to a subsystem within the ego which took over the operation of only certain ego apparatuses, having no control of the overall ego. Lower[86] called depersonalization a regressive defense against the threat of masochistic surrender, also serving to gratify a sadomasochistic Oedipal wish. Arlow[87] writes of a disowning fantasy, specific for depersonalization, which he formulated as, "this is not really happening to me, but to another person; therefore, I have nothing to worry about." Bradlow[88] considered the fantasy to be "this is not really being experienced by me, but by someone else. That other person is not human. I am. Therefore, I have nothing to be anxious about." The practical uses of such formulations are less than clear.

Yap[63] has made a special study of self-mutilators from the point of view of an existential psychotherapist. He stresses that all of his patients experienced "a crippled existence," and, being significantly unsure of their 'Dasein,' lacked a positive, self-confident feeling of being in the world. He felt that this non-experiencing or experiencing of a crippled 'Sein' is caused by negation in early childhood, by neglect or by over-protection which also negates the gratification of wants; by hurting or belittling, especially in the course of an education which involves physical and psychical assault; or because a child's demand for affection is greater than normal. Yap's description of self-mutilation in the context of needing to affirm the reality of self is similar to the descriptions we have derived above. The self-mutilation may improve the experience of a 'Sein' but not lead to a positive 'Dasein.' This is sufficient to encourage them to continue with the attempts, though the continued nonaffirmation of their 'Dasein' confirms their central existential doubt.

Finally, one can note the possibility that these episodes could in part represent complex seizure phenomena, as they resemble in several ways some manifestations of temporal lobe epilepsy. An assiduous EEG search for temporal lobe abnormalities could be fruitful.

MANAGEMENT

Everyone who has written any clinical account of cutting behavior has agreed that it is very difficult to manage or treat; on no single point is there greater agreement. This relatively common condition probably constitutes one of the most difficult treatment and management problems in clinical psychiatry. Few of the studies that have been reported have much useful advice to offer, but on the basis of the better understanding of the phenomenology of self-mutilation which this review provides, we should be able to discern some general therapeutic principles. Most slashers are seen in a hospital, having been admitted after an episode of slashing or having cut in the course of an admission, and it is in this context that we will discuss treatment. Attempting to manage a chronic cutter without admitting that person to a hospital can be even more difficult.

Many of the management problems arise from the effects that wrist-slashing produces among the staff. Pao[25] has pointed out that just as cutting can be concerned with castration anxiety in the patient, it can evoke castration anxiety among the members of the staff. They may also feel menaced by the rapidity with which the patient regresses to the intensely self-engrossed, object-unrelated state. Suddenly, you find yourself having completely lost touch with the patient, quite alone in her company. The primitive aggression of the regressed state is also menacing. After a slash, staff attitudes are usually highly aroused and fluctuate between feelings of rage, guilt, shame, sympathy, understanding and solicitude, resentment, aloneness, and the bitter sensation of feeling quite unable to cope effectively with a clinical situation, frustration, and the urge to retaliate. The rapidity with which the patient's mood may swing down unpredictably, apparently without cause is especially upsetting to staff who have come to rely on their ability to understand a patient and to predict behavior. The patient can learn to use brittleness defensively in relations with such a staff.

Offer and Barglow[59] remark that the great anxiety of the personnel makes the patient still more fearful and might lead her to fail to exercise whatever controls she has, thinking "If they think I can't control myself, it must be so."

Over a period of weeks, if the patient continues to cut, she tends to become the center of staff conflict and often intense disagreement as to proper diagnosis and management, with a special focus on the amount of supervision needed and the restrictions to be applied. This has to be considered very cautiously, as some of the suggestions are retaliatory rather than therapeutic, and may actually lead to an increase in the patient's disturbance. It is essential to communicate to the patient, verbally and non-verbally and with impressive consistency, that her welfare is the genuine and non-punitive concern of the staff; that they understand how alarming her state can be, but that they feel confident of their ability to cope with it and that they believe that she can assume responsibility for her own life and actions.

Strauss et al.[90] have discussed how such patients challenge the usual team approach. Members of the team can be enticed into considering themselves better able to handle the patient than is the therapist, especially, as Grunebaum and Klerman[31] emphasize, if the therapist is a young, inexperienced resident. They often regard his plans as too permissive for the patient, and want more exacting limit-setting. The patient becomes a "special patient" with the attendant draw-backs of this status, as Burnham[91] and Main[92] have described. Such patients tend to be rejected by most staff members, although this is often rationalized medically by describing the patient pejoratively as "manipulative" or "attention-seeking" (though it is only attention-getting behavior that we notice) as if such labels automatically absolve us of our responsibility to understand the patient or justify increasingly arbitrary administrative decisions. The other staff may become so hostile that the therapist is forced into an adversary position, taking the patient's part in all confrontations.

The patient may seek out relatively junior staff members to confide in especially and usually asks them to promise not to divulge to others what she may tell them, forming what Grunebaum and Klerman have called a co-conspiratorial dyad,[31] maneuvering the staff members into a position in which they are caught between professional and personal obligations. They may also form such dyads with another patient, who is sworn not to reveal that she knows the patient intends to cut. The other patient may feel in such conflict over this, as to cut herself, and nurses have been known to cut under similar circumstances.[36]

The patient often regards her family with disfavor and so too frequently the family members may be excluded from the treatment process. Yet a resolution of family impasse may be necessary if the patient is to return to the family and have any real chance of remaining well.

Nelson and Grunebaum[23] have reported some of the features of those patients who had done well in their follow-up study. Half had been helped by individual psychotherapy, and 9 out of 10 related their improvement to having gotten married, to their relationships with their spouses, and their responsibility as parents. Increasing self-esteem was also important. Two major components of improvement seemed to be increased verbal expression of feelings and learning to use constructive behavioral alternatives. They had often learned to discharge their feelings—angry, sad, or anxious—by talking about them, often in the context of a long-term relationship with a therapist who she perceived as someone who would not reject her. Identification with significant emotionally healthy figures who behaved in socially acceptable ways, including, hopefully, the therapist, helped some who were not able to verbalize well. They specifically commented that "insight into the genesis of slashing behavior usually was not helpful" and one can imagine how unhelpful it could be to offer some of the tentative and speculative interpretations we have reviewed above to a patient under the guise of insight.

Graff and Mallin[24] comment that some periods of cutting were ended or staved off by the therapist putting an arm around the patient, for the cutters' methods of relief are physical, pre-verbal messages and may need qualitatively similar replies. "The therapist must remember," they add, "that the patient wishes physical contact as a little child; therefore, he must avoid presenting sexual stimulation," and suggest that she be treated with the same concern, attendance, and discipline "as if she were his little daughter." Other therapists would not accept the use of physical contact in this way.

Burnham and Giovacchini[65] regard it as a major task of therapy "to invade the isolation" and to help the patient develop awareness of her emotional interactions with others. The staff should not collaborate in maintaining an aloof distance from the patient, but confront her with the very disturbing emotional effect she has on others, for such patients often seem genuinely unaware of the extent of the effect they have on others. She can learn that she is capable of more satisfying relationships with others. Easson[94] has stressed similar features in describing the management of cutting episodes in the seriously disturbed adolescent. Crabtree,[45] a proponent of

intensive psychotherapy, even proposes the establishment and maintenance of "an interactional transference psychosis," insisting that the
patient is responsible for her own behavior and its consequences;
stressing delay of impulses, consideration of alternatives, and the
existence of a genuine choice of actions. He, too, proposes the honest
and clear expression to the patient of the feelings she arouses. Loomis
and Horsley,[93] though speaking from a behavioral point of view,
propose broadly similar action. Pro-social behavior incompatible with
harming oneself should be reinforced. Following a cut, a patient should
not be excused from her responsibilities. Necessary medical treatment
of the injury should be carried out with minimal interpersonal reinforcement. Suturing, if needed, should be done with minimal expression
of verbal concern and, if practical, the patient should be provided
with gauze and tape to apply herself. In such ways, reinforcement
of self-destructive behavior can be avoided or minimized. Gardner
and Gardner[58] have proposed that behavioral techniques such as
autogenous relaxation training or aversive conditioning might be
effective. Wilbur, Chandler, and Carpenter,[95] among others, have
described the modification of self-mutilative behavior among severely
retarded children by adversive conditioning, but the rationale for
aversive conditioning in adults such as we have described is obscure,
and relaxation-based deconditioning of anxiety responses would seem
more likely to succeed.

Individual psychotherapy needs to deal with impulse control and
enable the patient to abandon pathological techniques including projection and acting-out that perpetuate self-defeating interpersonal relations.[31] The positive aspects of the personality should be emphasized
and nurtured. Setting limits is a major problem. Firmness and consistency are needed, but one must distinguish between appropriate
restrictions and the retaliation that is aroused by acting-out that
challenges conventional societal mores. Especially as discharge nears,
the patient may act in such a way as to force the doctor to keep
her in the hospital. Further slashing, drinking, or similar episodes
should not lead to reimposition of special attention and restrictions.
The patient's continuing responsibility for her actions must still be
stressed, while plans for the future proceed.

Other modes of treatment may become available in time if a
biological basis for the syndrome is found. There are several faint
evidences of such a possibility. An animal model for the condition
may emerge. Tinkelpaugh[96] has described self-mutilation in a male
rhesus monkey separated from his mate, and the author, in conjunction
with Levinson[97] has seen self-mutilation in a depressed chimpanzee.

Genovese, Napoli, and Bolego-Zonta[98] have reported the production of self-mutilating behavior in rodents by injecting pemoline gastrically, and Peters[99] produced similar effects in rats with intra-gastric caffeine. Another possible model exists in the Lesch-Nyhan syndrome,[100] an inborn error metabolism (specifically a defect in hypoxanthine-guanine-phosphoribosyl-transferase) leading to hyperuricaemia, choreoathetoid movements, mental retardation, and persistent and grossly disfiguring self-mutilation. Several reports have shown that hyperaggressive behavior induced in rats (by isolation, or transection of the olfactory bulbs) was alleviated by giving them L-5 hydroxytrytophan. Mizuno and Yugari[101] gave this substance orally to four patients with the Lesch-Nyhan syndrome. Self-mutilation stopped in every case, after 1 to 3 days, and was controlled on maintenance doses. They postulate that the faulty purine metabolism leads to decreased serotonin levels in some parts of the brain, somehow producing the self-mutilation. The possibility of related but more minor metabolic anomalies in the common typical cutter warrants serious study. Cooper and Fowlie[102] describe gross self-mutilation in a severely subnormal girl unhelped by any therapy. On lithium carbonate in typical clinical doses and to the usual blood-levels, she became quieter and cooperative within a week, stopped mutilating, and has shown no recurrence in 5 years on lithium. This report also deserves further study, as does the possible implication of temporal lobe phenomena, which could respond to the use of anticonvulsant medication.

CONCLUSION

We have attempted to demonstrate that there exists a clearly identifiable condition of self-mutilation, usually involving wrist-cutting, which exhibits much of the stability of a syndrome. This synthesis of the results of many disparate studies shows that much more is known about these puzzling patients than is generally recognized and a more rational approach to treatment can be attempted. While self-mutilators represent a significant problem group within the territory of suicide and para-suicide, they can be clearly distinguished from other similar presentations with significantly higher lethality, and thus warrant different treatment.

REFERENCES

1. Battacharyya NN: Indian puberty rites. Indian Studies Past and Present. Calcutta, 1968
2. Montagu MFA: Ritual mutilation among primitive people. Ciba Symposia 8:421–436, 1946

3. Phillips RH, Muzaffer A: Some aspects of self-mutilation in the general population of a large psychiatric hospital. Psychiatr 35:421–423, 1961

4. Ressman AA, Butterworth T: Localized acquired hypertrichosis. Arch Dermatol Syphilis 65:418–423, 1952

5. Barter JR, Swaback DO, Todd D: Adolescent suicide attempts: A follow-up study of hospitalized patients. Arch Gen Psychiatry 19:523–527,1968

6. Ballinger BR: Minor self-injury. Br J Psychiatry 115:535–538, 1971

7. Whitehead PC, Ferrence RG, Johnson FG: Physicians reports of self-injury cases among their patients not seen in hospital. Life-Threatening Behavior 2:137–146, 1972

8. Whitehead PC, Johnson FG, Ferrence RG: Measuring the incidence of self-injury: Some methodological and design considerations. Am J Orthopsychiatry 1:142–148, 1973

9. Johnson FG, Ferrence RG, Whitehead PC: Self-injury: Identification and intervention. Can Psychiatr Assoc J 18:101–105, 1973

10. Johnson FG: (personal communication), London, Ontario, 1974

11. McKerracher DW, Loughnane T, Watson R: Self-mutilation in female psychopaths. Br J Psychiatry 114:821–823, 1968

12. Green AH: Self-destructive behavior in physically abused schizophrenic children. Arch Gen Psychiatry 19:171–179, 1968

13. Shodell MJ, Reiter HH: Self-mutilative behavior in verbal and non-verbal schizophrenic children. Arch Gen Psychiatry 19:453–455, 1968

14. Reiger W: Suicide attempts in a federal prison. Arch Gen Psychiatry 24:532–535, 1971

15. Fully G, Hivert PE, Schaub S: Suicides en mileau carceral en France depuis 1955. Annales Medecine Legale 45:108–115, 1965

16. Beto DR, Claghorn JL: Factors associated with self-mutilation within the Texas department of correction. Am J Correction 30:25–27, 1968

16a. Claghorn JL, Beto DR: Self-mutilation in a prison mental hospital. J Soc Therapy 13:133–141, 1967

17. Wilmotte JN, Plat-Mendlewicz J: Epidemiology of suicidal behavior in Belgian prisoners, in Danto BL (ed) Jail House Blues. Michigan, Epic, 1973, pp 57–82

18. Panton JH: The identification of predispositional factors in self-mutilation with a state prison population. J Clin Psychol, 18:63–67, 1962

19. Beigel A, Russell HE: Suicidal behavior in jail—prognostic considerations. Hosp Community Psychiatry 23:361–363, 1972

20. Danto BL: The suicidal inmate. Police Chief 8:64–71, 1971

21. Cooper HHA: Self-mutilation by Peruvian prisoners. Int J Offender Therapy 3:180–188, 1971

22. Rosenthal RJ, Rinzler C, Wallsh R, Klausner E: Wrist-cutting syndrome: The meaning of a gesture. Am J Psychiatry 11:1363–1368, 1972

23. Nelson SH, Grunebaum H: A follow-up study of wrist-slashers. Am J Psychiatry 10:1345–1349, 1971

24. Graff H, Mallin R: The syndrome of the wrist-cutter. Am J Psychiatry 1:36–41, 1967
25. Pao Ping-Nie: The syndrome of delicate self-cutting. Br J Med Psychol 42:195–206, 1969
26. Novotny P: Self-cutting. Bull Menninger Clin 36:505–514, 1972
27. Fabian JJ, Maloney MP, Ward MP: Self-destructive and suicidal behaviors in a neuropsychiatric inpatient faculty. Am J Psychiatry 12:1383–1385, 1973
28. Clendenin WW, Murphy GE: Wrist-cutting: New epidemiological findings. Arch Gen Psychiatry 25:465–469, 1971
29. Ferrence RG, Whitehead P: (personal communication), London, Ontario 1974
30. Lester D: Attempts to predict suicidal risk using psychological tests. Psychol Bull 74:1–17, 1970
31. Grunebaum HU, Klerman GL: Wrist-slashing. Am J Psychiatry 124:4, 1967
32. Siomopoulos V: Repeated self-cutting: An impulse neurosis. Am J Psychother 28:85–94, 1974
33. Rinzler C, Shaprio D: Wrist-cutting and suicide. Mt Sinai J Med NY 35:485–488, 1968
34. Asch SS: Wrist-scratching as a symptom of anhedonia: A predepressive state. Psychoanal Q 40:603–617, 1971
35. Goldwyn RM, Cahill JL, Grunebaum HU: Self-inflicted injury to the wrist. Plas Reconstr Sur 39:583–589, 1967
36. Simpson MA: The phenomenology of self-mutilation in a general hospital setting. Canad Psychiat Ass J 20:429–434,1975
37. Clanon TL: Persecutory feelings and self-mutilation, in prisoners. Correct Psychiatry J Soc Ther 11:96–102, 1965
38. Balduzzi E: Contributo alla psicopatologia degli stati ossessivi (a proposito di un caso clinica con impulsivita auto lesiva) [Contribution to the psychopathology of obsessive states (Apropos of a clinical case with self-mutilating impulse)] Rivista Sperimentale di Freniatria e Medicina Legale della Alienazioni Mentali 85:314–333, 1961
39. Stinnet JL, Hollender MH: Compulsive self-mutilation. J Nerv Ment Dis 5:371–375, 1970
40. Scullica L: Acute post-traumatic keratoconus caused by self-mutilation. Bollention Oculist 11:581–588, 1962
41. Gerhard JP: Apropos of ocular self-mutilation. Bulletins et Memoires de la Societe Francaise d'Ophtalmologie 68:622–626, 1968
42. Rosen DH, Hoffman AM: Focal suicide: Self-enucleation by two young psychotic individuals. Am J Psychiatry 8:1009–1012, 1972
43. McEvedy C: Self-inflicted injuries. (Ph.D. dissertation, Univ London), 1963
44. Waldenberg SSA: Wrist-cutting—A psychiatric injury. (Ph.D. dissertation, London Univ), 1972

45. Crabtree LH: A psychotherapeutic encounter with a self-mutilating patient. Psychiatry 30:91–100, 1967
46. Friedman M, Glasser M, Laufer E, Laufer M, Wohl M: Attempted suicide and self-mutilation in adolescence: Some observations from a psychoanalytic research project. Int J Psychoanal 53:179–183, 1972
47. Malcove L: Bodily mutilation and learning to eat. Psychoanal Q 2:557–561, 1933
48. Nogami Y: On binge-eating in adolescence. (personal communication, Tokyo, 1974)
49. Shinosaka N: (personal communication, Japan, 1974)
50. Bettelheim B: Symbolic Wounds. New York, Free Press, 1962
51. Lester D: Self-mutilating behavior. Psychol Bull 2:119–128, 1972
52. Bach-y-Rita G: Habitual violence and self-mutilation. Am J Psychiatry 9:1018–1020, 1974
53. Mason WA, Sponholz RR: Behavior of rhesus monkeys reared in isolation. J Psychiatr Res 1:299–306, 1963
54. Kafka JS: The body as transitional object: A psychoanalytic study of a self-mutilating patient. Br J Med Psychol 42:207–212, 1969
55. Vereecken JL: Recidiverende automutilatie. Nederlaudse Tijdschrift Geneeskunde 109:2280–2284, 1965
56. Dorn RM: (personal communication, Beverly Hills, California, 1974)
57. Taylor AJW: A search among Borstal girls for the psychological and social significance of their tattoos. Br J Criminol 4:170–185, 1968
58. Gardner AR, Gardner AJ: Self-mutilation, obsessionality, and narcissism (synopsis). Br J Psychiatry 125:419, 1974
59. Offer D, Barglow P: Adolescent and young adult self-mutilation incidents in a general psychiatric hospital. Arch Gen Psychiatry 3:194–204, 1960
60. Battle RJ, Pollitt JD: Self-inflicted injuries. Br J Plas Surg 17:400–412, 1964
61. Clark HE, Campbell JD: Self-inflicted gunshot wounds. Am J Psychiatry 104:565–569, 1948
62. Watson JP: The relationship between a self-mutilating patient and her doctor. Psychother Psychosom 18:67–73, 1970
63. Yap KB: Automutilatie. Holland, Van Loghum Slaterus, Deventer, 1970
64. Gero G, Rubinfine D: On obsessive thoughts. J Am Psychoanal Assoc 3:222–243, 1955
65. Burnham RL, Giovacchini PL: Symposium on impulsive self-mutilation: Discussion. Br J Med Psychol 42:223–229, 1969
66. McKerracher DW, Street DRK, Segal LJ: A comparison of the behavior problems presented by male and female subnormal offenders. Br J Psychiatry 112:891–897, 1966
67. Simpson MA: Female genital self-mutilation. Arch Gen Psychiatry 29:508–510, 1973

68. Simpson MA, Anstee BH: Female genital self-mutilation as a cause of vaginal bleeding. Postgrad Med J 50:308–309, 1974
69. Gerstle ML, Guttmacher AF, Brown F: A case of recurrent malingered placenta praevia. Mt Sinai J Med NY 24:641–646, 1957
70. Goldfield M, Glick I: Self-mutilation of the female genitalia. Dis Nerv Syst 31:843–845, 1970
71. Lowy FH, Kolivakis TL: Autocastration by a male transsexual. Can Psychiatr Assoc J 16:399–405, 1971
72. Vedrinne J, Moine C, Guillemin G, et al: Voluntary genital mutilation in women. Medecine Legale et Dommage Corporel 2:156–157, 1969
73. Simpson MA: Blood as a transitional object (in preparation)
74. Conn JF: A case of marked self-mutilation presenting a dorsal root syndrome. J Nerv Ment Dis 3:251, 1932
75. Richardson P: (personal communication, London, 1973)
76. Menninger K: Man against Himself. New York, Harcourt, 1938
77. Deutsch, H: Psychology of Women, vol 1. New York, Grune & Stratton, 1944, p 168
78. Rado S: Fear of castration in women. Psychoanal Q 2:425–475, 1933
79. Hoffer W: Oral aggressiveness and ego development. Int J Psychoanal 31:45, 1950
80. Stengel E: Pain and the psychiatrist. Br J Psychiatry 111:795–802, 1965
81. Declich M: Some considerations on the problem of self-mutilation. Rassegna Studia Psychiatria 45:603–621, 1956
82. Dabrowski C: Psychological bases of self-mutilation. Genet Psychol Monogr 19:1–104, 1937
83. Matthews PC: Epidemic self-injury in an adolescent unit. Int J Soc Psychiatry 14:125–133, 1968
84. Plath S: 'Cut' in Ariel. London, Faber & Faber, 1965
85. Wahl CW: Suicide as a magical act, in Shneidman ES, Farberow NL (eds): Clues to Suicide. New York, McGraw-Hill, 1957
86. Lower RB: Depersonalization and the masochistic wish. Psychoanal Q 40:584–602, 1971
87. Arlow JA: Panel report: Depersonalization. J Am Psychoanal Assoc 12:171–186, 1964
88. Bradlow PA: Depersonalization, ego-splitting, non-human fantasy, and shame. Int J Psychoanal 54:487–492, 1973
89. Glauber JP: Observations on a primary form of anhedonia. Psychoanal Q 18:67–78, 1949
90. Strauss A, Shatzman L, Bucher R, Ehrlich D, Sabshin M: Psychiatric Ideologies and Institutions. Glencoe, Illinois, Free Press, 1964, pp 317–329
91. Burnham DL: The special-problem patient: Victim or agent of splitting? Psychiatry 29:105–122, 1966
92. Main TF: The ailment. Br J Med Psychol 30:129–145, 1957

93. Loomis ME, Horsley JA: Interpersonal Change: A Behavioral Approach to Nursing Practice. New York, McGraw-Hill, 1974
94. Easson WH: The Severely Disturbed Adolescent. International Universities Press, New York, 1964
95. Wilbur RL, Chandler PJ, Carpenter BL: Modification of self-mutilative behavior by aversive conditioning. Behav Engineering 3:14-25, 1974
96. Tinkelpaugh OL: The self-mutilation of a male macacus rhesus monkey. J Mammal 9:293, 1928
97. Levinson B: (personal communication, Johannesburg, South Africa, 1974)
98. Genovese E, Napoli PA, Bolego-Zonta N: Self-aggressiveness. Life Sci 8:513-515, 1969
99. Peters JM: Caffeine-induced hemorrhagic auto-mutilation. Arch Int Pharmacodyn Ther 169:139-146, 1967
100. Nyhan WL: Clinical features of the Lesch-Nyhan syndrome. Fed Proc 27:1022-1033, 1968
101. Mizuno TI, Yugari Y: Self-mutilation in the Lesch-Nyhan syndrome. Lancet 1:761, 1974
102. Cooper AF, Fowlie HC: Control of gross self-mutilation with lithium carbonate. Br J Psychiatry 122:370-371, 1973
103. Waltzer H: Depersonalization and self-destruction. Am J Psychiatry 3:399-401, 1968

Herbert Hendin

10
Growing Up Dead: Student Suicide

This chapter has two introductory passages—Henry A. Murray's paper
Dead to the World: The Passions of Herman Melville, *Essays in
Self Destruction* (1967), E. S. Shneidman (ed), reproduced here with
the kind permission of Jason Aronson, Inc., and excerpts from Chapter
2 of Herman Melville's early novel *Redburn* (1849).

When I chose the phrase "dead to the world," I was thinking of a variety
of somewhat similar psychic states characterized by a marked diminution
or near-cessation of affect involving both hemispheres of concern, the inner
and the outer world. Here it is as if the person's primal springs of vitality
had dried up, as if he were empty or hollow at the very core of his being.
There is a striking absence of anything but the most perfunctory and superficial
social interactions; output as well as intake is at a minimum. The person
is a nonconductor. To him the human species is wholly uninviting and
unlovable, a monotonous round of unnecessary duplicates; and since everything he sees and every alternative opportunity for action seems equally
valueless and meaningless, he has no basis for any choice. In fact, to make
even a small decision and to execute it calls for an exhausting effort. Sometimes,
he unresistingly and automatically falls in with somebody else's decision;
but he is more likely to respond to suggestions with a blanket No, keeping
his thoughts hidden from others behind a deaf-and-dumb reserve, the impen-
etrable wall of a self-made prison.
I was thinking particularly of Melville's forty-year withdrawal from his
society—the "Great Refusal" as Weaver called it—and of a patient of mine
who resembled Melville in this respect but whose cessation of affect was

more total, suffering as he was from what we used to call the "feeling of unreality." His sensations and perceptions of nature and of people he encountered were unusually acute and vivid, but he did not experience other persons as animate beings: they resembled puppets, automatons, mechanical contrivances without any feelings or desires to which anyone could appeal. He saw eyes that were as bright as the glass eyes of a manufactured doll, but he received no intimations of a soul, or consciousness, behind these eyes. Primitive people and children spontaneously animate the inanimate—see a man in the moon who follows them on their walks, as Piaget has described; but here was a man who reversed the process; he inanimated the animate. All empathy was dead in him; he was inert as a stone, unmoved by any of the events or confrontations which moved others.

Then I thought of *The Stranger*, that landmark book by Camus in which the psychic condition of a man who is untouched by his mother's death is hauntingly portrayed. This condition of affectlessness—which has been expertly analyzed by Nathan Leites—was almost immediately recognized as representative for our time, representative at least of the root mood of an articulate depth-sensitive minority, the Ishmaels of today. This brought to mind scores of other modern authors of whose views of the contemporary world Melville's writings were prophetic; their obsession with darkness, death, and leanings toward self-destruction epitomized in Malraux's affirmation: man is dead. But none of these seemed quite so revealing as Meursault, the nonhero of *The Stranger*, whose outburst of antitheistic rage near the end of the story showed that a volcano of resentful passion had been simmering all along beneath that crust of emotional inertia. What had once looked like an apathetic indifference to the surrounding world, an all-pervasive ennui, could now be more dynamically understood as an alternative to murder, namely ostracism of mankind contrived by an unforgiving heart that had been turned to stone by experiencing an intolerable offense.

At this point what psychoanalyst could resist coming forth with a battery of concepts to explain it all?—say, as nothing but a perseveration of the child's global reaction to his mother at a time when she quite literally constituted the child's whole known world and its culture. In the case of Camus as well as of Melville, for example, there is evidence that a virtually deaf-and-dumb, ostracising mother generated resentment in the child which was followed by a reciprocal, retaliative withdrawal. A conventional psychoanalyst would be likely to assume, if he were confronted by a patient in whom this state of being had persisted into adulthood, that it was his office to get his patient to look homeward, and like an angel melt with ruth. Once having reconciled himself to either his mother or his father, as the case might be, the patient would more readily become reconciled to the culture in which he was imbedded and less reluctantly adjust to it. But if the culture—society and its churches—was actually inimical to the realization of the fullest potentialities of an individual's personal life, as Melville and Camus believed it to be, the question is, should a man who saw the culture as the Enemy be persuaded by the implications of a seductive professional technique to throw in his sponge and surrender to it?

I have been talking about a diminution or cessation of feeling, one component of consciousness, on the assumption that this condition is somewhat analogous to a cessation of the whole of consciousness. If the cessation of feeling is temporary it resembles sleep; if it is permanent (a virtual atrophy of emotional life) it resembles death, the condition of the brain and body after the home fires of metabolism in the cortex have gone out. In a feelingless state the home fires are still burning but without glow or warmth. The implication here is that an intensive, detailed study of affective states in connection with suicidal phenomena should be fruitful in "fresh leads and new insights." This seems too obvious to require mention. For what is suicide in most instances but an action to interrupt or put an end to intolerable affects? But do we know all we need to know about the nature of intolerable affects? Is there not more to learn about the different varieties of feelings, combinations of feelings, and temporal sequences of feelings which are conducive to suicide on the one hand or, on the other hand, make suicide unthinkable?

As one standing-stone for my proposal let me quote from William James, whose books and letters abound in all sorts of uncommon common sense. "Individuality," he affirms, "is founded in feeling; and the recesses of feeling, the darker, blinder strata of character, are the only places in the world in which we catch real fact in the making, and directly perceive how events happen and how work is actually done." Not very long after the avowal of this judgment, John B. Watson's swift invasion and conquest of a good deal more than half of the terrain of American academic psychology, committed James to such an outcast state that one leading physiological psychologist announced—to the President of Harvard, of all people—that Professor James had done more harm to psychology than any man who had ever lived. But there are indications that the exile of James and of feelings as phenomena worthy of investigation was only temporary. They have recently named the Cambridge habitat of the behavioral sciences William James Hall, and throughout the country there have been an increasing number of studies of those negative affects—anxiety, anger, resentment, and guilt—whose vicissitudes and dynamics were revealed to us by Freud and his successors, Dr. Franz Alexander for one. And now, to do justice to some of the feelings and emotions omitted by psychoanalysis, we have the prospect of the completion in the near future of the intricate three-volume work by Silvan S. Tomkins, *Affect, Imagery, Consciousness.* Besides, there is burgeoning in this country, as an antithetical reaction to strict behaviorism, an enthusiastic though still amorphous aggregate of phenomenological, existential, and humanistic psychologists who question the assumption that evolutionary processes fashioned human nature for the special advantage of technocratic behaviorists of this century, setting forth all its most important determinants on the surface and leaving nothing of any consequence inside. In short, a concentrated study of affects in relation to suicidal inclinations would have a sufficient array of facts and theories to start with and should break new ground, provided the investigators were prepared to make much finer distinctions than current terminology, or even the English language, permits, envisaging as an ideal, let us say, the power of an Indian (Hindu) language to differentiate, as we learn from Coomaraswamy, "three hundred and sixty kinds of the fine emotions of a lover's heart."

* * * * *

It was with a heavy heart and full eyes, that my poor mother parted with me; perhaps she thought me an erring and a willful boy, and perhaps I was; but if I was, it had been a hardhearted world, and hard times that had made me so. I had learned to think much and bitterly before my time; all my young mounting dreams of glory had left me; and at that early age, I was as unambitious as a man of sixty.

Yes, I will go to sea; cut my kind uncles and aunts, and sympathizing patrons, and leave no heavy hearts but those in my own home, and take none along but the one which aches in my bosom. Cold, bitter cold as December, and bleak as its blasts, seemed the world then to me; there is no misanthrope like a boy disappointed; and such was I, with the warm soul of me flogged out by adversity. But these thoughts are bitter enough even now, for they have not yet gone quite away; and they must be uncongenial enough to the reader; so no more of that, and let me go on with my story.

"Yes, I will write you, dear mother, as soon as I can," murmured I, as she charged me for the hundredth time, not to fail to inform her of my safe arrival in New York.

"And now, Mary, Martha, and Jane, kiss me all round, dear sisters, and then I am off. I'll be back in four months—it will be autumn then, and we'll go into the woods after nuts, and I'll tell you all about Europe. Good-by! Good-by!"

So I broke loose from their arms, and not daring to look behind, ran away as fast as I could, till I got to the corner where my brother was waiting. He accompanied me part of the way to the place, where the steamboat was to leave for New York; instilling into me much sage advice above his age, for he was but eight years my senior, and warning me again and again to take care of myself; and I solemnly promised I would; for what cast-away will not promise to take care of himself, when he sees that unless he himself does, no one else will.

We walked on in silence till I saw that his strength was giving out, he was in ill health then, and with a mute grasp of the hand, and a loud thump at the heart, we parted.

It was early on a raw, cold, damp morning toward the end of spring, and the world was before me; stretching away a long muddy road, lined with comfortable houses, whose inmates were taking their sunrise naps, heedless of the wayfarer passing. The cold drops of drizzle trickled down my leather cap, and mingled with a few hot tears on my cheeks.

I had the whole road to myself, for no one was yet stirring, and I walked on, with a slouching, dogged gait. The gray shooting-jacket was on my back, and from the end of my brother's rifle hung a small bundle of my clothes. My fingers worked moodily at the stock and trigger, and I thought that this indeed was the way to begin life, with a gun in your hand!

Talk not of the bitterness of middle-age and after life; a boy can feel all that, and much more, when upon his young soul the mildew has fallen; and the fruit, which with others is only blasted after ripeness, with him is nipped in the first blossom and bud. And never again can such blights be made good; they strike in too deep, and leave such a scar that the air of Paradise might not erase it. And it is a hard and cruel thing thus in early youth to taste beforehand the pangs which should be reserved for the stout time of manhood when the gristle has become bone, and we stand up and fight out our lives, as a thing tried before and foreseen; for then we are veterans used to sieges and battles, and not green recruits, recoiling at the first shock of the encounter.

Growing Up Dead: Student Suicide*

More and more young people in this culture believe that feeling itself is a danger and life's best achievement is the fastest, and highest possible flight from emotion. Many young people escape into sensation—into drugs, casual sex, or the acquisition of a variety of experiences without emotional involvement. But an increasing number of young people look elsewhere for relief. When Vonnegut wrote "how nice—to feel nothing, and still get full credit for being alive." † he expressed as a wry joke what many college students, tragically, are actually doing. The trend is toward a diminished involvement in life, and attempt to find in numbness and limited experience, some escape from the anger and turmoil without and within. There is a rising tide of college students who try to blot out their pain, anger, and frustration with the ultimate numbness.

Suicide among young people and among college students in particular has been steadily and alarmingly rising during the past 20 years. Over 4,000 of the 25,000 annual suicides in the country are now in the 15-24 age group. The suicide rate for this group has increased over 250 percent in the past 2 decades, from 4.2 in 1954 to 10.6 in 1973.§ Among these figures, one of the most dramatic

*This chapter is adapted from Dr. Hendin's book *The Age of Sensation*. New York, W. W. Norton, 1975.

† Slaughterhouse five, Kurt Vonnegut, Jr., Delacorte Press, New York, 1969.

§ Rates are calculated by the National Center for Health Statistics per 100,000 of the age group.

322

is the increase in the suicide rate of young men aged 15–24 which has gone from 6.7 in 1954 to 17.0 in 1973. As these figures show, the suicide trend was evident through the quiet 1950s, persisted through the political activism of the 1960s and the many shifts in the drug culture and continues on campuses today. Underlying these shifts are the more profound changes that have occurred in people over the past 20 years. Why do increasing numbers of college students want to end their lives? What does their behavior say about changes in American life?

For the past 6 years, I have been studying and treating young people who have made suicide attempts, as part of a study of culture, character, and crisis among college students.† Psychoanalytic interviewing techniques emphasizing free associations, dreams, and fantasies provide access to the inner life, the inner significance for these students of both living and dying. What was revealed in the lives of young people who had made suicide attempts were the ways in which death, depression, and misery had been part of their lives since childhood and had been built into their relationships with their parents.

It is no accident that death as a motivating force in human behavior is now a major preoccupation. As parents become less able to accept or enjoy children, as young men and women find their contacts with each other infused with anger, we become preoccupied with the small and large forms of destructiveness. For a nation that has been described as death-denying, we are becoming one that is death-obsessed. For Freud there was a fairly even balance between the forces of death and life,[1] but for contemporary writers as brilliant as Ernest Becker,[2] the struggle with death is seen as the ultimate cause of all human behavior. Many American families are so filled with tension and rage, so unable to adjust happily to children, that in order to survive, parents and children have to deaden themselves.

For many young people, life is a grueling war of attrition in which depression is the best available accomplice, the only way to ward off the impact of their daily lives. Such students experience death daily in their attempts to bury their anger, rage, and pain deep within themselves. As the lives of students who make suicide attempts suggest, the fascination with death is often the climax of having been emotionally dead for a lifetime.

---

† Over 50 students who made suicide attempts were studied in depth in the course of a 6-year period of this project. The study was supported by a grant from the National Insititute of Mental Health (MH 20818-02).

The students I saw were drawn to death as a way of life. The most seriously suicidal were those whose absorption and preoccupation with their own extinction were an integral ongoing part of their daily experience. These students see their relationships with their parents as dependent on their emotional if not physical death and become tied to their parents in a kind of death knot. Coming to college, graduating, becoming seriously involved with another person, and enjoying an independent existence have the power to free them. In fact the meaning of suicide and depression lies in their encounter with the forces that might unleash their own possibilities for freedom.

The question is often asked: Can the psychology of suicide be understood from those who made attempts and survived? My own belief is that it can. The attempted-suicide population contains the majority of the eventual suicide population in addition to many whose involvement with suicide will not be fatal. Some of the students I saw died from the consequences of injuries sustained in their attempts. Some, such as a student who lived after a 7-story jump, survive fortuitously. This young woman had, as do a majority of actual suicides of all ages, a history of prior attempts.

It is often said that suicidal students have been destroyed by the strain of competition and work and by parental pressure toward success. But far from being harmed by their work, many students used it as a barricade. "Work," as one student put it, was his "main defensive army." Nor were the parents of these students more achievement-oriented than most. Their own problems had led them to need their children to be quiet drones. They often opposed the work that their children found fascinating because they were so unable to cope with pleasure and excitement. Dull, demanding mental labor was often the nexus of the suicidal students' existence. It did not have to lead to success or any pleasurable sense of achievement, but rather functioned as another link in the chain of emotional deadness that bound them to their parents.

It has been thought that the literal death or physical loss of a parent was crucial in producing suicidal people. Zilboorg,[3] in 1936, applied to the study of suicide Freud's observations on the importance of "ambivalent identification" with a "lost loved object" in causing depression.[4] He called attention to the frequency of the actual death of a parent before or during the adolescence of suicidal patients. In my own work I found that a significantly high proportion of seriously suicidal students had lost a parent. But what even these students made clear is that more than ambivalent identification with a dead parent is involved. What is crucial is the quality of feeling that flows between the student and his parents. The bond of emotional death was as powerful in suicidal students who had not experienced the actual death of a parent as it was in those who had. Both groups were pulled toward their own death primarily by the bond that had defined their relationship with their parents while their parents had lived, and continued to control their lives even if their parents died.

Case 1

Leon* had lost neither of his parents, although it could be said that he never really had them either. He had gotten along with them by burying himself alone in his room studying, listening to music, and having suicidal thoughts. At 18 he had already been thinking of suicide for years and in high school had compiled a list of reasons why he should not kill himself. He enumerated them to me in the mechanical manner he usually adopted: first, things were so bad that they could only get better; second, he had no right to take his life; third, his parents had made a great investment in his education and it would cost a lot to bury him; fourth, his parents would blame themselves; and fifth, they would be devastated and would miss him. When he had spent some time at college he added a sixth reason—his friends would feel very bad if he did it. Leon had been able to resist his suicidal preoccupations during his lonely high school years, but after a few months at college in which he had grown close to his roommates, his need to kill himself became overwhelming. The challenge to his past isolation and deadness from his new friendships was finally pushing him toward suicide.

Leon wanted to hold onto his depression far more than he realized. He saw himself as always having been on the losing side of the law of averages. He gave his dissatisfaction with his own average at college after studying hard all term as cause of his depression and sign of his bad luck. After a college mixer at which he met no one, he rode the subways and stood for a long time at one station in Harlem in a challenge to fate to see if he would be mugged. He considered it a bad omen that two of his favorite professional football teams lost on the day after he was admitted to the hospital. During the time I saw him, after his favorite team won a crucial game, he dreamed that they lost in the last minute.

Leon saw defeat as preferable to victory, but for the most part he sought an impregnability that prevented both. He had a recurring fantasy in which he was a medieval citadel under attack. He drew a map to illustrate the deployment of his protective armies. Areas were indicated in different colors to mark his social, academic, spiritual, and emotional defenses. Most of his forces were concentrated in the academic realm. Leon's map is a powerful symbol of his emotional state. He felt that he would survive only as long as his defenses held.

* All names have been changed.

Leon saw life as war and himself as the ultimate weapon. It was easier for him to see danger as an outside attack than to see his own destructiveness. After an incident in which his roommates had disappointed him, he dreamed that he was an executioner who had to decide whether people should live or die. He condemned them to death and "some kind of angel came and killed them all." Leon clearly saw himself as the Angel of Death. His suicidal preoccupations and his depression mask an image he had of himself as sitting on a time bomb that was "getting ready to explode." When I questioned him about the anger and destructiveness suggested in this image, he was quick to tell me that the most that would happen is that he would "quietly and non-violently" kill himself.

Leon's need to hide his anger was bound up with his need not to blame his parents for his problems. He insisted that he had had little relationship with them and liked them from afar but was always irritated with them when at home. All the incidents he related about his childhood cast his mother in the role of dampener of his or his father's pleasure or excitement. His father handled the situation by being away much of the time, leaving his mother to rule the house. Leon felt that he and his parents had never been able to talk about anything, but expressed no anger or bitterness over this. His suicide note conveys the quality of his family life.

Addressing his letter to both his parents, Leon wrote that by the time they read it he would be dead and that they were not responsible for his act. (In suicide notes, such statements specifically freeing particular people of any blame or responsibility are usually to be read psychologically as meaning the opposite.) He added that he was depressed and could see nothing coming out of his life. He went on to dispose of his possessions, leaving his tapes and tape-recording equipment to his mother and requesting that his favorite tape be buried with him. From beginning to end, Leon's note is about communication from beyond life. He tells his parents that it is too late to reach him but goes on to leave them equipment which permits him to speak to them, like the Angel of Death he dreamed he was, as a voice from beyond the grave. In asking to be buried with the tape of melancholy songs he played again and again as accompaniment to his suicidal thoughts, Leon was almost literally asking to be cemented for all eternity in his unhappy, isolated relation to his mother.

Although preoccupied with suicide for a long time, the next student only became overtly suicidal after the death of his mother. His story makes clear that because of his tie to her when she was alive, her death required his own emotional death. When he said with a flat, depressed intensity, "I don't think life should be lived if it isn't worth living for its own sake. No one should stay alive for anyone else's sake," it is clear that he felt he had lived or not lived for her sake, not his own.

Case 2

Larry is a 26 year-old graduate student referred for evaluation following a serious suicide attempt which he barely survived. He had been preoccupied with suicide since his sophomore year in college and had made 3 previous attempts. Neatly groomed and casually dressed, he seemed alternately fearful and lifeless. He said he tried to have the least possible contact with people, had only the few friends he made in high school and spent most of his time studying in his room. While he shared an apartment with 2 other students, they merely lived together and did not "socialize." He protected himself against letting me know or reach him by attempting to stop any observation or interpretation of his behavior by quickly saying "it is possible." Insisting on the futility of our talking and on the futility of his life, he said he could stand back and listen to our conversation and that it was like a grade Z movie. Standing back, listening while grading himself and others, were characteristic ways in which he defended himself against involvement. He kept insisting that nothing could change his life to any degree, suggesting a determination to see to it that nothing did.

Larry's one close relationship with a woman was shaped by his need to retain his deadness and estrangement. He lived with a woman named Jill for 6 months, which he described as the liveliest, happiest, and most spontaneous time of his life. Nevertheless, when the time came for Jill to leave for Europe where she had planned to live, he made no attempt to persuade her to stay and did not seriously consider going with her.

Larry met Jill when his mother was dying of cancer. When I asked him if the fact that his mother was dying made him more willing to get involved with Jill he said he had wondered many times if that were the case. During the 6 months after his mother had died and Jill had left, Larry made serveral suicide attempts. While he felt they had more to do with Jill than his mother, he insisted that he was not bothered by missing Jill, but by his lack of control over the situation. The need to deny her importance to him and the pain of losing her were further expressions of Larry's general deadness.

Larry attributed the origins of his lifeless, isolated existence to being the only child of an overbearing mother and to having had a father who was "removed and out of things." One of his earliest memories vividly dramatizes his family situation. When he was about 7 his father was away for a day and his mother was going to a wedding shower. He did not recall what he was doing, but felt he must have "been playing in a way my mother didn't like." His mother screamed at him that she would not go to the shower because of him. He later thought she was looking for an excuse not to go. But the situation conveys not only her use of the martyr role, but her message to Larry that if he is playful, mischievous, or alive, she will not live or enjoy anything.

Larry saw his mother as refusing to let him grow up. Until he moved into the dorms when a college sophomore, she refused to let him have a door on his room and insisted on her right to open his mail. She seemed to have been particularly fearful of his involvement with girls. Larry felt his mother tried to live her life through him. As he spoke it was clear he felt he had performed at school and lived for his mother and not for himself. Yet he had felt lost and out of control in the unstructured life in the dorms and felt depressed and cut off without his mother while he attempted to bury himself in his studies. It was in this period that he first became preoccupied with suicidal thoughts.

Nothing outside of his family had much deep, living reality for Larry. In all his dreams, he was back where he grew up with his parents. After our first session he dreamed of Jerry, a lively, out-going boy he knew as a child and whom he associated with fun. He saw himself as rarely capable of having fun and enjoyed himself only when he had had a couple of drinks or smoked pot. It is also clear that he associated fun with separating from his mother, which he was clearly afraid to do. He said, "What's the use of talking about her? She's dead and I'm alive." Psychologically speaking, the reverse seemed truer.

Larry dreamed he had a heart attack. In actuality, not he but his father had had a heart attack a few months earlier. His father had remarried a year before that and seemed much happier than when Larry's mother was alive. Larry had been afraid since the attack that his father would die and leave him alone. In dreaming that he and not his father had the attack, Larry felt he was saying "better me than you."

Larry felt that one life can be sacrificed to keep another alive and that his "death" had been a way of keeping his mother alive. He acknowledged at times he had wished she would die, thinking her death might liberate him. He became tearful in talking of how her death had liberated his father. When I pointed out that he seemed unable to bury her, he replied he would not know how to take the first step with the shovel. His numbness minimized the distinction between living and dying and created a middle state in which he figuratively did keep his mother alive through his own emotional death. Suicide is but the final dramatization of this process.

Larry's suicide attempt was not simply a journey toward reunion with a lost love object. His whole life had been a death tie to an object both needed and hated. In not living he keeps his mother alive, atones for his rage towards her, and preserves their past relationship. What overwhelmed Larry is not simply her loss but the fact that her loss constituted an invitation to life—an invitation his father could accept but he could not.

Leon and Larry were typical of suicidal students whose intense concentration on academic work was the means they used to deal with existence and served to conceal their sense that they had no right to live. They were typical of suicidal students who had come from families in which the relationship between their parents and family life as a whole were essentially dead. Their sense of family life was rooted in this deadness and fixed in their perception of their parents as requiring their lifelessness. While they often appeared to be concerned over failure in school, they turned out to be more concerned with being drones and not being very successful or finding too much pleasure in what they were doing. Like Leon, who saw his academic efforts as a defensive army, these students used the continued deployment of uninteresting and methodical work as a withdrawal from either satisfaction or rage. Their withdrawal signified for them a holding on to the past and strengthened the tie of numbness they had forged in their relations with their family.

When a parent actually died—as Larry's mother—many suicidal students felt they had no right to continue to live or tried to keep the parent alive and preserve the relationship through their own death. But living independent lives was a stimulus to death whether or not a parent had actually died. Suicidal students were generally lifeless and outwardly compliant in manner. What lay beneath this compliant surface was an enormous fury. They dreamed of themselves as forces that can and do murder the people who let them down, or as people held in the grip of a rage beyond their own control. Suicide and suicidal preoccupation was for them a way of extinguishing their anger.

Many students in college continued to use contacts with their parents to control their own enthusiasm and ensure their lifelessness. Elated by a new relationship, excited by school, they would call their parents when they were feeling best, knowing that their parents' lack of response would kill their mood. When happiest, one student described having the impulse to "throw myself in front of a train or call my mother," equating the death-dealing power of both with a wry seriousness. Being happy for these students meant giving up the past; giving up sadness meant relinquishing the securest part of themselves.

What overwhelms these students is not simply grief over separating from or losing a parent, but the fact that the separation or loss constitutes an invitation to freedom. These students perceive inhibition of their power to live as the price of existing. The long-observed phenomena of depressed patients becoming more suicidal as they overcome their depression takes on new significance in this light. It is said that depression operates to paralyze action and that a lessening depression makes possible an overt, actual suicide attempt. But this is an inadequate explanation for what takes place with these students.

Depression is actually a form of protective deadness which can shield the individual and may even make suicide unnecessary for some. Larry and Leon became acutely suicidal when life beckoned most and challenged their familiar depression. They broke down under the stress of possible pleasure, success, and independence. Suicide and suicidal desire are means of recapturing the depression that seems to be slipping away, the means these students used to cling to the deadness they see not merely as their best defense but as the basic human bond.

Suicide is a way of life for the many students I saw who continually killed their enthusiasm, their hope, their freedom, and finally attempted to kill themselves. It is the climax of the ongoing drama they play out with parents in which emotional death is seen as the price of domestic peace.

The method many students chose was not only their last message to their parents, but the climactic gesture that also expressed how they had lived and how they hoped to resolve the conflicts that plagued them in life. One student who spent the night on the roof of his dorm thinking of jumping, spoke of it in terms of the tragic fame that suicide had given to Marilyn Monroe. He had the fantasy that he would call to tell his parents he was going to jump and while they got upset he would leave the receiver hanging and go up on the roof. They would call someone at school but it would be too late. The fantasy reflects the blocked communication that had always existed in his family and his wish to make his parents experience the frustration he had always endured in trying to reach them. He clenched and wrung his fists as he spoke of how much he wanted to strike back.

Perhaps most important is the meaning of his preoccupation with Marilyn Monroe's suicide—the grotesque, grim wish to make a splash by jumping in a notorious death. The student who had unaccountably survived a 7-story jump had wanted the attention a spectacular death would bring. But the need such students have for a dramatic, newsworthy attempt derives from the intense experience of having been passed over by their parents. "Do I have to die before you'll notice me?" "Do you have to read it in the news before you know I'm dead?" is the cry such students are making. And they are willing to die to be noticed.

Physical agony was a last resort for students whose parents never cared about their emotional problems, but might respond to them if they were literally hurt. Sandra, who severed an artery in a dramatic wrist-cutting suicide attempt, told of less severe wrist-cutting in high school which had gone unnoticed by her parents. (Several students had similar experiences in which they never told their parents what they had done, but seemed disappointed that their parents had not noticed their scars.) After her recent suicide attempt, Sandra dreamed that she had on dungarees streaming with blood and her mother watched her without saying a word. In discussing the dream she bitterly said her mother would never acknowledge that she felt pain and was hurt. The vivid childhood memory of another suicidal student is of being unjustly punished by her mother and sent to her room. She spent an hour working loose a tooth that was not quite ready to come out so as to have an excuse to leave her room and be forgiven by her mother.

Suicide for love, the wish to die when love and need are not requited are traditionally causes of suicide attempts in the young. Moreover, suicide in response to rejection suggests a strong desire for love, life, and involvement and unbearable disappointment over the frustration of such needs. It would seem to be quite different from the deathly tie to parents and the resistence to involvement that has been described.

Yet relationships that lead to disappointment and suicide often have death, disappointment, and depression built into them. The "I won't live without you" message to an unwilling partner is a restatement of earlier disappointments relived with and through a lover who remains aloof. The suicidal person often makes conditions for life: If I don't succeed, I'll kill myself; if you don't want me, I won't live. Such conditions are not only self-fulfilling, they are meant to be. Just as conditions for love set by one individual on another are designed to kill affection, so are conditions for living designed to kill life, not sustain it. Such conditions are, for the suicidal invariably admissions reducible to the message "I can't love you or live with you, but through my death there can be an enduring bond between us."

One student had shot himself in the heart; the bullet grazed his heart, pierced his lung, and came to rest close to his spine. He came into treatment telling me that he would give me 6 months to make him less lonely, isolated, and depressed before he killed himself. This kind of ultimatum, whether given to a therapist, a girlfriend, or to yourself is designed not merely to bring about the end, but to kill whatever relationship comes before it. This young man was treatable only by focusing on the way in which he tried to make our relationship one in which he could be dead and challenge or resist my efforts to bring him back to life. Life is not, as it seems, or as the patient often says, unbearable with depression, but is inconceivable without it.

Suicidal students destroy any possibility for pleasure, often believing they are searching for affection at the same moment they are destroying it. Their inability to tolerate or find positive experiences reflects the extreme emotional hardships they have experienced in childhood. But the more severe conflicts of the families of suicidal students only dramatize the problems shared by the families of many students today. Pleasure and enjoyment are casualties in the modern war of the family. Too many children are growing up feeling that their parents did not regard them as sources of pleasure. Young people today with diminished capacity for enjoyment or diminished sense of their own ability to give pleasure, have for the most part grown up feeling they gave little to their parents. Even in cases where the parents did the right thing, the sense of joyless duty was often communicated.

We tend to regard the capacity for pleasure as a biological fact in which experience determines only the particular sources of pleasure for the individual. But it is not. Children who see that they are not a source of pleasure to their parents become unable to be a source of pleasure to themselves and have few expectations of happiness with others. The unrelieved numbness of the depressed and suicidal students dramatizes how profoundly the lack of parental desire for an emotionally alive child can make the child feel that emotional lifelessness is a price of any relationship with their parents and of survival itself. Unfortunately, we are gearing more and more people for numbness.

Society is fomenting depression in the trend toward the devaluation of children and the family. The increasing emphasis on solitary gratification and immediate, tangible gain from all relationships encourages an unwillingness in parents to give of themselves or tolerate the demands of small children. It is not surprising that the family emerges through the eyes of many students as a jail in which everyone is in solitary confinement, trapped within their own particular suffering. The frequent absence of intimacy, affection, warmth, or shared concern, the prevalence of families in which no one had gotten what he needed or wanted has had a profound impact on this generation.

Out of this disaffection has come a rising number of young people who are drawn to numbness because it has been their only security for a lifetime. Whenever the newness of coming to college, of graduating, of finding a person or a pursuit interferes with that security and threatens to break the bond of deadness that theld them to their parents, these students may be over-whelmed by suicidal desires.

Certainly in their suicidal attempts these young people are moving toward becoming finally and forever what they felt they were meant to be.

REFERENCES

1. Freud S: Civilization and Its Discontents, Strachey J (trans, ed). New York, Norton, 1962
2. Becker E: The Denial of Death. New York, Free Press, 1973
3. Zilboorg G: Differential diagnostic types of suicide. Arch Gen Psychiatry 35:270-291, 1936
4. Freud S: Mourning and melancholia (1916), in Collected Papers, vol. IV. London, Hogarth, 1949, pp. 152-170

Edwin S. Shneidman

11
Suicide Among The Gifted

The introductory passages to this chapter are from Mortality, *The Gifted Child Grows Up, Vol. IV Genetic Studies of Genius* (1947), Lewis M. Terman and Melita H. Oden. They are reproduced with the kind permission of Mrs. Oden and the Stanford University Press. The chapter itself a reproduction of E. S. Shneidman: Perturbation and Lethality as Precursors of Suicide in a Gifted Group, *Life-Threatening Behavior* and is reproduced with the permission of Behavioral Publications 1: 23–45, 1971.

There had been 61 deaths among the gifted subjects by 1940 (35 males and 26 females). The incidence for males was 4.14 percent and for females 3.98 percent. For the sexes combined the mortality rate was 4.07 percent. These proportions are based on the 1,500 subjects for whom information was available; that is, the 28 subjects (11 men and 17 women) with whom we have lost contact are excluded from the calculations of mortality rate. As pointed out in the preceding chapter, there is no reason to believe that our loss of contact with these subjects has been due to greater mortality among them.

The mortality rate for the generality in a particular age span can be determined from a life table by finding the number out of an arbitrarily large number of live births who are living at a given age, and the proportion of those who survive to a specified older age. We used the life tables from Dublin and Lotka, based on the mortality rate in 1929–31. Age 11 was chosen as the initial age on the table and 30 as the upper limit, since these ages closely approximated the mean age of the gifted group at the time of the original survey and at the 1940 follow-up, respectively. The mortality rate for the generality of white population is this age period was 5.37 percent for males, 4.68 percent for females, and 5.02 percent for the sexes combined. As noted above, of the 1,500 gifted subjects for whom we had information, 4.07 percent died between 1922 and 1940. It appears, therefore, that the death rate among the gifted subjects was definitely below that of the general population.

CAUSES OF DEATH

The causes of death to 1940 are summarized in Table 7, which gives both the N and percentage incidence for each category. It will be noted that the death rate from accident was much higher for males than for females. This is true also in the general white population, for whom the accidental death rate among males in recent years has been nearly twice as great as that among females. According to Dublin and Lotka, at age 10 the chances per 1,000 general population of eventually dying from accidental causes are 80.8 for males and 44.9 for females.

TABLE 7

Causes of Death to 1940, with Percentage Incidence

	Males (N = 846)		Females (N = 654)		Total (N = 1,500)	
	N	%	N	%	N	%
Natural causes	18	2.13	21	3.21	39	2.60
Accidents	12	1.42	3	0.46	15	1.00
Suicides	5	0.59	1	0.15	6	0.40
No information as to cause	. .	. . .	1	0.15	1	0.07
Deaths from all causes	35	4.14	26	3.98	61	4.07

Suicide in the gifted group follows the pattern of the general population in its greater frequency among males, the ratio of men to women in both cases being more than 3 to 1. Dublin and Lotka's calculations of the probability of dying from specified causes offer the most nearly comparable data we have found on the incidence of suicide in the general population. Their estimate of the probability of eventual suicide is based on the mortality conditions of 1930. According to these authors, 2.13 percent of the generality of males alive at age 10 will eventually die by suicide. The corresponding figure for females is 0.59 percent. In the gifted group 0.59 percent of males and 0.15 percent (one case) of females had committed suicide by 1940 when the average age of the group was about 30 years. If our group is ever to equal the rate for the generality as estimated by Dublin and Lotka, 3.61 as many men and 3.93 as many women as had committed suicide by 1940 will have to take their own lives in the years to come. The incidence of suicide in our group may be expected to increase since, in the general population, the median age of those committing suicide is 49, with about two-thirds of the deaths from this cause occurring between the ages of 33 and 65. If the gifted group should follow this pattern of increase with age, the ultimate number of suicides would be only a little over three times the number in 1940. As stated above, to reach the ultimate rate for the generality, the 1940 incidence would have to be multiplied by 3.61 for males and 3.93 for females, which on the basis of present evidence appears unlikely. In this connection, attention should be called to the probability that estimates for the general population are too low; not only does the individual committing suicide often take pains to make his death appear accidental, but also relatives and friends sometimes prefer to conceal the fact of suicide. So far, except for one case, we have had full information regarding the circumstances and causes of death of all deceased gifted subjects.

ADDITIONAL DEATHS TO END OF 1945

With 1945 reports in from more than 90 percent of the subjects, the following deaths are known to have occurred between 1940 and the end of 1945:

	Men	Women
Natural causes	2	2
Accidents	3	. .
Suicides	. .	1
War deaths	5	. .
All causes	10	3

In addition to the five men who lost their lives in military service, two of the accidental deaths are indirectly attributable to the war. One man, a chemical engineer, was engaged in work in an atomic bomb laboratory when he came in contact with materials which proved fatal. The other was overcome by fumes while working as a welder in a war plant.

We estimate that the total number of deaths reported here would not be increased by more than one or two if all returns were in. At the end of 1945 the mean age of the group was close to 35 years. It would appear that the incidence of mortality in the group, as compared with that of the generality, was no less favorable at the later date than in 1940.

SUBJECTS WHO HAVE DIED

The mean age at death of gifted subjects deceased by 1940 was 21.9 years for males (S.D. 5.5 years) and 21.8 years for females (S.D. 6.5 years), and the age range was from 8 to 35 years. Of the 35 deceased men, 20 were still in school at the time of death—16 in college and 4 in high school or below. The 15 who had completed their schooling included 13 college graduates and 2 who had completed a year or more of college but had not graduated.

Nine of the 26 women had died before completing their education. Among the 17 who had finished their schooling were 6 college graduates, 1 who had finished high school and taken nurse's training, and 10 who had not gone beyond high school.

The average IQ of deceased subjects who had been given the Binet test was 149, and the IQ range was from 135 to 184. Space does not permit case notes on all who have died, but the following paragraphs give brief descriptions of several who are fairly representative of those deceased after the age of seventeen years. . . .

Deaths by suicide. Our case notes on the subjects who committed suicide have been made purposely brief and in some instances have been disguised in order to prevent identification. The five men in this category ranged at the time of their deaths from eighteen to thirty-five years of age. All had been in the study from the beginning, three having been admitted on the basis of a Binet test, and two on a Terman Group Test. None of the five had been married.

M 1314 was the youngest of our suicides. His hereditary background, especially on the maternal side, was streaked with insanity and constitutional inferiority. The parents were divorced following the father's desertion of the family when our subject was only three, and the father died a few years later. The subject was reared in an orphanage and attended public schools. His Binet IQ at the age of eleven was 165, and his achievement test scores were all several grades above his school placement. In high school his marks ranged from A in the subjects he liked to D in those he disliked. Although rather unsocial in his interests, he was rated by both the school and the orphanage as being above average in popularity and leadership, and in his junior year at high school he was elected class treasurer. Soon thereafter he got into trouble and was sent by the juvenile court to a detention home. He escaped, was found in another city, and escaped from the detention home there. After a year or so of wandering, he settled in an Eastern city and took up sculpturing. Shortly afterward he became despondent over a disappointment in love and committed suicide at the age of eighteen.

M 913 was admitted to the gifted group on a Terman Group Test at the age of fourteen. His IQ was 141. The parents were divorced when he was ten years old, and thereafter he lived with his mother and two siblings on a very restricted family income. The only case of mental difficulty reported in the family background was a paternal uncle who was described as "decidedly queer." When he was located, it was noted that the subject was rather undeveloped socially, and was in danger of becoming overly introverted. In high school he grew somewhat more sociable, but was shy with girls and disliked parties. He graduated at sixteen with a very superior record despite the fact that he had to work for self-support most of his free time. He then worked full time for two years to earn money for college, but after entering college he had to drop out several times to help support the family. Although an honor student in science, he was constantly afraid of failing. However, he got his Bachelor's degree at age twenty-three, and continued for graduate study while working part time. Worry over his responsibilities and the outlook for his future was accentuated by several weeks of illness from pneumonia. It was while convalescing from this illness that his depression led him to commit suicide. He was twenty-four years old at the time.

M 131 earned an IQ above 180 when tested by us at the age of seven. Subsequent tests substantiated this early superiority. At eleven years his score on the Army Alpha exceeded by a wide margin the median for university graduate students, and at twelve years his score on the Thorndike test for high-school graduates equaled that of superior Ph.D. candidates. His family background included a number of relatives who had won distinction in such fields as law, finance, the ministry, music, and literature. Five cousins who were tested had IQ's of 157, 156, 150, 130, and 122. At the age of five he could read fluently and perform complicated arithmetic problems. He never attended the elementary school, but entered a junior high school at the age of nine, and the following year was advanced to the tenth grade. He graduated from high school at thirteen and from college at sixteen. After getting his Master's degree in science, he took a position in industry that allowed him to use both his scientific and business talents. He advanced rapidly and was soon earning $500 per month. This was in a depression period when a large proportion of men, including many college graduates, were unable to find jobs at all. Quite unexpectedly and without his friends being aware of his personal difficulties, he committed suicide before the age of thirty.

M 249 qualified for the group at the age of seventeen with a very high score on the Terman Group Test. He finished high school at eighteen, and was considered by his teachers a very superior student as well as a fine all-round boy who enjoyed both fun and work. He got his B.S. *cum laude*, took both a Master's degree and a Ph.D. degree in the biological sciences, was awarded a postdoctorate fellowship, and was soon appointed an assistant professor in a large university. He was well liked by his students, and was considered an exceptional teacher and able research man. He published a number of scientific articles and was listed in *American Men of Science*. His heredity was apparently clear of mental disease or defect, and the subject himself had shown no signs of instability in his earlier years. At the age of twelve years he developed an organic disorder, but the condition was later arrested and he was able to live a normally active life. The cause of his suicide, which occurred when he was in the middle thirties, is unknown.

M 57 was twenty when he committed suicide. A review of his case history up to 1930 revealed little of significance in his background or development except that he was somewhat overprotected and dependent. At the time of our 1927-28 follow-up he was eleven years old and in the eighth grade. He was described by the field assistant as a fine-looking boy with great personal charm. His IQ on the Stanford-Binet was 162 as compared with an IQ of 140 when he was originally tested at the age of five. Both home and school reports rated him above average in all traits, and particularly in the intellectual and social traits. He finished high school at sixteen and attended college for two years. Because of ill health and financial handicaps he left school and worked at various jobs for the next two years. At this time he developed marked traits of egocentricity and dissatisfaction which were evidenced both at home and at work. His self-centeredness and lack of consideration for others alienated both family and friends and cost him several jobs, but his desire for friends and social approval was strong, and the consequent conflict resulted eventually in suicide.

Only two women are known to have committed suicide; one of these committed suicide after 1940 and so is not included in Table 7.

F 502 earned an IQ of 143 when she was first tested in childhood. There was a history of insanity and suicide on both sides of the family. She graduated from high school at an early age with a fine record both in scholarship and extracurricular activities. After entering college she suffered a nervous breakdown that kept her out of school for a time. Apparently recovered, she returned to college, but had another breakdown and later committed suicide.

F 878, deceased after 1940 and therefore not included in Table 7, had given no indications of mental instability or maladjustment prior to the act that caused her death. There was no history of mental disease of any kind in her family background. She was one of several children in a well-to-do, cultured, and very congenial home with close family ties. Her IQ at the age of seven was 153. Her score on the Terman Group Test six years later was equally superior. She attended college for two years, but financial difficulties in the family caused her to drop out. She was married in her early twenties to a college man well started on a professional career. She herself was a strikingly beautiful and talented girl with many cultural and intellectual interests. The only known cause for unhappiness was her inability to bear children. In a period of depression, following a series of miscarriages, she committed suicide at the age of thirty.

The mean IQ (Binet) of the suicide cases was 157.0, as compared with 147.2 for those who died of natural causes and 150.1 for those who died of accidents, but these differences are not statistically reliable. Of the 7, only one (F 502) had a history of mental breakdown serious enough to require hospitalization before suicide occurred, although in the case of 2 of the 5 men there had been recognized difficulties in social or mental adjustment dating from early adolescence. Three of the 7 cases had a record of insanity or suicide, or both, in the immediate family. The amount of school acceleration was extreme in only one of the suicide cases (M 131).

Suicide Among The Gifted

INTRODUCTION AND BACKGROUND

The two principal assertions in this paper are (1) that discernible early prodromal clues to adult suicide may be found in longitudinal case history data and (2) that it is useful to conceptualize these premonitory clues in terms of *perturbation* and *lethality*.

The data from which evidence for these assertions was obtained are those of the longitudinal study of 1528 gifted people initiated by Lewis M. Terman in 1921.* Terman and his coworkers searched the public schools of the cities of California for exceptionally bright youngsters. His purposes were "to discover what gifted children are like as children, what sort of adult they become, and what some of the factors are that influence their development."[1] That study, begun a half-century ago, continues to this day.

Of the original 1528 subjects, 857 were males and 671 were females. The sample was composed of children (mean age 9.7 years) with

*This study was conducted while the author was a Fellow at the Center for Advanced Study in the Behavioral Sciences, 1969-1970. Arrangements were made for confidential access to the research records by Professor Robert R. Sears who, with Professor Lee J. Cronbach, is one of the two scientific executors of the Terman Study. The data themselves are the property of Stanford University. The author is especially grateful to Mrs. Melita Oden and Mrs. Sheila Buckholtz, long-time staff members of the Gifted Study, for their extensive help in preparing relevant data for his use and for advice and guidance along the way.

Stanford-Binet I.Q.s of 140 or higher—mean I.Q. was over 150—and an older group of high school students (mean age 15.2 years) who scored within the top 1 percent on the Terman Group Test of Mental Ability. The present analysis will be limited to male subjects, of whom approximately 80 percent were born between 1905 and 1914.

An enormous amount of data has been collected. At the time of the original investigation in 1921-1922, the information included a developmental record, health history, medical examination, home and family background, school history, character trait ratings, and personality evaluations by parents and teachers, interest tests, school achievement tests, and the like. Subsequently, there has been a long series of systematic followups by mail or by personal field visits: in 1924, 1925, 1936, 1940, 1945, 1950, 1955, and 1960. Another follow-up study is planned for the near future. In the field studies (1921, 1927, 1940, and 1950), subjects and their families were interviewed and data from intelligence tests, personality tests, and questionnaires were obtained.

The Terman studies have catalyzed two generations of thought, research, attitudinal changes, and educational developments. Detailed descriptions of the subjects at various ages, as well as summaries of the important findings, are available in a series of publications authored by Professor Terman and his chief coworker, Melita Oden.[1-5] Among longitudinal studies[6] the Terman Study is unique in many ways, including the extent to which its staff has continued to maintain contact with the subjects for nearly half a century. As of 1960, only 1.7 percent of the 1528 subjects had been lost entirely.

Almost everyone in the psychological and pedagogical worlds now knows the basic findings of the Terman Study: that intellectually gifted children—far from being, as was once thought, spindly, weak, and maladjusted or one-sided—are, on the whole, more physically and mentally healthy and successful than their less-than-gifted counterparts. An unusual mind, a vigorous body, and a well-adjusted personality are not incompatible.*

A mortality summary for the Terman gifted group is as follows: in 1960 when the median age was 49.6 there had been 130 known

---

*As part of the Terman Study of the Gifted, Catharine M. Cox[7] completed a comprehensive retrospective study of the childhood intelligence of 301 historically eminent men born after 1450. Of the individuals discussed in her study, 119 were thought to have I.Q.s of 140 or higher. (As examples—1 person in each of the five-step I.Q. intervals from 140 to 190: Carlyle, Jefferson, Descartes, Hume, Pope, J. Q. Adams, Voltaire, Schelling, Pascal, Leibnitz, and J. S. Mill.) As to suicide among this extraordinary group, so far as can be ascertained, only 1 of the 301 eminent men died by killing himself, Thomas Chatterton, at age 17.

deaths, 83 male and 47 female. The mortality rate was 9.8 percent for males and 7.2 percent for females—8.6 percent for the total group. According to Dublin's life tables,[8] 13.9 percent of white males, 10.1 percent of white females, and 12 percent of a total cohort who survive to age 11 will have died before age 50. In 1960, the figures indicated a favorable mortality rate in the Terman group lower than the general white population of the same age.

By 1960, 110 of the 130 Terman group deaths, 61 percent, had been due to natural causes. (Cardiovascular diseases ranked first with males and cancer was first among females.) Accidents accounted for 19 male deaths, while only 5 females died in accidents. Five men had lost their lives in World War II. There were no homicide victims. One death was equivocal as to mode and could not be classified. As of 1960, suicide was responsible for 14 male and 8 female deaths; by 1970 there were 28 known deaths by suicide—20 men and 8 women.

An inspection of the listing of suicidal deaths (Table 11-1) suggests that there were several subgroups: student suicides, 30- and 40-year suicides, and middle-age suicides. Among the 28 suicides, of both sexes, ranging in age from 18 to 63 (a 45-year span), year of death from 1928 to 1968 (40 years), using a variety of lethal methods (pills, poison, drowning, guns), there was a subgroup of 5 persons, numbers 14 to 18, all of whom were male, Caucasian, with I.Q.s over 140, born about the same time (between 1907 and 1916), 4 of whom committed suicide within a year of each other (1965 or 1966), were in the "middle period" of their lives (ages at death 43, 50, 51, 53, and 58), and used the same method (all gunshot). This special subgroup seemed to offer a unique opportunity for an especially intensive investigation.*

A listing of all those subjects who had died indicated that there were 10 other males, born about the same time (1910 to 1914) as the 5 suicides, who had died of natural causes (either cancer or heart disease) during the same years that 4 of the 5 suicides had killed themselves (1965-1966). The opportunity for a natural experiment, using blind analyses, was evident.

Thirty cases were selected to include the 5 suicides, the 10 natural

---

*In the technical literature on suicide, one does not find many anamnestic or case history reports for individuals who have *committed* suicide. (Materials for attempted suicides are another story; the data on them are far more plentiful.) Only 4 sources, spread over a half-century, come to mind: Ruth Cavan's[9] extensive diaries of two young adults, Binswanger's[10] detailed report of 33-year-old Ellen West, Kobler and Stotland's[11] extensive reports of 4 hospitalized patients—ages 23, 34, 37, and 56—in a "dying hospital," all of whom committed suicide within the same month, and Alvarez'[12] annotated bibliography.

Table 11-1
The 28 Suicides in the Terman Study as of 1970

	Age at Suicide	Year of Birth	Year of Suicide	Marital Status	Education	Occupational Level*	Method of Suicide
Men							
1	18	1910	1928	S	High School	S	Poison
2	19	1916	1935	S	2 yrs. college	V	Gunshot
3	24	1908	1932	S	AB+	Grad S	Drowning
4	28	1910	1938	S	MA	II	Poison
5	33	1913	1946	M,D,M	High school	III	Barbituate
6	34	1913	1947	S	2 yrs. college	III	Carbon monoxide
7	35	1904	1939	S	Ph.D.	I	Gunshot
8	37	1909	1946	M	1-1/2 yrs. coll.	II	Poison
9	42	1905	1947	M	2 yrs. college	II	Not known
10	42	1916	1958	M,D,M,D	AB + 3 yrs.	I	Barbituate
11	45	1911	1956	M	3 yrs. college	II	Barbituate
12	45	1911	1956	M	AB,MA,LLB	IV	Carbon monoxide
13	45	1913	1958	M	MD+	I	Poison
14	43	1910	1953	M⁴,D⁴	2 yrs. college	II	Gunshot

	Age	Year	Year	Status	Education	Occupation	Method
15	50	1916	1965	M,D	BS	Inc.	Gunshot
16	51	1915	1966	M,D,M	High school	III	Gunshot
17	53	1913	1966	M	LLB	I	Gunshot
18	58	1907	1966	M^3,D^2	2 yrs. college	I	Gunshot
19	61	1905	1966	S	MA	Ret (I)	Barbituate
20	63	1905	1968	M,D,M	Ph.D.	I	Barbituate
Women							
1	22	1914	1936	S	2 yrs. college	S	Gunshot
2	30	1905	1935	S	AB	A (librarian)	Carbon monoxide
3	30	1913	1943	M	2 yrs. college	H	Gunshot
4	32	1917	1949	W	3 yrs. college	A (physical therapist)	Barbituate
5	37	1916	1953	M^5,D^4	2 yrs. college	A (writer)	Barbituate
6	40	1915	1955	M,D	3 yrs. college	H	Barbituate
7	44	1910	1954	M	MA	H	Barbituate
8	44	1910	1954	M,D	BS	A (social worker)	Barbituate

*Occupational levels—Men: I. professional; II. official, managerial, and semiprofessional; III. retail business, clerical, sales, skilled trades, and kindred; IV. agricultural and related; V. minor business, minor clerical, and semiskilled occupations. Occupational groupings—Women: A. professional and semiprofessional; B. business (includes secretarial and office work as well as work in other business fields); H. housewife.

deaths, and the 15 individuals who were still alive. The latter two subgroups were matched with the 5 suicides in terms of age, occupational level, and father's occupational level. That these three subgroups are fairly well matched is indicated by the information in Table 11-2. (The reader should keep in mind that all 30 subjects were male, Caucasian, Californian, middle- and upper-middle-class, had I.Q.s over 140, and were members of the Terman Gifted Study.) Each folder was edited by Mrs. Oden so that I could not tell whether the individual was dead or still alive. (Death certificates, newspaper clippings, and other "death clues" were removed.) The cases came to me, one at a time, in a random order. Although I was "blind" as to the suicide-natural death-living identity of each case, I did know the total numbers of cases in each subgroup.

Table 11-2

Occupations and Ages for the Suicide, Natural Death, and Living Subjects

	Suicide (N = 5)	Natural Death (N = 10)	Living (N = 15)
Occupational level			
I—Professional	2	5	7
II—Official, managerial, semiprofessional	2	4	6
III—Retail business, clerical and sales, skilled trades	1	1	2
Fathers' occupational level			
I—Professional	—	2	5
II—Official, managerial, semiprofessional	4	6	6
III—Retail business, clerical and sales, skilled trades	—	1	4
IV—Agricultural and related occupations	—	—	—
V—Minor business or clerical and semiskilled	1	1	—
Year of birth			
1907	1	—	—
1908	—	—	—
1909	—	—	—
1910	1	1	3
1911	—	3	3
1912	1	1	4
1913	—	2	1
1914	—	3	3
1915	1	—	1
1916	1	—	—

RATING OF PERTURBATION (THE LIFE CHART)

The cases were analyzed in terms of two basic continua (by which every life can be rated): perturbation and lethality. Perturbation refers to how upset (disturbed, agitated, sane—insane, discomposed) the individual is, rated on a 1 to 9 scale,* to determine how likely it is that he will take his own life. (Lethality is discussed below.) For each of the 30 cases a rough chart of the individual's perturbation in early childhood, adolescence, high school, college, early marriage, and middle life was made. Clues were sought relating to tranquility—disturbance, especially evidences of any *changes* and variations in the levels of perturbation. An attempt was made to classify the materials under such headings as early prodromata, failures, and signatures (each explained below).

A life chart was constructed for each case, roughly following the procedures developed by Adolf Meyer.[13,14] In each case the folders were examined more or less chronologically in an attempt to order the materials in a temporal sequence while keeping in mind a number of related skeins.

One example of perturbation (from an individual who turned out to be among the five homogeneous suicides) is as follows.

A high school counselor wrote about one young man that was "emotionally unstable, a physical roamer and morally erratic, excellent to teachers who treat him as an adult but very disagreeable to others." At the same time, the home visitor wrote: "I like him tremendously; he is better company than many teachers." Ten years later the subject himself wrote: "My gifts, if there were any, seem to have been a flash in the pan."

Early Prodromata

Under this category were included early important interpersonal relationships, especially with the subject's father and mother. The folder materials contained ratings by the subject of his attitudes and

---

*The following point must be strongly emphasized: a basic assumption in this entire scheme is that an individual's orientations toward his cessation are biphasic, that is, any adult, at any given moment, has (*a*) more or less long-range, relatively chronic, pervasive, habitual, characterological orientations toward cessation as an integral part of his total psychological makeup (affecting his philosophy of life, need systems, aspirations, identification, conscious beliefs, etc.); and (*b*) is also capable of having acute, relatively short-lived, exacerbated, clinically sudden shifts of cessation orientation. Indeed, this is what is usually meant when one says that an individual has become suicidal. It is therefore crucial in any complete assessment of an individual's orientation toward cessation to know both his habitual *and* his at-that-moment orientations toward cessation. (Failure to do this is one reason why previous efforts to relate suicidal state with psychological test results have been barren.)

interactions with each of his parents. Some information relating to relationships with parents may be of special interest. In the 1940 questionnaire materials, when the modal age of the male subjects was 29.8 years, there was a series of questions concerning earlier conflict and attachment to mother and father. The responses of the 5 individuals who, as it turned out, made up the homogeneous suicide group, seemed to have three interesting features: (1) in answer to the question "Everything considered, which was your favorite parent—father, mother, had no favorite?" only 1 of the 5 answered "father"; (2) in answer to the question about the amount of conflict between the individual and his father and the individual and his mother, 2 of the 5 indicated moderate to severe conflict with the father, whereas none of the 5 indicated moderate or severe conflict with the mother; (3) the 1 suicide who was most obviously rejected by his father (and who indicated that he had had conflict with him) was the only 1 to indicate that "there has been a person . . . who had had a profound influence on his life." He wrote "My father, I think, has been responsible for a code of ethics stressing honesty and fair dealing in all relations." It was this man's father who insisted that he come into the family business and then called him stupid when he, for reasons of his own temperament, did not show the same amount of aptitude for business that his older brother demonstrated.

In general, for the 5 suicidal subjects, for reasons that are not completely clear, it seemed that the relationships with the father were more critical than the relationships with the mother. It may be that an exceptionally bright, handsome young child tends to be mother's darling and, for those same reasons, tends to be father's rival, hence the built-in psychological tendency for there to be more friction between father and son than between mother and son.

In the perusal of the records, evidence of trauma or stress in early life was sought: the death of a parent, divorce of the parents, stress (either overt or subtle) between the parents, or rejection of the subject by either parent. In retrospect, I had in mind a continuum ranging from tranquil and benign at one end to stressful and traumatic at the other.

The folder materials indicated that at the time the study began practically all of the subjects were described in essentially positive terms. For example, among the 5 subjects who, as it turned out, were the 5 homogeneous suicides, the following early descriptions by the home visitor appeared: "Attractive boy, well built, attractive features, charming." "Round chubby boy; very sweet face." "Winning little fellow, very fine all-around intelligence. The mother has excellent common sense and much is due to her." "Friendly, cheerful, freckled boy." "Tall for his age."

At the beginning, the psychological picture for most Terman youngsters was benign. However, in 2 of 5 homogeneous suicide cases there were, at an early age, already subtle prodromal clues of things to come: "He is the constant companion of his father but he is not father's favorite." (A few years later, at age 14, a teacher wrote about this child, "This boy's parents are of two minds; his mother is for college, his father thinks that college is of no value to a person who expects to take up the business. The boy does not show very much hardmindedness. His type is more the theoretical, he prefers ideas to matter.") During the same year, his mother wrote that the child's worst faults were "his lack of application and irresponsibility"—perhaps not too unusual at age 14.

Example: A child is ranked by his mother as "average" in these traits—prudence, self-confidence, optimism, permanence of mood, egotism, and truthfulness. We do not know, of course, how much of this is accurate perception or how much is self-fulfilling prophecy.

Example: At age 14 there is a series of letters from the head of his boarding school. (The parents were away on an extended trip.) The headmaster wrote letters having to do with the boy's veracity, perhaps revealing his own special emphases, "We have every hope of making him a straightforward young man. We are people he cannot bluff, and with consistent vigilance the boy will be able to overcome his difficulties." A few years later his mother wrote: "His success will depend a good deal on his associates."

Least Successful

In Melita Oden's [1] monograph she presented a number of measures and comparisons between the 100 Terman subjects ranked as most successful and an equal number adjudged to be least successful. For each of the 30 cases that I have analyzed, I tried to make some judgment along a success–failure continuum. In the end, 8 cases were labeled as conspicuous successes and 5 as failures. As it turned out, none of those cases rated by me as "most successful" subsequently committed suicide, whereas 3 of the cases rated as "least successful" killed themselves.*

---

* Among the 20 men who committed suicide, at least 3 were considered outstandingly successful by gifted group standards: 2 in the 1960 study and 1 who died in 1938 who had a brilliant record until his death at the age of 28. Conversely, 3 were considered least successful: 2 in 1940 (they had died before 1960) and 1 in the 1960 evaluation. [1]

Example: a very bright young boy (I.Q. 180) who did very well
in high school, both academically and in extracurricular activities.
When he was 15 years old Professor Terman wrote of him, "I think
there is no doubt that he would make a desirable student at Stanford."
Within a year, at age 16, he had entered Stanford and flunked out.
Eventually, after working as a clerk, he returned to college after
1 year and graduated. He earned a law degree going to school at
night and upon completion, became an attorney in a large law firm.
He was described as unsocial and shy. In his forties he says he
was inclined to drink rather heavily, but not sufficiently to interfere
with his work. His wife is described as vivacious, he as withdrawn.
After a heart attack, his income suddenly became half of what he
had been earning. He described himself as much less interested than
his peers in vocational advancement or financial gain.

Signatures

In each case, I looked for some special (albeit negative) indicators
that might in themselves, or in combination, be prodromatic to suicide.
For example, alcoholism, homosexuality, suicide threats, conspicuous
achievement instability, depression, neurasthenia, and dyspnea could
be listed. All 5 of the homogeneous suicides had one or more of
these signature items. An additional 8 (of the 30 cases) also had
signature items. These items in themselves did not necessarily point
to suicide, but when taken in combination with other features in
the case they constituted an important aspect of the total prodromal
picture.

Example, this one emphasizing the lifelong instability of the
individual: at age 7 his mother wrote that "he is inclined to take
the line of least resistance." At the same time, the teacher rated
him high in desire to excel, general intelligence, and originality, average
in prudence, generosity, and desire to know, and low in willpower,
optimism, and truthfulness. She indicated that, although he came from
a good home, he was inclined to be moody and sulky. At age 8
his mother said he was strong-willed and liked to have his own way,
that school was easy, and that he was making excellent grades. At
age 10 his parents divorced. At age 12 the teacher reported that he
was not a very good student and was doing only fair work, that he
had rather lazy mental habits. At age 16 he graduated from high
school with a C average. He did not attend college. In his twenties
he became an artist and was married. He was in the army during
World War II and afterwards was unemployed and described by his

wife as "immature, unstable, irresponsible, and extravagant." Because of his many affairs, his wife, although stating she was fond of him, left him. She called him impulsive, romantic, and unstable. In his thirties he worked for a while as a commercial artist. He wrote to Professor Terman, "I am a lemon in your group." He indicated, as a joke, that his "hobby" was observing women from a bar stool. He remarried. He wrote to Professor Terman in relation to his artwork that he "received much acclaim from those in the immediate audience," but that his works had not yet been displayed in any shows. His life was a series of up and downs, some impulsive behaviors, and lifelong instability, although his status improved markedly in the late 1950s.

Apropos "up and downs" in general, any sudden *changes* in life status or life style can be looked upon as suspicious, i.e., prodromal to suicide, especially a change which marks a decline of status, position, or income. Generally, in suicide prevention work, one views any recent changes in life style as possible serious indicators of suicidal potential.

RATING OF LETHALITY (THE PSYCHOLOGICAL AUTOPSY)

In addition to the life chart, the second procedure employed was one that I had some years before labeled "the psychological autopsy." This procedure is a retrospective reconstruction of an individual's life that focuses on lethality, that is, those features of his life that illuminate his intentions in relation to his own death, clues as to the type of death it was, the degree (if any) of his participation in his own death, and why the death occurred at that time. In general, the main function of the psychological autopsy is to help clarify deaths that are equivocal as to the *mode* of death—usually to help coroners and medical examiners decide if the death (which may be clear enough as to cause of death, e.g., asphyxiation due to drowning or barbiturate overdose) was of an accidental or suicidal mode. Clearly, the *psychological* autopsy focuses on the role of the decedent in his own demise.

In the last few years, a number of individuals have written on this topic. Litman and his colleagues[15] have presented a general overview of its clinical use, Curphey[16] has written of the use of this procedure from the medicolegal viewpoint of a forensic pathologist, and Weisman and Kastenbaum[17] have applied this procedure to study and terminal phase of life. Elsewhere,[18] I have indicated that 3 separate types (and uses) of the psychological autopsy can be discerned. Each is tied to answering a different primary question: (1) why did the

individual commit suicide? (2) why did the individual die at this time?
and (3) what is the most accurate mode of death in this case? Given
a death which is clear as to *cause* of death but which is equivocal
as to *mode* of death, the purpose of this type of psychological autopsy
is to clarify the situation so as to arrive at the most accurate or
appropriate mode of death—what it truly was. This original use of
the psychological autopsy grew out of the joint efforts of the Los
Angeles County chief medical examiner-coroner (then Dr. Theodore
J. Curphey) and the staff of the Los Angeles Suicide Prevention
Center as an attempt to bring the skills of the behavioral sciences
to bear relevantly on the problems of equivocal deaths. In those
10 percent of coroner's cases where the mode of death is questionable
or equivocal, this equivocation usually lies between the modes of
accident and suicide. Here are 3 simplified examples.

1. *Cause of death:* asphyxiation due to drowning. Woman found
    in her swimming pool. Question: did she "drown" (accident),
    or was it intentional (suicide)?
2. *Cause of death:* multiple crushing injuries. Man found at the foot
    of a tall building. Question: did he fall (accident), or did he jump
    (suicide)? Or, even, was he pushed or thrown (homicide)?
3. *Cause of death:* barbiturate intoxication due to overdose. Woman
    found in her bed. Question: would she be surprised to know
    that she was dead (accident), or is this what she had planned
    (suicide)?

An outline for a psychological autopsy is presented in Table 11-3.

In the usual application of the psychological autopsy, the procedure
is to interview close survivors, relatives and friends of the decedent
in order to reconstruct his role in his own death. In the present
study, I was, of course, limited to an examination of folder materials.

All the criteria that have been discussed above—perturbation,
including early prodramata, failure, and signatures—were combined
into one judgment of that individual's lethality, that is, the probability
of his committing suicide in the present or the immediate future.
In this process of judgment I was guided by 2 additional governing
concepts (1) the key role of the significant other and (2) the concept
of a partial death or chronic suicide or "burned-out" life.

The Crucial Role of the Significant Other

In an adult who is suicide prone, the behavior of the significant
other, specifically the wife, seems either lifesaving or suicidogenic.
My reading of the cases led me to feel that the wife could be the

Table 11-3
Outline for Psychological Autopsy

1. Identifying information for victim (name, age, address, marital status, religious practices, occupation, and other details)
2. Details of the death (including the cause or method and other pertinent details)
3. Brief outline of victim's history (siblings, marriage, medical illnesses, medical treatment, psychotherapy, previous suicide attempts)
4. "Death history" of victim's family (suicides, cancer, other fatal illnesses, ages at death, and other details)
5. Description of the personality and life style of the victim
6. Victim's typical patterns of reaction to stress, emotional upsets, and periods of disequilibrium
7. Any recent—from last few days to last 12 months—upsets, pressures, tensions, or anticipations of trouble
8. Role of alcohol and drugs in (1) overall life style of victim and (2) in his death
9. Nature of victim's interpersonal relationships (including physicians)
10. Fantasies, dreams, thoughts, premonitions, or fears of victim relating to death, accident, or suicide
11. Changes in the victim before death (of habits, hobbies, eating, sexual patterns, and other life routines)
12. Information relating to the "life side" of victim (upswings, successes, plans)
13. Assessment of intention, i.e., role of the victim in his own demise
14. Rating of lethality
15. Reactions of informants to victim's death
16. Comments, special features, etc.

difference between life and death. In general, a wife who was hostile, independent, competitive, or nonsupporting of her husband who had some of the suicidal prodromata seemed to doom him to a suicidal outcome, whereas a wife who was helpful, emotionally supportive, and actively ancillary seemed to save a man who, in my clinical judgment at least, might otherwise have killed himself.

To the extent that these global clinical impressions of the important role of the spouse, in some cases, are correct then, in those cases there is an equal implication for suicide prevention, specifically that one must deal actively with the significant other. A regimen of therapy or a program of education must not fail to include the spouse, indeed it might be focused primarily on the wife and only secondarily on the potential suicide himself. Of course, the conscious and unconscious attitudes of the wife toward her husband must be carefully assessed.

In a situation where the wife is deeply competitive (and might unconsciously wish him dead), using her as an auxiliary therapist would at best be an uphill climb. It is possible that in some cases a separation might be a lifesaving suggestion. All the above is not to impugn the wife, but rather appropriately to involve her. It could very well be that, had the study focused on female suicides, the above prescription would be in relation to the complementary role of the husband.

The Concept of a Partial Death

This concept is well known in suicidology. In the technical literature it was given its most well known presentation by Karl Menninger.[19] On valid psychological grounds he denies the dichotomous nature of psychological death and asserts that there are some lives that are moieties and only partial existences. Henry Murray[20] expands this theme in his paper "Dead to the World."

When I chose the phrase "dead to the world," I was thinking of a variety of somewhat similar psychic states characterized by a marked diminution or near-cessation of affect involving both hemispheres of concern, the inner and the outer world. Here it is as if a person's primal springs of vitality had dried up, as if he were empty or hollow at the very core of his being. There is a striking absence of anything but the most perfunctory and superficial social interactions; output as well as intake is at a minimum. . . . I have been talking about a diminution or cessation of feeling, one component of consciousness, on the assumption that this condition is somewhat analogous to a cessation of the whole of consciousness. If the cessation of feeling is temporary it resembles sleep; if it is permanent (a virtual atrophy of emotional life) it resembles death, the condition of the brain and body after the home fires of metabolism in the cortex have gone out. In a feelingless state the home fires are still burning but without glow or warmth.

That last statement about the home fires burning led me to think of a "burned-out" person—one whose whole life was a kind of chronic suicide, a living death, a life without ambition and seemingly without purpose.

In the lethality ratings of the 30 cases, those that gave me the greatest difficulty were the chronic, nonachieving, "partial death" lives. I decided that I would rate this type of person among the first 12 in lethality, but not among the first 5. I did this with the conviction that this very style of living was in itself a kind of substitute for overt suicide; that in these cases; the *raison d'être* for committing overt suicide was absent, in that the truncated life itself was the significant inimical act.[21]

RESULTS OF BLIND CLINICAL ANALYSES

On the day that I completed the blind analysis of the 30th case I wrote a memorandum to Professor Sears that included the following

My analysis of the data and possibly the data themselves do not permit me to state with anything like full confidence which 5 cases were suicidal. The best that I can do—from my subjective ratings of each individual's perturbation and lethality—is to rank order 11 of the cases as the most likely candidates for suicidal status. I should be somewhat surprised if any of the other 19 individuals committed suicide. The rank order for suicide potential is as follows . . .

Then we—Mrs. Oden, Mrs. Buckholtz, and I—met to "break the key."

The facts revealed that the individual whom I had ranked as number 1 had, in fact, committed suicide, my number 2 had committed suicide, number 3 was living, number 4 had committed suicide, number 5 had committed suicide, and number 6 had committed suicide. Numbers 7 and 9 were living; numbers 8, 10, and 11 had died natural deaths. For the statistical record, the probability of choosing four or five of the five suicide cases correctly by chance alone is 1 out of 1,131—significant at the .000884 level. Obviously, a null hypothesis that there are no discernible prodromal clues to suicide can be discarded with a fair degree of confidence.

Table 11-4 presents a summary of the blind analysis data in terms of a brief vignette, signature items, success-failure ratings, perturbation ratings, lethality ratings, and suicide probability ranking for all 30 subjects. (The "Postscript" information was not available to me when I made these ratings and was added to the chart after all the other ratings and rankings had been made.)

Much of my analysis of these 30 cases was inferential, sometimes even intuitive—which is to say that not every clue or cognitive maneuver can be recovered, much less communicated. But for what it is worth, I deeply believe that a number of experienced professional persons could have done as well. Indeed, I feel that the volumes of information generated in the past 20 years by suicidologists furnish the working concepts and the background facts for making precisely this kind of (potentially lifesaving) judgment every day of the year in the practical clinical situation. Knowledge of this sort is now an established part of the new discipline of suicidology.

One striking result was that among those who committed suicide in their fifties, the pattern of life consistent with this outcome seemed clearly discernible *by the time they were in their late twenties*. The data subsequent to age 30 served, in most cases, primarily to strengthen

Table 11-4
Blind Ratings and Outcomes for 30 Matched Male Terman Study Subjects

No.	Notable Characteristics	Signatures	Life Success	Perturbation	Lethality	Suicide Rank	Postscript
1	NP hospitalization; divorced; great perturbation; talks of suicide at 15 and 20	Suicide threats	C−	7-8	High	1	Committed suicide
2	Deaf; professional; low drive for worldly success	Nonachiever	C	3-4	Low	12+	Living
3	Flunked out of college; obtained LLB; shy; ups and downs; drop in income; alcohol	Alcohol; ups and downs	C	6-7	High	2	Committed suicide
4	Insurance man in heart attack rut	—	B	3-4	Low	12+	Died—heart
5	Ambitious bank officer	—	B	3-4	Low	12+	Died—cancer
6	Brilliant professor of medicine; textbook author; good life	—	A	1-2	Low	12+	Died—cancer
7	Set back at adolescence by home stresses; obese; no college aspirations; withdrawn; low-level job; underachiever; stabilized	Underachiever; stabilized	C−	6-7	?	11	Died—heart

#	Description	Note	Grade	Range	Level	Score	Outcome
8	Physician; too high standards for people; tones down	—	B+	5-6	Low	12+	Died—heart
9	Hand-driving rancher; dominated by mother	—	B	5-6	Low	12+	Died—cancer
10	Stable geologist; steady life	—	A	1-2	Low	12+	Living
11	Lithographer; brilliant; no family back-up; underachiever	Underachiever	C	5-6	Low	12+	Living
12	Multimarried; emphysemic; inventor; ups and downs	Dyspnea; failure	C	6-7	High	4	Committed suicide
13	Scion of business fortune; straight success line; father helpful and supportive	—	A	4-5	Low	12+	Living
14	Quietly successful in own small business; tranquil life	—	B	3-4	Low	12+	Living
15	Had all advantages; did rather well but not superlatively	—	B	3-4	Low	12+	Living
16	Neurasthenic; esoteric mother; underachiever; chronic suicide	Depression; neurasthenia	C−	6-7	?	7	Living

357

Table 11-4 (continued)
Blind Ratings and Outcomes for 30 Matched Male Terman Study Subjects

No.	Notable Characteristics	Signatures	Life Success	Perturbation	Lethality	Suicide Rank	Postscript
17	Artist; unstable; flighty; impetuous; willful	Instability	B−	7-8	?	5	Committed suicide
18	Insurance man; stable life; interesting siblings	—	B	3-4	Low	12+	Living
19	Brilliant child and siblings; needed a father; stabilized by second wife	—	B	4-5	Low	12+	Living
20	Pleasant man; pleasant life; pleasant family; likes work	—	B	2-3	Low	12+	Living
21	Early genius; hiatus; never fully recovers; wife commits suicide	—	B	5-6	Mdn	12+	Died—heart
22	Shy, depressed artist; multiple illnesses; making it	Depression; ill	B	6-7	?	9	Living
23	Unhappy; forced into father's business; rejected by father; always second to sibling; 4	Depression; instability	B+	7-8	?	6	Committed suicide

divorces;unstable; downhill; alone						
24 Average school administrator; ordinary stresses	—	B	4-5	Low	12+	Living
25 Well-adjusted, stable attorney; great relationship with father; good life success	—	A	2-3	Low	12+	Living
26 Depressed engineer; hypomanic wife; his job holds him	Depression	B	6-7	Mdn+	8	Died—cancer
27 Scientist; brilliant beginning; wife drains him; good but not great	—	B+	3-4	Low	12+	Living
28 Engineer; overcame adolescent crisis and parents' divorce; good marriage; has grown steadily	—	B	4-5	Low	12+	Died—heart
29 Author; asthmatic; depressed; strong support from wife	Dyspnea; depression	A-	5-6	?	10	Died—cancer
30 Professional; stormy life; alcoholic; competing wife	Alcohol; instability	B-	6-7	?	3	Living

the impression of suicidal outcome that I had formulated at that point. Those relatively few cases in which this earlier impression was reversed in the thirties and forties had one or two specific noteworthy elements within them: (1) a psychologically supporting spouse or (2) a "burning-out" of the individual's drive and affect. In the latter cases, this condition of psychological aridity and successlessness seemed to be the price for continued life.

What were some of the main clinical impressions relating to adult suicide in this gifted male group? In the briefest possible vignette, my main overall clinical impression might be formulated in this way: the *father*, even in his absence, *starts* the life course to suicide; *school and work* (and the feelings of inferiority and chronic low-grade hopelessness) *exacerbate* it; and the *wife* can, in some cases, effect the *rescue* from it (or otherwise play a sustaining or even a precipitating role in it).

Among the 5 homogeneous suicides, 3 types of suicidal prodromata relating to instability, trauma, and control could be differentiated.

Instability

In general, suicide is more likely to occur in a life where there has been instability (rather than stability). As used here, instability is practically synonymous with perturbation.

CHRONIC INSTABILITY

Evidences of chronic, long-term instability would include neuro-psychiatric hospitalization, talk or threat of suicide, alcoholism, multiple divorces, and any unusually stressful psychodynamic background—even though these bits of evidence occurred in as few as 1 of the 5 cases. Examples: Mr. A: NP hospitalization, divorce, talk of suicide at 15 and at 20; Mr. B: unstable personality, divorced, flighty behavior, few stabilizing forces; Mr. C: unhappy man, rejected by father, always second-best, 4 marriages, highly perturbed.

RECENT DOWNHILL COURSE

A recent downhill change that occurs in a career marked by ups and downs, that is a generally unstable life course, was characteristic of suicidal persons. Specifically, these changes include a marked sudden decrease in income, sudden acute alcoholism, a change in work, and divorce or separation, especially where the wife leaves the husband for another man. In general, a sudden, inexplicable change for the worse is a bad augury. This means that in an individual with an up and down history, the most recent bit of information can be singularly irrelevant, if not outright misleading. Examples: Mr. D: highly recommended for university, flunked out of college, went back to school, earned an LL.B. degree, shy, alcoholic, sudden drop in income, up and down course, does not "burn out"; Mr. E: inventor, multiple marriages, up and down course, severe emphysema. (N.B., dyspnea can be an especially incapacitating symptom and has been related to suicide in special ways.[22]

Trauma

EARLY CHILDHOOD OR ADOLESCENT TRAUMA

Examples would include acute rejection by one or both parents, lack of family psychological support, and separation or divorce of the parents. A crisis in adolescence can turn a life toward lower achievement.

ADULT TRAUMA

This includes poor health, such as asthma, emphysema, severe neurosis, obesity, and multiple illnesses. Another major type of adult trauma relates to the spouse, either rejection by the wife for another man or being married to a hyperactive (and competing) wife, who has changed from the woman he married. Examples: Mr. F, a depressed engineer whose top security job in aerospace holds him together; and Mr. G, who has a complicated, hypomanic, and successful wife toward whom he is deeply ambivalent.

Controls

OUTER CONTROLS

These are the compensations or stabilizing influences in individuals who, without these assets from other than within themselves, would be more perturbed than they are and might commit suicide. Examples: the stabilizing work of Mr. F, mentioned above; the stabilizing wife of asthmatic Mr. H, a woman who nurses him and keeps the world from inappropriately intruding upon him or exhausting him. She husbands his limited energies.

INNER CONTROLS

These inner controls are not the usual strengths or positive features or assets of personality or character. They are the negative inner controls of default. One such is what occurs in some individuals who are perturbed early in their lives, who, if they survive, stabilize or simmer down or "burn out" in their fifties or sixties. Examples: Mr. J: He was psychologically traumatized during adolescence by home stresses. He has no hobbies, no college aspirations, is withdrawn, and works as a mechanic and caretaker.

Mr. K: Extremely high I.Q. He is neurasthenic, has a mother with esoteric tastes, experiences back and shoulder pains just like his father, and is unable to hold a job as a professional. He calls himself "an unsuccessful animal." He ends up working as a clerk in a large company. His stance is that—to use an example from Melville—of the contemporary Bartleby ("I prefer not to"), what Menninger[19] has called a "chronic suicide," where the truncated life itself can be conceptualized as a partial death.

DISCUSSION

Whereas the clinical challenge is to be intuitive, to display diagnostic acumen, and to manifest therapeutic skill, the scientific challenge is to state theory and to explicate facts in a replicable way. I feel obligated to address myself to the theoretical side of this issue.

I shall begin with low-level theory, that is, an explication of the specific items that guided my thinking in choosing the individuals whom I believed had committed suicide. Some 10 items were in my mind (1) early (grammar school, adolescence, or college age) evidences of instability, including dishonesty; (2) rejection by the father; (3) multiple marriages; (4) alcoholism; (5) an unstable occupational history; (6) ups and downs in income; (7) a crippling physical disability, especially one involving dyspnea; (8) disappointment in the use of one's potential, that is, a disparity between aspiration and accomplishment; (9) any talk or hint of self-destruction; and (10) a competitive or self-absorbed spouse. In summary, this low-level theoretical explication states that a bright male Caucasian who committed suicide in his fifties was apt to be rejected by his father, adolescently disturbed, multimarried, alcoholic, occasionally unsettled or unsuccessful, disappointed in himself and disappointing to others, unstable, lonely, and perturbed with a penchant for precipitous action.

At a somewhat deeper level, and thus more theoretical, are the elements of rejection, disparity between aspiration and accomplishment, instability, and perturbation. At a still deeper level (and even more theoretical) is the notion that the suicidal person is one who believes that he has not had his father's love and seeks it symbolically without success throughout his life, eventually hoping, magically, to gain it by a singular act of sacrifice or expiation. The most theoretical formulation might be stated as: those gifted men who committed suicide in their fifties did not have that internalized viable approving parental homunculus that, like a strong heart, seems necessary for a long life.

It is interesting to reflect that the 5 gifted suicidal persons of this study constituted an essentially nonpsychotic group. This assertion is not to gainsay that each of them was severely perturbed at the time of the suicide, but that they were not "crazy"; that is, they did not manifest the classical hallmarks of psychosis such as hallucinations, delusions, dereistic thinking, and the like. Their perturbation took the form—prior to the overt suicidal act—of alcoholism, other than one marriage (single, divorced, or multiple marriages), chronic loneliness, occupational ups and downs, impetuosity and impulsivity, and inner (as well as overt) agitation. Although, as it is in most suicidal persons, one can suppose that their thought processes were circumscribed ("tunnel vision") and tended to be dichotomous ("either a happy life or death"), there was no direct evidence to indicate that they were psychotically bizarre or paleological.[23]

As has been noted by Oden,[1] the magic combination for life success among the gifted is not a simple one. for suicide also the equation is a combination of obvious and subtle elements. Many factors, none of which seems to be sufficient alone, appear to coexist in a suicidal case. And, as in any equation, there are factors on both the positive (life-loving, biophilic, suicide-inhibiting) and the negative (death-loving, necrophilic, suicide-promoting) sides.

In the algebra of life and death, the wife may play an absolutely vital role, holding her spouse to life or, at the worst, stimulating or even provoking him to suicide. Every suicidologist knows that suicide is most often a two-person event, a dyadic occurrence, and for this reason, if no other, the management and prevention of suicide almost always has to involve the significant other. With high suicide risk gifted males, my impression is that the most important lifesaving task is not directly to the potentially suicidal person, but through the wife—especially in concert with the family physician.

Currently, there is a small number of retrospective studies seeking to establish some of the early precursors of suicide among special populations presumed to be intellectually superior, specifically physicians and university graduates. A few words about each.

Blachly and his colleagues[24] have made an analysis of 249 suicides by physicians reported in the obituary columns of the *Journal of the American Medical Association* between May 1965 and November

Table 11-5

Summary of Findings of Three Studies of Precursors to Suicide among Intellectually Superior Subjects

Present Clinical Impressions*	Blachly's Tabular Results	Paffenbarger's Statistical Findings
a. early (before 20) evidences of instability, including dishonesty	a. mentally depressed or disturbed	a. college education of father
b. actual or felt rejection by the father	b. prior suicidal attempt or statement of suicidal intent	b. college education of mother
c. multiple marriages	c. heavy drinker or alcoholic	c. father professional
d. alcoholism	d. drug addiction or heavy drug user	d. father dead
e. an unstable occupational history	e. "inadequate" financial status	e. parents separated
f. ups and downs in income (not to mention ups and downs in mood)	f. death of close relative in decedent's childhood	f. cigarette smoker in college
g. a crippling physical disability, especially one involving dyspnea	g. suicide of relative	g. attended boarding school
h. disappointment in the use of	h. seriously impaired physical health	h. college dropout

potential, i.e., a disparity between aspiration and accomplishment

i. any talk or hint of self-destruction
j. a competitive or self-absorbed spouse

i. nonjoiner in college
j. allergies
k. underweight
l. self-assessed ill health
m. self-consciousness
n. subject to worries
o. feelings of being watched or talked about
p. insomnia
q. secretive-seclusiveness
r. "anxiety-depression" index (including nervousness, moodiness, exhaustion, etc.)

---

*Of course, not all of these features occurred in any one suicidal case; conversely, some of these features occurred in as few as one suicidal case. It was the "total impression" that counted most.

1967. Deaths from suicide exceeded the combined deaths from automobile accidents, airplane crashes, drowning, and homicide. The mean age of the suicidal group was 49. Blachly and his associates mailed questionnaires to the next of kin (usually the widow); about 30 percent of the inquiries were returned, many with extensive comments. The suicide rate varied greatly among the medical specialties, ranging from a low of 10 per 100,000 among pediatricians to a high of 61 per 100,000 among psychiatrists. A résumé of Blachly's main findings is presented in Table 11-5.

Paffenbarger and his associates [25,26] have completed analyses of over 50,000 medical and social histories (including physical and psychological evaluations) of former male students at the University of Pennsylvania and at Harvard covering a 34-year period from 1916 to 1950. Their original focus was on individuals who subsequently died of coronary heart disease. The data drew their attention to those who had committed suicide whom they then compared with their nonsuicidal cohorts. The 4000 known deaths included 225 suicides. Their findings relative to suicide point to paternal deprivation through early loss or death of the father, loneliness and underjoining in college, dropping out of college, and feelings of rejection, self-consciousness, and failure during the college years.

Dr. Caroline Thomas,[27] a cardiologist like Paffenbarger, is studying the causes of death among 1337 former medical students of the Johns Hopkins University School of Medicine from 1948 to 1964. Her present project, as did Paffenbarger's, began as a study of the precursors of coronary heart disease but, in light of the data (14 suicides among the 31 premature deaths) shifted to include precursors of suicide. That project is currently in the hypothesis stage. Interesting results should be forthcoming.

What may be of especial interest in Table 11-5 are the common elements or threads in the findings of the 3 projects and the clinical findings of this present study. To what extent these findings relate only to the intellectually superior and to what extent they are ubiquitous is a matter for further study. Nonetheless it is not premature to say that, on the basis of currently known data, it would appear that the common findings would seem to have general application.

REFERENCES

1. Oden MH: The fulfillment of promise: 40-year follow-up of the Terman gifted group. Genet Psychol Monogr, 77:3–93, 1968
2. Terman LM: Genetic Studies of Genius: I. Mental and Physical Traits

of a Thousand Gifted Children. Stanford, Stanford Univ Press, 1925

3. Terman LM: Psychological approaches to the biography of genius. Science 92:293-301, 1940

4. Terman LM, Oden MH: Genetic Studies of Genius: IV. The Gifted Child Grows Up. Stanford, Stanford Univ Press, 1947

5. Terman LM, Oden MH: Genetic Studies of Genius: V. The Gifted Child at Mid-Life. Stanford, Stanford Univ Press, 1959

6. Stone AA, Onque GC: Longitudinal Studies of Child Personality. Cambridge, Massachusetts, Harvard Univ Press, 1959

7. Cox CM: The early mental traits of three hundred geniuses, in Genetic Studies of Genius, vol. 2. Stanford, Stanford Univ Press, 1926

8. Dublin LI, Lotka AJ, Spiegelman M: Length of Life. New York, Ronald Press, 1949

9. Cavan RS: Suicide. Chicago, Univ Chicago Press, 1928

10. Binswanger L: The case of Ellen West, in May R, Angel E, Ellenberger HF (eds): Existence. New York, Basic Books, 1958, p 237-364

11. Kobler AL, Stotland E: The End of Hope. New York, Free Press, 1964

12. Alvarez WC: Minds That Came Back. Philadelphia, Lippincott, 1961

13. Meyer A: The life chart and the obligation of specifying positive data in psychopathological diagnosis, reprinted in Winters EE (ed): The Collected Works of Adolf Meyer, vol. 3. Baltimore, Johns Hopkins, 1951, p. 52-56

14. Meyer A: Mental and moral health in a constructive school program, reprinted in Winters EE (ed); The Collected Works of Adolf Meyer, vol. 4. Baltimore, Johns Hopkins, 1952, p. 350-70

15. Litman RE, Curphey TJ, Shneidman ES, Farberow NL, Tabachnick ND: Investigations of equivocal suicides. JAMA 184:924-29, 1963

16. Curphey TJ: The role of the social scientist in the medicolegal certification of death from suicide, in Farberow NL, Shneidman ES (eds): The Cry for Help. New York, McGraw-Hill, 1961

17. Weisman AD, Kastenbaum R: The psychological autopsy: A study of the terminal phase of life. Comm Ment Health J 4:1-59, 1968

18. Shneidman ES: Suicide, lethality and the psychological autopsy, in Shneidman ES, Ortega MJ (eds): Aspects of Depression. Boston, Little, Brown, 1969

19. Menninger KA: Man against Himself. New York, Harcourt, 1938

20. Murray HA: Dead to the world: The passions of Herman Melville, in Shneidman ES (ed): Essays in Self-Destruction. New York, Science House, 1967

21. Shneidman ES: Orientations toward death: A vital aspect of the study of lives, in White RW (ed): The Study of Lives. New York, Atherton, 1963

22. Farberow NL, McKelligott W, Cohen S, Darbonne A: Suicide among patients with cardiorespiratory illnesses. JAMA 195:422-28, 1966

23. Shneidman ES: Logical content analysis: An explication of styles of

"Concludifying," in Gerbner G, Holsti OR, Krippendorff K, Paisley WJ, and Stone PJ (Eds.): The Analysis of Communication Content. New York, Wiley, 1969

24. Blachly PH, Disher W, Roduner G: Suicide by physicians. Bull Suicidol 1–18, 1968

25. Paffenbarger RS, Jr, Asnes DP: Chronic disease in former college students. III. Precursors of suicide in early and middle life. Am J Public Health 56:1026–36, 1966

26. Paffenbarger RS, Jr, King SH, Wing AL: Chronic disease in former college students. IX characteristics in youth that predispose to suicide and accidental death in later life. Am J Public Health 59:900–908, 1969

27. Thomas CB: Suicide among us: Can we learn to prevent it? Johns Hopkins Med J 125:276–85, 1969

PART V

Philosophic and Legal Aspects of Suicide

Richard Brandt

12
The Morality and Rationality of Suicide

The introductory piece to this chapter is from David Hume's famous essay, Of Suicide (1777).

One considerable advantage that arises from Philosophy, consists in the sovereign antidote which it affords to superstition and false religion. All other remedies against that pestilent distemper are vain, or at least uncertain. Plain good sense and the practice of the world, which alone serve most purposes of life, are here found ineffectual: History as well as daily experience furnish instances of men endowed with the strongest capacity for business and affairs, who have all their lives crouched under slavery to the grossest superstition. Even gaiety and sweetness of temper, which infuse a balm into every other wound, afford no remedy to so virulent a poison; as we may particularly observe of the fair Sex, who, tho' commonly possest of these rich presents of nature, feel many of their joys blasted by this importunate intruder. But when sound Philosophy has once gained possession of the mind, superstition is effectually excluded; and one may fairly affirm, that her triumph over this enemy is more complete than over most of the vices and imperfections incident to human nature. Love or anger, ambition or avarice, have their root in the temper and affections, which the soundest reason is scarce ever able fully to correct; but superstition being founded on false opinion, must immediately vanish when true philosophy has inspired juster sentiments of superior powers. The contest is here more equal between the distemper and the medicine, and nothing can hinder the latter from proving effectual, but its being false and sophisticated.

It will here be superfluous to magnify the merits of philosophy, by displaying the pernicious tendency of that vice of which it cures the human mind.

The superstitious man, says Tully, is miserable in every scene, in every incident of life; even sleep itself, which banishes all other cares of unhappy mortals, affords to him matter of new terror; while he examines his dreams, and finds in those visions of the night prognostications of future calamities. I may add, that tho' death alone can put a full period to his misery, he dares not fly to this refuge, but still prolongs a miserable existence from a vain fear lest he offend his maker, by using the power, with which that beneficent being has endowed him. The presents of God and nature are ravished from us by this cruel enemy; and notwithstanding that one step would remove us from the regions of pain and sorrow, her menaces still chain us down to a hated being, which she herself chiefly contributes to render miserable.

'Tis observed by such as have been reduced by the calamities of life to the necessity of employing this fatal remedy, that if the unseasonable care of their friends deprive them of that species of Death, which they proposed to themselves, they seldom venture upon any other, or can summon up so much resolution a second time, as to execute their purpose. So great is our horror of death, that when it presents itself, under any form, besides that to which a man has endeavoured to reconcile his imagination, it acquires new terrors and overcomes his feeble courage: But when the menaces of superstition are joined to this natural timidity, no wonder it quite deprives men of all power over their lives, since even many pleasures and enjoyments, to which we are carried by a strong propensity, are torn from us by this inhuman tyrant. Let us here endeavour to restore men to their native liberty by examining all the common arguments against Suicide, and shewing that that action may be free from every imputation of guilt or blame, according to the sentiments of all the ancient philosophers.

If Suicide be criminal, it must be a transgression of our duty either to God, our neighbour, or ourselves.—To prove that suicide is no transgression of our duty to God, the following considerations may perhaps suffice. In order to govern the material world, the almighty Creator has established general and immutable laws by which all bodies, from the greatest planet to the smallest particle of matter, are maintained in their proper sphere and function. To govern the animal world, he has endowed all living creatures with bodily and mental powers; with senses, passions, appetites, memory and judgment, by which they are impelled or regulated in that course of life to which they are destined. These two distinct principles of the material and animal world, continually encroach upon each other, and mutually retard or forward each others operations. The powers of men and of all other animals are restrained and directed by the nature and qualities of the surrounding bodies; and the modifications and actions of these bodies are incessantly altered by the operation of all animals. Man is stopt by rivers in his passage over the surface of the earth; and rivers, when properly directed, lend their force to the motion of machines, which serve to the use of man. But tho' the provinces of the material and animal powers are not kept entirely separate, there results from thence no discord or disorder in the creation; on the contrary, from the mixture, union and contrast of all the various powers of inanimate bodies and living creatures, arises that surprizing harmony and proportion which affords the surest argument of supreme wisdom. The providence of the Deity appears not immediately in any operation, but governs everything by those general and immutable laws, which have been established from the beginning of time. All events, in one sense, may be pronounced the action of the Almighty; they all proceed from those powers with which he has endowed his creatures. A house which falls by its own weight is not brought to ruin by his providence more than one destroyed by the hands of men; nor are the human faculties less his workmanship, than the laws of motion and gravitation. When the passions play, when the judgment dictates, when the limbs obey; this is all the operation of God, and upon these animate principles, as well as upon the inanimate, has he established the government of the universe. Every event is alike important in the eyes of that infinite being, who takes in at one glance the most distant regions of space and remotest periods of time. There is no event, however important to us, which he has exempted from the general laws that govern the universe, or which he has peculiarly reserved for his own immediate action and operation. The revolution of states and empires depends upon the smallest caprice or passion of single men; and the lives of men are shortened or extended by the smallest accident of air or diet, sunshine or tempest. Nature still continues her progress and operation; and if general laws be ever broke by particular volitions of the Deity, 'tis after a manner which entirely escapes human observation. As, on the one hand, the elements and other inanimate parts of the creation carry on their action without regard to the particular interest and situation of men; so men are entrusted to their own judgment and discretion, in the various shocks of matter, and may employ every faculty with which they are endowed, in order to provide for their ease, happiness, or preservation. What is the meaning then of that principle, that a man who, tired of life, and hunted by pain and misery, bravely overcomes all the natural terrors of death and makes his escape from this cruel scene; that such a man, I say, has incurred the indignation of his Creator by encroaching on the office of divine providence, and disturbing the order of the universe? Shall we assert that the Almighty has reserved to himself in any peculiar manner the disposal of the lives of men, and has not submitted that event, in common with others, to the general laws by which the universe is governed? This is plainly false; the lives of men depend upon the same laws as the lives of all other animals; and these are subjected to the general laws of matter and motion. The fall of a tower, or the infusion of a poison, will destroy a man equally with the meanest creature; an inundation sweeps away every thing without distinction that comes within the reach of its fury. Since therefore the lives of men are for ever dependant on the general laws of matter and motion, is a man's disposing of his life criminal, because in every case it is criminal to encroach upon these laws, or disturb their operation? But this seems absurd; all animals are entrusted to their own prudence and skill for their conduct in the world, and have full authority, as far as their power extends, to alter all the operations of nature. Without the exercise of this authority they could not subsist a moment; every action, every motion of a man, innovates on the order of some parts of matter, and diverts from their ordinary course the general laws of motion. Putting together, therefore, these conclusions, we find that human life depends upon the general laws of matter and motion, and that it is no encroachment on the office of providence to disturb or alter these general laws: Has not every one, of consequence, the free disposal of his own life? And may he not lawfully employ that power with which nature has endowed him? In order to destroy the evidence of this conclusion, we must shew a reason, why this particular case is excepted; is it because human life is of so great importance, that 'tis a presumption for human prudence to dispose of it? But the life of a man is of no greater importance to the universe than that of an oyster. And were it of ever so great importance, the order of nature has actually submitted it to human prudence, and reduced us to a necessity in every incident of determining concerning it. Were the disposal of human life so much reserved as the peculiar province of the Almighty that it were an encroachment on his right, for men to dispose of their own lives; it would be equally criminal to act for the preservation of life as for its destruction. If I turn aside a stone which is falling upon my head, I disturb the course of nature, and I invade the peculiar province of the Almighty by lengthening out my life beyond the period which by the general laws of matter and motion he had assigned it.

A hair, a fly, an insect is able to destroy this mighty being whose life is of such importance. Is it an absurdity to suppose that human prudence may lawfully dispose of what depends on such insignificant causes? It would be no crime in me to divert the *Nile* or *Danube* from its course, were I able to effect such purposes. Where then is the crime of turning a few ounces of blood from their natural channel?—Do you imagine that I repine at providence or curse my creation, because I go out of life, and put a period to a being, which, were it to continue, would render me miserable? Far be such sentiments from me; I am only convinced of a matter of fact, which you yourself acknowledge possible, that human life may be unhappy, and that my existence, if further prolonged, would become ineligible: but I thank providence, both for the good which I have already enjoyed, and for the power with which I am endowed of escaping the ill that threatens me. To you it belongs to repine at providence, who foolishly imagine that you have no such power, and who must still prolong a hated life, tho' loaded with pain and sickness, with shame and poverty.—Do you not teach, that when any ill befalls me, tho' by the malice of my enemies, I ought to be resigned to providence, and that the actions of men are the operations of the Almighty as much as the actions of inanimate beings? When I fall upon my own sword, therefore, I receive my death equally from the hands of the Deity as if it had proceeded from a lion, a precipice, or a fever. The submission which you require to providence, in every calamity that befalls me, excludes not human skill and industry, if possibly by their means I can avoid or escape the calamity: And why may I not employ one remedy as well as another?—If my life be not my own, it were criminal for me to put it in danger, as well as to dispose of it; nor could one man deserve the appellation of *hero* whom glory or friendship transports into the greatest dangers, and another merit the reproach of *wretch* or *miscreant* who puts a period to his life from the same or like motives.—There is no being, which possesses any power or faculty, that it receives not from its Creator, nor is there any one, which by ever so irregular an action can encroach upon the plan of his providence, or disorder the universe. Its operations are his works equally with that chain of events, which it invades, and which ever principle prevails, we may for that very reason conclude it to be most favoured by him. Be it animate, or inanimate, rational, or irrational; 'tis all a case: Its power is still derived from the supreme creator, and is alike comprehended in the order of his providence. When the horror of pain prevails over the love of life; when a voluntary action anticipates the effects of blind causes; 'tis only in consequence of those powers and principles, which he has implanted in his creatures. Divine providence is still inviolate and placed far beyond the reach of human injuries. 'Tis impious, says the old Roman superstition, to divert rivers from their course, or invade the prerogatives of nature. 'Tis impious, says the French superstition, to inoculate for the small-pox, or usurp the business of providence, by voluntarily producing distempers and maladies. 'Tis impious, says the modern *European* superstition, to put a period to our own life, and thereby rebel against our creator; and why not impious, say I, to build houses, cultivate the ground, or sail upon the ocean? In all these actions we employ our powers of mind and body, to produce some innovation in the course of nature; and in none of them do we any more. They are all of them therefore equally innocent, or equally criminal.—*But you are placed by providence, like a centinel in a particular station, and when you desert it without being recalled, you are equally guilty of rebellion against your almighty sovereign, and have incurred his displeasure.*—I ask, why do you conclude that providence has placed me in this station? For my part I find that I owe my birth to a long chain of causes, of which many depended upon voluntary actions of men. *But Providence guided all these Causes, and nothing happens in the universe without its consent and Co-operation.* If so, then neither does my death, however voluntary, happen without its consent; and whenever pain or sorrow so far overcome my patience, as to make me tired of life, I may conclude that I am recalled from my station in the clearest and most express terms. 'Tis Providence surely that has placed me at this present moment in this chamber: But may I not leave it when I think proper, without being liable to the imputation of having deserted my post or station? When I shall be dead, the principles of which I am composed will still perform their part in the universe, and will be equally useful in the grand fabric, as when they composed this individual creature. The difference to the whole will be no greater than betwixt my being in a chamber and in the open air. The one change is of more importance to me than the other; but not more so to the universe.

'Tis a kind of blasphemy to imagine that any created being can disturb the order of the world or invade the business of providence! It supposes, that that Being possesses powers and faculties, which it received not from its creator, and which are not subordinate to his government and authority. A man may disturb society no doubt, and thereby incur the displeasure of the Almighty: But the government of the world is placed far beyond his reach and violence. And how does it appear that the Almighty is displeased with those actions that disturb society? By the principles which he has implanted in human nature, and which inspire us with a sentiment of remorse if we ourselves have been guilty of such actions, and with that of blame and disapprobation, if we ever observe them in others.—Let us now examine, according to the method proposed, whether Suicide be of this kind of actions, and be a breach of our duty to our *neighbour* and to *society*.

A man, who retires from life, does no harm to society: He only ceases to do good; which, if it is an injury, is of the lowest kind.—All our obligations to do good to society seem to imply something reciprocal. I receive the benefits of society and therefore ought to promote its interests, but when I withdraw myself altogether from society, can I be bound any longer? But, allowing that our obligations to do good were perpetual, they have certainly some bounds; I am not obliged to do a small good to society at the expence of a great harm to myself; why then should I prolong a miserable existence, because of some frivolous advantage which the public may perhaps receive from me? If upon account of age and infirmities I may lawfully resign any office, and employ my time altogether in fencing against these calamities, and alleviating as much as possible the miseries of my future life: Why may I not cut short these miseries at once by an action which is no more prejudicial to society?—But suppose that it is no longer in my power to promote the interest of society; suppose that I am a burthen to it; suppose that my life hinders some person from being much more useful to society. In such cases my resignation of life must not only be innocent but laudable. And most people who lie under any temptation to abandon existence, are in some such situation; those, who have health, or power, or authority, have commonly better reason to be in humour with the world.

A man is engaged in a conspiracy for the public interest; is seized upon suspicion; is threatened with the rack; and knows from his own weakness that the secret will be extorted from him: Could such a one consult the public interest better than by putting a quick period to a miserable life? This was the case of the famous and brave *Strozi of Florence*.—Again, suppose a malefactor is justly condemned to a shameful death; can any reason be imagined, why he may not anticipate his punishment, and save himself all the anguish of thinking on its dreadful approaches? He invades the business of providence no more than the magistrate did, who ordered his execution; and his voluntary death is equally advantageous to society by ridding it of a pernicious member. That suicide may often be consistent with interest and with our duty to ourselves, no one can question, who allows that age, sickness, or misfortune may render life a burthen, and make it worse even than annihilation. I believe that no man ever threw away life, while it was worth keeping. For such is our natural horror of death, that small motives will never be able to reconcile us to it; and though perhaps the situation of a man's health or fortune did not seem to require this remedy, we may at least be assured, that any one who, without apparent reason, has had recourse to it, was curst with such an incurable depravity or gloominess of temper as must poison all enjoyment, and render him equally miserable as if he had been loaded with the most grievous misfortunes.—If suicide be supposed a crime, 'tis only cowardice can impel us to it. If it be no crime, both prudence and courage should engage us to rid ourselves at once of existence, when it becomes a burthen. 'Tis the only way that we can then be useful to society, by setting an example, which, if imitated, would preserve to every one his chance for happiness in life and would effectually free him from all danger or misery.[1]

[1] It would be easy to prove that Suicide is as lawful under the Christian dispensation as it was to the Heathens. There is not a single text of Scripture which prohibits it. That great and infallible rule of faith and practice which must controul all philosophy and human reasoning, has left us in this particular to our natural liberty. Resignation to Providence is indeed recommended in Scripture; but that implies only submission to ills that are unavoidable, not to such as may be remedied by prudence or courage. *Thou shalt not kill*, is evidently meant to exclude only the killing of others over whose life we have no authority. That this precept, like most of the Scripture precepts, must be modified by reason and common sense, is plain from the practice of magistrates, who punish criminals capitally, notwithstanding the letter of the law. But were this commandment ever so express against suicide, it would now have no authority, for all the law of *Moses* is abolished, except so far as it is established by the law of Nature. And we have already endeavoured to prove, that suicide is not prohibited by that law. In all cases Christians and Heathens are precisely upon the same footing; *Cato* and *Brutus*, *Arria* and *Portia* acted heroically; those who now imitate their example ought to receive the same praises from posterity. The power of committing suicide is regarded by *Pliny* as an advantage which men possess even above the Deity himself. 'Deus non sibi potest mortem consciscero si velit, quod homini dedit optimum in tantis vitæ pœnis.'—Lib. ii. cap.5.

The Morality and Rationality of Suicide *

"Suicide" is conveniently defined, for our purposes, as doing something that results in one's death, from the intention either of ending one's life or to bring about some other state of affairs (such as relief from pain) that one thinks it certain or highly probable can be achieved only by means of death or will produce death. It may seem odd to classify an act of heroic self-sacrifice on the part of a soldier as suicide. It is simpler, however, not to try to define "suicide" so that an act of suicide is always irrational or immoral in some way; if we adopt a neutral definition like the above we can still proceed to ask when an act of suicide in that sense is rational, morally justifiable, and so on, so that all evaluations anyone might wish to make can still be made.

The literature in anthropology makes clear that suicide has been evaluated very differently in different societies, and philosophers in the Western tradition have been nearly as divergent in their evaluative views of it. I shall not attempt to review these evaluations but rather to analyze the problem and appraise some conclusions from the viewpoint of contemporary philosophy.

*This paper was written while the author was a Fellow at the Center for Advanced Study in the Behavioral Sciences and also a Special Fellow in the Department of Health, Education, and Welfare. Parts of it appear in S. Perlin (ed), *Handbook for the Study of Suicide*, Oxford University Press, 1975 and are reprinted with the permission of the editor and publisher.

I wish to discuss three questions, of which the first is in my opinion of least importance and the last of most importance. First, if an agent takes his own life when it is objectively morally wrong for him to do so, was his action necessarily morally blameworthy, or, to use a theological term, sinful? Second, when is it objectively morally right or wrong for an agent to take his own life? Third, when is it rational, from the point of view of an agent's own welfare, for him to commit suicide? What these questions mean, and how they differ, will be explained.

THE MORAL BLAMEWORTHINESS OF SUICIDE

In former times the question whether suicide is sinful was of great interest because the answer to it was considered relevant to how the agent would spend eternity. At present the practical issue is not great, although a normal funeral service may be denied a person judged to have sinned by committing suicide. At present the chief practical issue seems to be that persons may disapprove morally of a decedent for having committed suicide and his friends or relatives may wish to defend his memory against moral charges. The practical issue does not seem large, but justifies some analysis of the problem.

The question whether an act of suicide was sinful or morally blameworthy is not apt to arise unless it is already believed that morally the agent should not have done it; this question will be examined in the following section. But sometimes we do believe this, for instance, if he really had very poor reason for doing so and his act foreseeably had catastrophic consequences for his wife and children. At least, let us suppose that we do so believe. In that case we might still think that the act was hardly morally blameworthy or sinful if, say, the agent was in a state of great emotional turmoil at the time. We might then say that, although what he did was wrong, his action is excusable, just as in criminal law it may be decided that, although a person broke the law, he should not be punished because he was not responsible, e.g., was temporarily insane, did what he did inadvertently, and so on.

These remarks assume that to be morally blameworthy or sinful for an act is one thing, and for the act to be wrong is another. But what after all does it mean to say that a person is morally blameworthy on account of an action? We cannot say there is agreement among philosophers on this matter, but I suggest the following account as being safe from serious objection: X is morally blameworthy on account of an action A may be taken to mean that X did A, and

X would not have done *A* had not his character been in some respect below standard, and in view of this it is fitting or justified for *X* to have some disapproving attitudes including remorse toward himself and for some other persons *Y* to have some disapproving attitudes toward *X* and to express them in behavior.

In case the above definition does not seem obviously correct, it is worthwhile pointing out that it is usually thought that an agent is not blameworthy or sinful for an action unless it is a reflection on him; the definition illustrates this fact and makes clear why this act did not manifest any defect of character. It may be thought that the definition introduces terms as obscure as the one we are defining, e.g., "character" and "below standard," and it is true these need explanation which cannot be provided here. But I think we are able to proceed more easily with them than with the original term; the definition is really clarifying. For instance, if someone charges that a suicide was sinful, we now properly ask, What defect of character did it show? Some writers have claimed that suicide is blameworthy because it is cowardly, and since being cowardly is generally conceded to be a character defect, if an act of suicide is admitted to be both objectively wrong and also cowardly, the claim to blameworthiness is supported, if the above definition is correct. Of course, most people would hesitate to call taking one's own life a cowardly act, and there will certainly be controversy about which acts are cowardly and which are not. But at least we can see part of what has to be done to make a charge of blameworthiness plausible.

The most interesting question is Which types of suicide in general are ones that, even if objectively wrong, are not sinful or blameworthy? Or, in other words, When is a suicide morally excused even if it is objectively wrong? We can at least identify some types of cases: (1) Suppose I think I am morally bound to commit suicide because I have a terminal illness and continued medical care will financially ruin my family. Suppose, however, that I am mistaken in this belief, and that suicide in such circumstances is not right. But surely I am not morally blameworthy, for I may be doing, out of a sense of duty to my family, what I would personally prefer not to do and is hard for me to do. What character defect might my action show? Suicide from a genuine sense of duty is not blameworthy, even when the moral conviction in question is mistaken, (2) Suppose that I commit suicide when I am temporarily of unsound mind, either in the sense of the M'Naghten rule that I do not know that what I am doing is wrong, or of the Durham rule that, owing to a mental defect, I am substantially unable to do what is right. Surely any suicide in an unsound state of mind is morally excused, (3) Suppose I commit suicide when I could not be said to be temporarily of unsound mind, but simply because I am not myself. For instance, I may be in an extremely depressed mood. Now a person may be in a highly depressed mood and commit suicide on account of being in that mood when there is nothing the matter with his character or, in other words, his character is not in any relevant way below standard. What are other examples of being "not myself," that might be states of a person responsible for his committing suicide, and that would or might render the suicide excusable even if wrong? Being frightened, distraught, or in almost any highly emotional frame of mind—anger, frustration, disappointment in love, or perhaps just being terribly fatigued. So there are at least three types of suicide that are morally excused even if objectively wrong.

The main point is this. Mr. *X* may commit suicide and it may be conceded that he should not have done so. But it is another step to show that he is sinful, or morally blameworthy, for having done so. To support this further charge, it must be shown that his act is attributable to some substandard character trait; so, after the suicide Mrs. *X* can concede that her husband should not have done what he did, but point out that it is no reflection on him.

WHEN SUICIDE IS MORALLY JUSTIFIED OR OBJECTIVELY RIGHT

Let us now consider our second topic, when a suicide is objectively right or morally justified. It may help the reader if I say at the outset that what I mean by "is objectively wrong" or "is morally unjustified" is "would be prohibited by the set of moral rules the currency of which in the consciences of persons in his society, a rational personal would choose to support and encourage, as compared with any other set of moral rules or none at all."

First, I wish to eliminate some confusions which have plagued discussions of this topic. The distinctions I am about to make are no longer controversial, and can be accepted by sceptics on the fundamental issues as well as by anyone else.

Persons who say suicide is morally wrong must be asked which of two positions they are affirming. Are they saying that every act of suicide is wrong, *everything considered?* Or are they merely saying that there is always *some* moral obligation, doubtless of serious weight, not to commit suicide, so that very often suicide is wrong, although it is possible that there are countervailing considerations

which in particular situations make it right or even a moral duty?
It is quite evident that the first position is absurd; only the second
has a chance of being defended.

In order to illustrate what is wrong with the first view, we may
begin with an example. Suppose an army pilot's single-seater airplane
goes out of control over a heavily populated area; he has the choice
of either staying in the plane and bringing it down where it will do
little damage but at the cost of certain death for himself, or of bailing
out and letting the plane fall where it will, very possibly killing a
good many civilians. Suppose he chooses to do the former, and so,
by our definition, commits suicide. Can anyone say that his action
was morally wrong? It is improbable that even Immanuel Kant, who
opposed suicide in all circumstances, would say that it is but rather
would claim that this act is not one of suicide, "It is no suicide
to risk one's life against one's enemies, and even to sacrifice it,
in order to preserve one's duties toward oneself."[1] St. Thomas
Aquinas[2] may claim it would be wrong, for he says, "It is altogether
unlawful to kill oneself," admitting as an exception only the case
of being under special command of God. But most likely St. Thomas
would say that the act is right because the basic intention of the
pilot was to save the lives of civilians, and whether an act is right
or wrong is a matter of the basic intention.* I think a good reformulation
of St. Thomas' view, consistent with his basic intentions, would be
to assert that he recognizes that in this case there are two obligations,
one to spare the lives of innocent civilians and the other not to destroy

---

*He says,[2] "Nothing hinders one act from having two effects, only one of which
is intended, while the other is beside the intention. Now moral acts take their species
according to what is intended, and not according to what is beside the intention,
since this is accidental as explained above." [Q. 43, Art. 3: I.-II., Q. 1, Art. 3,
ad 3] Mr. Norman St. John-Stevas, the most articulate contemporary defender of
the Catholic view, writes as follows, "Christian thought allows certain exceptions
to its general condemnation of suicide. That covered by a particular divine inspiration
has already been noted. Another exception arises where suicide is the method imposed
by the State for the execution of a just death penalty. A third exception is *altruistic*
suicide, of which the best known example is Captain Oates. Such suicides are justified
by invoking the principle of double effect. The act from which death results must
be good or at least morally indifferent; some other good effect must result: the death
must not be directly intended or the real means to the good effect: and a grave
reason must exist for adopting the course of action."[3] Presumably the Catholic doctrine
is intended to allow suicide when this is required for meeting strong moral obligations;
whether it can do so consistently depends partly on the interpretation given to "real
means to the good effect." Readers interested in pursuing further the Catholic doctrine
of double effect and its implications for our problem should read Philippa Foot.[4]

one's own life, and that of the two obligations the former is the stronger, and therefore the action is right.

In general, we have to admit that there are things there is some moral obligation to avoid which, on account of other morally relevant considerations, it is sometimes right or even morally obligatory to do. There may be some obligation to tell the truth on every occasion, but there are surely many cases in which the consequences of telling the truth would be so catastrophic that one is obligated to lie. To take simple cases: Should one always tell an author truthfully how one evaluates his book, or tell one's wife truthfully whether she looks attractive today? The same applies to promises. There seems to be some moral obligation to do what one has promised (with some exceptions), but if one can keep a trivial promise only at serious cost to another (e.g., keep an appointment only by failing to give aid to someone injured in an accident), it is surely obligatory to break the promise.

The most that the moral critic of suicide could say, then, is that there is *some* moral obligation not to do what a person knows will cause his death, but he surely cannot say there are *no* circumstances in which there are obligations to do things which in fact will result in one's death—obligations so strong that it is at least right, and possibly morally obligatory, to do something that will certainly result in one's own death. Possibly those who argue that suicide is immoral do not intend to contest this point, although if so they have not expressed themselves very clearly.

If this interpretation is correct, then in principle it would be possible to argue that in order to meet my obligation to my family, I might take my own life as the only course of action which could avoid catastrophic hospital expenses in a terminal illness. I suspect critics may not concede this point, but in principle it would seem they must admit arguments of this type; the real problem is comparing the gravity of the obligation to extend my own life and of the obligation to see to the future welfare of my family.

The charitable interpretation of suicide critics on moral grounds, then, is to attribute to them the view that there is a strong moral obligation not to take one's own life, although this obligation may be superseded by some other obligations, say to avoid causing the death of others. Possibly the main point they would wish to make is that it is never right to take one's own life for reasons of one's own personal welfare, of any kind whatsoever.

What reasons have been offered for believing that there is a strong moral obligation to avoid suicide, which cannot be superseded

by any consideration of personal welfare? The first arguments may
be classified as theological. St. Augustine and others urged that the
fifth commandment (Thou shalt not kill) prohibits suicide, and that
we are bound to obey a divine commandment. To this reasoning
one might reply that it is arbitrary exegesis of the fifth commandment
to assert that it was ever intended to prohibit suicide. A second type
of theological argument with wide support was accepted by John
Locke, who wrote, " . . . men being all the workmanship of one
omnipotent and infinitely wise Maker; all the servants of one sovereign
Master, sent into the world by His order and about His business;
they are His property, whose workmanship they are made to last
during His, not one another's pleasure. . . . Every one . . . is bound
to preserve himself, and not to quit his station wilfully. . . ."[5] Kant
wrote, "We have been placed in this world under certain conditions
and for specific purposes. But a suicide opposes the purpose of his
Creator; he arrives in the other world as one who has deserted his
post; he must be looked upon as a rebel against God. So long as
we remember the truth that it is God's intention to preserve life,
we are bound to regulate our activities in conformity with it. . . .
This duty is upon us until the time comes when God expressly
commands us to leave this life. Human beings are sentinels on earth
and may not leave their posts until relieved by another beneficent
hand."[6] Unfortunately, however, even if it were granted that it is
the duty of human beings to do what God commands or intends
them to do, more argument is required to show that God does *not*
permit human beings to quit this life when their own personal welfare
would be maximized by so doing. How does one draw the requisite
inference about the intentions of God? The difficulties and contradictions in arguments to reach such a conclusion are discussed at
length and perspicaciously by David Hume in his essay "On Suicide."*

A second group of arguments may be classed as arguments from
natural law. St. Thomas says, "It is altogether unlawful to kill oneself,
for three reasons. First, because everything naturally loves itself,
the result being that everything naturally keeps itself in being, and
resists corruptions so far as it can. Wherefore suicide is contrary
to the inclination of nature, and to charity whereby every man should
love himself. Hence suicide is always a mortal sin, as being contrary
to the natural law and to charity."[2] Here St. Thomas ignores two

---

*This essay was first published in 1777, and appears in collections of Hume's
works. For an argument similar to Kant's, see also St. Thomas Aquinas[2] (II, II,
Q. 64, Art. 5).

obvious points. First, it is not obvious why a human being is morally bound to do what he has some inclination to do. (St. Thomas did not criticize chastity.) Second, while it is true that most human beings do feel a strong urge to live, the human being who commits suicide obviously feels a stronger inclination to do something else. The inclination of the deliberate suicide is not to cling to life, but to do something else instead. It is as natural for a human being to dislike and to take steps to avoid, say, great pain, as it is to cling to life. A somewhat similar argument by Kant may seem better. In a famous passage Kant writes, "[The maxim of a person who commits suicide] is 'From self-love I make it my principle to shorten my life if its continuance threatens more evil than it promises pleasure.' The only further question to ask is whether this principle of self-love can become a universal law of nature. It is then seen at once that a system of nature by whose law the very same feeling whose function is to stimulate the furtherance of life should actually destroy life would contradict itself and consequently could not subsist as a system of nature. Hence his maxim cannot possibly hold as a universal law of nature and is therefore entirely opposed to the supreme principle of all duty."[7] What Kant finds contradictory is that the motive of self-love (interest in one's own long-range welfare) should sometimes lead one to struggle to preserve one's life, but at other times to end it. But where is the contradiction? One's circumstances change, and, if the argument of the following section is correct, one sometimes maximizes one's own long-range welfare by trying to stay alive, but at other times by bringing about one's demise. So, if one's consistent motive is to maximize one's long-term welfare, sometimes (usually) one will do one thing, but sometimes another.

A third group of arguments, a form of which dates at least to Aristotle, has a more modern and convincing ring. These arguments purport to show that, in one way or another, a suicide necessarily does harm to other persons, or to society at large. Aristotle says that the suicide treats the *state* unjustly.[8] Partly following Aristotle, St. Thomas says, "Every man is part of the community, and so, as such, he belongs to the community. Hence by killing himself he injures the community."[2] Blackstone held that a suicide is an offense against the king "who hath an interest in the preservation of all his subjects," perhaps following Judge Brown in 1563, who argued that suicide cost the king a subject, "he being the head has lost one of his mystical members."[9] The premise of such arguments is, as Hume pointed out, obviously mistaken in many instances. It is true that Freud would perhaps have injured society had he not finished his last book (as he did), instead of committing suicide to escape the pain of throat cancer. But surely there have been many suicides whose demise was not a noticeable loss to society; an honest man could only say that in many instances society was better off without them.

It need not be denied that suicide is often injurious to other persons, especially the family of a suicide; clearly it sometimes is. But we should notice what this fact establishes. Suppose we admit that there is some obligation not to perform any action which will probably or certainly be injurious to other people, the strength of the obligation being dependent on various factors, notably the seriousness of the expected injury. Then there is some obligation not to commit suicide, when that act would probably or certainly be injurious to other people—a conclusion which will probably not be disputed. But the fact that there is some obligation not to commit suicide when it will probably injure others does not show that suicide as such is something there is some obligation to avoid. There is an obligation to avoid injuring others, and to avoid suicide when it will probably injure others, but this is very different from showing that suicide as such is something there is some obligation to avoid in all instances.

Is there any way in which we could give convincing argument, establishing that there is or is not some moral obligation to avoid suicide as such, an obligation, of course, which might be over-ridden by other obligations in some or many cases?

To give all the argument that would provide a convincing answer to this question would take a great deal of space. I shall therefore present one answer to it that seems plausible to some contemporary philosophers and, I suspect, will seem plausible to the reader. Suppose it could be shown that it would maximize the long-run welfare of everybody affected if people were taught that there is a moral obligation to avoid suicide, so that people would be motivated to avoid suicide just because they thought it wrong, and so that other people would be inclined to disapprove of persons who commit suicide unless there were some excuse (such as those mentioned in the first section). One might ask, How could it maximize utility to mould the conceptual and motivational structure of persons in this way? To which the answer might be, Feeling this way might make persons who are impulsively inclined to commit suicide in a bad mood or a fit of anger or jealousy, take more time to deliberate; hence some suicides that have bad effects might be prevented. In other words, it might be a good thing for people to feel about suicide in the way they feel about breach of promise or injuring others, just as it might be a good thing for people to feel a moral obligation not to smoke or to wear seatbelts. I do not say this would be a good thing; all I am saying is that *if* it were welfare-maximizing for people's consciences to trouble them at the very thought of suicide, then there would be some moral obligation not to commit this act. I am not at all sure whether it *would* be welfare-maximizing for people to have negative moral feelings about suicide as such; maybe what is needed is just for them to have negative moral feelings about injuring others in some way, and perhaps negative moral feelings about failing to deliberate adequately about their own welfare before taking any serious and irrevocable course of action. It might be that negative moral feelings about suicide as such would stand in the way of courageous action by those persons whose welfare really is best served by suicide, and whose suicide is, in fact, the best thing for everybody concerned. One highly relevant piece of information concerning what should be instilled into people's consciences in this regard is why people do commit suicide and how often the general welfare (and especially their own welfare) is served by so doing. If among those people who commit suicide and are intellectually able to weigh pros and cons are many who commit suicide in a depression and do not serve anybody's welfare by so doing, then it could be beneficial to teach people that suicide as such is wrong.

WHETHER AND WHEN SUICIDE IS BEST OR RATIONAL FOR THE AGENT

We come now to a topic which, for better or worse, strikes me as of considerable practical interest: whether and when suicide is the rational or best thing for a person from the viewpoint of his own welfare. If I were asked for advice by someone contemplating suicide, it is to this topic that I would be inclined primarily to address myself. Some of the writers who are most inclined to affirm that suicide is morally wrong are quite ready to believe that from the agent's own selfish viewpoint suicide would sometimes be the best thing for him, but they do not discuss the point in any detail. I should like to clarify when it is and is not. What I hope to do is produce a way of looking at the matter that will help an individual see whether suicide is the best thing for him from the viewpoint of his own welfare—or whether it is the best thing for someone being advised, from the viewpoint of that person's welfare.

It is reasonable to discuss this topic under the restriction of two

388   Richard Brandt

assumptions. First, I assume we are trying to appraise a successful suicide attempt disregarding unsuccessful attempts. The second assumption is that when a person commits suicide, he is dead, that is, we do not consider that killing himself is only a way of expediting his departure to an afterlife. I shall assume there is no afterlife. I believe that at the present time potential suicides deliberate on the basis of both these assumptions, so that in making them I am addressing myself to the real problem as prospective suicides see it. What I want to produce is a fresh and helpful way of looking at their problem.

The problem is a choice between future world courses—the world course which includes my demise, say, an hour from now, and several possible ones which contain my demise at a later point. We cannot have precise knowledge about many features of the latter group. One thing we usually cannot have precise knowledge about is how or when I shall die if I do not commit suicide now. One thing is certain: it will be sometime, and it is almost certain that it will be before my one-hundredth birthday. So, to go on the rational probabilities, let us look up my life expectancy at my present age from the insurance tables, making any corrections that are called for in the light of full medical information about my recent state of health. If I do not already have a terminal illness, then the choice is between a world course with my death an hour from now and several world courses with my death, say, 20 years from now. The problem is to decide whether the expectable utility to me of some possible world course in which I live for another 20 years is greater than or less than the expectable utility to me of the one in which my life stops in an hour.

Why say the choice is between world courses and not just a choice between future life courses of the prospective suicide, the one shorter than the others? The reason is that one's suicide has some impact on the world (and one's continued life has some impact on the world), and that how the rest of the world is will often make a difference to one's evaluation of the possibilities. We are interested in things in the world other than just ourselves and our own happiness. For instance, we may be interested in our children and their welfare, our future reputation, the contribution we might make to the solution of some problems, or possible effects of the publication of a book we are completing.

What is the basic problem for evaluation? It is the choice of the expectably best world course from my viewpoint. One way of looking at the evaluation, although in practice we cannot assign the specific numbers it is suggested we assign, is that we compare the suicide world course with the continued life world course (or several of them) and note the features in which they differ. We then assign numbers to these features, representing their utility to us if they occur, and then multiply this utility by a number which represents the probability that this feature will occur. (Suppose I live and am certain that either P or Q will occur, and that there is an equal chance that each could occur. I then represent this biography as containing the sum of the utility of P multiplied by one-half and the utility· of Q multiplied by one-half.) We then sum these numbers, which will represent the combined expectable utility of that world course to us. The world course with the highest sum is the one that is rationally chosen. But of course it is absurd to suppose that we can assign these numbers in actual fact; what we can actually do is something in a sense simpler but less decisive.

If we look at the matter in this way, we can see that there is a close analogy between an analysis of the rationality of suicide and a firm's analysis of the rationality of declaring bankruptcy and going out of business. In the case of the firm, the objectives may be few and simple, and indeed for some boards of directors the only relevant question is Will the stockholders probably be better off or worse off financially if we continue or if we declare insolvency? More likely the question considered will be a bit more complex, since an enlightened firm will at least wonder what will happen to its officers and employees and customers and even possibly the general public if it goes out of business, and how their utilities will be affected.

Perhaps a closer analogy to this choice between world courses is the choice between a life course in which I get 12 hours of sleep tonight and one in which I live through one (the best) of the various possible experiences open to me.

Since, as I have suggested, we cannot actually perform the operation of assigning personal utility numbers to anticipated distinctive outcomes, reduce these by a fraction representing their probability, and then sum in order to find which course of action will maximize expectable utility of a world course, what then can we do to determine which world course is best, from the viewpoint of our own welfare? I think the answer is—that the prospective suicide has to determine whether he wants the world course as it will be with his death occurring now or shortly or the best option open to him with his life continuing; whether he would want one or the other if he had these alternatives, envisaged correctly, clearly, vividly, and in a normal not emotional or depressed frame of mind. I agree at once that it is a large order to get anything as complex as even the outlines of your prospective best life option before you vividly, but anyone can do what we all do from time to time—take pencil and paper and set down features of the prospective best life that one would want and features of it one would not want, do some matching of the good ones and the bad ones, and see where one comes out. The frame of mind of a prospective suicide is not apt to be one ideal for calm deliberation of this sort, and for this reason it will usually be helpful to have some discussions. But I want to explain why the particular sort of preferential comparison I have described is basic, and how in particular, failure to come to it will lead to wrong decisions in the emotional situation of the prospective suicide.

However, first let me say that I do not for a moment suggest that a person who takes this view of alternative world courses is necessarily going to prefer to continue living. On the contrary, when a person is seriously ill the probability is that he is going to feel worse and worse until sedations are so extensive that he is incapable of clear thought or emotional reaction toward anything and his physical condition is such that he cannot act to end his life even if he prefers to do so. If a person knows that this situation exists and has the prospect of his life being more and more undesirable, as each day passes, he may fulfill all my conditions of normal and fully informed wanting and elect quite rationally (at least in the absence of unusual situations such as Freud's) to choose the world course which contains as short a life span for himself as possible.

There are two other misconceptions I wish to eliminate. It is often argued that one can never be certain what is going to happen, and so one is never rationally justified in doing anything as final, drastic and irreversible as taking one's life. And it is true that certainties are hard to find; strictly speaking they do not exist even in the sciences. Unfortunately for the critic who makes use of this line of argument, it works both ways. I might say, when I am very depressed about my life, that the one thing I am certain of is that I am now very depressed and prefer death to life, and there is only some probability that tomorrow I shall feel differently. So, one might argue if one is to go only by certainties, I had better end it now. No one would take this seriously; we always have to live by probabilities, and make our estimates as best we can. People sometimes argue that one should not commit suicide in order to escape excruciating pain because they are not certain that a miraculous cure for terminal illness will not be found tomorrow—a logical possibility. But if everyone had argued in this way in the past hundred years, many persons would have waited until the bitter end and suffered excruciating pain; the line of argument that ignores probabilities and demands certainty would not have paid off in the past, and there is no good reason to think it will pay off any better in the future. Indeed, if the policy were generally adopted that probabilities in practical decisions should be ignored when they are short of certainty, it can be demonstrated that the policy for action *cannot* pay off. The second misconception is reliance on the argument that if you are alive tomorrow you can always decide to end it all then, whereas if you are dead tomorrow you cannot then decide that it is better to live. The factual point is correct, of course. But the argument has practical bearing only if there is reason to think that tomorrow you might find life good and want to live; sometimes it is as nearly certain as matters of this sort can be, that you will not. It is true that one can always bear another day, so why not delay? But this argument can be used for every succeeding day, with the result that one never takes action. One would think that, as soon as it is clear beyond reasonable doubt not only that death is preferable to life today, but that life is going to be so bad that one would prefer to be dead every day from here on out, the rational thing to do is to act promptly.

Let us not pursue the question whether it is rational for a person with a painful terminal illness to commit suicide; obviously it is, unless there are some special activities or responsibilities that are more important to the patient than his pain. However, the issue seldom arises, because patients of this sort seldom take suicide seriously, perhaps because matters get worse so slowly that no particular time seems to be the one calling for action, or because sedation makes it impossible for complex decisions to be made. Let us rather turn to the practically much more important problem, whether it is rational for persons to commit suicide for reason other than painful physical illness. Most persons who commit suicide do so, apparently, because they face some nonphysical problem which depresses them. It is to them that the conception mentioned a few moments ago is addressed— that a rational decision is the one in favor of the life course which one would prefer, comparing death with the best option open to one if he had the alternatives correctly and vividly before him in a normal frame of mind. Let me mention some problems which bother people, and which apparently are among the most important reasons for suicide. For example, some event which has made one feel ashamed or involved loss of prestige and status, such as reduction from affluence to poverty, the loss of a limb or of physical beauty, the loss of sexual capacity, the occurrence of some event that makes it impossible to achieve something important, loss of a loved one, disappointment in love, loneliness and the prospect of increasing loneliness, or the infirmities of increasing age. One cannot deny that such things can be sources of serious unhappiness.

I am assuming that a rational choice is one that a person makes with full and vivid awareness of the facts, so that he avoids making a choice he would not have made but for a factual misconception. (There are other requirements that would be mentioned in a second approximation.) These first simple requirements for a rational choice are exceedingly important in the case of a prospective suicide for the reason that must suicides take place at a time of severe depression, that often or always means that these requirements are very hard for the person to meet. Let me pursue several points the prospective suicide should bear in mind in deciding whether it is rational for him to take his life.

First, the prospective suicide should be aware of the fact that depression, like any severe emotional experience, tends to primitivize intellectual processes. It restricts the range of one's survey of the possibilities. The reason for reflection is to compare the world course of suicide with that of the best alternative. But the best alternative is precisely what will not come to mind if, as so often happens in a depressed mood, one's mind is obsessed only with thoughts of how badly off he is. You cannot both occupy yourself exclusively with thoughts of your present painful state of affairs and of how nice it would be to get out of the discomfort easily, and also reflect on your alternatives. If you are disappointed in love, you are apt to give your mind wholly to speeches you might make to your beloved, reflection on where you made mistakes in the past, or to how empty life is going to be without her; you are not going to consider vigorous courses of action you might take to replace this person with activities or other persons you will in time like just as well. The prospective suicide should not delude himself that he is acting rationally when he has not taken the trouble to give serious thought to his full range of options.

There is a second insidious influence of a state of depression. It seriously affects one's judgment on probabilities. A person disappointed in love is likely to take a dim view of himself, his prospects, and his attractiveness; he thinks that, because he has been rejected by one person, he will probably be rejected by anyone who looks desirable to him. Probably in a less gloomy frame of mind he would make different estimates. Part of the reason for such gloomy probability estimates is that depression tends to repress one's memory evidence which supports an optimistic prediction. Thus a rejected lover tends to forget all the cases in which he has elicited enthusiastic response from members of the opposite sex, and of the cases in which he was the rejector. Thus his pessimistic self-image is based upon a highly pessimistically selected set of data. Even when he is reminded of the data, however, he is apt to resist an optimistic inference. He resembles students who have come to think that nothing but failure is in store for them, even when it is pointed out that they often succeeded academically in the past. In a depressed mood one is apt to refuse to do the rational thing of projecting past successes and expecting probable future successes; but rather argue that past successes were lucky flukes and cannot be relied upon for a prognosis of the future. Obviously, however, there is such a thing as a reasonable and correct prognosis on the basis of an accurate account of past experience, and it is the height of irrationality not to estimate the future on that basis.

What a person must do, then, is make himself vividly aware of the alternatives that are really open to him, and consider what they will be like, including whether he will be happy with them. Of course, a person cannot have as precise a picture of what he can have a year from now as of what he cannot have now, how well off he is, and how he feels right now. But if he makes proper use of past experience he can have a fairly accurate knowledge of what is probably in store for him. If he uses knowledge of himself, he can know whether he will like it.

Suppose he envisages a probable future life and honestly admits that in all probability he will like it. How will this affect whether he will now want this alternative future or to commit suicide?

One effect should be guarded against as far as possible—one which is pervasive and not distinctive of depressed states. Future events seem quite distant just as objects distant in space look small. That is, the prospect of a distant event does not have the effect on motivational processes that it would have if it were expected in the immediate future. In that sense, all animals are impatient. Rat psychologists call essentially this fact the *goal-gradient* phenomenon; a rat will run faster toward a food box when it is close enough so that he can actually see it and does not do as well when he can only represent it in some nonperceptual way, as presumably he does in the early stages of a maze. In the same way, the commuter anxious to return home finds his footsteps quicken when he turns a corner and can actually see his home. Things in the future seem less important; it is always difficult for a weight-reducer to decline a tempting chocolate even while visualizing the future benefits of being slender unless he remembers he has to make a confession before a weight-watchers group tomorrow night. When comparing present unpleasant states with probable pleasant future ones, this phenomenon of the reduction of the motivational size of distant events is like looking at the future through the wrong end of binoculars. This effect probably is the result of deficiency in vividness of the imagination or representation of the future event. Thus there is a cognitive defect if one makes one choice rather than another merely because of unequal awareness of the two events. A rational person will take precautions to see the future in its proper perspective and compensate for this unfortunate phenomenon of human nature. How to accomplish this is no small problem; apparently appropriate verbalizing can be successful.

There is a final and very important effect of depression in decision-making—that of the emotional state on the motivational machinery. For instance, when we are hungry and think of bacon and eggs for breakfast, our mouths water and the idea seems attractive; we find ourselves tending to move toward the refrigerator. Similarly, when we have had many weeks of books and papers, the thought of vegetating in a deckchair seems most appealing. The grass looks green, as it were, in many directions. And, when we think of something like suicide, there are all sorts of things we might do or bring about that seem attractive in this way; the idea of suicide, at the cost of not looking at tomorrow's *Times* or football game, foregoing tomorrow's evening out, or not reading some books long unread, seems a very repellent idea. The trouble with a state of depression is that it simply shuts off all this motivational machinery. The only thought that moves one is about the source of the depression. When we are depressed about something, nothing else is attractive and the normally unattractive features of the things we have lost either fail to strike our attention or lose their repulsive force. We tend to emphasize, out of proportion, the unpleasant aspects of the situation. Why this is so is not so obvious; but in general, just as the thought of bacon and eggs, when we have just finished breakfast, leaves us cold, so the idea of anything we would normally want leaves us cold in a depressed frame of mind.

We know that this effect is temporary and should be allowed for, just as we know that when we have finished a good meal our satiety is temporary and we should make provision for another meal a few hours later. So, a rational person will want to take into account this temporary infirmity of his sensory machinery. To say this does not tell us how to do it, since to know that the machinery is out of order is not to tell us what results it would give us if it were working. One maxim is to refrain from making important decisions in a depressed frame of mind, and one of the important decisions is surely suicide. If decisions have to be made, at least one should use inductive inference from recollection of how certain sorts of outcomes were wanted in the past when in a normal frame of mind.

Most irrational suicides seem to be due to temporary despair. When a person is contemplating suicide in a moment of despair, he must be aware of all the factors which tend to make suicide temporarily attractive. He must see that if he is to be rational he must avoid impulsive acts which are contrary to the way he would normally act. He should see that the probability is very high that it is irrational for him to end his life. Rather in a moment of despair when one is seriously contemplating suicide, he should realize that a reassessment of goals and values is in order—one which it is difficult to make objectively because of his very state of mind.

Let us consider in an example what form such a reassessment might take, based on a consideration of the "errors" we have been considering.

Suppose the president of a company is ousted in a reorganization and, to make matters as bad as possible, let us suppose he has made unwise investments so that his income from investments is small and, to cap it off, his wife has left him for another man. His children are already grown, and he is too old for appointment to a comparable position in another business. So his career and home life are gone. Here we have the makings of a suicide. Let us suppose he is right about the main outlines of his prospects: that there is no comparable future open to him in business, and that his wife is really gone. He must move from a luxurious home into a modest apartment; he will be unable to entertain his friends in the manner to which he has been accustomed; he is not going to have the affection of his wife and is going to be lonely at least for a time. Is all this bearable?

What sort of reflection is in order? First he has to deal with his personal life. If he does not fall victim to pessimistic deflation of his self-image, he will know that he is an interesting man and can find women with whom he can be close and who can mean as much to him as his wife did, or he may find several with whom he can find a life-style which he can enjoy more than the traditional married life. All this, however, will take some time and he will know that he has to be patient. He will also look at a textbook on behavior therapy and will find how he can remove the pain of his wife's departure in a very brief space of time. The matter of career is more serious.

Even Kant, who condemned suicide in all cases, says, inconsistently, that a man unjustly convicted of a crime who was offered a choice between death and penal servitude, would certainly, if honorable, choose death rather than the galleys. "A man of inner worth does not shrink from death; he would die rather than live as an object of contempt, a member of a gang of scoundrels in the galleys." Kant may have been right about what it is rational to do in this extreme instance. Would death be better for the ex-president of a company than accepting a job, say, as a shoe salesman? (An older man might not find employment even here, but with a bit of imagination, entrepreneurial opportunities are open to any talented man in a capitalist society!) This might at first seem repellent, but on reflection one will see there are some good points. He may be able to remember how he enjoyed doing somewhat similar things as a boy. An intelligent man might find it interesting to engage in conversation with a variety of customers from all walks of life. He could try out his psychological knowledge by using devices to play on the vanity of women (or men!) as a motivation for buying expensive shoes. Further, he will not require sleeping pills in this new job, pills he has been taking because he could not get company problems off his mind. He may see that after a time he could enjoy the new job, perhaps not as much as the old one, at least after he gets over contrasting it with a past career no longer open to him. One thing he will surely bear strongly in mind: that his real friends are not going to change their attitudes toward him because of his new career, his less ostentatious circumstances, or the loss of his wife. On the contrary, these new circumstances are apt to make them like him better. Of course, all these considerations may not seem attractive to him at first, but he will know that they *will* be attractive to him after some little time has passed, and he has thought through a realistic comparison of his new life with his old life situation.

At this point David Hume was not his usual perspicuous self—nor Plato before him.[10] In "On Suicide," Hume speaks of the propriety of suicide for one who leads a hated life, "loaded with pain and sickness, with shame and poverty." Pain and sickness are one thing; they cannot be enjoyed and cannot be escaped. But shame and poverty are another matter. For some situations Hume might be right. But Hume, accustomed as he was to the good things of life, was too short with shame and poverty; a life which he would classify as one of shame and poverty might be a tolerable life, inferior to Hume's life style, but still preferable to nothing.

A decision to commit suicide for reasons other than terminal illness may in certain circumstances be a rational one. But a person who wants to act rationally must take into account at least the various possible "errors" mentioned above, and make appropriate rectifications in his initial evaluations.

THE ROLE OF OTHER PERSONS

We have not been concerned with the law, or its justifiability, on the matter of suicide, but we may note in passing that for a long time in the Western world suicide was a felony and in many states attempted suicide is still a crime. It is also a crime to aid or encourage a suicide in every state; one who makes a lethal device available for a suicidal attempt may be subject to a prison sentence— including physicians, if they provide a lethal dose of sedatives.*

The last mentioned class of statutes raises a question worth our consideration, What are the moral obligations of other persons toward those who are contemplating suicide? I ignore questions of their moral blameworthiness, and of what it is rational for them to do from the viewpoint of personal welfare as being of secondary concern. I have no doubt that the question of personal interest is important particularly to physicians who may not wish to risk running afoul of the law, but this risk is, after all, something which partly determines what their moral obligation is, since moral obligation to do something may be reduced by the fact that it is personally dangerous to do it.†

The moral obligation of other persons toward one who is contemplating suicide is an instance of a general obligation to render aid to those in serious distress, at least when this can be done at no great cost to one's self. I do not think this general principle is seriously questioned by anyone, whatever his moral theory, so I feel free to assume it as a premise. Obviously the person contemplating suicide is in great distress of some sort; if he were not, he would not be seriously considering terminating his life.

How great a person's obligation is to one in distress depends on a number of factors. Obviously a person's wife, daughter, and

---

*For a proposal for American law on this point see the *Model Penal Code*, Proposed Official Draft, The American Law Institute, 1962, pp. 127-128; also Tentative Draft No. 9, p. 56.

†The law can be changed, and one of the ways in which it gets changed is by responsible people refusing to obey it and pointing out how objectionable it is on moral grounds. Some physicians have shown leadership in this respect, e.g., on the matter of dispensing birth control information and abortion laws. One wishes there were more of this.

close friend have special obligations to devote time to helping this sort of person—to going over his problem with him, to think it through with him, etc.—which others do not have. But that anyone in this kind of distress has a moral claim on the time of anyone who knows the situation (unless there are others more responsible who are already doing what should be done) is obvious.

What is there an obligation to do? It depends, of course, on the situation and how much the second person knows about the situation. If the individual has decided to terminate his life if he can, and it is clear that he is right in this decision, then, if he needs help in executing the decision, there is a moral obligation to give him help. If it is sleeping pills he needs, then they should be obtained for him. On this matter a patient's physician has a special obligation.

On the other hand, if it is clear that the individual should not commit suicide, from the point of view of his own welfare, or if there is a presumption that he should not, when the only evidence is that a person is discovered unconscious with the gas turned on, it would seem to be the individual's obligation to intervene and prevent the successful execution of the decision, see to the availability of competent psychiatric advice and temporary hospitalization, if necessary. Whether one has a right to take such steps when a clearly sane person, after careful reflection over a period of time, comes to the conclusion that an end to his life is what is best for him and what he wants, is very doubtful, even when one thinks his conclusion a mistaken one. It would seem that a man's own considered decision about whether he wants to live must command respect, although one must concede that this could be debated.

The more interesting role in which a person may be cast, however, is that of adviser. It is often important to one who is contemplating suicide to go over his thoughts with another and to feel that a conclusion, one way or the other, has the support of a respected mind. One thing one can obviously do, in rendering the service of advice, is to discuss with the person the various types of issue discussed above, made more specific by the concrete circumstances of his case, and help him find whether, in view, say, of the damage his suicide would do to others, he has a moral obligation to refrain and whether it is rational or best for him, from the viewpoint of his own welfare to take this step or adopt some other plan instead.

To get a person to see what is the rational thing to do is no small task. Even to get a person, in a frame of mind when he is seriously contemplating or perhaps already unsuccessfully attempted suicide, to recognize a plain truth of fact may be a major operation.

If a man insists, "I am a complete failure," when it is obvious that by any reasonable standard he is far from that, it may be tremendously difficult to get him to see the fact. The relaxing quiet of a hospital room may be a prerequisite of ability to think clearly and weigh facts with some perspective.

But there is another job beyond that of getting a person to see what is the rational thing to do, and that is to help him *act* rationally or *be* rational after he has determined what course of action is rational.

How either of these tasks may be accomplished effectively may be discussed more competently by an experienced psychiatrist than by a philosopher. But it may not be inappropriate to point out that sometimes an adviser can cure a man's problem in the course of advising. Loneliness and the absence of human affection are states which exacerbate any other problems; disappointment, reduction to poverty, etc., seem less impossible to bear in the presence of the affection of another. Hence simply to be a friend, or to find someone a friend, may be the largest contribution one can make either to helping a person be rational or see clearly what is rational for him to do; this service may make one who was contemplating suicide feel that there is now a future for him which is possible to face.

REFERENCES

1. Kant I: Lectures on Ethics, New York, Harper Torchbook, 1963, p 150
2. St. Thomas Aquinas: Summa Theologica, Second Part of the Second Part, Q. 64; see also Art. 5
3. John-Stevas N St: Life, Death and the Law, Bloomington, Indiana, Indiana Univ Press, 1961, pp 250-251
4. Foot P: The problem of abortion and doctrine of double effect, Oxford Rev, 5; 5-15, 1967
5. Locke J: Two Treatises of Government, Chap. 2
6. Kant I: Lectures on Ethics, Harper Torchbook, 1963, p 154
7. Kant I: The Fundamental Principles of the Metaphysic of Morals, Paton, HJ, trans. London, The Hutchinson Group, 1948, Chap. 2 (First German edition, 1885)
8. Aristotle: Nicomachaean Ethics, Bk 5, Chap 10, p 1138a
9. Blackstone: Commentaries, IV: 189; Brown in Hales v. Petit, I Plow. 253, 75 ER 387 (CB 1563)
10. Plato: The Laws, Bk IX

Thomas L. Shaffer

13
Legal Views of Suicide

The introductory passages to this chapter are from *Blackstone's Commentaries on the Laws of England*, Vol. IV (1769). The edition used here was published in 1836.

III. Felonious homicide(36) is an act of a very different nature from the former, being the killing of a human creature, of any age or sex, without justification or excuse. This may be done either by killing one's self, or another man.

Self-murder,(37) the pretended heroism, but real cowardice, of the Stoic philosophers, who destroyed themselves to avoid those ills which they had not the fortitude to endure, though the attempting it seems to be countenanced by the civil law,(o) yet was punished by the Athenian law with cutting off the hand which committed the desperate deed.(p) And also the law of England wisely and religiously considers that no man hath a power to destroy life but by commission from God, the author of it: and, as the suicide is guilty of a double offence; one spiritual, in invading the prerogative of the Almighty and rushing into his immediate presence uncalled for; the other temporal, against the king, who hath an interest in the preservation of all his subjects; the law has therefore ranked this among the highest crimes, making it a peculiar species of felony, a felony committed on one's self. And this admits of accessories before the fact, as well as other felonies; (38) for if one persuades another to kill himself, and he does so, the adviser is guilty of murder.(q) A *felo de se*,(39) therefore, is he that deliberately puts an end to his own existence, or commits any unlawful malicious act, the consequence of which is his own death: as if, attempting to kill another, he runs upon his antagonist's sword; or, shooting at another, the gun bursts and kills

401

402   Legal Views of Suicide

himself.(*r*)(40) The party must be of years of discretion and in his senses, else it is no crime. But this excuse ought not to be strained to that length to which our coroner's juries are apt to carry it, viz., that the very act of suicide is an evidence of insanity; as if every man who acts contrary to reason had no reason at all: for the same argument would prove every other criminal *non compos*, as well as the self-murderer. The law very rationally judges that every melancholy or hypochrondriac fit does not deprive a man of the capacity of discerning right from wrong; which is necessary, as was observed in a former chapter(*s*) to form a legal excuse. And, therefore, if a real lunatic kills himself in a lucid interval, he is a *felo de se* as much as another man.(*t*)

But now the question follows,—What punishment can human laws inflict on one who has withdrawn himself from their reach? They can only act upon what he has left behind him, his reputation and fortune; on the former by an ignominious burial in the highway, with a stake driven through his body;(41) on the latter by a forfeiture of all his goods and chattels to the king; hoping that his care for either his own reputation or the welfare of his family would be some motive to restrain him from so desperate and wicked an act. And it is observable that this forfeiture has relation to the time of the act done in the felon's lifetime, which was the cause of his death. As if husband and wife be possessed jointly of a term of years in land, and the husband drowns himself, the land shall be forfeited to the king and the wife shall not have it by survivorship. For by the act of casting himself into the water he forfeits the term; which gives a title to the king prior to the wife's title by survivorship, which could not accrue till the instant of her husband's death.(*u*) And though it must be owned that the letter of the law herein borders a little upon severity, yet it is some alleviation that the power of mitigation is left in the breast of the sovereign, who upon this, as on all other occasions, is reminded by the oath of his office to execute judgment in mercy.(42)

The other species of criminal homicide is that of killing another man. But in this there are also degrees of guilt which divide the offence into *manslaughter* and *murder,* the difference between which may be partly collected from what has been incidentally mentioned in the preceding articles, and principally consists in this,—that manslaughter, when voluntary, arises from the sudden heat of the passions, murder from the wickedness of the heart.

(36) See 2 Bishop's New Crim. Law, 353 *et seq.,* for an enumeration of homicides that are indictable felonies. Kerr's Law of Homicide, p. 29 (1891), on intent as an element of the crime.

(37) It has been said that the distinctions between murder and manslaughter attach to suicide, so far as they are capable, as well as to the killing of others; but there is high authority for saying that a man cannot commit manslaughter on himself. Kerr's Law of Homicide, 49 (1891).

(38) Suicide is held to be murder so fully that every one who aids or abets in the act is guilty of murder. Kerr's Law of Homicide, 52 (1891). There are English cases which lay down the principal that where parties mutually agree to commit suicide and one only accomplishes that object, the survivor will be guilty of murder in point of law.—KERR.

If a person who has attempted to commit suicide accidentally kills another who tries to prevent its accomplishment, he is guilty of at least manslaughter, if not murder.—KERR.

(39) [A self-murderer.]

(40) He who kills another upon his desire or command is in the judgment of the law as much a murderer as if he had done it merely of his own head; and the person killed is not looked upon as a *felo de se*, inasmuch as his assent was merely void, being against the law of God and man. I Hawk. P. C. c. 27, s. 6. Keilw. 136. Moor. 754. And see Rex *v.* Sawyer, I Russell, 424. Rex *v.* Evans, id. 426—CHITTY.

(41) But now, by 4 Geo. IV. c. 52, s. I, it shall not be lawful for any coroner, or other officer having authority to hold inquests, to issue any warrant or other process directing the interment of the remains of persons agaunst whom a finding of *felo de se* shall be had in any public highway; but such coroner or other officer shall give directions for the private interment of the remains of such person *felo de se*, without any stake being driven through the body of such person, in the churchyard or other burial-ground of the parish or place in which the remains of such person might by the laws or customs of England be interred if the verdict of *felo de se* had not been found against such person, such interment to be made within twenty-four hours from the finding of the inquisition, and to take place between the hours of nine and twelve at night. Proviso, (s. 2,) not to authorize the performing of any of the rites of Christian burial on the interment of the remains of any such person, nor to alter the laws or usages relating to the burial of such person, except so far as relates to the interment of such remains in such yard or burial-ground at such time and in such manner.—CHITTY. In the United States there is no punishment for suicide. See Kerr's Law of Homicide, 62 (1891). An attempt to commit suicide is made an offence by statute in New York. See Darraw *v.* Family Fund Society, 116 New York, 542 *et seq.* As it is also in Pennsylvania.

(42) As to *what* a *felo de se* shall forfeit, it seems clear that he shall forfeit all chattels real or personal which he has in his own right; and also all chattels real whereof he is possessed, either jointly with his wife, or in her right; and also all bonds and other personal things in action belonging solely to himself; and also all personal things in action, and, as some say, entire chattels in possession, to which he was entitled jointly with another, or any account, except that of merchandise. But it is said that he shall forfeit a moiety only of such joint chattels as may be severed, and nothing at all of what he was possessed of as executor or administrator. I Hawk. P. C. c. 27, s. 7. The blood of a *felo de se* is not corrupted, nor his lands of inheritance forfeited, nor his wife barred of her dower. I Hawk. P. C. c. 27, s. 8. Plowd 261, b., 262, a. I Hale, P. C. 413. The will of a *felo de se* therefore becomes void as to his personal property, but not as to his real estate. Plowd. 261. No part of the personal estate of a *felo de se* vests in the king before the self-murder is found by some inquisition, and consequently the forfeiture thereof is saved by a pardon of the offence before such finding. 5 Co. Rep. 110, b. 3 Inst 54. I Saund. 362. I Sid. 150, 162. But if there be no such pardon, the whole is forfeited immediately after such inquisition, from the time of the act done by which the death was caused, and all intermediate alienations and titles are avoided. Plowd. 260. I Hale, P. C. 29. 5 Co. Rep. 110. Finch, L. 216. See also, upon this subject, Lambert *v.* Taylor, 6 D. & R. 188, 4 B. & C. 138.—CHITTY.

Legal Views of Suicide

KITTY JAY'S FLOWERS

In South Devon, not far from Plymouth, two obscure country lanes cross on the moor near Hound Tor. The place is a forbidding bit of wilderness; it was the site of Sherlock Holmes' adventure with the hound of the Baskervilles. In the center of this crossroad is the grave of Kitty Jay. The grave is distinct, complete with headstone and large rocks from the moor to mark where the body lies. The grave has been there for well over 200 years. I have a picture of the grave as it appeared on July 6, 1974. Beneath the headstone there is a Folger's coffee jar filled with fresh white daisies and foxglove from the field nearby. There is an oral tradition behind the flowers; this the way my colleague Frank Booker describes it.

Kitty Jay was a foundling girl. In the middle of the eighteenth century, she was taken on at one of the great houses in the vicinity of Hound Tor, just above Manaton, on the moor. She was quite a young girl, although her exact age we do not know. As matters fell out, she grew overly fond of one of the sons of this great house where she was employed. Matters progressed, and, before too long, Kitty Jay was with child. Now, there was no question at that time of marriage. The position of the two people was too diverse. But it was not at all uncommon for some provision to be made for the girl and her child in such cases. In Kitty Jay's case, however, the young man and his family would make no provision for her. It was plain that soon she was going to be turned out to the tender mercies of

404

the society of that time and place. In despair, Kitty Jay went down to one
of the barns and hanged herself.

The coroner's jury was called in to sit upon the case. This was not
because there was any question of foul play. It was perfectly clear that
Kitty Jay had hanged herself. The function of the coroner's jury was to
decide whether, at the time that she hanged herself, Kitty Jay was of sound
mind or of unsound mind. For, if she was of unsound mind when she hanged
herself, she could be buried in the churchyard at Manaton, in consecrated
ground. If, on the other hand, the coroner's jury found that she was of
sound mind when she took her own life, she could not be buried in the
churchyard. The coroner's jury sat at the old Half Moon Inn, which is beside
the village green in Manaton, just above St. Winifred's Church, next to
the churchyard in which she would have been buried.

It would have been a harmless charity for them to have found that
this girl was of unsound mind. After all, who could say, anyway? However,
for whatever reason, they found that Kitty Jay was of sound mind when
she took her life. Therefore, according to the law and the custom of the
time and place, Kitty Jay was taken out to a crossroads, and there buried,
where every beggar's foot might pass over her grave.

For some reason, the local people could not and did not forget or acquiesce
in what had happened. Someone put a headstone up, there in the crossroads,
and surrounded the grave with protective stones. This was certainly not
Kitty Jay's family, for she had no family; she was a foundling. The most
remarkable part of the story, however, is that, while Kitty Jay died and
was buried over 225 years ago, the local tradition and folklore is that every
day since then someone has placed fresh flowers on Kitty Jay's grave.

Frank Booker has visited the grave several times since 1970.
He says it is in a remarkably remote place—"on the backside of
nowhere." The flowers have always been fresh, he says, invariably
"whatever is growing at the time in that vicinity," and placed in
a jar or can on the grave. "I have been there on a windy Tuesday
in February, when the wind was blowing in sheets, and there found
fresh-cut greenery placed there that very day."

The tradition is not that ghosts place the flowers on the grave.
"Ghosts don't use coffee cans. The idea is that a succession of human
beings have taken the trouble, every day, for two centuries and more,
to place fresh flowers on Kitty Jay's grave." The locals either don't
know, or won't tell Frank, who does it. Frank believes
that the ancestors of the great family, whose illegitimate child Kitty
Jay carried to her grave with her, are responsible. "I believe that
some of them may have felt that Kitty Jay was badly treated." Badly
treated, I suppose, in life and in death.

Kitty Jay's crossroads' grave expresses the strain that suicide presents to sentiment and to law. In one sense, the law has judged about suicide, and the community, as it sometimes does, has rejected the judgment. In a better sense, the law, which finally expresses what the community wants expressed, cannot make up its mind. The body at the crossroads is there because the woman who possessed it was a deviant of some kind, but the community has never really been able to decide what to think about her. Such are the perils of deciding that a sane person killed herself or that an insane person, because insane, did not.

The body would not be at the crossroads unless the law, the people, considered the woman somehow malicious. A suicide, being at common law a felon, caused his goods to be forfeited to the Crown and thereby punished his family; punishment of survivors is probably not the malice the law had in mind, but was possibly sometimes the malice which was there in fact. Common law required that malice be shown or there could not be a judgment of suicide. The law dictionary defines suicide as "the deliberate termination of one's existence, while in the possession and enjoyment of his mental faculties," that is, with malice. Attempted suicide was punished as an attempt to commit a felony (i.e., an act which was intrinsically wrong). Modern American law treats suicide as a wrong, but does not usually even bother to say it is a crime, since the social object is not either the redemption or the condemnation of the victim, but social consequences for others. The only modern reason to regard suicide as a crime (given the fact that we no longer provide graves for beggar's feet or take away the family's property) is to exert social coercion on people who attempt suicide but do not succeed. The reason for coercion is in every case perceived deviance, by definition, and in some cases malicious deviance.

Malicious, for example, when *A* tries to kill himself and fails, but kills *B* in the process. The "better rule" in that case is that the attempter has committed manslaughter or murder, even though his act might, without his intent (to kill himself), be no more than an accident.

But in other circumstances the attempter is treated as morally inert. For instance, it is a crime to induce another to commit suicide. In reasoning, judges have usually said that it is as if the inducer had himself inflicted death. "If the prisoner furnished the poison to the deceased for the purpose and with the intent that she should with it commit suicide," stated the Ohio Supreme Court, "then. . . he administered the poison to her. . ." In other words, the victim was not a moral agent, but a conduit. This is apparently true whether or not the victim was mentally capable of making a decision about suicide.

In other circumstances, the act of suicide is seen as an act of sickness, not malicious deviance, but deviance—subtopic mental illness. Even in states where attempted suicide is a crime, or is treated as an attempt at crime, one finds no modern record of prosecution or conviction. Legal commentators tend to say such things as, "Modern notions of mental health would certainly indicate that these persons possess anything but the requisite criminal or felonious intent to commit a crime. . . The more enlightened and humane approach of curing rather than punishing the person set on self-destruction, and the punishment of those encouraging such, should be the trend for the future."

It might be useful to look at the ambivalence in suicide law— to look at the melancholy poetry of Kitty Jay's flowers—in reference to these three inconsistent legal views of suicide: that the suicidal person is malicious, inert, and sick.

RONALD PORSON'S ASPIRIN

This is a legal discussion and needs legal verisimilitude. The traditional way to provide that is to pose a hypothetical problem— something like one the manipulated law student in the novel, *The Paper Chase* might have had to cope with—and then to discuss cases and legal principles in reference to the problem. Here is the problem (using characters from C. P. Snow's novels and a style which has become traditional in examination for first-year courses in torts).

Ronald Porson is a middle-aged business executive, married and the father of two adult children. Roy Calvert is his principal business associate; Porson is secretly indebted to Calvert for $50,000. Last March, Porson and Calvert spent two heated hours discussing this debt. Calvert threatened to expose the debt, sue Porson, expose Porson's extramarital affairs with secretaries, and, if necessary, beat him up. Porson said he did not know what he would do, that he could not pay the debt and that he did not know what would happen if Calvert carried out any of his threats. Calvert said, "The thing for you to do, Ron, is to go home and kill yourself and then I can collect what I am owed out of your life insurance."

Porson went home, ingested a 98-cent bottle of aspirin, and lay down next to his wife, Helen, saying to her, "I've always loved you, Helen. Give my love to the kids." Helen was half asleep but, even in that condition, found this communication remarkable. After reflecting a while, she decided that the situation called for action. She ran into the street in front of the Porson apartment building and summoned two passersby, Francis Getliffe and Walter Luke (both nuclear physicists who lived on the same street).

Luke ran into the apartment. Getliffe, who said he refused to get involved with another kook, stayed in the street. (Investigation will reveal that Getliffe knows how to administer first aid for aspirin poisoning, and that he also knows how to induce vomiting.)

Helen told Luke she thought Ronald had taken an overdose of aspirin. Luke rolled Porson over; Porson was by then comatose. Luke got astride Porson and began administering vigorous, 1940s-style artificial respiration. This produced no visible progress and Luke finally decided that Porson should be taken to a hospital. He hauled Porson out of bed, picked him up, gunny-sack fashion, carried him to his (Luke's) car, and drove to the hospital.

The doctor on duty decided at first that Porson was on a bad trip and treated him for overdose of LSD a hallucinatory drug. When Helen arrived at the hospital half an hour later with the empty aspirin bottle, the doctor said, "Oh, that's it." He administered an antidote for the LSD antidote and pumped Porson's stomach.

Porson recovered, Helen believes, through the intervention of the Holy Ghost. As soon as he was out of the hospital, Porson consulted a lawyer. He is angry and litigation minded. His lawyer is cooperative. Porson wants to sue Calvert for provoking him into attempting suicide. He wants to sue Helen for interfering with his right to commit suicide. He wants to sue Luke for a bad job of rescue (which resulted, by the way, in two broken ribs, three bad bumps on the head, and, assuming Luke should have said something to the doctor about the aspirin, the effects of being first cured and then uncured for taking LSD). Finally, he wants to sue Getliffe for not getting involved.

PORSON V. LUKE (MALICE)

Morally it seems Porson should not be able to recover money from Luke, who, after all, can be said to have saved his life, even if that cost Porson a broken rib or two. That moral instinct seems to depend on a feeling that Porson was engaged in conduct which imperiled him, that the humane thing for another person to do was to rescue him, and that the risk involved was created not by Luke (who did his best), but by Porson himself. "The risk of rescue," the great Cardozo once said, "is born of the occasion." The implicit judgment about Porson in all of this is that he invited Luke's intervention in such a way that we should hold Porson, not Luke, responsible for the consequences of the invitation. In other words, Porson created a peril and knew he was doing it. This is a view of the suicidal person as malicious; it enjoys much support in the law.

Formerly common law held that it was against public policy to permit the beneficiary of a suicide victim to recover on the victim's life insurance (this is now obviated in most places by statutes controlling the language of insurance contracts). Suicide was unnatural, the English judges said, because it is contrary to instincts of self-preservation, it should not be the occasion of profit, it was contrary to the commandment against homicide, and it was antisocial because the King had lost a subject ("he being the head has lost of one of his mystical members"). This view was said to accord with Aristotelian and Thomistic "natural law" jurisprudence.

Modern insurance contracts often contain language precluding recovery on the policy if the death was due to "suicide, sane or insane." (These defenses are usually limited to the first two or three years of the policy.) American courts, which tend not to favor insurance companies, have made a distinction, in cases involving these policies, between suicide and accidental death. In Texas an intoxicated man who stepped in front of a bus, his condition aggravated by despondency, was held to have died accidentally. The same was true of one who took poison as a result of distress, one who shot himself when subject to "an overdraft of whiskey," and one who jumped from a window because he thought he was being pursued by his enemies. The cases almost suggest the generalization that a person who thinks he has a good reason to kill himself is seen as the victim of an accident. They are, of course, illogical—as the flowers on Kitty Jay's grave, given the choice to put the grave at a crossroads, are illogical.

Both sets of legal precedents admit, though, that it is possible to commit suicide as the result of a calculating choice and agree in that, if death is the result of that sort of choice, the suicide himself, and his family, must bear the consequences of his act. Both lines of cases, even though they are largely inconsistent in result, turn on a principle which would support Luke's defense in the suit by Porson.

A line of cases from the law of evidence also seems to support Luke (as does moral intuition). These involve attempted suicide as an admission of guilt. In a California case the defendant, shortly after he had allegedly killed someone, was seen to point a pistol at his head. This was held to be an admission of guilt. In another case, the defendant, awaiting trial for crime, smuggled poison into his cell. In a third case, the defendant slashed his wrists, and a fourth drank acid after arrest. In each case the suicidal act was treated as evidence of guilt. The idea is that an attempt at suicide is similar to the act of flight to avoid arrest—both are evidence of a bad conscience. The underlying principle is that suicide is the result of conscious choice, and the conscious choice is evidence for a jury to consider.

PORSON V. *CALVERT* (INERT)

If Porson loses his suit against his inept rescuer, Luke, logic might extend the reasoning of that result to say that he should not be able to prevail against Calvert either. If Porson acted consciously (maliciously), surely another person, who may have caused him distress, or even one who suggested suicide to him, is beyond what tort lawyers call "the chain of causation." But one's moral instinct somehow rebels against that result. Calvert ought to lose, because what Calvert did is wrong.

I can think of two ways to rationalize Calvert's losing: (1) to see him as associated in the wrong, as sharing the guilt with Porson or being *in pari delicto* with Porson (this theory would preserve the view of Porson as acting deliberately) and (2) to rationalize Calvert's losing would be to say that Porson had no moral agency when he took the aspirin, and that the reason he lacked moral agency was that Calvert created in him a state of moral inertia; Porson did not intend to do what he did. The cases, by and large, support the second rationalization more than the first. But there is some authority for either theory.

In *Bogust* v. *Iverson*, a college girl killed herself after her school counselor terminated his professional relationship with her. In a suit for damages, the family argued that he had made her dependent on him and then failed to care for her in her helplessness. The court held for the counselor, noting, as I did in discussing the claim against Luke, that the act of a suicide is a conscious (malicious) act that creates moral consequences. In this case, the counselor was not responsible for the consequences because, as the court saw it, the conscious act of the college girl was an intervening cause between his (alleged) negligence and her death. The court indicated that the result would be different if it were shown that the counselor's conduct had caused the girl to become insane (because then her act would not be malicious).

The court also said its decision would be different if the counselor had known that the girl intended to commit suicide. That sounds promising as supporting the first theory against Calvert, with the warning that the point was little more than musing by the Wisconsin judges (*obiter dicta*), and the further warning that the two cases are somewhat different in that the college girl was under the counselor's professional care.

In *Cauverien* v. *DeMetz* a lower court judge held in favor of facts pleaded (hypothesized) by the suicide's family. The alleged conduct there was as outrageous as Calvert's. Henry Cauverien was a diamond dealer. He consigned a diamond to Sam DeMetz and Manuel Pola. DeMetz and Pola told Henry they would not return the diamond and would deny he had given it to them. A month later Henry killed himself. The family offered to prove that he did so because of the conduct of DeMetz and Pola. The court decided that if these facts were true, there was enough in the family's theory to justify recovery. The judge noted that the defendant's conduct was intentional and that Henry was so upset about the situation that he had become insane.

Absent the two points noted by the judge—intentional misconduct and the creation of insanity—the dominant rule has been that the family cannot recover damages from one who provokes suicide. The classic case is *Scheffer* v. *Washington City*, an 1882 decision of the US Supreme Court. The defendant was a railroad company; the decedent was injured in an accident involving one of its trains. The pain from his injury was so bad that he killed himself eight months later. The court conceded the fact of causation (which might have been arguable), but held against the family on the ground that the railroad could not have foreseen this consequence of its negligence. Cases involving intentionally inflicted trauma, as was alleged in the New York case, tend to reach a different result. The difference turns on whether the wrong-doing is intentional.

These precedents sound against Calvert and turn on the principle that insanity or mental distress *is* a foreseeable result of intentional wrongdoing, and that the suicide is a foreseeable result of insanity or distress. They avoid the independent-agency argument because the suicide was not himself when he took his own life (or, in our case, attempted to do so). A leading, modern California decision is authority for this position and, inferentially at least, authority for the first theory suggested. (The first theory is that Porson's attempt to kill himself was wrong and that Calvert was associated in the wrong-doing; it is a malice theory of suicide and is consistent with the result I labored over in the unsuccessful suit by Porson against Luke).

In the California case, *Tate* v. *Canonica* the defendant threatened, accused, harassed, and humiliated the decedent so much that he killed himself. The family argued that the defendant's conduct caused the decedent to become disturbed and that as a result of the disturbance he took his own life. The court found for the family. The judges said they thought that the reason for the rule against recovery in other states was that suicide was considered a crime in those states—in this case a crime which intervened to break a chain of causation. Since suicide is not a crime in California, that reason did not apply, and modern tort (civil wrong) law, to the effect that intentional affliction of mental suffering is an actionable wrong, did apply. The court went beyond the insanity theory to hold that the mental state of the suicide victim is irrelevant. Calvert would, in other words, be liable as a coconspirator whether or not Porson was insane. Calvert would be treated, either way, as if he were inert.

A commentator on the California decision notes that the usual law on infliction of mental suffering requires a connection between the injury the victim suffered and the injury the wrongdoer intended to inflict. One could therefore say that if the wrongdoer did not intend his victim's suicide, this requirement is not met. However, one could say that great emotional distress is necessarily present in one who commits suicide, and that suicide is a foreseeable result of great emotional distress. This rationale becomes even more plausible under a revision of the authoritative national compilation on the law of torts, published after the California decision. That modern revision turns on illness. If the wrongdoer inflicts illness and the illness causes some unforeseen result, the wrongdoer is nonetheless responsible for the result (as well as for the illness). "The section," the commentator says, "discounts the presence of actual intention to inflict the ultimate illness or harm. This rationale would avoid the problem in *Tate*, in which the defendants did not intend to cause the deceased to commit suicide." This new section will not apply, however, unless the disease could have been caused by the harrassment. And, of course, the new theory does not apply at all unless one regards suicidal behavior as a disease.

The older law on civil recovery for suicide tended to assume that suicide is an unthinkable act. The basic problem, in discussing recovery—denying recovery—on the basis of causation, is the insight that not even an intentional wrongdoer would guess that his victim would commit suicide. *Tate* v. *Canonica* and the new compilation on tort law are thought to avoid this result because they do not require contemplation of suicide, but only contemplation of disease. The idea is that you should be able to tell that you can annoy someone so much that he will get sick, even though you can't be expected to foresee that he might be so annoyed he will kill himself. It is important, though, to note that *Tate* did not turn solely on this theory. Recovery against Calvert would be justified, under the *Tate* rule, whether or not Porson was sick. The law, thus applied, regards Porson as inert.

PORSON V. PORSON (SICK)

It is conventional in modern discussions of liberal ethics to say that a person has a right to kill himself if he wants to. I, for example, do not believe that suicidal people should be involuntarily confined to a mental institution in order to prevent their committing suicide. But my principle slackens a bit, as liberal ethics sometimes tend to do, when the tables are turned. Porson wants to sue his wife because she prevented the success of his attempted suicide and my moral intuition is that he should not be able to punish her for what she did.

This case illustrates a common concern among those working professionally with suicidal people, that forceful intervention to prevent suicide will result in legal liabilities. We really do not mean what we say about a right to commit suicide, if what we say means that a well-meaning spouse (or even a passerby for that matter) acts at his peril in saving life. Our moral instinct in Helen's case is therefore against allowing Porson to recover damages from her.

We may be able to effectuate our instinct in Helen's case under bars of recovery, such as the common-law rule that one cannot recover damages from his spouse, but it is expedient here to explore its merits. We would not agree with Helen if she were seeking to put Ronald in a mental institution against his will, or to have him declared incompetent, or both. It is important to consider this second point because the best modern legal theory we can find to save Helen from damages is the theory that Ronald was sick.

The defendant in a homicide prosecution occasionally offers evidence that the victim threatened suicide. Most courts admit this evidence, if other facts make suicide a tenable explanation of death and if the threat was within a reasonable time before death. This dominant rule in the law of evidence appears to argue that suicidal people are not sick; if a rational person, a well person, says he will kill himself, one's reaction ought to be that he means what he says.

It is not the sort of thing one says insincerely, if only because the proposed conduct is unexpected. It is even, as the lawyers say, "conduct against interest." It is a bit like the Archbishop of Canterbury saying he does not believe in God.

If the statement comes from a person who is not well (not rational), whose conduct is expected to be bizarre, the statement is less believable. One of the things we expect from disturbed people is that their utterances will not comport with our perceptions. They are out of it, seeing things, disoriented, or even mentally ill. If he is sick, it is less likely that a person means it when he threatens suicide, than it would be if he were well. If the law of evidence allows legal fact finders (juries) to consider a suicide threat as evidence, it must therefore be because it considers such a statement to be the credible utterance of a person who is more or less well, at least as regards the issue of intention to commit suicide.

A similar line of authority allows fact finders to consider statements in suicide notes—not only the threat of suicide in them, but incriminating statements (of, say, theft) commonly given as a reason for suicide, and even statements which implicate survivors in wrongdoing. These rules of evidence are not imposed without opposition. One commentator says that statements in suicide notes proceed from motives to falsity caused by aggressive drives, guilt feelings, and exaggerated or groundless self-depreciation. Therefore, they should not be credited. But judges make the rules, not commentators, and judges appear to regard suicidal statements as credible and, therefore, arguably, as statements of well persons.

The evidence cases do not argue in Helen's favor, but they are perhaps too far from the issue here to be persuasive anyway. One might also complain that these are unrealistic. They do not, for instance, distinguish among suicidal dispositions. Some suicide is accompanied by bizarre behavior suggesting irrationality, for example the person who publicly leaps from a window. Others are performed after lonely deliberation. It is possible that bizarre behavior suggests sickness more than lonely deliberation does.

Claims under workmen's compensation statutes are more discriminating and closer to Porson's situation. In the typical case, a modern statute provides benefits for the family of a worker whose death is caused by an injury incurred in the course of his employment. Many statutes provide an exception where death is "the result of intentional self injury." The issue for the court, in a case where suicide is obviously the cause of death, is what *intentional* means. Courts tend to find that suicide performed in a bizarre manner is intentional, and that suicide after deliberation is not. The idea here is similar to the idea of the old torts cases finding that conduct which is the product of delusion is not intentional conduct.

This theory might suggest that Porson's attempt was unintentional. Helen, therefore, saved him from something he really did not want to do, and he can hardly complain about that. If she rescued him from a delusion, he should thank her. If she resisted an impulse he was unable to resist, she only did for him what he would have done for himself. Of course, Helen's theory here is tenuous. Ronald's opportunity for deliberation on his way home from Calvert's may have been enough to make him a deliberative suicide rather than an impulsive one. The Illinois court, in somewhat similar circumstances, said of the deceased, "His morbid mental condition had not. . . progressed to the stage of insane frenzy. He still had moderately intelligent mental power, rational knowledge of the consequences of his act, and the capacity for conscious volition."

Sickness may, after all, be a thin reed for Helen's defense. We chose it in her behalf because we suspect that the modern liberal mind believes in a person's right to kill himself and would therefore countenance interference only if the suicidal person was not himself and therefore wanted (or so we suppose) to be rescued. In other words, our operative theory of deviance in Helen's behalf has been subtopic-mental illness, and our operative principle of freedom permits interference with the mentally ill to some extent short of involuntary commitment. Progressive mental-health professionals appear to favor temporary interference with suicidal people even when they oppose involuntary commitment. Typically, the explanation is that suicide is a sudden crisis and that the interference is merely a matter of helping the person through the crisis.

It might be better to return to the older, more rigid view that suicidal behavior is deviance-subtopic-wrong and to vindicate Helen on the theory that she acted to prevent the commission of a crime, sin, or act against the best interests of Porson or of others.

PORSON V. GETLIFFE (THE BAD SAMARITAN)

Students in torts and jurisprudence have haggled over the situation Getliffe presents since the days when law schools were in courthouse attics. The reason for haggling is not so much that they doubt their intuitive disapproval of him as that they don't know what to do about it.

In the typical hypothetical situation, *A*, a good swimmer, stands on the shore and watches *B* drown. *A* could have saved *B* without incurring significant risk and without much effort. The student is supposed to concede that *A* is a bad Samaritan, but the issue is whether *A* is liable to *B*'s survivors for *B*'s wrongful death. The legal rule is said to be that *A* is not liable, the rationale being that *A* owes *B* no duty of rescue.

This rule is generally thought to be unfortunate. Perceptive scholars note a trend toward requiring people to be good Samaritans, and attribute the bad-Samaritan rule to excessive nineteenth century individualism. Judges tend to find relationships which impose a duty of rescue while they affirm *in dicta* the principle that a "stranger" owes no duty. "For example," Edmond Cahn stated, "no matter how careful one may be in exercising control over a piece of machinery, if a 'stranger' happens to become entangled in it, there arises an affirmative duty to halt the machine." The tendency is, he says, "to compel men to act like good neighbors and to leave heroism to individual option."

Cahn, who is as sensitive a moralist as American legal education has produced, favors retaining the old rule because "instances of such wholesale callousness . . . are extremely infrequent among Americans, and . . . the penalties imposed would be divided so fine as to lose any deterrent effect." In a deeper sense, he feels that one who acts wrongfully, as Getliffe did, when confusion is great and panic possible, has to be forgiven. The best the law can do is encourage rescue and protect good impulses. If, for example, Getliffe has rushed to rescue Porson and had been hurt as a result, Porson or Calvert or both of them would be liable to Getliffe for his damages. "The risk of rescue . . . is born of the occasion." The vulnerability to legal liability was created by the inducement to suicide and the attempt at it.

It is an unsatisfactory solution, somehow, if only because we expect better of ourselves than Getliffe's apathy on the sidewalk. In the last analysis, I suppose, we can best rationalize the result by saying that some things are better left to generous impulse.

Luke should be encouraged and protected in his efforts, and immune from suit as a result of them ("if only," as Cardozo said, his conduct "be not wanton"). And Calvin should be subject to whatever sanctions the law maintains against one who provokes homicide.

Helen should be protected in her efforts—no more, or less, than if she were a stranger rather than Porson's wife—and Getliffe should be disapproved of as much as the administration of justice will allow.

My own jurisprudence of suicide would, I think, be old fashioned. In fact, I borrow it from an old-fashioned moralist, G. K. Chesterton:

> Not only is suicide a sin, it is the sin. It is the ultimate and absolute evil, the refusal to take an interest in existence; the refusal to take the oath of loyalty to life. The man who kills a man, kills a man. The man who kills himself, kills all men. . . . His act . . . destroys all buildings: it insults all women. The thief is satisfied with diamonds; but the suicide is not: that is his crime. . . . The suicide insults everything on earth by not stealing it. . . . If it comes to clear ideas and the intelligent meaning of things, then there is much . . . rational and philosophic truth in the burial at the crossroads. . . . The man's crime is different from other crimes—for it makes even crimes impossible.

Helen was right to act as she did because her husband's act was a wrong, a wrong she was entitled to prevent. It was a wrong to her and to all persons. To her, first, because she has a narrow, specific interest in the survival of the person to whom she is bound by law and custom. But Porson's self-destruction would be a wrong to Helen even if she had never met him. Her right to stop him is nothing less than a right of self-defense. Porson's death would have diminished her life. We all, inevitably, have an investment in one another. If life defeats one of us, defeats so much that life is not even preferable to death, it defeats each of us. It deprives each of us of one who might have taught, supported, and inspired, and therefore makes life worse for those who are left. Sir Thomas Browne said he was indebted to every man he met because that man did not kill him. There is, in that grim recollection of man's inhumanity to man, a realistic hope that the debt will grow, that the stranger will not only spare my life but share it and make it better. My destruction of myself would deprive him of that claim on me, as his self-destruction would deprive me of his brotherhood. Perhaps the law cannot in every case, and perhaps God does not, punish this wrong, but it is a wrong nonetheless in the most elementary and interpersonal meaning of wrong. The site of suicide is a place without good; it is a place of lost possibility. It is important to civilization to say that suicide is not acceptable, in whatever lame way it can, and, of course, law is one of civilization's means of communication.

We simply must disapprove of Getliffe's aloofness for much the same reason. His refusal to rescue makes him a collaborator in wrong. The community, the law, develops clumsy remedies for civil wrong (money damages, for example) because it is a crude science, but the clumsiness of the remedy should not obscure the fact that the remedy is social. The law may soon be ready to require Getliffe to pay for some of Porson's misery, even though money seems a vulgar way to express a moral value. (Money is more convincing as a symbol than it is borne of high impulse). But the law needs to convince as much as to inspire. The impulse, I suppose, is that indifference to pain is an unworthy attitude, regardless of where the pain comes from.

Getliffe's money expresses that impulse less practically than Kitty Jay's flowers. The relation between law and beauty is like that; beauty calls law to its best self. Beauty mourns what men did to Kitty Jay when she was alive, and what they declined to do to keep her alive, more than it mourns the disposition of her corpse. The flowers near the moor say something sad about what Kitty might have been, and of the lost nobility she might have brought to the noblemen of eighteenth-century Manaton—something sad about them, about her, and about all the rest of us.

REFERENCES

Treatises

American Law Institute: Second Restatement of the Law of Torts. St. Paul, West, 1965-1966, Sections 279-80, p 312

Black HC: Black's Law Dictionary (ed 4). St. Paul, West, 1957

Cahn E: The Moral Decision. Bloomington, Indiana, Indiana Univ Press, 1960, ch. VII

Chesterton GK: Orthodoxy. New York, Dodd, Mead, 1949, pp 131-133

Herdon D: Death as a Fact of Life. New York, Norton, 1973

Holmes OW: The Common Law. Boston, Little, Brown, 1881

Rodes RE, Jr: The Legal Enterprise. New York, Dunellen, 1975

Shaffer TL: Death, Property, and Lawyers. New York, Dunellen, 1970

Cases

Aetna Life Ins. Co. v. McLaughlin, 380 Texas S.W.2d 101 (1964)

Barber v. Industrial Comm'n, 241 Wis. 462, 6 N.W.2d 199 (1942)

Blackburn v. State, 23 Ohio 146 (1872)

Bogust v. Iverson, 10 Wis. 2d 129, 102 N.W.2d 228 (1960)

Cauverein v. DeMetz, 188 N.Y.S. 2d 627 (1951)

Harper v. Industrial Comm'n 24 Ill. 2d 103, 180 N.E.2d 480 (1962)

Scheffer v. Washington City, 105 U.S. 249 (1882)

State v. Campbell, 146 Mont. 251, 405 P.2d 978 (1965)

Tate v. Canonica, 5 Cal. Rep. 28 (1960)

Wagner v. International R. Co., 232 N.Y. 176 (1921)

Articles in Legal Periodicals

Annotation, Admissability of evidence relating to accused's attempt to commit suicide. Am Law Rep 22:840, 1968

Annotation, Insurance: construction of "sane or insane" provision of suicide exclusion. Am Law Rep 9:1015, 1966

Grieshober DW: Suicide—criminal aspects. Villanova Law Rev 1:316, 1956

Note, The judicial interpretation of suicide. Univ Penn Law Rev 105:391, 1957

O'Sullivan R: The ethics of suicide. Catholic Lawyer: 147, 1956

Schulman RE: Suicide and suicide prevention: A legal analysis. Am Bar Assoc J 54:855, 1968

Shaffer TL: Judges, repulsive evidence, and the ability to respond. Notre Dame Lawyer 43:503, 1968

Robert Kastenbaum

14
Suicide as the Preferred
Way of Death

The introductory piece to this chapter is Albert Camus' famous essay, The Myth of Sisyphus (1940). Permission of Alfred A. Knopf to reprint is gratefully acknowledged.

There is but one truly serious philosophical problem, and that is suicide. Judging whether life is or is not worth living amounts to answering the fundamental question of philosophy. All the rest—whether or not the world has three dimensions, whether the mind has nine or twelve categories—comes afterwards. These are games; one must first answer. And if it is true, as Nietzsche claims, that a philosopher, to deserve our respect, must preach by example, you can appreciate the importance of that reply, for it will precede the definitive act. These are facts the heart can feel; yet they call for careful study before they become clear to the intellect.

If I ask myself how to judge that this question is more urgent than that, I reply that one judges by the actions it entails. I have never seen anyone die for the ontological argument. Galileo, who held a scientific truth of great importance, abjured it with the greatest ease as soon as it endangered his life. In a certain sense, he did right. That truth was not worth the stake. Whether the earth or the sun revolves around the other is a matter of profound indifference. To tell the truth, it is a futile question. On the other hand, I see many people die because they judge that life is not worth living. I see others paradoxically getting killed for the ideas or illusions that give them a reason for living (what is called a reason for living is also an excellent reason for dying). I therefore conclude that the meaning of life is the most urgent of questions. How to answer it? On all essential problems (I mean thereby those that run the risk of leading to death or those that intensify the passion of living) there are probably but two methods of thought: the method of La Palisse and the method of Don Quixote. Solely the balance between evidence and lyricism can allow us to achieve simultaneously emotion and lucidity. In a subject at once so humble and so heavy with emotion, the learned and classical dialectic must yield, one can see, to a more modest attitude of mind deriving at one and the same time from common sense and understanding.

Suicide has never been dealt with except as a social phenomenon. On the contrary, we are concerned here, at the outset, with the relationship between individual thought and suicide. An act like this is prepared within the silence of the heart, as is a great work of art. The man himself is ignorant of it. One evening he pulls the trigger or jumps. Of an apartment-building manager who had killed himself I was told that he had lost his daughter five years before, that he had changed greatly since, and that that experience had "undermined" him. A more exact word cannot be imagined. Beginning to think is beginning to be undermined. Society has but little connection with such beginnings. The worm is in man's heart. That is where it must be sought. One must follow and understand this fatal game that leads from lucidity in the face of existence to flight from light.

There are many causes for a suicide, and generally the most obvious ones were not the most powerful. Rarely is suicide committed (yet the hypothesis is not excluded) through reflection. What sets off the crisis is almost always unverifiable. Newspapers often speak of "personal sorrows" or of "incurable illness." These explanations are plausible. But one would have to know whether a friend of the desperate man had not that very day addressed him indifferently. He is the guilty one. For that is enough to precipitate all the rancors and all the boredom still in suspension.

But if it is hard to fix the precise instant, the subtle step when the mind opted for death, it is easier to deduce from the act itself the consequences it implies. In a sense, and as in melodrama, killing yourself amounts to confessing. It is confessing that life is too much for you or that you do not understand it. Let's not go too far in such analogies, however, but rather return to everyday words. It is merely confessing that that "is not worth the trouble." Living, naturally, is never easy. You continue making the gestures commanded by existence for many reasons, the first of which is habit. Dying voluntarily implies that you have recognized, even instinctively, the ridiculous character of that habit, the absence of any profound reason for living, the insane character of that daily agitation, and the uselessness of suffering.

What, then, is that incalculable feeling that deprives the mind of the sleep necessary to life? A world that can be explained even with bad reasons is a familiar world. But, on the other hand, in a universe suddenly divested of illusions and lights, man feels an alien, a stranger. His exile is without remedy since he is deprived of the memory of a lost home or the hope of a promised land. This divorce between man and his life, the actor and his setting, is properly the feeling of absurdity. All healthy men having thought of their own suicide, it can be seen, without further explanation, that there is a direct connection between this feeling and the longing for death.

The subject of this essay is precisely this relationship between the absurd and suicide, the exact degree to which suicide is a solution to the absurd. The principle can be established that for a man who does not cheat, what he believes to be true must determine his action. Belief in the absurdity of existence must then dictate his conduct. It is legitimate to wonder, clearly and without false pathos, whether a conclusion of this importance requires forsaking as rapidly as possible an incomprehensible condition. I am speaking, of course, of men inclined to be in harmony with themselves.

Stated clearly, this problem may seem both simple and insoluble. But it is wrongly assumed that simple questions involve answers that are no less simple and that evidence implies evidence. A *priori* and reversing the terms of the problem, just as one does or does not kill oneself, it seems that there are but two philosophical solutions, either yes or no. This would be too easy. But allowance must be made for those who, without concluding, continue questioning. Here I am only slightly indulging in irony: this is the majority. I notice also that those who answer "no" act as if they thought "yes." As a matter of fact, if I accept the Nietzschean criterion, they think "yes" in one way or another. On the other hand, it often happens that those who commit suicide were assured of the meaning of life. These contradictions are constant. It may even be said that they have never been so keen as on this point where, on the contrary, logic seems so desirable. It is a commonplace to compare philosophical theories and the behavior of those who profess them. But it must be said that of the thinkers who refused a meaning to life none except Kirilov who belongs to literature, Peregrinos who is born of legend, and Jules Lequier who belongs to hypothesis, admitted his logic to the point of refusing that life. Schopenhauer is often cited, as a fit subject for laughter, because he praised suicide while seated at a well-set table. This is no subject for joking. That way of not taking the tragic seriously is not so grievous, but it helps to judge a man.

In the face of such contradictions and obscurities must we conclude that there is no relationship between the opinion one has about life and the act one commits to leave it? Let us not exaggerate in this direction. In a man's attachment to life there is something stronger than all the ills in the world. The body's judgment is as good as the mind's, and the body shrinks from annihilation. We get into the habit of living before acquiring the habit of thinking. In that race which daily hastens us toward death, the body maintains its irreparable lead. In short, the essence of that contradiction lies in what I shall call the act of eluding because it is both less and more than diversion in the Pascalian sense. Eluding is the invariable game. The typical act of eluding, the fatal evasion that constitutes the third theme of this essay, is hope. Hope of another life one must "deserve" or trickery of those who live not for life itself but for some great idea that will transcend it, refine it, give it a meaning, and betray it.

Thus everything contributes to spreading confusion. Hitherto, and it has not been wasted effort, people have played on words and pretended to believe that refusing to grant a meaning to life necessarily leads to declaring that it is not worth living. In truth, there is no necessary common measure between these two judgments. One merely has to refuse to be misled by the confusions, divorces, and inconsistencies previously pointed out. One must brush everything aside and go straight to the real problem. One kills oneself because life is not worth living, that is certainly a truth—yet an unfruitful one because it is a truism. But does that insult to existence, that flat denial in which it is plunged come from the fact that it has no meaning? Does its absurdity require one to escape it through hope or suicide—this is what must be clarified, hunted down, and elucidated while brushing aside all the rest. Does the Absurd dictate death? This problem must be given priority over others, outside all methods of thought and all exercises of the disinterested mind. Shades of meaning, contradictions, the psychology that an "objective" mind can always introduce into all problems have no place in this pursuit and this passion. It calls simply for an unjust—in other words, logical—thought. That is not easy. It is always easy to be logical. It is almost impossible to be logical to the bitter end. Men who die by their own hand consequently follow to its conclusion their emotional inclination. Reflection on suicide gives me an opportunity to raise the only problem to interest me: is there a logic to the point of death? I cannot know unless I pursue, without reckless passion, in the sole light of evidence, the reasoning of which I am here suggesting the source. This is what I call an absurd reasoning. Many have begun it. I do not yet know whether or not they kept to it.

When Karl Jaspers, revealing the impossibility of constituting the world as a unity, exclaims: "This limitation leads me to myself, where I can no longer withdraw behind an objective point of view that I am merely representing, where neither I myself nor the existence of others can any longer become an object for me," he is evoking after many others those waterless deserts where thought reaches its confines. After many others, yes indeed, but how eager they were to get out of them! At that last crossroad where thought hesitates, many men have arrived and even some of the humblest. They then abdicated what was most precious to them, their life. Others, princes of the mind, abdicated likewise, but they initiated the suicide of their thought in its purest revolt. The real effort is to stay there, rather, in so far as that is possible, and to examine closely the odd vegetation of those distant regions. Tenacity and acumen are privileged spectators of this inhuman show in which absurdity, hope, and death carry on their dialogue. The mind can then analyze the figures of that elementary yet subtle dance before illustrating them and reliving them itself.

Suicide as the Preferred
Way of Death

Within a few years suicide will not be regarded as crime, weakness, failure, or pathology. I do not mean that suicide will be tolerated or passively sanctioned but rather that it will have become the model, ideal, or preferred mode of death in our society.

The possibility that this situation might come to pass—and why—will be explored in this paper. The analysis is not based upon rates of attempted or completed suicide, nor is an attempt made to pass judgment upon the desirability of the development that is forecast. It is simply an effort to see where we might be going by looking around at what is happening now, chiefly in our own thoughts and feelings.

BACKGROUND DEFINITIONS AND CONSIDERATIONS

By *suicide* I mean what people usually mean: an instrumental act or series of actions through which a person intentionally terminates his or her own existence. Certainly there are problems with this traditional sort of definition. It can be difficult to determine the existence of intention in a particular instance or, if one looks even more closely, the type of intention. It is also possible to question the general value or validity of intention as a concept. But for the purposes of this exploration it is important to retain the idea of deliberate, knowing actions taken specifically to terminate one's own life. Society still tends to interpret suicide as a planned consequence rather than simply an outcome of action. It is this assumed intentional component that makes it possible for us to repeatedly ask Why?—A question which otherwise would be an empty verbalism. The assumption of intention also lends credence to our tendency to make moral judgments about suicide in general or any one suicide in particular. These characteristics of our response to suicide are likely to prove significant in any forthcoming transformation of its status in society.

We also adhere closely to common usage by setting aside another problem that has come to be of much concern to clinicians and researchers. Certifiable suicide will be our focus, despite the high probability that many other deaths involve self-destructive components as well. Tabachnick[1] and his colleagues, for example, have probed into suicidal dynamics that show up as automobile "accidents." Other modes of accidental death, unnecessary risk-taking, and excessive use of alcohol and drugs are among the pathways to annihilation that have been examined as possible suicide-equivalents. Yet important as these forms of self-destruction may be, it is suicide in the narrow and straightforward usage that is our prime focus here.

Preferred mode of death is another term that needs explanation. We are not indifferent to the conditions under which death occurs. Did death come too soon, too late, or right on time? Did it occur in the right place? Was the total dying-unto-death process marked by an acceptable style? And was the cause of death itself acceptable?

Granted, we are not usually cognizant of these questions. Most physically healthy, non-depressed people do not dwell upon details of the death scene. Nevertheless, both as individuals and as a society we do have our preferences. These express themselves clearly enough when the presence or prospect of death imposes itself upon us. The demise of one person perturbs us greatly, while another death may not have so jarring an impact. Leaving aside our relationship to the deceased (which may be the single most important factor), we still are likely to respond differentially depending upon time, place, style, and cause. Some of the specifics will be considered later. Our point for now is that it is probable that most individuals and societies prefer certain modes of death to others. These preferences tell us something about a culture's broad pattern of values and dynamics. But there is no reason to suppose that preferred modes of death are simply the expression or outcome of cultural dynamics; more likely, orientations toward death also exert considerable influence in the shaping of cultural dynamics in general.

While I believe the considerations to be presented are quite in touch with our current state of knowledge and ignorance, the position itself goes beyond what can be fully documented at present. I am trying to suggest a way of viewing suicide within the larger context of changing cultural preferences for mode of death and drawing those implications that seem most justified under the circumstances.

IS SUICIDE A PREFERRED MODE OF DEATH?
A FIRST LOOK

By and large, we do not think of suicide as a preferred mode of death. There have been both religious and legal condemnations of suicidal behavior in our society. Even those who believe that suicide is not necessarily sinful or criminal tend to disapprove of or be alarmed by self-destruction. It is something to be prevented; people are to be talked out of suicidal frames of mind and, if necessary, supervised closely when in an acute suicidal crisis. Further, there appear to be few people in the general population who presently regard suicide as their own death-oriented behavior of choice. Of approximately 30,000 readers of a national magazine who responded to his questionnaire, Shneidman[2] found that only 2 percent indicated "suicide" as the answer to his question, "If you had a choice, what kind of death would you prefer?"

However, notice what happens to our perspective when the term *suicide* is invoked. A powerful process of selection and condensation takes place. All the many dimensions of the total dying-death situation telescope into causation and a few related concerns. Suicide provides a critical aspect of the "cause-of-death" specification. It also tells us that a person has seized control of his or her life, seeming to have wrenched free from established patterns of expectation and control to which we are all expected to be faithful.

I wonder, then, if we truly object to all dimensions of that action known officially as suicide. Perhaps we become so impressed with the causation-control dimension that we tend to dismiss the entire death as wrong or unpalatable. Let us, at least, suspend final judgment regarding our total view of suicidal death until a few other considerations have been advanced.

SOME DIMENSIONS OF DYING AND DEATH

A brief survey of selected dimensions of the total dying-death process will advance our understanding of suicide as preferred or nonpreferred modality.

Cause of Death

It seems to me that in our society we prefer to think that (1) death does have a cause, (2) it is very important to know the cause, and (3) the cause can be stated and understood in objective, rational terms. These propositions may appear so obvious that one can hardly imagine alternatives. The self-evident nature of these assumptions, however, simply attests to their deep embeddedness in our cultural patterns of thinking and valuing. Any and all of these assumptions could be challenged or ignored had we the inclination to do so. I am suggesting, then, that emphasis upon cause of death (and thus upon suicide as one particular cause among others) is an expression of preferred modalities of thought rather than metaphysical necessity. This also suggests that we might just change our thinking about causation and death as the general conditions of our life and experience change.

Turning to specific causes of death, it will take but a moment to remind ourselves that suicide is not the only type that has been strongly disapproved of. Syphilis has been a stigmatized cause for many years—check out popular biographies of famous people whose probable cause of death has been evaded because of the discredit it might bring. Syphilis represented a shameful, immoral way to die because of the manner in which the condition was contracted. By contrast, a variety of other causes have been literally unspeakable in certain contexts because they are so frightening. There are known instances in which cholera and plague victims have been officially miscertified to avoid public panic (or to avoid reduced attendance at a prestigious event). The fate of a particular cause may stem largely from real or imagined danger of contagion and contamination, or from real or imagined suffering induced by the condition itself. Today's biggest fright word seems to be cancer, although it is spoken more openly than in past years. A thorough understanding of suicide as preferred or nonpreferred way to die, then, would require a more careful analysis of its status with respect to many other causes of death that also arouse strong feeling.

Control of Life and Death

Bringing about one's own death is only one manifestation of the desire or capacity to influence the duration of life. Murder, hunting, and warfare are among some of the other expressions, besides the suicidal, of the inclination to take somebody's life and death into one's own hands in some way or other.

Life-death control operates in the other direction as well. The attempt to circumvent death or to prolong life (the emphases are different) has taken many forms over the centuries.[3] The central point here is that people frequently have disagreed about both the moral and practical ramifications of life-extending ventures. Should we take life into our own hands, or is it best to leave control to the powers of nature, chance, or deity? Responses to this kind of question have been truly variable. Religious orientation, socioeconomic status, and the structure of the immediate situation have been among the variables, as well as the question of precisely whose life is involved and what particular modalities for avoiding what particular pathway to death. In our own time, for example, many types of heroic measure are advocated and practiced, yet other approaches, such as cryogenic suspension, meet with considerable antagonism.[4] As a society, we are far from equal-handed in efforts to strengthen the chances of life against death.[5]

The control dimension must be taken into account, although it is not the only dimension involved. In other words, we are not necessarily in favor of seizing control over life-death forces for purposes of prolonging life. We may hesitate to take responsibility or consider it to be unwise or immoral. Ambivalence and disagreement are not characteristics of suicide alone. Any movement to take control of life in either direction is likely to generate a mixed response. I suggest, then, that some of the aversion to suicide already touched upon in this paper might be attributable to a more general tendency to shrink from control (and responsibility) over any manipulation of life expectancy.

Place of Death

Every death certificate includes an entry for the place of death. It is well known that death (along with birth and other significant life events) has been occurring in places outside the home with increasing frequency during recent decades. This has led to a shifting expectation. More and more people now associate the death scene with a specialized environment that is clearly distinct both from the home and the daily sociophysical structure in which the individual had functioned most of his or her life.

A typical admixture of attitudes and values might be described as, "I want to die in a place that has meant something to me, rather than in an essentially sterile public institution. But I do not want to impose my death upon those who would be unprepared for it, or disturbed by the process. Perhaps I should breathe my last in a hospital to spare my family this burden." Attitudes and expectations regarding the death of persons other than ourselves also tend to be patterned. From an outsider's view, a hospital might seem to be the place for the sick and the old to die. But within the more differentiated framework of the hospital staff, the correct place is not the institution in general (where many patients survive and function well), but a particular ward or unit. Furthermore, the better place on this unit is the side-room with screens carefully in place.[6]

Where death occurs does seem to make a difference to most people. The outsider prefers to avoid death places when he can, and certainly does not want to be surprised by death when it occurs in the wrong place. When the outsider has become an insider (his own death or that of a person close to him), the preference will reflect very personal orientations toward both life and death.

The place or setting in which suicide occurs has not been completely ignored. Those who conduct psychological autopsies, for example, usually take the setting into account.[7,8] In general, however, place has been of interest chiefly for its clue value in determining causation rather than as a dimension of preference in itself. I am suggesting that suicide can be a method of assuring that death occurs in the right place.

Duration and Experience of the Dying Process

The American way of death emphasizes speed and unawareness; the curtain of darkness descends rapidly, silently. This clinical impression is supported by studies of expectations and preferences for mode of demise.[9] We want to spend a long time living, and as little time as possible dying.

For most people, the ideal death comes softly and unexpectedly during sleep. The person goes to bed without pain, fear, or knowledge of death and simply does not awaken again.

By contrast, an illness that tends to involve a long period of living with death alarms even many of the professionals who specialize in its treatment. Experience with clinical workshops, for example, has led the author and his colleagues to the conclusion that personnel who work with cancer patients are themselves especially fearful of experiencing this particular terminal pathway. However, this is not the place to evaluate such an attitude. Rather, I wish only to propose that we do have in our society a fairly decisive preference for the quick and easy death (exceptions readily granted). Suicide, then, can recommend itself as a way to achieve this desired ending.

Time of Death

It is not that uncommon to encounter people who believe that there is a certain time to die, or even that their own time is now ripe or rapidly approaching. Such an orientation often surfaces among both staff and patients in geriatric facilities,[10] but is not restricted to any one age group. Glaser and Strauss[11] have shown how influential the expectations of another person's time-to-die can be in the response they elicit from health-providers. The timing of death can be of more concern than place or any other variable because one might be caught off guard if the patient dies too soon (just as one might be distressed and impatient if the patient dies far behind schedule).

In our own continuing studies of death attitudes, it is common for respondents (in good health) to express a readiness to die at whatever age they believe themselves most likely to reach. It is an appropriate or acceptable time to die (at least in advance perspective). In most samples, between 10 percent and 20 percent of the respondents would prefer to die at an earlier age than they expect to die.[9] Others set their preferred time of death some distance beyond the probable age of death. Whatever the particular choice, most respondents find it natural to contemplate a certain time of death as being more acceptable or appropriate than others.

Suicide is obviously one way of attempting to make sure that death comes at the right time, regardless of the specific factors that make a time right for a particular individual.

Style of Death

Some of the dimensions already noted contribute to what might be called the style of a death. But there are other facets of the dying-unto-death process that can be significant to all those involved. One person might seek a brave death, while for another it is the serene death that is desired. In both instances there may be the hope of setting good examples for others. We have seen deaths where the individual was attempting to emulate the style of a person much admired and influential in his own life. The possible styles are numerous and capable of much variation. For a person who does have a certain sense of the kind of death he or she wants to achieve, this motivation can be the shaping force that organizes timing, place, duration, etc. of the dying experience. Even the person who is not clearly aware of preferring one particular death style is likely to have values and aversions that express themselves during the process. Similarly, those who are intimately associated with the dying person are likely to have their own ideas and feelings about the style this death should follow.

Again, perhaps the best proof we can have that style of death (as with the other dimensions) does exist as a potent influence is the observation of our own response when a death goes right or goes wrong. And, again, suicide offers the possibility of terminating one's life in an acceptable or most preferred style.

Siding with Death

Let us now touch upon several developments that have the effect of supporting death against life. It is time to make explicit the concept of death system that has influenced material already presented. The death system has been characterized as "the sociophysical network by which we mediate and express our relationship to mortality."[4] All cultures, past and present, have had death systems, which include objects, symbols, times, places, and people, some permanently and structurally embedded in the system, others recruited as the occasion demands. The death system has several vital functions to perform. These include warnings and anticipations, the effort to prevent death or prolong life, response to the dying, disposal and ritualization of the dead, establishment of equilibrium between living and dead, explanation of death, and the deliberate delivery of the living over to death.

Cultures differ in many ways, including their relative emphases upon these various functions. Furthermore, the death system in any given culture is subject to change over time, We will be looking at some of the more relevant ways in which our own death system seems to be changing.

Moral Sanction for Death

During the past two decades or so there has been a surfacing of influential views to the effect that death can be a morally acceptable or even preferable alternative to continuing life. Most often raised within the context of new sociomedical conditions, these views seem to be meeting with an increasingly favorable response from both the health-care provider and the general public.

One of the most persistent advocates of the new morality has been Joseph Fletcher, an Episcopal theologian. Of his many writings on this subject, it is probably "The Patient's Right to Die" that has received most attention because of its initial appearance in a national magazine.[12] But he started his challenge to tradition in *Morals and Medicine*[13] and has continued to write and speak on this topic.

Much of Fletcher's concern has centered around that modern nightmare, the vision of a person transfixed indefinitely between life and death by elaborate medical technology. He sees this as a new phenomenon, raising new questions and requiring new answers from the perspective of morality.

In truth, the whole problem of letting people 'go' in a merciful release is a relatively new one. It is largely the result of our fabulous success in medical science and technology. Not long ago, when the point of death was reached, there was usually nothing that could be done about it. Now, due to the marvels of medicine, all kinds of things can keep people 'alive' long after what used to be the final crisis. For example, there is the cardiac 'pacemaker,' a machine that can restart a heart that has stopped beating. Turn off the machine, the heart stops. Is the patient alive? Is he murdered if it is taken away? Does he commit suicide if he throws it out of the window? Artificial respirators and kidneys, vital organ transplants, antibiotics, intravenous feeding—these and many other devices have the double effect of prolonging life and prolonging dying. The right to die in dignity is a problem raised more often by medicine's successes than by its failures. Consequently, there is a new dimension in the debate about 'euthanasia.' The old-fashioned question was simply this: 'May we morally do anything to put people mercifully out of hopeless misery?' But the issue now takes a more troubling twist: 'May we morally omit to do any of the ingenious things we *could* do to prolong people's suffering?'[12]

Fletcher anticipated some of the objections that arose from his position that the patient has a moral right to die. He argues[13] that voluntary euthanasia is neither suicide nor murder, and dismisses the contention that only God has the right to control life and death by asking us to abandon all medical practice if we really hold to that interpretation. The argument, pro and con, is of considerable interest. But the basic point here is that the moral dimension has been brought clearly to the fore, has taken account of emerging sociomedical circumstances, and has come down (though with qualifications) on the side of death.

Other clergymen and philosophers have also added their voices to the moral sanctioning of death. Theologian Daniel C. Maguire[14] finds indications of a shift in the traditional Catholic approach to life-and-death morality. He cites, for example, the conviction expressed by Bishop Francis Simons after his experiences in India. Bishop Simons would rely upon the concensus of good and intelligent people to determine when an unborn infant should be killed to save the life of its mother. He denies that the unborn have a fundamental right to life, unrelated to the jeopardy of the mother. This is quite a different problem from the euthanasia or death with dignity issue raised by Fletcher. It is concerned more with the exercise of control in a life-and-death priority situation. Nevertheless, the bishop's challenge to tradition unsettles the certitude that the right to life of a certain class (the unborn) has absolute precedence.

Perhaps of even more interest here is the bishop's willingness to consider certain acts of suicide morally acceptable. He specifies a context in which the alternative is severe torture that would result in divulging damaging secret information. The traditional Catholic position had been unequivocally against suicide. As Maguire observes, "Perhaps the revealing thing about Bishop Simons' article was that it did not create a big stir among Catholic moralists. Many Catholic moralists today would come to the same conclusions, each by his individual method."[14]

Advocates of the new morality often claim that their views are shared by many others. To date, no critical review of findings in this area has been attempted (to my knowledge). Nevertheless, it does seem evident that these moralists are not just speaking to or for themselves. There is a general, ongoing dialogue in the media, in death education courses, and in other contexts where life and death issues are raised. At the least, there is a mood and a movement that favors positive moral sanctions for death under particular (or sometimes, not very particular) circumstances. Much of this concern still pivots around the death with dignity issue, but it does not take much imagination to interpret the continuing developments in the area of abortion as a liberalization of the traditional moral stance against the deliberate decision to mete out death. The answer to the question, Who dies? may be quite different in the case of abortion as contrasted with voluntary euthanasia. But the question is relevant in both instances, and it is obvious that more than one kind of answer can be given in both instances. More importantly, the differences between particular forms of death (e.g., abortion, voluntary euthanasia, suicide) should not entirely obscure the fact that moral sanctions in general are in process of revision, with the shift emphasizing approbation of actions that have death as consequence.

Pragmatic Sanction for Death

It is not entirely wise to separate the moral from the pragmatic, and I do not mean to imply that those who advocate one of these perspectives are necessarily unmindful of the other. However, for our purposes it is useful to shift focus, concentrating now upon some of the applied or practical factors that are leading to death advocacy.

"Intelligent use of available resources" would be one way of stating a position that can now be encountered in many quarters. There is much precedent, of course, for the circumstance of many lives trying to survive where few can be supported by a barren or hostile environment. But in our own times there can be seen a gradual emergence of a new configuration of facts and attitudes. Let us take two examples, both of which are included in the particular advocacy of a man who combines the authority of doctor and law-maker. Walter W. Sackett, a physician and a member of the Florida legislature, was perhaps the first of contemporary law-makers and officials to introduce a bill favoring euthanasia. Of particular interest here are certain of his reasons as well the examples he most frequently cites.

Sackett shares the concern of many others in arguing for death with dignity in general. But he also has spoken of the desirability of conserving public resources by discontinuing the existence of deeply retarded state wards. I do not know if his position on this topic has remained firm, but he has indicated that those in a chronic and hopeless situation should not be supported. He also argues for the merciful discontinuation of life of the aged. Sackett claims that many elders fully support this approach, fearing prolonged dying more than death *per se.*

The net is thus cast wider than in the usual advocacy. A retarded and disabled child and an aged adult are not necessarily in danger of imminent death or even of a protracted terminal course. Sackett's views on this subject have met with quite a divided response. What particularly strikes this writer is the number of people who say, "Yes, he has something there . . . Why keep them alive?" It often seems as though Sackett's prestige and open advocacy has permitted attitudes of others to rise to the surface that already were pointed in that direction.

The case is pragmatic because both the retarded and the aged person are seen as having negligible value to society (in the eyes of at least some beholders). How do they produce or contribute? Both draw vital resources that could be utilized more productively and efficiently elsewhere and both are not much good to themselves either; they are better off dead. This latter argument is more articulate in the case of elders (or those who volunteer to speak for elders) who express a readiness or preference for death. What a deeply retarded individual thinks, feels, and values is seldom recorded.

In a way, Sackett's advocacy is but a logical extension of well established tendencies in our society to allocate life-support resources according to certain priorities. He is more explicit than most who publicly speak about this and does not completely shy away from instrumental actions that would terminate life. Otherwise, what he offers is quite in keeping with our inclination to select some lives for safeguarding and support, others for hazard and death. The aged and the chronically ill are generally less favored than the young and the acutely ill (see, for example, recent documents prepared by the US Senate Special Subcommittee on Aging[15]).

This is not the place to explore all the dimensions of priority and preference. I just wish to propose that we have already entered an era in which tacit and inarticulate priorities are being raised to explicit propositions that demand discussion and resolution.

IS SUICIDE A PREFERRED MODE OF DEATH?
A SECOND LOOK

We return to suicide and a reevaluation of self-destruction as a preferred or soon-to-be-preferred mode of death. Our first look gave little support for this view, but since that time we have considered a variety of factors that might impact upon our culture's *modus terminalis.*

Pressure for Designing a "Good Death"

I suggest we are approaching a situation in our culture in which increasing pressure will be brought to bear upon the design of an ideal form of death. Awareness of the dying process and criticism of how the total dying-unto-death scene is managed has become widespread. Although concepts of appropriate death[16] have circulated among a small number of professionals and scientists in recent years, the mounting concern of the public at large might well lead to a rather different design. Death talk and awareness make most people anxious even though some anxiety often is dispelled in the process of articulation and communication. Anxiety reduction would be served by the establishment of an agreed-upon ideal. In this sense, Kubler-Ross[17] has both raised and partially reduced the general anxiety level; raised anxiety by opening the door to the death-bed scene and lowered anxiety by proposing that there is a more or less fixed sequence of stages that culminates in a type of acceptance. Again, however, we cannot assume that the culture's choice of preferred death modality will be identical with any that have been proposed by the professionals.

We look now for those characteristics that might be most desired if our culture could design a mode of death to order.

Suicide as the Designed Death

According to our preceding analyses, among the characteristics which make a death acceptable or preferable in our culture are the following: (1) it has a rational, specifiable cause—suicide can be a raional, specifiable cause; (2) as a contemporary-spirited death, it embodies the element of control—suicide can provide the element of control; (3) it occurs in a favored setting, probably non-institutional—suicide can be enacted in a favored setting; (4) it is over quickly—suicide can be a quick route to death; (5) it involves little or no suffering or experiencing—suicide can involve little or no suffering or experiencing; (6) it comes at the right time—suicide can come precisely at the right time; and (7) it expresses the individual's most characteristic or valued style—suicide can express individual style.

There is probably no other mode of death that can so adequately meet these emerging criteria. It is suggested, then, that suicide will gradually become the culturally sanctioned mode of death as the tendencies already noted here gain more access to the establishment (media, legislation, influence on programs in the governmental and commercial sectors, etc.).

Moral and Pragmatic Sanctions

The foregoing is based chiefly upon individual preference writ large. What about broader moral and pragmatic sanctions that go beyond individual preference?

The growing moral support for death with dignity expresses concern for what is considered to be unnecessary suffering of the dying person, and often, family and loved ones as well. Precisely how termination is to be accomplished is a problem with legal and pragmatic as well as moral implications, but this problem arises in the first place because of the desire to bring a life to its end. Once the principle of death on demand is accepted, the particular means can then be evaluated. For some individuals in some contexts of terminal illness, suicide might be both the moral and pragmatic technique of choice. A person who has always valued independence, for example, might be considered right in taking responsibility for this final act which also carries through his or her life style.

In an even larger spectrum of cases, the dying person might be counted virtuous for the willingness to take this obligation into his own hands rather than have it passed more directly to physician, family, or committee. Many physicians, for example, fear that any medical participation in the termination process would interfere with their role and image when they are engaged in life-saving procedures.

The alternative of a medical person with a specialty in killing or releasing the terminally ill does not seem to have aroused much enthusiasm.

A suicide carried out in an approved manner could be the most satisfactory alternative to the moralist and the pragmatist in all persons concerned. One of the first shifts in attitude necessary for this development is already in process. Suicide is not regarded as wrong for all people under all circumstances by most people in our society today. As we have seen, influential spokesmen for the historically conservative Catholic position have started to specify circumstances under which suicide might be preferable to other types of action. Among both the population in general and those who comprise the specialized suicide-prevention or mental-health community, frequently there is a belief that some suicides were less unfortunate than others. We do tend to distinguish among specific suicidal acts, e.g., the parent whose suicide involves first the murder of his or her children and spouse is less likely to meet with our approval than the terminally-ill and despondent individual who goes off some place and quietly arranges for a quick and simple exit.

In other words, we would exchange the global idea of "suicide is wicked or unacceptable" for a more differentiated proposition. "*This* kind of suicide meets with the highest expectations of our culture . . . but *that* kind of suicide is not recommended or condoned." "*This* suicide was accomplished with great craftmanship;" "*That* one had the right idea, but it didn't work out very well." We can have our morality and our pragmatics—and our suicide, too.

Typical characteristics of an appropriate suicide would probably include an anticipatory period during which usual sociomedical techniques have been given a reasonable chance. Enough advance warning would be given to avoid inflicting the trauma of surprise upon the survivors. Further, the exit scene would comfort rather than disturb the survivors. Another important point should be noted: the suicide will be acceptable because it does follow certain cultural guidelines, no matter what these particular guidelines turn out to be. This marks one of the major differences between the unacceptable suicides that occur today, and the modal or ideal suicides that may occur tomorrow. The person who commits suicide today may be flaunting society, telling us that the kind of life we have made for ourselves is not worth keeping. More specifically, the sanctions against suicide are rejected and this rejects part of the governance of our culture in general. The person who commits suicide as part of the designed death in the future would, by his careful and considerate execution of the total act, affirms his respect and participation in our culture's value system. This kind of suicide strengthens rather than assaults the social fabric.

Suicide as a preferred mode of death may go well beyond the death with dignity scene. Elders and any other individuals who accept the judgment of their culture that they are used up, unproductive, expendable, etc. might be strongly motivated to attain a last moment of stature through voluntary termination of life. This process might become fairly rigid and institutionalized. Self-termination might be clearly expected of a person who finds him- or herself in a particular situation. Or it might remain as an option; one does not have to commit suicide, but the strong, virtuous, socially-conscious person would. For many individuals, the choice of going out beautifully, boldly, and in the national interest might appeal more than lingering on the fringes as a secondary or resented figure.

TO THE SUICIDOLOGIST

It is for reasons such as the above that I am proposing the possibility that suicide could become the most preferred mode of death in our culture. This notion has been toyed with by others; it is too available a theme not to have been taken up and varied in imaginative literature. But a different chord may be struck when one person identified with death- and suicide-concern encounters the argument seriously presented by another. It may also be the case that the suicidologist is the person who will have the greatest difficulty in evaluating this possibility on its own merits. If much of one's time, energy, and emotions are given over to the prevention of suicide and other forms of self-destructive behavior, it can be perturbing to encounter the prediction that has been presented here. But the suicidologist might also use this as an opportunity to reevaluate his or her relationship to the phenomena of self-destruction.

Precisely what is it about suicide that has earned our enmity? Each person can work toward answering that question for himself. However, part of the answer could be that we object to facets of suicide that disturb us when they occur in any form of death. Did this suicide take us by surprise? We usually are upset when any death takes us by surprise. Was pain and suffering involved? Was it messy? Did the person die at the wrong time? Should a particular suicide involve several of these components we are likely to be perturbed, somewhat apart from the fact that the specific cause has been classified as self-initiated.

Let us take another moment to think about the wrong-time characteristic of some suicides. The time can be wrong because the victim–aggressor was too young (often defined in relationship to the observer's own age and certainly to his or her expectations). This is as much a commentary upon our own value system, linked with the prevailing value system of the culture, as anything else. Instead of automatically responding in one way to the death of the young and another to the death of the old, we might pause to examine the basis for this common distinction.[18] But the wrong time can also mean that we believed there was more that might have been done to prevent the fatal action, to help the individual through the crisis and on to a life-cherishing course. In this sense, the suicidologist's attitude brings him into line with the physician who is frustrated and upset when a patient dies before the treatment plan has exhausted its options. There was still another maneuver or two the physician might have used to keep this person alive, but death foreshortened this plan, perhaps through some secondary complication. We are left feeling mournful, helpless, and angered. The person did not have to die at that moment, but he did, and so deprived us of the opportunity to do what still might have been done on the side of life. An important dimension of the bad death, then, is the one in which we did not have full opportunity to influence for the better (either to circumvent death or improve the circumstances). It is very likely that our definitions of death are intimately related to what we can and will do in our practical encounters, whether with suicide or terminal illness.[5]

Should suicide become the preferred mode of death in our society, this would not necessarily mean that all suicides would be condoned, any more than it would mean that all medical practice would cease. Certain types of suicide would have high status and other suicidal attempts would still invoke negative sanctions. Suicidology would have two distinct aspects—a continuation of the present effort to understand, predict, and prevent self-destructive behavior, and a sensitive new approach designed to help people in certain circumstances attain the particular form of death recommended to them both by cultural idealizations and their own promptings. Should this come to pass, the challenges to suicidology would be, if anything, even greater than those we have already been facing.

REFERENCES

1. Tabachnick N (ed): Accident or Suicide? Springfield, Illinois, Charles C Thomas, 1973

2. Shneidman ES: Deaths of man. New York, Penguin, 1974
3. Gruman G: A history of ideas about the prolongation of life. Transactions of the American Philosophical Society. Philadelphia, American Philosophical Society, 1966
4. Kastenbaum R: On the future of death: Some images and options. Omega 3:306–318, 1972
5. Kastenbaum R, Aisenberg RB: The Psychology of Death. New York, Springer, 1972
6. Kastenbaum R: Multiple perspectives on a geriatric 'death valley'. Community Ment Health J 3:21–29, 1967
7. Shneidman ES: Suicide, lethality, and the psychological autopsy, in Shneidman ES, Ortega M (eds): Aspects of Depression. International Psychiatry Clinics, vol. 6, Boston, Little, Brown, 1969, pp 225–250
8. Weisman AD: The Realization of Death. New York, Jason Aronson, 1974
9. Sabatini P, Kastenbaum R: The do-it-yourself death certificate as a research technique. Life-Threatening Behavior 3:20–32, 1973
10. Weisman AD, Kastenbaum R: The Psychological Autopsy: A Study of the Terminal Phase of Life. New York Behavioral Publications, 1968
11. Glaser BG, Strauss AL: Time for Dying. Chicago; Aldine Atherton, 1968
12. Fletcher J: The patient's right to die. Harpers, 1960
13. Fletcher J: Morals and Medicine. Boston, Beacon Press, 1954
14. Maguire DC: Death by Choice. New York, Doubleday, 1974
15. US Senate Special Committee on Aging: Nursing Home care in the United States: Failure in public policy. Washington, D.C., US Government Printing Office, 1974 (Part 1), 1975 (Part 2)
16. Weisman AD: On Dying and Denying. New York, Behavioral Publications, 1972
17. Kubler-Ross E: On Death and Dying. New York, Macmillan, 1969
18. Kastenbaum R: Is death a life crisis? in Datan N, Ginsberg L (eds): Life Span Developmental Psychology: Normative Crises and Interventions. New York, Academic Press, 1976

PART VI

Responses to Suicide

Ari Kiev

15
Crisis Intervention and Suicide Prevention

The introduction piece to this chapter is the landmark piece, Symptomatology and Management of Acute Grief (1944) by Erich Lindemann, reproduced here with the kind permission of the *American Journal of Psychiatry.*

At first glance, acute grief would not seem to be a medical or psychiatric disorder in the strict sense of the word but rather a normal reaction to a distressing situation. However, the understanding of reactions to traumatic experiences whether or not they represent clear-cut neuroses has become of ever-increasing importance to the psychiatrist. Bereavement or the sudden cessation of social interaction seems to be of special interest because it is often cited among the alleged psychogenic factors in psychosomatic disorders. The enormous increase in grief reactions due to war casualties, furthermore, demands an evaluation of their probable effect on the mental and physical health of our population.

The points to be made in this paper are as follows:

1. Acute grief is a definite syndrome with psychological and somatic symptomatology.
2. This syndrome may appear immediately after a crisis; it may be delayed; it may be exaggerated or apparently absent.
3. In place of the typical syndrome there may appear distorted pictures, each of which represents one special aspect of the grief syndrome.
4. By appropriate techniques these distorted pictures can be successfully transformed into a normal grief reaction with resolution.

Our observations comprise 101 patients. Included are (1) psychoneurotic patients who lost a relative during the course of treatment, (2) relatives of patients who died in the hospital, (3) bereaved disaster victims (Cocoanut Grove Fire) and their close relatives, (4) relatives of members of the armed forces.

The investigation consisted of a series of psychiatric interviews. Both the timing and the content of the discussions were recorded. These records were subsequently analysed in terms of the symptoms reported and of the changes in mental status observed progressively through a series of interviews. The psychiatrist avoided all suggestions and interpretations until the picture of symptomatology and spontaneous reaction tendencies of the patients had become clear from the records. The somatic complaints offered important leads for objective study. Careful laboratory work on spirograms, g.-i. functions, and metabolic studies are in progress and will be reported separately. At present we wish to present only our psychological observations.

SYMPTOMATOLOGY OF NORMAL GRIEF

The picture shown by persons in acute grief is remarkably uniform. Common to all is the following syndrome: sensations of somatic distress occurring in waves lasting from twenty minutes to an hour at a time, a feeling of tightness in the throat, choking with shortness of breath, need for sighing, and an empty feeling in the abdomen, lack of muscular power, and an intense subjective distress described as tension or mental pain. The patient soon learns that these waves of discomfort can be precipitated by visits, by mentioning the deceased, and by receiving sympathy. There is a tendency to avoid the syndrome at any cost, to refuse visits lest they should precipitate the reaction, and to keep deliberately from thought all references to the deceased.

The striking features are (1) the marked tendency to sighing respiration; this respiratory disturbance was most conspicuous when the patient was made to discuss his grief. (2) The complaint about lack of strength and exhaustion is universal and is described as follows: "It is almost impossible to climb up a stairway." "Everything I lift seems so heavy." "The slightest effort makes me feel exhausted." "I can't walk to the corner without feeling exhausted." (3) Digestive symptoms are described as follows: "The food tastes like sand." "I have no appetite at all." "I stuff the food down because I have to eat." "My saliva won't flow." "My abdomen feels hollow." "Everything seems slowed up in my stomach."

The sensorium is generally somewhat altered. There is commonly a slight sense of unreality, a feeling of increased emotional distance from other people (sometimes they appear shadowy or small), and there is intense preoccupation with the image of the deceased. A patient who lost his daughter in the Cocoanut Grove disaster visualized his girl in the telephone booth calling for him and was much troubled by the loudness with which his name was called by her and was so vividly preoccupied with the scene that he became oblivious of his surroundings. A young navy pilot lost a close friend; he remained a vivid part of his imagery, not in terms of a religious survival but in terms of an imaginary companion. He ate with him and talked over problems with him, for instance, discussing with him his plan of joining the Air Corps. Up to the time of the study, six months later, he denied the fact that the boy was no longer with him. Some patients are much concerned about this aspect of their grief reaction because they feel it indicates approaching insanity.

Another strong preoccupation is with feelings of guilt. The bereaved searches the time before the death for evidence of failure to do right by the lost one. He accuses himself of negligence and exaggerates minor omissions. After the fire disaster the central topic of discussion for a young married woman was the fact that her husband died after he left her following a quarrel, and of a young man whose wife died when he fainted too soon to save her.

In addition, there is often disconcerting loss of warmth in relationship to other people, a tendency to respond with irritability and anger, a wish not to be bothered by others at a time when friends and relatives make a special effort to keep up friendly relationships.

These feelings of hostility, surprising and quite inexplicable to the patients, disturbed them and again were often taken as signs of approaching insanity. Great efforts are made to handle them, and the result is often a formalized, stiff manner of social interaction.

The activity throughout the day of the severely bereaved person shows remarkable changes. There is no retardation of action and speech; quite to the contrary, there is a push of speech, especially when talking about the deceased. There is restlessness, inability to sit still, moving about in an aimless fashion, continually searching for something to do. There is, however, at the same time a painful lack of capacity to initiate and maintain organized patterns of activity. What is done is done with lack of zest, as though one were going through the motions. The bereaved clings to the daily routine of prescribed activities; but these activities do not proceed in the automatic, self-sustaining fashion which characterizes normal work but have to be carried on with effort, as though each fragment of the activity became a special task. The bereaved is surprised to find how large a part of his customary activity was done in some meaningful relationship to the deceased and has now lost its significance. Especially the habits of social interaction—meeting friends, making conversation, sharing enterprises with others—seem to have been lost. This loss leads to a strong dependency on anyone who will stimulate the bereaved to activity and serve as the initiating agent.

These five points—(1) somatic distress, (2) preoccupation with the image of the deceased, (3) guilt, (4) hostile reactions, and (5) loss of patterns of conduct—seem to be pathognomonic for grief. There may be added a sixth characteristic, shown by patients who border on pathological reactions, which is not so conspicuous as the others but nevertheless often striking enough to color the whole picture. This is the appearance of traits of the deceased in the behavior of the bereaved, especially symptoms shown during the last illness, or behavior which may have been shown at the time of the tragedy. A bereaved person is observed or finds himself walking in the manner of his deceased father. He looks in the mirror and believes that his face appears just like that of the deceased. He did show a change of interests in the direction of the former activities of the deceased and may start enterprises entirely different from his former pursuits. A wife who lost her husband, an insurance agent, found herself writing to many insurance companies offering her services with somewhat exaggerated schemes. It seemed a regular observation in these patients that the painful preoccupation with the image of the decease described above was transformed into preoccupation with symptoms or personality traits of the lost person, but now displaced in their own bodies and activities by identification.

COURSE OF NORMAL GRIEF REACTIONS

The duration of a grief reaction seems to depend upon the success with which a person uses the *grief work*, namely emancipation from the bondage to the deceased, readjustment to the environment in which the deceased is missing, and the formation of new relationships. One of the big obstacles to this work seems to be the fact that many patients try to avoid the intense distress connected with the grief experience and to avoid the expression of emotion necessary in it. The men victims after the Cocoanut Grove fire appeared in the early psychiatric interviews to be in a state of tension with tightened facial musculature, unable to relax the fear they might "break down." It required considerable persuasion to yield to the grief process before they were willing to accept the discomfort of bereavement. One assumed a hostile attitude toward the psychiatrist, refusing to allow any references to the deceased and rather rudely asking him to leave. This attitude remained throughout his stay on the ward, and the prognosis of his condition is not good in the light of other observations. Hostility of this sort was encountered on only occasional visits with the other patients. They became willing to accept the grief process and to embark on a program of dealing in memory with the deceased person. As soon as this became possible there seemed to be a rapid relief of tension and the subsequent interviews were rather animated conversations in which the deceased was idealized and in which misgivings about the future adjustment were worked through. . . .

With eight to ten interviews in which the psychiatrist shares the grief work, and with a period of from four to six weeks, it was ordinarily possible to settle an uncomplicated and undistorted grief reaction. This was the case in all but one of the Cocoanut Grove fire victims.

MORBID GRIEF REACTIONS

Morbid grief reactions represent distortions of normal grief. The conditions mentioned here were transformed into "normal reactions" and then found their resolution.

a. *Delay of Reaction.*—The most striking and most frequent reaction of this sort is *delay* or *postponement*. If the bereavement occurs at a time when the patient is confronted with important tasks and when there is necessity for maintaining the morale of others, he may show little or no reaction for weeks or even much longer. . . .

That this delay may involve years became obvious first by the fact that patients in actual bereavement about a recent death may seem upon exploration be found preoccupied with grief about a person who died many years ago. In this manner a woman of 38, whose mother had died recently and who had responded to the mother's death with a surprisingly severe reaction, was found to be but mildly concerned with her mother's death but deeply engrossed with unhappy and perplexing fantasies concerning the death of her brother, who died twenty years ago under dramatic circumstances from metastasizing carcinoma after amputation of his arm had been postponed too long. The discovery that a former unresolved grief reaction may be precipitated in the course of the discussion of another recent event was soon demonstrated in psychiatric interviews by patient who showed all the traits of a true grief reaction when the topic of a former loss arose.

The precipitating factor for the delayed reaction may be a deliberate recall of circumstances surrounding the death or may be a spontaneous occurrence in the patient's life. A peculiar form of this is the circumstance that a patient develops the grief reaction at the time when he himself is as old as the person who died. For instance, a railroad worker, aged 42, appeared in the psychiatric clinic with a picture which was undoubtedly a grief reaction for which he had no explanation. It turned out that when he was 22 his mother, then 42, had committed suicide.

b. *Distorted Reactions.*—The delayed reactions may occur after an interval which was not marked by any abnormal behavior or distress, but in which there developed an *alteration* in the patient's *conduct* perhaps not conspicuous or serious enough to lead him to a psychiatrist. These alterations may be considered as the surface manifestations of an unresolved grief reaction, which may respond to fairly simple and quick psychiatric management if recognized. They may be classified as follows: (1) *overactivity without a sense of loss*, rather with a sense of wellbeing and zest, the activities being of an expansive and adventurous nature and bearing semblance to the activities formerly carried out by the deceased, as described above; (2) *the acquisition of symptoms belonging to the last illness of the deceased*. This type of patient appears in medical clinics and is often labelled hypochondriasis or hysteria. To what extent actual alterations of physiological functions occur under these circumstances will have to be a field of further careful inquiry. I owe to Dr. Chester Jones a report about a patient whose electrocardiogram showed a definite change during a period of three weeks, which started two weeks after the time her father died of heart disease.

While this sort of symptom formation "by identification" may still be considered as conversion symptoms such as we know from hysteria, there is another type of disorder doubtessly presenting (3) a recognized *medical disease*, namely, a group of psychosomatic conditions, predominantly ulcerative colitis, rheumatoid arthritis, and asthma. Extensive studies in ulcerative colitis have produced evidence that 33 out of 41 patients with ulcerative colitis developed their disease in close time relationship to the loss of an important person. Indeed, it was this observation which first gave the impetus for the present detailed study of grief. Two of the patients developed bloody diarrhea at funerals. In the others it developed within a few weeks after the loss. The course of the ulcerative colitis was strikingly benefited when this grief reaction was resolved by psychiatric technique.

At the level of social adjustment there often occurs a conspicuous (4) *alteration in relationship to friends and relatives*. The patient feels irritable, does not want to be bothered, avoids former social activities, and is afraid he might antagonize his friends by his lack of interest and his critical attitudes. Progressive social isolation follows, and the patient needs considerable encouragement in re-establishing his social relationships.

While overflowing hostility appears to be spread out over all relationships, it may also occur as (5) *furious hostility against specific persons;* the doctor or the surgeon are accused bitterly for neglect of duty and the patient may assume that foul play has led to the death. It is characteristic that while patients talk a good deal about their suspicions and their bitter feelings, they are not likely to take any action against the accused, as a truly paranoid person might do.

(6) Many bereaved persons struggled with much effort against these feelings of hostility, which to them seem absurd, representing a vicious change in their characters and to be hidden as much as possible. Some patients succeed in hiding their hostility but become wooden and formal, with affectivity and conduct *resembling schizophrenic pictures*. A typical report is this, "I go through all the motions of living. I look after my children. I do my errands. I go to social functions, but it is like being in a play; it doesn't really concern me. I can't have any warm feelings. If I were to have any feelings at all I would be angry with everybody." This patient's reaction to therapy was characterized by growing hostility against the therapist, and it required considerable skill to make her continue interviews in spite of the disconcerting hostility which she had been fighting so much. The absence of emotional display in this patient's face and actions was quite striking. Her face had a mask-like appearance, her movements were formal, stilted, robot-like, without the fine play of emotional expression.

(7) Closely related to this picture is a *lasting loss of patterns of social interaction*. The patient cannot initiate any activity, is full of eagerness to be active—restless, can't sleep—but throughout the day he wil not start any activity unless "primed" by somebody else. He will be grateful at sharing activities with others but will not be able to make up his mind to do anything alone. The picture is one of lack of decision and initiative. Organized activities along social lines occur only if a friend takes the patient along and shares the activity with him. Nothing seems to promise reward; only the ordinary activities of the day are carried on, and these in a routine manner, falling

apart into small steps, each of which has to be carried out with much effort and without zest.

(8) There is, in addition, a picture in which a patient is active but in which most of his activities attain a coloring which is *detrimental to his own social and economic existence.* Such patients with uncalled for generosity, give away their belongings, are easily lured into foolish economic dealings, lose their friends and professional standing by a series of "stupid acts," and find themselves finally without family, friends, social status or money. This protracted self-punitive behavior seems to take place without any awareness of excessive feelings of guilt. It is a particularly distressing grief picture because it is likely to hurt other members of the family and drag down friends and business associates.

(9) This leads finally to the picture in which the grief reaction takes the form of a straight *agitated depression* with tension, agitation, insomnia, feelings of worthlessness, bitter self-accusation, and obvious need for punishment. Such patients may be dangerously suicidal. . . .

It is remarkable that agitated depressions of this sort represent only a small fraction of the pictures of grief in our series.

PROGNOSTIC EVALUATION

Our observations indicate that to a certain extent the type and severity of the grief reaction can be predicted. Patients with obsessive personality make-up and with a history of former depressions are likely to develop an agitated depression. Severe reactions seem to occur in mothers who have lost young children. The intensity of interaction with the deceased before his death seems to be significant. It is important to realize that such interaction does not have to be of the affectionate type; on the contrary, the death of a person who invited much hostility, especially hostility which could not well be expressed because of his status and claim to loyalty, may be followed by a severe grief reaction in which hostile impulses are the most conspicuous feature. Not infrequently the person who passed away represented a key person in a social system, his death being followed by disintegration of this social system and by a profound alteration of the living and social conditions for the bereaved. In such cases readjustment presents a severe task quite apart from the reaction to the loss incurred. All these factors seem to be more important than a tendency to react with neurotic symptoms in previous life. In this way the most conspicuous forms of morbid identification were found in persons who had no former history of a tendency to psychoneurotic reactions.

MANAGEMENT

Proper psychiatric management of grief reactions may prevent prolonged and serious alterations in the patient's social adjustment, as well as potential medical disease. The essential task facing the psychiatrist is that of sharing the patient's grief work, namely, his efforts at extricating himself from the bondage to the deceased and at finding new patterns of rewarding interaction. It is of the greatest importance to notice that not only over-reaction but under-reaction of the bereaved must be given attention, because delayed responses may occur at unpredictable moments and the dangerous distortions of the grief reaction, not conspicuous at first, be quite destructive later and these may be prevented.

Religious agencies have led in dealing with the bereaved. They have provided comfort by giving the backing of dogma to the patient's wish for continued interaction with the deceased, have developed rituals which maintain the patient's interaction with others, and have counteracted the morbid guilt feelings of the patient by Divine Grace and by promising an opportunity for "making up" to the deceased at the time of a later reunion. While these measures have helped countless mourners, comfort alone does not provide adequate assistance in the patient's grief work. He has to accept the pain of the bereavement. He has to review his relationships with the deceased, and has to become acquainted with the alterations in his own modes of emotional reaction. His fear of insanity, his fear of accepting the surprising changes in his feelings, especially the overflow of hostility, have to be worked through. He will have to express his sorrow and sense of loss. He will have to find an acceptable formulation of his future relationship to the deceased. He will have to verbalize his feelings of guilt, and he will have to find persons around him whom he can use as "primers" for the acquisition of new patterns of conduct. All this can be done in eight to ten interviews . . .

Since it is obvious that not all bereaved persons, especially those suffering because of war casualties, can have the benefit of expert psychiatric help, much of this knowledge will have to be passed on to auxiliary workers. Social workers and ministers will have to be on the look-out for the more ominous pictures, rerring these to the psychiatrist while assisting the more normal reactions themselves.

ANTICIPATORY GRIEF REACTIONS

While our studies were at first limited to reactions to actual death, it must be understood that grief reactions are just one form of separation reactions. Separation by death is characterized by its irreversibility and finality. Separation may, of course, occur for other reasons. We were at first surprised to find genuine grief reactions in patients who had not experienced a bereavement but who had experienced separation, for instance with the departure of a member of the family into the armed forces. Separation in this case is not due to death but is under the threat of death. A common picture hitherto not appreciated is a syndrome which we have designated *anticipatory grief*. The patient is so concerned with her adjustment after the potential death of father or son that she goes through all the phases of grief—depression, heightened preoccupation with the departed, a review of all the forms of death which might befall him, and anticipation of the modes of readjustment which might be necessitated by it. While this reaction may well form a safeguard against the impact of a sudden death notice, it can turn out to be of a disadvantage at the occasion of reunion. Several instances of this sort came to our attention when a soldier just returned from the battlefront complained that his wife did not love him anymore and demanded immediate divorce. In such situations apprently the grief work had been done so effectively that the patient has emancipated herself and the readjustment must now be directed towards new interaction. It is important to know this because many family disasters of this sort may be avoided through prophylactic measures.

Crisis Intervention and Suicide Prevention

INTRODUCTION

Despite the availability of potent antidepressant medications, a humanitarian approach to psychiatric disorder, and an increased number of people in the public-aid professions, the suicide rate has not changed significantly in the past 15 years and there is no reason to assume that the rate of suicide attempts has declined.

The number of completed suicides in the United States is estimated at approximately 20,000 to 40,000 annually without counting indirect forms of self-destruction resulting from auto accidents, industrial accidents, narcotic addiction, and chronic alcoholism. It is the second most common cause of death in the college-age population and the most common cause of death among young black women and American Indian youths, and is gradually becoming more and more prominent as a major cause of death among teenagers and young adults.

Suicide risk is considerable in the elderly, the alcoholic, those with suicidal histories, and those with severe psychiatric disorders. The availability of lethal weapons, contact with others who have made attempts, and recent major catastrophic stresses also increase suicide risk.

The magnitude of suicidal behavior is such as to constitute a major health problem. Except for the fluctuations during the Depression and world wars, the suicide rate has remained rather stable in this country. It has been the 12th most common cause of death since

1950. Since 1900, this rate has ranged from 18.4 per 100,000 in 1932 to a low of 9.8 per 100,000 in 1957.

The persistence of a similar rate over time is particularly striking in view of the major advances in psychiatry which have occurred in the past 15 years, especially the advent of the psychotropic drugs, the development of open-door hospitals, and the resurgence of interest in community psychiatry.

Perhaps the most critical factors leading to suicide are not sufficiently identified so that even when intervention occurs, little impact is made on prognosis. This is most dramatically illustrated by the fact that patients who have made suicide attempts and entered into treatment still have the highest suicide rates of any specific patient grouping. Perhaps the critical variables are not really approached in treatment or in prevention programs, in part because of the stigma associated with suicide and because of the turmoil associated with the suicidal episode, such that when the patient settles down and has passed the peak of crisis, there is a tendency to think that the risk has passed.

Elsewhere I have considered some of the myopic tendencies of existing programs and the need for expanding into new areas of activity, so as to reach larger segments of the high risk population by the development of outreach programs and the like.

Many people, by virtue of their social class membership or life situation have ready-made explanations for their distress and as such, may not seek appropriate help and may for this reason be considered at high risk. One such group is the patients who attempt suicide, are evaluated as non-serious and summarily discharged from emergency rooms without any provision made for followup. Suicidal patients must be adequately treated and their families counseled as to the significance of the act even when it appears to be of low risk. The first 3 months following an attempt is the greatest risk period, since improvement may mean that the individual has the energy to put his morbid thoughts and feelings into effect.

Additional vulnerable groups outside the treatment network include college students, Indians on reservations, blacks in ghettoes, and the elderly, all of whom are often inclined to attribute their distress to their life circumstances. Each group requires different therapeutic and support systems as well as different types of environmental modification. Techniques must be developed to approach these population groups with specific educational efforts which will enlighten them to the manifestations of treatable psychiatric conditions. More investigation of specific factors and recurrent stresses for these groups will aid these efforts. More specific knowledge of these different subcultures will facilitate the development of plans to deliver appropriate care.

EVALUATING SUICIDAL POTENTIAL

The depressed suicidal patient, not unlike many other types of psychiatric patients, is overwhelmed by feelings of despair, fear, and uncertainty. His usual methods of coping having failed; he is plagued by thoughts of guilt and overwhelming anxiety sometimes masked by lethargy. His judgment and reality-testing may be poor and he may be trying to meet his responsibilities with decreasing efficiency and success. Suicide, if considered at all, is usually viewed as a way out or as an end to suffering rather than as a clear decision to die.

Immediately after an attempt, the patient's resources are mobilized, and he often appears healthier than he really is. The rationale he presents of the causal factors leading to the attempt frequently leads the attending physician or nearest relative to conclude that the attempt was primarily motivated to elicit sympathy and/or attention. This attitude most probably accounts for the pattern of rapidly discharging patients from hospital emergency rooms after treating the physical results of the attempt. The probability of a subsequent, more dangerous attempt is highest under such conditons when the patient remains depressed or involved in relatively unchanged life circumstances.

There is a crucial need in crisis-intervention work to develop a means for intervening in the critical areas of patient's life so as to actually prevent recurrent episodes—identify recurrent factors, assist the patient to cope with subsequent stresses and not to be caught up by crisis itself, or allow it to calm down so that the previous situation reestablishes itself. The issues have been resolved when in fact it is at that moment that intervention should really begin. Right from the outset one must delineate those factors which may be modified so as to improve prognosis when the patient returns to his home and old situation. Attention must be paid to such general questions as the difference between patients in terms of the most critical variables affecting their suicidal behavior, be it diagnosis, life situation, whatever. In particular it is crucial to identify social factors which influence outcome and which should be more carefully assessed for possible ways of intervening at the time of admission along with the assessment of maladaptive patterns and clinical psychopathological phenomena.

The Role of Social Factors in the Causation of Psychiatric Disorders

The stresses of life associated with changes in the life cycle such as adolescence, menopause and increasing age, the adjustment to new life situations such as marriage, death of a loved one, graduation from school, retirement, or the onset of a new career may complicate psychiatric illnesses because of the extra demands they place on people. However, to the extent that such experiences are used to rationalize the presence of symptoms, they may lead to the failure to recognize a treatable illness. For this reason, it is important to distinguish between natural life stresses and symptoms of emotional illness. Even if one ought to feel depressed because of a dreadful experience, adequate treatment can strengthen the individual's capacity to cope.

The Onset of Psychiatric Illness

Most persons, particularly in this society, tend to blame themselves or circumstances for these symptoms, consequently they do not or cannot recognize them as early signs of psychiatric illness. Family, friends, colleagues, or the ill person himself are much more apt to feel that the symptoms are due to lack of will power, laziness, inadequacy, or personal failure. Less puritanical unlookers may blame the pressures of work, school, or family stresses. Loneliness, isolation, or recent stressful experiences are even more acceptable explanations for symptoms, at least less moral blame seems to be attached to them. But numerous studies have begun to suggest that symptoms first develop as a result of as yet unspecified physiological or biochemical changes in the nervous system. According to this view, interpersonal and psychological difficulties then follow the development of the symptoms. Furthermore, old problems tend to be magnified and handled less effectively when someone is already emotionally ill. If the symptoms are successfully treated and relieved, however, the problems that seemed so overwhelming are reduced in magnitude, and the patient regains the ability to cope as well as he was able to before the onset of the illness.

Sick Role

While the assessment of psychiatric symptoms constitutes an accepted phase in the evaluation of suicide potential, the social and psychological responses to symptoms and the juxtaposition of symptoms in relationship to other variables must also be assessed in determining what specific treatment is indicated, the likelihood of treatment being accepted, and the possibility of support or sabotage by the relevant people in the patient's social world.

The patient's acceptance of treatment obviously has crucial significance for prognosis. Prognosis is guarded to the extent that a negative attitude towards treatment, a tendency to attribute psychological problems and distress to external circumstances which cannot be controlled or to specific events which have passed, reduces the likelihood that a patient will accept treatment. This is particularly true in patients who have attempted suicide but express unwillingness to accept the notion that they have a problem and require treatment.

Some patients who refuse to assume the sick role improve simply because of the passage of time. But others, not accepting the fact of their illness or problem and incorrectly attributing depressive symptoms to lack of will power, may put themselves under tremendous pressure to continue working, and to the extent that they are symptomatic, may continue to experience excessive guilt over failure to perform up to par and at times, additional pressure from significant others who also do not recognize his need for treatment. All this increases suicide risk.

Further substantiation of the concept of the sick role resulted from analyses which showed that the patient's concept of his illness correlated with the duration of treatment contact. Patients who denied the presence of illness or who attributed it to personal weakness remained in treatment for a shorter duration of time than patients who acknowledged the presence of illness.

Some Causes Leading People To Attempt Suicide

Why do people attempt suicide? There can be a chain of reasons. A person experiencing the inner distress of emotional illness without recognizing that it is an illness that requires treatment like pneumonia or flu is apt to find it almost impossible to explain what is happening to him or to explain his inability to perform. If he attempts to control the symptoms or makes a greater effort and still fails, his sense of guilt and despair will increase. Added to his own feelings of self-blame may be the judgments of others in his immediate environment who, not recognizing his real distress or the fact that his disturbances in sleep, appetite, energy, and drive are out of his control, may either criticize him or minimize his distress. The may insist that there is no real cause for his feelings and urge him to force himself to work and enjoy things. This kind of advice, well-meant as it may be, will only deepen the ill person's sense of helplessness and guilt. He may develop a pressing need to escape from both his own feelings and the additional guilt of being a burden to others. It is true that most people want to live, but not in a state of crippling distress. The tension that precedes the actual suicide attempt turns minutes into hours and days into unending nights; it so alters the person's capacity for rational judgment that he cannot even imagine that this tension state is really brief and self-limited.

Efforts to Get Relief

The person suffering from these symptoms may try in many ways to get some relief. He may use tranquilizers, either prescribed or purchased over the counter, to reduce his anxiety and tension. He may get barbiturates or non-prescription sleeping pills to combat insomnia, and energy tonics for temporary and partial relief, but these stop-gap remedies can in the end be harmful if the underlying psychiatric illness is not recognized and treated. Some persons will search for new meanings to life or security through religion or philosophical movements; again, what for one person would be a rich, enlarging experience can, to the unrecognized psychiatric patient, be a potentially harmful experience, because the search has been motivated by an illness which will not be cured by these otherwise normal activities. When the search does not bring the longed-for relief, despair may deepen. Still others turn to excessive alcohol, or experiment with LSD or other potent, dangerous, and sometimes addicting drugs which not only bring no relief, but can lead to secondary complications more serious than the original illness.

The Early Recognition and Treatment of Potentially Suicidal Persons

Practitioners in psychiatry and related fields have focused much effort on developing techniques for the early recognition and treatment of psychiatric illness, commonly known as mental disturbances or emotional disorders. Certain basic principles have emerged from this work, knowledge of which may help clients, their families, and others to cope more effectively and less fearfully with psychiatric illness.

Difficulty in Recognizing Psychiatric Illness

It is often difficult for people to recognize that they are in fact suffering from an abnormality of mood, thought, or behavior. The subjective experiences of normal life events may be so similar to the subjective experiences of emotional disorder that it is difficult for an individual to perceive any difference between the two. Some of the clients who visit therapists have been suffering from various symptoms for considerable periods of time, but the symptoms are so common in everyday life experience that they were not recognized as clinically treatable problems. People look for help only when they begin to find it difficult to function.

Even today, thousands of people associate psychiatric illness with the notion of someone going stark raving mad or having a nervous breakdown and being placed in a hospital (usually conceived of as a snakepit) in order to protect society from potential violence. This is a grossly unrealistic picture of psychiatric illness. Most psychiatric illnesses are temporary and self-limiting and do not become apparent even to the close, untrained onlooker except when he sees the person's social abilities and work performance decline.

The early symptoms of mental illness include very common experiences—difficulty in falling asleep, restless sleep, early morning awakening, loss of appetite or compulsive overeating (with resultant weight gain), or feeling blue or down in the dumps. The person, or his family, may blame noisy streets, a heavy dinner, fatigue, or work worries for such sleep difficulties and brush them off as temporary and unimportant. Loss of appetite, sudden distaste for food, and loss of weight may go unnoticed or be rationalized as the result of a change in diet, a desire to lose weight, or gastric indigestion. The person's energy may drop so that simple, routine tasks become burdensome or even impossible; he may find it slowly and progressively more difficult to concentrate, lose interest in work and hobbies, find that his sexual drive has dropped off and he may become preoccupied with morbid thoughts, excessive worry, anxiety, fears, and pessimism coupled with guilt over being unable to perform or feel joy and other emotions. Sometimes the ill person will perceive the environment inaccurately and decide that coworkers or family and friends are either unsympathetic or actively hostile to him. He may find reasons to blame outside forces for the distress he feels. One of the difficulties in recognizing such a condition as a psychiatric illness is that the rationalizations sound quite plausible; he might indeed be under genuine stresses that would disturb anyone to some degree. As a matter of fact, it is precisely the degree that determines the line between normal reaction to stress and the onset of a psychiatric condition.

Other individuals may find their thinking markedly disturbed, so that they cannot adequately express ideas or they misunderstand the ideas of others. They may then react by withdrawing from ordinary life experiences rather than suffer the strain caused by attempting to function.

To the extent that many of these symptoms can be temporary exaggerations of normal experiences, they often go unrecognized as the early signs of mental illness.

Characteristics of Previous Attempt

The gravity of a suicidal intent, the dangerousness of the attempt, the efforts made by the patient to prevent assistance from appearing on the scene, the presence of precipitating stresses, the use of alcohol and other factors must be weighed in evaluating risk of a subsequent attempt. The seriousness of a previous attempt is an indicator of the patient's disturbance, as well as the patient's capacity to act impulsively and self-destructively.

Impulsivity

The degree of impulsivity underscores the patient's capacity to act impulsively in a self-destructive way should the various events and circumstances such as stresses and illness be present at a later date. In our own experiences, patients with the highest scores on impulsivity have the poorest outcome. Seriousness of method employed in a previous attempt has some prognostic significance with those choosing irreversible methods having the poorest prognosis.

Method of Attempt

Individuals who attempt suicide in the presence of others, do not take a sufficient quantity to produce coma, or call for help after the attempt have better prognoses than those who isolate themselves from the world, take precautions not to be discovered, or are accidentally discovered. Alcohol contributes to suicidal risk because of its synergistic interaction with drugs and its disinhibitory effects.

Repeated Attempts

The 300 patients in our series made repeated attempts, which ranged from gestures to dangerous attempts ending in coma, and in several instances, death. Repeated sub-intentioned overdoses resulting in hospitalization were the most common pattern. Unsuccessful resolution of turbulent life situations, denial of suicidal intent, and treatment refusal were common background factors. These patients also demonstrated a tendency to explosive emotional outbursts lasting several minutes to hours and associated with impairments of reality-testing ability. These states, often provoked by interpersonal conflict, generated intense urges to escape the situation, eliminate the tension or uncomfortable emotional state, or strike out at others by harming themselves.

A physical illness often served as the precipitant for the elderly who lacked supportive social groups. Those who were integrated into social groups often experienced excessive guilt over failure to live up to the group's expectations.

The majority of repeated attempts occurred shortly after entry into treatment in patients who remained symptomatically distressed or involved in the same life circumstances which had led to the attempt which brought them to our attention. The predisposition to repeated attempts often increased as a result of the negative attitudes of others toward the patient's behavior. Delusional thought often induced fear and revulsion in others, while withdrawal induced anger and guilt, and manipulativeness induced resentment.

Evaluating Significant Others

Our own clinical studies have pointed to the relevance of such variables as interpersonal conflict, social isolation, and major life changes as contributing to suicidal risk. In our study of suicide attempts, we have determined that the social world of the patient, specifically his relationships, plays a far more critical role in the subsequent clinical course than does diagnosis or the severity of the patient's psychiatric condition. For both depressed and attempted suicide patients, the attitudes of significant others as to the presence or absence of a treatable illness and the recognition of the fact that the patient was isolated and not functioning, were important aspects of the outcome.

In the depressed control group, a better prognosis was associated with concerned relatives who were calm and not panicked in the face of increased symptoms and suicidal thoughts and who recognized the need for professional care. Prognosis was unfavorable where there were few symptoms, conflicts, the denial model of the sick role was selected, and panic and confusion occurred despite recognition of isolation and nonfunctioning.

Low scores on the significant others factor in the attempted suicide group correlated with unfavorable clinical outcome at the end of one year. The responses of significant others predicted all outcomes except for major changes in the attempt group. Low scores on the significant others factor correlated with increased conflict, hospitalization, subsequent attempts, and increased symptomatology. In fact, the results of this analysis tend to substantiate the importance of the role of attitudes toward illness both of the patient and significant others in both attempts and depressed controls. However, the attitudes of significant others proved to be the major prognostic factor in the attempt group. Indeed this variable predicted all outcomes, except for major changes. In the depressed group, the attitudes of significant others also proved to have prognostic significance although other variables also proved to be significant as well in predicting one year outcome. Clinically, expressions of distress about symptoms, excessive concern of significant others, and interpersonal conflict correlated with subsequent suicide attempts, hospitalization and the recurrence of symptoms. One must pay special attention to the quiet patients who slip past the attention of significant others by virtue of their relatively low profile or reduced social impact.

The data emphasize the importance of consulting with significant others at the time of admission or first contact with suicidal or potentially suicidal individuals. They emphasize the importance of considering the long-term relationship and attitudes toward the patient rather than considering the nature of the immediate responses which are often highly conditioned by the anxiety of the moment following the suicide attempt. The data make a strong case for the value of crisis intervention efforts at the time of the attempt and the importance of engaging significant others in the therapeutic process, so as to assist them in developing constructive attitudes and approaches to the patient.

Where negative attitudes once prevailed, they are likely to reappear once the immediate crisis is over unless appropriate intervention is introduced. While more work remains to determine which attitudes can and should be modified and the ways in which this might be done, special emphasis should be attached to attitudes about the sick role.

IDENTIFYING LIFE STRESSES

A variety of changes in the patient's illness, life situation, and attitude to treatment occur prior to and following an attempt. Some patients face custody fights, divorce proceedings, and unemployment. Others encounter prejudice and feel stigmatized. Explaining new relationships to children and friends proves stressful for many.

Some patients discover the secondary gains of being treated as sick and continue to remain dependent. Some friends and relatives of patients compete with the therapist of therapeutic team, challenging the value of the medicine or criticizing the patient's efforts to improve. This creates confusion and obstructs the development of feasible objectives and goals.

Patients who cannot limit the demands of others often feel guilty about suicidal thoughts or behavior. Resentment and hostility develop from this, creating more guilt and the generation of new crises. Significant others sometimes respond to independence strivings with oppressiveness.

Some patients create crises by threatening suicide and involving others in their experience. Knowing only part of the story, such friends often act at cross purposes, adding more turbulence to the situation. The anxiety and undisciplined response of others in turn reinforce the patient's passive dependency and manipulativeness and give some patients who fail to realize their own role in the crisis, a feeling of being victimized.

Persisting social and environmental problems also create significant stress. Inadequate or noxious social relationships contribute to the patient's demoralization, sense of worthlessness, and conviction of suicide as a valid release from distress.

Increased isolation and the disruption of interpersonal relationships commonly occur in the lives of patients, making the assumption of personal responsibility more of a burden than a challenge. Where a suicide attempt results from a loss of significant relationships, as in the death of a loved one, the post-attempt period is often very stressful, although some patients are challenged by new circumstances to become independent and self-reliant.

Highly dependent individuals tolerate bereavement much worse than independent and resourceful individuals. The elderly often need the assistance of social services, particularly when they have built their life around a spouse. Serious physical illness and fewer social roles in the older age groups reduce flexibility and adaptability and are likely to persist after an attempt, thus contributing to the continued suicidal risk of elderly patients.

The patient's behavior subsequent to attempt intensifies social stress and keeps the patient at high risk. In this sense, chronic persistent stresses create more serious management problems than do discrete episodes of objective stress which do not persist. Persisting noxious relationships is perhaps the most troublesome type of stress that sometimes necessitate hospitalization to protect the patient.

Maladaptive patient patterns include excessive confessions to others, efforts to amend for past wrongdoings, and failure to pursue self-interest and involvement in complicated relationships. An increase in risk-taking behavior, alcohol abuse, or drug abuse often reflect a deflection of self-destructive trends into less obvious forms.

Reality factors such as job pressures and housing shortages add extra burdens to the recovering individual. Important parameters of employment status include length of employment, frequency, and regularity of unemployment and discrepancies between educational level and job status. Unemployment contributes to insecurity as do highly responsible jobs or ones which restricted autonomous activity. Unemployment frequently coincides with downward social and residential mobility, advancing age, and changing attitudes of young people toward work, all of which may indirectly contribute to suicidal risk.

Those outside the usual network of friendships and relationships such as the isolated, the alcoholic, the elderly, and the chronically ill, experience considerable stress. Social and environmental factors influence whether patients enter into treatment, and/or encounter acute conflicts. Depressed patients experienced more objective stress in their lives but enjoyed better relationships than patients diagnosed as having psychotic or character disorders, the latter experiencing more interpersonal conflict than the other diagnostic groups. Interpersonal conflict creates more stress for younger patients than older ones, whose relationships often seem more stabilized. The stresses predominating in the older age groups include the death of loved ones, physical illness, physical handicaps, and employment problems.

Difficult interpersonal relationships with significant others also prove stressful for many, and must be assessed. Sympathetic at first, relatives often become unsympathetic, rejecting and negativistic when their efforts fail to obtain favorable responses from the patient.

The parameters of relationships that can be clinically assessed include number, duration, activities, sentiments, values, and rules or characteristic patterns of the relationships. These parameters reflect stability, dependency, and intensity of involvement in the relationship.

Changes in personality and in the role assumed subsequent to an attempt occasionally lead to shifts in the environment and new pressures that often precipitate new crises. Significant others, willing to allow others to take responsibility for the patient's welfare, sometimes reduce their own efforts which the patient interprets as rejection. Some patients improve to a better level of functioning than prior to their illness, others regress, fearful of being stigmatized or of losing control of themselves. Still others marry, divorce, leave home, or make other major changes in their lives. Difficulties persist when such decisions are viewed as solutions to unresolved problems. The requirements of new living situations tax the patient's adaptive resources, especially if others deny the validity of the patient's illness and emphasize the need for more assertions of will power.

Scapegoating and threats of rehospitalization by significant others occur most often in relation to the patient's independence strivings. Excessive protectiveness may be manifested in efforts to check up on the patient or discourage healthy activity. Such protectiveness blends into partial infantilism as in efforts to screen the patient's mail (this generated explosive rifts and often led to hospitalization), or as in one case, the creation of an institutional setting at home by the inclusion or 'round the clock baby-sitters. Increased reliance on social agencies also creates feelings in inadequacy, excessive dependency, and resentment in patients.

Some pathological relationships appear innocent enough on the surface. Patients may become over involved with parents who believe themselves to be dutiful and respectful. Such parents continually seek reassurance and demand regular telephone calls, visits, and favors from the patient, with little regard for the patient's neglect of his or her life. Such parents expect to be consulted on all decisions and rationalize their instructions as a willingness to help which could not be rejected. They find a host of reasons for almost continual interaction, continually pressuring the patient to confide all personal matters.

Changes in the patient's behavior often lead to manipulative responses in significant others, who often mistakenly interpret these changes as evidence of disturbance. The patient's rights and the significant other's obligations have to be clarified continually so that the family can learn to interact in a healthy way. Relatives, anxious for the patient's difficulties to pass, often press patients to improve, function better at their job, or to return to school prematurely, failing to realize the undue burden of such expectations to the patient. Some angry spouses doubt the desirability of treatment, and make efforts to undermine the patient's faith in the value of treatment. Inappropriate expectations also undermine the patient's self-confidence. Some parents unwittingly encourage others to adopt infantile attitudes towards the patient by focusing on his helplessness, not on his performance. Such patients soon learn not to take the initiative. Checking out plans with others fosters dependency and an uncertainty about capabilities.

TREATMENT OF DEPRESSION

Unrecognized and untreated depressive illness all too often leads to suicide, or at least attempted suicide. Anxiety, agitation, apprehension, and a pervasive feeling of worthlessness are the components of a depressive illness that may drive the patient to attempt to take his or her own life. Recent efforts to cope with this major public health problem have led to the development of various suicide prevention programs, relying heavily on emergency telephone hot lines, brief psychotherapeutic techniques, patient-led groups, as well as the development of comprehensive crisis intervention clinics.

As much as such programs may have ameliorative effects on the life crises which may have precipitated the suicide attempt, by themselves they rarely have significant effects in reducing the distressing symptomatology that characterizes depressive reactions, regardless of whether they result from tangible environmental factors or develop as psychobiological responses to nonspecific life stresses. For symptomatic relief and rapid reduction of suicide potential, more specific measures, such as effective psychopharmaceuticals are indicated.

The antidepressant drugs available today, principally the tricyclics, have proven useful in controlling the specific target symptoms of depressive illness in a rapid, economical, and relatively simple fashion. Antidepressant medication is especially useful for relieving insomnia, loss of appetite, lack of energy, depressed mood, hypochondriasis, reduced sexual drive, and feelings of emotional emptiness when these are part of the depressive state.

In our experience at the suicide prevention clinic of the Cornell Program of Social Psychiatry in New York City, one important finding related to drug therapy has been that the risk of suicide is greatest when a period of improvement occurs before the end of a discrete period of depression. This is so because depression is a cyclic entity. For this reason, the antidepressant medication employed should provide not only prompt, but sustained symptomatic relief until the patient has returned to his to her premorbid status.

To substantiate the value of chemotherapy as part of an overall approach to treating potentially suicidal patients, we undertook a double-blind placebo-controlled study which demonstrated that doxepin and amitriptyline were significantly better than placebo in the treatment of neurotic depression among adult outpatients attending the clinic.

Method and Materials

This double-blind placebo-controlled study involved 89 adult outpatients attending our clinic. The study design called for all patients to have a working diagnosis of neurotic depression based on the criteria set forth in the Diagnostic and Statistical Manual of Mental

Table 15-1
Changes in Hamilton Depression Scale (Total Score)
Baseline to Final

Group	Total Patients Evaluated	Baseline Score	Final Score	Difference	% Improvement
Amitriptyline	25	24.96	14.92	10.04	40
Doxepin	26	24.12	11.92	12.19	51
Placebo	19	23.26	16.79	6.47	28

Disorders (DSM-II) of the American Psychiatric Association, and to exhibit manifest signs of depression as determined by clinical evaluation.

In all, 79 percent (22 of 28) of the patients in the doxepin group and 63 percent (19 of 30) of the patients in the amitriptyline group showed improvement relative to baseline versus 54 percent (15 of 28) of the patients in the placebo group. The difference in percentage between the doxepin group and the placebo group is statistically significant.

Hamilton Depression Scale

Table 15-1 shows the results for the three therapeutic modalities in total Hamilton Depression Scale scores, baseline versus final. The difference in score from baseline to final was statistically significant at the p. $< .05$ level for both the doxepin and amitriptyline groups, but not for the placebo group.

Analysis of change from baseline to final for Factor 1 (general depression) on the Hamilton Scale revealed significant improvement at the $p < .05$ level for both the doxepin and amitriptyline groups, but not for the placebo group (see Table 15-2).

Table 15-2
Change in Factor 1 (General Depression) Hamilton
Depression Scale Baseline to Final

Group	Total Patients Evaluated	Baseline Score	Final Score	Difference	% Improvement
Amitriptyline	25	11.48	7.09	4.39	33
Doxepin	26	12.10	5.94	6.16	51
Placebo	19	10.31	7.09	3.22	31

Maximum versus Final Improvement

A measure of the efficacy of the active medications employed was also provided via a comparison of the maximum improvement observed over the course of the study versus the improvement observed at the termination of therapy. Among the placebo group, this difference (the magnitude of relapse) was significant ($p < .05$) for 3 of the 4 measures utilizing the Hamilton Depression Scale: total score, Factor

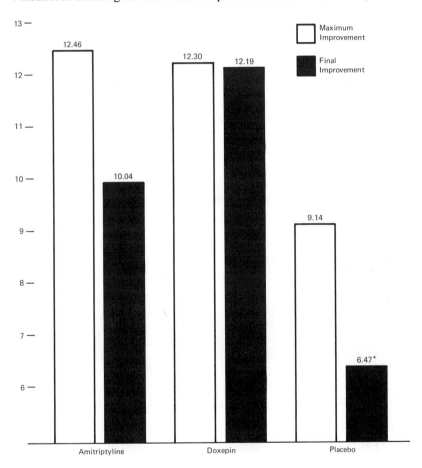

*The final score was significantly lower ($p<0.05$) than that observed at point of maximal improvement.

The statistical method employed to determine significance was a two-sample test.

Fig. 15-1. Hamilton Depression Rating Scale—maximum improvement versus final improvement.

2 and the anxiety component of Factor 2. Among the patients receiving active medication, the degree of improvement appears to have been sustained throughout the duration of the therapy (see Fig. 15-1).

It is interesting to note that the time required to reach maximum improvement, 3-1/2 weeks, was the same for all 3 groups.

Medicine must be taken in adequate doses for a reasonable period of time. Some of the medicines require 10 days to 3 weeks to reach an effective level in the body; to stop taking a medicine because it does not work immediately is a serious mistake. Side effects such as perspiration, dry mouth, constipation, sluggishness, dizziness, and blurring of vision may occur occasionally in the initial stages, but they are usually temporary. They are no cause for alarm, but they should be reported to the doctor who will adjust the dosage if he feels it necessary. In no case should the patient stop taking the medicine without consulting his doctor, nor should he take medicines the doctor has not prescribed. Uncontrolled use of sleeping medications, tranquilizers, or stimulants such as dexedrine is potentially harmful and may complicate an unrecognized illness.

Do's and Don'ts for Patients on Medicine

DO'S
1. The patient, his family, and friends must recognize the importance of obtaining treatment for a diagnosed illness.
2. Report all symptoms to your physician. Any change of mood, appetite, sleep pattern, drive, energy, concentration, etc.
3. Follow the doctor's advice.
4. Report all side effects from medicine.
5. Keep a record of all medication taken. Should it be necessary to take other medicines, undergo surgery or dentistry, or be fitted for eye glasses, these records will ensure that undesirable mixtures will not be prescribed and the source of side effects will be understood.

DON'TS
1. Don't stop medicine unless specifically directed to do so by the doctor.
2. Don't decrease or increase a medicine except at the doctor's direction.
3. Don't use any form of alcohol which may produce undesirable side effects and/or complications and which may diminish the effectiveness of the medicine. Certain foods must be avoided

when taking some types of antidepressant medicine. It is important to follow the recommendations of the doctor who will advise you on this.

4. Don't take on unnecessary burdens while in treatment until it is apparent that you are definitely ready to do so.

5. Don't take responsibility for the illness. The patient's only responsibility is to recognize the illness, obtain competent professional help, and cooperate with the doctor or others on the medical team. This is especially important for those who feel that they have caused their illness and are beyond help.

6. Avoid any major life change until you discuss this with the doctor, who may be better able to objectively assess the decision in relationship to the illness.

The magnitude and intensity of social and psychological problems and conflicts generally decrease as the patient's symptoms are relieved and he is restored to his normal emotional state. It is much easier to assess his problems at this stage. Difficulties on the job, at home, or in interpersonal relationships produce much guilt and may seem insoluble and overwhelming to the patient; nevertheless, as the patient improves they may disappear, become completely manageable, or be reduced to just one problem area.

Still, efforts are made to alter any environmental circumstances that are clearly contributing to the person's illness. The frequency of visits to the therapist is based upon the extent of the person's distress and need for support during crisis periods. Sometimes it is desirable to see the patient every day if only for brief periods. At other times, it is enough to maintain telephone contact with the patient during crisis periods. For most patients a weekly visit over a period of 1 or 2 months will carry them through until their distress is sufficiently relieved so that they are coping adequately again.

Personality changes do not come about in the therapy session, but in real life situations, particularly when patients are able to experiment with new ways of being and behaving. This is particularly true for those individuals with chronic difficulties in adjustment and getting along. For this reason, treatment moves most rapidly when patients can focus on concrete problems in work, at home, or in interpersonal relationships, for these areas offer the greatest opportunity for trying out new ways of dealing with others, which can in turn lead to new attitudes and greater opportunities for self-realization.

The therapists act as guides in solving problems and try to assist the patient to help himself overcome those early learned habits and inhibitions which block him from pursuing his goals. While the professionals certainly do not have answers to all problems, there is good evidence that the effects of an individual's success in solving a previously insoluble problem are generalized to other areas of his life.

The vast majority of psychiatric illnesses, especially the depressive disorders, last some 3 to 4 months. Generally, it takes 2 to 3 weeks for medication to begin to work. The course of improvement may zig-zag, with good periods being followed sometimes by a temporary return of symptoms. However, the odds are that once the patient has begun to improve, overall progress will be uphill.

It takes considerably longer for attitudes and relationships to change. Once the patient discovers that each day is a new one affording him countless ordinary situations where he can try to realize himself and his potential by behaving in new ways, he can continue to progress on his own, periodically consulting with his therapist when and if new problems arise.

The recent addition of lithium carbonate to the psychiatrist's armamentarium for the first time provides a prophylactic agent potentially useful in a range of conditions often unresponsive to conventional antidepressants and tranquilizers. Lithium has been claimed to be of value in the treatment of a number of conditions including excitement states, manic states, premenstrual tension, phobias and obsessive–compulsive behavior. It has also been demonstrated to be an effective prophylactic agent against recurrent manic states, manic depressive mood swings, and recurrent depressions. The majority of the patients in our clinic who have been treated with lithium have suffered from mild forms of manic depressive mood swings characterized principally by recurrent depressions that have occurred independent of life circumstances. Often, these patients have experienced periods of elation when the depression lifted, which has proved to be a clue to the existence of this mood-swing disturbance even when the elation has been of a very short duration.

REEDUCATION FOR LIVING

The objective here is to prevent further crises by patient education concerning early recognition of depressive symptoms, strengthening adaptive skills, and intervention into noxious habits and spheres of influence.

Simultaneously with stress on symptom relief, we begin a program of patient reeducation. This program is based on the assumption that positive changes in an individual's life adaptation can take place at any point in his life and that growth and development are not restricted to the early years of life. Recent life experiences, relevant past experiences and, most important, the nature of the patient's relationship with other people are reviewed periodically. We focus on ways of improving daily functioning by attempting to increase the patient's awareness of personal habits which may limit effective interaction with others. The patient is assisted in redefining goals; assets and liabilities of personality are reassessed. Better ways of coping with stress and interpersonal relationships are developed to maximize patient security and satisfaction.

The second phase of treatment focuses on ways for improving the present life situation. The patient is actively discouraged from concentrating on either the past or the future. Attention to past negative experiences only conditions the patient to anticipate future recurrences, rendering him so cautious and circumspect that he may be unable to function adequately in the present. Failure to assert himself leads to withdrawal from effort, preoccupation with details and fantasies, and increasing dependency on the wishes of others. This state of mind fosters an exaggerated fear of the consequences of action and so breeds inaction. Therapy focuses on strengthening the ego defenses and reducing fantasy and illusion on the assumption that reality creates more problems than fantasy.

In general, it is desirable to have some therapeutic plan which can be implemented. To decide on the best plan, we follow a several-step inquiry: What factors prevent the patient from reaching his objectives or goals? The elucidation of this may reveal that the patient may have assumed burdens and responsibilities on behalf of others which so consume his energies that he is unable to find sufficient time for pursuing his own goals, replenishing energy, and maintaining self-confidence. A second question, if the patient has no goals, is to inquire about the burdens the patient has assumed. We have invariably found that faulty strategies for the relief of distress relate to pent-up feelings of resentment developed in relationships where people believe they have no chance of changing. Recognizing that ultimately all one can control or change is oneself, a major focus of the second phase of crisis-intervention therapy is to ascertain what the patient can do to modify his life situation. Focusing on alternative life strategies thus becomes the focus of treatment. This then becomes the arena of struggle to the extent that efforts to constrain one's self or modify behavior are likely to be experienced as change by others, and as such, will be resisted, since most change produces anxiety and efforts to stop whatever is viewed as the source of anxiety. Treatment at this stage explores obstacles to the achievement of personal goals and seeks to help the patient to develop feasible strategies of living based on his strengths and the development of greater mastery over self. A major premise of this therapy is that the patient must learn to take care of himself. Patients are encouraged to learn the value of not assuming responsibilities for others greater than they can assume for themselves. An individual may fail to move toward his goals because of lack of skill or training, fear of error, self-doubt, misperception of the opposition of others, and preoccupation with trivial matters or the priorities set by others. Once he moves toward a goal, the patient may be stymied by the passive resistance of those whom he has tried to influence or manipulate, by new cues in a changing situation, and by the abnegation of responsibility associated with excessive reliance on others. Threats, cajolery, flattery, and the commands of others may halt him in his tracks or incline him to rebel and act contrary to his objectives. Envy, competitiveness, and other moods may distract him from his objectives. A desire to please may conflict with the goal or consume time. Failure to prepare for changing options and to plan stepwise objectives may lead to maintenance efforts, the avoidance of new activities, and the perpetuation of a state of inertia.

Too close attention to cultural myths, for example, about special connections needed to reach a goal, as well as the pessimism of others, may handicap the individual's efforts to give his wholehearted attention to the task. Excessive reliance on others may also impede progress toward a goal, either because the individual feels guilty when he makes demands on others or because they are equally unreliable in setting themselves a task and accomplishing it.

Certain characteristics of goals foster failure. A goal may be unreasonable, unfeasible, or unavailable in relationship to the individual's abilities. He may select goals set by others which are not suited for him. Abstract or mythical goals such as happiness or success have little to do with human satisfaction and do not set practical guidelines for individual action. Too many goals foster confusion, an absence of goals apathy, and the goals of others—dissatisfaction. Frustration results when efforts to reach the goal involve misguided efforts to modify the behavior of others. The wise individual refrains from criticizing or dominating others that reinforces lack of faith in themselves and the expectation of failure. Instead, the wise individual seeking to lead others changes his own behavior, stops supporting those things he wishes to see changed, and allows others to take responsibility for themselves. People learn more from emmulating others and from pursuing goals appropriate to their age.

Masochistic efforts to fail and suffer often derive from unrealistic needs to meet the expectations of others, and/or from fear to seek one's own objectives. Such involvement with others takes various forms and produces varying effects on the individual. Unexpressed resentments may sabotage productive efforts through passive resistance or open conflict. Frequently, methods and procedures become so routinized and even bureaucratized that original objectives cannot be reached, the emphasis being placed on maintenance of the system and adherence to procedural methodological details. Administrative tasks and responsibilities may multiply and distract all efforts from concrete objectives. Next to personal distractions, excessive attention to administrative details accounts for the greatest reduction of the freedom to pursue one's initiative toward one's objectives. Perfectionist strivings, the doubt created by helpful advice or the critical censorship of "experts" most often intrude on the methods taken to reach an objective. The less focus given to the single objective the more vulnerable people become to the views of others that may be sought after with the main expectation that goal achievement will be facilitated.

Corrective steps include periodic assessment of progress toward a goal, a pruning of obsolescent methods, and a periodic determination of daily steps or increments which operationalize strategy. Continual adjustments to maintain one's course on target may reduce the confusion deriving from the acquisition of additional goals. At times, corrective steps themselves become the primary motivational forces guiding action into repetitive, compulsive, automatic circular patterns of behavior which impede progress. Excessive alertness to obstacles accentuates their significance and leads to unproductive diversionary activities. Excessive concern for details and efforts to prevent error may lead to unnecessary doubt, uncertainty, and sometimes, paralysis of action. Preoccupation with detail may create boredom, tension, and a need to change activities entirely to create new interest and excitement. Excessive preoccupation with detail and method may also heighten anxiety and stir up introspective fantasies unrelated to the original objective. Too much attention directed toward others engaged in similar activities and in pursuit of similar goals may foster envy, competitiveness, self-doubt, and a neglect of available resources.

Audiovisual Aids

The process of reeducation and remotivation of patients is facilitated by the use of a variety of educational and motivational aids including the use of videotaped playback of individual therapy sessions during the course of treatment. Particularly effective have been a series of audio-cassettes to reinforce certain of the concepts considered during treatment.

DISCHARGE

Duration of Treatment Contact

Treatment contact obviously varies from center to center. In our cohort of treated patients 57 percent of the attempters remained in treatment for 3 months or less, 26 percent remained in treatment for 6 months, and 20 percent of the attempters who were offered treatment dropped out after 1 or 2 visits. Patients who visited the clinic at least 5 times were more likely to remain in treatment for longer periods, 45 percent of the patients visited the clinic at least 11 times.

Disposition

Of the 140 patients 22 percent improved sufficiently to discontinue treatment, an additional 13 percent was referred for long-term therapy, 3 percent was referred to other medical, vocational, or rehabilitative services, 9 percent was referred to medical or psychiatric hospitals, and 51 percent (72/140) of the patients dropped out of treatment. The disposition of a matched group of depressed patients treated in our clinic paralleled the attempt cases, 51 percent of these patients also dropped out of treatment.

Patients diagnosed as having character disorders were more frequently referred for further psychiatric treatment and for medical, social, or rehabilitative services than patients with diagnoses of depressive or psychotic reaction. Twenty-five percent of the character disorders, 16 percent of the psychotic group, and 9 percent of the depressed group were so referred. Only 2 percent of the character disorders versus 16 percent of the psychotic and 12 percent of the depressed groups were referred for hospitalization. Character disorders also tended to stay in treatment for longer periods of time than patients in the other 2 diagnostic categories. The depressed attempters had a higher percentage of dropouts (58 percent) than the other 2 diagnostic groups. The majority of patients gave no satisfactory explanation for dropping out, 18 percent refused to take medication, and a smaller percentage moved out of the city.

SUMMARY

The social impact of attempted suicide can be broadly measured in terms of psychiatric morbidity, divorce, separation, unemployment, and other manifestations of conflict and shifts in interpersonal or family relationships.

The most striking characteristic of the social environment of most patients is the degree of life difficulties, stressful relationships, and frequent crises. Suicide attempts are generally indicative of overall maladjustments in functioning, not isolated episodic or chance occurrences. Viewed as responses to a relationship, symptoms of depression often became the focus of sadomasochistic relationships, making it difficult at times to differentiate treatable symptoms from the effects of unsatisfactory relationships. The onset of symptoms often creates much friction in relationships leading in turn to rejection, separations, and repeated suicidal attempts as a result of inability to handle tense interpersonal conflicts while in a guilt-ridden, self-derogating depressed state.

Good treatment consists of appropriate medication and a meaningful patient–therapist relationship. The therapist's theoretical orientation counts for less than his warmth, sympathy, understanding, and orientation to reality. Treatment efforts seek to increase self-reliance, strengthen the capacity to tolerate rejection, and help to develop alternative ways of tension reduction. Patients require help in accepting reality and discovering strengths in themselves which can be maximally utilized. Crisis-intervention therapy avoids intensive examination of sensitive areas which reduces the patient's sense of self-confidence. Where self-destructive behavior has become habitual, prognosis remains guarded and resocialization is required.

Crisis intervention helps patients to cope with increased stress by learning to anticipate and plan for difficult situations; reduces the duration of the recovery phase in instances of repeated attempts, the incidence of complications, and the speed of adjustment to difficult stresses; and reduces the incidence of overreaction and interpersonal conflict which often follows an initial attempt. To the extent that others believe problems are being handled, treatment reduces the concerns of others to the significance of the attempts and to the underlying distress of the individual.

The techniques and the results of successful treatment vary with different psychiatric disorders. Personality factors influence the response to both psychotherapy and chemotherapy. Some hysterical and immature patients exaggerate their distress over minimal depressive symptoms and the side effects of medication. Obsessive perfectionist patients often show little tolerance for symptoms and never believe they have improved. They judge themselves perfectionistically and rarely compare their progress to their initial depressed or disturbed state. Schizoid patients often become increasingly withdrawn.

In general, where the patient accepts help and maintains contact over time with a psychiatrist or therapeutic team, the outcome is more favorable than when the patient attends sporadically or evokes rejecting attitudes in others which renforce the misperceptions that others don't care.

To the extent that successful treatment depends on the establishment of a working relationship between patient and therapist, positive outcome relates to maturity. The healthiest patients obtain the best results and benefit most from the therapeutic relationship. The families of patients whose illness resulted from stress changed more readily. Relationships stabilize around the patient's psychopathology and efforts to change them in the families of schizophrenics and character disorders who have developed a longstanding life style to fit the patient's special needs. Impulsive patients rapidly respond to support. Patients suffering endogenous depressions require support but respond less to suggestions or encouragement. Both groups tolerate intensive psychotherapy poorly.

REFERENCES

1. Kiev A: New directions for suicide prevention centers. Am J Psychiatry 127:87–88. 1970
2. Kiev A: The chemotherapy of depressive illness. Drug Therapy 1:9–14, 1971
3. Kiev A: A Strategy for Daily Living. New York, Free Press, 1973
4. Kiev A: The role of chemotherapy in managing potentially suicidal patients. Dis Nerv Sys 35:108–111, 1974
5. Kiev A: Lithium—drug in search of an illness. Drug Therapy 4:63–65, 1974
6. Kiev A: Prognostic factors in attempted suicide. Am J Psychiatry 131:9, 1974
7. Kiev A (ed): Somatic Manifestations of Depressive Disorders. Princeton, Excerpta Medica, 1974

Richard K. McGee

16
The Volunteer Suicidologist: Current Status and Future Prospects

The introduction section to this chapter is Louis I. Dublin's Suicide Prevention, *On the Nature of Suicide*, edited by E. S. Shneidman, and reproduced with the kind permission of Jossey-Bass, Inc. © 1969 and 1973.

I propose to comment on four aspects of the suicide prevention problem which I believe have bearing on where we may go in the future development of the program.

The change in the climate of interest in suicide prevention. The current interest in suicide prevention in the United States is a fairly new development. Early in this century there was scarcely any interest in this area. Such interest as there was was almost altogether confined to theoretical considerations among the professional groups, particularly the psychiatrists, the clergy, and the lawyers. The general attitude was, on the whole, a negative one. Little, if any, hope was held out for the prevention of suicide. The medical profession, which one might suppose would be most concerned, showed the least interest. The psychiatrists, dominated by Freud and his disciples, were launched into considerations that often led down blind alleys. With rare exceptions, the clergy saw only a sin against God and the lawmakers saw only a crime against the state, which had to be expiated through reprisals in jail or penalties on the next-of-kin. Even the health officers, who had a legal mandate to prevent unnecessary sickness and death, made virtually no provision for the control of suicide.

This was the more surprising because Morselli and Durkheim had already published their classic studies and had outlined some of the possibilities of useful intervention. Nevertheless, there were a few brave spirits who, without special learning or skills, were moved by simple compassion for those in distress and here and there made significant efforts to serve them. Sometimes they were individuals acting independently; sometimes they were representatives of unorthodox religious groups, such as the Salvation Army in England, Germany, and the United States. The Ethical Society of Vienna made an especially valuable demonstration of the possibilities for preventive service. At the same time, studies by the statisticians and sociologists brought together a body of substantial knowledge concerning the victims. They showed that patterns of personality, social relations, and methods existed in the most widely separated places. Their findings outlined the anatomy of suicide or, perhaps better, the epidemiology of suicide, on the basis of which a preventive program might be started.

The discovery of the possibilities of prevention. This apparently was the platform from which the activities of the National Institute of Mental Health were launched. Step by step, the work supported by the institute, through grants in support of intensive research and of preventive efforts in various localities, has finally led to what we have today—a nationwide awareness of the importance of suicide as a health and social problem and a determination on the part of our mental health leaders to bring it under control. Out of these sporadic humanitarian efforts grew the confidence that potential suicides could be effectively served. Sometimes these efforts reached as many as several thousand persons a year, each with his own particular problem. Through a process of trial and error it was not long before techniques developed that could be safely followed. In this way the concept of the suicide prevention center took form, although its type of organization varied somewhat from place to place. Soon it was recognized that many social services were often needed and that the center must, therefore, be closely associated with all the official and voluntary health and welfare agencies of the community, acting often as a focal point for the referral of cases to those organizations that could best handle a particular problem. This is essentially the type of agency that has crystallized to serve the needs of suicide prevention in various parts of the country.

The importance of the lay volunteer. The lay volunteer was probably the most important single discovery in the fifty-year history of suicide prevention. Little progress was made until he came into the picture. The lay volunteer had the time and the qualities of character to prove that he cared. With proper training he can make a successful approach to the client, and by his knowledge of the community services available for useful referral he can often tide the client over his crisis. This is not the theoretical construct of an effective organization; it is rather the day-to-day story of a large number of such organizations. It is essentially the story of the Samaritans of Britain who, in fourteen years, stretched the one-man experiment of Chad Varah into the fifty-four units now operating in virtually every large center of population in England and Scotland, involving thousands of dedicated volunteers and thousands of suicidal persons who come under their care. And it is likewise the story of many suicide prevention centers in the United States and in other parts of the world.

The need for a firm base of support. The recent progress of the movement has clearly been the result of the interest and support of the National Institute of Mental Health. It has made it possible for a few local groups to organize and launch their preventive operations, freed of most of the financial burdens involved. But this support is a hazard as well as a benefit. The National Institute of Mental Health has made it clear that its support has been intended to demonstrate the feasibility of the various efforts. It is, in the last analysis, up to the local communities to take over and finance the organizations which have so fully proved their worth. It has been my hope over the years that the local health departments, supported through local budgets, would take on this function; but, unfortunately, they have not, except in a very few areas. In most instances, the support has been assumed in part, if not altogether, by the local mental health association. The time has now come when the financing of the suicide prevention centers will once and for all have to be placed on a sound financial basis. This means that it must be assumed by the local communities as a part of their regular operating budgets, very much as they support their health departments, mental health clinics, and other governmental agencies. If, as seems likely, the suicide prevention centers of the future will function through the comprehensive mental health clinics, that too would carry with it a guarantee of continuity and of freedom to operate without the embarrassing difficulties of raising funds each year through voluntary contributions from the public. However, this problem of financial support is still wide open for solution and the experience of the next decade will indicate what are probably the most feasible and practicable procedures.

The Volunteer Suicidologist: Current Status and Future Prospects *

The past 10 years have witnessed far-reaching developments in the philosophy and the practice of delivering community social and health services generally and suicide prevention services specifically. While the merits of these developments may be argued, there is a substantial segment of the suicidology profession which espouses the belief that none of them is greater in significance than the utilization of the paraprofessional volunteer as the key element in the service delivery system. The role of the volunteer has been widely discussed in other places, and it is not necessary here to rehearse facts which are now well established. The volunteer suicidologist has become a vital component of the suicide prevention scene throughout the world, and anyone who cares to trace the course of this development has ample resources available in the literature.[1-7]

This chapter is concerned primarily with a review of the current state of the use of volunteers and secondarily with an attempt to focus attention on some of the possibilities which are emerging from the maximum utilization of volunteers in the future.

*Portions of this chapter were presented in a paper prepared for a symposium, "Issues in the Utilization and Evaluation of Paraprofessionals," chaired by J. Kalafat at the American Psychological Association, New Orleans, Louisiana, 1974.

THE CURRENT STATUS OF VOLUNTEER
SUICIDOLOGISTS

A fact upon which this discussion is based is that volunteers are now being utilized in nearly all of the community suicide prevention and crisis intervention services throughout America. It was for this reason that the American Association of Suicidology, meeting in Detroit in 1972, dropped the associate membership classification for volunteer workers and simultaneously invested them with full membership status, privileges, and responsibilities, including representative membership on the Board of Directors.

Yet, the current status of the volunteer suicidologist is deeper and more significant than the extent of his utilization or his official recognition in an association. It can be appreciated in terms of the mass of research data which has been accumulated and methods which have been developed to form a systematic technology of volunteer selection and evaluation. It is not an exaggeration to say that more is known about the functioning of volunteers in suicide and crisis centers than is known about the functioning of professional personnel in mental health clinics and hospitals.

To understand the relevance of this new technology, it is only necessary to recall what suicide prevention programs were like in 1964 when the movement began to spread across the country. Then there was an absolute minimum of reliable information on how to recruit, select, predict performance, and evaluate performance of telephone crisis workers. Quality control was not being ignored, it was simply that, during this time of early development, communities were moving ahead to initiate new programs in order to meet a prevalent social need without waiting for the development of a new technology for volunteer utilization. Every program director knew who was a good volunteer worker, and a recitation of the evaluation criteria sounded much like the 12 parts of the boy scout law (A good worker is: Trustworthy, Loyal, Helpful, Friendly. . . .). It was left entirely to the individual program coordinator to determine how these virtues were identified and assessed in applicants, trainees, and workers. It was within this context that the Center for Crisis Intervention Research (CCIR) was created within the Department of Clinical Psychology at the University of Florida in 1969. The purpose of the center was to establish a research program to investigate, as thoroughly as possible in 5 years time, the parameters of the volunteer worker on the suicide prevention telephone. This research was conducted through the voluntary cooperation of crisis workers at the Suicide and Crisis Intervention Service (SCIS), a local community agency in Gainesville, Florida. It was the expectation that the findings of these investigations would be general and would have relevance for several forms of human services offered by volunteers in a variety of community agencies.

Prior to this project, a few programs had been seeking answers to questions involving the management of volunteers. For example, McGee, Pennington, and Hegert[8] had evaluated the utility of the Minnesota Multiphasic Personality Inventory (MMPI) for predicting the degree of involvement volunteers would show in the program once they were selected. They were forced to conclude that the efficiency of the method was still unknown because some dependent variable categories contained so few subjects that the results of appropriate statistical procedures were suspect.

In another report, McGee[9] discussed the results of a correlational analysis involving 71 personality test scores, personal history data, and independent rating by qualified judges of the volunteers' on-the-job performance. The results led to a clinical interpretation of the personality test profiles which differentiated the 7 best volunteers from the 7 worst volunteers. Four traits were said to characterize the best workers: (1) they are comfortable with themselves; (2) they love life and live it to the fullest; (3) they experience an active social existence; and (4) they have a capacity for influential leadership.

These 4 characteristics were later adopted by the Nashville Crisis Call Center for the content of rating scales completed by local professionals on all volunteer applicants. Used as selection criteria, these scales have served the Nashville program for several years, but, nevertheless, it is evident that the early work was more poetic than scientific.

Beginning in 1970, the CCIR defined a series of problem areas to constitute the foci of its investigations. Some general research questions were posed.

1. What are the criteria for evaluating the performance of volunteers on the job? What do they do that really makes a difference with callers in crisis?
2. What variables present at initial recruitment predict these later performance criteria?
3. What are the dynamic factors which facilitate or disrupt a volunteer's identification and service to a crisis intervention center? What are the motivations and rewards for volunteers?
4. How do paraprofessional workers compare to the traditional

professionals in performing the work of a crisis intervention program?

5. What kinds of people are attracted to volunteer service in crisis intervention programs?

Only the first of these areas, the development of performance criterion measures, will be discussed in this chapter. *

THE DEVELOPMENT AND USE OF A TECHNICAL EFFECTIVENESS SCALE

Rationale

The concept of technical effectiveness (TE) is defined as the extent to which a person performs those tasks that he has been explicitly trained to perform, and which the suicide prevention and/or crisis intervention center recognizes as the fundamental duties of the worker performing the telephone crisis intervention function.[10] The variables included in TE pertain to those functions of the crisis worker which are considered necessary, but not sufficient, in the opening of every case handled by a telephone crisis agency: (1) securing the communication; (2) assessing the caller's condition (especially lethality); and (3) formulating a plan of action for treatment.

Method

The TE scale was developed through a process of item elimination. It is a 9-item sclae composed of dichotomous items uniquely relevant to the crisis call situation. The basic instrument contains 9 items when used for suicide calls, but only 7 are relevant when potential suicide is not a prominent aspect of the call.

The Kendall Coefficient of Concordance was computed on three separate sets of data in order to determine the reliability of the scale across several raters. Two groups of 3 independent raters judged the value of TE in 2 independent taped samples of 14 and 11 calls. Reliability values ranged from .904 to .992 on these 4 sets of data. In another study, 10 new raters attained an interrater reliability of .923 rating 10 tapes independently. These results clearly demonstrate the interrater reliability of this instrument to be exceptionally high; all 3 coefficients attained significance at the .001 level.

---

*A complete report of this project (which includes the TE, CE, and SE scales) has been prepared; copies may be obtained from the author upon request.

It has also been shown that the scale can be used meaningfully by only 1 person, making it practical for any suicide prevention and crisis intervention program director to use this performance assessment device in his own organization. Spearman rank-order correlations comparing the TE ratings of one judge with those of 3 others have ranged from .960 to .997.

Results

Two additional questions have received considerable attention in the analyses of large quantities of data. Can the TE scale discriminate between volunteers in a manner that would allow assessment of telephone crisis worker performance over a group of volunteers? Further, what is the nature of intra-volunteer change in TE over time? A sample of 400 scores were compiled in an attempt to answer these questions.

To answer the first question, data were collected early in the research project from a sample of 76 workers. The frequency distribution of scores obtained on ratings of these 76 first calls* proved to be distributed evenly along the range of possible TE scores. At a later point in the project, mean TE scores were computed over the 3 most recent first calls taken by 133 volunteers. A frequency array of these means was observed to closely approximate a normal distribution, with the 3-call averages ranging through more than 5 standard deviations.

The volunteer coordinator at a particular suicide prevention and / or crisis intervention center might ask very practical questions such as "How often should I check a particular volunteer worker's TE scores in order to assure he is providing effective service to our clients?" A rank-order correlation between the average TE score of the last 3 rated calls and the average TE score of all rated calls taken by each worker was computed for the sample of 133 volunteers, and found to be .79 ($p < .001$). This may be seen as a particularly useful finding. Since there seems to be a highly positive correlation between these 2 sets of data, suicide prevention or crisis center personnel, if TE scores are used as a quality control check, would only have to check the volunteer's performance occasionally, perhaps once every 6 months. Three calls, rated at this frequency, would be sufficient

---

*A first call is defined as the initial telephone contact between a particular client and the SCIS. Only these calls were recorded and preserved for research analysis.

to give an accurate check on how each worker is performing the critical function of opening new cases.[11]

An investigation of intra-volunteer variance failed to identify any common pattern of change over time. One important factor should be kept in mind—no attempt was made to control for variance associated with the caller in these data. The most probable cause for the lack of intra-volunteer consistency is the fact that the crisis worker is continuously presented with a wide variety of types of caller situations in his work. These calls include the quick single contact in which the caller is seeking information rather than counseling and is therefore highly protective of significant information. There is also the longer, more intensive call in which the caller is seeking help, and is oriented to engage in a trusting relationship with the volunteer.

The TE scale is an assessment instrument with face validity, but its application must be constantly tempered against the situation presented by the call and the caller. If TE ratings should become a source of status ranking among volunteers, they may become, in their pursuit to please the evaluators, overly restricted in their response to clients. High TE scores are probably of minimal value if the caller does not receive a response from the crisis worker that does more than simply satisfy the technical expectations of the program administration.

MEASURING THE THERAPEUTIC FUNCTIONING OF CRISIS WORKERS

Rationale

Although the TE scale offers a means of measuring desirable behaviors of volunteer crisis workers in a suicide prevention center, inadequacies in this method have been noted. It cannot be used alone for identifying effective crisis workers. Obviously, there are certain clinical qualities which must be present for the most competent technical skills to result in an effective engagement between client and counselor.

A review of the literature reveals the qualities which people should possess in order to be judged as clinically effective.[12-17] An operational definition to encompass these qualities, and a method of rating behavior according to that definition have emerged from the Rogerian client-centered school of psychotherapy.

Most prominent in this field of research in the area of psycho-therapy are the studies of Truax and Carkhuff and their associates and Lister[18] at the University of Florida. Their investigations have promoted confidence in the ability of judges to rate the level of empathy, genuineness, and warmth which is provided by the counselor. These traits have become identified as the conditions of the therapeutic encounter which facilitate client change—hence the term "facilitative conditions" is used for the aggregate of empathy, genuineness, and warmth.

Method

Knickerbocker[19] initiated and stimulated a series of investigations on the clinical effectiveness (CE) of volunteers. The subjects of these investigations came from 2 distinct populations of workers at the SCIS, the service agency associated with CCIR. The first sample included 65 volunteer paraprofessional workers from the local commu-nity. The other sample consisted of 27 workers who were professionally trained in one of the usual clinical or couseling roles. Both advanced doctoral trainees and practicing professionals were included in the second group.

Ratings of worker performance were made by trained raters on 2 sets of scales designed to measure empathy, genuineness, and warmth. Reliability coefficients were computed for the ratings of each scale, and all were within the range of .78 to .83.

Results

Analysis of variance methods were employed to determine if there are observable differences between professional and paraprofes-sional crisis workers in level of offered facilitative conditions. Tests of significance of differences between group means were also measured by t tests.

The paraprofessional volunteers were rated significantly higher than the professionals on both tests of warmth, and on one measure of empathy. There was no measure on which the professionals exceeded the nonprofessionals.

Therapeutic responses of a humanistic nature, which focus on the affective content and personal meaning of the client, correspond to the realities of the day-to-day proceedings in a crisis intervention delivery system. The measures of empathy, genuineness, and warmth naturally combine to offer the best judgment about the clinical effectiveness of people who work in this setting.

THE RELATIONSHIP OF PERSONALITY TO CLINICAL
EFFECTIVENESS IN CRISIS INTERVENTION

Method

Galvin[20] attempted a replication of Knickerbocker's earlier work by once more comparing professionals to paraprofessionals in therapeutic effectiveness. He also investigated the personality of subjects in the professional and paraprofessional group using the Myers-Briggs Type Indicator, which is based upon Jung's theory of psychological types.

Subjects for the professional group were drawn from the staff of a typical comprehensive community mental health center. Those for the paraprofessional group served in an equally representative telephone crisis intervention service.

Results

Paraprofessionals were found to be functioning at a higher level than professionals on all facilitative conditions. These differences were statistically significant for all conditions except empathy. It was further observed that there was no statistical difference in the typological makeup of the professionals and paraprofessional groups. Previous research had found professional therapists to be predominately of the NF (intuitive and feeling) type. In Galvin's data, 71 percent of the professionals and 81 percent of the paraprofessionals were of the NF preference. This finding shows that the paraprofessional volunteers resemble professional therapists in their personality characteristics to a much greater extent than they resemble the general population of adults.

Discussion

Findings such as these by Knickerbocker and Galvin reinforce the belief that it is the personality rather than years of professional training that the helper brings to a therapeutic situation that is of greatest relevance in explaining the therapeutic effect of a helper on his client.

In a related study involving the personal characteristics of crisis intervention personnel, Harkey[21] performed follow-up interviews with clients within 24 hours of their first call to the SCIS. The purpose of these interviews was to elicit statements and reaction which could be rated by a panel of judges to denote the level of satisfaction and/or relief experienced by the caller as a result of having called for help. After establishing the reliability of the judges ratings of client satisfaction, Harkey correlated these judgments with ratings made of the volunteers' verbal behavior during the original call by applying the dimensions of the Bales Interaction Process Analysis system.[22,23] Some surprising results emerged from this analysis. The Bales dimension which consistently correlated with the caller satisfaction variables (confidence in the center, feeling better after the call, and total satisfaction score) was worker friendliness. Furthermore, the judged degree of friendliness in the volunteer also distinquished significantly between high- and low-scoring workers on the empathy and warmth scales of the CE measure. (Different sets of judges rated the Bales and the CE measures.)

While it is not unreasonable that friendly-appearing workers would also seem empathic and warm and would promote positive responses in clients, it was considered surprising that worker friendliness, reliably judged by independent raters, would show so much variance within a group of volunteer telephone counselors. The findings clearly show that there were some unfriendly-appearing workers who prompted feelings of dissatisfaction in clients as well. Variance in this trait might never have been identified unless an analysis of call-taking performance was made.

It is too easy to assume that all workers selected for duty would be evaluated as friendly to clients or automatically eliminated. Thus, not only objective screening for selection, but follow-up performance evaluations are necessary for quality control of volunteer personnel. Research investigations such as this demonstrates that this type of evaluation is possible within a suicide prevention program; the findings demonstrate that it is essential.

THE EFFECT OF HELPER BEHAVIOR ON MODIFYING CLIENT AFFECT AND SELF-DISCLOSURE DURING A CALL

Knickerbocker and Brasington[24] performed 2 independent studies in which they developed subjective methods for rating anxiety and depression in callers and assessed changes in these affective states from the beginning to the end of crisis calls. Their second study expanded on the first by investigating client self-disclosure as a third outcome variable, and relating all 3 of these dimensions to the clinical effectiveness (CE) dimensions of empathy, genuineness, and warmth.

Method

The investigators randomly selected tapes of first contact calls from the tape library. A segment lasting 2 minutes was extracted from the beginning and the end of each call. In each case, these segments were edited to remove all information that would identify the client. They were then coded and transferred in a random sequence to master tapes. The original calls were preserved for the rating of CE variables in the second study.

Raters were trained to judge anxiety and depression using a subjective 5-point scale ranging from 1 = no anxiety (or depression) to 5 = extremely anxious (or depressed).

Results

In the first study, it was observed that the levels of anxiety and depression diminshed significantly when mean values of first-of-call and last-of-call ratings were compared by t tests. The t value was significant at the .005 level for the decrease in anxiety and at the .025 level for depression.

The second investigation correlated diminished anxiety, diminished depression, and self-disclosure with the CE variables and found all of them to be significantly related at the .02 level or better. Further, to verify the anxiety and depression reduction as a function of the client's ability to freely explore and disclose himself, correlations of .44 ($p < .01$) and .39 ($p < .01$) were observed between self-disclosure and anxiety and depression respectively.

Discussion

It is clearly evident from the data of these 2 investigations that changes in anxiety and depression levels can be used effectively for judging outcome in crisis calls. The 2 dimensions may be rated reliably on a simple, subjective 5-point scale. Moreover, observing client change by this method enables a judgment to be made about the quality of the helping relationship offered by the telephone counselor. It is evident that the more the crisis worker offered a positive human relationship, the more the caller's level of anxiety and depression diminished.

It seems then that there is evidence of dynamic links between the personal behaviors of the crisis worker and what happens to the caller as a result of his interaction.

A COMPREHENSIVE METHOD FOR EVALUATING
SUICIDE AND CRISIS INTERVENTION WORKERS:
THE SITUATION EFFECTIVENESS SCALE

Rationale

The technical effectiveness (TE) and clinical effectiveness (CE) measures of volunteer performance are both useful when assessing the worker on certain types of calls. However, there are some cases that occur with high frequency in a crisis center caseload when TE and CE are not adequate, either alone or combined.

The TE scale is applicable only to the first-contact call where a new case is being opened. Similarly, in highly lethal emergency situations where authoritative action is the key to intervention, empathic behaviors are probably the least relevant to the demands of the task.

Steinberger and Slutzky[25] have conceptualized a more realistic approach to performance measurement that they define as *comprehensive*. This method treats each call as an event which involves several worker, caller, and problem variables interacting to form a unique, complex behavioral setting. The worker's performance in relationship to this specific caller-problem context is the crucial concern. It is this worker-caller-problem interaction that defines the situation in which the worker's performance is to be observed and measured.

The situation effectiveness (SE) scale was developed to improve upon the limitations of TE and CE. It is composed of 34 items, grouped into 2 major parts. The first part contains 5 items which are considered essential to a crisis worker's performance on every call. They deal with the worker's initial approach to the caller, clarity of communication, and patience or understanding. The second part of the scale is more flexible and contains 29 items which may or may not be relevant to any particular call. Items judged as not applicable are omittted in tabulating the performance score. The scale yields 4 scores including sub-scales which measure (1) the worker's level of communicating acceptance and concern, (2) the worker's ability to assess the case, (3) the worker's approach to treatment, and (4) the total score which defines the general level of effectiveness in the situation presented by that call.

Reliability

After the items were developed and rewritten for optimum clarity, 2 groups of raters were trained to rate 13 randomly selected calls.

It was observed that the average reliability over 8 raters ranged from .74 to .85 when measured by the intra-class correlation method.

OVERVIEW OF TECHNOLOGICAL DEVELOPMENTS

The preceding pages relate a series of research activities designed to develop and standardize methods for making meaningful evaluations of the performance of volunteer suicidologists at work in a crisis intervention agency. It is recognized that the basic method employed, namely pooled judgments of independent raters, is not without its limitations as a rigorous scientific procedure. The performance dimensions studied, with the possible exception of the items of the TE scale, involved the presence (and the degree) or absence of qualitative behaviors, or styles of behaving, which have been shown in other research to facilitate client change following clinical intervention. They were applied in this series of investigations because of their obvious relevance and appropriateness. The investigators were and still are unable to conceptualize a creative or innovative methodology for assessing these performance variables which escapes the shortcomings of even reliable ratings.

However, it should be noted that Powell and his associates have pioneered and documented a highly precise and scientifically sophisticated method of studying worker behaviors. Two published articles [27,28] and 7 unpublished manuscripts of papers presented at professional meetings from 1972 to 1974 contain reports on the development and utilization of the Caller-Worker Interaction Program (CWIP). This is a complex system for codifying categories of verbal behaviors and computing both the frequency and sequential ordering of these events during a call to the crisis center. A trained technician either listens to a tape or, with sufficient experience and proficiency, monitors a live call and enters each codable thought unit into a computer using a terminal incorporating either a lightpen and TV screen, or a typewriter to feed 11-digit data chunks to the memory banks. If a volunteer asks the caller "Well, are you feeling badly enough now to consider harming yourself?", the technician would code this thought unit into 8 verbal events as 1WORKER, 2RESPOND, 2ELICIT, 1QUESTION, 2NOW, 2EMOTION, 2NEGATIVE, 1THINK. The computer would store the notation 12212220010 for analysis. [27] By contrast, a judge applying the TE scale [10,11] to the same conversation would, upon hearing the volunteer ask this question, merely check "yes" to item No. 7 and note that if the caller responds in the affirmative, the volunteer should be held responsible for 2 more behaviors related to assessing lethality.

The CWIP system clearly makes up in precision what the TE/CE/SE Scale ratings sacrifice in favor of decreased expense and increased universal adaptability and practicality. Whereas one method has been likened to the act of using a yardstick to measure the thickness of a razor blade, the other is akin to swatting flies with atomic missles. As the technology for assessing volunteer performance continues to develop, the large middle range between these current methodologies will obviously be narrowed. Nonetheless, it is significant that as of the mid-1970s the undeniably important role of the volunteer suicidologist has fostered the development of an evaluative technology to undergird his continued contribution to clinical intervention in self-destructive and life-threatening behavior.

A LOOK INTO THE FUTURE

The ultimate value of systematically developing methods to observe the behaviors of volunteers in emergency-oriented, suicide and crisis related, service delivery systems must not be thought of in terms of the measurement technology *per se*. While sophistication, precision, and accuracy are indeed important, the real value is of the possibility of introducing a practical quality control system by which to set and certify compliance with at least minimum standards of operation.

It has been proposed that perhaps the most significant of the many current developments in suicidology will be the establishment of standards for the certification of individual community programs. It is presently unclear how actual accreditation site visits will be made, but the American Association of Suicidology (AAS) will become the agency to set the standards for quality service and issue the official certification. The AAS has already published its official statement regarding this.[28] There is still much deliberation to be done before these standards are ready to be applied. It is apparent that there are relatively few centers in the country today which could meet various standards which have been developed for some areas.[29,30] The Samaritans in England have been certifying their branches for several years, and in the US the programs associated with CONTACT Teleministries, Inc. are certified by the parent corporation for having met established standards. This should become universal practice for crisis intervention programs by the end of this decade. By 1980, anyone who calls a suicide-prevention or a crisis service should be as certain of receiving quality service as he is when he enters a general hospital or visits a licensed practitioner of any healing profession.

In the beginning, only the agencies will be evaluated and granted certification for their adherence to each of a set of broad areas of center operation. The first draft of an evaluation instrument produced by an AAS Task Force on Center Accreditation includes the following 7 areas: (1) administration; (2) training procedures; (3) general service delivery; (4) suicide services; (5) ethical issues; (6) community integration; and (7) program evaluation.

These areas are further subdivided into a total of 41 components, each of which is assessed by a 4-level rating scale. The procedure is adapted from the Program Analysis of Service Systems (PASS) methods developed by Wolfensberger and Glenn.[31] It may be realistically anticipated that this center accreditation program will be operational sometime in 1976.

But what of individual personnel working in the telephone rooms and serving on the Outreach CARE Teams in the certified agencies? The initial plan requires only that all individual workers are periodically evaluated as to their performance by some definitive procedure. No attempt has been made to articulate the methods, content, or sophistication to be followed in meeting this criterion. Eventually this also should be done. It may represent a third or even fourth phase of perhaps a 10-year program of enhancing the quality of services rendered by suicide prevention and crisis intervention agencies. But the time is surely coming when every volunteer suicidologist will be given the opportunity to earn the right to wear that title by demonstrating his proficiency on some form of national competency examination. Perhaps suicidology training programs will eventually be standardized and made available by community colleges, adult education departments of local public schools, or regional institutes conducted by the AAS. Passing the course will entitle each worker to his own personal certification as a competent crisis worker. The various levels of training and certification in first aid given by the American National Red Cross are a model for this procedure. Another example is the recently developed emergency medical technician training program which has been promoted by the US Department of Health, Education, and Welfare. These standards have been written into law by several state legislatures for ambulance attendants and such training is provided by many community colleges.

When the volunteer suicidologist has evolved to this status in the care-giving systems of the community, he will never again be called a non- or a paraprofessional. He may not even still be a volunteer, but as a suicidologist, his potential will have been realized and his contribution will have been fully recognized by the society he serves.

REFERENCES

1. Dublin LI: Suicide prevention, in Shneidman ES (ed): On the Nature of Suicide. San Francisco, Jossey-Bass, 1969, p 45
2. Farberow NL: The selection and training of nonprofessional personnel for the therapeutic roles in suicide prevention. Paper read at Southeastern Psychological Association, 1966
3. Heilig SM: Manpower: Utilization of nonprofessional crisis workers, in McGee RK (ed): Planning Emergency Services for Comprehensive Community Mental Health Centers. Gainesville, Florida, Univ Florida, Department of Clinical Psychology, 1967, p 46
4. Heilig SM, Farberow NL, Litman RE, Shneidman ES: The role of nonprofessional volunteers in a suicide prevention center. Community Ment Health J 4:287-295, 1968
5. McGee RK: An Evaluation of the Volunteer in Suicide Prevention: Final Project Report. Gainesville, Florida, Univ Florida, Department of Clinical Psychology, 1974
6. McGee, RK, Jennings B: Ascending to "lower levels": The case for nonprofessional crisis workers, in Lester D, Brockopp GW (eds): Crisis Intervention and Counseling by Telephone. Springfield, Illinois, Charles C Thomas, 1973, p 223
7. Varah C: The Samaritans. New York, Macmillan, 1965
8. McGee RK, Pennington J, Hegert T: Criteria for selecting and evaluating nonprofessional crisis workers in a suicide prevention center. Unpublished research report, Univ Florida, Department of Clinical Psychology, 1967
9. McGee RK: An approach to the selection of volunteers for suicide prevention centers. Paper presented at American Association of Suicidology, Chicago, 1968
10. Fowler DE, McGee RK: Assessing the performance of telephone crisis workers: The development of a technical effectiveness scale, in Lester D, Brockopp GW (eds): Crisis Intervention and Counseling by Telephone. Springfield, Illinois, Charles C Thomas, 1973, p 287
11. Freeman D, Fowler DE: The development and use of a technical effectiveness scale, in McGee RK (ed): An Evaluation of the Volunteer in Suicide Prevention: Final Project Report. Gainesville, Florida, Univ Florida, Department of Clinical Psychology, 1974, p 108
12. Bergin AE, Solomon S: Personality and performance. Am Psychol 18: 393, 1963
13. Carkhuff, RR: The Counselor's Contribution to the Facilitative Process. Urbana, Illinois, Parkinson, 1967

14. Carkhuff RR: Differential functioning of lay and professional helpers. J Counsel Psychol 15:117–126, 1968
15. Truax CB, Carkhuff RR: Significant developments in psychotherapy research, in Abt LE, Reiss BF (eds): Progress in Clinical Psychology. New York, Grune & Stratton, 1964
16. Truax CB, Carkhuff RR: Toward Effective Counseling and Psychotherapy: Training and Practice. Chicago, Aldine Atherton, 1967
17. Truax CB, Wargo DG, Frank JD, Imber SB, Battle CC, Hoehn-Saric R, et al: Therapist's contribution to accurate empathy, non-possessive warmth, and genuineness in psychotherapy. J Clin Psychol 22:331–334, 1966
18. Lister JL: Scales for the measurement of empathic understanding, facilitative genuineness, and facilitative warmth, in McGee RK (ed): An Evaluation of the Volunteer in Suicide Prevention: Final Project Report. Gainesville, Florida, Univ Florida, Department of Clinical Psychology, 1974
19. Knickerbocker DA: Lay volunteer and professional trainee therapeutic functioning and outcomes in a suicide and crisis intervention service (Ph.D. dissertation, Univ Florida, Fla), 1972
20. Galvin M: Facilitative conditions and psychological type in client interaction by professionals and paraprofessionals (Ph.D. dissertation, Univ Florida), 1975
21. Harkey KB: Determinants of the satisfaction level of callers to the suicide and crisis intervention service (masters thesis, Univ of Florida), 1972
22. Bales RF: Interaction Process Analyses: A Method for the Study of Small Groups. Reading, Massachusetts, Addison-Wesley, 1950
23. Bales RF: Personality and Interpersonal Behavior. New York, Holt, 1970
24. Knickerbocker DA, Brasington GT: The effect of helper behavior on modifying client affect and self-disclosure during a call, in McGee RK (ed): An Evaluation of the Volunteer in Suicide Prevention: Final Project Report. Gainesville, Florida, Univ Florida, Department of Clinical Psychology, 1974, p 142
25. Steinberger J, Slutzky GN: A comprehensive method of evaluating crisis intervention workers: The development of the situation effectiveness scale, in McGee RK: An Evaluation of the Volunteer in Suicide Prevention: Final Project Report. Gainesville Florida, Univ Florida, Department of Clinical Psychology, 1974, p 124
26. Powell ER, Ashton PT, Heaton ME: Initial observations of dyadic interaction in crisis intervention centers. J Community Psychol 1:330–334, 1973
27. Powell ER, Heaton ME, Ashton PT: Systematic observation of crisis center telephone interactions. Life-Threatening Behavior 4:224–239, 1974
28. Motto JA, Brooks RM, Ross CP, Allen NH: Standards for Suicide Prevention and Crisis Centers. New York, Behavioral Publications, 1974

29. Motto JA: Development of standards for suicide prevention centers.
     Bull Suicidol 33–37, 1969
30. Ross CP, Motto JA: Implementation of standards for suicide prevention
     centers. Bull Suicidol 1971, 19–21
31. Wolfensberger W, Glenn L: PASS: Program Analysis of Service Systems
     (ed 3). Toronto, National Institute on Mental Retardation, 1972.

Richard Fox

17

The Recent Decline of Suicide in Britain: The Role of the Samaritan Suicide Prevention Movement

The introductory passage to this chapter is from Jacques Choron's
Suicide, reproduced here with the kind permission of Charles Scribner's
Sons © 1972.

It has been suggested that suicide "troubles and appalls us because it
so intransigently rejects our deeply held conviction that life must be worth
living."

While there is undoubtedly some truth in this, in more cases than one
would like to admit the reason for the shock may not be the challenges
to the belief that life is good, but the fact that one is not really quite sure
that it is. As the modern Spanish philosopher José Ortega y Gasset has
pointed out, for most people at all times "life" meant limitation, obligation,
dependence, and oppression. They go on living simply because they happen
to have been born, sustained by the force of habit, sometimes out of curiosity
or vague hopes for a better future, and because they are afraid of the
alternative—death. But the suicide seems to have conquered this fear. Thus
he confirms not only the suspicion that life may not be the highest good
but the one that death may not be the greatest evil. In challenging the usual
attitudes toward both life and death, the suicide is not merely a nonconformist
but also a seducer, and this is one of the reasons that most civilized societies
consider him almost as dangerous as he appeared to primitive man when
his unappeased ghost was thought to threaten the welfare of the tribe.

This accounts for the strict condemnation of suicide in most cultures.
However, people did commit suicide, sometimes for motives that were
laudable, or at least under circumstances that were understandable. The
indiscriminate condemnation had to admit some exceptions. Moreover, with

growing sophistication, intermittent "failure of nerve," and spreading philosophical reflection on life and death, man's ability to take his own life began to appear in a different light. Some even saw it as a great boon, a precious privilege. The only real questions were under what circumstances this privilege might be exercised, or what exceptions could be tolerated. When was suicide good and when was it evil? When was it right and when wrong? From classical antiquity until the nineteenth century all thought and writing on suicide were dominated by this issue. In other words, suicide was treated as a religioethical and legal problem.

By comparison with suicide as a problem, the problem of suicide—that is, the question of why some people kill themselves while most others in similar circumstances do not—came to the fore much later. This does not mean that some, even among the ancients, did not seek an explanation other than that given by the suicides themselves. The connection between melancholia and suicide goes back to Hippocrates, and to Galen's theory of the four humors. The search for the real causes of suicide was resumed as soon as it became possible to see it not exclusively, as Christianity did, in terms of sin and the Devil's work. Burton's *Anatomy of Melancholy* (1628), Jean Dumas' *Traité du suicide ou du meurtre volontaire* (1773), Esquirol's *Sur la monomanie suicide* (1827), Bourdin's *du suicide considéré comme maladie* (1845), and Brierre de Boismont's *Du suicide et de la folie suicide* (1856) represent the most important efforts to explain suicidal behavior as resulting from mental disorders. In the last third of the nineteenth century students of society also turned their attention toward suicide. The basis of their investigations was the gradually accumulated statistics on suicide, and the motive of their studies was the desire to discover "laws" in the seemingly capricious human behavior similar to the laws of nature. The relatively stable suicide rates in a given society which the statistics made apparent were assumed to result from extraindividual (social) forces. This was the thesis defended by Enrico Morselli in his *Il suicido* (1879). In the same year Thomas Masaryk, the future founder of the Czechoslovak Republic, then a candidate for a chair at the University of Vienna, submitted a dissertation, *Suicide as a Social Mass-Phenomenon (Selbstmord als soziale Massenerscheinung,* published in 1881), in which, under the false impression that suicide does not occur in primitive societies, he maintained that the increase in the incidence of suicide was due to modern civilization and the decline of religion. Toward the end of the century, in 1897, appeared Emile Durkheim's *Le Suicide,* the basic sociological study of suicide. None of the works mentioned in this paragraph, however, was morally neutral, and the suicide statistics underlying them went under the name of "moral statistics." It is only in the twentieth century that moral bias was completely eliminated from scientific—psychiatric or sociological—studies of suicide. And it is only since the mid-1950s that any unprecedented upsurge of interest in suicidal phenomena has taken place, not only among psychiatrists but also among psychologists, sociologists, and anthropologists . . .

The first known document dealing with suicide is an ancient Egyptian text known as "The Dialogue of a Misanthrope with His Own Soul" or simply as "Dispute over Suicide." A man tired of life because of a series of misfortunes and contemplating suicide wants to convince his soul to accompany him into death, but the soul hesitates because it is afraid that in committing suicide the man will be deprived of a proper funeral and thus forsake the soul's chances of a blissful afterlife. It tries therefore to induce him to abandon his project and to turn instead to a life of hedonistic pleasures. This the man refuses to do because life has no rewards to offer, and particularly because a life of indulgence would bring his name into "evil odor."

The misanthrope of the dialogue emerges as a decent person unable to adjust to the violence and injustice of his times and the dog-eat-dog morality, as evidenced by the second of the four poems of the text:

> To whom can I speak today?
> [One's] fellows are evil;
> The friends of today do not love . . .
> Hearts are rapacious:
> Every man seizes his fellow's goods . . .
> The gentle man has perished,
> [But] the violent man has access to everybody . . .
> There are no righteous;
> The land is left to those who do wrong . . .
> To whom can I speak today? I am laden with wretchedness
> For lack of intimate friends. . . .

In this work social isolation and loneliness emerge as the main reason for contemplating suicide. It is interesting that the prominent role of loneliness in the causation of suicide has been recently emphasized by several students. Because of it death becomes irresistibly attractive:

> Death is in my sight today
> Like the recovery of a sick man . . .
> Like the longing of a man to see his house again
> After many years of captivity. . . .

But death is attractive also because it leads to another existence in which justice prevails and the dead share divine privileges:

> Why surely, he who is yonder,
> shall seize [the culprit] like a living god
> . . . He shall stand in the celestial bark. . . .

It is not easy to determine the respective shares of the psychological and sociological factors in any particular instance of suicide, or even in attempted suicide where the psyche and circumstances of the subject are available for scrutiny. One such factor is loneliness, which many consider to be the common denominator of most suicides and which Walter Pöldinger demonstrated to be a deeper motive in suicides arising from unhappy love affairs, marital discord, and sickness. Sometimes social factors—widowhood, divorce, unemployment, imprisonment—are the principal causes of loneliness, but the psychological makeup of the individual also may prevent him from establishing normal social relationships when these are possible. Whatever its roots, loneliness is certainly an important precipitating factor or motive of suicide. (Actually, the term "precipitating factor" is more correctly applied, not to a complex like "marital discord," but to a single act, such as one partner's leaving the house after a violent argument.) However, the role of interpersonal conflicts and the suffering that people inflict upon one another should also not be underestimated. Thus, when Pöldinger finds confirmation of Paul Valery's dictum, "Suicide is the absence of the others," it would be well to remember Jean-Paul Sartre's statement, "Hell is the others."

Both loneliness and interpersonal conflicts are motives for suicide, rather than causes, a distinction which Robert Gaupp insisted upon at the beginning of the twentieth century. For Gaupp the causes of suicide are the biopsychical driving forces, which often do not even rise to the consciousness of the individual and thus cannot constitute motives, but which are related to race, age, sex, work, and social status. This valuable distinction has been narrowed down among the psychiatric profession to refer only to abnormal mental states . . .

A much more realistic problem in connection with suicide prevention is its effectiveness. Actually, this comprises two problems. One is the overall effect of the activity of suicide prevention centers on lowering the suicide rate of a nation, the ideal target being its reduction to zero. The other is the evaluation of the effectiveness of a given center.

In a recent British study, Christopher Bagley tried to evaluate the effect of the Samaritans on the suicide rate by "an ecological method"—that is, by comparing the changes in suicide rates of towns where the Samaritans operate with an equal number of "control" towns, which are generally similar, "given present knowledge of urban characteristics," but in which Samaritans do not as yet operate. He found that in Halifax the pre-Samaritan rate was 17.7 per 100,000; five years after the Samaritans became active the rate dropped to 12.97. In the "control" town of Leeds, in the same period, the previous rate of 11 per 100,000 rose to 13.2. Bagley concludes that "the evidence points to the possibility, although it by no means offers proof, that Samaritan schemes may directly lower suicide rates." . . .

Whatever the motives and causes of suicidal behavior may be in a given case, people who contemplate, attempt, or carry out the act of killing themselves often complain that their lives have lost meaning or are no longer worth living. These statements presuppose that their lives did have meaning or were felt to be worth living until certain events brought on a radical change. In the late 1930s the Austrian psychologist Margarete von Andics, a disciple of Alfred Adler, interviewed 100 survivors of attempted suicides at the Vienna Clinic of Psychiatry and Neurology with the view of determining what human beings take to be the meaning of life, or, put negatively, in what circumstances does a person consider that life is meaningless? What is the "thing" without which one does not desire to live any longer? Beginning appropriately with an analysis of what "life" in the biographical meaning of the word consists of, she distinguishes two "spheres." The "personal sphere" comprises childhood and parental home; society, friendship and exchange of ideas; love, marriage, home; family and relatives; reputation and esteem. The "material sphere" consists of possessions, control of body (health, sexuality, ability to work), talents and school, profession and achievements.

Impeded satisfaction in one or the other sphere assumes the character of deprivation and can become a motive for suicide by making life appear meaningless or intolerable. In particular, a childhood devoid of affection can be said to create a predisposition to suicide. Loneliness, the lack of someone to whom one can unburden onself, is one of the latent ills in most of those lives which turn to suicide. But Andics attaches the greatest importance to the fact that none of the persons examined by her belonged, at the time of the attempt to commit suicide, to any community of a wider scope than family, love affair, or friendship. She found that the "thing" without which life becomes meaningless was not necessarily "someone" but most prominently a "something" in the form of integration and participation in a larger social context. She quotes Rabindranath Tagore as saying: "He who does not help turn the wheel of the world lives in vain." In other words, in order to feel that his existence has a meaning "the individual must have a part in the practical and surrounding world" . . .

The Recent Decline of Suicide in Britain: The Role of the Samaritan Suicide Prevention Movement

Suicide rates in Britain, as in most countries, have been remarkably stable over the past four decades.* The rate per 100,000 ran fairly consistently between 10 and 12 with a peak of around 15 during the years of industrial recession with its massive unemployment, and a steady drop as the war clouds gathered and industry picked up leading to an all time low of 9 during the early years of World War II (see Figs. 17-1, 17-2). There are speculations as to why war correlates with suicide rates, but those of us who recall that time of almost incredible national unity and purpose in the face of overwhelming danger can have little doubt as to the reasons.

After the war, as society returned to normal, the rate predictably climbed to its usual level with a relatively increasing tendency in the young and in females (in common with other Western countries) reaching a post-war peak of 12.2 in 1963, i.e., 5714 recorded suicides in England and Wales. What happened thereafter is one of the most striking facts in the post-war British social scene. A step-like drop of about 200 recorded deaths per year occurred to a low of 3772 in 1972, a rate of 7.7 per 100,000 (see Fig. 17-3). The 1973 and 1974

*The figures quoted relate to England and Wales (48 million) and are taken from the various Registrar General's Reports on Causes of Death, London, Her Majesty's Stationary Office. Scotland, with about 10 percent of the population, has its own method of ascertaining causes of death and its (until recently) lower suicide rate was probably accounted for on the basis of more open verdicts. The Scottish rates, as published, have changed little of recent years.

504

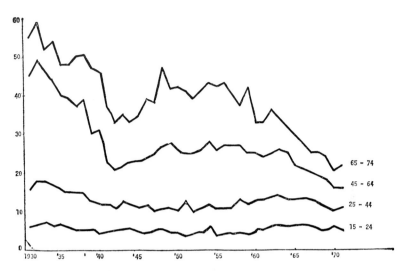

Fig. 17-1.   Suicide per 100,000 in England and Wales for males, 1930–1971.

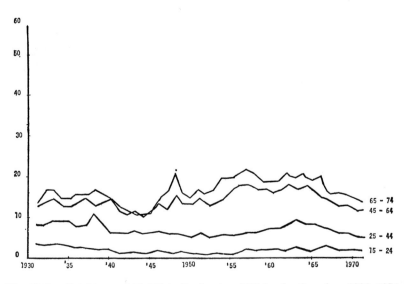

Fig. 17-2.   Suicide per 100,000 in England and Wales for females, 1930–1971.

505

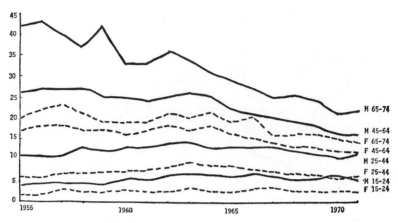

Fig. 17-3. Suicide per 100,000 in England and Wales for males (solid line) and females (dotted line), 1955–1971.

figures were almost identical and what makes the decline particularly significant is that the social conditions prevailing at this time, with one economic crisis heaped upon another, were much more those of the early 1930s than the early 1940s, massive unemployment excepted. Suicide is, of course, underreported everywhere but no one can doubt, especially since the work of Sainsbury and Barraclough,[1,2] that comparisons of the rates between countries can be made and that changes within one country over a relatively short span of years are based more on fact than on artifact.

The reason most commonly adduced for this decline is the changeover from lethal coal gas to low carbon monoxide natural gas for domestic purposes and the drop in suicidal gas poisoning (formerly the commonest method). Those who agree with Durkheim[3] that the suicide rate is an index of the quality of life in its widest sense in a particular society will be dissatisfied with this explanation and not surprised to discover that other places switching to natural gas have shown no such decline. In Basel, Switzerland, for example, Stengel,[4] stated that people started drowning themselves instead, and in Holland, a high gas-using country and the first to completely exploit the North Sea gas fields in the mid-1960s, experienced a slight rise in suicide in both sexes between 1961 and 1969.[5]

Overdose now being the major method of suicide, it has been suggested that many suicides are hidden in verdicts of accidental poisoning (see Fig. 17-4). Bearing in mind the massive increase in doctors prescribing drugs during this period,[6] it is no surprise to note

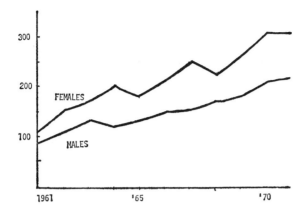

Fig. 17-4.   Accidental deaths by medical agents, in England
and Wales (whole numbers) Overall rise for 1961-1971 = 338.

an upward trend, however, the 1972 total exceeds the 1962 total by
only 243 which does little to account for a suicide decline nearly
10 times that amount. The homicide increase (on the theory that
people may act out their aggression on others instead of themselves)
was of much the same order. The new category of "injury undetermined
whether accidentally or purposely inflicted" which was first recorded
in England and Wales in 1967 shows virtually no change between
then and 1972 (see Fig. 17-5).* The unique reversal in 1967 by the
High Court of a suicide verdict seems, therfore, to have had no
influence on the coroners.[7] The repeal of the law in 1961 in England
against attempting suicide seems to have had little or no influence
on suicidal behavior.

Other possible intervening variables have been examined in more
detail elsewhere[8] but whether one takes better intensive care, makes
changes in medical treatment, provides housing for the elderly, etc.,
it is hard to find anything which does not apply equally or even
better in countries where suicide has remained static or risen. The
percentage of Gross National Product spent on medical services is
less in the United Kingdom than in most Western countries and the
pattern of medication prescribing by doctors who changed from lethal
barbiturates to drugs of low lethality, notably benzodiazepines, seems

*As footnote 1, Table 7, International Classification of Disease No. E850-E859,
for 1972, published 1974. Ditto homicide, ICD No. E960-969. Ditto open verdicts,
ICD No. E980-989.

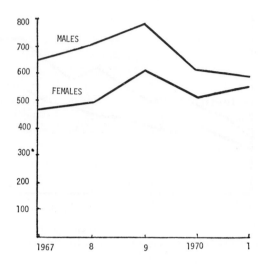

Fig. 17-5.   Death by injury in England and Wales; unknown
whether accident or suicide (whole numbers).

to have been almost identical throughout Western countries—one index
of the influence of multinational pharmaceutical corporations.*
    The one variable that does appear confined to the British scene
is the nationally known and publicly accepted network of 156 suicide
prevention centers known as the Samaritans.[9,10] A National Opinion
Poll survey of over 2,000 people in Britain in September 1975 revealed
a 92 percent level of knowledge of Samaritans in people aged 16
and over. The "image" of the organization proved overwhelmingly
favorable. Several European countries have centers operating on
similar lines but lacking not only the saturation (there are approximately
as many suicide prevention centers in Britain as in the rest of Europe)
but also the technique of "befriending," regarded as essential by
Samaritans. The American suicide prevention thrust has perhaps been
blunted by the lack of a national cohesion and image that must hamper
large scale publicity exercises and make the services less well known.
In the United States ground coverage is less (e.g., 1 suicide prevention
center for all of Los Angeles versus 12 for London) and client ratios
are correspondingly reduced, drop-in centers are scarce, befriending
has only just begun, and the plethora of emergency telephone services
run by and for all kinds of groups, sometimes overtly evangelistic,
may cause confusion in potential clients who may call several agencies

* From unpublished data presented in Washington, May 3, 1974.

and receive conflicting advice. Further, in the United States the occasional association of suicide prevention centers with compulsory treatment orders or the police becomes known among groups of high-risk clients who inevitably gather in places as such psychiatric admission wards. While the term *Samaritans* undoubtedly does deter some clients because of its religious overtones, there are speculations that the term *suicide prevention center* may alienate some clients by being too clinical, and appeal little to those who are in distress but do not consider themselves at that time as a suicide case. It is surprising that the controversial dispute over titles does not seem to have been subject to research. It should not be difficult to ascertain consumer reaction.

It is not known which of these differences between the British service and others plays the largest part, if any, in the differences in suicide rates among countries. However, the factors that stand out are ground coverage and, linked with this, the level of national knowledge and public image. Clearly the volunteer principle of using unpaid professionals in a consultant capacity only, makes the Samaritan program remarkably inexpensive to run and therefore easier to propagate.

In addition, Bagley[11,12] conducted a statistical evaluation of the role of Samaritans in suicide prevention, the only controlled study of a suicide preventive effort to date. In 1964 he took all the Samaritan branches that had been in operation for at least 2 years (15 in all), recorded the suicide numbers in those towns during those years, and compared them with suicide numbers during the same number of years preceding the opening of the branch.

Moser and Scott[13] had carried out a correlation analysis of 157 towns in England and Wales of populations over 50,000 using 57 demographic health, social, and economic variables. Four factors, extracted from the correlation matrix which accounted for 60 percent of the total variance were social class, population structure and change, percentage of new houses built, and poor housing conditions. These correlated highly with half the remaining factors and from an ecological map, Bagley was able to extract the 15 control towns most closely resembling each experimental one, on which to conduct identical suicide calculations.

Overall, the Samaritan towns showed a suicide decrease of 5.8 percent and the controls a rise of 19.8 percent—statistically significant beyond any chance effect (see Figs. 17-6 and Table 17-1). The most pointed criticism of this research was based upon the appropriateness of the matching. In light of this, Bagley rematched the next 2 groups

Fig. 17-6.   Samaritan branches, 1974.

of 15 control towns in rank ordering and still came up with significant results.[14] The Samaritans had lower suicide rates than their matched non-Samaritan controls. Bagley did concede that there could very well be some common factors, some subtle ethos, about a town which might lie behind both the development of a Samaritan branch *and* the drop in suicide rate, but the current national coverage being what it is, over 150 centers in Great Britain, this possible criticism is now hard to sustain. It is of interest to note that probably the biggest town without a Samaritan branch (Merthyr Tydfil) has a population of 60,000.

The fact that deliberately self-injuring behavior has increased strikingly since the WW II underlines the claims by Stengel[4] that suicides and attempted suicides are different groups, although they overlap to some degree. Admissions to hospital after overdose exceeded 100,000 in 1972[15] giving a suicide/attempted suicide ratio of 1:26. Adding those treated in casualty departments and sent home, by family doctors, or unreported, it is clear that the usual textbook figure of

Table 17-1
Samaritan Branches

Samaritan branches operating at least two years prior to 1964	= 15
Average rates of suicide calculated for years operating, and for same number of years before Samaritans started	
Average change in suicide rate in Samaritan towns	down 5.8%
Average change in suicide rate in "control" towns	up 19.8%
Statistically significant at 0.1 level	

8 to 10 suicide attempts to one suicide is greatly outdated, for Britain anyway. Overdosing is the overwhelmingly predominant method of self-injury in Britain and is also the method, permitting discovery in time and a second chance, Stengel's "gamble with death." In the writer's view, the majority represent semi-suicidal cries for help; conscious or unconscious manipulations; unplanned, impulsive acts (the motive for which even the victim is sometimes unable to explain later); or just the wish to "opt out" for a while, for example, the overstressed young housewife whose children are out of hand and whose husband is unhelpful. Less common cases are the confused elderly on multiple medications, the malingerer who claims to have overdosed in order to escape into the hospital, and the person who has not overdosed but appears drowsy and sedated and so is wrongly thought to have done so. There are clear virtues to the use of terms other than attempted suicide for cases that are not. Parasuicide is the term most canvassed in Europe and researchers such as Kreitman[16] now use no other.

Interesting new work on the geographical distribution of self-injuring behavior in both Bristol and Edinburgh has shown that it does not occur randomly.[17,18] The central, overcrowded areas of the towns appeared to contribute most cases and a factor of social contagion may be postulated, suggesting promising research possibilities for the future. Overdosing, the primary cause of admission to medical wards, has reached epidemic proportion and must be related in part to the demand by patients for psychotropic drugs to relieve distress, and pressure on physicians by pharmaceutical houses to prescribe such drugs. It is a decreasing minority of homes that is without a ready supply of tranquilizers in the bathroom cabinet, but perhaps the picture is not entirely black. Unsuccessful suicide attempts can call attention to a crisis situation and mobilize help. Drugs prescribed to psychiatric patients whether in the hospital or the doctor's office are mostly of low lethality. To remove this particular outlet for the ultimate discharge of emotional stress could lead to a rise in methods less likely to allow the crucial second chance, and the opportunity for postvention.

ORIGIN AND DEVELOPMENT OF SAMARITANS

The use of a publicised telephone number to allow contact by people in distress started in 1953 in London when the Reverend Chad Varah became Rector of St. Stephen's Church in central London, a post with virtually no parochial responsibilities other than ceremonial ones connected with the Lord Mayor. Therefore, he had time to develop what he first envisaged as a counseling service directed in particular to people with sexual problems. The public media showed great interest, the service became well known, and along with increasing numbers of clients, came offers of help. After a while Chad Varah noticed that some of the clients queuing up outside seemed to get much of what they needed by talking either to other clients or to the volunteers making the coffee, and could leave without having to see him at all. Thus was initiated the cornerstone of Samaritan work, the concept of *befriending* lonely people by other ordinary people, without obligations and with no strings attached; not a form of therapy or counseling and with an absolute taboo on evangelisation whether religious, political, or whatever.

Expansion of the work led to a grant by the Gulbenkian Foundation allowing the addition of 2 deputy directors and a fully qualified psychiatric social worker. Procedures for selecting and training volunteers evolved through experience and appreciation that distress was often at its worst during the long, lonely hours of darkness led to the center being manned for 24 hours. Little was done through the 1950s by way of data collecting, but an experienced psychiatrist, Dr. Louis Rose of St. Batholomew's Hospital went through the records kept on all clients in the course of 1 year and estimated that some 40 percent represented significant suicidal risk. He and other psychiatrists had been brought in (again in an entirely voluntary capacity) to assist with general guidance, training, and securing hospital admission for those who needed it. By the time I was called on in 1959 to arrange for the admission of psychotic clients via the emergency clinic at the Maudsley Hospital, the leadership in the London Samaritans had already become skilled and experienced. I was among the first psychiatrists to refer aid for Samaritan befriending psychiatric patients whose problems were more lack of companionship than mental illness, their psychiatric symptoms filling, as it were, the vacuum in their lives.

The Samaritans' first development outside London came in 1958 when a young Scottish schoolmaster read a newspaper article and wrote to Reverend Chad Varah. He received a telephone call asking him to visit immediately a recently bereaved and suicidal widow who had just called London from a hotel room in Edinburgh. The second branch of the Samaritans opened in Edinburgh the following year. Branches in Liverpool, Glasgow, Aberdeen, and Manchester soon followed, and by the time the first national conference took place in 1961, 15 were in operation. Church of England influence in the organization was at that time strong partly because of the way in which the organization had started and because clergy were among the few people with the time and experience with troubled people in a position to establish a branch and partly because there were so many individuals who were trying to find a more significant role in a society where the Church appeared to be becoming increasingly irrelevant. Samaritan membership was, however, at no time limited to Church people and it is important to record that when the 13th branch opened in Belfast in 1961, its director the Reverend Bill Thomson (who later became the second chairman of the organization) had a Roman Catholic Priest as a deputy director—somewhat in advance of the change in Vatican policy allowing closer cooperation with non-Catholic agencies. It is interesting to note that the religious sectarian troubles that have tragically torn apart the unhappy province of northern Ireland have never arisen in any of the 11 Samaritan branches currently functioning in both parts of Ireland.

The people who came together to start these early branches were not always those best suited by energy and personality; 1 branch rather quickly dissolved and others struggled on with too few volunteers and inadequate services. The need for a national organization became apparent and Samaritans became incorporated under the Companies Act in 1963 on terms that gave them a patent on the use of the word *Samaritan* in connection with an emergency telephone service. It also provided for a council of management consisting of all directors of full branches meeting at least 3 times a year and an Executive Committee (currently 16, plus consultants in publicity, psychiatry, and the law, and an honorary bursar) which meets every two months. Branches continued to open at a steady rate because Samaritans moving from one city to another took their experiences and enthusiasm to new places, and volunteers who lived in towns adjacent to existing branches formed themselves into "befriending groups," coping with the problems arising in their area. When they reached a sufficient size, they formed an independent branch. Reading, for example, fostered groups in Basingstoke, Bracknell, Slough, and Amersham, all of which later became full branches. More experienced volunteers became available to help new branches in selection and training, and the Executive Committee, discovering through bitter experience that branches which started in a small way tended to stay that way but those which began from a position of strength succeeded, decreed that no new branch could start until its premises had been inspected and found adequate and it had sufficient trained volunteers to open with a full 24-hour service.

A branch remains on probation for a year and could then be granted full status with a vote on the Council of Management subject to a further panel (i.e. accreditation) visit. Branches are visited at least every 3 years or as problems arise (e.g., assessing the suitability of a new director) by 2 visitors selected from a special panel. All Executive Committee members are active practicing Samaritans at the grass roots level, including the consultants and those who represent the 12 regions into which Great Britain is divided (north and south Ireland form one such). The inauguration of the service in southern Ireland with Branch No. 110 in Dublin was a particularly poignant occasion for the author (who joined the Executive Committee as Honorary Psychiatric Consultant in 1965). It was apparent that the Samaritans was an organization of ordinary people offering to help other ordinary people irrespective, of race, politics, color or creed; acts which may underlie the present enthusiasm in even very small Irish towns to set up branches.

The number of branch directors who are members of the clergy has declined steadily over the years and for 2 years they have been in the minority. The number of women in positions of leadership and direction has steadily increased and at the beginning of 1975 there were 36 women directors (of about 150).

Volunteer numbers were first recorded in 1965 when the 68 branches had 6537. They increased steadily to 18,020 at the end of 1974 in 147 branches with, in addition, a large number of befriending groups in towns insufficiently large to support a full branch.

In 1973 there were overseas branches of the Samaritans in 9 countries, mostly former colonial territories, and in 1974 the first Samaritan branch opened in the United States. Founded in Boston and directed by novelist Monica Dickens, an experienced London branch volunteer, it is run on the standard pattern of other branches and its first year seems to have been a highly successful one. (The profile of the clients and their problems seem similar to those in Britain and their lethality was high.)

HOW A SAMARITAN BRANCH WORKS

Volunteer recruitment may be by personal contact, the branch speakers' panel, or by actual advertising. Ex-clients, those who have made suicide attempts, and those who have received psychiatric treatment are not automatically excluded. An application form is required that includes a solemn commitment to observe complete secrecy in relation to all matters concerning clients. Two references are also required. There is no age limit and recent years have seen a swing toward youth among both volunteers and leaders from what was in many branches a predominantly middle-age movement.

The initial interview is conducted in the center or the volunteer's home and the successful applicant then goes into mandatory preparation classes that introduce them to the structure and working of the organization; the befriending of people with sexual, marital, and psychological problems; the recognition of those in need of medical care; and legal aspects of the work. Role play is increasingly used with mock telephones and there is a national cassette library of training tapes. People unsuited to this type of service usually eliminate themselves during the training process.

A period of observation of supervised telephone duty and a final interview follow. The acceptance rate varies widely from branch to branch and from time to time. Of a particular sample of 100 consecutive volunteers to the London branch, only 7 made it to full Samaritan status but the national average is about one-third acceptance.

At any one branch, 100 volunteers are considered the minimum for a full 24-hour manned service. A decreasing minority of branches has the phone switched automatically to a volunteer's house at night and branches such as central London and Birmingham can have as many as 200 or 300 volunteers so that the administrative problems become complex. Only 3 of the largest branches have salaried staff (apart from occasional part-time secretarial help) so a complex system of especially experienced leaders supervise the work sometimes on a daily basis, sometimes a week at a time, sometimes on a group basis as, e.g., geographically according to where the volunteers live. Other volunteers specialize in publicity (there is usually a special publicity committee), preparing the schedules, fund raising, on matters concerning the premises, etc. It may be that half or more of the total membership is involved in some kind of administrative or leadership function in addition to befriending and telephone duty which is likely to average about one 4-hour or overnight shift every two weeks, although some branches expect more.

Volunteers are of all ages from 17 years upward and from all walks of life. Ideally they will reflect the local population structure as to age and social class, but basic educational qualifications are required for some aspects of the work, such as the completion of the client form, and there is a middle- and upper-class tradition of voluntary and charitable work that is slow to permeate downwards. Material values and aspirations did so more quickly. Only one systematic study of volunteers has been done, in a fairly new Scottish branch, showing the majority to have left school early, had some personal experience of suicide at some time in their lives, and to be of varied ages. Motivation toward the work fell into 3 categories:— from personal involvement as above; because their ordinary work lacked inter-personal involvement, and to repay the debt they felt to society through their own good fortune. They were also the achievers in life in other ways.

Dr. George Day,[19] a retired psychiatrist, former volunteer, and branch director, has done over 400 Maudsley Personality Inventories on volunteers, although not on a precisely random basis, with the finding that they were a highly significantly stable group as measured on the neuroticism dimension but average on introversion/extroversion; leaders, however, were more likely to be extraverted. My inquiry of all branches as to its history of volunteer suicide shows, with two-thirds of the results in, an average or perhaps slightly above average expectancy. The better organized branches allocate a leader or leaders specifically to attend to problems that volunteers may have. Turnover seems to average about 20 percent a year, the reasons for which have not been studied.

Local publicity is invariably by local newspaper advertising (often obtained free), posters, and helping reporters with news stories whenever possible. Client material, of course, is always kept strictly confidential. Funds are raised by the usual round of teas, bazaars, flag days, donations, legacies, door-to-door collections, and subscriptions from local councils, businesses, and voluntary organizations. Having no paid staff, the average branch budget is low, about £2,000 per year (approximately $4100).

"Friends of the Samaritans" are usually established to carry out the fund raising, most of the money going to rent, upkeep, utilities, publicity and telephones. There is a 5 percent levy on the branch budget to support the central office, the 2 full-time general secretaries (both ex-Samaritan volunteers of long and distinguished standing) and their secretarial help. The central office is a modest suburban house at 17 Uxbridge Road, Slough, Bucks. In training great stress is placed on the right of any client at any time to determine his own destiny. About 1 percent of clients come after committing a crime and volunteers have to get used to the idea that these are *never* handed over to the police, although of course the offenders are encouraged to give themselves up, in which case the befriender goes with them to the station, legal representation is arranged, and so on. Similarly, Samaritans are never party to compulsory orders and a client may even leave the center with the announced intent of committing suicide; however, almost all of these change their minds and return later. Clients are not pursued if they break contact, although a friendly note expressing interest may be sent or a phone call made to people considered to be at high risk.

A further word about befriending: in order to protect the volunteer and his family, he or she is known only by first name and branch number (e.g., Richard, 690), although his identity and home phone number may be revealed with the consent of the director. Experience has taught that clients with severely inadequate personalities stand to gain little by befriending and those with aggressive psychopathic traits could actually be harmed. If a relationship were allowed to develop with emotional dependency and the development of unrealistic expectations, there could be negative results when the client felt let down. Training is directed at recognizing those who must not be befriended as well as those who can be. Decisions like this and referral to doctors are made only by branch leaders.

The classic befriending situation is in a case of sudden loss in which the befriender stands in for the absent friend or relative and helps the client first to see some purpose in life and second to reestablish links with it. The relationship between social isolation, loneliness, and anomie with suicidal states is one of the cornerstones of the befriending philosophy.

Decisions whether systematic befriending is to be offered, and by which volunteer, are made by a branch leader. Regular reports are made and the volunteer understands that the leader can terminate the relationship or switch to another befriender if he fears something is awry. This happens very seldom, the author being a national trouble-shooter for major psychiatric problems involving clients, and aware of very few.

Another service that branches supply is a *flying squad,* or emergency team consisting of specified volunteers with cars, able to drive immediately to a crisis situation which can vary from one of homicide in a family to an overdose case in a telephone booth. The squad may be a man and a woman, but single females are sent by some branches as representing the least threatening kind of person and one who can best defuse a situation fraught with tension. If a client, having overdosed, becomes unconscious on the end of a phone an ambulance may be called—a service which is free in Britain. The police are called only with the client's consent or in the event of a major crime. Samaritans have been called by the aggressor after murder has been committed.

Branch premise were, in earlier days mostly on church property because of cost, but about half of the branches currently own their own places, usually a small house or apartment near the city center, unobtrusively advertised. The branches have a duty room with files and telephones, a waiting area, tea-making facilities, restrooms, and a number of client-interview rooms appropriate to the workload of the branch. The branch may be lucky enough to have a larger room for committees and training classes and the decor is likely to be simple to make the client feel at home; most of the furnishings are second-hand donations and the decorating is done by the volunteers.

The professional's work in Samaritans is advisory rather than directoral, the inspiration and drive coming from the voluntary effort. While in the rest of Europe, psychiatrists, psychologists, and social workers become involved intimately in volunteer selection, training and supervision, this scarcely happens in Britain. One or 2 branches have psychiatric consultants who are trying special techniques such as T-groups or personality inventories on an experimental basis but it has been my view that though I, as a psychiatrist, may be competent to spot the mentally disturbed, the person most likely to select the right sort of Samaritan volunteer will be an experienced leader. All branches have honorary consultants in general practice and law and most also have consultants in psychiatry. The latter is available (via the director only) for consultation but the vast bulk of clients in need of psychiatric care are referred to specialists by the family physician. An important part of the psychiatrist's job is to refer lonely patients for befriending so that volunteers are optimally occupied. An underoccupied branch falls in morale and one under some strain is stimulated into more vigorous recruitment, the provision of extra emergency lines, extension of facilities, etc.[20-22] In the early days more stress was placed upon the need for psychiatric consultants partly because of the lack of experience within the organization and partly in search of respectability. Even though a 1966 study of 101 professors of psychiatry and medical superintendents in areas where branches were in operation showed two-thirds in favor of and only 10 percent opposed to Samaritans there are still those who see Samaritans as interfering, amateur do-gooders. There is an element of rivalry here, the thought that only professionally qualified people are capable of coping with human distress, of which the reluctance to admit that Samaritans may have helped prevent suicide is a part. By now, however, the organization is sufficiently accepted as to be perhaps too respectable for some clients and, since many long-serving Samaritans have more practical experience of being with and helping suicidal people than most professionals, the need for psychiatric help has become less. What is more important is that trainers should know what Samaritans are about, which may come better from a local general practitioner, social worker, or from within the movement, than from a sceptical psychiatrist. In 1969, we knew of approximately 350 physicians and psychiatrists who were actively involved with the organization.

THE SAMARITAN CLIENTS

Client numbers were first recorded in 1964 when there were over 12,000. Thereafter recording has always been of new clients such that total calls and repeat contacts with clients of previous years are not known. The number of new clients, however, rose by a remarkably consistent 30 percent annually until 1971 when the number increased 75 percent, from 89,000 to 156,000 in 1972. This was due beyond a doubt, to an 11-episode documentary based on Samaritans and using the name, screened on one of the 3 national TV networks at peak viewing times on Saturday evening. The audience averaged around 7-1/2 million out of a total viewing population of 50 million (15 percent).[21] Branch work increased to about double what would have been expected, even allowing for the usual increase from February to April when the series ran. One feature of this bulge of extra clients was the large number of young including school children who presented problems varying from a lost school book to the most alarming of family crises. A recent school girl suicide, Tina Wilson, was a result of bullying and called forth a public inquiry. One recommendation was that Samaritan services be made better known to school children. This group had presumably been little touched by previous publicity techniques and it is interesting to note that an $18,000 advertising campaign in mass circulation newspapers produced not one single client, so far as could be judged by comparing client numbers with previous years at a number of cooperative branches. Experience suggests that editorial material in national papers, especially an article by a popular columnist, gets results but advertising does not. In local papers, however, it is another matter. Before, during, and after the TV series, which was competently made with our cooperation by the British Broadcasting Corporation studies were made from 5 psychiatric centers of patients admitted with deliberate self-injury.[21] The advent of the program had no influence on admissions, of which incidentally, 96 percent were due to overdose. Knowledge of the Samaritans (40 percent) was less in this group than what was then regarded as the national level of around 70 percent. Those who had known of Samaritans had not contacted them mostly because of the impulsive nature of their act.

After the 1972 increase in client numbers, the 1973 figure was virtually unchanged at 157,000, but 1974 saw a further surge to 192,284. This is about 1 out of every 250 in the total population and guessing that an equal number of old clients stay in touch, it comes to 1 out of every 125 or about 1 family in 40.

For each new client a report form is completed as far as possible. Data collection takes second place to the creation of a trusting relationship with the distressed person. Though this form includes most of the features found in most lethality scales, formal scores are not made. The aim is always to persuade the client to come to the center for a face-to-face interview and most of them do. Although the overwhelming majority of clients make initial contact by phone many start by coming to the center, most are open from early morning to 11:00 P.M. Data from the report forms, coded for computing in 1966; 1969 and 1972, showed primarily a fairly consistent age spread obviously excepting a deficiency in those under 15 years of age. The age group 15-24 had many more females than expected as had the group 25-34 though less so. Sex ratios evened up thereafter but there were fewer than expected of both sexes over 65, our clients amounting to 6 percent of the total against an average of 13 percent over 65 in the general population. It seems universally the experience of helping agencies that the elderly are likelier to suffering, stoically, in silence. There is also the lesser likelihood of having, and even knowing how to use, a telephone. Social class spread showed that in 1972, a surprising double the expected number of professional people as clients and a still larger number of the unskilled. There is the usual preponderence of single (28 percent), separated (8 percent), divorced (4 percent) and widowed (7 percent). The highest risk clients judged by the code "attempt now" was between 1:00 A.M. and 2:00 A.M. when 1 call in 30 was thus coded against 1:200 average. The call peak was from 8:00 P.M. to 9:00 P.M. and not, as might be predicted, 90 minutes later when the bars closed. As to problems presented, marital was the most common (12 percent) with loneliness, depression, worry over third party looming large among the 40 categories coded. Acute mental illness was just under 1 percent. The sex ratio in 1966 was 1:1 but, with expansion of the work, had changed by 1972 to 1 male to 1.34 females.[22] Barraclough and Shea[23] have shown a suicide rate 30-40 times the expected rate during the following year in clients who default, especially during the month after contact is lost.

SERVICES FOR THE YOUNG

Although suicide in the under 25 age group has at least not increased in Britain as it has in some other countries, this is the one group for which no decline has been recorded and suicide in that group remains probably the second-highest cause of death. Students of certain universities were known as particularly high-risk groups[24] so that the development of student-manned emergency nightline or contact services was of interest. Essex University pioneered this in Britain in 1970 and the service received 80 calls in their first 101 nights. Yet Colchester Samaritans, an efficient branch just 2 miles away, had not received one student call during the 5 years of its existence. Student services grew and spread so rapidly that almost all universities now have one. Some are closely linked with the local Samaritans with combined training and nightliners doing duty also at the Samaritan center. Other nightlines remain fiercely independent if not paranoid and either keep no records or burn them ceremoniously every term as at Keele. This, plus the seeming reluctance of university authorities to reveal suicide or self-injury figures, makes the evaluation of these services difficult. They undoubtedly serve a need. However, Samaritans, as an organization, have so far avoided advertising to, or providing special services for, any special group with the intent that they exist for all types of distress in any sort of person but one branch has now started, and a second soon intends to start, a special youth line separately advertised and on a different number from the Samaritan emergency number answered, however, in the same office. These are not in university towns and if it becomes clear that they get clients otherwise deterred by a Samaritan middle-class establishment image, they will doubtless spread.

FUTURE TRENDS IN SAMARITANS

An important question is: Just how big will the organization get? Will it, to paraphrase Lady Wootton's remark about psychiatry, end up with one half of the population befriending the other half?[25] There exist, especially in northern Ireland, branches in towns as small as 12,000 population with sparsely populated country around, yet they seem to find work to do. New functions may well emerge as, for example, routine visiting of the elderly, or those living alone, whether clients or not. A branch in Scotland operating from a post office box number covers great areas of the Highlands, and another eccentric branch operates only from a tent at pop festivals. Doubtless new departures will occur such as these. Following the Los Angeles example, about 5 branches are currrently carrying out group work with especially high-risk clients, either as their own drop-ins or more intensively in cooperation with professionals.

The pattern of service for towns or parts of cities without the resources or needs for a full service may well be satellite groups or sub-offices manned only part of the 24 hours and with limited premises but having an emergency number of their own which can be made to ring directly to the main center at other times. Unfortunately, this is expensive. We need to work out better publicity techniques to reach the elderly and less well-educated and perhaps to review the policy on third party calls. Until 1966, these calls were not taken; the client had to approach the Samaritans of his own volition. When the first print-out revealed the deficit of persons over 65 this rule was relaxed to accept third party calls from competent persons (doctors, social workers, clergy) with the clients' consent. This is being reviewed in the light of American experience perhaps to widen this form of referral, subject to appropriate safeguards.

Whatever developments the future may hold, one thing to be avoided at all costs is to be absorbed in any way into the state or any other official scheme. Branches are increasingly often approached by official sources to cooperate, for example to send a representative to Community Health Councils (the watchdogs of the National Health Service), to assist with preventive schemes directed at those bereaved in middle-age, and to help with research rehabilitation prevention projects for patients after self-injury. Samaritans do try to help as far as is compatible with strict confidentiality but such participation is kept as secret as possible and though a Samaritan's name may appear on a document, his affiliation will hopefully be omitted.

Clients often come to Samaritans because they are just ordinary people, outside officialdom, and no part of any computer-linked record system. There are the sensitive, those who feel their troubles too trivial for the busy doctor, those afraid of what they have read or heard of psychiatric treatments and of being "taken away," and the paranoids who think the doctors are plotting against them. Samaritans provide a caring, unthreatening alternative. They must stay that way.

CONCLUSION

The growth, development, and function of the Samaritan suicide prevention service in the British Isles have been described. The remarkable decline in recorded suicide by about a third during the decade following 1963 to the lowest British rate ever, is discussed in relation to possibly related factors. The notion is put forward that the Samaritan organization may be responsible to a major extent for this reduction. If one subscribes to Durkheim's belief that suicide rates reflect in some way the subtle elements that contribute in a society to the quality of life, then one may conclude that a nationally-known network of suicide prevention centers such as the Samaritans—offering immediate 24-hour help on a strictly confidential basis, the systematic befriending of the lonely and anomic person, and dedicated exclusively to the welfare of the individual human being in distress—can significantly change the quality of life for the better.

REFERENCES

1. Sainsbury P, Barraclough BM: National suicide statistics, in Proceedings 5th International Conference for Suicide Prevention, London, 1969, pp. 176-179
2. Sainsbury P: Suicide: opinion and facts. Proc R Soc Med 66:6, 579-587, 1973
3. Durkheim E: Suicide. Glencoe, Illinois, Free Press, 1951
4. Stengel E: Suicide and Attempted Suicide. Baltimore, Penguin, 1964
5. Brooke EM (ed): Suicide and Attempted Suicide. Geneva, World Health Organization, 1974
6. Dunnell K, Cartwright A: Medicine Takers, Prescribers and Hoarders. London, Routledge & Kegan Paul, 1972
7. Lancet 2:326, 1967
8. Fox R: The Suicide Drop—Why? R Soc Health J 95:1, 9-13, 1975
9. Varah C (ed): The Samaritans. London, Constable, 1965. New York, Macmillan, 1966

10. Varah C (ed): Samaritans in the '70's. London, Constable, 1973
11. Bagley C: The evaluation of a suicide prevention scheme by an ecological method. Soc Sci Med 2:1, 1-14, 1968
12. Bagley C: An evaluation of suicide prevention agencies. Life-Threatening Behavior 1:245-259, 1971
13. Moser C, Scott W: British Towns. Edinburgh, Oliver and Boyd, 1961
14. Bagley C: News and notes. Br J Psychiatry: April and May, 1972
15. Report on Hospital Inpatient Enquiry for the year 1972: Preliminary Tables. London, Her Majesty's Stationery Office, 1973, p 15
16. Kreitman N, Philip AE, Green S, and Bagley CR: Parasuicide. Br J Psychiatry 115:746, 1969
17. Morgan HG, Pocock H, and Pottle S: The Urban distribution of non-fatal deliberate self-harm. Br J Psychiatry 126:319-328, 1975
18. McCulloch JW, Philip AE: Social variables and attempted suicides. Acta Psychiatr Scand 43:341-346, 1967
19. Day G: The Samaritan movement in Great Britain, Perspectives in Biology and Medicine, vol. 17. Chicago, Univ Chicago Press, 1974, pp 507-512
20. Fox R: Samaritans and the medical profession, in Proceedings 5th International Conference for Suicide Prevention, London, 1969, pp 152-156
21. Fox R: The Samaritan contribution to suicide prevention, in Proceedings 6th International Conference for Suicide Prevention, Mexico City, 1971, pp 343-351
22. Fox R: Soap opera and suicide prevention, in Proceedings 7th International Conference for Suicide Prevention, Amsterdam, 1973, pp 632-636
23. Barraclough, BM, Shea M: Suicide and Samaritan clients. Lancet 2:868-870, 1970
24. Fox R: Suicide among students and its prevention. R Soc Health J, 91:4, 181-185, 1971
25. Wootton B: Social Science and Social Pathology. London, Allen & Unwin, 1959

Robert E. Litman
and Carl I. Wold

18
Beyond Crisis Intervention

The introduction to this chapter are from the concluding section of Freud's *Beyond the Pleasure Principle* (1920), translated by C. J. M. Hubback, and reproduced here with the kind permission of Boni and Liveright © 1924; copyright renewed 1952.

If this attempt to reinstate an earlier condition really is so universal a characteristic of the instincts, we should not find it surprising that so many processes in the psychic life are performed independently of the pleasure-principle. This characteristic would communicate itself to every part-instinct and would in that case concern a harking back to a definite point on the path of development. But all that the pleasure-principle has not yet acquired power over is not therefore necessarily in opposition to it, and we have not yet solved the problem of determining the relation of the instinctive repetition processes to the domination of the pleasure-principle.

We have recognised that one of the earliest and most important functions of the psychic apparatus is to 'bind' the instreaming instinctive excitations, to substitute the 'secondary process' for the 'primary process' dominating them, and to transform their freely mobile energy-charge into a predominantly quiescent (tonic) charge. During this transformation no attention can be paid to the development of 'pain', but the pleasure-principle is not thereby annulled. On the contrary, the transformation takes place in the service of the pleasure-principle; the binding is an act of preparation, which introduces and secures its sovereignty.

Let us distinguish function and tendency more sharply than we have hitherto done. The pleasure-principle is then a tendency which subserves a certain function—namely, that of rendering the psychic apparatus, as a whole free from any excitation, or to keep the amount of excitation constant or as low as possible. We cannot yet decide with certainty for either of these conceptions, but we note that the function so defined would partake of the most universal tendency of all living matter—to return to the peace of the inorganic world. We all know by experience that the greatest pleasure it is possible for us to attain, that of the sexual act, is bound up with the temporary quenching of a greatly heightened state of excitation. The 'binding' of instinct-excitation, however, would be a preparatory function, which would direct the excitation towards its ultimate adjustment in the pleasure of discharge.

In the same connection, the question arises whether the sensations of pleasure and 'pain' can emanate as well from the bound as from the 'unbound' excitation-processes. It appears quite beyond doubt that the 'unbound', the primary, processes give rise to much more intense sensations in both directions than the bound ones, those of the 'secondary processes'. The primary processes are also the earlier in point of time; at the beginning of mental life there are no others, and we may conclude that if the pleasure-principle were not already in action in respect to them, it would not establish itself in regard to the later processes. We thus arrive at the result which at bottom is not a simple one, that the search for pleasure manifests itself with far greater intensity at the beginning of psychic life than later on, but less unrestrictedly: it has to put up with repeated breaches. At a maturer age the dominance of the pleasure-principle is very much more assured, though this principle as little escapes limitations as all the other instincts. In any case, whatever it is in the process of excitation that engenders the sensations of pleasure and 'pain' must be equally in existence when the secondary process is at work as with the primary process.

This would seem to be the place to institute further studies. Our consciousness conveys to us from within not only the sensations of pleasure and 'pain', but also those of a peculiar tension, which again may be either pleasurable or painful in itself. Now is it the 'bound' and 'unbound' energy processes that we have to distinguish from each other by the help of these sensations, or is the sensation of tension to be related to the absolute quantity, perhaps to the level of the charge, while the pleasure-pain series refers to the changes in the quantity of charge in the unit of time? We must also be struck with the fact that the life-instincts have much more to do with our inner perception, since they make their appearance as disturbers of the peace, and continually bring along with them states of tension the resolution of which is experienced as pleasure; while the death-instincts, on the other hand, seem to fulfil their function unostentatiously. The pleasure-principle seems directly to subserve the death-instincts; it keeps guard, of course, also over the external stimuli, which are regarded as dangers by both kinds of instincts, but in particular over the inner increases in stimulation which have for their aim the complication of the task of living. At this point innumerable other questions arise to which no answer can yet be given.

We must be patient and wait for other means and opportunities for investigation. We must hold ourselves too in readiness to abandon the path we have followed for a time, if it should seem to lead to no good result. Only such 'true believers' as expect from science a substitute for the creed they have relinquished will take it amiss if the investigator develops his views further or even transforms them.

For the rest we may find consolation in the words of a poet for the slow rate of progress in scientific knowledge:

Whither we cannot fly, we must go limping.

The Scripture saith that limping is no sin.

Beyond Crisis Intervention

A major current development at the suicide prevention center in Los Angeles is the increased emphasis that is being placed on expanding anti-suicide efforts, over time, to continue well beyond the usual limits of crisis intervention. In this paper we will describe the background for these developments and report on the operation and evaluation of a special continuing relationship program which we recently completed.

LIMITATIONS OF CONVENTIONAL CRISIS INTERVENTION

The principal activities of emergency or crisis counseling services, and of suicide prevention centers, are not preventive in the public health or epidemiological sense. These services provide anti-suicide intervention according to a crisis therapy model. Most observers agree that a great deal of short-term benefit results and probably that some lives are saved. However, this saving of lives is, in the United States at least, nowhere reflected in reduced suicide rates. Of course, there are problems associated with using the suicide rate as an index of effectiveness, since criteria for certifications of suicide, as presently reported, are variable and uncontrolled. Still, a dramatic response to crisis intervention, the introduction of anti-depressant drugs, or the development of new health care facilities has not occurred. An explanation was suggested by Kiev[1] who speculated that persons at high risk for suicide are less likely to use suicide prevention services, therefore, most calls to suicide prevention centers do not relate to suicide or represent low suicidal risks. The facts contradict that contention. Wherever follow-up studies of persons who are in touch with suicide prevention centers have been done, a significantly high suicide rate of 250 to 1000 (per 100,000 population at risk per year) has been determined. Wilkins[2] checked the names of 1100 callers to the Chicago Call-For-Help Clinic with death certificates from the county coroner's office and the Bureau of Vital Statistics. After an average follow-up period of 18 months, Wilkins located 8 certified suicides plus 4 equivocal deaths (which were quite probably suicide) and 5 deaths due to alcohol with strong self-destructive components. Sawyer, Sudak, and Hall[3] discovered 53 suicides who had contacted the Cleveland Suicide Prevention Center over a period of 4 years, and they reported an average annual suicide rate of 288 suicides per 100,000 population over 4 years. This figure is approximately 25 times higher than the suicide rate of 11.9 for the general population of the Cleveland area. The Cleveland center had been in contact with almost 6 percent of the total officially recognized suicides in the county.

In a 1964 review[4] of Los Angeles Suicide Prevention Center cases there were 9 suicides among 238 patients who had been seen 2 years before. A 1970 follow-up study of a randomly selected sample of 1968 callers revealed that 16 of 417 subjects were dead, 9 of these by suicide. In a comparison of suicide prevention center contacts and certified committed suicides in Los Angeles conducted in 1972, approximately 8 percent of the certified suicides had been in touch previously with the suicide prevention center.

One conclusion from these follow-up studies is that suicide prevention centers are in contact with large numbers of low-, medium-, and high-risk suicidal individuals. A second conclusion is that before measures are taken to increase services by reaching out in new directions toward high-risk groups, we should stop to evaluate the services being provided for the persons who are now in touch.

In the early follow-up study, Litman[4] reported that patients who had been in touch with the suicide prevention center, because of acute situational stress and acute suicidal problems, had received considerable help through crisis intervention and had made a good recovery. By contrast, people who were chronically suicidal and had no special acute situational stress at the first contact tended to have further difficulties, and a number of them continued to be suicidal after the contact with the suicide prevention center was discontinued.

The following hypothesis was offered. About half of the people who commit suicide are chronically suicidal with little acute situational stress. Crisis intervention has been only partially or temporarily effective in preventing the eventual suicide of such people. Apparently, suicide intervention is appropriate for suicidal patients who conform to the theoretical model for crisis therapy in that they have had a previous period of stable adjustment and have fallen into disequilibrium because of some acute stress. For suicidal patients who do not conform to the crisis model, supplementary types of intervention are indicated.

More recently, Wold and Litman[5] reviewed extensive psychological autopsies on 8 persons who committed suicide after being in touch with the suicide prevention center, and concluded that the subjects' deaths resulted from their lifestyles and were relatively independent of any crisis that existed at the time they were originally in touch with the center. The suicides were associated more with gradual exhaustion of their resources, energy, and hope than with sudden stress or loss. It was noted that current suicide prevention activities based on the model of crisis intervention tend to overemphasize the importance of the caller's current situation. The emergency telephone workers tend to focus on the emergency risk—the danger of immediate acts of severe, irreparable destruction—and to relatively neglect the suicide risk over the foreseeable future of 1 or 2 years. Yet, individual crisis interventions are relatively ineffective as suicide prevention with persons who have a long history of chronic or repetitive suicidal behavior as part of a self-destructive life style. Such persons are chronically depressed, make repeated suicide attempts, have masochistic personal relationships, and abuse drugs and alcohol. For these persons a rational treatment plan should emphasize the gradual amelioration of self-destructive lifestyles with rather less emphasis on active intervention to ensure the temporary safety of the patients.

Studies using statistical methods point toward the same conclusions as the clinical reviews of psychological autopsies. For example, in one study 52 persons who had committed suicide within 2 years after their contact with the Los Angeles Suicide Prevention Center were compared with 465 randomly selected persons who were still alive 2 years after their contact with the center.[6] The statistical analysis consisted of a step-wise discriminant function analysis of 75 items of information which were collected with a mean reliability of 85 percent. The items which contributed to high suicidal risk referred to long-range, chronic, relatively slow-to-change issues rather than acute or crisis issues. In one version of the prediction scale the weighted items appeared in the order shown in Table 18-1.

Table 18-1
Discriminant Function Analysis

Variable in Rank Order	Items Predicting Suicide
1	Older age
2	Chronic alcoholism
3	Absence of recent irritation, rage, violence
4	Lethal prior behavior
5	Male sex
6	Not willing to accept help now
7	Longer duration of current episode
8	No prior in-patient psychiatric treatment
9	No recent loss or separation
10	Depression with somatic symptoms
11	No loss of physical health
12	Higher occupational level

Note that items 3, 9 and 11 indicate an absence of stress or crisis, and items 6 and 8 indicate an unwillingness to accept help.

Currently, only 40 percent of suicide prevention center callers conform to the classical descriptions of people in crisis states. For most of the highest risk suicidal persons the suicide danger can be predicted ahead as a long-range, recurrent problem which can be ameliorated by repeated crisis interventions, but tends to recur. One has the impression that suicide prevention center interventions are postponing rather than preventing suicides.

CONTINUING RELATIONSHIP MAINTENANCE (CRM)

These research findings led us to develop a reaching-out service we called continuing relationship. High-risk suicidal individuals, identified by their call-for-help to the emergency telephone service and evaluated as high-risk by the lethality rating scales, were assigned to the program for an average time period of 18 months. The service was not considered therapy; it was conducted by teams of volunteers led by paraprofessional workers, trained and supervised by professional staff. It was planned that each client in the program would receive at least 1 telephone call a week as minimum relationship, however, for most persons there was more contact than that. The program included occasional home visits and other befriending contacts, and there were individual and group meetings at the suicide prevention center and other meeting places. The clients were encouraged to use all community and personal resources that seemed appropriate. In this intervention model, the emphasis was on rehabilitation rather than crisis, and our goals were to build up the clients' strengths, developing increased competence and use of community resources over an extended period of time. Of course, the long-range goal was to decrease suicidal behavior and, thus, suicide. The intermediate goals were to decrease aloneness in the clients and to help them increase their networks of friends and family.

The rationale for this program is derived from sociological and clinical observations. Sociologists have pointed out that suicide is most likely to occur in settings where individuals feel isolated and alienated, and when they are in fact alone. According to sociological theorists, the greater the degree of social relationships, the less the susceptibility to suicide. For example, Maris[7] advances the concept of external constraints provided by relationship as a major postulate in a developing theory of suicide. Living alone is a leading clinical indicator of high suicidal potentiality in some populations.[8,9] Aloneness may be by personal choice (as in depressive reactions), or because of a hostile interpersonal interaction (as in divorce). A variety of helping groups from the Salvation Army to the Samaritans have emphasized that extended personal relationships are the most potent of anti-suicide remedies.

An effort was made to select and train a group of volunteers representative of the Los Angeles community. The group was heterogeneous, including men and women with varied ethnic and socioeconomic backgrounds. In screening interviews with senior staff members, the motivation and potential effectiveness of volunteer workers were evaluated. Efforts were made to eliminate volunteers who were excessively narcissistic (Always know by instinct the right thing to do), or if they had preconceived ideas about the approach to other persons (for example, through astrology, scientology, sex therapy, graphology) or if they were psychotic. Volunteers with a history of a prior suicide episode from which they were currently distant in both time and feeling, were not automatically rejected. During the 8-week training program, the training staff had the opportunity to become familiar with the volunteers, and importantly, the volunteers had an opportunity to anticipate the actual work and discontinue training if they felt that it was not suitable for them. Approximately 80 percent of the volunteers initially screened and selected for training went on to complete the training and offer service. The training program combined some didactic presentations by professional staff with direct clinical experiences using case examples and role-playing.

On the average, volunteers chose to stay in contact with 3 or 4 clients, spending about an hour per week with each. At the end of the program, there were about 40 volunteer workers making contact with approximately 160 clients. On the average, the clients were in relationship with the workers for 18 months. Every effort was made to keep the program flexible and client-centered. Contacts were primarily by telephone, with supplementary meetings at the suicide prevention center or in the subject's home. Workers were trained to keep their expectations for the clients at a low level and not to expect miraculous improvements. The goals were limited and realistic. Clients varied greatly in the degree of relationship that they were willing to tolerate. For some, there was relatively intense involvement and for others only a brief or superficial contact could be sustained. Most clients were tentative at first, gaining increased trust in the workers over time. Often the clients would fluctuate from an enthusiastic response to receiving calls to suspicion, withdrawl, or overt hostility. Sometimes people found it difficult to communicate by telephone and they would prefer to write to the volunteer worker.

The CRM relationship was not seen as therapy in the formal sense. However, the relationship between worker and client had its therapeutic aspects. The suicidal persons learned they could discuss their hopelessness, anxieties, suicidal fantasies and acts, even delusions and hallucinations without alienating their workers. The worker strove to empathize with rather than negate those feelings, or to collude with the client in masking or repressing them. Often it was appropriate for the worker to refer the client to other community resources. In this way, volunteers helped their clients tolerate the anxieties they were likely to feel when venturing into therapy, rehabilitation training, a new job, or feared social and sexual relationships.

Once each week the volunteers met in small groups of 6 or 8 with a paraprofessional team leader and a professional staff member for the purpose of consultation and continuing training. At these weekly clinical meetings, individual cases were discussed, ideas exchanged, and responsibility for the clients shared by the group as a whole, including supervisors.

Experience demonstrated that chronically suicidal persons were so needy, dependent, and demanding that they easily exhausted the energy and good will of friends, family, and therapists. It was recognized in the design of the program that in order to maintain relationships with these distressed and chaotic people for a prolonged period, workers would have to pace themselves, not for a sprint, but for a long-distance run. Therefore, new workers were cautioned to conserve their energies and not to become depleted by responding to each new situation as if it were an acute crisis. At first, CRM volunteers found it difficult not to respond to the client's sense of constant emergency. In a way, this is natural because of their previous training and experience in crisis intervention. However, this is one area in which the support of the group, and particularly of the experienced anti-suicide workers, was of help to the new CRM worker.

In the weekly anti-suicide meetings workers discussed the anxieties they were having in their relationships with clients as well as reporting on trends which suggested improvement.

CONTROLLED STUDY OF AN ANTI-SUICIDE PROGRAM

There is an impressive professional consensus about how acutely suicidal persons should be treated. Obviously, mental health professionals feel with subjective certainty that their clinical interventions have prevented suicides in some cases. Yet, there is no direct, scientifically objective proof that any suicide has ever been prevented by clinical interventions, including hospitalization, psychiatric treatment, and crisis therapy. The basic question is How does one measure events which never happened, i.e., a prevented suicide? The classic answer is a controlled study. The difficulties which interfere with carrying out a classic, controlled study with suicide as an outcome criterion are many and serious. Consider the following.

1. The ethical issues must be confronted directly. Everyone involved in the controlled study must give their voluntary, informed consent to participate. How does the investigator justify not providing an anti-suicide service for the subjects in the control group? What are the potential benefits of the special service, and do these benefits clearly outweigh the potential harmful effects?

2. How will subjects be selected? Even if extremely high-risk suicidal subjects are selected and followed for 2 years, the maximum rate of suicide that could be anticipated might be 5 to 6 percent. As a result, the study must include several hundred subjects to be statistically significant. If low or moderate-suicide risk subjects are included, then, in order to use committed suicide as an outcome criterion, several thousand subjects would be required.

3. How do we design an anti-suicide program for several hundred or several thousand subjects to meet the expectation that the program has an effective impact, yet, at the same time, conduct it at reasonable financial and personnel expense?

4. Finally, there are a number of unsolved technical problems connected with measuring instruments. In comparing the surviving members of 2 groups, how do we determine who has improved? Even body counts of deaths and suicides in the 2 groups are subject to some distortions due to faulty certifications. Many suicidal populations are transient and difficult to follow up.

Bagley[10] has used indirect approaches to evaluate anti-suicide efforts in England. He found that communities with Samaritan anti-suicide services had slightly lower suicide rates than communities without Samaritans. He also found that a group of suicide attempters who did not have psychiatric treatment had slightly more suicide attempts subsequently than did a group of suicide attempters who had intensive psychiatric treatment. These are creative approaches to the evaluation problem but they do not carry the authority of controlled experiments. We are aware of only one controlled study using committed suicide as an outcome criterion and that was conducted by Motto.[11]

Motto reported a controlled study of patients who were discharged from hospitals after suicide attempts. They received no other treatment but they were divided into 2 sub-groups, contact and no contact. Those in the contact group received a regular communication from the staff member who interviewed them when they were in the hospital. Contact was made in the form of a telephone call or, more often, a brief letter. The content of the message was simply an expression of concern that the person's life situation was reasonably satisfactory and inviting a reply from the person if the person wished to send one. An effort was made to personalize the letters as much as possible and to avoid a form letter impression. At the end of an 18 month follow-up period, the suicide rate in the 2 groups was the same (1.5 percent). Motto felt that possibly the length of the contacts and the frequency of contacts were too small to generate a feeling of attachment and relationship.

RESEARCH DESIGN AND METHODS

A high suicide risk sub-population was selected from among suicidal callers to the Los Angeles Suicide Prevention Center (mostly during 1972). The screening process began with the notes and clinical judgment of suicide risk made by volunteer workers on each call. These notes were reviewed by staff and when signs of high suicide risk were present, the individual was called back approximately 1 week later. The call-back interview was structured to provide answers to some 68 items. Some of these items collectively supplied an assessment of suicide risk, including scores on 2 measures of suicide risk; the remaining items helped to identify the subject for later follow up. A final screening was then conducted, with all of the materials reviewed by the senior research psychologist and an experienced paraprofessional to make the final selection of subjects. Four hundred subjects who had been identified as high-risk were assigned either to the continuing relationship maintenance (CRM) group or to a comparison group (control), using a table of random numbers. As soon as a subject was assigned to the CRM group, a trained volunteer worker began to establish a continuing relationship with him.

Early in 1974 efforts began to bring the continuing relationships to a conclusion. There was some resistance to this and about 20 percent of the clients had to be transferred to other suicide prevention center programs. In June of 1974, the program was closed and a new group of research assistants (medical students on vacation) were hired to conduct the follow-up study which included interviews (usually by telephone) with 271 of the original 400 high-risk subjects.

Observations and Results

The following observations were made during the course of this program.

1. Both groups received a great deal of counseling from the suicide prevention center (SPC). It proved to be impossible to adhere to the strict study design, which would have required that people in the control group not receive further help from the SPC. Certainly it would have been a breach of ethical standards to have turned away high-risk suicidal persons because they had been selected as subjects of an experiment. The process of identifying and evaluating high-risk callers by a lengthy call-back interview promoted an attachment to the SPC, even though the clients were not contacted again by a continuing relationship worker. In the final analysis, we discovered that we had 2 groups of high suicide risk persons, divided into group 1, the study group, which received CRM on a "we-call-you" schedule, and group 2 which received on-going intermittent crisis counseling on a "you-call-us" basis, at their option. Almost 70 percent of group 2 was in touch with the SPC at one time or another after their initial designation.
2. Conducting this project had a definite effect on the workload

of the SPC. The effect was to increase greatly the number of chronically suicidal persons calling repeatedly on the crisis counseling telephone lines. While the project was being conducted, the number of repeat callers increased dramatically, from an average of 2 or 3 such callers in any week in 1969, to an average of 20 repeat callers in any given week in 1973. The number of calls made by people who had called the center more than 20 times increased from 20 percent to 40 percent of the total calls. (The total of all calls per month averaged 1000.) For SPC telephone workers, trained in crisis intervention attitudes and techniques, these chronic and repetitive callers posed unanticipated challenges and concerns. We are now evaluating the effectiveness of long-term telephone contacts on a "you-call-us" basis for chronic high suicide risk persons.

3. In debriefing the volunteer workers at the end of the project, it was discovered that many of the workers had felt overwhelmed in relationship with their clients, who were often severely disturbed, feeling hopeless, pessimistic, ineffective, failure-prone, alcoholic, and repeatedly suicidal. There was a tendency for the volunteer workers to wish to turn over the most difficult cases to paraprofessional supervisors and to the professional staff, and a reciprocal tendency on the part of the professionals to accept these cases. We concluded that the task of being in relationship with chronic, high-risk suicidal persons over a time span of many months was probably too demanding for volunteer workers and would be accomplished more effectively by salaried paraprofessionals and professionals.

The data from the follow-up study are presented in Tables 18-2 through 18-5.

It is apparent that the intermediate objectives of the CRM program were achieved, but the ultimate objectives were not. The study group was significantly improved as compared to the other group, in that there was reduced loneliness, improved love relationships, better use of professional help, less depression, and more confidence in using community resources. There was a general trend, but not statistically significant, for relative improvement in the study group in many other items. On the other hand, the stage-2 goals of the project, which were to reduce suicidal ideation, suicide attempts, and committed suicides, were not achieved. There were 10 deaths (7 suicides) in the study group, and 6 deaths (2 suicides) in the other group. This was not a statistically significant difference, and it represented a failure

Table 18-2

Comparison of Two Groups at Follow Up:
Current Relationships

Current Relationship Items	Differences	Significance Level*
1. Current work involvement (includes school and homemaking)	CRM group has more work involvement	.06
2. Living arrangement	CRM group slightly less living alone	.34
3. Eating alone	CRM group less eating alone	.06
4. All sources of help used in last month	About the same	.53
5. Subjects perception of sources of help for problems	CRM group perceives many more sources of help	.0006
6. Current love relationships	CRM group have more	.36
7. Family relationships	About the same	.53
8. Have used professional help within last year	Same	.94
9. Are willing to accept help now	CRM group are more help-accepting	.19

*Based upon a chi-square comparison.

to reach hoped-for goals. Moreover, the 2 groups were equivalent at the end of the study in suicidal ideation and suicide attempts. Psychological autopsies of those persons in both groups who had committed suicide revealed that 8 of the 9 suicides occurred in persons who chronically abused alcohol. The 7 others who died, not by suicide, were alcoholics as well. This is an important finding since less than 50 percent of the high-risk clients in the study were involved in alcohol abuse.

Tentative conclusions are (1) continuing relationship is a low cost, post-crisis intervention which helps improve the quality of life for chronic, high-risk suicidal persons who have poor personal relationships and are not alcoholic, but, (2) continuing relationship as we offered it through volunteer befrienders was "too little and too late" to have a significant life-change effect sufficient to prevent suicide and suicide attempts in high risk suicidal persons who abused alcohol, and (3) for high risk suicidal alcoholics, a program of intense crisis

Table 18-3
Comparison of Two Groups at Follow Up:
Alcohol Abuse

Alcoholism Items	Difference	Significance Level*
1. Report of change in degree of alcoholism during project	CRM group report slightly less alcoholism	.18
2. Recent (1 month before follow up) drinking behaviors	About the same	.50
3. Recent problem drinking	About the same	.24
4. Recent professional help for alcoholism	No difference	.81
5. Recent contact with Alcoholics Anonymous	About the same	.47
6. Report of other substance abuse	About the same	.56

*Based upon a chi-square comparison.

Table 18-4
Comparison of Two Groups at Follow Up:
Suicidal Behavior

Suicidal Behavior Items	Difference	Significance Level*
1. Suicidal behaviors during period of project	No difference in frequency or lethality	.99
2. Recent suicidal behaviors (within last month before follow up)	No difference	.75
3. Recent frequency of suicidal ideation	CRM group less frequent suicidal ideation	.10
4. Recent urgency of suicidal ideation	No difference	.81

*Based upon a chi-square comparison.

Table 18-5

Comparison of Two Groups at Follow Up: Life Events

Intercurrent Life Events	Differences	Significance Level*
1. Separation (divorce, death) from loved one	About the same	.28
2. Development of new love relationship	CRM group made more new love relationships	.02
3. Received professional help	CRM group received more professional help	.06
4. Received help from non-professional persons	CRM group received more help	.004
5. Physical illness during project	CRM group had less physical illness	.03

*Based upon a chi-square comparison.

intervention effort achieving some change in the immediate life situation is recommended rather than the on-going, low-level of relationship maintenance.

Psychological Autopsies

Table 18-6 shows some brief descriptions of the 16 deaths which occurred among both CRM and control subjects.

More detailed descriptions of 2 of the 9 people who committed suicide are given below. Information was derived from notes at the time of their contact with the suicide prevention center telephone service, working notes during the period of CRM service for those subjects in that group, and psychological autopsies[12-16] during which survivors who had been significant others in the life of the deceased, were interviewed.

CASE 1

S.X. was the first person in the CRM group to commit suicide. He was 47 years old when he killed himself. Although he had made a suicide attempt about 20 years before his death, his life remained fairly stable prior to his initial contact with the suicide prevention center, about 5 years before he committed suicide. His love relationships were homosexual. He lived

Table 18-6
Sixteen Deaths among CRM and Other Subjects

Initials	Age	Sex	Mode of Death	Alcoholism	Research Group	Date of Death	Months on Program
DX	25	F	Suicide	No	Control	6/72	<1
SX	47	M	Suicide	Yes	CRM	4/73	4
GI	49	F	Natural	Yes	Control	4/73	12
DC	44	F	Suicide	Yes	CRM	7/73	1
SJ	39	M	Natural	Yes	CRM	7/73	<1
HW	56	M	Natural	Yes	CRM	7/73	4
KH	37	M	Suicide	Yes	CRM	8/73	18
FN	50	F	Suicide	Yes	CRM	8/73	2
UX	72	M	Suicide	Yes	CRM	9/73	6
IL	50	F	Suicide	Yes	CRM	10/73	19
SB	49	M	Natural	Yes	CRM	12/73	23
DI	61	M	Natural	Yes	Control	1/74	14
SD	49	M	Natural	Yes	Control	4/74	9
NX	29	F	Suicide	Yes	CRM	5/74	10
KN	57	M	Natural	Yes	Control	7/74	11
XX	44	M	Suicide	Yes	Control	8/74	14

Totals:

15 Alcoholics
10 Men
10 CRM Subjects
9 Suicides
8 Alcoholic Suicides
7 CRM Suicides

541

with the same man for 14 years until that relationship ended. At the same time, other important parts of his life had begun to disintegrate. He had been employed as a dress designer and had worked for a major department store for many years. He lost his job when he was about 42 years of age, and began drinking more heavily in combination with barbiturate abuse. The pattern of his love relationships became unstable and transitory; for a time he was a male prostitute. During this period he exhausted and lost his few friends and he was alienated from his half sister, his only available family member. The CRM worker was in contact with her, but she refused to talk with S.X. and would not allow him to live with her as he wished.

During the 4 months he was in contact with the CRM worker he was initially distant and demanding, and subsequently gradually responded to the concern and interest and began to welcome the telephone calls and the eventual home visit by the worker. He complained of various physical ailments and symptoms, including stomach ulcers, a disintegrating spinal disc, Padget's disease, rectal bleeding, and inability to digest his food or to sleep at night. The home visit was arranged when he reported his telephone was disconnected for non-payment. He wrote, "I'm in terrible trouble. The owners want me out by April 1st. I have no money, 5 rooms full of furniture, no car, no phone and really no one to help me." During the visit the worker reported that S.X. was very depressed. He was facing eviction, his current roommate had left and he was unable to feed himself properly. He was on welfare because of his emotional and physical disability. The CRM worker was in contact with the welfare workers in an effort to provide an appropriate living arrangement. S.X. moved to a small run-down apartment without a telephone, which severely limited contact with the CRM worker. The worker was very concerned and made concerted efforts to arrange medical, psychiatric, and financial assistance through other community resources. When he was 43 years of age, S.X. had a year of outpatient psychotherapy which culminated in about a year of inpatient care in a state mental hospital. Efforts by the worker to reestablish mental health help were unsuccessful. About 10 days prior to his death the worker had the last contact with S.X. by telephone. The worker learned of the death when he went to the new apartment and was told by the manager that S.X.'s body had been found 2 days earlier. S.X. had been dead for 4 days without being discovered. The physical autopsy was complicated by the advanced state of decomposition of the body. Numerous empty wine bottles and 3 prescription vials for Nembutal and Phenobarbital were found throughout the apartment. It was most likely that S.X. died by ingesting an overdose of barbiturates and alcohol. The CRM worker experienced grief and frustration at the death, with the feeling that S.X. had been cut off from the world during the last 6 weeks of his life. The worker was most aware of the difficulty in maintaining contact with S.X. with an accompanying sense of helplessness.

In summary, S.X.'s life had been on an accelerated downhill course for the last 5 years prior to his death. His relationships became transitory and unstable in the context of alcoholism and barbiturate abuse. Efforts to get help from mental health resources failed to interrupt this pattern. His intense and chronic feelings of hopelessness interfered with his ability to establish the human relationships necessary for his survival.

CASE 2

A newspaper reporter called the suicide prevention center about D.C., and 44 year old woman, after he received a suicide note from her. A volunteer worker contacted D.C., who told the worker that the night before, fortified by a large amount of brandy, she had tried to drown herself in the ocean. Two efforts were unsuccessful and she called a friend. She said that she had been depressed over money problems, was receiving welfare aid, and was in therapy with a psychiatrist with whom she had not discussed her suicidal plans out of fear of going back to the hospital again. The volunteer persuaded D.C. to discuss her suicidal feelings with her psychiatrist. When a call was made some 4 weeks later, D.C. continued to feel hopeless. She said, "I don't think I'll ever find meaning in my life again." The call-back worker reported some improvement in mood by the end of the interview. The interview data were assessed, and based on the high suicide risk, D.C. was assigned to the CRM program; her random assignment was the CRM group. The CRM worker recontacted D.C. to establish an extended relationship. At that time the worker reported that D.C. had frequent suicidal thoughts and that she was considering some specific details relating to suicide. She continued in regular therapy with her psychiatrist. The next week when the CRM worker called, the woman who answered explained that D.C. had committed suicide. She had checked into a motel, overdosed on medication, and tied a plastic bag over her head. During subsequent interviews with D.C.'s survivors, the following information was gathered. The woman with whom D.C. had been living had been her companion for over 20 years; they had lived together with this woman's mother and sister. Her companion felt that D.C. had "never been comfortable in this world" and that her death was inevitable. D.C.'s poetry revealed her view of death as a pleasurable event and her wish that society could see suicide as a dignified alternative to life. On one occasion she explained that she was very depressed and wanted to kill herself, but she would not because death should be an act of joy, not despondency. D.C. was described as very bright with a brilliant mind, and she had been a good student. At college she performed well but inexplicably dropped out prior to completion. She had a pattern of difficulty in reaching any of the goals she had set for herself. There had been an early marriage when she was 20, but it was annulled. Her relationship with her companion was described as spiritual and not physical. D.C. was described as outwardly happy with a good sense of humor. She disguised her depression from those around her. For many years she drank excessively, yet her friend claimed that it had not excessively interfered with her life. D.C.'s first suicide attempt was 13 years prior to her death. It was an overdose of medication in the context of repetitive work failures, masked depression, and much time spent in writing poetry. D.C.'s father died when she was about 35 years of age and her subsequent suicide attempts were an expressed effort to join him. About 2 years prior to her suicide, D.C. voluntarily entered a state hospital for psychiatric help. She improved after about 6 weeks, and continued in outpatient psychotherapy with a psychiatrist until her death.

D.C. had been severely emotionally disturbed for much of her life. Her poetry revealed her love affair with death. In spite of close and stable relationships with a girlfriend and a psychiatrist, she committed suicide.

Discussion

If we had not had 2 groups, this report on continuing relationship maintenance might have been a great deal more optimistic. One should note that the clients liked it and only a small minority had hostile feelings about it. Because we felt that we had selected a truly high-risk study group, and would not have been surprised at as many as 10 suicides out of the 200, we might have felt that 7 suicides was a partial success. It is especially puzzling to note the low number of suicides in the comparison group.

There are several alternative explanations: There was a selection defect, so that more highly suicidal persons were put into the study group. Every effort was made to prevent this. The difference between the 2 groups in the number of suicides is not statistically significant and is a matter of chance. Supporting this is the fact that from the standpoint of suicidal behaviors, other than committed suicide, the 2 groups are the same. The CRM program, while somewhat helpful to many of the clients, was a toxic element to a small minority. For them it played into their tendency to have unrealistic expectations followed by frustration, disappointment, and an aggravation of suicidal tendencies. Many of these situations have in common the feature that the CRM workers were discouraged and depressed over the relationship. It was possible too that the depression and hopelessness of the CRM worker was communicated to the client and was an additional element which contributed to the client's hopelessness. Another possibility is that the comparison program serendipitously turned out to be an innovative anti-suicide program on its own. The elements of the program were a call-back evaluation and a promise for another call-back 2 years later, a willingness to accept repeated calls on a "you-call-us-at-your-option" basis, giving crisis-oriented intervention and more-or-less ignoring the chronic nature of the caller, for those persons who called frequently, a concentrated effort was made for a transfer to some appropriate helping agency, and a willingness, if the caller was persistent, to see the client in face-to-face ancillary therapies or groups at the Suicide Prevention Center.

Previous studies of committed suicides, particularly those of Murphy and Robins[17], have demonstrated that 2 major psychiatric diagnoses can be assigned to most suicides—depressive reaction and alcohol abuse. Persons in these 2 categories commit suicide under different circumstances. Alcoholics are especially vulnerable to difficulties in their personal relationships.

The Los Angeles Suicide Prevention Center experience indicates that at present, most of the suicides of individuals who had contacted the center occur in chronic alcohol abusers. Continuing relationships benefited non-alcoholic depressives, but were ineffective with suicidal alcoholics. We have the impression that suicidal alcoholics make the best use of time-limited intensive or expanded crisis-oriented interventions aimed at introducing or reintroducing the clients into appropriate existing intervention programs.

SUMMARY

The suicide prevention center attracts many persons at high risk for suicide. With few exceptions, clients who are in acute suicidal crises make good recoveries. Suicides, after contact with the SPC, occur in substantial numbers among chronically suicidal callers. Recognizing this, the SPC has conducted a number of programs for intervention over time averaging 18 months, with chronic depressives, drug abusers, and alcohol abusers. One special program of continuing relationship has been described and evaluated here in some detail. In the SPC population the suicidal chronic alcoholics are at highest risk and provide the greatest challenge for helpful intervention.

REFERENCES

1. Kiev A: New directions for suicide prevention centers. Am J Psychiatry 74:87–88, 1970
2. Wilkins J: A follow-up study of those who called a suicide prevention center. Am J Psychiatry 127:155–161, 1970
3. Sawyer J, Sudak H, Hall S: A follow-up study of 53 suicides known to a suicide prevention center. Life-Threatening Behavior 2:227–238, 1972.
4. Litman R: Suicide prevention center patients: A follow-up study. Bull Suicidol 6:12–17, 1970

5. Wold C, Litman R: Suicide after contact with a suicide prevention center. Arch Gen Psychiatry 28:735-739, 1973

6. Litman R, Farberow NL, Wold C, Brown T: Prediction models of suicidal behaviors, *in* Beck A, Resnick H, Lettieri D, (eds): The Prediction of Suicide. Bowie, Maryland, Charles Press, 1974

7. Maris RE: Social Forces in Urban Suicide. Homewood, Illinois, Dorsey, 1969

8. Tuckman J, Youngman WF: A scale of assessing suicide risk of attempted suicide. J Clin Psychol 24:17-19, 1968

9. Wold CI: Characteristics of 26,000 suicide prevention center patients. Bull Suicidol 6:24-28, 1970

10. Bagley C: The evaluation of a suicide prevention scheme by an ecological method. Soc Sci Med 2:1-14, 1968

11. Motto J: Contact as a suicide prevention influence: A method and a preliminary report, in Proceedings 6th International Conference for Suicide Prevention. Los Angeles, 1972, p 337

12. Litman RE, Curphey T, Shneidman ES, Farberow NL, and Tabachnick ND: Investigations of equivocal suicides. JAMA 184:924-929, 1963

13. Shneidman ES: Suicide, lethality and the psychological autopsy, in Shneidman ES, and Ortega M (eds): Aspects of Depression. Boston, Little, Brown, 1969

14. Shneidman ES: Deaths of Man. New York, Penguin, 1974

15. Weisman AD: The Realization of Death. New York, Jason Aronson, 1974

16. Weisman AD, Kastenbaum R: The Psychological Autopsy. Community Mental Health Journal Monograph, No. 4. New York, Behavioral Publications, 1968

17. Murphy G, Robins E: Social factors in suicide. JAMA 199:303-308, 1967

Author Index

547

Subject Index

Body image of self-mutilators, 290-291
Bogust v. *Iverson*, 410-411
Borderline personality state, 289-290
Borstal girls, study of, 302
Boston (Massachusetts), 514
Bristol (England), 511
British Broadcasting Corporation, 520
Bulletin of Suicidology, 7
Bulletin of the Atomic Scientist, 265
"Burned-out" person, 354

California, 171, 342
  court decision on suicide, 411-412
California *F* Scale, 241
California State Death Registry, 171
Caller-Worker Interaction Program (CWIP), 493-494
Calvert, Roy (fictional character), 407, 408, 410-413, 415, 416
Cancer, 158, 265
Catalogical reasoning, 236-238
Catholic view (Catholic doctrine; Catholic position), 382n, 433, 438, 513
Causes of suicide, 502
Cauverien v. *DeMetz*, 410-411
CCIR (Center for Crisis Intervention Research), 483, 484
Center for Crisis Intervention Research (CCIR), 483, 484
Cessation, orientations toward, 382n
Chairs, The (Ionesco), 264
Changes in life style, 351
Chemotherapy, *see* Medication
Chicago Call-For-Help Clinic, 529
Childhood, self-mutilation and deprivation in, 292-293
Children, self-mutilation among, 288, 293-294
Christianity (Christian ethics; Christian law; Christian dispensation; Christian tradition), 3, 233, 377n, 382n

See also Religion
Christians, 7-8, 377n
Chronic suicide (chronically suicidal persons), 155, 355, 530, 533
Church of England, 512-513
Class, socioeconomic, 143, 152
Cleveland Suicide Prevention Center, 529
Clinical effectiveness (CE) of volunteers, 487-488, 489-490
Clinical Psychology, University of Florida Department of, 483
Co-conspiratorial dyad, 307
Cognition
  self-destructive, 246-249
  suicide and, 203-277
  See also Reasoning; Thinking
Cognitive maneuvers, 211, 225
Cognitive variables, 235
Cohort mortality, study of, 45-46
College-age population, 454
College students, *see* Students
Color differentials ic suicide, 87-88
  See also Blacks; Nonwhites; Race; Whites
Commitment, as component of suicide syndrome, 115-116
Common law, 406, 409
Common sense, 232
Community, suicide as injury to, 385-386
Community Health Councils (Great Britain), 522
Community Mental Health Center population, 185, 189
Concurrent validity, 165
Confession, as autobiographical motive, 255
Confessions (Rousseau), 268-269
Consciousness, narrowing of, *see* Constriction in suicidal thinking
Constriction in suicidal thinking, 240-243, 261-263, 275-276
Construct validity, 165-168

of Health, Education, and
Welfare), 18
Suicide notes
  addressee of, 266
  ambithetical, 269, 271
  antithetical, 269
  athetical, 271
  causes for suicide discussed in,
      265n
  compared with writings of those
      facing other deaths, 272–275
  emphases in analysis of, 260
  as evidence, 414–415
  Los Angeles study of, 259, 266
  motives for writing, 266–267
  psychological state and, 261–265
  ambithesis, 269, 271
  reasoning patterns in, *see*
      Reasoning—patterns of, in
      suicide notes
  studies using, 259–261
  synthetical, 270
  thetical, 269
  as well persons' statements, 414
Suicide prevention, *see* Prevention,
    suicide
"Suicide Prevention" (Dublin), 479
Suicide rates
  age-specific, *see* Age—suicide
      statistics related to
  for blacks, 99–100, 103, 106,
      111–113, 115–119, 126–127
  in England and Wales
      (1886-1905),4
  in European countries, 3
  in Great Britain, 505–507, 509–511
  trend analysis of, *see* Trend
      analysis
  United States, 25–55, 82–83, 454,
      528–529
  See also Demography of suicide;
      Statistics, suicide
Suicide statistics, *see* Statistics,
    suicide
Suicide syndrome, 115–117, 124, 157
Suicido, Il (Morselli), 71, 500

Suicidologist, volunteer, *see*
    Volunteer suicidologist
Supportive spouse, 360, 361
  See also Significant other
Suttee, 9, 16
Sweden, 18, 19
Switzerland, 72
Symptom acquisition, as grief
    reaction, 449
Symptomatology, in self-mutilators,
    289
"Symptomatology and Management
    of Acute Grief"
    (Lindemann), 445

t tests, 488, 491
TAT (Thematic Apperception Test),
    142
Tate v. *Canonica*, 412–413
Tavistock Inventory, 302
Technical effectiveness (TE) scale,
    485–487, 492, 493–494
*Technical Recommendations for
    Psychological Tests and
    Diagnostic Techniques*
    (Cronbach et al.), 163–169
Technological developments in crisis
    intervention worker
    evaluation, 494–494
Telephone crisis calls, 485–493
Tension
  relief from, as autobiographical
      motive, 254
  self-mutilation and, 297–298, 301
Terman Group Test of Mental
    Ability, 338–340
Terman Study (Terman Gifted
    Study), 341–346, 356, 361
  blind ratings and outcomes for
      subjects of, 356–359
Terminal illness (fatal disease), 261,
    265–266, 273–275, 390–392,
    437, 438
  See also Euthanasia
Terminality-Lethality Index, 148

a
b
c
6 d
7 e
8 f
9 g
0 h
1 i
8 2 j